How Optical Sensors and Deep Learning Enhance the Production Management in Smart Agriculture

How Optical Sensors and Deep Learning Enhance the Production Management in Smart Agriculture

Guest Editors

Jibo Yue

Meiyan Shu

Chengquan Zhou

Haikuan Feng

Fenghua Yu

MDPI

Basel • Beijing • Wuhan • Barcelona • Belgrade • Novi Sad • Cluj • Manchester

Guest Editors

Jibo Yue
College of Information and Management Science
Henan Agricultural University
Zhengzhou
China

Meiyan Shu
College of Information and Management Science
Henan Agricultural University
Zhengzhou
China

Chengquan Zhou
Institute of Agricultural Equipment
Zhejiang Academy of Agricultural Sciences
Hangzhou
China

Haikuan Feng
Information Technology Research Center
Beijing Academy of Agriculture and Forestry Sciences
Beijing
China

Fenghua Yu
College of Information and Electrical Engineering
Shenyang Agricultural University
Shenyang
China

Editorial Office
MDPI AG
Grosspeteranlage 5
4052 Basel, Switzerland

This is a reprint of the Special Issue, published open access by the journal *Agriculture* (ISSN 2077-0472), freely accessible at: https://www.mdpi.com/journal/agriculture/special_issues/GA46OO8W4L.

For citation purposes, cite each article independently as indicated on the article page online and as indicated below:

Lastname, A.A.; Lastname, B.B. Article Title. *Journal Name* **Year**, *Volume Number*, Page Range.

ISBN 978-3-7258-6548-2 (Hbk)
ISBN 978-3-7258-6549-9 (PDF)
https://doi.org/10.3390/books978-3-7258-6549-9

Contents

agriculture

Editorial

How Optical Sensors and Deep Learning Enhance the Production Management in Smart Agriculture

Jibo Yue [1,*], Meiyan Shu [1], Chengquan Zhou [2], Haikuan Feng [3] and Fenghua Yu [4]

1 College of Information and Management Science, Henan Agricultural University, Zhengzhou 450002, China; smy511@henau.edu.cn
2 Institute of Agricultural Equipment, Zhejiang Academy of Agricultural Sciences, Hangzhou 310004, China; zhoucq@zaas.ac.cn
3 Information Technology Research Center, Beijing Academy of Agriculture and Forestry Sciences, Beijing 100097, China; fenghk@nercita.org.cn
4 College of Information and Electrical Engineering, Shenyang Agricultural University, Shenyang 110866, China; adan@syau.edu.cn
* Correspondence: yuejibo@henau.edu.cn

The advent of smart agriculture marks a paradigm shift from experience-driven to data-driven decision-making, fundamentally reshaping centuries-old farming practices. At the heart of this transformation lies the synergistic integration of optical sensors and deep learning (DL) technologies [1]. Modern optical sensors range from cost-effective RGB cameras and near-infrared-modified consumer devices to sophisticated multispectral, hyperspectral, and fluorescence imaging systems [2]. These sensors are now routinely deployed on unmanned aerial vehicles (UAVs), unmanned ground vehicles (UGVs), fixed-wing aircraft, tractors, and stationary phenotyping platforms. These sensors deliver unprecedented spatiotemporal resolution and spectral richness, capturing subtle physiological signals (chlorophyll fluorescence, water stress indices, and anthocyanin accumulation) that remain invisible to the human eye [3]. Rich optical datasets collected by these sensors can be paired with DL architectures, particularly convolutional neural networks (CNNs), vision transformers (ViTs), and hybrid models. When combined with these powerful DL approaches, the datasets are transformed into actionable intelligence, enabling precise yield forecasting at the individual plant or plot level, automated phenotyping of thousands of genotypes per day, and real-time variable-rate application of water, fertilizers, and pesticides. By the end of 2024, an estimated 400,000 DJI Agriculture drones were in operation worldwide, representing a 90% increase since 2020 [4]. Meanwhile, the market for AI-enabled precision agriculture solutions is expanding at an extraordinary pace [5], driven by technological maturity as well as urgent global needs stemming from climate variability, labor shortages, and the necessity to feed a projected population of 10.3 billion by the mid-2080s [6].

Nevertheless, significant scientific and engineering hurdles continue to impede seamless transition from laboratory prototypes to robust, farmer-ready systems. Spectral saturation in dense canopies, bidirectional reflectance distribution function (BRDF) effects, mixed pixels in low-altitude imagery, and rapid illumination changes (such as cloud passage and diurnal variation in solar angle) routinely degrade data quality and model reliability. Additionally, occlusion by leaves, overlapping fruits, and dense weed canopies further complicates the detection of small targets. Perhaps most critically, the computational footprint of state-of-the-art DL models often exceeds the thermal and power constraints of edge devices carried by lightweight drones or solar-powered field robots [7]. These challenges are further compounded by the notorious difficulty of collecting large, well-annotated, and geographically diverse agricultural datasets. Unlike urban or indoor scenes,

 https://doi.org/10.3390/agriculture15242612

crop appearance varies dramatically across cultivars, growth stages, management practices, and stress conditions. In response, the research community has pursued multiple convergent strategies: (i) lightweight yet expressive architectures (Ghost, ShuffleNet, MobileViT, EfficientFormer); (ii) knowledge distillation and neural architecture search tailored to agricultural tasks; (iii) advanced feature selection and band-reduction techniques for hyperspectral data; (iv) domain adaptation and self-supervised pretraining on massive unlabeled satellite/drone imagery; and (v) hybrid physics-informed neural networks that embed radiative transfer principles to improve generalization under varying atmospheric and canopy conditions [8]. These innovations have collectively pushed mean average precision (mAP) beyond 90% in many real-world tasks while reducing inference latency to tens of milliseconds on embedded GPUs, bringing fully autonomous optical-DL pipelines within practical reach.

This Special Issue, entitled "How Optical Sensors and Deep Learning Enhance the Production Management in Smart Agriculture," assembles thirteen high-quality contributions that exemplify the current state-of-the-art and illuminate viable paths forward (Table 1). The collected works span staple crops (rice, maize, wheat), high-value horticultural species, and complex real-world field scenarios. They comprehensively address the entire pipeline, from sensor selection and flight planning to model optimization and on-farm validation. Methodologically, the collected works showcase the full spectrum of contemporary deep learning and machine learning approaches. These include heavily optimized YOLO variants for real-time detection and ripeness grading [9], attention-augmented lightweight CNNs for disease severity assessment, random forest and extreme gradient boosting ensembles fused with vegetation indices for yield prediction, dual-branch spectral–spatial networks for hyperspectral anomaly detection, and transfer-learning frameworks that dramatically reduce the annotation burden. Crucially, nearly all studies include rigorous field experiments conducted under commercial or near-commercial conditions across multiple continents, with quantitative metrics (R^2 > 0.85 for regression tasks, mAP@0.5 > 0.90 for detection, overall accuracy > 95% for classification) that meet or exceed the thresholds required for operational deployment. By bridging the gap between algorithmic sophistication and agricultural practicality, this Special Issue not only documents tangible progress but also establishes a benchmark and inspiration for the next wave of optical-DL innovations in global food production.

Table 1. Summary of publications featured in this Special Issue.

Articles	Models	Optical Sensors	Platforms	Authors	References
1	YOLO	Zenmuse P1	UAV	Sun et al.	[10]
2	YOLO	Canon EOS 5D Mark IV	Field	He et al.	[11]
3	YOLO	Digital camera	Field	Sun et al.	[12]
4	DNN	HeadWall MV.C VNIR	UAV	Chen et al.	[13]
5	DCFM	ImSpector V10E	Field	Qi et al.	[14]
6	RF	GaiaSky-mini	UAV	Wang et al.	[15]
7	VisLAI	Mavic 3M	UAV	Fu et al.	[16]
8	LAINet	Sony IMX707	Field	Yang et al.	[17]
9	RF	Sentinel-2 MSI	Satellite	Lu et al.	[18]
10	RF, XGBoost	Sentinel-2 MSI	Satellite	Simeón et al.	[19]
11	CFD	-	UAV	Xu et al.	[20]
12	QY-SE-MResNet34	iPhone 14 Pro	Field	Li et al.	[21]
13	DRL	-	Review	Zhao et al.	[22]

The YOLO series, renowned for its real-time detection capabilities, has been extensively adapted for agricultural tasks involving optical imagery. Researchers have introduced targeted enhancements to address issues like small-target detection [23], background complexity, and model efficiency. Sun et al. [4] proposed YOLOv8n-SSDW, a lightweight model incorporating separable residual CoordConv, spatio-channel enhanced attention, and dynamic upsampling for barnyard grass detection in rice fields. This achieved an mAP@0.5 of 0.851, with a 10.6% reduction in parameters, proving effective in occluded paddy environments during drone-based field tests. Similarly, He et al. [5] developed a sparse parallel attention mechanism integrated with CNN for passion fruit disease detection using optical sensing, attaining a precision of 0.93, a recall of 0.88, an accuracy of 0.91, an mAP@0.5 of 0.90, and outperforming baselines like Faster R-CNN and YOLO in handling multi-scale lesions under complex backgrounds. Sun et al. [6] advanced a GCSS-YOLO variant for classifying four tomato ripening stages in greenhouses, embedding RepNCSPELan for feature extraction and Shape_IoU loss, resulting in an mAP@0.5 of 0.853 and successful mobile deployment via NCNN for real-time monitoring.

Hyperspectral and multispectral optical data, combined with DL, have shown promise in quantitative trait estimation. Chen et al. [7] employed E2D-COS feature selection with DNN and transfer learning to estimate maize leaf chlorophyll content from UAV hyperspectral imagery, identifying key bands (e.g., 418 nm, 688 nm) and improving R^2 by up to 0.11 across growth stages. Qi et al. [8] introduced a dual-channel feature fusion model (DCFM) for hierarchical rice blast detection, fusing spectral features via successive projections and spatial features from MobileNetV2-CBAM, yielding an overall accuracy of 96.72% and a Kappa of 95.97%. Wang et al. [9] fused days after transplanting and meteorological factors with UAV hyperspectral data for rice LAI inversion, using RF on preprocessed spectra to achieve R^2 = 0.8015 and RMSE = 0.5745, enhancing stability under small-sample conditions.

In crop monitoring and yield prediction, DL models optimized for optical inputs have addressed phenological variations and environmental stressors. Fu et al. [10] developed VisLAI, a computer vision-based model using UAV visible light imagery and HSV optimization for maize LAI estimation, reaching R^2 values up to 0.92 across stages and surpassing machine learning alternatives like Gradient Boosting (R^2 = 0.88). Yang et al. [11] proposed LAINet, an improved CNN with triplet attention and growth-stage integration for corn LAI, attaining R^2 = 0.81 on a regional dataset. Lu et al. [12] integrated Sentinel-2 multispectral data with soil salt content using RF for winter wheat yield under saline stress, improving R^2 to 0.78 and reducing RMSE by incorporating salinity indices. Simeón et al. [13] applied machine learning classifiers (e.g., RF, XGBoost) to Sentinel-2 temporal spectra for rice variety mapping, achieving 0.94 accuracy during reproduction using red-edge and NIR bands.

Further innovations extend to specialized applications. Xu et al. [14] simulated rotor airflow and droplet deposition in plant protection UAVs, optimizing nozzle distances for maximal deposition (0.766 $\mu L/cm^2$ at 360 mm) via optical sensing validation. Li et al. [15] enhanced ResNet34 with SE blocks and kernel adjustments for wheat powdery mildew severity classification, reaching 89% accuracy on leaf images. Zhao et al. [16] reviewed deep reinforcement learning (DRL) trends in agricultural machinery, highlighting hybrid architectures for navigation and UAV operations.

Despite the remarkable progress achieved, several persistent challenges continue to hinder the large-scale deployment of optical sensors and deep learning in real-world agricultural systems. First, data scarcity and poor generalization remain critical bottlenecks: field-collected optical datasets are often limited in size, imbalanced across growth stages or stress conditions, and heavily influenced by site-specific factors (soil type, cultivar, management practices), making models prone to overfitting or failure when transferred to new regions. Second, spectral overlap and environmental interference significantly degrade the signal-to-noise ratio in multispectral and hyperspectral imagery. Key sources of this interference include cloud cover, varying solar angles, leaf inclination angles, and soil background. Third, computational constraints on edge devices mounted on drones, robots, or tractors demand models that are not only accurate but also extremely lightweight, low-power, and capable of real-time inference under strict latency requirements.

To tackle these obstacles, the contributions in this Special Issue comprise a rich portfolio of innovative solutions. Transfer learning and domain adaptation techniques, often initialized from large-scale natural image-pretrained backbones or simulated spectra, have dramatically reduced the need for large, labeled field datasets while improving cross-region robustness. Attention mechanisms (channel, spatial, triplet, and dynamic sparse attention) have been strategically inserted into both CNN and transformer architectures to suppress background noise, enhance discriminative spectral-spatial features, and focus computational resources on disease lesions, small fruits, or subtle phenological changes. Model lightweighting strategies, including structured/unstructured pruning, knowledge distillation, and dynamic inference, have successfully reduced parameter counts, enabling smooth deployment on resource-constrained platforms such as NVIDIA Jetson series and mobile CPUs [24]. Furthermore, multimodal data fusion has emerged as a powerful paradigm, integrating optical/hyperspectral imagery with meteorological records, soil salinity indices, and growth-day information, which can significantly mitigate the impact of occlusion, illumination variation, and spectral saturation [25].

The thirteen articles assembled in this Special Issue collectively provide evidence of the maturity and practical viability of optical sensor–deep learning pipelines in smart agriculture. Through rigorous field validation across diverse crops, geographic regions, and sensing platforms (UAVs, ground robots, fixed-wing aircraft, handheld spectrometers), these studies demonstrate how state-of-the-art systems can operate reliably in unstructured, dynamic environments with accuracy, speed, and robustness values that meet or exceed the requirements of commercial farming operations [26]. More importantly, they establish a clear technical roadmap for the next generation of agricultural intelligence: edge–cloud collaborative inference for ultra-low latency decision-making; meta-learning and few-shot adaptation for rapid deployment to new cultivars or climates; continual learning frameworks that evolve with seasonal data streams; and deeper interdisciplinary fusion of optical sensing, robotics, agronomy, and economics [27]. These advancements are expected to drive not only incremental improvements but also achieve transformative leaps in resource-use efficiency, early-warning capability, and climate resilience, ultimately contributing to global food security and agricultural sustainability in an era of increasing environmental uncertainty.

Conflicts of Interest: The authors declare no conflicts of interest.

References

1. LeCun, Y.; Bengio, Y.; Hinton, G. Deep learning. *Nature* **2015**, *521*, 436–444. [CrossRef] [PubMed]
2. Jha, K.; Doshi, A.; Patel, P.; Shah, M. A comprehensive review on automation in agriculture using artificial intelligence. *Artif. Intell. Agric.* **2019**, *2*, 1–12. [CrossRef]
3. Lee, G.; Hossain, O.; Jamalzadegan, S.; Liu, Y.; Wang, H.; Saville, A.C.; Shymanovich, T.; Paul, R.; Rotenberg, D.; Whitfield, A.E. Abaxial leaf surface-mounted multimodal wearable sensor for continuous plant physiology monitoring. *Sci. Adv.* **2023**, *9*, eade2232. [CrossRef] [PubMed]
4. DJI. *Agricultural Drone Industry Insight Report*; DJI: Shenzhen, China, 2025.
5. Tong, X.; Zhang, X.; Fensholt, R.; Jensen, P.R.D.; Li, S.; Larsen, M.N.; Reiner, F.; Tian, F.; Brandt, M. Global area boom for greenhouse cultivation revealed by satellite mapping. *Nat. Food* **2024**, *5*, 513–523. [CrossRef]
6. United Nations Department of Economic and Social Affairs. Population Division. In *World Population Prospects 2024: Summary of Results*; United Nations Department of Economic and Social Affairs: New York, NY, USA, 2024.
7. Wang, Y.; Feng, L.; Sun, W.; Wang, L.; Yang, G.; Chen, B. A lightweight CNN-Transformer network for pixel-based crop mapping using time-series Sentinel-2 imagery. *Comput. Electron. Agric.* **2024**, *226*, 109370. [CrossRef]

8. Yue, J.; Li, T.; Feng, H.; Fu, Y.; Liu, Y.; Tian, J.; Yang, H.; Yang, G. Enhancing field soil moisture content monitoring using laboratory-based soil spectral measurements and radiative transfer models. *Agric. Commun.* **2024**, *2*, 100060. [CrossRef]
9. Ouf, N.S. Leguminous seeds detection based on convolutional neural networks: Comparison of faster R-CNN and YOLOv4 on a small custom dataset. *Artif. Intell. Agric.* **2023**, *8*, 30–45. [CrossRef]
10. Sun, Y.; Guo, H.; Chen, X.; Li, M.; Fang, B.; Cao, Y. YOLOv8n-SSDW: A Lightweight and Accurate Model for Barnyard Grass Detection in Fields. *Agriculture* **2025**, *15*, 1510. [CrossRef]
11. He, Y.; Zhang, N.; Ge, X.; Li, S.; Yang, L.; Kong, M.; Guo, Y.; Lv, C. Passion Fruit Disease Detection Using Sparse Parallel Attention Mechanism and Optical Sensing. *Agriculture* **2025**, *15*, 733. [CrossRef]
12. Sun, H.; Zheng, Q.; Yao, W.; Wang, J.; Liu, C.; Yu, H.; Chen, C. An Improved YOLOv8 Model for Detecting Four Stages of Tomato Ripening and Its Application Deployment in a Greenhouse Environment. *Agriculture* **2025**, *15*, 936. [CrossRef]
13. Chen, R.; Ren, L.; Yang, G.; Cheng, Z.; Zhao, D.; Zhang, C.; Feng, H.; Hu, H.; Yang, H. Estimation of Leaf Chlorophyll Content of Maize from Hyperspectral Data Using E2D-COS Feature Selection, Deep Neural Network, and Transfer Learning. *Agriculture* **2025**, *15*, 1072. [CrossRef]
14. Qi, Y.; Liu, T.; Guo, S.; Wu, P.; Ma, J.; Yuan, Q.; Yao, W.; Xu, T. Hyperspectral Imaging Combined with a Dual-Channel Feature Fusion Model for Hierarchical Detection of Rice Blast. *Agriculture* **2025**, *15*, 1673. [CrossRef]
15. Wang, N.; Li, S.; Qi, X.; Liu, M.; Yang, J.; Zhou, J.; Yu, L.; Yu, F.; Chen, C.; Wang, Y. Accurate Inversion of Rice LAI Using UAV-Based Hyperspectral Data: Integrating Days After Transplanting and Meteorological Factors. *Agriculture* **2025**, *15*, 2335. [CrossRef]
16. Fu, W.; Chen, Z.; Cheng, Q.; Li, Y.; Zhai, W.; Ding, F.; Kuang, X.; Chen, D.; Duan, F. Maize Leaf Area Index Estimation Based on Machine Learning Algorithm and Computer Vision. *Agriculture* **2025**, *15*, 1272. [CrossRef]
17. Yang, C.; Lei, J.; Liu, Z.; Xiong, S.; Xi, L.; Wang, J.; Qiao, H.; Shi, L. Estimation Model of Corn Leaf Area Index Based on Improved CNN. *Agriculture* **2025**, *15*, 481. [CrossRef]
18. Lu, C.; Yang, M.; Dong, S.; Liu, Y.; Li, Y.; Pan, Y. Improving Winter Wheat Yield Estimation Under Saline Stress by Integrating Sentinel-2 and Soil Salt Content Using Random Forest. *Agriculture* **2025**, *15*, 1544. [CrossRef]
19. Simeón, R.; Masslouhi, K.E.; Agenjos-Moreno, A.; Ricarte, B.; Uris, A.; Franch, B.; Rubio, C.; San Bautista, A. Machine Learning Applied to Crop Mapping in Rice Varieties Using Spectral Images. *Agriculture* **2025**, *15*, 1832. [CrossRef]
20. Xu, X.; Chen, S.; Li, Z.; Wu, Z.; Tan, Y.; Huang, S.; Lan, Y. Distribution Characteristics of Rotor Airflow and Droplet Deposition of Plant Protection UAVs Under Varying Rotor–Nozzle Distances. *Agriculture* **2025**, *15*, 1995. [CrossRef]
21. Li, M.; Guo, Y.; Guo, W.; Qiao, H.; Shi, L.; Liu, Y.; Zheng, G.; Zhang, H.; Wang, Q. Wheat Powdery Mildew Severity Classification Based on an Improved ResNet34 Model. *Agriculture* **2025**, *15*, 1580. [CrossRef]
22. Zhao, J.; Fan, S.; Zhang, B.; Wang, A.; Zhang, L.; Zhu, Q. Research Status and Development Trends of Deep Reinforcement Learning in the Intelligent Transformation of Agricultural Machinery. *Agriculture* **2025**, *15*, 1223. [CrossRef]
23. Tian, Y.; Wang, S.; Li, E.; Yang, G.; Liang, Z.; Tan, M. MD-YOLO: Multi-scale Dense YOLO for small target pest detection. *Comput. Electron. Agric.* **2023**, *213*, 108233. [CrossRef]
24. Li, H.; Chen, J.; Gu, Z.; Dong, T.; Chen, J.; Huang, J.; Gai, J.; Gong, H.; Lu, Z.; He, D. Optimizing edge-enabled system for detecting green passion fruits in complex natural orchards using lightweight deep learning model. *Comput. Electron. Agric.* **2025**, *234*, 110269. [CrossRef]
25. Chang, W.; Gu, S.; Wang, B.; Hu, S.; Li, R.; Guo, X. Estimating water use efficiency in maize: A UAV-based approach integrating multisensory data with SEBAL evapotranspiration modeling. *Comput. Electron. Agric.* **2025**, *237*, 110695. [CrossRef]
26. Guo, J.; Yang, Z.; Karkee, M.; Duan, J.; He, Y. Robotization of banana de-handing under multi-constraint scenarios: Challenges and future directions. *Artif. Intell. Agric.* **2025**, *15*, 1–11. [CrossRef]
27. Jung, J.; Maeda, M.; Chang, A.; Bhandari, M.; Ashapure, A.; Landivar-Bowles, J. The potential of remote sensing and artificial intelligence as tools to improve the resilience of agriculture production systems. *Curr. Opin. Biotechnol.* **2021**, *70*, 15–22. [CrossRef]

agriculture

MDPI

Article

Accurate Inversion of Rice LAI Using UAV-Based Hyperspectral Data: Integrating Days After Transplanting and Meteorological Factors

Nan Wang [1], Shilong Li [1], Xin Qi [1], Meihan Liu [1], Jiayi Yang [1], Jiulin Zhou [1], Lihong Yu [2], Fenghua Yu [1], Chunling Chen [1,*] and Yonghuan Wang [2,*]

[1] College of Information and Electrical Engineering, Shenyang Agricultural University, Shenyang 110866, China
[2] Liaoning Agriculture and Rural Development Service Center, Shenyang 110034, China
* Correspondence: chenchunling@syau.edu.cn (C.C.); gbzxflk@163.com (Y.W.)

Abstract: The leaf area index (LAI) is a key physiological parameter characterizing rice canopy structure and growth status. To face the limits of traditional destructive sampling, which is time-consuming, labor-intensive, and difficult to achieve large-scale dynamic detection, this study proposes a precise UAV-based hyperspectral inversion method for rice LAI using the fusion of Days After Transplantation and Meteorological Factors data (DATaMF). The study framework consisted of three key components: spectral preprocessing (smoothing-R_{SG}, resampling-R_{RS}, first derivative transformation-R_{FD}), spectral feature selection (SPA, CARS, Relief-F), and the construction and assessment of LAI inversion models (RF, ELM, XGBoost) that integrated DATaMF. The results show that (1) the three-level data preprocessing procedure—comprising R_{SG}, R_{RS}, and R_{FD}—coupled with the feature subset selected by the CARS method, demonstrates strong performance in LAI inversion; (2) the incorporation of DATaMF significantly improves rice LAI estimation, leading to improved model accuracy and robustness; and (3) the optimal LAI inversion model is achieved with the RF-based CARS-R_{FD}-DATaMF approach, yielding test set R^2, RMSE, and RPD values of 0.8015, 0.5745, and 2.2857, respectively. In conclusion, the hyperspectral LAI inversion method developed in this study, which integrates DATaMF, significantly enhances the model's accuracy and stability under small-sample conditions. This approach provides reliable technical support for efficient, precise, and dynamic monitoring of rice growth.

Keywords: LAI inversion; UAV; feature band selection; first derivative transformation; machine learning; rice

1. Introduction

Leaf area index (LAI) is a critical physiological parameter for characterizing rice canopy structure and growth [1], with significant influences on photosynthetic efficiency [2], transpiration rate [3,4], and final yield [5]. Conventional methods for obtaining LAI, including destructive sampling and canopy analyzers, are accurate [6] but limited by their time-consuming and labor-intensive procedures. These drawbacks make them impractical for the large-scale, high-frequency dynamic monitoring required in modern rice production systems.

In recent years, UAV-based hyperspectral remote sensing has emerged as a key technology in modern smart agriculture, owing to its unique capability for rapid, non-destructive, and multi-temporal acquisition of spectral information in the field [7]. In contrast to

https://doi.org/10.3390/agriculture15222335

multispectral data, hyperspectral data provide richer and more continuous spectral characteristics [8], which capture finer details on the physiological, biochemical, and structural properties of the rice canopy. This provides essential data support for the accurate and efficient inversion of rice LAI.

The precise inversion of LAI using UAV remote sensing has evolved through significant paradigm shifts, progressing from empirical statistical models to complex machine learning algorithms, and from broadband vegetation indices to narrowband hyperspectral features [9,10]. Early studies primarily estimated LAI by establishing statistical relationships between the parameter and traditional vegetation indices, such as the Normalized Difference Vegetation Index (NDVI) and the Enhanced Vegetation Index (EVI) [11]. Advances in sensor technology, along with a detailed understanding of the spectral response to crop physiological mechanisms, have gradually shifted the focus of remote sensing toward the refined mining and application of spectral features [12,13]. Studies indicate that the choice of bandwidth is a critical factor, as narrowband, mid-frequency, and broadband vegetation indices yield varying levels of accuracy in LAI inversion [14]. Meanwhile, the rapid development of machine learning algorithms such as Random Forests (RF) and Extreme Learning Machine (ELM) has demonstrated powerful nonlinear modeling capabilities [15], effectively establishing complex nonlinear mapping relationships between spectra and growth and physiological indicator, such as rice LAI, significantly improving the inversion accuracy of the model.

However, several challenges persist in inverting rice LAI using hyperspectral data. First, the stability of the canopy spectrum–LAI relationship can be compromised by complex field conditions, such as variations in soil background and illumination, as well as dynamically changing meteorological factors including temperature, wind speed, and relative humidity [16]. These factors adversely affect the accuracy and robustness of inversion models. Second, the high dimensionality and strong multicollinearity of the original UAV canopy spectral data, combined with a limited sample size, can induce the Hughes phenomenon [17], which reduces the model's generalization capability, obscures the true spectral–LAI interaction mechanisms, and limits the model's applicability across different rice varieties and growing environments. Furthermore, given that LAI is a dynamic parameter that evolves throughout the rice growth cycle, the integration of temporal phase information into inversion models becomes a critical consideration.

Therefore, to address the aforementioned challenges, this study proposes a precise UAV-based hyperspectral inversion strategy for rice LAI, driven by the integration of Days After Transplantation and Meteorological Factors (DATaMF) data, providing an effective solution for rice LAI inversion under small-sample conditions. The core contents of this study are as follows: (1) to extract key spectral information related to LAI through systematic spectral preprocessing and feature dimensionality reduction; (2) to investigate the influence of DATaMF incorporation on the inversion performance of different machine learning models; (3) to determine the optimal inversion model for rice LAI under small-sample conditions.

2. Materials and Methods

2.1. Trial Design and Research Area Overview

The experiment was conducted from June to September 2023 at the experimental field of the Precision Agriculture Aviation Research Base of Shenyang Agricultural University, Gengzhuang Town, Haicheng City, Anshan City, Liaoning Province, China (40°58′45″ N, 122°43′35″ E). The region is characterized by fertile soil, distinct seasons, and abundant rainfall, providing an ideal environment for rice cultivation. The rice cultivar used was 'Shennong 9816' (Shenyang, China). The layout of the experimental field is shown in

Figure 1. A total of five nitrogen fertilizer gradients were set, namely, zero nitrogen fertilizer, low nitrogen fertilizer, medium nitrogen fertilizer, standard nitrogen fertilizer, and high nitrogen fertilizer, which were, respectively, recorded as N0, N1, N2, N3, and N4, among which N3 was 220.5 kg/ha. The fertilizer was applied in a base-tillering-panicle ratio of 5:3:2. The application rates for N1, N2, and N4 were set at −50%, −25%, and +25% of N3, respectively. All plots received consistent field management practices. The field sampling period was from the tillering stage to the heading stage of rice, with a sampling interval of 4 days. A total of 141 sets of UAV canopy spectra and corresponding LAI data were collected.

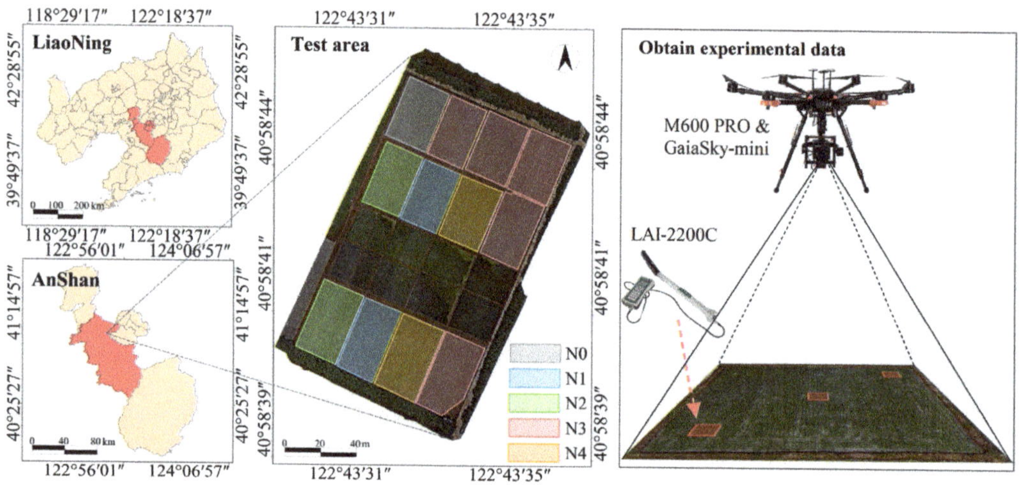

Figure 1. Schematic diagram of the study area location, nitrogen gradient experimental design, and data acquisition.

The overall technical route of this study is shown in Figure 2. Firstly, a three-level data preprocessing process, including Savitzky–Golay smooth denoising (R_{SG}), resampling (R_{RS}), and First derivative transformation (R_{FD}), is utilized to process the spectral data (R_{UAV}) collected by the UAV. The key feature bands in R_{RS} and R_{FD} are screened by combining three feature selection methods: Successive Projection Algorithm (SPA), Competitive Adaptive Reweighted Sampling (CARS), and Relevant Features (Relief-F). Meanwhile, DATaMF was introduced to construct the rice LAI inversion model based on three machine learning algorithms: Random Forests (RF), Extreme Learning Machine (ELM), and eXtreme Gradient Boosting (XGBoost), and the performance of the model was systematically evaluated and comparatively analyzed.

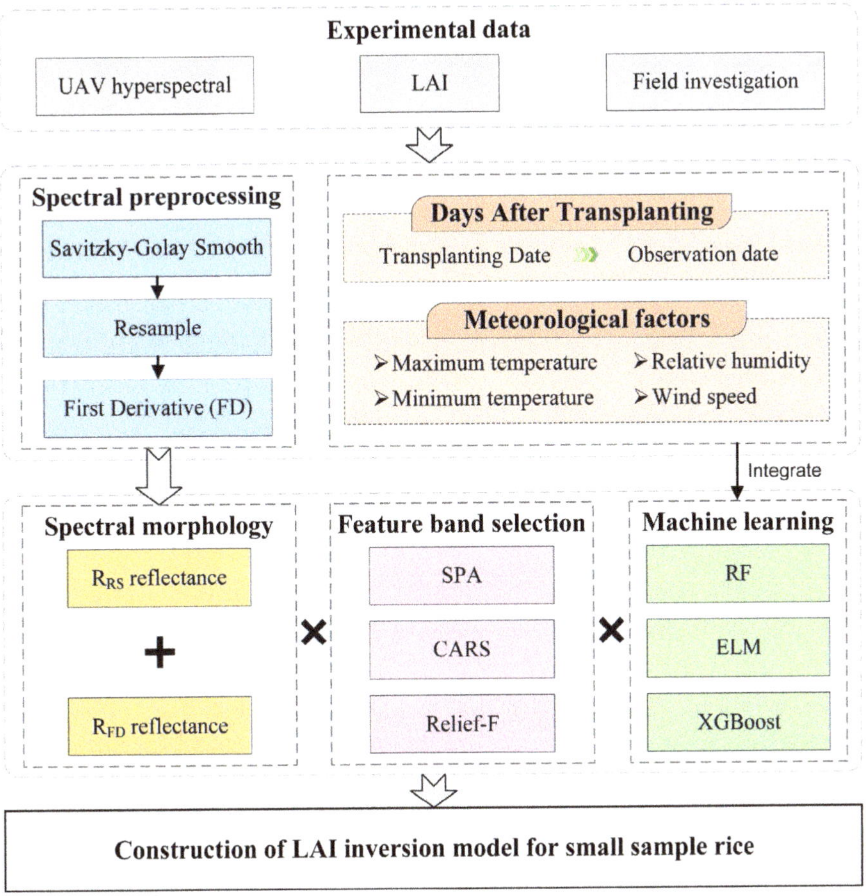

Figure 2. Technical flowchart for rice LAI inversion integrating DATaMF. Among them, the '+' indicates that spectral morphology includes R_{RS} (resampled reflectance) and R_{FD} (first derivative transformation); the '×' indicates that spectral morphology, Feature band selection, and Machine learning interact in combination.

2.2. Data Acquisition

2.2.1. Acquisition of UAV-Based Canopy Hyperspectral Data

In this study, the M600 PRO hexacopter UAV from Shenzhen DJI Innovation Co., Ltd. (Shenzhen, China) was used as the remote sensing platform, and at the same time, the GaiaSky-mini built-in push-broom hyperspectral imaging system from Dualix Spectral Imaging Co., Ltd. (Wuxi, China) was equipped to collect the data of hyperspectral images on the canopy of the rice UAV. The UAV was operated at a flight altitude of 100 m. The hyperspectral imager has a spectral resolution of 3.5 nm, covering a range of 400–1000 nm with 170 effective bands. The spatial resolution was 7 cm, with a single image acquisition time of 15 s and a frame rate of 162 fps. All data were acquired between 10:00 and 14:00 local time. Prior to each flight, dark current and whiteboard corrections were performed. At the same time, a 1.5 m × 1.5 m diffuse reflector with a reflectivity of 60% was placed simultaneously in the rice canopy observation area for the correction of reflection data in the later stage. Based on the SpectraVIEW spectral processing software (Dualix Spectral Imaging, Wuxi, China), the collected hyperspectral images were preprocessed for lens, uniformity, reflectance, etc. The ENVI5.3 + IDL tool software (GeoScene Information

Technology Co., Beijing, China) was used to extract the spectral reflectance data of the canopy layer of the rice UAV at the sampling points.

2.2.2. Acquisition of Rice Leaf Area Index (LAI) Data

In this study, the LAI-2200C plant canopy analyzer (Li-Cor, Inc., Lincoln, NE, USA) was used to measure the LAI of the rice canopy at ground level. The instrument determines LAI values by measuring radiation above and below the canopy using fisheye lens sensors. To ensure the reliability of the data, three measurement points were established in each test field. At each measurement point, three repeated measurements were carried out strictly in accordance with the instrument operation specifications, and the final average value was taken as the effective LAI value of the sampling area [18].

2.2.3. Acquisition and Organization of Data on Days After Transplantation and Meteorological Factors

In this study, data of Days After Transplantation and Meteorological Factors (DATaMF) were collected. Among them, the number of days after transplanting is defined as the growth days of rice from the date of transplanting. It was primarily calculated manually based on the recorded transplanting date and the dates of experimental observations. Meteorological factors, including minimum temperature, maximum temperature, wind speed, and relative humidity, were obtained from the ERA5 hourly data on single levels from 1979 to present [19]. The daily data used in this study were derived from hourly data processed and organized by the WheatA system. The detailed statistical results of meteorological factors are shown in Figure 3.

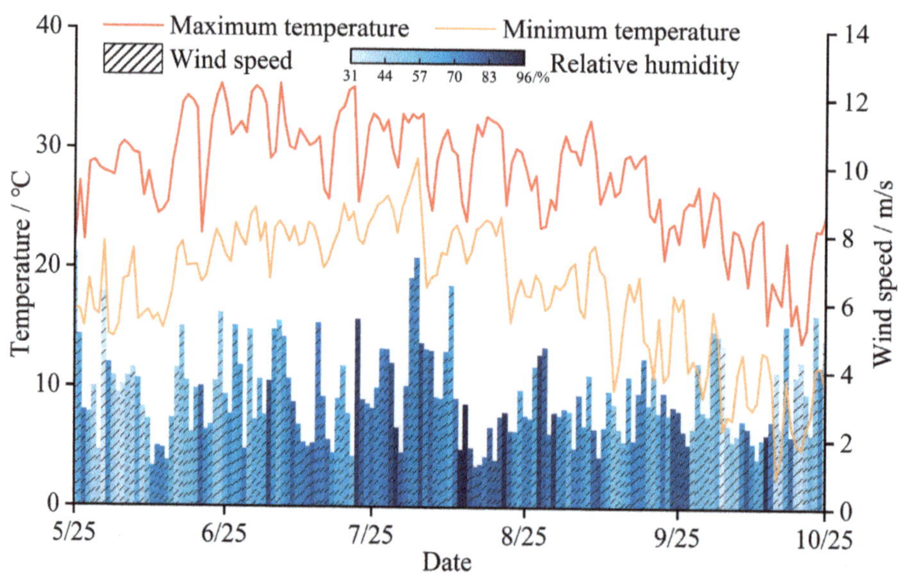

Figure 3. Time series of meteorological factors during the experimental period. Among them, the temperature data corresponds to the left-axis scale, the wind speed data corresponds to the right-axis scale, and the relative humidity data corresponds to the shade of blue.

2.3. *Spectral Preprocessing*

In the field of rice growth monitoring using UAV remote sensing, the accuracy of spectral data analysis is crucial. However, the collection of field spectral data is prone to interference from various environmental factors such as cloud cover, wind speed, and soil moisture content, resulting in a large amount of redundant noise information being mixed into the spectral curve and limiting the inversion accuracy of physical and chemical parameters of rice [20]. Therefore, in this study, Savitzky–Golay smoothing (R_{SG}) was applied to the UAV-collected spectral curves (R_{UAV}) using MATLAB R2024 [21].

In addition, the first derivative transformation represents the rate of change in the spectral curve and is one of the commonly used spectral transformation methods. It can enhance the spectral response characteristics to a certain extent [22–24], and its calculation formula is shown in Equation (1). Considering that the error in derivative calculation is directly related to the band interval $\Delta\lambda$, to ensure the calculation accuracy of derivative transformation, the spectral resolution of R_{SG} is resampled to a 1 nm interval (R_{RS}), and the first derivative transformation (R_{FD}) is performed on the spectral curve based on R_{RS}.

$$R_{FD}(\lambda_i) = \frac{dR_{RS}}{d\lambda} \approx \frac{R_{RS}(\lambda_{i+1}) - R_{RS}(\lambda_{i-1})}{2\Delta\lambda} \tag{1}$$

Among them, the $R_{FD}(\lambda_i)$ represents the wavelength λ_i reflectivity value after the first derivative transform, $R_{RS}(\lambda_i)$ represents the wavelength λ_i reflectivity, and $\Delta\lambda$ represents the adjacent wavelength interval.

2.4. Spectral Feature Extraction by Multi-Feature Band Selection Method

Considering that the spectral data obtained has a high dimension and strong correlation between bands, when dealing with the inversion problem in the small sample scenario, the computational complexity is relatively large, and it is prone to cause the "Hughes phenomenon" [25], which in turn affects the inversion accuracy of the physical and chemical parameters of rice. To improve computational efficiency and mitigate the interference of high-dimensional redundancy on feature selection, the spectral data of R_{RS} and R_{FD} are extracted at intervals of 5 nm before the selection of feature bands, reducing the spectral dimension.

In this study, three characteristic band selection methods, namely, SPA (Successive Projection Algorithm) [26], CARS (Competitive Adaptive Reweighted Sampling) [27] and Relief-F (Relevant Features) [28], were utilized—primarily implemented in MATLAB using the spa, carspls, and relief functions—to start from band independence, model contribution, and category separability, respectively, to achieve the characteristic band selection of multi-dimensional spectral data. SPA employs an iterative vector projection optimization approach to select band combinations with maximal information and minimal redundancy, making it suitable for handling strongly correlated spectral data [29]. CARS integrates an exponential decay function with adaptive reweighted sampling, emulating the "survival of the fittest" principle, which enhances model stability under small-sample conditions [30]. Relief-F is an instance-based filter feature selection method designed for multiclass problems [31]. It does not rely on a specific model and is relatively computationally efficient. Therefore, in this study, the above three methods were used to analyze the R_{RS} and R_{FD} at 5 nm intervals, and the characteristic band combinations that could effectively characterize the changes in rice LAI were screened out, providing key inputs for the subsequent construction of a small-sample hyperspectral inversion model of rice LAI.

2.5. Construction of Rice LAI Inversion Models Based on Different Machine Learning Algorithms

In order to systematically evaluate the impact of different machine learning algorithms on LAI inversion performance, this study selected three machine learning algorithms—Random Forests (RF) [32,33], Extreme Learning Machine (ELM) [34,35], and eXtreme Gradient Boosting (XGBoost) [36,37]—for constructing rice LAI inversion models. Prior to model construction, input data were normalized. Based on the experimental design, the input features were divided into two categories: one consisted of a subset of feature bands selected by feature selection methods from R_{RS} and R_{FD}; the other incorporated an extended feature set formed by adding DATaMF to the aforementioned inputs. By developing inversion models under these different feature combinations, this study aimed to capture the complex nonlinear relationships between spectra and rice LAI. Furthermore, to facilitate clearer comparison of inversion results across models, the R_{RS}, R_{FD}, R_{RS}-DATaMF, and R_{FD}-DATaMF datasets were split into training and testing sets in an 8:2 ratio, with consistent datasets ensured for the RF, ELM, and XGBoost models. The RF and ELM models were implemented in the MATLAB environment, primarily utilizing the built-in functions TreeBagger and elmtrain for model development, while XGBoost was implemented in Python 3.10.2 using the xgboost package 3.0.5.

2.6. Model Evaluation Method

In this study, the model performance was evaluated using the coefficient of determination (R^2), Root Mean Square Error (RMSE), and Relative Prediction Deviation (RPD) as the evaluation indicators for the rice LAI inversion model [38,39], and the calculation formulas are shown in Equations (2)–(4). The size of R^2 is mainly used to evaluate the fitting effect of the inversion model. The closer it is to 1, the better the fitting effect. RMSE serves as an evaluation criterion for the degree of difference between the predicted values and the true values of the inversion model. The smaller the value, the higher the accuracy of the model. RPD assesses the stability of the inversion model by comparing the ratio of RMSE to the standard deviation of the true value. When RPD < 1.4, the reliability of the inversion model is insufficient. Conversely, the model has better stability.

$$R^2 = 1 - \frac{\sum_{j=1}^{N}\left(y_{real_j} - \hat{y}_{pred_j}\right)^2}{\sum_{j=1}^{N}\left(y_{real_j} - \overline{y}_{real}\right)^2} \tag{2}$$

$$\text{RMSE} = \sqrt{\frac{\sum_{j=1}^{N}\left(\hat{y}_{pred_j} - y_{real_j}\right)^2}{N}} \tag{3}$$

$$\text{RPD} = \frac{SD}{\text{RMSE}} \tag{4}$$

Among them, y_{real_j} is the true value of the physicochemical parameter, $\overline{y}_{real}$ is the average value of the true value, $\hat{y}_{pred_j}$ is the predicted value of the inversion model, N is the total number of samples, and SD is the standard deviation of the true value of the samples.

3. Results

3.1. Results of Spectral Pretreatment

In this study, the acquired UAV spectral curves were preprocessed using the Savitzky–Golay smoothing, resampling, and first derivative transformation. The results are shown in Figure 4 (taking five samples as examples). Compared with Figure 4a, the Savitzky–Golay smoothing in Figure 4b significantly reduces the perturbation caused by moisture and environmental noise in the near-infrared region. It can be seen from Figure 4b,c that the spectral curve shape remains relatively stable after resampling. The result of the first derivative transformation is shown in Figure 4d. The spectral curve presents distinct peaks and troughs. That is, in the band region where the spectrum is relatively smooth and the rate of change is low in Figure 4c, the corresponding R_{FD} reflectance value approaches zero, forming a sharp and clear peak at the 720 nm band.

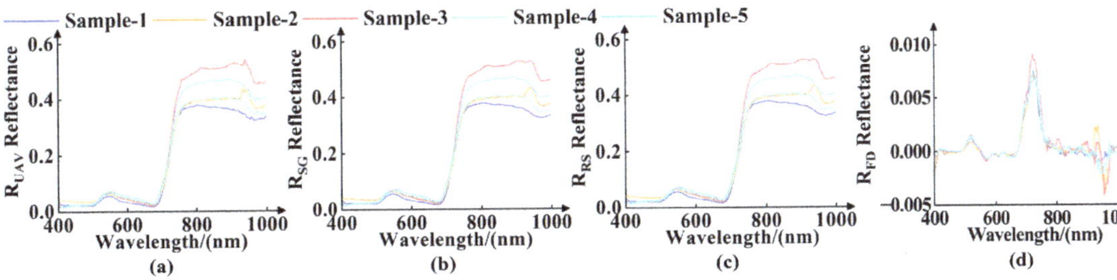

Figure 4. Preprocessing results of the spectral curve. (**a**) Spectral curves collected by UAV; (**b**) Savitzky–Golay smoothing results of spectral curves; (**c**) resampling results of the spectral curve; (**d**) the result of the first derivative transformation of the spectral curve.

3.2. Spectral Feature Extraction Results Based on the Multi-Feature Band Selection Method

In this study, three feature selection methods, namely, SPA, CARS, and Relief-F, were used to extract the characteristic bands of LAI in the R_{RS} and R_{FD} spectra, respectively. The specific results are as follows:

The feature bands selected by SPA are shown in Figure 5. It can be seen from Figure 5a,b that the overall trend of RMSE changes is roughly the same, first rapidly declining and then stabilizing. Moreover, the minimum RMSE is achieved when the number of variables is 5. The corresponding selected bands are indicated in Figure 5c,d. That is, five LAI characteristic bands were screened out from the R_{RS} and arranged in ascending order of the band sequence as 460, 535, 630, 675, and 770 nm, respectively. Five LAI characteristic bands were also screened out in the R_{FD} and arranged in ascending order of the band sequence as 835, 855, 910, 920, and 960 nm, respectively.

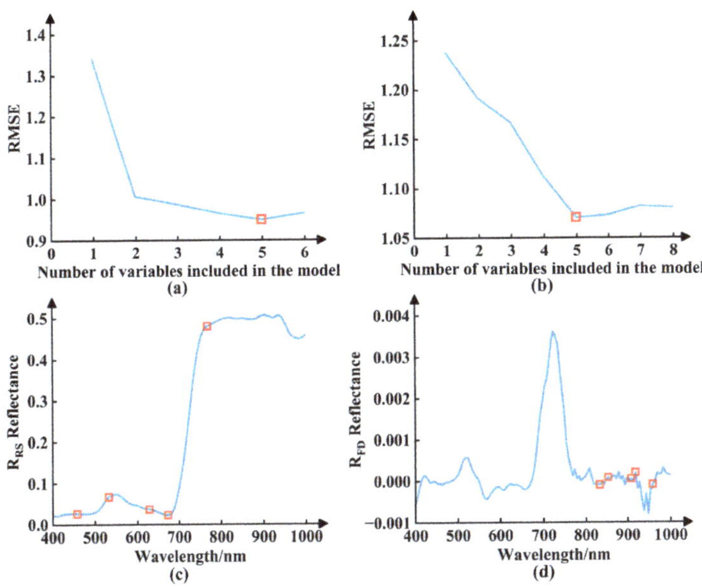

Figure 5. The results of SPA band screening. (**a**,**b**) are, respectively, the relationship graphs between RMSE and the number of variables under R_{RS} and R_{FD}; the red boxes highlight the optimal number of variables, which corresponds to the minimum RMSE. (**c**,**d**) represent R_{RS}, R_{FD} and the selected characteristic bands, respectively; the red boxes mark the specific wavelengths identified as the most sensitive to LAI variations.

The feature bands selected by CARS are shown in Figure 6. It can be seen from the figure that as the number of iterations increases, the number of variables based on R_{RS} and R_{FD} feature selection represented in Figure 6a,d both decline rapidly and then stabilize. Their RMSECV values reach the minimum at the 66th and 63rd iterations, respectively, and the optimal iteration points are marked in Figure 6c,f. In this study, the CARS feature selection method was utilized to screen out seven LAI feature bands in R_{RS}. Arranged in ascending order of the band sequence, they were 685, 805, 810, 815, 820, 840, and 845 nm, respectively. Nine LAI characteristic bands were screened out from the R_{FD} and arranged in ascending order of the band sequence as 425, 665, 670, 755, 775, 810, 835, 910, and 985 nm.

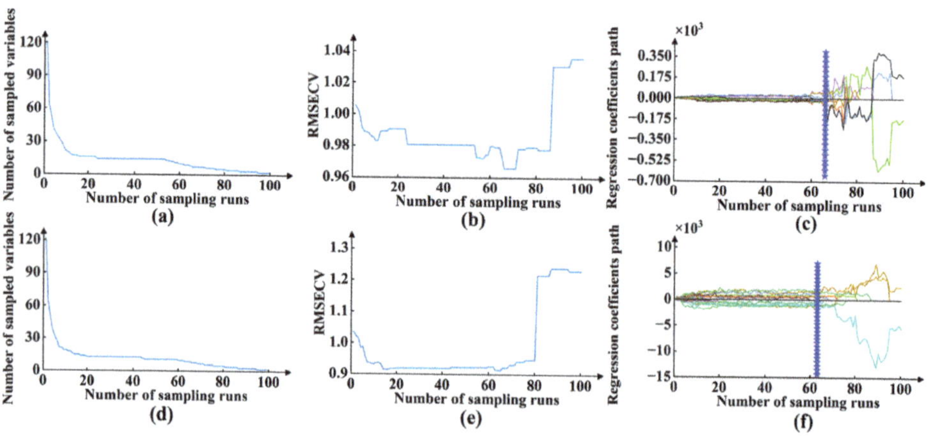

Figure 6. The results of CARS band screening. (**a**,**d**) are, respectively, the variation curves of the number of bands based on R_{RS} and R_{FD}; (**b**,**e**) are, respectively, the RMSECV variation curves based on R_{RS} and R_{FD}; (**c**,**f**) show the regression coefficient paths of each band derived from R_{RS} and R_{FD}, respectively. Each colored line traces the change in the regression coefficient of an individual wavelength variable throughout the algorithm's iterations. The blue stars on the x-axis indicate the optimal iteration points where the RMSECV reaches its minimum value during the CARS feature selection process.

Relief-F assigns weights to features by comparing the categories of neighboring samples. The positive and negative values and their magnitudes, respectively, represent the correlation (positive and negative) between the spectral bands and LAI, as well as the strength of the correlation between the two. It then ranks them in importance and retains the top 10% of the characteristic bands with the highest weights. The band screening results are shown in Figure 7. The upper and lower red lines in the figure represent the weight thresholds, dividing the image into upper, middle, and lower parts. The positive and negative correlated feature bands selected are, respectively, located in the upper and lower parts of the figure. That is, in this study, twelve LAI characteristic bands were screened out in R_{RS} based on Relief-F, and they were arranged in ascending order of the band sequence as 480, 485, 490, 495, 500, 505, 650, 655, 660, 665, 670, and 675 nm. Twelve LAI characteristic bands were screened out from the R_{FD} and arranged in ascending order of the band sequence as 465, 470, 870, 895, 910, 915, 930, 955, 975, 990, 995, and 1000 nm.

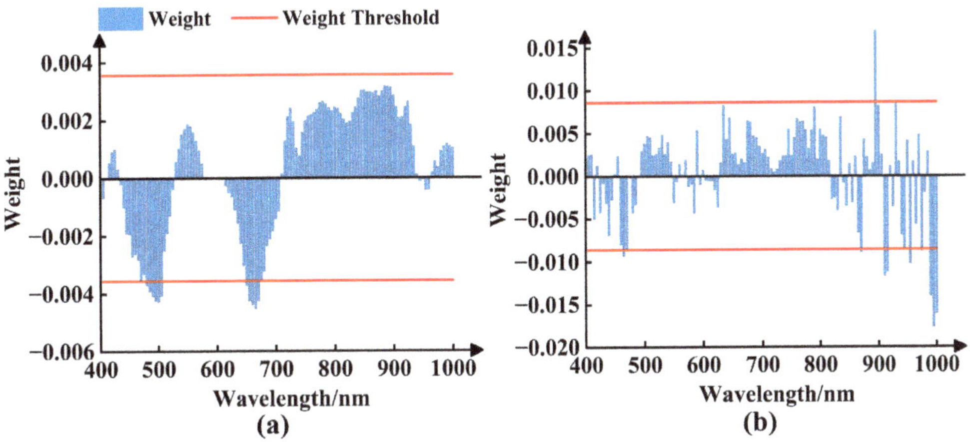

Figure 7. Relief-F band screening result graph. (**a**) represents the band weight values of R_{RS} and the screening results; (**b**) represents the band weight values of the R_{FD} and the screening results.

In summary, by comparing three different feature selection methods, namely, SPA, CARS, and Relief-F, this study found that they showed significant differences in R_{RS} and R_{FD}. The comparison results of the feature band screening are shown in Figure 8. In contrast, the SPA method can effectively capture the core spectral information of LAI inversion with very few bands. The screening results of the CARS method show obvious "cluster" characteristics, to a certain extent, retaining the synergy effect among continuous spectra. The screening results of the Relief-F method on R_{RS} are concentrated between 400 and 700 nm, while most of the screening results in R_{FD} are distributed between 800 and 1000 nm, indicating that the first derivative transformation can significantly enhance the spectral characteristics of the canopy structure in the near-infrared band.

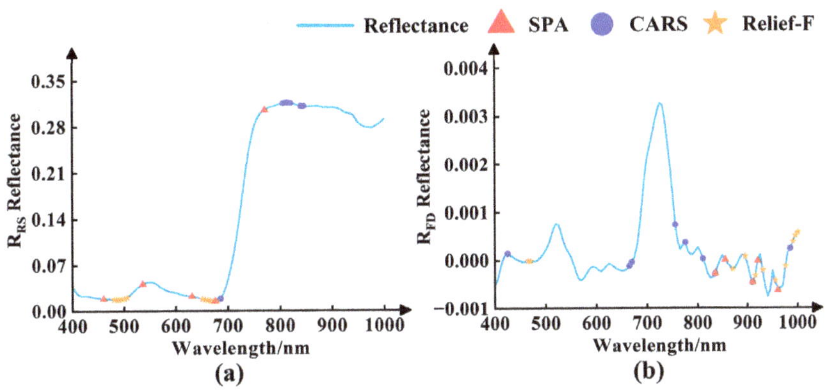

Figure 8. Comparison of multi-feature selection results. (**a**) The feature screening results based on R_{RS} for SPA, CARS, and Relief-F; (**b**) feature screening results based on R_{FD} for SPA, CARS, and Relief-F.

3.3. Inversion Results of Rice LAI Models Based on Different Machine Learning Algorithms

3.3.1. Summary of Rice LAI Inversion Results Based on Different Machine Learning Algorithms

To systematically evaluate the impact of different input features and machine learning algorithms on the performance of rice LAI inversion, this study constructed LAI inversion models using RF, ELM, and XGBoost. The models were built using spectral data R_{RS} and

R_{FD} processed by three feature selection methods (SPA, CARS, Relief-F), along with their fused versions with DATaMF (R_{RS}-DATaMF and R_{FD}-DATaMF). The inversion results of the top three optimal models under different machine learning algorithms are shown in Table 1, and the detailed fitting results of the models are shown in Figures 9–11.

Table 1. Statistical performance comparison of the three best-performing rice LAI inversion models for different machine learning algorithms.

Machine Learning Algorithm	Input Features	Training Set			Test Set		
		R^2	RMSE	RPD	R^2	RMSE	RPD
RF	CARS-R_{FD}-DATaMF	0.8560	0.5166	2.6466	0.8015	0.5745	2.2857
	SPA-R_{FD}-DATaMF	0.8026	0.6047	2.2610	0.7568	0.6360	2.0648
	CARS-R_{FD}	0.8413	0.5423	2.5214	0.7497	0.6451	2.0355
ELM	SPA-R_{FD}-DATaMF	0.7460	0.6860	1.9932	0.7069	0.6981	1.8810
	CARS-R_{FD}-DATaMF	0.7469	0.6848	1.9965	0.6969	0.7099	1.8498
	SPA-R_{RS}-DATaMF	0.7259	0.7127	1.9184	0.6857	0.7229	1.8166
XGBoost	CARS-R_{FD}-DATaMF	0.7409	0.6929	1.9732	0.6610	0.7508	1.7489
	Relief-F-R_{RS}-DATaMF	0.7456	0.6865	1.9916	0.6468	0.7664	1.7134
	SPA-R_{FD}-DATaMF	0.7334	0.7028	1.9455	0.6337	0.7805	1.6825

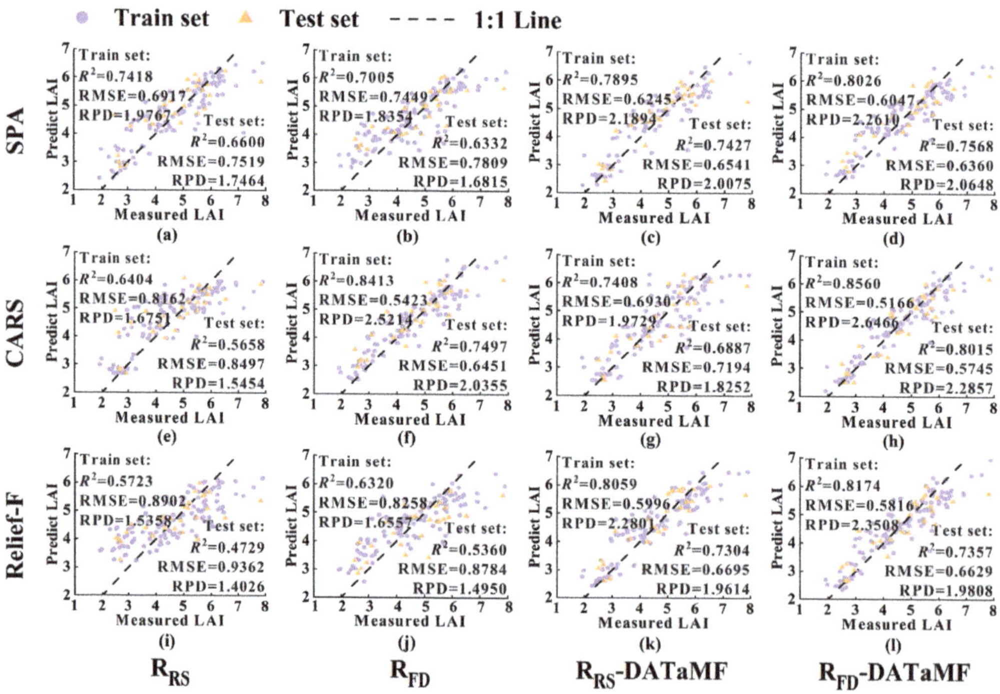

Figure 9. Results of rice LAI inversion based on the RF model under different input features. The feature selection method and the input data used for each subfigure are determined by the row and column labels of the overall figure.

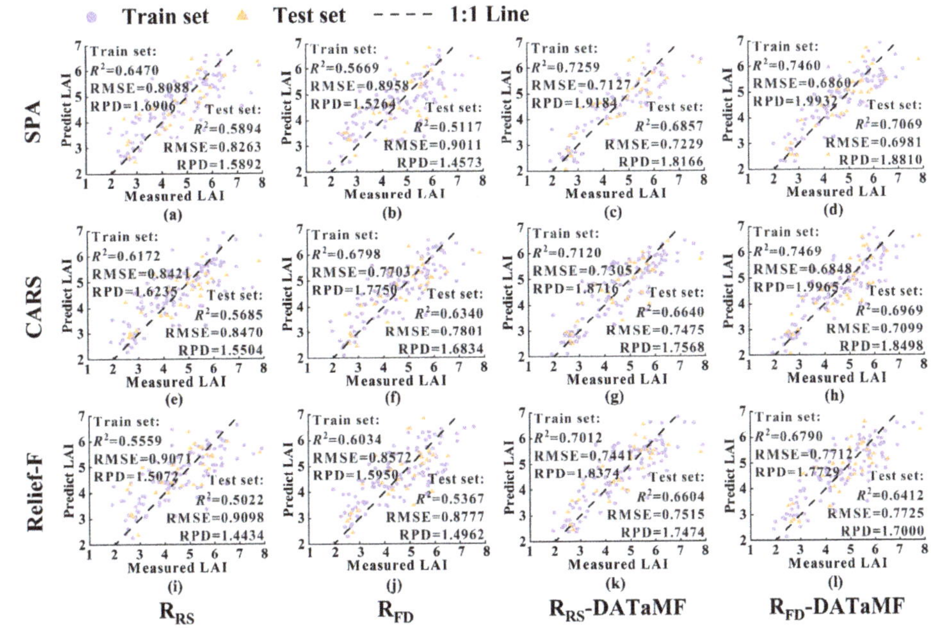

Figure 10. Results of rice LAI inversion based on the ELM model under different input features. The feature selection method and the input data used for each subfigure are determined by the row and column labels of the overall figure.

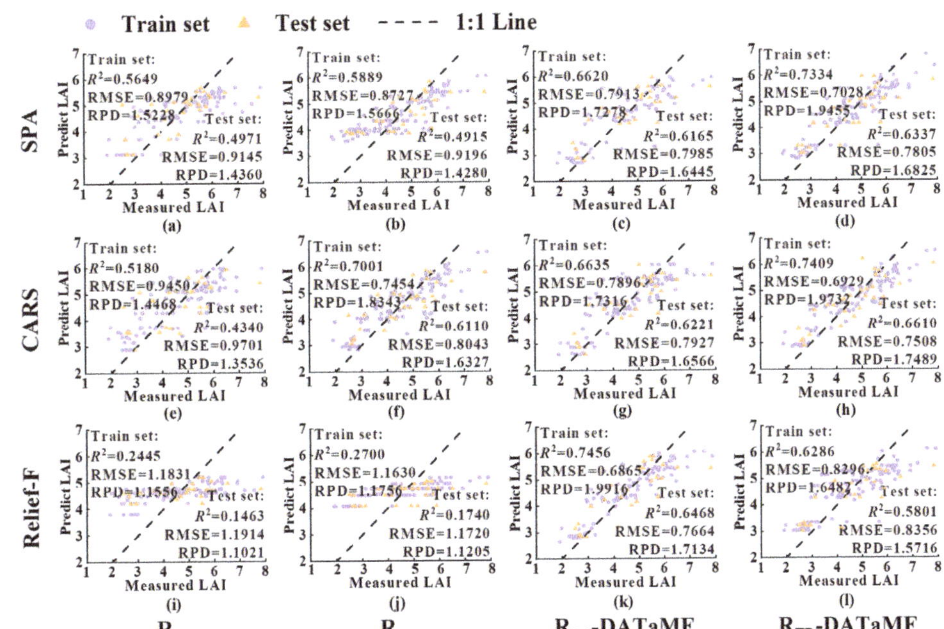

Figure 11. Results of rice LAI inversion based on the XGBoost model under different input features. The feature selection method and the input data used for each subfigure are determined by the row and column labels of the overall figure.

Overall, from the comprehensive inversion results in the figures, different spectral data preprocessing methods, feature selection algorithms, and the introduction of DATaMF significantly affected the performance of the LAI inversion models. Analyzing the nine inversion models in Table 1 from the perspective of feature selection methods reveals that only a few models were built based on feature bands selected by the Relief-F method. Furthermore, the inversion models built based on the CARS method generally outperformed those based on SPA. This indicates that the CARS method may have greater advantages in screening key features from the high-dimensional spectral data in this study.

A horizontal comparison of the three machine learning algorithms—RF, ELM, and XGBoost—showed that the inversion model built based on RF achieved the best fitting performance, with R^2, RMSE, and RPD values of 0.8015, 0.5745, and 2.2857, respectively, for the test set. In contrast, the best LAI inversion models under the ELM and XGBoost algorithms had test set R^2 values of 0.7069 and 0.6610, respectively, which were significantly lower than that of RF. This phenomenon preliminarily proves that when processing the fused data of spectrum and DATaMF, the RF algorithm may possess stronger anti-overfitting capabilities and a better ability to capture complex nonlinear relationships.

Additionally, another clear pattern emerged: among the top three inversion models for each of the RF, ELM, and XGBoost algorithms, the input features almost included the newly introduced DATaMF feature. This result indicates that introducing the DATaMF feature, which characterizes the rice growth process and meteorological data, has a significant positive incentive for improving the fitting performance of the LAI inversion model and substantially enhances the model's explanatory power for the rice growth process.

3.3.2. Comprehensive Comparison of Inversion Performance of Rice LAI Models Based on Different Machine Learning Algorithms

To sum up, by comparing the results of Section 3.3.1 in this study, it can be known that the optimal LAI inversion model is RF-based CARS-R_{FD}-DATaMF, and the R^2, RMSE, and RPD of its training set are 0.8560, 0.5166, and 2.6466, respectively; the R^2, RMSE and RPD of the test set are 0.8015, 0.5745, and 2.2857, respectively. This study further provides a comprehensive analysis of the rice LAI inversion models from three perspectives: feature selection, machine learning algorithms, and the inclusion of DATaMF, as follows:

The average performance of models grouped by feature selection method is summarized in Tables 2 and 3. Among them, "With R_{RS}" represents the LAI inversion model constructed based on the two-input data of R_{RS} and R_{RS}-DATaMF. "With R_{FD}" represents the LAI inversion model constructed based on two types of input data: R_{FD} and R_{FD}-DatAMF. It can be seen that the characteristic bands based on the CARS method combined with R_{FD} screening exhibit the best fitting performance, and the inversion result of LAI is the best. Based on the above analysis, it can be known that the selection of feature selection methods needs to be combined with the actual requirements of the model and through specific research and analysis, which is consistent with the research conclusions of relevant scholars [40].

Table 2. The training set results of LAI inversion models using different feature selection methods.

Performance Metrics	SPA		CARS		Relief-F	
	With R_{RS}	**With R_{FD}**	**With R_{RS}**	**With R_{FD}**	**With R_{RS}**	**With R_{FD}**
R^2	0.6885	0.6898	0.6487	0.7608	0.6042	0.6051
RMSE	0.7545	0.7511	0.8028	0.6587	0.8351	0.8380
RPD	1.8376	1.8547	1.7202	2.1245	1.7180	1.6997

Table 3. The test set results of LAI inversion models using different feature selection methods.

Performance Metrics	SPA		CARS		Relief-F	
	With R_{RS}	With R_{FD}	With R_{RS}	With R_{FD}	With R_{RS}	With R_{FD}
R^2	0.6319	0.6223	0.5905	0.6924	0.5265	0.5339
RMSE	0.7780	0.7860	0.8211	0.7380	0.8708	0.8665
RPD	1.7067	1.6992	1.6147	1.7901	1.5617	1.5607

The average performance of models grouped by machine learning algorithms is summarized in Tables 4 and 5. From the results, whether "With R_{RS}" or "With R_{FD}", RF achieved the best LAI inversion performance on both the training set and the test set. ELM's performance is second, while XGBoost's performance is relatively weak. This might be because RF can effectively reduce the model variance by constructing multiple decision trees and adopting the Bagging strategy. The random initialization weights of ELM may limit its full mining of complex nonlinear spectral features, while XGBoost, under a limited data scale, the mechanism of minimizing losses by constantly learning residuals is more susceptible to noise and outliers in the data. In conclusion, the rice LAI inversion model based on RF demonstrates superior robustness.

Table 4. The training set results of LAI inversion models using different machine learning algorithms.

Performance Metrics	RF		ELM		XGBoost	
	With R_{RS}	With R_{FD}	With R_{RS}	With R_{FD}	With R_{RS}	With R_{FD}
R^2	0.7151	0.7750	0.6598	0.6703	0.5664	0.6103
RMSE	0.7192	0.6360	0.7909	0.7775	0.8822	0.8344
RPD	1.9383	2.2118	1.7415	1.7765	1.5960	1.6906

Table 5. The test set results of LAI inversion models using different machine learning algorithms.

Performance Metrics	RF		ELM		XGBoost	
	With R_{RS}	With R_{FD}	With R_{RS}	With R_{FD}	With R_{RS}	With R_{FD}
R^2	0.6434	0.7021	0.6117	0.6212	0.4938	0.5252
RMSE	0.7635	0.6963	0.8008	0.7899	0.9056	0.8771
RPD	1.7481	1.9239	1.6506	1.6779	1.4844	1.5307

The average performance of models grouped by the inclusion of DATaMF is summarized in Tables 6 and 7. Among them, the LAI inversion models based on R_{RS}-DATaMF and R_{FD}-DATaMF are denoted as "DATaMF", and the LAI inversion models based on R_{RS} and R_{FD} are denoted as "No DATaMF". It can be seen that for the three machine learning algorithms of RF, ELM and XGBoost, the number of days after transplanting and meteorological factors, as the new feature sets introduced in this study, have both improved the robustness and accuracy of the rice LAI inversion model to a certain extent. Therefore, the introduction of DATaMF can provide new ideas for monitoring crop growth in dynamic environments.

Table 6. Results of the LAI inversion model training set before and after the introduction of DATaMF.

Performance Metrics	RF		ELM		XGBoost	
	No DATaMF	DATaMF	No DATaMF	DATaMF	No DATaMF	DATaMF
R^2	0.6880	0.8020	0.6117	0.7185	0.4811	0.6957
RMSE	0.7518	0.6033	0.8469	0.7216	0.9679	0.7488
RPD	1.8667	2.2835	1.6196	1.8983	1.4503	1.8363

Table 7. Results of the LAI inversion model test set before and after the introduction of DATaMF.

Performance Metrics	RF		ELM		XGBoost	
	No DATaMF	DATaMF	No DATaMF	DATaMF	No DATaMF	DATaMF
R^2	0.6029	0.7426	0.5571	0.6758	0.3923	0.6267
RMSE	0.8070	0.6527	0.8570	0.7337	0.9953	0.7874
RPD	1.6511	2.0209	1.5366	1.7919	1.3455	1.6696

4. Discussion

4.1. Analysis of the Results of Spectral Preprocessing and Characteristic Band Selection

This study implemented a three-stage preprocessing procedure comprising Savitzky–Golay smoothing (R_{SG}), resampling (R_{RS}), and first derivative transformation (R_{FD}). As can be seen from Figure 4a, R_{UAV} exhibits significant high-frequency fluctuations in the near-infrared region. This finding is consistent with the research results of Hong et al. [41], indicating that the process of collecting spectral data using UAVs is susceptible to unavoidable environmental factors such as leaf swaying caused by wind speed, cloud layer changes, and differences in soil background moisture [42]. The smoothed spectra R_{SG} effectively reduced noise while largely preserving the original spectral profile, thereby minimizing signal distortion and providing a more reliable basis for subsequent analysis. The effectiveness of this spectral smoothing method in the field of agricultural remote sensing has been widely verified by numerous scholars [43,44]. The calculation accuracy of the first derivative transformation depends on the uniformity and precision of the wavelength segment interval ($\Delta\lambda$) [45], which has been confirmed by scholars to be an effective spectral processing method [46]. Resampling the smoothed R_{SG} to a high-resolution interval of 1 nm can fundamentally reduce the computational error introduced by the band interval problem and further magnify the spectral details related to the physical and chemical parameters of rice.

As can be seen from the comparison of multi-feature selection results in Figure 8, there are significant differences in location and quantity among the three feature selection methods, namely SPA (Successive Projection Algorithm), CARS (Competitive Adaptive Reweighted Sampling), and Relief-F (Relevant Features). For example, SPA only selects spectral bands with low collinearity, resulting in relatively discrete selected bands, which is consistent with the findings of Li et al. [47]. Judging from the distribution of characteristic bands selected by CARS in R_{RS} and R_{FD}, the spectral features are distributed in different regions, corroborating the results of Wang et al. [48] that CARS can screen the band combinations with the greatest contribution to the model across the full band range. In contrast, the Relief-F method obtains spectral features containing more bands, and its selection results in R_{RS} and R_{FD} are concentrated in the visible light region and near-infrared region, respectively, showing a certain clustering phenomenon, which aligns with the conclusions of Ren et al. [49] regarding dimensionality reduction in hyperspectral images. From the results in Tables 2 and 3, it can be seen that the reason why the inversion model constructed by CARS combined with R_{FD} can achieve the best fitting effect may be that R_{FD} amplifies the features of the near-infrared region, and the adaptive re-weighted sampling mechanism of CARS can effectively deal with the overfitting problem under small sample data. The results of this study are consistent with the findings of Liu et al. [50], that is, the feature selection strategy combined with derivative transformation performs better than the inversion using R_{RS}.

4.2. The Influence of Different Machine Learning Algorithms and the Introduction of DATaMF on the Performance of Rice LAI Inversion Models

This study systematically evaluated the LAI inversion performance of three machine learning algorithms, namely, Random Forests (RF), Extreme Learning Machine (ELM), and eXtreme Gradient Boosting (XGBoost), before and after the introduction of the Days After Transplantation and Meteorological Factors (DATaMF) after rice transplantation. The results in Tables 4 and 5 show that, under the same input data, there are significant differences in the LAI fitting effects based on different machine learning algorithms. This phenomenon is similar to that observed by Zhang et al. [51] in estimating grassland aboveground biomass based on multiple machine learning algorithms. Among the inversion results of this study, RF demonstrated superior inversion performance. This might be because RF improves its generalization performance for small-sample data and high-dimensional features and is less affected by the noise and multicollinearity present in spectral data. This is consistent with the findings of Zhou et al. [52], that is, no inversion method is always optimal, but RF usually demonstrates a strong fitting ability.

One of the core innovations of this study is to input DATaMF as an additional new feature set along with the spectrum into the inversion model. The results in Tables 6 and 7 indicate that the introduction of DATaMF can enhance the accuracy and robustness of the model regardless of the machine learning algorithm used. It is worth affirming that this conclusion is consistent with that of Zare et al. [53], who introduced weather data for crop yield prediction. This is mainly because LAI increases significantly from the tillering stage to the heading stage [54], and the number of days after transplanting is an effective data that can characterize the physiological stage differences in rice. This highly resembles the view of Graf et al. [55] that phenological information is an important support for agricultural decision-making. Secondly, meteorological conditions of high temperature and low humidity are prone to cause rice to curl. Strong wind conditions will increase the disturbance of the canopy structure, leading to spectral noise and subsequently affecting the canopy spectrum. In the study of Fan et al. [56] on estimating potato yield, the importance of environmental variables was also recognized, and these data were successfully used to achieve the most accurate potato yield estimation [57].

However, this study also has some limitations. The limited diversity of meteorological factors and rice varieties may limit the generalizability of the model. Secondly, the quantification of the contributions from meteorological factors and their interactions requires further in-depth analysis. Future research could be extended to multiple regions and varieties to further validate the model's transferability.

5. Conclusions

In this study, to improve the accuracy of UAV hyperspectral inversion of rice LAI under the condition of small samples, we proposed an inversion method integrating Days After Transplanting and Meteorological Factors (DATaMF) data. By systematically comparing different spectral preprocessing schemes, feature selection algorithms, and machine learning models, the following main conclusions are drawn:

(1) The three-level preprocessing procedure—comprising the Savitzky–Golay smoothing (R_{SG}), resampling (R_{RS}), and first derivative transformation (R_{FD})—effectively

eliminates environmental noise and enhances spectral features, thereby providing high-quality input for subsequent modeling. The spectral subset selected by Competitive Adaptive Reweighted Sampling (CARS) in combination with R_{FD} further improves the model's performance in estimating rice LAI.

(2) The introduction of the DATaMF feature set significantly enhances the accuracy and robustness of the LAI inversion model. Results indicate that after integrating DATaMF, the test set exhibits an average increase in R^2 of approximately 0.1643, an average decrease in RMSE of approximately 0.1618, and an average increase in RPD of 0.3164.

(3) Among the three machine learning algorithms—RF, ELM, and XGBoost—the RF-based CARS-R_{FD}-DATaMF model achieves the best inversion performance, with test set R^2, RMSE, and RPD values of 0.8015, 0.5745, and 2.2857, respectively. This model is capable of meeting the requirements for precise and dynamic monitoring of LAI throughout the rice growth process.

Author Contributions: Conceptualization, M.L.; methodology, X.Q.; software, J.Y.; validation, J.Z.; formal analysis, N.W.; investigation, S.L.; resources, F.Y.; data curation, M.L.; writing—original draft preparation, N.W.; writing—review and editing, S.L.; visualization, N.W.; supervision, F.Y. and L.Y.; project administration, C.C.; funding acquisition, F.Y., C.C. and Y.W. All authors have read and agreed to the published version of the manuscript.

Funding: This research was funded by the Science and Technology Plan Project of Inner Mongolia Autonomous Region (Grant No. 2025SYFDZ0411), and the National Key R&D Program of China (Grant No. 2024YFD2300100).

Institutional Review Board Statement: Not applicable.

Data Availability Statement: The raw data supporting the conclusions of this article will be made available by the authors on request.

Acknowledgments: We would like to thank the editors and reviewers for their professional advice on this manuscript.

Conflicts of Interest: The authors declare no conflicts of interest.

References

1. Liu, Y.; Wang, B.; Tao, J.F.; Tian, S.J.; Sheng, Q.H.; Li, J.; Wang, S.W.; Liu, X.L.; He, H.L. Canopy structure dynamics constraints and time sequence alignment for improving retrieval of rice leaf area index from multi-temporal Sentinel-1 imagery. *Comput. Electron. Agric.* **2024**, *227*, 109658. [CrossRef]
2. Jin, Z.Y.; Liu, H.Z.; Cao, H.N.; Li, S.L.; Yu, F.H.; Xu, T.Y. Hyperspectral Remote Sensing Estimation of Rice Canopy LAI and LCC by UAV Coupled RTM and Machine Learning. *Agriculture* **2025**, *15*, 11. [CrossRef]
3. Yuan, W.S.; Meng, Y.; Li, Y.; Ji, Z.G.; Kong, Q.M.; Gao, R.; Su, Z.B. Research on rice leaf area index estimation based on fusion of texture and spectral information. *Comput. Electron. Agric.* **2023**, *211*, 108016. [CrossRef]
4. Wei, H.H.; Geng, X.Y.; Zhang, X.; Zhu, W.; Zhang, X.B.; Chen, Y.L.; Huo, Z.Y.; Zhou, G.S.; Meng, T.Y.; Dai, Q.G. Grain Yield, Biomass Accumulation, and Leaf Photosynthetic Characteristics of Rice under Combined Salinity-Drought Stress. *Rice Sci.* **2024**, *31*, 118–128. [CrossRef]
5. Wu, T.Z.; Zhang, Z.W.; Wang, Q.; Jin, W.J.; Meng, K.; Wang, C.; Yin, G.F.; Xu, B.D.; Shi, Z.H. Estimating rice leaf area index at multiple growth stages with Sentinel-2 data: An evaluation of different retrieval algorithms. *Eur. J. Agron.* **2024**, *161*, 127362. [CrossRef]
6. Du, R.Q.; Chen, J.Y.; Xiang, Y.Z.; Zhang, Z.T.; Yang, N.; Yang, X.Z.; Tang, Z.J.; Wang, H.; Wang, X.; Shi, H.Z.; et al. Incremental learning for crop growth parameters estimation and nitrogen diagnosis from hyperspectral data. *Comput. Electron. Agric.* **2023**, *215*, 108356. [CrossRef]
7. Yu, F.H.; Bai, J.C.; Jin, Z.Y.; Guo, Z.H.; Yang, J.X.; Chen, C.L. Combining the critical nitrogen concentration and machine learning algorithms to estimate nitrogen deficiency in rice from UAV hyperspectral data. *J. Integr. Agric.* **2023**, *22*, 1216–1229. [CrossRef]
8. Guo, A.T.; Ye, H.C.; Huang, W.J.; Qian, B.X.; Wang, J.J.; Lan, Y.B.; Wang, S.Z. Inversion of maize leaf area index from UAV hyperspectral and multispectral imagery. *Comput. Electron. Agric.* **2023**, *212*, 108020. [CrossRef]

9. Zhou, Y.X.; Li, X.J.; Chen, C.; Zhou, L.; Zhao, Y.Y.; Chen, J.J.; Tan, C.; Sun, J.Q.; Zhang, L.J.; Hu, M.C.; et al. Coupling the PROSAIL Model and Machine Learning Approach for Canopy Parameter Estimation of Moso Bamboo Forests from UAV Hyperspectral Data. *Forests* **2024**, *15*, 946. [CrossRef]
10. Li, J.T.; Wijewardane, N.K.; Ge, Y.F.; Shi, Y.Y. Improved chlorophyll and water content estimations at leaf level with a hybrid radiative transfer and machine learning model. *Comput. Electron. Agric.* **2023**, *206*, 107669. [CrossRef]
11. Kamal, M.; Phinn, S.; Johansen, K. Assessment of multi-resolution image data for mangrove leaf area index mapping. *Remote Sens. Environ.* **2016**, *176*, 242–254. [CrossRef]
12. Garofalo, S.P.; Ardito, F.; Sanitate, N.; De Carolis, G.; Ruggieri, S.; Giannico, V.; Rana, G.; Ferrara, R.M. Robustness of Actual Evapotranspiration Predicted by Random Forest Model Integrating Remote Sensing and Meteorological Information: Case of Watermelon (*Citrullus lanatus*, (Thunb.) Matsum. & Nakai, 1916). *Water* **2025**, *17*, 323. [CrossRef]
13. Duan, B.; Liu, Y.; Gong, Y.; Peng, Y.; Wu, X.; Zhu, R.; Fang, S. Remote estimation of rice LAI based on Fourier spectrum texture from UAV image. *Plant Methods* **2019**, *15*, 124. [CrossRef] [PubMed]
14. Liang, L.; Huang, T.; Di, L.P.; Geng, D.; Yan, J.; Wang, S.G.; Wang, L.J.; Li, L.; Chen, B.Q.; Kang, J.R. Influence of Different Bandwidths on LAI Estimation Using Vegetation Indices. *IEEE J. Sel. Top. Appl. Earth Obs. Remote Sens.* **2020**, *13*, 1494–1502. [CrossRef]
15. Kganyago, M.; Adjorlolo, C.; Mhangara, P.; Tsoeleng, L. Optical remote sensing of crop biophysical and biochemical parameters: An overview of advances in sensor technologies and machine learning algorithms for precision agriculture. *Comput. Electron. Agric.* **2024**, *218*, 108730. [CrossRef]
16. Qi, H.M.; Chen, A.; Yang, X.C.; Xing, X.Y. Estimation of crude protein content in natural pasture grass using unmanned aerial vehicle hyperspectral data. *Comput. Electron. Agric.* **2025**, *229*, 109714. [CrossRef]
17. Liu, K.; Zhou, Q.B.; Wu, W.B.; Xia, T.; Tang, H.J. Estimating the crop leaf area index using hyperspectral remote sensing. *J. Integr. Agric.* **2016**, *15*, 475–491. [CrossRef]
18. Li, S.L.; Jin, Z.Y.; Bai, J.C.; Xiang, S.; Xu, C.Y.; Yu, F.H. Research on fertilization decision method for rice tillering stage based on the coupling of UAV hyperspectral remote sensing and WOFOST. *Front. Plant Sci.* **2024**, *15*, 1405239. [CrossRef]
19. Hersbach, H.; Bell, B.; Berrisford, P.; Biavati, G.; Horányi, A.; Muñoz Sabater, J.; Nicolas, J.; Peubey, C.; Radu, R.; Rozum, I.; et al. ERA5 hourly data on single levels from 1940 to present. *Copernic. Clim. Change Serv. C3S Clim. Data Store CDS* **2023**. [CrossRef]
20. Gao, C.R.; Li, H.; Wang, J.C.; Zhang, X.; Huang, K.M.; Song, X.Y.; Yang, W.D.; Feng, M.C.; Xiao, L.J.; Zhao, Y.; et al. Combined use of spectral resampling and machine learning algorithms to estimate soybean leaf chlorophyll. *Comput. Electron. Agric.* **2024**, *218*, 108675. [CrossRef]
21. Lu, B.; Liu, N.; Li, H.; Yang, K.; Hu, C.; Wang, X.; Li, Z.; Shen, Z.; Tang, X. Quantitative determination and characteristic wavelength selection of available nitrogen in coco-peat by NIR spectroscopy. *Soil Tillage Res.* **2019**, *191*, 266–274. [CrossRef]
22. Song, G.M.; Wang, Q.; Jin, J. Estimation of leaf photosynthetic capacity parameters using spectral indices developed from fractional-order derivatives. *Comput. Electron. Agric.* **2023**, *212*, 108068. [CrossRef]
23. Jin, J.; Wang, Q. Hyperspectral indices developed from the low order fractional derivative spectra can capture leaf dry matter content across a variety of species better. *Agric. For. Meteorol.* **2022**, *322*, 109007. [CrossRef]
24. Xiao, B.; Li, S.Z.; Dou, S.Q.; He, H.C.; Fu, B.L.; Zhang, T.X.; Sun, W.W.; Yang, Y.L.; Xiong, Y.K.; Shi, J.K.; et al. Comparison of leaf chlorophyll content retrieval performance of citrus using FOD and CWT methods with field-based full-spectrum hyperspectral reflectance data. *Comput. Electron. Agric.* **2024**, *217*, 108559. [CrossRef]
25. Hughes, G. On the mean accuracy of statistical pattern recognizers. *IEEE Trans. Inf. Theory* **1968**, *14*, 55–63. [CrossRef]
26. Zhang, B.Y.; Gu, L.M.; Dai, M.L.; Bao, X.Y.; Sun, Q.; Zhang, M.Z.; Qu, X.Z.; Li, Z.H.; Zhen, W.C.; Gu, X.H. Estimation of grain filling rate of winter wheat using leaf chlorophyll and LAI extracted from UAV images. *Field Crops Res.* **2024**, *306*, 109198. [CrossRef]
27. Zhou, X.F.; Sun, R.J.; Zhang, Z.J.; Song, Y.Y.; Jin, L.J.; Yuan, L. Improved Leaf Chlorophyll Content Estimation with Deep Learning and Feature Optimization Using Hyperspectral Measurements. *Phyton-Int. J. Exp. Bot.* **2025**, *94*, 503–519. [CrossRef]
28. Zhang, H.Y.; He, L.; Chen, Q.W.; Abdulraheem, M.I.; Ma, G.; Zhang, Y.F.; Gu, J.J.; Hu, J.D.; Wang, C.Y.; Feng, W. Multi-angular spectroscopic detection of winter wheat nitrogen fertilizer utilization status using integrated feature selection and machine learning. *Comput. Electron. Agric.* **2025**, *231*, 109916. [CrossRef]
29. Yan, K.T.; Song, X.B.; Yang, J.; Xiao, J.Q.; Xu, X.D.; Guo, J.; Zhu, H.Y.; Lan, Y.B.; Zhang, Y.L. Citrus huanglongbing detection: A hyperspectral data-driven model integrating feature band selection with machine learning algorithms. *Crop Prot.* **2025**, *188*, 107008. [CrossRef]
30. Wang, Z.L.; Huang, W.Q.; Li, J.B.; Liu, S.Q.; Fan, S.X. Assessment of protein content and insect infestation of maize seeds based on on-line near-infrared spectroscopy and machine learning. *Comput. Electron. Agric.* **2023**, *211*, 107969. [CrossRef]
31. Spolaôr, N.; Cherman, E.A.; Monard, M.C.; Lee, H.D. ReliefF for Multi-label Feature Selection. In Proceedings of the 2nd Brazilian Conference on Intelligent Systems (BRACIS), Fortaleza, Brazil, 19–24 October 2013; pp. 6–11.

32. Ihalainen, O.; Sandmann, T.; Rascher, U.; Mottus, M. Illumination correction for close-range hyperspectral images using spectral invariants and random forest regression. *Remote Sens. Environ.* **2024**, *315*, 114467. [CrossRef]
33. Guo, S.; Feng, Z.; Wang, P.; Chang, J.; Han, H.; Li, H.; Chen, C.; Du, W. Mapping and Classification of the Liaohe Estuary Wetland Based on the Combination of Object-Oriented and Temporal Features. *IEEE Access* **2024**, *12*, 60496–60512. [CrossRef]
34. Huang, G.B.; Zhu, Q.Y.; Siew, C.K. Extreme learning machine: Theory and applications. *Neurocomputing* **2006**, *70*, 489–501. [CrossRef]
35. Li, S.; Jin, Z.; Wang, N.; Guo, S.; Bai, J.; Yu, F.; Tian, M. Research on the optimal fertilization decision method for rice economy based on PROSAIL-WOFOST optimal coupling unit. *Comput. Electron. Agric.* **2025**, *238*, 110840. [CrossRef]
36. Ye, M.; Zhu, L.; Li, X.; Ke, Y.; Huang, Y.; Chen, B.; Yu, H.; Li, H.; Feng, H. Estimation of the soil arsenic concentration using a geographically weighted XGBoost model based on hyperspectral data. *Sci. Total Environ.* **2023**, *858*, 159798. [CrossRef]
37. Guan, Q.; Qiao, S.; Feng, S.; Du, W. Investigation of Peanut Leaf Spot Detection Using Superpixel Unmixing Technology for Hyperspectral UAV Images. *Agriculture* **2025**, *15*, 597. [CrossRef]
38. Xu, L.C.; Su, X.Y.; Wang, K.T.; Zhou, T.; Lu, C.H.; Niu, J.Q.; Jin, X.C.; Huang, J.Q.; Feng, H.L. Enhancing canopy nitrogen estimation in Torreya Grandis based on advanced SLIC-EVI and HMT-seCNN methods using hyperspectral UAV data. *Comput. Electron. Agric.* **2025**, *231*, 109977. [CrossRef]
39. Xiang, S.; Bai, J.C.; Jin, Z.Y.; Li, S.L.; Yu, F.H.; Xu, T.Y. PIOSL-5 With Nitrogen as an Independent Input Parameter and Accurate Estimation of Leaf Nitrogen. *IEEE Trans. Geosci. Remote Sens.* **2025**, *63*, 5513813. [CrossRef]
40. Bai, J.; Zhu, S.Y.; Hao, Y.C.; Li, X.Z.; Yang, C.B.; Wang, C.; Qiao, X.X.; Feng, M.C.; Xiao, L.J.; Song, X.Y.; et al. Comparative analysis of the effects of different dimensionality reduction algorithms on hyperspectral estimation of total nitrogen content in wheat soils. *Eur. J. Agron.* **2025**, *168*, 127660. [CrossRef]
41. Hong, Y.; Guo, L.; Chen, S.; Linderman, M.; Mouazen, A.M.; Yu, L.; Chen, Y.; Liu, Y.; Liu, Y.; Cheng, H.; et al. Exploring the potential of airborne hyperspectral image for estimating topsoil organic carbon: Effects of fractional-order derivative and optimal band combination algorithm. *Geoderma* **2020**, *365*, 114228. [CrossRef]
42. Gao, J.; Meng, B.; Liang, T.; Feng, Q.; Ge, J.; Yin, J.; Wu, C.; Cui, X.; Hou, M.; Liu, J.; et al. Modeling alpine grassland forage phosphorus based on hyperspectral remote sensing and a multi-factor machine learning algorithm in the east of Tibetan Plateau, China. *ISPRS J. Photogramm. Remote Sens.* **2019**, *147*, 104–117. [CrossRef]
43. Tan, J.; Ding, J.; Wang, Z.; Han, L.; Wang, X.; Li, Y.; Zhang, Z.; Meng, S.; Cai, W.; Hong, Y. Estimating soil salinity in mulched cotton fields using UAV-based hyperspectral remote sensing and a Seagull Optimization Algorithm-Enhanced Random Forest Model. *Comput. Electron. Agric.* **2024**, *221*, 109017. [CrossRef]
44. Yang, Z.; Tian, J.; Wang, Z.; Feng, K. Monitoring the photosynthetic performance of grape leaves using a hyperspectral-based machine learning model. *Eur. J. Agron.* **2022**, *140*, 126589. [CrossRef]
45. Tsai, F.; Philpot, W. Derivative Analysis of Hyperspectral Data. *Remote Sens. Environ.* **1998**, *66*, 41–51. [CrossRef]
46. Yu, Y.; Yu, H.; Li, X.; Zhang, L.; Sui, Y. Prediction of Potassium Content in Rice Leaves Based on Spectral Features and Random Forests. *Agronomy* **2023**, *13*, 2337. [CrossRef]
47. Song, L.; Wang, L.; Yang, Z.; He, L.; Feng, Z.; Duan, J.; Feng, W.; Guo, T. Comparison of algorithms for monitoring wheat powdery mildew using multi-angular remote sensing data. *Crop J.* **2022**, *10*, 1312–1322. [CrossRef]
48. Wang, Y.; Chen, S.; Hong, Y.; Hu, B.; Peng, J.; Shi, Z. A comparison of multiple deep learning methods for predicting soil organic carbon in Southern Xinjiang, China. *Comput. Electron. Agric.* **2023**, *212*, 108067. [CrossRef]
49. Ren, J.; Wang, R.; Liu, G.; Feng, R.; Wang, Y.; Wu, W. Partitioned Relief-F Method for Dimensionality Reduction of Hyperspectral Images. *Remote Sens.* **2020**, *12*, 1104. [CrossRef]
50. Liu, H.; Chen, J.Y.; Xiang, Y.Z.; Geng, H.S.; Yang, X.Z.; Yang, N.; Du, R.Q.; Wang, Y.; Zhang, Z.T.; Shi, L.S.; et al. Improving UAV hyperspectral monitoring accuracy of summer maize soil moisture content with an ensemble learning model fusing crop physiological spectral responses. *Eur. J. Agron.* **2024**, *160*, 127299. [CrossRef]
51. Zhang, R.; Feng, Q.; Zhang, Y.; Mai, J.; Liang, T. Estimation and trend analysis of grassland aboveground biomass on the Qinghai-Xizang Plateau based on machine learning. *Ecol. Indic.* **2025**, *177*, 113715. [CrossRef]
52. Zhou, X.J.; Liang, B.; He, J.N.; He, W. Accurate leaf area index estimation for Eucalyptus grandis using machine learning method with GF-6 WFV-A case study for Huangmian town, China. *Front. For. Glob. Change* **2024**, *7*, 1420533. [CrossRef]
53. Zare, H.; Viswanathan, M.; Weber, T.K.D.; Ingwersen, J.; Nowak, W.; Gayler, S.; Streck, T. Improving winter wheat yield prediction by accounting for weather and model parameter uncertainty while assimilating LAI and updating weather data within a crop model. *Eur. J. Agron.* **2024**, *156*, 127149. [CrossRef]
54. Fukuda, S.; Koba, K.; Okamura, M.; Watanabe, Y.; Hosoi, J.; Nakagomi, K.; Maeda, H.; Kondo, M.; Sugiura, D. Novel technique for non-destructive LAI estimation by continuous measurement of NIR and PAR in rice canopy. *Field Crops Res.* **2021**, *263*, 108070. [CrossRef]
55. Graf, L.V.; Merz, Q.N.; Walter, A.; Aasen, H. Insights from field phenotyping improve satellite remote sensing based in-season estimation of winter wheat growth and phenology. *Remote Sens. Environ.* **2023**, *299*, 113860. [CrossRef]

56. Fan, Y.; Liu, Y.; Yue, J.; Jin, X.; Chen, R.; Bian, M.; Ma, Y.; Yang, G.; Feng, H. Estimation of potato yield using a semi-mechanistic model developed by proximal remote sensing and environmental variables. *Comput. Electron. Agric.* **2024**, *223*, 109117. [CrossRef]
57. Yang, J.; Zhang, Y.-Z.; He, H.-H.; Li, Y.-C.; Chen, X.-R.; Bian, J.-M.; Jin, G.-H.; Li, X.-X.; Huang, S.-E. Current status and research advances of high-temperature hazards in rice. *Ying Yong Sheng Tai Xue Bao J. Appl. Ecol.* **2020**, *31*, 2817–2830. [CrossRef]

agriculture

MDPI

Article

Machine Learning Applied to Crop Mapping in Rice Varieties Using Spectral Images

Rubén Simeón [1], Kenza El Masslouhi [2], Alba Agenjos-Moreno [1], Beatriz Ricarte [3], Antonio Uris [4,*], Belen Franch [5], Constanza Rubio [4] and Alberto San Bautista [1]

1 Centro Valenciano de Estudios Sobre el Riego (CVER), Universitat Politècnica de València, 46022 Valencia, Spain; rusibro@etsiamn.upv.es (R.S.); alagmo@etsiamn.upv.es (A.A.-M.); asanbau@prv.upv.es (A.S.B.)
2 Department of Plant Production, Protection and Biotechnology (DPPBV), Institut Agronomique et Vétérinaire Hassan II (IAV Hassan II), Rabat 16000, Morocco; elmasslouhikenza@gmail.com
3 Institut de Matemàtica Multidisciplinar, Universitat Politècnica de València, 46022 Valencia, Spain; bearibe@mat.upv.es
4 Physics Technologies Research Centre, Universitat Politècnica de València, 46022 Valencia, Spain; crubiom@fis.upv.es
5 Global Change Unit, Image Processing Laboratory, Universitat de València, 46980 Valencia, Spain; belen.franch@uv.es
* Correspondence: auris@fis.upv.es

Abstract: Global food security is increasingly challenged by climate change and the availability of arable land. This situation calls for improved crop monitoring and management strategies. Rice is a staple food for nearly half of the world's population and a significant source of calories. Accurately identifying rice varieties is crucial for maintaining varietal purity, planning agricultural activities, and enhancing genetic improvement strategies. This study evaluates the effectiveness of machine learning algorithms to identify the most effective approach to predicting rice varieties, using multitemporal Sentinel-2 images in the Marismas del Guadalquivir of Sevilla, Spain. Spectral reflectance data were collected from ten Sentinel-2 bands, which include visible, red-edge, near-infrared, and shortwave infrared regions, at two key phenological stages: tillering and reproduction. The models were trained on pixel-level data from the growing seasons of 2021 and 2024, and they were evaluated using a test set from 2022. Four classifiers were compared: random forest, XGBoost, K-nearest neighbors, and logistic regression. Performance was assessed based on accuracy, precision, recall, specificity and F1 score. Non-linear models outperformed linear ones. The highest performance was achieved with the Random Forest classifier during the reproduction phase, reaching an exceptional accuracy of 0.94 using all bands or only the most informative subset (red edge, NIR, and SWIR). This classifier also maintained excellent accuracy (0.93 and 0.92) during the initial tillering phase. This fact demonstrates that it is possible to perform reliable varietal mapping in the early stages of the growing season.

Keywords: Sentinel-2; rice; machine learning; pixel classification; variety mapping; precision agriculture; crop mapping; remote sensing

1. Introduction

Global food security faces increasing challenges as climate change and limited arable land place greater pressure on food systems. Consequently, effective land and water management is crucial for sustaining food production [1]. According to the FAO [2], food production must rise by 50% by 2050 to meet the growing demands of an expanding population, yet climate change is already affecting key crop yields, complicating strategic planning and operational management in agriculture [3].

Among staple crops, rice remains the most important, particularly in developing countries [4,5], serving as a fundamental energy source for nearly half of the global population. It accounts for over 21% of human caloric intake, with even higher dependence in Southeast Asia, where it makes up more than 76% [6,7]. Around three billion people rely on rice as a dietary staple, making it one of the most essential crops in global agriculture worth studying [8].

Recent advances in satellite technology have greatly improved the monitoring of crops, the prediction of yields, and the detection of diseases [9–11], with initiatives such as NASA Harvest (established in 2017) playing a key role in supporting global food security [9]. In this context, crop mapping is essential for yield estimation and resource management [12], although spatial and temporal variability still hinder accurate classification [13]. Reliable identification depends on phenological differences that influence spectral and structural responses [14], which makes the timely generation of precise crop distribution maps indispensable [15,16].

Sentinel-2 time-series data have proven highly effective for crop mapping, thanks to their high spatial, temporal, and spectral resolution. Spectral bands in the visible, red-edge, and infrared regions provide insights into vegetation properties such as chlorophyll content, canopy structure, and water status. These raw spectral bands can be used directly or combined into vegetation indices (VIs) such as the Normalized Difference Vegetation Index (NDVI) and Enhanced Vegetation Index (EVI), which highlight plant vigor and greenness. Several studies have reported the utility of these time-series observations for early and accurate crop classification [17–19]. In addition to identifying crop types, remote sensing technologies also support yield forecasting [20], monitoring nutrient deficiencies [21], detecting rice diseases for timely interventions [22], and following plant growth dynamics and phenology [23]. All these advantages combined strengthen the foundation for precision agriculture [24].

Traditional crop-mapping methods often rely on expert knowledge and fixed, rule-based systems, such as spectral or phenological thresholds, and they involve intensive-labor field inspections. These approaches are time-consuming and prone to misclassification when crops have similar growth patterns (e.g., Triticum aestivum vs. Triticum durum). They also often fail to generalize across regions [13,14]. Therefore, there is a need for more flexible, accurate, and automated classification techniques.

Machine learning classifiers such as decision trees, K-Nearest Neighbor (k-NN), Gradient Boosting, and Support Vector Machines (SVMs) have become widely used for crop classification using remote sensing data. They can process large datasets and achieve good accuracy in cropland mapping [25–27]. Random forest and SVM have achieved excellent results in distinguishing crop types in heterogeneous agricultural landscapes [28,29]. Wavelength bands, which capture the spectral reflectance of vegetation, serve as the primary input for these models. When combined into vegetation indices (VIs), such as NDVI or EVI, they enhance the sensitivity to plant physiological traits at different phenological stages, thereby improving classification accuracy [30,31].

Building on this framework, several studies have demonstrated that integrating time-series remote sensing data with machine learning models improves classification accuracy [32]. This combined approach has been successfully applied worldwide—for example, in Uzbekistan, where it was used to classify crop rotations involving irrigated cotton, winter wheat, and rice with an overall accuracy of 80% [29], and in the United States for distinguishing between corn and soybean crops [33]. However, the studies have begun to address rice variety discrimination using satellite data, usually using higher computational cost and then only one growth year, a limited number of varieties, and a limited area of study. Guo et al. [34], demonstrated that a deep CNN applied to a Sentinel-2 image time series could separate five rice varieties within a single growing season in Australia. Similarly, Rauf et al. [35] proposed a multi-temporal Sentinel-2 approach to classify two major rice cultivars ("Basmati" and "IRRI") in Pakistan, achieving an accuracy of 98.6% using a Conv2D (CNN analysis). Saadat et al. [36] combined Sentinel-1/2 time series with a multistream CNN to map two rice varieties and the non-rice areas, achieving an overall accuracy (OA) of 97%. López-Andreu et al. [37], studied various machine learning (ML) classification models for rice crop in Murcia, Spain, in 2019, covering an area of 336 hectares. The Extra Trees, Random Forest, and K-Neighbors models achieved an accuracy of 0.93 in the 2019 trial. However, tests in the new year (2020) reduced the accuracy to 0.86 in specific weeks of the growing season.

This study investigates the potential of machine learning models, applied to Sentinel-2 multispectral imagery, to accurately classify the common rice varieties using spectral reflectance bands. The research aims to evaluate the performance of different supervised machine learning models in distinguishing rice varieties. The ultimate goal is to identify the most effective approach to predicting varietal classes. This will support the improved monitoring and management of rice cultivation in the region, as well as constraining variety-specific yield models. This will improve rice production forecasts at the field and regional levels.

2. Materials and Methods

2.1. Study Area

The present study was conducted during the 2021, 2022, and 2024 rice-growing seasons in the Marismas del Guadalquivir, a major rice-producing region in southern Spain. In 2023, no rice was cultivated due to drought conditions. The study area is situated within the municipalities of Isla Mayor, La Puebla del Río, and Los Palacios y Villafranca (Figure 1), and it is approximately bounded by the following WGS 84 coordinates: 37.2602° N, 6.3647° W (northwest) and 36.9962° N, 5.9345° W (southeast). This relatively flat and homogeneous agricultural landscape spans about 350 km^2 (roughly 15 × 23 km) and is almost entirely dedicated to flooded rice cultivation, with a total rice field area of approximately 39,635 hectares. Figure 1 shows the spatial distribution of rice plots in the study area.

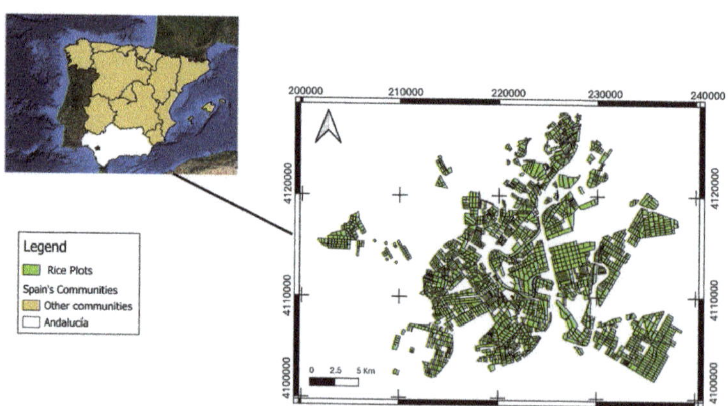

Figure 1. Situation of Sevilla and spatial distribution of rice plots in the study area.

The Guadalquivir River, the main source of irrigation, flows for about 657 km from its origin in the Sierra de Cazorla (Jaén province) to the Atlantic Ocean at Sanlúcar de Barrameda, passing through Córdoba and Seville. It drains a basin of around 58,000 km^2 and is essential for sustaining agriculture in Andalusia. Rice in the Marismas is cultivated under flood irrigation, with water depths ranging from 10 to 20 cm. Despite moderate salinity levels (EC = 2.3 dS m^{-1}) [38], the region's subtropical Mediterranean climate—characterized by hot, dry summers and mild winters—provides ideal conditions for rice growth [39].

The soils in the study area are primarily clay to silty clay, with a pH between 7.9 and 8.3 and organic matter content ranging from 1.5% to 3.2%. Compared to northern rice-growing regions such as Aragón and Navarre, the Marismas del Guadalquivir achieves higher yields, largely due to the warmer irrigation water, as northern fields are supplied via colder rivers originating in the Pyrenees, an environmental factor that can limit photosynthetic efficiency and reduce crop productivity [38].

2.2. Experimental Setup

The present study focused on eight rice varieties that are widely cultivated and consistently present across the 2021, 2022, and 2024 seasons in the Marismas del Guadalquivir region. The varieties "Puntal", "Hispalong", "J Sendra", "Copsemar7", "Guadiagrán", "Bomba", "Hispagran", and "Piñana" represent a significant portion of the regional rice production and are commonly sown by local farmers. Table 1 presents the number of parcels, corresponding to cultivated areas (in hectares). The final matrix consists of 670,277 rows, 10 bands per year, and as many columns as the number of dates available in each year, for a total of 49,135,100 values. Table 2 presents the number of pixels per variety for the years 2021, 2022, and 2024, as well as for the total study period.

Table 1. Rice parcels and cultivated area (ha) used in the study across seasons 2021, 2022, and 2024.

Season	Number of Parcels	Area (ha)
2021	587	2215.7
2022	408	2130.5
2024	648	2356.6

Table 2. Number of pixels per variety in 2021, 2022, and 2023 and the total for the study.

Variety	2021	2022	2024	Total
Puntal	36,337	34,225	37,280	107,842
Hispalong	29,957	25,565	58,027	113,549
J Sendra	40,208	44,584	38,580	123,372
Copsemar 7	17,038	17,730	20,215	54,983
Guadiagrán	34,980	7943	22,103	65,026
Bomba	18,262	23,464	17,213	58,939
Hispagran	20,816	31,380	26,935	79,131
Piñana	38,057	28,160	1218	67,435
Total	235,655	213,051	221,571	670,277

2.3. Satellite Data

This study utilized Sentinel-2 satellite imagery, accessed and processed through Google Earth Engine (GEE), a robust cloud-based platform designed for large-scale spatial analysis. GEE facilitated the efficient selection, filtering, and export of imagery based on specific spatial and temporal parameters. The dataset was derived from the Sentinel-2 Level 2A product, which provides surface reflectance values corrected for atmospheric interference.

Imagery was acquired over the rice-growing region, but only for cloud-free days' images, within tile 29SQB of the Military Grid Reference System (MGRS), covering the study area across the 2021, 2022, and 2024 rice-growing seasons. Central to data acquisition was the multi-spectral instrument (MSI) aboard the Sentinel-2A satellite. This sensor captures reflected sunlight across 13 spectral bands; however, this study focused on a subset of 10 bands, primarily those with the highest spatial resolutions of 10 and 20 m (Table 3).

Table 3. Bands and their resolution (m) from Sentinel-2 and each Wavelength (nm) resolution and regions.

Band Number	Name	Central Wavelength (nm)	Spatial Resolution (m)	Spectral Region
B02	Blue	490	10	Visible
B03	Green	560	10	Visible
B04	Red	665	10	Visible
B08	Near-Infrared (NIR)	842	10	Near-Infrared
B05	Vegetation Red Edge 1	705	20	Red Edge
B06	Vegetation Red Edge 2	740	20	Red Edge
B07	Vegetation Red Edge 3	783	20	Red Edge
B8A	Narrow NIR	865	20	Near-Infrared
B11	Short Wave Infrared 1	1610	20	Short Wave Infrared
B12	Short Wave Infrared 2	2190	20	Short Wave Infrared

Only cloud-free Sentinel-2 images were processed for each rice-growing season studied, covering the entire period from sowing to harvest. The selected image acquisition dates were aligned across all years based on days after sowing (DAS) and corresponding key crop phenological stages, ensuring consistency in crop development monitoring. Detailed download dates and relatively corresponding days after sowing are summarized in Table 4. All images provide surface reflectance data.

Table 4. Dates of downloaded Sentinel-2 images across seasons and corresponding days after sowing (DAS) and phenological stage.

Phenological Stage	DAS	2021	2022	2024
Germination	0	10 June	5 June	4 June
	20	30 June	25 June	24 June
Tillering	35	15 July	10 July	9 July
	40	20 July	15 July	14 July
	45	25 July	20 July	19 July
Inflorescence emergence	75	18 August	19 August	18 August
Flowering	80	-	-	23 August
	90	28 August	3 September	2 September

2.4. Variety Data

Field boundaries were obtained from the Spanish Cadastre INSPIRE portal [40]. Rice parcel data and varietal information were sourced from official Red de Alerta e Información Fitosanitaria (RAIF) maps provided by the Federación de Arroceros de Sevilla [41] for the

2021, 2022, and 2024 seasons. These maps identified more than 20 cultivated rice varieties and served as the basis for the selection of ground truth data.

2.5. Statistics and Machine Learning Algorithms

The objective of this study was to evaluate the spectral separability of rice varieties using Sentinel-2 satellite imagery. A Principal Component Analysis (PCA) was applied to the dataset, combining days after sowing (DAS) and spectral bands, to identify the most relevant features contributing to varietal discrimination. The analysis was conducted at the pixel level, with each pixel labeled according to its corresponding rice variety, based on the official parcel maps. The spectral reflectance values corresponding to DAS in Table 3 served as input for the machine learning models used in the classification process.

2.5.1. Principal Component Analysis

Principal Component Analysis (PCA) is a statistical method used to simplify large datasets by reducing their dimensionality while preserving as much of the original information (variance) as possible.

Given a dataset with n samples and p correlated variables $X_1, X_2, \ldots, X_p$, PCA seeks to transform these into a smaller set of k new uncorrelated variables $Z_1, Z_2, \ldots, Z_k$ (where $k \leq p$). These new variables, called principal components, are linear combinations of the original variables:

$$Z_j = v_{1j} \cdot X_1 + v_{2j} \cdot X_2 + \ldots + v_{pj} \cdot X_p \tag{1}$$

where the coefficients v_{ij} reflect the weight or contribution of each original variable X_i to the principal component Z_j, providing information about their correlations.

Principal components are constructed to be mutually uncorrelated and are ordered by the amount of variance they explain. The first principal component captures the greatest variance, while the last captures the least. By reducing dimensionality, PCA facilitates visualizing enormous and complex data in two or three dimensions, aiding in the identification of possible clusters or groups within the dataset. In this case, groups of pixels with similar characteristics.

In this study, PCA was applied using reflectance values of the bands listed in Table 2 across the following seven days after sowing (DAS): 20, 35, 40, 45, 75, 80, and 90. The purpose was to cluster both DAS and bands simultaneously, identifying patterns of variation over time and spectral variables.

2.5.2. Machine Learning Models

Different machine learning models were applied to classify pixels according to rice varieties. Training and validation were performed using combined data from the 2021 and 2024 seasons, with an 80/20 split for training and validation, respectively. All pixels from the 2022 season were reserved exclusively for testing. Stratified random sampling was employed during the training and validation data selection to ensure the balanced representation of all varieties and avoid bias.

For classification, four supervised learning algorithms were employed: k-nearest neighbors (k-NN), extreme gradient boosting (XGBoost), random forest (RF), and logistic regression (LR). The selected algorithms have been widely applied in comparable classification studies (Table 5). Models were trained with standard hyperparameters widely used in the literature. Random forest and XGBoost employed 100 estimators, KNN used 5 neighbors, and logistic regression was run with the lbfgs solver and 1000 maximum iterations.

Table 5. Representative studies using machine learning algorithms for the classification of different crops in multiple countries.

Crop	Algorithm	Study Area	Reference
Rice, cotton, pepper, peanut, tomato, maize, eggplant, gram, millet, sorghum	RF	India	[42]
Boro rice, vegetables, betel vine	RF and k-NN	India	[43]
Cotton, maize, wheat, barley, lucerne, groundnuts, canola, and pecan nuts	RF and XGBoost	South Africa	[44]
Tobacco, rice, winter wheat, rapeseed/canola	XGBoost	China	[45]
Barley, rice, corn (maize), wheat, rapeseed (Canola), alfalfa, sunflower, legumes, oats, vineyards, cherry trees, shrub grass, broad beans	RF and XGBoost	Navarre province, Spain	[46]
Tea, fruit plantations, mulberry	LR	China	[47]

k-Nearest Neighbors (k-NN)

Cover and Hart [48] introduced the nearest-neighbor classification rule, which assigns a class label to an unknown sample, x, based on the class of its closest training sample, x_i, in a metric space.

The k-NN algorithm assigns a class to a data point based on the majority class among its k-closest neighbors in the feature space. k-NN does not require explicit training; instead, it stores the entire training dataset, and when a new instance needs to be classified, the algorithm finds the k-nearest neighbors (with the smallest distances) and then assigns the class that is most frequent among them.

A small value of k (e.g., 1 or 3) makes the algorithm sensitive to noise and outliers. A large value of k may include too many irrelevant points and may reduce accuracy [49].

Extreme Gradient Boosting (XGBoost)

XGBoost is an ensemble machine learning algorithm that extends the gradient boosting framework by building a series of decision trees sequentially for classification and regression tasks [50]. Gradient boosting iteratively fits new models to the residual errors of prior models, refining predictions over time.

Random Forest (RF)

RF is an ensemble learning algorithm introduced by Leo Breiman in 2001 [51]. It combines two key concepts: bootstrap aggregating (bagging), which Breiman had introduced earlier in 1996 [52], and random feature selection at each node split, a technique influenced by the work of Amit and Geman [53] in image recognition. In RF, multiple decision trees are built using random subsets of the training data (via bootstrapping) and random subsets of features, which introduces diversity among the trees. The final prediction is made by aggregating the outputs of all trees, through majority voting in classification tasks.

Logistic Regression (LR)

LR is a statistical classification method originally developed for binary outcomes, with roots tracing back to the early 20th century in biological studies. It models the probability of a binary response by applying the logistic (sigmoid) function to a linear combination of input features. The method was formalized through the work of David Cox in 1958 [54], who framed it within the context of generalized linear models.

LR estimates parameters by maximizing the likelihood of the observed data, via iterative optimization techniques like gradient descent. It remains effective for linearly separable classes and offers interpretable coefficients representing the effect of each predictor.

2.5.3. Performance Evaluation

The confusion matrix is a powerful tool for analyzing the performance of a multi-classifier [55] since it allows us to easily obtain the number of correct and incorrect answers for a classification algorithm. Thus, with a $k \times k$ confusion matrix, as shown in Figure 2, there are k correct classifications and $k^2 - k$ possible errors.

Real Variety \ *Predicted Variety*	V_1	V_2	$\cdots$	V_j	$\cdots$	V_k	a_i
V_1	n_{11}	n_{12}	$\cdots$	n_{1j}	$\cdots$	n_{1k}	a_1
V_2	n_{21}	n_{22}	$\cdots$	n_{2j}	$\cdots$	n_{2k}	a_2
$\vdots$	$\vdots$	$\vdots$	$\ddots$	$\vdots$	$\vdots$	$\vdots$	$\vdots$
V_i	n_{i1}	n_{i2}	$\cdots$	n_{ij}	$\cdots$	n_{ik}	a_i
$\vdots$	$\vdots$	$\vdots$	$\vdots$	$\ddots$	$\vdots$	$\vdots$	$\vdots$
V_k	n_{k1}	n_{k2}	$\cdots$	n_{kj}	$\cdots$	n_{kk}	a_k
p_j	p_1	p_2	$\cdots$	p_j	$\cdots$	p_k	N

Figure 2. Confusion matrix of N elements for pairwise comparison.

Particularly for this work, the following applies:

- $V_1, V_2, \ldots, V_k$: the different rice varieties.
- n_{ij}: the number of samples that truly belong to class V_i and were predicted as class V_j.
- a_i: total number of samples that truly belong to class V_i (i = 1, 2. . ., 8).
- P_j: total number of samples that were predicted as class V_j (j = 1, 2. . ., 8).
- N: total number of samples.

In general, for each class V_i, $i = 1, 2, \ldots, k$, the correct classifications, called true positives (TP_i), is the number of samples correctly classified as belonging to this class, so it is obtained as follows:

$$TP_i = n_{ii} \tag{2}$$

On the other hand, there are two kinds of errors:

- False positives (FP_i), which are the samples that have been incorrectly classified as belonging to class V_i, that is

$$FP_i = \sum_{\substack{j=1 \\ j \neq i}}^{k} n_{ji} = p_i - n_{ii} \tag{3}$$

- False negatives (FN_i), which are the samples that have been incorrectly classified as not belonging to class V_i; thus,

$$FN_i = \sum_{\substack{j=1 \\ j \neq i}}^{k} n_{ij} = a_i - n_{ii} \tag{4}$$

Moreover, there is a fourth type of samples, true negatives (FN_i), which are those that do not actually belong to class V_i. They are calculated by adding the entries of the submatrix that results from eliminating row and column i in the confusion matrix, that is

$$TN_i = N - a_i - p_i + n_{ii} \tag{5}$$

When the values of these four types of samples are known, several commonly used metrics can be generated, as shown in Table 6, to evaluate the performance of the classifier with different evaluation approaches. These metrics must be computed for each class, V_i, and then, the model metrics will be the average of them.

Table 6. Definitions and formulas of common classification performance Metricsmetrics.

Statistical Parameters	Explanation	Equation
Accuracy	Proportion of correct predictions over the total number of samples	$\frac{TP_i+TN_i}{TP_i+TN_i+FP_i+FN_i}$ (6)
Precision	Proportion of correctly classified positive from the total predicted positive	$\frac{TP_i}{TP_i+FP_i}$ (7)
Recall (sensitivity or true positive rate)	Proportion of correctly classified positive from the total truly positive	$\frac{TP_i}{TP_i+FN_i}$ (8)
Specificity (or true negative rate)	Proportion of correctly classified negative from the total truly negative	$\frac{TN_i}{TN_i+FP_i}$ (9)
F1-score (or F-measure)	Harmonic mean between Precision and recall values	$2 \cdot \frac{Precision \cdot Recall}{Precision+Recall}$ (10)

2.6. Software

Processing of satellite images obtained from Google Earth Engine (GEE) for Sentinel-2 was carried out using QGIS 3.10.14 software (QGIS, 2025). Statistical analyses and model evaluations were conducted in a Python 3.11.9 environment using Visual Studio Code (Microsoft, 2025). The analysis employed machine learning libraries (Scikit-learn, Pandas, Joblib, and Numpy) for data handling and classification tasks.

3. Results

3.1. PCA Results

In order to optimize the classification framework, the PCA technique was applied to the joint data matrix in order to establish an exploratory analysis that would guide the selection of the most informative DAS intervals and spectral bands for the classification of varieties. Rather than analyzing each available date independently, PCA enabled the temporal data grouping into two agronomically significant phenological stages, as defined by the Biologische Bundesanstalt, Bundessortenamt und Chemische Industrie (BBCH) scale for rice development [56]. The first group encompassed the tillering phase (35, 40, and 45 days after sowing, DAS; BBCH 21-29), a stage marked by active shoot proliferation. The second group corresponded to the reproductive phase (75, 80, and 90 DAS; BBCH 74-89), during which panicle initiation and flowering occur.

The first three principal components cumulatively accounted for an average of 83.22% of the total variance across both phenological stages analyzed, with the first component explaining, on average, 58.60%, followed by 16.20% and 8.42% for the second and third components, respectively. PCA of DAS showed limited varietal separability in early stages (20 to 45 DAS) due to overlapping clusters, while between 75 and 90 DAS the groups became compact and well separated, confirming this as the optimal window for discrimination. Similarly, PCA of Sentinel-2 bands indicated that near-infrared (B08, B8A) and red-edge bands (B05–B07) contributed most to varietal separability, whereas visible and SWIR bands played a minor role. These results are depicted in Supplementary Figures S1 and S2. These results combine both the tillering and early reproductive phase (35,40 and 45 DAS) and the later reproductive phase (75, 80, and 90 DAS). Spectral bands exhibiting the highest loading coefficients within these components were interpreted as the most informative for discriminating varietal differences.

Subsequently, a set of classification scenarios was developed, each defined by a distinct combination of Sentinel-2 bands selected based on their statistical contribution during the tillering and reproductive phases. These scenarios, detailed in Table 7, include spectral subsets from the visible, red-edge, near-infrared (NIR), and shortwave infrared (SWIR) regions. The final selection aimed to optimize the balance between dimensionality reduction and information preservation, thereby enhancing the discriminative power of the spectral inputs used in the subsequent machine learning classification models.

Table 7. Band combinations used for machine learning models as input features.

Scenario	Bands Combinations			Selection Criteria
	Visible Bands	Red-Edge & NIR Bands	SWIR Bands	
1	B02, B03, B04	B05, B06, B07, B08, B08A	B11, B12	A baseline scenario was created using all bands, to retain over 92% of the total variance and ensure maximum spectral information was included.
2	–	B05, B06, B07, B08, B08A	B11, B12	Focus on Red-Edge, NIR and SWIR regions based on PCA loadings.
3	–	B05, B06, B07, B08, B08A	–	Only Red-edge and NIR bands are used, relevant for canopy reflectance.
4	–	–	B11, B12	Only SWIR bands, useful for water content and stress indicators.

3.2. Results of Machine Learning Models

Tables 7, 8, 9, and 10 present, respectively, the classification performance of the k-NN, XGBoost, random forest, and logistic regression models across tillering (35–45 DAS) and reproductive (75–90 DAS) stages, evaluated under four spectral band combinations. Due to a lack of space and because no significant differences have been observed between the metric values of the different varieties, these values are the average of the metrics obtained for each of the eight varieties. As an example, the Supplementary Materials show the results obtained for Scenario 1 in Supplementary Figures S3–S6.

In Table 8, the consistently superior results observed in Scenario 1 across both phenological stages underscore the importance of leveraging the full Sentinel-2 spectral range. Specifically, validation accuracy reached 0.98 during tillering (35–45 DAS) and improved further to 0.99 during reproduction (75–90 DAS). Corresponding test accuracies of 0.93 and 0.94, indicating that the combined information from visible, red-edge, NIR, and SWIR bands captures complementary physiological traits that discriminate rice varieties effectively.

The gradual decline in classification metrics from Scenario 2 to Scenario 4 illustrates the detrimental impact of spectral band reduction. Scenario 2, which excludes visible bands but retains red-edge, NIR, and SWIR, maintains high validation accuracy (0.98 at both stages) but shows a slight drop in test accuracy to 0.91 during tillering and 0.93 in reproduction. The further restricted spectral inputs in Scenario 3 caused test accuracy to drop to 0.84 at tillering and 0.88 at the reproductive stage.

Scenario 4, limited to SWIR bands, suffered the most substantial performance degradation, with test accuracies of 0.62 and 0.67 during the two stages. Despite high specificity values (>0.94), the low recall (~0.62) indicates that the model frequently failed to identify true positives, reflecting a tendency toward false negatives.

Table 8. Test and validation results (accuracy, precision, recall, specificity, and F1-score) of the k-NN model to map rice varieties in the different scenarios and DAS.

DAS	Scenario	Analysis	Accuracy	Precision	Recall	Specificity	F1-Score
35–40–45	Scenario 1	Validation	0.98	0.98	0.98	0.99	0.98
		Test	0.93	0.93	0.93	0.99	0.93
	Scenario 2	Validation	0.98	0.98	0.98	0.99	0.98
		Test	0.91	0.91	0.91	0.98	0.91
	Scenario 3	Validation	0.96	0.96	0.96	0.99	0.96
		Test	0.84	0.84	0.84	0.97	0.84
	Scenario 4	Validation	0.88	0.88	0.88	0.98	0.88
		Test	0.62	0.66	0.62	0.94	0.63
75–80–90	Scenario 1	Validation	0.99	0.99	0.99	0.99	0.99
		Test	0.94	0.94	0.94	0.99	0.94
	Scenario 2	Validation	0.98	0.98	0.98	0.99	0.98
		Test	0.93	0.93	0.93	0.99	0.93
	Scenario 3	Validation	0.96	0.96	0.96	0.99	0.96
		Test	0.88	0.88	0.88	0.98	0.88
	Scenario 4	Validation	0.89	0.89	0.89	0.98	0.89
		Test	0.67	0.68	0.67	0.95	0.67

Table 9. Test and validation results (accuracy, precision, recall, specificity, and F1-score) of the XGBoost model to map rice varieties in the different scenarios and DAS.

DAS	Scenario	Analysis	Accuracy	Precision	Recall	Specificity	F1-Score
35–40–45	Scenario 1	Validation	0.96	0.96	0.96	0.99	0.96
		Test	0.85	0.86	0.85	0.97	0.85
	Scenario 2	Validation	0.96	0.96	0.96	0.99	0.96
		Test	0.80	0.81	0.80	0.97	0.80
	Scenario 3	Validation	0.96	0.96	0.96	0.99	0.96
		Test	0.68	0.72	0.68	0.95	0.68
	Scenario 4	Validation	0.79	0.79	0.79	0.97	0.78
		Test	0.49	0.54	0.49	0.92	0.50
75–80–90	Scenario 1	Validation	0.99	0.99	0.99	0.99	0.99
		Test	0.93	0.93	0.93	0.99	0.93
	Scenario 2	Validation	0.98	0.98	0.98	0.99	0.98
		Test	0.92	0.92	0.92	0.98	0.92
	Scenario 3	Validation	0.95	0.95	0.95	0.99	0.96
		Test	0.85	0.85	0.85	0.79	0.85
	Scenario 4	Validation	0.84	0.84	0.84	0.97	0.84
		Test	0.60	0.62	0.60	0.94	0.60

Table 10. Test and validation results (accuracy, precision, recall, specificity, and F1-score) of the random forest model to map rice varieties in the different scenarios and DAS.

DAS	Scenario	Analysis	Accuracy	Precision	Recall	Specificity	F1-Score
35–40–45	Scenario 1	Validation	0.98	0.98	0.98	0.99	0.98
		Test	0.92	0.93	0.92	0.98	0.92
	Scenario 2	Validation	0.99	0.99	0.99	0.99	0.99
		Test	0.91	0.92	0.91	0.98	0.91
	Scenario 3	Validation	0.98	0.98	0.98	0.99	0.98
		Test	0.84	0.85	0.84	0.97	0.84
	Scenario 4	Validation	0.97	0.97	0.97	0.99	0.97
		Test	0.73	0.74	0.73	0.96	0.73

Table 10. *Cont.*

DAS	Scenario	Analysis	Accuracy	Precision	Recall	Specificity	F1-Score
75–80–90	Scenario 1	Validation	0.99	0.99	0.99	0.99	0.99
		Test	0.94	0.94	0.94	0.99	0.94
	Scenario 2	Validation	0.99	0.99	0.99	0.99	0.99
		Test	0.94	0.94	0.94	0.99	0.94
	Scenario 3	Validation	0.99	0.99	0.99	0.99	0.99
		Test	0.89	0.93	0.89	0.98	0.89
	Scenario 4	Validation	0.98	0.98	0.98	0.99	0.98
		Test	0.73	0.74	0.73	0.96	0.74

The improved overall accuracies at the reproductive stage compared to tillering, rising by approximately 1–4% across scenarios, reflect the increased spectral reflectance separability as rice plants mature and physiological differences among varieties intensify.

The results in Table 9, obtained using the XGBoost model under various scenarios, show that Scenario 1, which incorporates the full spectral range, constantly achieves the highest validation and test performance metrics at both phenological stages. Validation accuracy reaches 0.96 during tillering and improves to 0.99 during the reproductive stage, with test accuracy correspondingly increasing from 0.85 to 0.93.

Spectral simplification, reflected in Scenarios 2 to 4, results in progressive declines in model performance. Scenario 2 maintains high validation accuracies (0.96 and 0.98) but exhibits moderate test accuracy reductions to 0.80 at tillering and 0.92 during reproduction.

Scenario 3, limited to red-edge and NIR bands, shows a marked drop in test accuracy to 0.68 during tillering, though performance improves to 0.85 during the reproductive stage. The relatively lower test specificity (0.95 at tillering and notably 0.79 at the reproductive stage) reveals the limitations in accurately distinguishing true negatives, which may reflect spectral ambiguity among certain varieties.

The most constrained spectral input, Scenario 4 (SWIR bands only), yields the poorest classification results, with test accuracies dropping to 0.49 at tillering and 0.60 at reproductive stage. The recall and F1-score values indicate frequent false negatives.

Table 10 shows that the RF model demonstrates strong and stable predictive capabilities, with high validation accuracies exceeding 0.97 across all scenarios under phenological stages. In the early phenological stage (35–45 DAS), Scenario 1 achieves a validation accuracy of 0.98 and test accuracy of 0.92. These metrics reflect near-perfect agreement beyond chance, implying the model can effectively differentiate rice varieties using comprehensive spectral inputs early in the growing season. Scenario 2 closely mirrors this performance with slightly higher validation accuracy (0.99) and comparable test accuracy (0.91), indicating that excluding visible bands but retaining red-edge, NIR, and SWIR still preserves most discriminative information.

As spectral complexity decreases in Scenarios 3 and 4, model performance declines. Scenario 3 still maintains a high validation accuracy value (0.98) and a test accuracy of 0.84. Scenario 4 (SWIR only) experiences a more pronounced drop, with test accuracy falling to 0.73.

During the reproductive stage, all scenarios show improved test accuracies relative to the tillering stage. Scenario 1 and Scenario 2 both attain test accuracy of 0. Scenario 3 shows a meaningful test accuracy increase to 0.89, while Scenario 4 remains the least accurate.

The results of the LR in Table 11 model exhibit inferior classification performance compared to the ensemble (RF and XGBoost) and instance-based (k-NN) classifiers analyzed previously. In the early phenological stage (35–45 DAS), validation accuracies range from 0.60 in Scenario 1 down to 0.33 in Scenario 4, with corresponding test accuracies declining further to as low as 0.16. Moreover, the results reveal that the LR model's predictive agreement is barely above chance levels, reflecting substantial misclassification and model instability. This is evident in the low values obtained for precision, recall, and F1-score across scenarios, all of which fall below 0.60, particularly in the test sets.

Table 11. Test and validation results (accuracy, precision, recall, specificity, and F1-score) of the logistic regression model to map rice varieties in the different scenarios and DAS.

DAS	Scenario	Analysis	Accuracy	Precision	Recall	Specificity	F1-Score
35–40–45	Scenario 1	Validation	0.60	0.59	0.60	0.94	0.59
		Test	0.33	0.34	0.33	0.90	0.31
	Scenario 2	Validation	0.56	0.55	0.56	0.93	0.54
		Test	0.31	0.34	0.31	0.90	0.31
	Scenario 3	Validation	0.49	0.49	0.49	0.92	0.48
		Test	0.23	0.28	0.23	0.89	0.19
	Scenario 4	Validation	0.33	0.30	0.33	0.90	0.39
		Test	0.16	0.14	0.16	0.88	0.13
75–80–90	Scenario 1	Validation	0.75	0.75	0.75	0.96	0.75
		Test	0.48	0.50	0.48	0.92	0.47
	Scenario 2	Validation	0.63	0.64	0.63	0.94	0.63
		Test	0.40	0.40	0.40	0.91	0.38
	Scenario 3	Validation	0.52	0.53	0.52	0.93	0.52
		Test	0.38	0.35	0.38	0.91	0.35
	Scenario 4	Validation	0.42	0.43	0.42	0.91	0.41
		Test	0.20	0.18	0.20	0.88	0.15

During the reproduction, the LR model performance improves moderately. Validation accuracies peak at 0.75 for Scenario 1 but declines to 0.42 for Scenario 4, while test accuracies are notably lower, with the highest reaching only 0.48.

Interestingly, despite relatively high specificity values (ranging from 0.88 to 0.96 across all scenarios), the low precision and recall values indicate that the LR model predominantly favors negative class predictions, leading to numerous false negatives and a failure to reliably detect true positive class instances.

Figure 3 compares model accuracies across five spectral scenarios and two growing stages for predicting rice varieties. RF and k-NN achieved the highest accuracies, particularly with full spectral input (visible–red-edge–NIR–SWIR) during the reproductive phase. RF is stable across all spectral combinations. Accuracy fell with reduced spectral bands. A significant drop was observed within the LR model. Overall, performance improved with richer spectral data and later phenological stages.

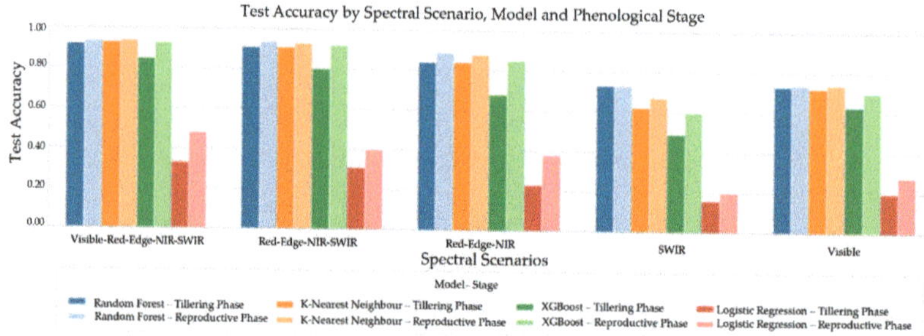

Figure 3. Comparative analysis of RF, K-NN, XGBoost, and LR for rice variety mapping using Sentinel-2 spectral bands across tillering and reproductive stages.

Figure 4 illustrates the spatial distribution using RF model predictions with Scenario 1 at the pixel level for the eight rice varieties. Green points indicate correct predictions, while red points highlight misclassified pixels. The model shows high pixel-level accuracy for varieties such as "Puntal", "Bomba", and "Piñana", for which nearly all pixels are correctly identified, and misclassifications are minimal and mostly confined to parcel edges. In contrast, varieties like "Guadiagrán", "Cosepmar 7", and "Hispagrán" exhibit more frequent errors. The overall spatial consistency across most varieties highlights the RF model's potential for reliable pixel-based varietal classification.

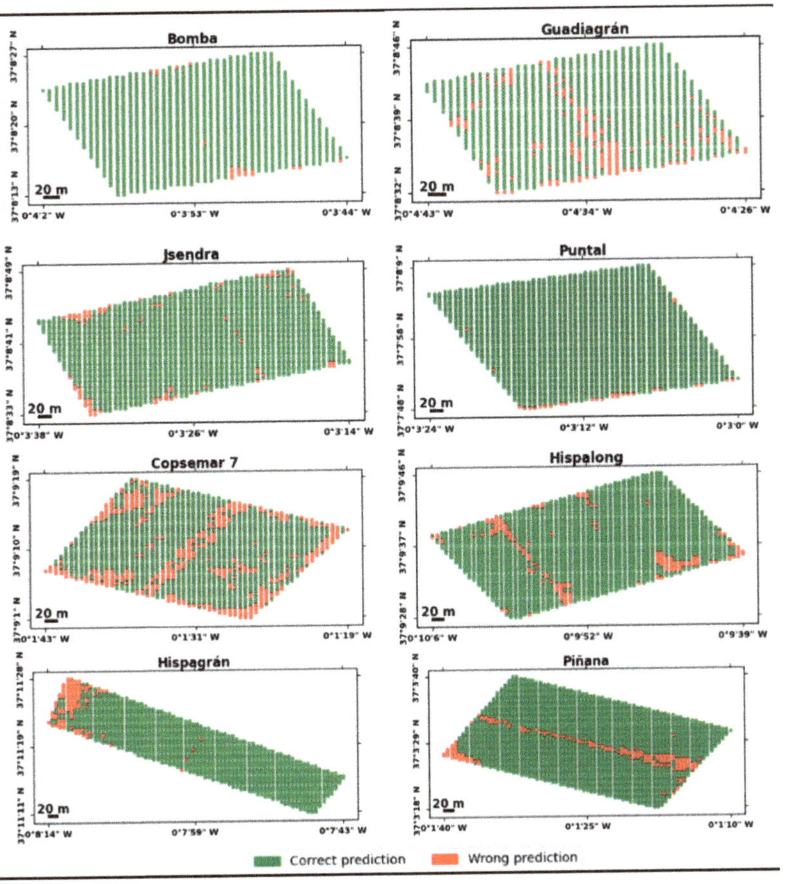

Figure 4. Geospatial assessment of pixel-level prediction accuracy by variety: test of Scenario 1 using RF Model Trained on 2021–2024 data and evaluated on independent 2022 parcels across the eight common rice varieties.

4. Discussion

4.1. Model Performance Comparison

The comparative analysis of the four supervised machine learning classifiers revealed a clear performance hierarchy in the task of classifying rice varieties using Sentinel-2 time-series data. As shown in Figure 2, RF emerged as the top-performing model across all configurations, followed by k-NN, XGBoost, and finally LR.

RF achieved the highest varieties' prediction accuracies. RF relies on an ensemble approach, which constructs multiple decision trees using random features and sample subsets, thereby reducing overfitting and increasing generalization [57]. RF handles high-dimensional data and multicollinearity, both of which are intrinsic to multispectral satellite imagery. A similar dominance of RF has been reported in land-cover studies; for instance, RF yielded overall accuracies up to 96.3% and demonstrated higher stability than XGBoost, even when trained on radar-optical fused inputs [58].

Despite its sensitivity to high-dimensional data, k-NN demonstrated solid classification accuracy, likely attributable to the discriminative structure of the selected spectral and temporal features. Such patterns were also noted by Asgari & Hasanlou [59], in whose work k-NN achieved an overall accuracy of 90% in crop-type mapping using vegetation indices derived from Sentinel-2, outperforming gradient boosting (GB) under similar input conditions.

XGBoost, being a "state-of-the-art" boosting method known for its high predictive ability [50], reflected moderate to good performance.

LR yielded the weakest results among all models, which proves its unsuitability for problems characterized by non-linear relationships and subtle spectral distinctions. LR's assumption of linear decision boundaries and its inability to model feature interactions significantly limited its performance in this study. Our results mirror the conclusions of Zhong et al. [60], who found LR to be ineffective for classifying spectrally similar crop types. Militino et al. [61] reported that logistic regression slightly outperformed XGBoost in terms of overall accuracy for the imbalanced binary classification task of burned area detection using multi-temporal satellite imagery.

This observed performance hierarchy, RF > k-NN > XGBoost > LR, underscores that ensemble-based (RF, XGBoost) and non-parametric (k-NN) models remain the most reliable for remote sensing-based varietal classification compared to simple linear statistical methods (LR).

Finally, while deep learning architectures such as PhenologyNet [62] offer fine-grained phenological classification via phenotypic similarity weighting, our findings show that high accuracy is achievable using classical machine learning methods. When training data is spectrally and temporally diverse and sampling is guided by phenological knowledge, ensemble models remain effective, interpretable, and operationally viable tools for rice variety classification using Sentinel-2 data.

4.2. Spectral Band Combination Analysis

The superior performance of models incorporating NIR and red-edge spectral bands, as observed in this study, is strongly supported by the physiological and structural relevance of these wavelengths in capturing vegetation and biophysical properties. Unlike models relying solely on visible or shortwave SWIR bands, NIR reflectance is tightly coupled with the leaf area index (LAI) and above-ground biomass, which serve as proxies for plant vigor and developmental stage [63].

Genotypic variability in rice varieties, manifested by tillering capacity, leaf orientation, and canopy density, modulates NIR reflectance patterns [64]. Equally important are the red-edge bands, positioned between the red and NIR regions (approximately 700–740 nm), which are uniquely sensitive to changes in chlorophyll content and photosynthetic activity [65,66]. These bands exhibit a steep reflectance gradient, known as the red-edge inflection point, which shifts in response to biotic stress, nutrient status, and phenological transitions. For instance, the shift from vegetative growth to the reproductive stage (marked by panicle emergence and floral development) can significantly alter chlorophyll distribution and spectral reflectance. Zhang et al. [45] demonstrated that prioritizing NIR and Red Edge enhances model generalizability and the classification precision by minimizing the influence of less informative spectral features. A detailed evaluation of Sentinel-2 and Sentinel-3 data by Imran et al. [67] revealed that red edge and NIR shoulder-based vegetation indices provide a consistent and scalable means of estimating LAI across spatial and temporal scales in heterogeneous grassland systems.

4.3. *Influence of Phenological Stages*

The best results were obtained when models were trained from the reproduction stage (DAS 75–90), corresponding to inflorescence emergence and flowering, rather than the tillering stage. During tillering (DAS 35–45), the minimal phenodata typic divergence of similarity is due to similar chlorophyll. In contrast, the reproductive stage is characterized by more heightened changes. Differences in panicle emergence timing, flag leaf angles, canopy openness, and the onset of senescence produce measurable changes in NIR, RE, and SWIR reflectance [68,69]. These variations may be intensified due to varietal responses to flowering stress. Moreover, flowering marks a transition in nutrient dynamics, with nitrogen remobilization and water redistribution within the plant, influencing SWIR signatures.

These findings match those of prior studies [70,71] that identify the flowering stage as optimal for crop classification and yield prediction. These findings are supported by Wang et al. [72], who pointed out that UAV-based hyperspectral fluorescence information collected during the flowering stage can enhance VIS based rice yield estimation models.

5. Conclusions

This study clearly demonstrates the power of combining Sentinel-2 multispectral imagery with machine learning classifiers to accurately discriminate between eight major rice varieties consistently cultivated in Seville. By training models on multi-season data from 2021 and 2024 and testing them on an entirely separate 2022 dataset, we confirm the strong potential for temporal generalization.

The PCA was utilized to guide the selection of the combination of growth stages and spectral bands most relevant for varietal classification analysis. Four machine learning classifiers were analyzed: random forest, XGBoost, K-nearest neighbors, and logistic regression. A clear performance hierarchy was revealed in the task of classifying rice varieties using Sentinel-2 time-series data. From the comparison of the four models, RF was revealed to be the best performing model across all configurations, followed by k-NN, XGBoost, and finally LR.

In terms of phenological stage, the highest accuracy, 0.94, was achieved during the reproduction phase with the random forest (RF) model, although even during the initial tillering phase, the model maintained excellent accuracy (0.93 and 0.92). This demonstrates that it is possible to perform reliable varietal mapping in the early stages of the growing season. This study also observed the superior performance of models incorporating NIR and red-edge spectral bands, unlike models based solely on visible or shortwave SWIR bands.

In conclusion, this research underscores the importance of combining phenologically timed spectral data with resilient machine learning frameworks. It not only enables early, accurate varietal mapping but also supports the development of scalable tools for precision agriculture. Our results highlight random forest as the most reliable approach, setting a strong foundation for future in seasonal variety mapping.

Furthermore, this work can be particularly valuable as a foundational step in the development and optimization of predictive models and algorithms. Accurately classifying rice varieties is a crucial prerequisite before applying models aimed at forecasting crop area, disease outbreaks, or yield estimation. As such, our approach offers a filtering mechanism to strengthen existing prediction models by integrating varietal information upfront. Ulti-

7. mately, the ability to distinguish between rice varieties enhances the interpretability and applicability of agronomic models, contributing to more reliable and actionable insights for farmers and stakeholders. This, in turn, may indirectly support improved field-level decision-making and better outcomes for the food industry, especially when deploying precision agriculture tools in operational contexts.

Supplementary Materials: The following supporting information can be downloaded at https://www.mdpi.com/article/10.3390/agriculture15171832/s1, Figure S1. Principal component analysis (PCA) of Sentinel-2 data grouped by days after sowing (DAS), showing the distribution of samples across PC1 (58.6%) and PC2 (16.2%); Figure S2. Principal component analysis (PCA) of Sentinel-2 data (Bands), showing the distribution of samples across PC1 (58.6%) and PC2 (16.2%); Figure S3. Confusion matrix of the random forest model for the test set at the tillering phase (Scenario 1); Figure S4. Confusion matrix of the K-nearest neighbor model for the test set at the tillering phase (Scenario 1); Figure S5. Confusion matrix of the XGBoost model for the test set at the tillering phase (Scenario 1); Figure S6. Confusion matrix of the logistic regression model for the test set at the tillering phase (Scenario 1).

Author Contributions: Conceptualization, R.S., A.A.-M., C.R. and A.S.B.; methodology, R.S., C.R., B.R., A.U., K.E.M., A.A.-M. and A.S.B.; software, R.S., K.E.M., B.F. and A.A.-M.; validation, R.S., A.A.-M., K.E.M., B.R., A.U., C.R. and A.S.B.; formal analysis, R.S., A.A.-M. and K.E.M.; investigation, R.S., A.A.-M., C.R., B.R., A.U., B.F. and A.S.B.; resources, C.R., B.R., A.U., B.F. and A.S.B.; data curation, R.S., K.E.M., A.A.-M. and A.S.B.; writing—original draft preparation, R.S., K.E.M., C.R., B.R., A.U., A.A.-M., B.F. and A.S.B.; writing—review and editing, C.R., B.R., A.U. and A.S.B.; visualization, R.S., C.R., B.R., A.U., B.F. and A.S.B.; supervision, R.S., K.E.M., A.A.-M., B.F. and A.S.B.; project administration, A.S.B. and C.R.; funding acquisition, C.R. and A.S.B. All authors have read and agreed to the published version of the manuscript.

Funding: This research was funded by the Algarrsen project SCPP2300C010708XV0 of the State Research Agency of the Ministry of Science, Innovation and Universities.

Institutional Review Board Statement: Not applicable.

Data Availability Statement: The raw data supporting the conclusions of this article will be made available by the authors upon request.

Conflicts of Interest: The authors declare no conflicts of interest.

References

1. Biradar, C.M.; Thenkabail, P.S.; Platonov, A.; Xiao, X.M.; Geerken, R.; Noojipady, P.; Turral, H.; Vithanage, J. Water productivity mapping methods using remote sensing. *J. Appl. Remote Sens.* **2008**, *2*, 023544.
2. Food and Agriculture Organization of the United Nations. *About FAO's Work on Plant Production and Protection*; Food and Agriculture Organization of the United Nations: Rome, Italy, 2022. Available online: https://www.fao.org/plant-production-protection/about/en (accessed on 31 May 2025).
3. Wolanin, A.; Mateo-García, G.; Camps-Valls, G.; Gómez-Chova, L.; Meroni, M.; Duveiller, G.; Liangzhi, Y.; Guanter, L. Estimating and Understanding Crop Yields with Explainable Deep Learning in the Indian Wheat Belt. *Environ. Res. Lett.* **2020**, *15*, 024019. [CrossRef]
4. Awika, J.M. Major cereal grains production and use around the world. In *Advances in Cereal Science: Implications to Food Processing and Health Promotion*, 1st ed.; Awika, J.M., Piironen, V., Bean, S., Eds.; American Chemical Society (ACS): Washington, DC, USA, 2011; pp. 1–13.
5. Farahzadi, F.; Ebrahimi, A.; Zarrinnia, V.; Azizinezhad, R. Evaluation of Genetic Diversity in Iranian Rice (*Oryza sativa*) Cultivars for Resistance to Blast Disease Using Microsatellite (SSR) Markers. *Agric. Res.* **2020**, *9*, 460–468. [CrossRef]
6. Zahra, N.; Hafeez, M.B.; Nawaz, A.; Farooq, M. Rice production systems and grain quality. *J. Cereal Sci.* **2022**, *105*, 103463. [CrossRef]
7. Zhao, M.; Lin, Y.; Chen, H. Improving nutritional quality of rice for human health. *Theor. Appl. Genet.* **2020**, *133*, 1397–1413. [CrossRef]
8. Cantrell, R.P.; Reeves, T.G. The rice genome. The cereal of the world's poor takes center stage. *Science* **2002**, *296*, 53. [CrossRef]

9. Becker-Reshef, I.; Bandaru, V.; Barker, B.; Coutu, S.; Deines, J.M.; Doorn, B.; Eilerts, G.; Franch, B.; Galvez, A.S.; Hosseini, M.; et al. The NASA harvest program on agriculture and food security. In *Remote Sensing of Agriculture and Land Cover/Land Use Changes in South and Southeast Asian Countries*; Springer International Publishing: Cham, Switzerland, 2022; pp. 53–80.
10. UN. Department of Economic and Social Affairs; UNCTAD; UN. ECA; UN. ECE; UN. ECLAC; UN. ESCAP; UN. ESCWA. *World Economic Situation and Prospects Executive Summary: 2015*; UN: New York, NY, USA, 2025. Available online: https://coilink.org/20.500.12592/5rsl4ww (accessed on 24 June 2025).
11. Sanyal, J.; Lu, X.X. Application of Remote Sensing in Flood Management with Special Reference to Monsoon Asia: A Review. *Nat. Hazards* **2004**, *33*, 283–301. [CrossRef]
12. Zhai, Y.; Wang, N.; Zhang, L.; Hao, L.; Hao, C. Automatic crop classification in northeastern China by improved nonlinear dimensionality reduction for satellite image time series. *Remote Sens.* **2020**, *12*, 2726. [CrossRef]
13. Bargiel, D. A new method for crop classification combining time series of radar images and crop phenology information. *Remote Sens. Environ.* **2017**, *198*, 369–383. [CrossRef]
14. Heupel, K.; Spengler, D.; Itzerott, S. A progressive crop-type classification using multitemporal remote sensing data and phenological information. *PFG—J. Photogramm. Remote Sens. Geoinf. Sci.* **2018**, *86*, 53–69. [CrossRef]
15. Bargiel, D.; Herrmann, S.; Lohmann, P.; Sörgel, U. Land use classification with high-resolution satellite radar for estimating the impacts of land use change on the quality of ecosystem services. *Int. Arch. Photogramm. Remote Sens. Spat. Inf. Sci. ISPRS Arch.* **2010**, *38*, 68–73.
16. Conrad, C.; Fritsch, S.; Zeidler, J.; Rücker, G.; Dech, S. Per-field irrigated crop classification in arid Central Asia using SPOT and ASTER data. *Remote Sens.* **2010**, *2*, 1035–1056. [CrossRef]
17. Wei, P.; Ye, H.; Qiao, S.; Liu, R.; Nie, C.; Zhang, B.; Song, L.; Huang, S. Early Crop Mapping Based on Sentinel-2 Time-Series Data and the Random Forest Algorithm. *Remote Sens.* **2023**, *15*, 3212. [CrossRef]
18. Wang, Y.; Zhang, Z.; Feng, L.; Ma, Y.; Du, Q. A New Attention-Based Cnn Approach for Crop Mapping Using Time Series Sentinel-2 Images. *Comput. Electron. Agric.* **2021**, *184*, 106090. [CrossRef]
19. Feng, S.; Zhao, J.; Liu, T.; Zhang, H.; Zhang, Z.; Guo, X. Crop Type Identification and Mapping Using Machine Learning Algorithms and Sentinel-2 Time Series Data. *IEEE J. Sel. Top. Appl. Earth Obs. Remote Sens.* **2019**, *12*, 3295–3306. [CrossRef]
20. Bellón, B.; Bégué, A.; Lo Seen, D.; de Almeida, C.; Simões, M. A Remote Sensing Approach for Regional-Scale Mapping of Agricultural Land-Use Systems Based on NDVI Time Series. *Remote Sens.* **2017**, *9*, 600. [CrossRef]
21. Ranjan, R.; Chopra, U.K.; Sahoo, R.N.; Singh, A.K.; Pradhan, S. Assessment of plant nitrogen stress in wheat (*Triticum aestivum* L.) through hyperspectral indices. *Int. J. Remote Sens.* **2012**, *33*, 6342–6360. [CrossRef]
22. Agenjos-Moreno, A.; Rubio, C.; Uris, A.; Simeón, R.; Franch, B.; Domingo, C.; Bautista, A.S. Strategy for Monitoring the Blast Incidence in Crops of Bomba Rice Variety Using Remote Sensing Data. *Agriculture* **2024**, *14*, 1385. [CrossRef]
23. Wang, B.; Fan, D. Research progress of deep learning in classification and recognition of remote sensing images. *Bull. Surv. Mapp.* **2019**, *2*, 99–102, 136.
24. Hatfield, J.L.; Gitelson, A.A.; Schepers, J.S.; Walthall, C.L. Application of Spectral Remote Sensing for Agronomic Decisions. *Agron. J.* **2008**, *100*, S-117–S-131. [CrossRef]
25. Forkuor, G.; Conrad, C.; Thiel, M.; Landmann, T.; Barry, B. Evaluating the sequential masking classification approach for improving crop discrimination in the Sudanian Savanna of West Africa. *Comput. Electron. Agric.* **2015**, *118*, 380–389. [CrossRef]
26. Chen, Y.; Lu, D.; Moran, E.; Batistella, M.; Dutra, L.V.; Sanches, I.D.A.; da Silva, R.F.B.; Huang, J.; Luiz, A.J.B.; de Oliveira, M.A.F. Mapping croplands, cropping patterns, and crop types using MODIS time-series data. *Int. J. Appl. Earth Obs. Geoinf.* **2018**, *69*, 133–147. [CrossRef]
27. Youssef, A.M.; Pourghasemi, H.R.; Pourtaghi, Z.S.; Al-Katheeri, M.M. Landslide susceptibility mapping using random forest, boosted regression tree, classification and regression tree, and general linear models and comparison of their performance at Wadi Tayyah Basin, Asir Region, Saudi Arabia. *Landslides* **2016**, *13*, 839–856. [CrossRef]
28. Hou, H.; Wang, R.; Murayama, Y. Scenario-based modelling for urban sustainability focusing on changes in cropland under rapid urbanization: A case study of Hangzhou from 1990 to 2035. *Sci. Total Environ.* **2019**, *661*, 422–431. [CrossRef]
29. Conrad, C.; Dech, S.; Dubovyk, O.; Fritsch, S.; Klein, D.; Löw, F.; Schorcht, G.; Zeidler, J. Derivation of temporal windows for accurate crop discrimination in heterogeneous croplands of Uzbekistan using multitemporal RapidEye images. *Comput. Electron. Agric.* **2014**, *103*, 63–74. [CrossRef]
30. Wardlow, B.D.; Egbert, S.L.; Kastens, J.H. Analysis of time-series MODIS 250 m vegetation index data for crop classification in the US Central Great Plains. *Remote Sens. Environ.* **2007**, *108*, 290–310. [CrossRef]
31. Simonneaux, V.; Duchemin, B.; Helson, D.; Er-Raki, S.; Olioso, A.; Chehbouni, A. The use of high-resolution image time series for crop classification and evapotranspiration estimate over an irrigated area in Central Morocco. *Int. J. Remote Sens.* **2008**, *29*, 95–116. [CrossRef]
32. Peña-Barragán, J.M.; Ngugi, M.K.; Plant, R.E.; Six, J. Object-Based Crop Identification Using Multiple Vegetation Indices, Textural Features and Crop Phenology. *Remote Sens. Environ.* **2011**, *115*, 1301–1316. [CrossRef]

33. Chang, J.; Hansen, M.C.; Pittman, K.; Carroll, M.; DiMiceli, C. Corn and soybean mapping in the United States using MODIS time-series data sets. *Agron. J.* **2007**, *99*, 1654–1664. [CrossRef]
34. Guo, Y.; Jia, X.; Paull, D. Mapping of rice varieties with sentinel-2 data via deep cnn learning in spectral and time domains. In Proceedings of the 2018 Digital Image Computing: Techniques and Applications (DICTA), Canberra, Australia, 10–13 December 2018; pp. 1–7.
35. Rauf, U.; Qureshi, S.; Jabbar, H.; Zeb, A.; Mirza, A.; Alanazi, E.; Rashid, N. A New Method for Pixel Classification for Rice Variety Identification Using Spectral and Time Series Data from Sentinel-2 Satellite Imagery. *Comput. Electron. Agric.* **2022**, *193*, 106731. [CrossRef]
36. Saadat, M.; Seydi, S.T.; Hasanlou, M.; Homayouni, S. A Convolutional Neural Network Method for Rice Mapping Using Time-Series of Sentinel-1 and Sentinel-2 Imagery. *Agriculture* **2022**, *12*, 2083. [CrossRef]
37. López-Andreu, F.J.; Erena, M.; Dominguez-Gómez, J.A.; López-Morales, J.A. Sentinel-2 Images and Machine Learning as Tool for Monitoring of the Common Agricultural Policy: Calasparra Rice as a Case Study. *Agronomy* **2021**, *11*, 621. [CrossRef]
38. de Barreda, D.G.; Pardo, G.; Osca, J.; Catala-Forner, M.; Consola, S.; Garnica, I.; López-Martínez, N.; Palmerín, J.; Osuna, M. An Overview of Rice Cultivation in Spain and the Management of Herbicide-Resistant Weeds. *Agronomy* **2021**, *11*, 1095. [CrossRef]
39. Fita, D.; Rubio, C.; Franch, B.; Castiñeira-Ibáñez, S.; Tarrazó-Serrano, D.; San Bautista, A. Improving Harvester Yield Maps Postprocessing Leveraging Remote Sensing Data in Rice Crop. *Precis. Agric.* **2025**, *26*, 33. [CrossRef]
40. Dirección General del Catastro. Sede Electrónica del Catastro: Visor cartográfico. Ministerio de Hacienda. 2025. Available online: https://www.sedecatastro.gob.es (accessed on 24 June 2025).
41. Federación de Arroceros de Sevilla. Sitio web Oficial de la Federación de Arroceros de Sevilla. 2025. Available online: https://www.federaciondearroceros.es/ (accessed on 24 June 2025).
42. Wang, S.; Di Tommaso, S.; Faulkner, J.; Friedel, T.; Kennepohl, A.; Strey, R.; Lobell, D.B. Mapping Crop Types in Southeast India with Smartphone Crowdsourcing and Deep Learning. *Remote Sens.* **2020**, *12*, 2957. [CrossRef]
43. Hudait, M.; Patel, P.P. Crop-type mapping and acreage estimation in smallholding plots using Sentinel-2 images and machine learning algorithms: Some comparisons. *Egypt. J. Remote Sens. Space Sci.* **2022**, *25*, 147–156. [CrossRef]
44. Prins, A.J.; Van Niekerk, A. Crop type mapping using LiDAR, Sentinel-2 and aerial imagery with machine learning algorithms. *Geo-Spat. Inf. Sci.* **2021**, *24*, 215–227. [CrossRef]
45. Zhang, P.; Jia, Y.; Shang, Y. Research and application of XGBoost in imbalanced data. *Int. J. Distrib. Sens. Netw.* **2022**, *18*, 15501329221106935. [CrossRef]
46. Arias, M.; Campo-Bescós, M.Á.; Álvarez-Mozos, J. Crop classification based on temporal signatures of Sentinel-1 observations over Navarre province, Spain. *Remote. Sens.* **2020**, *12*, 278. [CrossRef]
47. Rui, X.; Su, S.; Mai, G.; Zhang, Z.; Yang, C. Quantifying determinants of cash crop expansion and their relative effects using logistic regression modeling and variance partitioning. *Int. J. Appl. Earth Obs. Geoinf.* **2015**, *34*, 258–263.
48. Cover, T.; Hart, P. Nearest neighbor pattern classification. *IEEE Trans. Inf. Theory* **1967**, *13*, 21–27. [CrossRef]
49. Uddin, K.M.M.; Biswas, N.; Rikta, S.T.; Dey, S.K. Machine learning-based diagnosis of breast cancer utilizing feature optimization technique. *Comput. Methods Programs Biomed. Updat.* **2023**, *3*, 100098. [CrossRef]
50. Chen, T.; Guestrin, C. Xgboost: A scalable tree boosting system. In Proceedings of the 22nd ACM Sigkdd International Conference on Knowledge Discovery and Data Mining, San Francisco, CA, USA, 13–17 August 2016; pp. 785–794.
51. Breiman, L. Random Forests. *Mach. Learn.* **2001**, *45*, 5–32. [CrossRef]
52. Breiman, L. Bagging predictors. *Mach. Learn.* **1996**, *24*, 123–140. [CrossRef]
53. Amit, Y.; Geman, D. Shape quantization and recognition with randomized trees. *Neural Comput.* **1997**, *9*, 1545–1588. [CrossRef]
54. Cox, D.R. The Regression Analysis of Binary Sequences. *J. R. Stat. Soc. Ser. B* **1958**, *20*, 215–242. [CrossRef]
55. Tharwat, A. Classification assessment methods. *Appl. Comput. Inform.* **2020**, *17*, 168–192. [CrossRef]
56. Lancashire, P.D.; Bleiholder, H.; van den Boom, T.; Langelüddeke, P.; Stauss, R.; Weber, E.; Witzenberger, A. A Uniform Decimal Code for Growth Stages of Crops and Weeds. *Ann. Appl. Biol.* **1991**, *119*, 561–601. [CrossRef]
57. Belgiu, M.; Drăguţ, L. Random Forest in Remote Sensing: A Review of Applications and Future Directions. *ISPRS J. Photogramm. Remote Sens.* **2016**, *114*, 24–31. [CrossRef]
58. Thanh, D.K.; Ngoc, D.L.; Dieu, H.D.; Tran, V.A. Comparison of random forest and extreme gradient boosting algorithms in land cover classification in van yen district, Yen Bai Province, Vietnam. *J. Hydro-Environ. Res.* **2025**, *23*, 50–59.
59. Asgari, S.; Hasanlou, M. A Comparative Study of Machine Learning Classifiers for Crop Type Mapping Using Vegetation Indices. *ISPRS Ann. Photogramm. Remote Sens. Spat. Inf. Sci.* **2023**, *X-4/W1-2022*, 79–85. [CrossRef]
60. Zhong, L.H.; Gong, P.; Biging, G.S. Phenology-based crop classification algorithm and its implications on agricultural water use assessments in California's Central Valley. *Photogramm. Eng. Remote Sens.* **2012**, *78*, 799–813. [CrossRef]
61. Militino, A.F.; Goyena, H.; Pérez-Goya, U.; Ugarte, M.D. Logistic Regression versus XGBoost for Detecting Burned Areas Using Satellite Images. *Environ. Ecol. Stat.* **2024**, *31*, 57–77. [CrossRef]

62. Yang, H.-C.; Zhou, J.-P.; Zheng, C.; Wu, Z.; Li, Y.; Li, L.-G. PhenologyNet: A fine-grained approach for crop-phenology classification fusing convolutional neural network and phenotypic similarity. *Comput. Electron. Agric.* **2025**, *229*, 109728. [CrossRef]
63. Gitelson, A.A.; Viña, A.; Arkebauer, T.J.; Rundquist, D.C.; Keydan, G.; Leavitt, B. Remote estimation of leaf area index and green leaf biomass in maize canopies. *Geophys. Res. Lett.* **2003**, *30*. [CrossRef]
64. Zhang, H.; Duan, Z.; Li, Y.; Zhao, G.; Zhu, S.; Fu, W.; Peng, T.; Zhao, Q.; Svanberg, S.; Hu, J. Vis/NIR Reflectance Spectroscopy for Hybrid Rice Variety Identification and Chlorophyll Content Evaluation for Different Nitrogen Fertilizer Levels. *R. Soc. Open Sci.* **2019**, *6*, 191132. [CrossRef]
65. Frampton, W.J.; Dash, J.; Watmough, G.; Milton, E.J. Evaluating the Capabilities of Sentinel-2 for Quantitative Estimation of Biophysical Variables in Vegetation. *ISPRS J. Photogramm. Remote Sens.* **2013**, *82*, 83–92. [CrossRef]
66. Clevers, J.G.; Gitelson, A.A. Remote estimation of crop and grass chlorophyll and nitrogen content using red-edge bands on Sentinel-2 and -3. *Int. J. Appl. Earth Obs. Geoinf.* **2013**, *23*, 344–351. [CrossRef]
67. Imran, H.A.; Gianelle, D.; Rocchini, D.; Dalponte, M.; Martín, M.P.; Sakowska, K.; Wohlfahrt, G.; Vescovo, L. VIS-NIR, red-edge and NIR-shoulder based normalized vegetation indices response to co-varying leaf and Canopy structural traits in heterogeneous grasslands. *Remote Sens.* **2020**, *12*, 2254. [CrossRef]
68. Xie, Q.; Dash, J.; Huete, A.; Jiang, A.; Yin, G.; Ding, Y.; Peng, D.; Hall, C.C.; Brown, L.; Shi, Y.; et al. Retrieval of crop biophysical parameters from Sentinel-2 remote sensing imagery. *Int. J. Appl. Earth Obs. Geoinf.* **2019**, *80*, 187–195. [CrossRef]
69. Yang, J.; Jiang, J.; Fu, Z.; Wang, W.; Cao, Q.; Tian, Y.; Zhu, Y.; Cao, W.; Liu, X. Integrating phenology information with UAV multispectral data for rice nitrogen nutrition diagnosis. *Eur. J. Agron.* **2025**, *169*, 127696. [CrossRef]
70. Qiu, B.; Yu, L.; Yang, P.; Wu, W.; Chen, J.; Zhu, X.; Duan, M. Mapping Upland Crop–Rice Cropping Systems for Targeted Sustainable Intensification in South China. *Crop J.* **2024**, *12*, 614–629. [CrossRef]
71. Son, N.T.; Chen, C.F.; Chen, C.R.; Sobue, S.I.; Chiang, S.H.; Maung, T.H.; Chang, L.Y. Delineating and predicting changes in rice cropping systems using multi-temporal MODIS data in myanmar. *J. Spat. Sci.* **2017**, *62*, 235–259. [CrossRef]
72. Wang, F.M.; Yi, Q.X.; Hu, J.H.; Xie, L.L.; Yao, X.P.; Xu, T.Y.; Zheng, J.Y. Combining spectral and textural information in UAV hyperspectral images to estimate rice grain yield. *Int. J. Appl. Earth Obs. Geoinf.* **2021**, *102*, 102397. [CrossRef]

agriculture

MDPI

Article

Hyperspectral Imaging Combined with a Dual-Channel Feature Fusion Model for Hierarchical Detection of Rice Blast

Yuan Qi [1], Tan Liu [1,2,*], Songlin Guo [1], Peiyan Wu [1], Jun Ma [1], Qingyun Yuan [1], Weixiang Yao [1,2] and Tongyu Xu [1,2]

1 College of Information and Electronic Engineering, Shenyang Agricultural University, Shenyang 110866, China; qy06211121@163.com (Y.Q.); 15833032314@163.com (S.G.); 16671072683@163.com (P.W.); majun200108@163.com (J.M.); yuanqingyun@syau.edu.cn (Q.Y.); yaoweixiang@syau.edu.cn (W.Y.); xutongyu@syau.edu.cn (T.X.)

2 Key Laboratory of Smart Agriculture Technology in Liaoning Province, Shenyang 110866, China

* Correspondence: liutan0822@syau.edu.cn

Abstract: Rice blast caused by *Magnaporthe oryzae* is a major cause of yield reductions and quality deterioration in rice. Therefore, early detection of the disease is necessary for controlling the spread of rice blast. This study proposed a dual-channel feature fusion model (DCFM) to achieve effective identification of rice blast. The DCFM model extracted spectral features using successive projection algorithm (SPA), random frog (RFrog), and competitive adaptive reweighted sampling (CARS), and extracted spatial features from spectral images using MobileNetV2 combined with the convolutional block attention module (CBAM). Then, these features were fused using the feature fusion adaptive conditioning module in DCFM and input into the fully connected layer for disease identification. The results show that the model combining spectral and spatial features was superior to the classification models based on single features for rice blast detection, with OA and Kappa higher than 90% and 88%, respectively. The DCFM model based on SPA screening obtained the best results, with an OA of 96.72% and a Kappa of 95.97%. Overall, this study enables the early and accurate identification of rice blast, providing a rapid and reliable method for rice disease monitoring and management. It also offers a valuable reference for the detection of other crop diseases.

Keywords: rice blast; hyperspectral; deep learning; feature fusion; severity classification

1. Introduction

Rice is one of the most crucial crops in the world, and a main source of food for over half of the world's population [1]. Crop pests and diseases are among the serious threats to agricultural production in China. Diseases such as rice blast are increasingly affecting rice growers worldwide, posing a significant risk to global food security [2]. The incidence and severity of rice blast fluctuate annually based on geographical location and environmental factors [3], and can cause an annual yield loss of 10 to 30% [4]. During severe outbreaks, reductions in rice production can escalate from 40 to 50%. When the pathogen infects the crown, leaf blade, leaf neck, and spike, the onset of the disease is most pronounced [5]. Initially, the infection manifests as a small brown spot on the leaf tissue, gradually expanding into a fusiform shape, with a gray center and brown edges. These lesions may continue to grow, eventually merging and causing the death of the entire leaf [6,7]. Therefore, developing rapid and non-destructive methods for disease detection is indispensable for effectively monitoring rice growth.

Traditional methods for detecting rice diseases rely heavily on labor-intensive practices, including field inspections, surveys, and sample collection [8]. These approaches are time- and labor-intensive, highly dependent on subjective judgment, and often yield diagnostic accuracy. Moreover, they typically require inspectors with specialized expertise [9]. In large-scale or cross-regional farming, such methods are highly inefficient. Detecting early or latent signs of infestation also poses significant time and technical challenges [10]. Hyperspectral imaging technology (HSI) has emerged as a promising alternative to traditional methods. Owing to its high spectral resolution and the ability to capture both spectral and spatial information, it has become a research hotspot and has been widely applied in crop disease identification [11–13].

Technological advances in computer vision and machine learning have promoted the effective application of image processing in crop disease detection [14,15]. With the introduction of convolutional neural network (CNN) methods, crop disease detection based on deep learning has shown remarkable performance compared to traditional machine learning methods [16,17]. Even with limited labeled samples, semi-supervised models have been able to achieve high classification accuracy. You et al. [18] utilized hyperspectral microscope imaging combined with advanced chemometrics to recognize diseased Korla fragrant pears. The CNN model based on fusion datasets performed the best at differentiating between healthy pears and diseased pears, with a maximum accuracy of 96.72%. Chun et al. [19] developed a rapid and non-destructive method for determining the stage of botrytis cinerea infection in strawberry fruit using hyperspectral fluorescence imaging combined with multiple classification models. The 1D-CNN model, which was based on a ResNet-50, outperformed the other models with a precision of 96.88%, a recall of 96.87%, an F1-score of 96.85%, and an accuracy of 96.86%. Gui et al. [20] suggested a classification method using HSI technology for the early identification of soybean mosaic virus disease. This method combined a convolutional neural network with a support vector machine. The CNN-SVM model demonstrated 96.67% accuracy on the training set and 94.17% accuracy on the test set. Qi et al. [21] proposed a deep learning classification framework for effectively detecting potato late blight in hyperspectral images. The model integrated 2D and 3D convolutional neural networks (2D-CNN and 3D-CNN) with deep collaborative attention networks (PLB-2D-3D-A), achieving a maximum accuracy of 79%. Bu et al. [22] proposed ResNet-R&H, a novel classification model based on the ResNet architecture. By fusing RGB and hyperspectral images, the model was used to assess the freshness of vegetable soybean and achieved a test accuracy of 97.6%. Chen et al. [23] developed a deep learning model called the Rice Bakanae Disease-Visual Geometry Group (RBD-VGG) to detect rice bakanae disease. On the 21st day of infection, an accuracy of 92.2% was attained on average using this model.

Although HSI and image processing technologies have been widely used in agricultural production, most of the existing studies are still limited to modeling and analysis using spectral or image data. In contrast, relatively little attention has been given to the extraction and fusion of spatial structural features embedded within spectral images. Rice blast infestation often presents as a multilevel symptom ranging from microscopic pigment changes to macroscopic leaf morphology. Relying solely on biochemical response signals from spectral curves makes it difficult to fully capture the spatial distribution characteristics of the disease. Image information, on the other hand, can reveal structural changes in the shape, margins, and irregularities of disease spots. Therefore, relying only on single-dimensional features may lead to information loss and limited discriminative capability. The core of the HSI technique lies in its three-dimensional data, which include rich two-dimensional image information and one-dimensional spectral data. This necessitates utilizing the spectral and spatial information of the fusion features to distinguish different levels of rice blast.

Given these, this paper proposed a dual-channel deep learning feature fusion adaptive conditioning model. It employed the successive projection algorithm (SPA), random frog (RFrog), and competitive adaptive reweighted sampling (CARS) to determine spectral characteristic wavelengths associated with rice blast. In parallel, spatial features were extracted using the MobileNetV2 model combined with a dual-attention mechanism. Spectral and image data were input simultaneously and fused through a feature fusion adaptive conditioning module. This approach fully leveraged both internal and external features of disease identification, enabling high-precision classification of rice blast. Comparative analysis was conducted using support vector machine (SVM), particle swarm algorithm optimized support vector machine (PSOSVM), random forest (RF), residual neural network (ResNet50), and MobileNetV2 models with those in this study. This provides research ideas and methods for the application of hyperspectral images in rice blast detection.

2. Materials and Methods

2.1. Experimental Area

The experimental region of this study was situated in Liujiaohe Village, Shenyang New District, Shenyang, Liaoning Province (2020) (41°48′11″ N, 123°25′31″ E) and at the experimental base of Shenyang Agricultural University, Haicheng City, Liaoning Province (2021 and 2022) (40°85′43″ N, 122°74′33″ E). The study included both artificially stained experimental plots (2020 and 2021) and natural incidence areas (2022). Haicheng City is in the central part of the Liaodong Peninsula and belongs to the temperate semi-humid continental climate, with four distinct seasons and abundant rainfall. The average temperature in July and August is 25 °C, the average rainfall is 145 mm, the humidity is 78%, and there are 9 rainy days per month. The climatic conditions are favorable for rice cultivation, and the study area is shown in Figure 1.

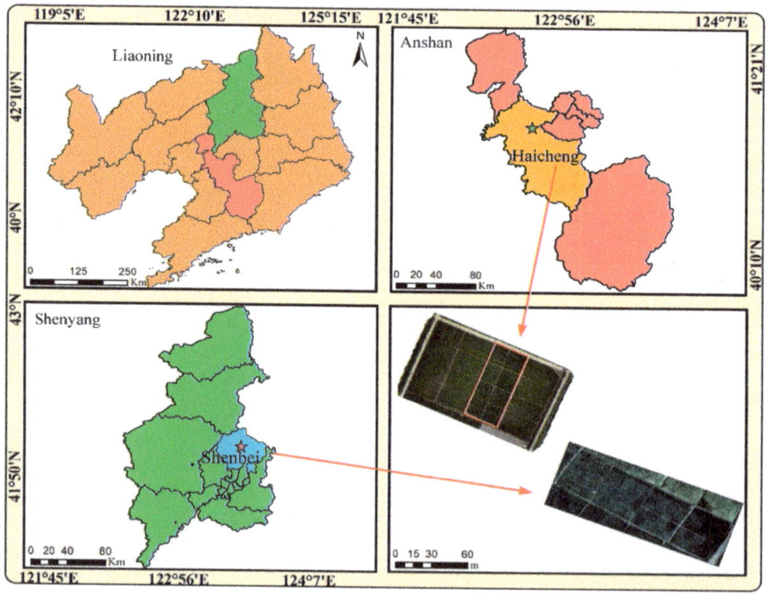

Figure 1. Study site.

Artificially stained experimental plots (2020 and 2021) are as follows: The test variety was Mongolian rice, which is susceptible to rice blast. During the rice cultivation period, the paddy fields were not sun-dried. The spore suspension was evenly sprayed on the leaf surface at 5:30 p.m. after sunset on 3 July 2020 and 6 July 2021, respectively. At the inoculation site, moistened black impermeable plastic bags were wrapped around the rice plants and removed at 6:30 a.m. the following day. To ensure the test results' reliability, plant protection experts were invited to provide guidance and assistance during the rice blast inoculation process. Through the experimental design of artificially inducing rice blast, rice in the infected area exhibited symptoms 6 days after inoculation. Trials were conducted at three critical fertility stages, namely the jointing, booting, and heading stages of rice, to collect healthy and diseased plants. Rice plants were randomly sampled from the selected area, focusing on only one leaf per plant below the flag leaf where symptoms were evident. These leaves were then manually collected and sent to the laboratory for hyperspectral image acquisition.

Natural incidence areas (2022) are as follows: With Yanfeng 47 as the planting rice variety and an area of 0.39 hm^2, the experimental plot produced a 30 $\times$ 20 cm density. The field looked to have an infestation of the rice blast on 12 July 2022, as discovered by the plant protection crew.

In addition, referring to the "GTB 15790-2009 rules of investigation and forecast of the rice blast" [24], the percentage of diseased area for the whole leaf blade was calculated to determine the disease level in the collected rice samples. The details are presented in Table 1. Figure 2 shows that level 0 refers to plots free from disease, while levels 1 to 4 denote progressively increasing infection severity.

Table 1. Disease classification standards and sample size statistics.

Disease Level	Standards for Spot Level	Size
Level 0	No disease spots.	96
Level 1	Disease spot area less than 1% of leaf area.	174
Level 2	Disease spot area of 1~5% of leaf area.	138
Level 3	Disease spot area of 5~10% of leaf area.	92
Level 4	Disease spot area of 10~50% of leaf area.	96

Figure 2. Ground images of rice blast at different levels of disease severity.

2.2. Hyperspectral Image Acquisition and Processing

Figure 3 demonstrates the process of hyperspectral image acquisition. The images of rice leaves were captured using this hyperspectral imaging system. The system consisted mostly of a hyperspectral imaging spectrometer (ImSpector V10E, Spectral Imaging Ltd., Oulu, Finland), a CCD camera (IGV-B1410, Antrim, Northern Ireland), a precision displacement console, a lightless dark box, two 150 W fiber optic halogen lamps (Ocean Optics, Dunedin, FL, USA), and a computer. The ImSpector V10E acquired an effective spectral range of 400–1000 nm, with 942 bands and a spectral resolution of 1.09 nm. The distance of the camera lens from the rice leaf surface was pre-set at 32 cm to capture images. Until the transition area was sharp and the black stripe was imaged, the focal length of the lens was adjusted using a white paper focusing plate with black stripes. For optimal image quality, the light source's exposure and intensity were adjusted, and the scanning speed was set to 1.2 mm/s.

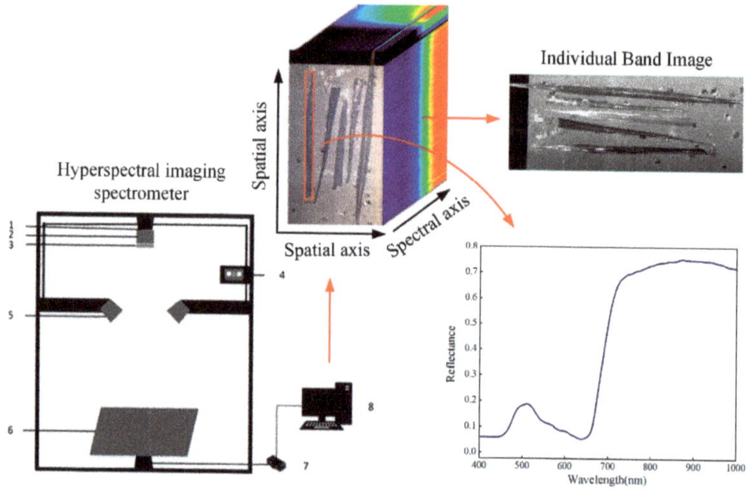

Figure 3. Hyperspectral imaging system: (**1**) CCD camera; (**2**) hyperspectral imaging spectrometer; (**3**) lens; (**4**) light source controller; (**5**) light source; (**6**) moving table; (**7**) displacement controller; (**8**) computer.

The intensity levels in different spatial hyperspectral images vary due to uneven illumination on the leaf surface and the dark current of the camera. Therefore, to acquire the final spectral reflectance, black and white plate reference correction must be applied to the raw hyperspectral images using the following equation.

$$I = \frac{R_S - R_D}{R_W - R_D} \tag{1}$$

where I represents the corrected spectral reflectance of rice leaves, R_S represents the spectral reflectance of the original hyperspectral images of rice leaves, and R_W and R_D are the spectral reflectance of the corrected white plate and corrected black plate, respectively.

2.3. *Data Extraction*

2.3.1. Spectral Feature Extraction

The whole rice leaves were used as a single region of interest (ROI), and the average spectral reflectance manually extracted around the ROI using the software ENVI 5.3 was used as one-dimensional spectral data of rice. Finally, 96 health data and 500 disease data were obtained. Due to the high dimensionality and strong correlation inherent in spectral data, a large amount of redundant information exists, which increases model complexity. To eliminate interfering classification variables and amplify spectral differences between sample categories, it is crucial to reduce the dimensionality of raw spectral data and extract key wavelengths for classification [25]. The SPA, CARS, and RFrog were employed in this paper to reduce the dimensionality of the data. These methods are widely used in the field of crop disease detection for selecting spectral characteristic wavelengths. This is because they are well-suited for scenarios involving high dimensionality, small sample sizes, and severe feature redundancy.

SPA is a forward feature-variable selection algorithm that eliminates the effect of collinearity between many wavelength variables and reduces model complexity [26]. The process begins by selecting an initial wavelength and calculating its projection onto the remaining unselected wavelengths. Wavelengths with the largest projection vectors are added to the wavelength subset and are iterated for N times. Each selected wavelength is linearly minimized to the previous one. Then the calibration correction model is used to select the spectral characteristic wavelengths.

CARS combines adaptive reweighted sampling (ARS) and exponentially decreasing function (EDF), which is a commonly utilized feature-variable selection method in crop disease identification. The spectral characteristic wavelengths are derived from the feature variables with the lowest root-mean-square error of cross-validation (RMSECV) through Monte Carlo interactive validation [27]. This method effectively enhances prediction accuracy while maximizing the retention of informative variables.

RFrog is a novel feature-variable extraction algorithm inspired by the modeling framework of Reversible Jump Markov Chain Monte Carlo [28]. This algorithm utilizes specific variables from the spectral data for continuous iteration and modeling. It simulates a Markov chain aligned with the steady-state distribution in space, calculates the selection probability of each spectral variable, and determines the spectral characteristic wavelengths based on the magnitude of these probabilities.

In this case, SPA is a fully deterministic method and does not require the setting of a random seed, whereas RFrog and CARS involve randomized processes during execution, which may lead to differences in the results of each run. To ensure the reproducibility of the experimental results, this paper sets a fixed random seed in the relevant algorithms.

2.3.2. Image Feature Parameter Extraction

The texture and shape feature parameters of rice samples were extracted from single-channel grayscale images. The spatial configuration and grayscale distribution of the image pixels were reflected in the texture features [29]. Extracting and incorporating these texture features helps improve the representation of spatial patterns in certain scenarios [30]. In the classification of rice blast, different disease classes may exhibit different texture patterns. Thus, extracting texture features can provide more distinguishing information. In addition to texture features, shape features serve as a basis for rice blast classification [31], and were used to characterize the shape of spots in rice blast images by extracting attributes such as area, perimeter, and width-to-height ratio. Finally, the feature parameters were combined with the original spectral data as fusion data to provide comprehensive and precise information for subsequent modeling.

2.4. *DCFM Model*

To accurately assess the severity of rice blast, it is necessary to combine spectral and spatial information of rice samples. Therefore, a dual-channel feature fusion model (DCFM) was constructed to effectively integrate spectral and spatial information. The model was based on deep learning and implemented using a convolutional neural network (CNN), as shown in Figure 4. The DCFM consisted of three main parts, namely a module for extracting features from one-dimensional spectral data of rice samples, a module for extracting spatial features from image data, and a module for feature fusion and adaptive conditioning classification. The effectiveness of the proposed DCFM was evaluated and examined by comparing it to the SVM, PSOSVM, RF, ResNet50, and MobileNetV2 model architectures. To ensure the fairness and scientific validity of the comparison, all baseline models (SVM, PSOSVM, RF, ResNet50, and MobileNetV2) underwent parameter tuning. Among them, the SVM model optimized the penalty coefficient c and kernel parameter g by grid search.

The number of decision trees in RF was set to 1000, and the rest of the parameters were default values. The PSOSVM model combined the particle swarm optimization algorithm to automatically search for the optimal hyperparameters. A variable inertia weight ω is introduced to enhance global search capability and reduce the risk of falling into local optima. For the deep learning models ResNet50 and MobileNetV2, the parameters were tuned based on empirical principles and performance in this study.

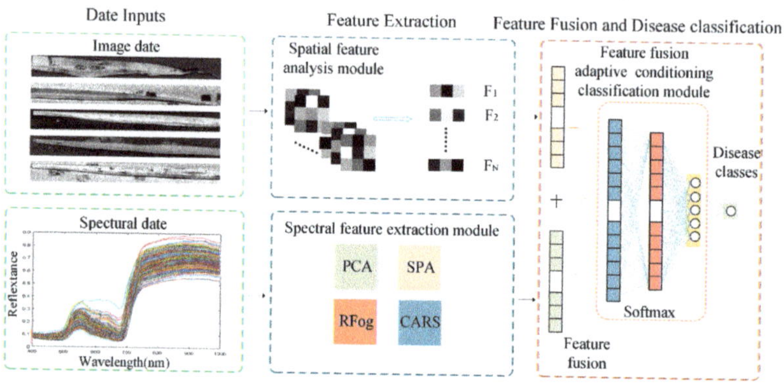

Figure 4. Structure of the DCFM model.

2.4.1. Spectral Feature Extraction Module

When crops are affected by diseases, their spectral responses change significantly, exhibiting distinct spectral characteristics. Therefore, in the spectral feature extraction module, traditional methods such as SPA, RFrog, and CARS are used to extract spectral features to help classify different disease levels.

2.4.2. Spatial Feature Extraction Module

In the spatial feature extraction module, the classical MobileNetV2 framework was used. Since feature fusion involves handling significantly more data than single-feature inputs, model input size and computational efficiency become critical. MobileNetV2, with its lightweight architecture, offers fewer parameters and lower computational complexity compared to the commonly used ResNet50 in hyperspectral images. This greatly reduces computational cost and hardware requirements. Therefore, MobileNetV2 was chosen as the backbone for spatial feature extraction in this study. The framework consisted of three convolutional layers, one fully connected layer, and one pooling layer. The pooling layer used maximum pooling, and the activation function was ReLU6. Due to different image sizes, all of the images were normalized to 1024 $\times$ 512, with blank spaces filled with zeros. The overall structure of MobileNetV2 is displayed in Table 2. Compared to the spectral feature extraction module, the spatial feature extraction module employed the CBAM [32], which consisted of two sub-modules connected in series, namely the channel attention module (CAM) and the spatial attention module (SAM), as shown in Figure 5. The overall network structure for spatial feature extraction is shown in Figure 6. This hybrid attention mechanism has the advantage of plug-and-play compatibility with the original network and can be integrated with any feedforward neural network. It can simultaneously acquire attention information in both channel and spatial dimensions, effectively improving the efficiency and accuracy of the network. The final SoftMax layer in MobileNetV2 was removed, eliminating its original classification function and allowing the model output to be converted into spatial feature representations. Subsequently, the extracted spatial features were mapped by adding a fully connected layer to convert them into one-dimensional vectors.

Table 2. MobilenetV2 model structure.

Input	Operator	t	c	n	s
2242 × 3	Conv2d	-	32	1	2
1122 × 32	bottlenneck	6	16	1	1
1122 × 16	bottlenneck	6	24	2	2
562 × 24	bottlenneck	6	32	3	2
284 × 32	bottlenneck	6	64	4	2
142 × 64	bottlenneck	6	96	3	1
142 × 96	bottlenneck	6	160	3	2
72 × 160	bottlenneck	6	320	1	1
72 × 320	Conv2d1 × 1	-	1280	1	1
72 × 1280	avgpool1 × 1	-	-	1	-
1 × 1 × 32	Conv2d1 × 1	-	k	-	-

Note: t is the multiplication factor, c is the number of output channels, n is the number of repetitions of the module, and s is the step size of the first layer of each module.

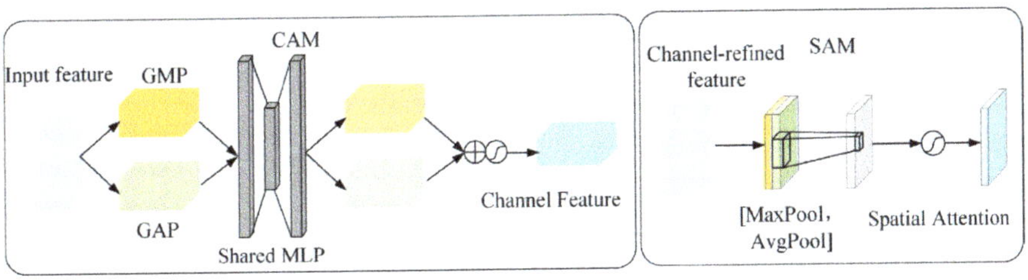

Figure 5. Hybrid attention mechanism structure.

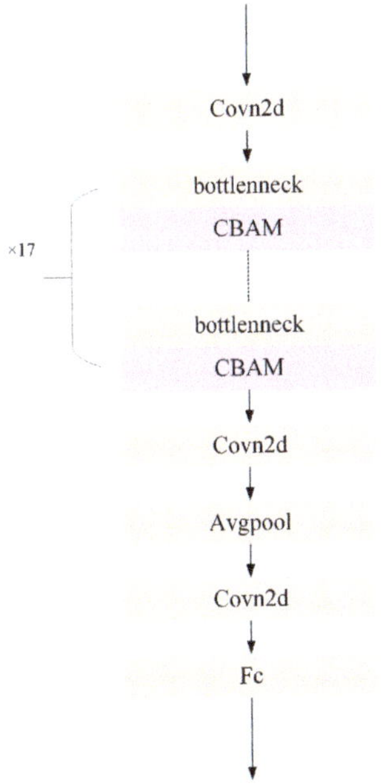

Figure 6. Spatial local convolutional network structure.

First, important channels were emphasized through CAM. The spatial dimensions of the input feature maps were compressed through parallel global max pooling (GMP) and global average pooling (GAP), while the original number of channels was preserved. Then, the two obtained feature maps were input into the multilayer perceptron (MLP) for compression and stretching. The features outputted from MLP were summed element by element, and the channel weight data were obtained after the sigmoid function. The sigmoid function maps the values to the range of (0, 1), making it well-suited for representing the degree of emphasis or suppression for each channel. For each channel's feature map, two 2D feature maps were obtained using maximum pooling and average pooling. These were then stacked along the channel dimension and fused through a convolutional layer. Finally, the resulting feature maps were passed through a sigmoid activation function to produce spatial weight maps, which highlight or suppress specific spatial positions. The process can be defined as follows:

$$M_c(F) = \rho(w_0(w_1(F^c_{avg})) + w_1(w_0(F^c_{max}))) \tag{2}$$

$$M_s(F') = \rho(f([F^s_{avg}; F^s_{max}]) \tag{3}$$

where F and F' represent the input feature map, $M_c(\bullet)$ denotes channel weights, $M_s(\bullet)$ denotes spatial weights, F_{avg} and F_{max} denote the average and maximum pooling layers, w_0 and w_1 denote the parameters of the MLP layer, f denotes the convolutional layer, and ρ denotes the sigmoid function.

2.4.3. Feature Fusion Adaptive Conditioning Module for DCFM Model

Feature fusion was the merging of one-dimensional feature vectors extracted from hyperspectral images and spectral data to enhance the utilization of features by the model and improve classification performance. Since the two input eigenvalues may differ in size, the data need to be normalized before fusion to effectively limit the range of the preprocessed data and reduce the impact of outliers on the accuracy of the model. Min–max normalization is a type of normalization that converts data from different value intervals to the same range from 0 to 1. Specifically, if one supposes the input data is $u = \{u_1, u_2, \ldots, u_C\}$, the normalization formula is Equation (4).

$$u' = \frac{u - \min(u)}{\max(u) - \min(u)} \tag{4}$$

Due to the different sources of the two features, there was no guarantee that they were not strongly correlated. Therefore, it was necessary to whiten each of these two types of input features. Suppose the input data is $y = \{y_1, y_2, \ldots, y_T\}$, the mean and variance of the data were first calculated for each feature by subtracting its corresponding mean and then dividing by its standard deviation so that each feature has zero mean and unit variance. This process not only helps to eliminate the correlation between features, but also helps to mitigate the problem of vanishing or exploding gradients, thus improving the model's performance and speeding up the convergence of the network. The principle is shown in Equations (5)–(7), below:

$$\mu \leftarrow \frac{1}{T}\sum_{i=1}^{T} y_i \tag{5}$$

$$\sigma^2 \leftarrow \frac{1}{T}\sum_{i=1}^{T} (y_i - \mu)^2 \tag{6}$$

$$y_{white} = \frac{y_i - \mu}{\sqrt{\sigma^2 + \epsilon}} \tag{7}$$

where y_i denotes the value taken by the i-th sample, T is the input data size, μ denotes the mean of the dataset, and σ^2 denotes the variance of the dataset.

The multiscale spatial features extracted from the hyperspectral image are $X_t = \{x_{t1}, x_{t2}, \ldots, x_{tn}\} \in R^n$, and the spectral data are $X_e = \{x_{e1}, x_{e2}, \ldots, x_{en}\} \in R^m$. In this experiment, feature fusion is performed by concatenating the spatial features X_t and X_e to obtain a new feature vector X_f; X_f is an m + n-dimensional feature vector. The feature fusion formula is expressed as follows:

$$X_f = X_t \oplus X_e = (x_{t1}, x_{t2}, \ldots, x_{tn}, x_{e1}, x_{e2}, \ldots, x_{em}), X_f \in R^{n+m} \tag{8}$$

In X_f, each feature vector not only contains the main features of the original spectral data, but also covers multi-scale spatial features in the neighborhood space and adjacent frequency bands. The centralized multi-scale features help reduce misclassification caused by similar single-scale features, thereby enhancing disease recognition. The fused feature X_f is input to the output layer for disease classification. Each neuron in the output layer was interconnected with each neuron in the previous layer to ensure sufficient information transmission and integration. The SoftMax function was used as the activation function for the final layer, converting the output into a probability distribution to facilitate the classification decision.

2.5. Experimental Settings

In this study, the experimental processing platform is i9-10980XE CPU, the main frequency is 2934 MHz, the memory is 64 G, and the GPU model is Quadro RTX 5000. All models were constructed using PyTorch 1.13.0 + Cuda 11.6 in Python 3.7. For reproducibility, a fixed random seed was set across all relevant libraries. The input image size for the experiment was 1024 × 512. Considering the potential negative impact of data augmentation on spectral curves, the model was trained using the original samples, without applying any augmentation techniques. To eliminate the uncertainty caused by dataset splitting on the model classification performance, all 596 samples were selected for model training in this study, and the model was evaluated using five-fold cross-validation. The models were trained using specific parameters, with a training batch size of 128 across 500 epochs. The SGD optimization algorithm was chosen, the initial learning rate of the algorithm was set to 0.001, and the momentum was set to 0.9. The loss function adopted weighted CrossEntropy. By assigning higher weights to the disease levels with fewer samples, the model was guided to pay more attention to the levels that were easily overlooked during the training, thus effectively mitigating the impact of imbalance across disease levels on performance. To comprehensively evaluate the performance of the rice blast recognition models, the overall accuracy (OA), precision, F1-score, and Kappa coefficient were used as the evaluation metrics. All metrics take values between 0 and 1, with larger values indicating better model performance. Ultimately, the best-performing model was determined based on the average performance of OA, Kappa, and F1-score in the five-fold cross-validation. These metrics were calculated as follows:

$$OA = \frac{TP + TN}{TP + TN + FP + FN} \tag{9}$$

$$\text{Precision} = \frac{TP}{TP + FP} \tag{10}$$

$$\text{F1-score} = \frac{2TP}{2TP + FN + FP} \tag{11}$$

$$P_e = \sum_{i=1}^{c} \frac{(TP_i + FN_i)(TP_i + FP_i)}{N^2} \tag{12}$$

$$\text{Kappa} = \frac{\text{OA} - P_e}{1 - P_e} \tag{13}$$

where TP denotes the correctly identified positive samples, TN denotes the correctly identified negative samples, FP denotes the falsely identified negative samples labeled as positive, and FN denotes the falsely identified positive samples labeled as negative.

3. Results

3.1. Spectral Analysis for Rice Blast

Figure 7 presents the average reflectance curves of rice blast infestation at different stages. In the visible region (500–600 nm), the reflectance of infected rice leaves slightly increases. In the red-edge region (630–720 nm), due to leaf damage and chlorophyll degradation caused by rice blast [33], the spectral curves exhibit a blue shift towards shorter wavelengths. In the NIR region (720–1000 nm), the spectral curves of diseased leaves significantly decrease. In the wavelength range of 400–450 nm, reflectance from diseased and healthy leaf regions of rice is noisy and has significant overlap [24].

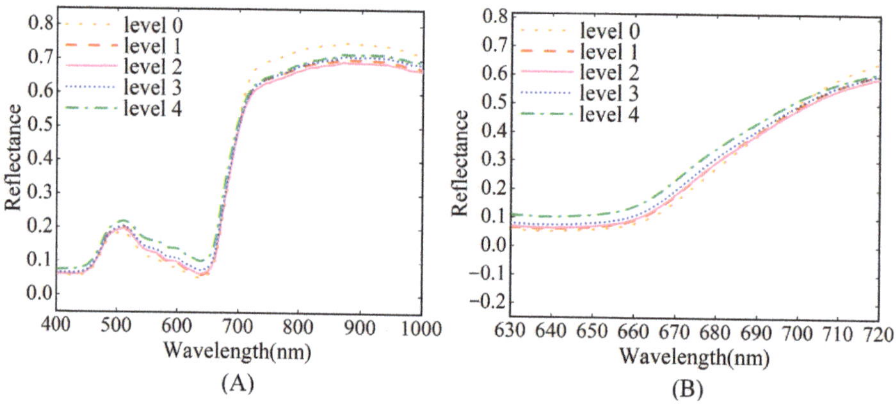

Figure 7. Comparison of average leaf reflectance curves. (**A**) Average leaf reflectance curves of diseases at 400 to 1000 nm; (**B**) average leaf reflectance curves of diseases at 630 to 720 nm.

3.2. Hyperspectral Image Result of Dimensionality Reduction

The hyperspectral image contains high-dimensional features and a large amount of information. However, this high dimensionality also increases the difficulty and complexity of image processing [34]. To simplify this process, principal component analysis (PCA) was utilized to reduce the dimensionality and generate principal component maps that retained substantial valid information [35]. The whole leaf of each sample was selected for PCA using the ROI tool. The first three principal component maps (PC1–PC3) of each hyperspectral image were retained for spatial feature extraction, and their cumulative variance contributions all exceeded 95%, as shown in Figure 8. Significant differences between healthy and diseased leaves were observed in the principal component images from PC1 to PC3. The diseased regions showed a noticeable texture difference from the surrounding areas, appearing with darker grayscale and lower brightness in PC2. Therefore, the spatial features extracted from the image after dimensionality reduction by PCA can clearly distinguish between the diseased area and the healthy ones.

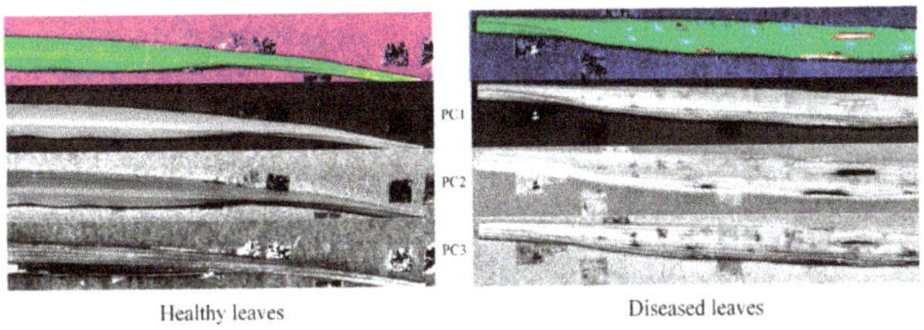

Figure 8. Principal component images of rice leaves.

3.3. Analysis of Spectral Feature Extraction Results

SPA was used to extract features from the spectral data to effectively capture information related to rice blast. The minimum and maximum numbers of features selected by the algorithm were set to 5 and 10, respectively, with RMSE used as the evaluation criterion. Figure 9A illustrates the RMSE plot used to determine the number of effective wavelengths. When the number of features was 1 to 4, the RMSE curve became steeper, indicating that these features significantly enhanced the model's predictive ability and represented a critical feature subset. For features 5 to 8, the curve became gentler, but continued to decline. This indicated that compared to the previous features, these features had less impact on model accuracy and remained stable at the 10th wavelength. Eventually, SPA screened out 10 optimal spectral characteristic wavelengths with a relatively uniform distribution across the spectrum, as shown in Figure 9B and Table 3.

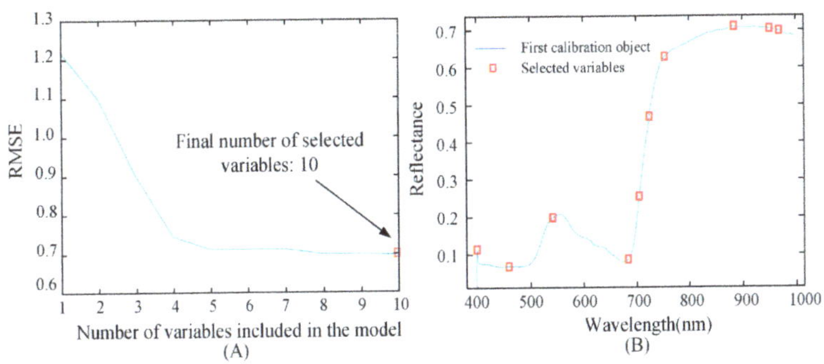

Figure 9. Selection process of wavelengths using SPA. (**A**) RMSE screen plot for determining the number of effective wavelengths; (**B**) distribution of effective wavelengths marked by each square.

Table 3. Spectral characteristic wavelength screening results.

Method	Characteristic Wavelengths/nm
SPA	401, 461, 543, 685, 706, 726, 756, 887, 983, 973
RFrog	514, 536, 547, 549, 572, 604, 623, 648, 674, 721, 736, 764, 773, 871, 917, 922, 925, 961
CARS	402, 410, 413, 418, 517, 543, 547, 548, 552, 572, 574, 575, 576, 622, 629, 630, 631, 632, 648, 649, 718, 752, 753, 764, 792, 794, 799, 803, 805, 816, 832, 836, 838, 865, 874, 890, 891, 893, 894, 895, 896, 903, 912, 923, 927, 938, 944, 946, 950, 959, 965, 966, 972, 974, 975, 976, 987, 988, 990

Feature extraction was performed using the RFrog, with the number of PLS components set to 6 and the number of iterations set to 100. The characteristic wavelengths were determined based on the probability value, with a screening threshold of 0.3. Wavelengths with a sampling probability greater than 0.3 were recognized as characteristic wavelengths, as shown in Figure 10A. A total of 18 key spectral characteristic wavelengths were successfully identified among 942 potential wavelengths, as shown in Table 3. These wavelengths showed a high correlation with the target variables in terms of both statistical relevance and biophysical significance.

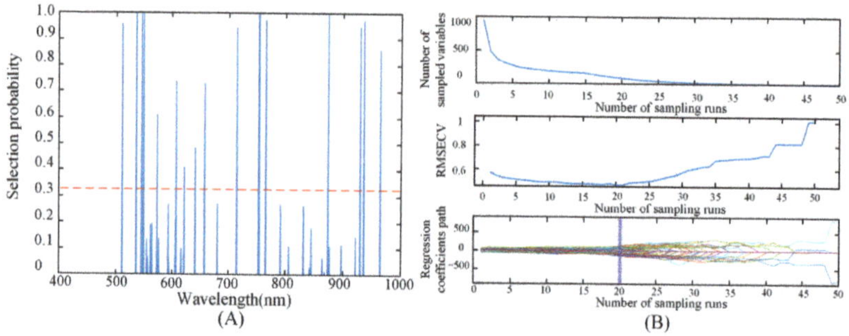

Figure 10. Extraction of characteristic wavelengths by RFrog, CARS. (**A**) RFrog; (**B**) CARS.

The CARS was utilized to reduce the dimensionality of spectral data, with the number of Monte Carlo runs set to 50, as shown in Figure 10B. The RMSECV initially decreased and then increased as the number of sampled variables changed, reaching its minimum at iteration 20. The best selection of wavelength variables was selected at this point, resulting in the final spectral characteristic wavelengths presented in Table 3.

3.4. Modelling Results for Single Features Input

To verify the advantages of DCFM in this study, the SVM, PSOSVM, and RF models based on single spectral features, as well as the ResNet50 and MobileNetV2 models based on single image features, were built. The feature maps extracted by the ResNet50 and MobileNetV2 models are shown in Figure 11. It can be observed that as the depth of the convolutional neural network increases, the spatial resolution of the feature maps gradually decreases. In the shallow convolutional layers near the input, the model typically extracts low-level features, such as edges and textures, and the feature maps at this stage retain almost all of the original image information. However, in the deeper convolutional layers closer to the output, the extracted features become increasingly abstract, containing less visual detail and more semantic information relevant to specific levels.

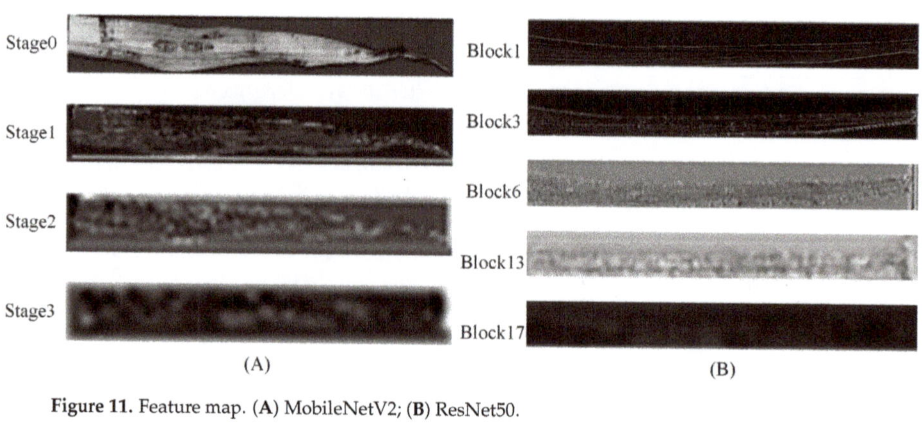

Figure 11. Feature map. (**A**) MobileNetV2; (**B**) ResNet50.

As detailed in Tables 4 and 5, among the models based on single spectral features, the PSOSVM model using spectral characteristic wavelengths by SPA achieved the best classification performance, with an OA of 94.31%, a Kappa of 92.97.%, and an F1-score of 94.14%. Figure 12 shows the heat map of the accuracy across different models and feature extraction methods for different disease levels. SVM and PSOSVM performed well when using SPA-based features, with an accuracy of 100% on level 4. RF performed better on levels 0 and 1 when using CARS, but misclassification was higher for level 2, resulting in a lower accuracy of 74.32%. ResNet50 and MobileNetV2 models constructed based on single image features have higher misclassification rates, with OA and Kappa of 85.81%, 86.90%, 82.43%, and 83.82%, respectively. This may be attributed to the spectral features' superior ability to reveal the intrinsic characteristics of crops, making it more effective in capturing subtle differences among rice blast severity levels compared to image data [36]. In addition, from the classification results, MobileNetV2 was more suitable as a backbone network for spatial feature extraction compared to ResNet50. Overall, the SVM, PSOSVM, and RF models constructed using spectral features outperformed the image-based ResNet50 and MobileNetV2 models in terms of classification accuracy.

Table 4. Recognition results under single spectral features input.

Methods	SVM			PSOSVM			RF		
	OA (0%)	Kappa(%)	F1-Score (%)	OA (%)	Kappa (%)	F1-Score (%)	OA (%)	Kappa (%)	F1-Score (%)
SPA	91.94	90.04	92.83	94.31	92.97	94.14	88.99	86.41	86.79
RFrog	88.60	85.91	88.69	87.36	84.55	87.82	88.99	86.38	88.70
CARS	88.27	85.54	88.90	91.74	89.80	91.10	92.66	90.94	93.09

Table 5. Recognition results under single image data input.

Input Features	Methods	OA (%)	Kappa (%)	F1-Score (%)
Image	ResNet50	85.81	82.43	84.04
	MobileNetV2	86.90	83.82	86.11

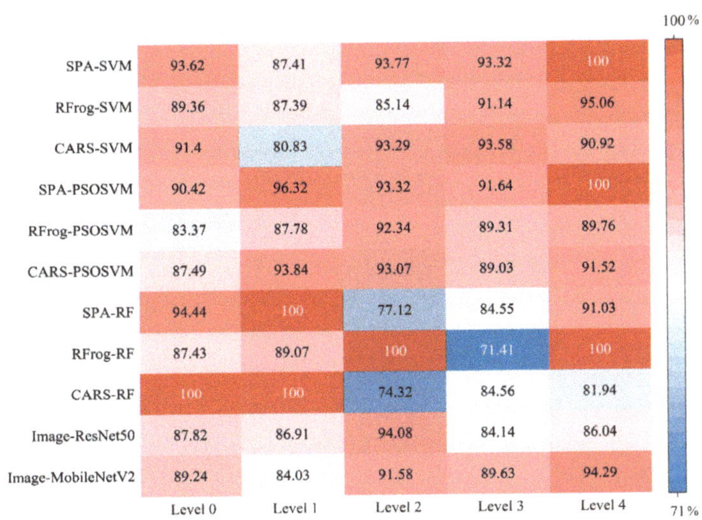

Figure 12. Accuracy heat map.

3.5. DCFM Modeling Results

The DCFM rice blast classification model was constructed using both spectral and spatial features, and the recognition results of the model are summarized in Table 6. The experimental results demonstrated that the DCFM model based on fused features achieved higher accuracy than models using a single feature input in identifying different rice blast severity levels, with OA and Kappa being higher than 90% and 88%, respectively. When the spectral characteristic wavelengths screened by SPA were fused with spatial features, the best classification result was obtained, with an OA of 96.72% and a Kappa of 95.97%. As displayed in Figure 13, the SPA-DCFM model was more accurate in classifying diseases at levels 1 and 4, with accuracies of 99.42% and 100%, respectively. The models in this paper outperformed traditional machine learning models (SVM, ELM, and RF) in terms of OA, Kappa, and F1-score. Compared to SPA-SVM, OA and Kappa increased by 4.78% and 5.93%, respectively. Compared to SPA-PSOSVM, OA and Kappa increased by 2.41% and 3%, respectively. Compared to SPA-RF, OA and Kappa increased by 7.73% and 9.56%, respectively. In comparison to the other two deep learning models, the classification accuracy of the ResNet50 and MobileNetV2 models was lower than that of the model proposed in this paper. When comparing and analyzing models built on single versus fused features, it was evident that the DCFM model using the effective fusion of spectral and spatial features had superior recognition accuracy for rice blast.

Table 6. Results of DCFM based on different features.

Input Features	Precision (%)					OA (%)	Kappa (%)	F1-Score (%)
	Level 0	Level 1	Level 2	Level 3	Level 4			
SPA+ Image	94.48	99.42	95.03	94.53	100	96.72	95.97	96.42
RFrog+ Image	94.26	98.33	87.92	91.23	100	90.88	88.79	90.53
CARS+ Image	95.37	95.76	94.92	91.84	100	94.74	93.55	94.47

Table 7 shows the model parameters and floating point operations per second (FLOPs) for DCFM, ResNet50, and MobileNetV2, as well as the results of the inference time comparison to the traditional methods, SVM, PSOSVM, and RF. Among the deep learning models, MobileNetV2 has the lowest number of parameters and FLOPs, with 3.5 M and 0.31 B. The DCFM model has the second highest number of parameters and FLOPs, with 3.9 M and 0.39 B. In contrast, ResNet50 has the highest number of parameters and FLOPs, 4.2 M and 0.67 B, respectively, suggesting a higher computational complexity. Therefore, for the proposed DCFM, MobileNetV2 was chosen as the backbone of spatial feature extraction, which has a lower number of parameters and better computational speed for this architecture. In terms of inference time, traditional machine learning methods (SVM, PSOSVM, and RF) significantly outperformed the deep learning models. SPA-RF takes only 0.08 ms, which is 5.5 times faster than the fastest deep learning model (MobileNetV2, 0.44 ms). However, DCFM may obtain higher classification accuracy through feature fusion, and thus was more advantageous in terms of overall performance.

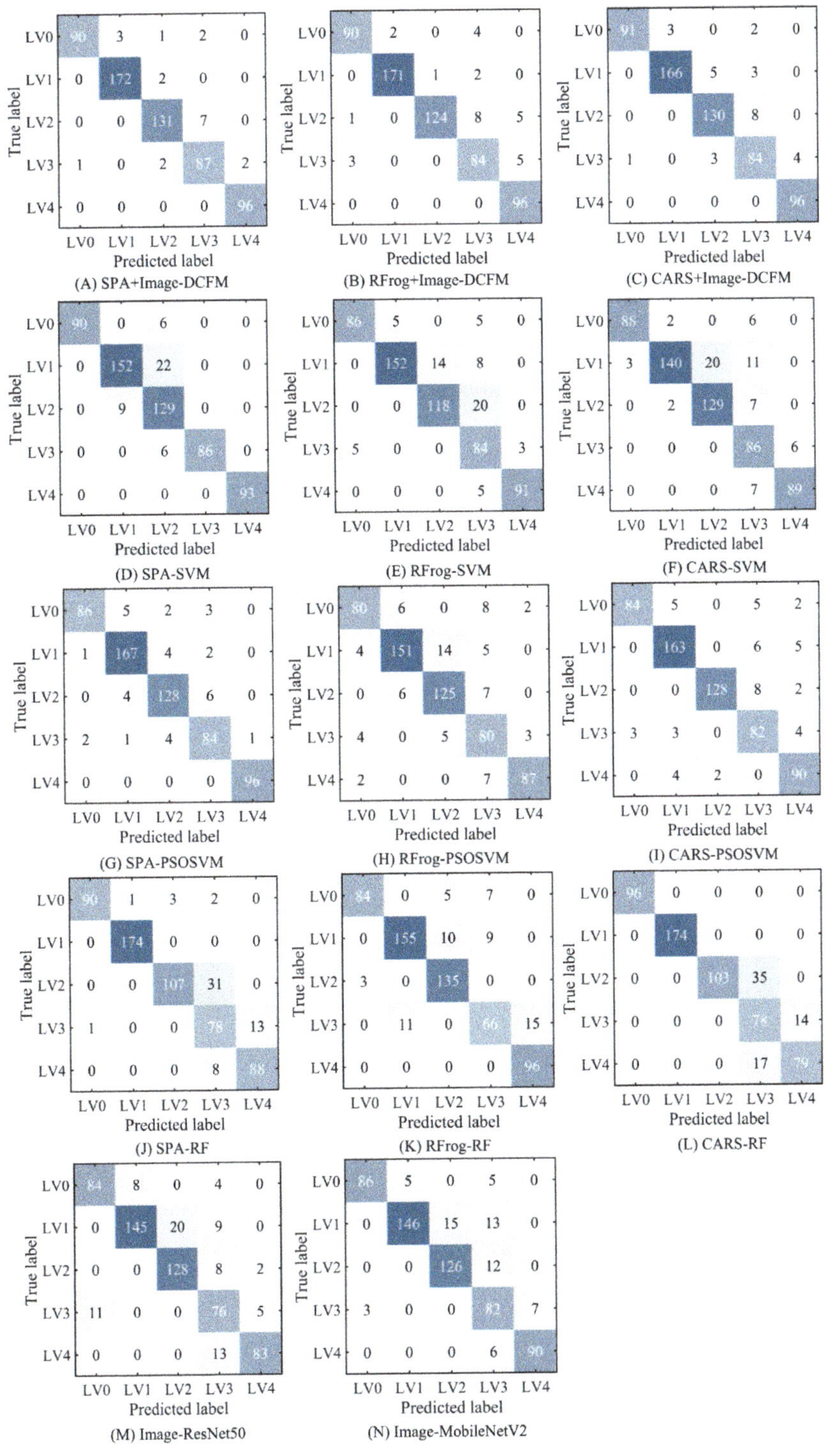

Figure 13. Confusion matrix for classification models with different input features.

Table 7. Comparison of model sizes and inference times of different models.

Methods	Parameters/Million	FLOPs/Billion	Inferencing Time (s)
SPA+ Image-DCFM	3.9	0.39	0.46
Image-ResNet50	4.2	0.67	0.58
Image-MobileNetV2	3.5	0.31	0.44
SPA-SVM	-	-	0.11
SPA-PSOSVM	-	-	0.17
SPA-RF	-	-	0.08

4. Discussion

Rice blast poses a serious threat to rice production, potentially leading to significant yield losses or possibly crop collapse [37]. Efficient and precise monitoring and control of rice blast are crucial for increasing rice production and quality. HSI is an emerging technology that has been widely applied in disease detection and agriculture due to its non-destructive, quick, and precise qualities.

4.1. Physiological Relevance and Mechanistic Interpretation of Selected Spectral Features

To eliminate the effect of nonlinear distortions and noise caused by the environment and equipment in the spectral images, and to obtain more accurate data, the Savitzky–Golay (SG) filter with nine points was first used to calibrate and process hyperspectral images [38]. Identifying the correct spectral features is essential for recognizing abnormal areas and disease lesions [39], as shown by the spectral reflectance curves corresponding to the different types of ROIs in Figure 7. Therefore, after pre-processing, the high-dimensional spectral data were analyzed to find characteristic wavelengths using SPA, RFrog, and CARS. As can be seen from Table 3, there were some differences in the wavelengths extracted by the three feature selection methods, but all of them were highly concentrated in the red-edge and NIR region. Specifically, seven of the ten characteristic wavelengths (685–973 nm) extracted by the SPA method were located in the red-edge and NIR bands. Similarly, 11 of the 18 wavelengths (648–961 nm) extracted by the RFrog method belong to the same wavelengths, while 44 of the 59 characteristic wavelengths (630–990 nm) extracted by the CARS method were in the red-edge and NIR bands. The red-edge band, located between 630–720 nm, was a unique spectral wavelength between the red absorption maximum and high reflectance [40], reflecting the conversion process between chlorophyll absorption and sheet scattering. Horler et al. [41] identified a peak, about 720 nm, attributed to leaf reflection scattering properties by derivative analysis. Table 3 shows that all three methods selected wavelengths near this peak, 726 nm, 721 nm, and 718 nm, respectively. In addition, the red-edge band was selected frequently, probably due to a decrease in leaf chlorophyll content caused by rice blast, which resulted in a shift of the red-edge position to shorter wavelengths (blueshift), a spectral change that provides reliable feature support for early disease detection [42]. With the deepening of the infestation process, the infestation filaments gradually penetrated the interior of the leaf cells, leading to a decrease in the reflective ability of water in the leaf to the NIR band and a weakening of the cellular water-holding capacity. At the same time, the plant produces reactive oxygen species (e.g., hydrogen peroxide) and deposits cellulose at the site of infection, eventually triggering tissue necrosis. Therefore, the selected characteristic wavelengths were highly concentrated in the NIR region, reflecting the sensitive response of water changes to spectral features [43].

4.2. Performance Assessment of Rice Blast Recognition Based on Spectral–Spatial Feature Fusion

Previous studies demonstrated that combining spectral features with image textural features enabled the identification of rice blast [44,45]. In contrast, the DCFM model proposed in this study directly input two-dimensional hyperspectral images, after PCA-based dimensionality reduction, into the network. MobileNetV2 was employed to extract spatial information, and the CBAM module was introduced to capture dependencies between spatial neighborhoods and salient features of the input feature maps. This enabled the model to extract more important spatial features. The last SoftMax layer of MobileNetV2 was removed, so its final output was the spatial information features of the image, eliminating the need to extract texture and shape features separately. Spatial features were mapped to one-dimensional data using a fully connected layer, which was then used for subsequent feature fusion with spectral data. This method utilized both spectral and image data obtained from hyperspectral images, enabling the simultaneous consideration of structural differences and spectral features associated with rice blast to improve classification accuracy. Based on different input features, three DCFM models were constructed, with the OA and Kappa being higher than 90% and 88%, respectively.

To further evaluate the classification model, the proposed DCFM model was compared to SVM, PSOSVM, RF, ResNet50, and MobileNetV2. The OA, Kappa, and F1-score of these models were lower than those of the DCFM model. When combined with the SPA feature extraction method, the DCFM achieved its best performance, with an OA of 96.72% and a Kappa coefficient of 95.97%. Additionally, it exhibited high precision in detailed disease classification, with accuracies of 94.48%, 99.42%, 95.03%, 94.53%, and 100% for levels 0, 1, 2, 3, and 4, respectively. Firstly, this may be because SPA selected fewer but more representative feature dimensions. It retained a set of wavelengths with minimal information redundancy among bands in the spectral data and effectively avoided multicollinearity. In contrast, CARS tended to select a set of spectral characteristic wavelengths that were highly correlated with the classification results. However, its stability was easily affected by the adaptive resampling strategy, resulting in a slightly lower performance compared to the SPA-based model. RFrog was a probability-based feature selection method, which was more likely to introduce redundant wavelengths or noise while capturing potential information. This reduced the purity of the feature set and weakened the model's generalization ability, making its overall performance the poorest among the three methods. In addition, the spatial attention mechanism added to the convolutional neural network emphasized important features and suppressed irrelevant information. This enhanced the network's capacity to extract features and facilitated the fusion of spatial and spectral features, thereby enabling the proposed model to achieve superior classification accuracy and robustness. This proved that the dual-channel feature fusion method in this study was effective and superior in rice blast classification.

Figure 13A–C show the prediction results of the fusion feature model compared to the actual categories. Figure 13D–L present the prediction results of models based solely on spectral features, while Figure 13M,N illustrate the results for models using only image features. When using spectral or image features alone, the model's misclassification on the mild disease levels (levels 1–3) was more obvious, indicating that the models have a problem of recognition ambiguity in identifying the early stages of the disease. In contrast, the number of missed and misclassified judgments by DCFM was significantly reduced. This indicated that the fused spatial information provided the model with more discriminative features. This enhanced the practicality and promotion potential of the DCFM model in complex field environments.

4.3. Advantages and Limitations

In small and medium sample data scenarios, complex feature fusion mechanisms may trigger problems such as unstable model training. To balance model performance and computational efficiency, this study adopted a simple tandem strategy to fuse the spectral features with the spatial features that were mapped into one-dimensional vectors. Although fusion methods based on the attention mechanism or weighted combination can theoretically enhance the interaction and representation between different features, they tend to incur huge computational costs. In practical agricultural applications, the model can be integrated into hyperspectral imaging systems and deployed on ground monitoring platforms or handheld portable devices for real-time field monitoring. Due to the low computational complexity of the model, it is suitable for resource-constrained agricultural production environments.

Meanwhile, it is undeniable that the number of training samples for different complex field environments has an important impact on the performance of deep learning models. To further improve the generalization ability and recognition accuracy of the rice blast detection model, future research will focus on expanding the sample sources to include rice blast samples from diverse geographical regions, cropping structures, and rice varieties. It will also aim to extend detection from the leaf scale to the canopy scale and incorporate more advanced feature fusion strategies to support broader field-level monitoring and management applications.

5. Conclusions

To efficiently and non-destructively identify rice blast levels and fully exploit the potential of HSI data, a dual-channel deep learning model (DCFM) combined with HSI was proposed. The model combined the CBAM spatial feature extraction module with MobileNetV2 to extract image features from rice samples, and then fused these features using a feature fusion adaptive conditioning module to classify rice blast. Compared to classical machine learning (SVM, PSOSVM, and RF) and deep learning (ResNet50 and MobileNetV2), DCFM achieved higher classification accuracy in disease classification. Among them, the combination of SPA and the DCFM model obtained the best identification performance, with an OA of 96.72% and a Kappa of 95.97%. Compared to classical algorithms using single features, spectral–spatial feature fusion better discriminated the differences between diseased rice samples of different varieties. The improvement highlighted the necessity and effectiveness of incorporating spatial information. This also provided a valuable reference for the accurate classification of other rice diseases using HSI. Additionally, the roles of different wavelengths and spatial information in the final classification are not equivalent. Therefore, constructing a spectral–spatial attention enhancement module using attention mechanisms to automatically highlight salient spectral features and spatial correlations between neighboring pixels is a direction worth further exploring.

Author Contributions: Conceptualization, Y.Q. and T.L.; methodology, Y.Q. and T.L.; software, Y.Q. and S.G.; validation, S.G. and W.Y.; formal analysis, S.G.; investigation, Q.Y.; resources, T.X.; data curation, Y.Q. and P.W.; writing—original draft preparation, Y.Q.; writing—review and editing, Y.Q., Q.Y. and T.L.; visualization, Y.Q., P.W. and J.M.; supervision, T.L., W.Y. and T.X.; project administration, T.L.; funding acquisition, T.L. and T.X. All authors have read and agreed to the published version of the manuscript.

Funding: This research was funded by the National Key R&D Program of China (2022YFD2002303-01, 2024YFD1501500), Liaoning Provincial Science and Technology Department Project (2023-MS-212).

Institutional Review Board Statement: Not applicable.

Data Availability Statement: The data presented in this study are available on request from the corresponding author.

Conflicts of Interest: The authors declare no conflicts of interest.

References

1. Peng, S.; Tang, Q.; Zou, Y. Current Status and Challenges of Rice Production in China. *Plant Pro. Sci.* **2009**, *12*, 3–8. [CrossRef]
2. Fukai, S.; Cooper, M. Development of Drought-Resistant Cultivars Using Physiomorphological Traits in Rice. *Field Crops Res.* **1995**, *40*, 67–86. [CrossRef]
3. Hossain, M.; Ali, M.; Hossain, D. Occurrence of Blast Disease in Rice in Bangladesh. *Am. J. Agric. Sci.* **2017**, *4*, 74–80.
4. Neupane, N.; Bhusal, K. A Review of Blast Disease of Rice in Nepal. *J. Plant Pathol. Microbiol.* **2020**, *11*, 528. [CrossRef]
5. Bonman, J.; Estrada, B.; Bandong, J. Leaf and Neck Blast Resistance in Tropical Lowland Rice Cultivars. *Plant Dis.* **1989**, *73*, 388–390. [CrossRef]
6. Larijani, M.R.; Asli-Ardeh, E.A.; Kozegar, E.; Loni, R. Evaluation of Image Processing Technique in Identifying Rice Blast Disease in Field Conditions Based on KNN Algorithm Improvement by K-Means. *Food Sci. Nutr.* **2019**, *7*, 3922–3930. [CrossRef] [PubMed]
7. Zarbafi, S.S.; Rabiei, B.; Ebadi, A.A.; Ham, J.H. Statistical Analysis of Phenotypic Traits of Rice (*Oryza Sativa L.*) Related to Grain Yield under Neck Blast Disease. *J. Plant Dis. Prot.* **2019**, *126*, 293–306. [CrossRef]
8. Zhang, Y.; Hao, X.; Li, F.; Wang, Z.; Li, D.; Li, M.; Mao, R. Unsupervised Domain Adaptation Semantic Segmentation Method for Wheat Disease Detection Based on UAV Multispectral Images. *Comput. Electron. Agric.* **2025**, *236*, 110473. [CrossRef]
9. Liu, T.; Qi, Y.; Yang, F.; Yi, X.; Guo, S.; Wu, P.; Yuan, Q.; Xu, T. Early Detection of Rice Blast Using UAV Hyperspectral Imagery and Multi-Scale Integrator Selection Attention Transformer Network (MS-STNet). *Comput. Electron. Agric.* **2025**, *231*, 110007. [CrossRef]
10. Sankaran, S.; Mishra, A.; Ehsani, R.; Davis, C. A Review of Advanced Techniques for Detecting Plant Diseases. *Comput. Electron. Agric.* **2010**, *72*, 1–13. [CrossRef]
11. Abdulridha, J.N.; Ampatzidis, Y.; Kakarla, S.C.; Roberts, P.D. Detection of Target Spot and Bacterial Spot Diseases in Tomato Using UAV-Based and Benchtop-Based Hyperspectral Imaging Techniques. *Precis. Agric.* **2019**, *21*, 955–978. [CrossRef]
12. Wu, G.; Fang, Y.; Jiang, Q.; Cui, M.; Li, N.; Ou, Y.; Diao, Z.; Zhang, B. Early Identifica-tion of Strawberry Leaves Disease Utilizing Hyperspectral Imaging Combing with Spectral Features, Multiple Vegetation Indices and Textural Features. *Comput. Electron. Agric.* **2023**, *204*, 107553. [CrossRef]
13. Hu, G.; Yao, P.; Wan, M.; Bao, W.; Zeng, W. Detection and Classification of Diseased Pine Trees with Different Levels of Severity from UAV Remote Sensing Images. *Ecol. Inform.* **2022**, *72*, 101844. [CrossRef]
14. Nazari, K.; Ebadi, M.J.; Berahmand, K. Diagnosis of Alternaria Disease and Leafminer Pest on Tomato Leaves Using Image Processing Techniques. *J. Sci. Food Agric.* **2022**, *102*, 6907–6920. [CrossRef]
15. Ahila, A.; Prema, V.; Ayyasamy, S.; Sivasubramanian, M. An Enhanced Deep Learning Model for High-Speed Classification of Plant Diseasesz0066 with Bioinspired Algorithm. *J. Supercomput.* **2024**, *80*, 3713–3737. [CrossRef]
16. Wang, H.; Nguyen, T.-H.; Nguyen, T.N.; Dang, M. PD-TR: End-to-End Plant Diseases Detection Using a Transformer. *Comput. Electron. Agric.* **2024**, *224*, 109123. [CrossRef]
17. Nagaraju, M.; Chawla, P.; Upadhyay, S.; Tiwari, R. Convolution Network Model Based Leaf Disease Detection Using Augmentation Techniques. *Expert Syst.* **2022**, *39*, e12885. [CrossRef]
18. You, S.; Li, Y.; Song, J.; Yu, X.; Tu, K.; Lan, W.; Pan, L. Evaluating the Microstructure and Physicochemical Properties of 'Korla' Fragrant Pear Disease Caused by Alternaria Alternata: Vis-NIR Hyperspectral Microscope Imaging Coupled with Convolutional Neural Network. *Postharvest Biol. Technol.* **2024**, *212*, 112913. [CrossRef]
19. Chun, S.-W.; Song, D.-J.; Lee, K.-H.; Kim, M.-J.; Kim, M.S.; Kim, K.-S.; Mo, C. Deep Learning Algorithm Development for Early Detection of Botrytis Cinerea Infected Strawberry Fruit Using Hyperspectral Fluorescence Imaging. *Postharvest Biol. Technol.* **2024**, *214*, 112918. [CrossRef]
20. Gui, J.; Fei, J.; Wu, Z.; Fu, X.; Diakite, A. Grading Method of Soybean Mosaic Disease Based on Hyperspectral Imaging Technology. *Inf. Process. Agric.* **2021**, *8*, 380–385. [CrossRef]
21. Qi, C.; Sandroni, M.; Cairo Westergaard, J.; Høegh Riis Sundmark, E.; Bagge, M.; Alexandersson, E.; Gao, J. In-Field Classification of the Asymptomatic Biotrophic Phase of Potato Late Blight Based on Deep Learning and Proximal Hyperspectral Imaging. *Comput. Electron. Agric.* **2023**, *205*, 107585. [CrossRef]
22. Bu, Y.; Hu, J.; Chen, C.; Bai, S.; Chen, Z.; Hu, T.; Zhang, G.; Liu, N.; Cai, C.; Li, Y.; et al. ResNet Incorporating the Fusion Data of RGB & Hyperspectral Images Improves Classification Accuracy of Vegetable Soybean Freshness. *Sci. Rep.* **2024**, *14*, 2568. [CrossRef]
23. Chen, S.; Lu, X.; Fang, H.; Perumal, A.B.; Li, R.; Feng, L.; Wang, M.; Liu, Y. Early Surveillance of Rice Bakanae Disease Using Deep Learning and Hyperspectral Imaging. *Abiotech* **2024**, *5*, 281–297. [CrossRef]

24. Zhao, D.; Feng, S.; Cao, Y.; Yu, F.; Guan, Q.; Li, J.; Zhang, G.; Xu, T. Study on the Classification Method of Rice Leaf Blast Levels Based on Fusion Features and Adaptive-Weight Immune Particle Swarm Optimization Extreme Learning Machine Algorithm. *Front. Plant Sci.* **2022**, *13*, 879668. [CrossRef] [PubMed]
25. Raghavendra, A.; Guru, D.S.; Rao, M.K. Mango Internal Defect Detection Based on Optimal Wavelength Selection Method Using NIR Spectroscopy. *Artif. Intell. Agric.* **2021**, *5*, 43–51. [CrossRef]
26. Zhang, M.; Chen, T.; Gu, X.; Kuai, Y.; Wang, C.; Chen, D.; Zhao, C. UAV-Borne Hyperspectral Estimation of Nitrogen Content in Tobacco Leaves Based on Ensemble Learning Methods. *Comput. Electron. Agric.* **2023**, *211*, 108008. [CrossRef]
27. Li, H.; Liang, Y.; Xu, Q.; Cao, D. Key Wavelengths Screening Using Competitive Adaptive Reweighted Sampling Method for Multivariate Calibration. *Anal. Chim. Acta* **2009**, *648*, 77–84. [CrossRef]
28. Li, H.-D.; Xu, Q.-S.; Liang, Y.-Z. Random Frog: An Efficient Reversible Jump Markov Chain Monte Carlo-like Approach for Variable Selection with Applications to Gene Selection and Disease Classification. *Anal. Chim. Acta* **2012**, *740*, 20–26. [CrossRef]
29. Wijayanto, A.K.; Prasetyo, L.B.; Hudjimartsu, S.A.; Sigit, G.; Hongo, C. Textural Features for BLB Disease Damage Assessment in Paddy Fields Using Drone Data and Machine Learning: Enhancing Disease Detection Accuracy. *Smart Agric. Technol.* **2024**, *8*, 100498. [CrossRef]
30. Balling, J.; Herold, M.; Reiche, J. How Textural Features Can Improve SAR-Based Tropical Forest Disturbance Mapping. *Int. J. Appl. Earth Obs. Geoinf.* **2023**, *124*, 103492. [CrossRef]
31. Shaodan, L.; Yue, Y.; Jiayi, L.; Xiaobin, L.; Jie, M.; Haiyong, W.; Zuxin, C.; Dapeng, Y. Application of UAV-Based Imaging and Deep Learning in Assessment of Rice Blast Resistance. *Rice Sci.* **2023**, *30*, 652–660. [CrossRef]
32. Woo, S.; Park, J.; Lee, J.-Y.; Kweon, I.S. CBAM: Convolutional Block Attention Module. In Proceedings of the Computer Vision—ECCV, Munich, Germany, 8–14 September 2018; Ferrari, V., Hebert, M., Sminchisescu, C., Weiss, Y., Eds.; Springer International Publishing: Cham, Switzerland, 2018; pp. 3–19. [CrossRef]
33. Zhang, J.; Huang, Y.; Pu, R.; Gonzalez-Moreno, P.; Yuan, L.; Wu, K.; Huang, W. Monitoring Plant Diseases and Pests through Remote Sensing Technology: A Review. *Comput. Electron. Agric.* **2019**, *165*, 104943. [CrossRef]
34. Bioucas-Dias, J.M.; Plaza, A.; Camps-Valls, G.; Scheunders, P.; Nasrabadi, N.; Chanussot, J. Hyperspectral Remote Sensing Data Analysis and Future Challenges. *IEEE Geosci. Remote Sens. Mag.* **2013**, *1*, 6–36. [CrossRef]
35. Feng, S.; Cao, Y.; Xu, T.; Yu, F.; Zhao, D.; Zhang, G. Rice Leaf Blast Classification Method Based on Fused Features and One-Dimensional Deep Convolutional Neural Network. *Remote Sens.* **2021**, *13*, 3207. [CrossRef]
36. Han, L.; Tian, J.; Huang, Y.; He, K.; Liang, Y.; Hu, X.; Xie, L.; Yang, H.; Huang, D. Hyperspectral Imaging Combined with Dual-Channel Deep Learning Feature Fusion Model for Fast and Non-Destructive Recognition of Brew Wheat Varieties. *J. Food Compos. Anal.* **2024**, *125*, 105785. [CrossRef]
37. Wu, X.-Y.; Dong, B.; Zhu, X.-M.; Cai, Y.-Y.; Li, L.; Lu, J.-P.; Yu, B.; Cheng, J.-L.; Xu, F.; Bao, J.-D.; et al. SP-141 Targets Trs85 to Inhibit Rice Blast Fungus Infection and Functions as a Potential Broad-Spectrum Antifungal Agent. *Plant Commun.* **2024**, *5*, 100724. [CrossRef]
38. Yu, R.; Ren, L.; Luo, Y. Early Detection of Pine Wilt Disease in Pinus Tabuliformis in North China Using a Field Portable Spectrometer and UAV-Based Hyperspectral Imagery. *For. Ecosyst.* **2021**, *8*, 44. [CrossRef]
39. Zhang, J.; Tian, Y.; Yan, L.; Wang, B.; Wang, L.; Xu, J.; Wu, K. Diagnosing the Symptoms of Sheath Blight Disease on Rice Stalk with an In-Situ Hyperspectral Imaging Technique. *Biosyst. Eng.* **2021**, *209*, 94–105. [CrossRef]
40. Curran, P.J.; Dungan, J.L.; Macler, B.A.; Plummer, S.E. The Effect of a Red Leaf Pigment on the Relationship between Red Edge and Chlorophyll Concentration. *Remote Sens. Environ.* **1991**, *35*, 69–76. [CrossRef]
41. Horler, D.N.H.; Dockray, M.; Barber, J. The Red Edge of Plant Leaf Reflectance. *Int. J. Remote Sens.* **1983**, *4*, 273–288. [CrossRef]
42. Zheng, Q.; Chen, Y.; Xia, Q.; Zhang, Y.; Li, D.; Jiang, H.; Wang, C.; Zhao, L.; Huang, W.; Dong, Y.; et al. New Hyperspectral Geometry Ratio Index for Monitoring Rice Blast Disease from Leaf Scale to Canopy Scale. *Remote Sens.* **2024**, *16*, 4681. [CrossRef]
43. Mandal, N.; Das, D.K.; Sahoo, R.N.; Adak, S.; Kumar, A.; Chinnusamy, V.; Mukherjee, J.; Rajashekara, H.; Ranjan, R.; Das, B. Assessing Rice Blast Disease Severity through Hyperspectral Remote Sensing. *J. Agrometeorol.* **2022**, *24*, 241–248. [CrossRef]
44. Guo, W.; Gong, Z.; Gao, C.; Yue, J.; Fu, Y.; Sun, H.; Zhang, H.; Zhou, L. An Accurate Monitoring Method of Peanut Southern Blight Using Unmanned Aerial Vehicle Remote Sensing. *Precis. Agric.* **2024**, *25*, 1857–1876. [CrossRef]
45. Zeng, T.; Zhang, H.; Li, Y.; Yin, C.; Liang, Q.; Fang, J.; Fu, W.; Wang, J.; Zhang, X. Monitoring the Severity of Rubber Tree Infected with Powdery Mildew Based on UAV Multispectral Remote Sensing. *Forests* **2023**, *14*, 717. [CrossRef]

agriculture

MDPI

Article

Distribution Characteristics of Rotor Airflow and Droplet Deposition of Plant Protection UAVs Under Varying Rotor–Nozzle Distances

Xiaojie Xu [1,2], Shengde Chen [1,2,*], Zhihong Li [1,2], Zehong Wu [1,2], Yuxiang Tan [1,2], Shimin Huang [1,2] and Yubin Lan [1,2,*]

1 College of Electronic Engineering (College of Artificial Intelligence), South China Agricultural University, Guangzhou 510642, China; connieyellow12@gmail.com (S.H.)
2 National Center for International Collaboration Research on Precision Agricultural Aviation Pesticides Spraying Technology, South China Agricultural University, Guangzhou 510642, China
* Correspondence: shengde-chen@scau.edu.cn (S.C.); ylan@scau.edu.cn (Y.L.)

Abstract: The rotor airflow intensity and distribution characteristics of plant protection UAVs vary significantly with spatial positions below the rotor. Consequently, changes in the rotor–nozzle distance directly affect droplet motion and deposition patterns. To optimize the spraying effect of UAVs, this study combined a numerical simulation of rotor airflow and droplet deposition at different vertical distances between rotor and nozzle with field validation tests. The simulation results revealed that airflow intensity initially increases and then decreases with greater rotor–nozzle distance, peaking at 300–400 mm below the rotor with a maximum airflow velocity of 8.1 m/s. At 360 mm, the droplet swarm achieved its highest average velocity, corresponding to optimal deposition effect. Field tests confirmed a non-linear relationship between rotor–nozzle distance and droplet deposition. Droplet deposition first increased but declined sharply beyond the optimal range. When the distance was 360 mm, the target area exhibited the highest droplet deposition of 0.766 $\mu L \cdot cm^{-2}$ and the lowest drift rate of 23.31%. Although a certain deviation existed between numerical simulation results and field test values, both methods consistently identified 360 mm as the ideal distance for balancing deposition efficiency and drift control. These findings provide actionable insights for field trial design and advance precision spraying strategies for plant protection UAVs.

Keywords: plant protection UAV; rotor–nozzle distance; rotor airflow; droplet deposition; precision spray

1. Introduction

In recent years, UAV technology has advanced rapidly, with plant protection applications gaining significant attention in agriculture [1]. As an innovative spraying method, plant protection UAVs employ low- or ultra-low-volume spray systems, offering high efficiency, intelligent operation, and rapid response to pest outbreaks. These capabilities make UAVs particularly effective for challenging terrains, such as tall crops, paddy fields, and hilly areas, where traditional machinery struggles [2]. Today, plant protection UAVs have become an indispensable component of modern agriculture, widely used for crops including rice, corn, wheat, fruit trees, and cotton, demonstrating their vital role in contemporary farming practices [3–5].

As an emerging agricultural technology, plant protection UAVs face challenges in maintaining consistent operation quality due to diverse product types and complex, variable working conditions [6]. Consequently, spraying effectiveness has become a primary concern for users. Initial studies on plant protection UAV spray technology identified flight operation parameters or spray components as the primary determinants of aerial spraying performance [7]. Researchers have conducted extensive experimental studies on plant protection UAV operational parameters and spray components to optimize performance and enhance spraying efficacy [8,9]. Zhang et al. [10] employed a thermal infrared camera in combination with a plant protection UAV to monitor the crop canopy temperature variations before and after spraying. The innovative approach enabled quantitative assessment of droplet deposition effects on rice canopies, facilitating investigation of how flight parameters influence spray deposition and subsequent optimization of plant protection UAV operational parameters. Qiu et al. [11] conducted a multi-level orthogonal test to evaluate the effects of flight speed and height on droplet deposition in plant protection UAV applications. Their experimental design systematically analyzed the influence of these operational parameters on spraying performance. Subsequently, the study established quantitative relationships between flight parameters (speed and height) and droplet deposition patterns for single-rotor UAVs, providing a basis for operational optimization. To provide practical guidance for agricultural applications, Qin et al. [12] investigated how the operating height of an N-3 oil-powered single-rotor UAV affects droplet deposition distribution in corn canopies. Their study determined optimal operational parameters of 7 m flight altitude and 3 m/s flight speed based on deposition analysis. Furthermore, employing Box–Behnken central composite design methodology, the researchers systematically analyzed the relationship between spray parameters and deposition performance. Through modeling, they identified the optimal parameter combination for the P20 plant protection UAV: 2.0 m flight height, 3.7 m/s flight speed, and 430 mL/min nozzle flow rate [13]. Similarly, in order to evaluate application potential for fruit tree spraying, Zhang et al. [14] conducted numerical simulations on the downwash airflow field of a six-rotor plant protection UAV during hover-based application in fruit trees; the airflow distribution characteristics under different hovering altitudes, various fruit tree growth stages, and varying natural wind speeds were analyzed. Lian et al. [15] proposed seven nozzle layout configurations for plant protection UAVs. Experimental spray tests revealed that the optimal deposition performance was achieved with two rear-mounted nozzles combined with outward-rotating propellers positioned above the nozzles. Xie et al. [16] conducted a comparative study of droplet deposition characteristics between DG11003 and SX11001VS nozzles using a DJI T20 plant protection UAV. The experimental results demonstrated that the DG11003 nozzle achieved superior droplet deposition distribution at higher application flow rates.

With the continuous deepening of the research on spraying technology of plant protection UAVs, the rotor airflow field generated by rotor rotation was gradually regarded as the most fundamental factor affecting droplet deposition distribution in aerial spraying [17]. The aerial spray operation is the process of pesticide droplet deposition under the action of rotor airflow. Therefore, Chen et al. [18] used a UAV wind field wireless measurement system to obtain and analyze the rotor airflow distribution of single-rotor and multi-rotor plant protection UAVs under varying flight conditions, and investigated the influence of rotor airflow on the characteristics of droplet deposition and drift. Yang et al. [19] simulated the rotor flow field and droplet movement of a six-rotor plant protection UAV in hovering state by using the computational fluid dynamics (CFD) method, and established a three-dimensional two-phase flow model. Zhan et al. [20] investigated the influence of the variable rotor airflow caused by progressively decreasing liquid loading on droplet deposition during the UAV-based spray operation.

As evidenced by these studies, the growing recognition of rotor airflow's role in plant protection UAVs has led to extensive research on its impact on droplet deposition. However, these studies primarily conducted measurements and analyses under fixed experimental conditions, where nozzle positions remained static beneath the rotor at constant distances [21]. In practice, both the intensity and distribution characteristics of rotor airflow vary significantly with different spatial positions under the rotor [22]. Variations in nozzle–rotor vertical spacing alter droplet motion and deposition distribution through rotor airflow interactions [23]. Therefore, to enhance the spraying performance of plant protection UAVs, this paper takes the nozzle–rotor vertical distance as the research object. The spatial distribution of rotor airflow and droplet deposition for a quadrotor plant protection UAV at varying nozzle–rotor distances were simulated based on CFD. Moreover, the influence of rotor airflow on droplet deposition and the simulation results were further analyzed and verified through field spraying tests. These results provide actionable insights for optimizing field trial design and advancing precision spraying strategies in plant protection UAV applications.

2. Physical Model

2.1. UAV Structure and Operating Parameters

In this study, a self-assembled EFT-410S four-rotor plant protection UAV was adopted. The parameters of this model are shown in Table 1.

Table 1. The main parameters of the plant protection UAV.

Main Parameter	Specifications and Values
Overall dimension	1470 × 1470 × 482 mm
Paddle size	21 inches (540 mm)
Operating height	1–5 m
Maximum drug load	10 L
Operating speed	0–8 m/s
Spray flow	2.1 L/min
Spray width	2–6 m

This model mainly includes a UAV frame, U-shaped pesticide liquid tank, micro water pump, retractable spray rod, pipeline, and four flat spray nozzles. The Lu120-02 fan-shaped nozzle (Lechler GmbH, Metzingen, Germany) was used for spraying with a spray angle of 120°. When operated at 0.3 MPa, the nozzle produced spray droplets exhibiting a median volumetric diameter (DV50) of 134.36 ± 1.74 μm [1]. As shown in Figure 1, different flight height, speed, and vertical distance between nozzle and rotor can be set according to the test requirements. To systematically evaluate effects, the nozzle–rotor vertical distance was controlled by using interchangeable connecting rods. The following image illustrates the vertical distance between the nozzle and rotor.

2.2. Modeling and Rotor Scanning

The modeling of the plant protection UAV is divided into two parts: the body and the rotor. First, the fuselage model is established according to the actual size of the UAV. Because the body part has little influence on the simulation results and its complex structure has a great influence on the difficulty of the numerical calculation process, the body part is appropriately simplified. Through the measurement of the fuselage entity, UG modeling software (v12.0) is used to draw the three-dimensional fuselage entity model, as shown in Figure 2a.

Figure 1. The vertical distance between the nozzle and rotor.

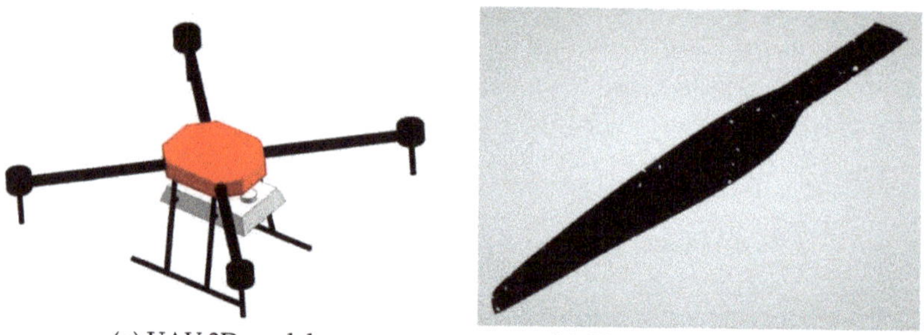

(**a**) UAV 3D model (**b**) 3D-scanned rotor model

Figure 2. UAV 3D model and rotor scanning.

Due to the critical role of rotor airfoil structure in air flow, all rotors were scanned by 3D scanning instruments, and reverse modeling was performed using Geomagic Design X software (v2019.0.1). The principle is that three-point matrix recognition is based on the three-dimensional spatial information of the scanned object, and the three-dimensional model of the scanned object is formed by the identification of 3 or more spatial matrix points. The modeling steps of the rotor are as follows: spray reflective enhancer into the rotor, paste the marking points on the complex area, and conduct three-dimensional scanning of the rotor using a GOM Optical Measuring Techniques scanner (GOM mbH, Braunschweig, Germany) and its supporting software, ATOS Professional (v2019), as shown in Figure 2b. Import the scanned point cloud data into the Geomagic Design X software, inversely build a 3D solid model according to the point cloud data, import the rotor model part and the body part into the UG 3D software for assembly, and output the stp format 3D model.

3. Numerical Simulation

CFD is the study of the interaction and flow of fluids at rest and in motion due to the relative motion of the fluid and the wall. As an important branch of modern fluid mechanics, CFD numerical simulation is based on the mass conservation equation, momentum conservation equation, and energy conservation. The three conservation laws form the basis of the continuity equation, the momentum equation (N-S equation), and the energy equation. In this paper, CFD theory and computational fluid dynamics software

Fluent (v2020 R2) were used to conduct numerical simulations. For different rotor–nozzle distances, the movement of spray droplets and the deposition distribution of droplets were numerically simulated.

3.1. Computing Domain Construction

In order to simulate the airflow distribution characteristics at different flight speeds and the influence of airflow on the droplet deposition distribution under different rotor–nozzle distances, and to facilitate the comparison and verification of later tests, it is necessary to first import the plant protection UAV body model, output in stp format and assembled in UG 3D software, into the workbench DM. The model calculation domain is constructed. Based on computational requirements, wrapping and Boolean operations were performed. Specifically, the entire fuselage was enveloped using a box-shaped domain, which was designed to balance computational performance while closely approximating the operational range of the agricultural UAV. A cylinder is used to wrap the four rotor parts, and the requirements for the rotation axis of the rotor and the central axis of the cylinder are consistent. According to the simulation requirements, the diameter of the rotor cylinder is 50 mm larger than the direct rotor and the thickness is 20 mm larger than the rotor pitch. The four rotor wings and the fuselage part of the UAV have independent spatial domains.

3.2. Turbulence Model

According to the simulation requirements, this paper adopts the transient simulation solution based on pressure and sets the gravity direction as -Z and the size as 9.81 m/s^2. In order to accurately simulate and describe the details of the flow field in the fluid domain from the perspective of airflow characteristics, the continuous phase turbulence model in the fluid domain uses the standard k-ε model, which is the standard for most practical engineering models in Fluent (v2020 R2) and has become the main modeling tool for computational fluid mechanics. The k-ε standard model establishes the model of turbulent kinetic energy (k) and its dissipation rate (ε) according to the continuity equation. In Reynolds (Ensemble) Averaging, the instantaneous N-S equation divides the velocity variable into mean and wave components, and the expression of the velocity component is as follows:

$$u = \overline{u}_i + u_i' \tag{1}$$

where $\overline{u}_i$ is the average velocity, u_i' is the fluctuation velocity, and (i = 1, 2, 3). The corresponding expression for a scalar quantity is as follows:

$$\varphi = \overline{\varphi} + \varphi_i' \tag{2}$$

where φ is the scalar. The flow rate is substituted into the instantaneous continuity equation and momentum equation, and the overall average momentum equation is derived as follows:

$$\frac{\partial \rho}{\partial t} + \frac{\partial}{\partial xi}(\rho u_i) = 0 \tag{3}$$

$$\frac{\partial}{\partial t}(\rho u_i) + \frac{\partial}{\partial x_j}(\rho u_i u_j) = -\frac{\partial \rho}{\partial t} + \frac{\partial}{\partial t}\left[\mu\left(\frac{\partial u_i}{\partial t} + \frac{\partial u_j}{\partial t} - \frac{2}{3}\delta_{ij}\frac{\partial u_i}{\partial x_i}\right)\right] + \frac{\partial}{\partial t}(-\rho u_i u_j) \tag{4}$$

Equations (3) and (4) mean that Reynolds-averaged Navier–Stokes (RANS) and N-S equations have the same expression. The value of k is derived from the continuity equation and the value of ε is derived from the energy equation. In the process of obtaining the two parameters, it is assumed that the fluid in the fluid domain is completely turbulent, so the simulation effect will be accurate and reliable. On this basis, the RNG k-ε model and

Realizable k-ε model are derived, and the turbulence kinetic energy k and dissipation rate ε can be deduced by the following equation:

$$\frac{\partial}{\partial t}(\rho k)+\frac{\partial}{\partial x_i}(\rho k u_i)=\frac{\partial}{\partial x_j}\left[(\mu+\frac{u_t}{\sigma_k})\frac{\partial k}{\partial x_j}\right]+G_k+G_b-\rho\varepsilon-Y_m+S_K \quad (5)$$

$$\frac{\partial}{\partial t}(\rho\varepsilon)+\frac{\partial}{\partial x_i}(\rho\varepsilon u_i)=\frac{\partial}{\partial x_j}\left[(\mu+\frac{u_t}{\sigma_\varepsilon})\frac{\partial \varepsilon}{\partial x_j}\right]+C_{1\varepsilon}\frac{\varepsilon}{k}(G_k+C_{3\varepsilon}G_b)-C_{2\varepsilon}\rho\frac{\varepsilon^2}{k}+S_\varepsilon \quad (6)$$

where G_K represents the turbulent kinetic energy of the average velocity; G_b represents the turbulent kinetic energy of the buoyancy; Y_m represents the total dissipation rate of the wave expansion in compressible turbulence; $C_{1\varepsilon}$, $C_{2\varepsilon}$, and $C_{3\varepsilon}$ are constants; σ_k and σ_ε are the Prandtl number of k and ε; and S_K and S_ε are user-defined.

The turbulent (or eddy) viscosity is calculated by the following combination:

$$\mu_t=\rho C_\mu\frac{k^2}{\varepsilon} \quad (7)$$

where C_μ is a constant.

3.3. Discrete Phase Model

In view of the movement and distribution of droplets under different distances from rotor to nozzle, Fluent selected the Discrete Phase Model to simulate the spraying of nozzle droplets. The DPM model could well simulate the separation and deposition of nozzle droplets. The Euler–Lagrange method provided in the DPM model is selected in this study. By solving the N-S equation, the fluid in the fluid domain is regarded as a continuous phase, while the discrete phase tracks its trajectory at unit time interval by exchanging momentum, mass, and energy with the continuous phase. Due to the continuous interaction energy between discrete phase droplets and continuous phase air, the continuous phase is set to be updated once every iteration. The droplet continuity equation adopts the form of Unsteady Particle dispersion and enables the Unsteady Particle Tracking discrete phase droplet continuity equation. The step size of the discrete phase particles is set to 0.001 s, and the solution method adopts the Euler–Lagrange method. The equation of motion of the discrete phase particles is expressed as follows:

$$\frac{d\vec{u}_p}{dt}=\frac{18\mu}{\rho_p d_p^2}\frac{C_D Re}{24}(\vec{u}-\vec{u}_p)+\frac{g_y(\rho_p-\rho)}{\rho_p}+\frac{\rho d}{2\rho_p dt}(\vec{u}-\vec{u}_p) \quad (8)$$

where $\vec{u}$ is the continuous phase velocity; $\vec{u}_p$ is particle velocity; ρ_p is the particle density; d_p is the particle diameter; g_y is the gravitational acceleration; Re is the relative Reynolds number; and C_D is the drag coefficient.

The spray numerical simulation also needs to consider the fragmentation and aggregation of droplets, and judge whether droplets merge and rebound. The judgment is mainly based on whether they reach the critical value of collision given by Rourke, which is a function of the collision Weber number and the radius of small droplets. The calculation formula is as follows:

$$b_{crit}=(r_1+r_2)\sqrt{\min(1,\frac{2.4f}{We})} \quad (9)$$

where b_{crit} is the critical value for judging the collision, merger, or rebound of droplets; r_1 and r_2 are the radius of small droplets; f is the ratio of r_1/r_2; and We is the collision Weber number.

3.4. Boundary Condition

The established computing domain model was imported into Fluent meshing (v2020 R2), and the computing domain model was meshed. In the process of meshing, the quality of the grid is particularly important. Due to the geometric complexity of both the external airflow field around the fuselage and the rotational domain, a tetrahedral mesh (Tetrahedrons) with Patch Conforming method was employed for grid generation. The physics preference was set to CFD with 100% relevance. The Relevance Center was set to Fine, Smoothing to Medium, and Span Angle Center to Fine to ensure computational accuracy. The mesh density of the outer drainage basin gradually decreases from the fuselage outward and the mesh size gradually increases from the fuselage outward. The mesh density of the rotation domain remains unchanged and the mesh size is uniform. The total number of mesh elements obtained is 14,628,887. The cell mass of the grid is 0.8453, and the average orthogonal mass of the grid is 0.78831, both of which meet the mesh division standards.

In order to simulate the air flow distribution characteristics under a certain flight speed and rotor speed, and the influence of air flow on the deposition distribution of droplets under different rotor–nozzle distances, the outer basin was designated as still fluid in the parameter setting of Fluent (Cell Zone Condition). The rotation domain of the four rotors were also divided into four fluids (fluid1, fluid2, fluid3, and fluid4). The rotation mode was set as the grid motion method, and the rotation center, rotation axis direction, and rotation speed of the four rotors were set according to the model size and numerical simulation requirements of the plant protection UAV. In order to simulate the flight speed of the four-rotor plant protection UAV, the upper, lower, front, and rear surfaces of the outer basin were set as walls. When the UAV was simulated in hover state, the left side of the outer basin was set as Pressure-inlet, and when different flight speeds were simulated, it was set as Velocity-inlet. The rear boundary was set as a pressure-outlet boundary with a gauge pressure of 0 Pa. Interfaces were defined between internal flow domains. Both the fuselage and rotor boundaries were configured as wall boundaries, where the fuselage remained stationary while the rotor wall moved at the same velocity as the rotating domain.

This simulation was mainly aimed at the research on the distribution characteristics of droplet deposition under the rotor–nozzle distance. Considering the requirements of later test verification, the flight speed of the UAV was 3 m/s and the rotor speed was 2000 r/min in the simulation test, and the mainstream model DJI-T30 plant protection UAV (Shenzhen DJI Innovation Technology Co., Ltd., Shenzhen, China) in the market was taken as a reference. The vertical rotor–nozzle distances were selected as 200, 280, 360, and 440 mm for the simulation test.

4. Simulation Result Analysis

4.1. Spatial Distribution Analysis of Rotor Airflow

The rotor airflow of a UAV can effectively promote the deposition movement of droplets and reduce drift. In order to study the intensity distribution of rotor airflow, the spatial airflow velocity distribution at 0, 0.25, 0.5, 0.75, 1.0, and 1.25 m directly below the rotor was selected at an interval of 0.25 m, as shown in Figure 3.

According to the distribution law of rotor airflow, it can be seen that the airflow around the center of the rotor was larger, decreasing from the center to the surrounding area. In addition, with the decrease of the space height, the rotor airflow first strengthened and then gradually weakened. Under the rotor within the range of 0.25–0.5 m, the rotor airflow intensity reaches its maximum value, with an airflow velocity of approximately 8 m/s. However, when the space height drops to 0.75 m, the rotor airflow intensity becomes significantly weaker. In order to accurately reflect the intensity distribution of rotor airflow in the horizontal direction, a horizontal coordinate line was set below rotor, and the diagram was drawn according to the speed results (Figure 4a). It can be seen that the intensity of airflow generated by the rear rotor was greater than that of the front rotor during the forward flight of the UAV, and the maximum difference of airflow intensity could reach 1.33 m/s. In addition, the airflow intensity below the center of the fuselage was significantly weaker than it was directly below the rotor; the difference between the airflow intensity below the fuselage and that of the rear rotor reached more than 4.89 m/s. Similarly, in order to accurately reflect the intensity distribution of rotor airflow in the vertical direction, the distribution of airflow intensity vertically downwards starting from the rotor plane was output, and the distribution of airflow velocity with spatial height was plotted. As can be seen from Figure 4b, the intensity of rotor airflow presented a trend of first strengthening and then weakening within a vertical spatial range of 600 mm directly below the rotor, which is consistent with the airflow velocity distribution in Figure 4. In the range of 0–360 mm directly below the rotor, the rotor airflow speed gradually increased, with the maximum airflow velocity reaching 8.1 m/s. When the vertical distance exceeded 360 mm, the rotor airflow velocity gradually decreased. Therefore, according to the preliminary analysis of the spatial distribution of rotor airflow, in order to obtain a large initial downward movement velocity of droplets sprayed by the nozzle for aerial spraying operation, the optimal installation position of the nozzle should be within the range of 300–400 mm directly below the rotor.

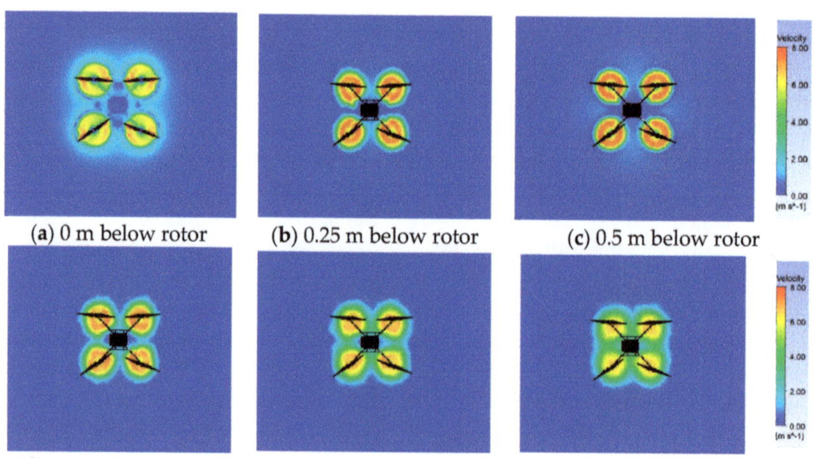

(**a**) 0 m below rotor (**b**) 0.25 m below rotor (**c**) 0.5 m below rotor
(**d**) 0.75 m below rotor (**e**) 1 m below rotor (**f**) 1.25 m below rotor

Figure 3. Airflow velocity distribution of cross-sections at different heights.

4.2. *Analysis of Droplet Deposition Movement*

In the simulation test of the droplet movement process, the rotor airflow distribution reached a stable state after 2 s, and an appropriate nozzle spraying time was set. Droplets were immediately entrained by rotor airflow and drifted towards the ground after being ejected by the nozzle, while also being affected by the relative wind field generated by the flight motion and moving backwards. As shown in Figure 5, the movement distribution of the droplet deposition at four different rotor–nozzle distances was simulated, including main view, side view, top view, and full view.

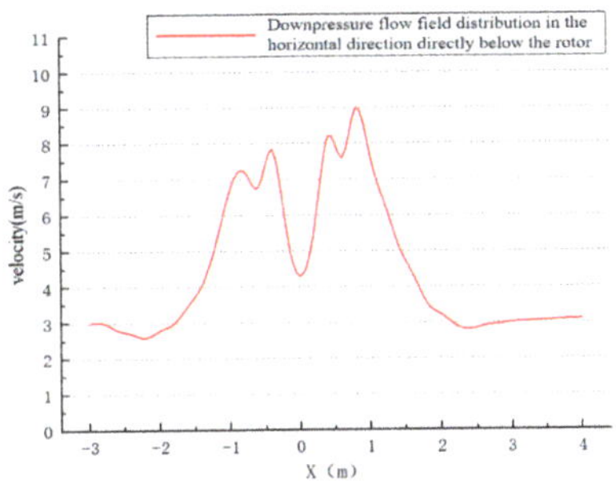

(**a**) Horizontal rotor airflow distribution

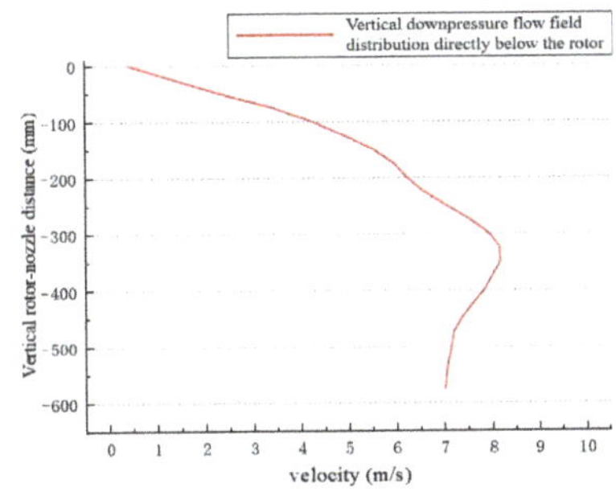

(**b**) Vertical rotor airflow distribution

Figure 4. Distribution of rotor airflow intensity.

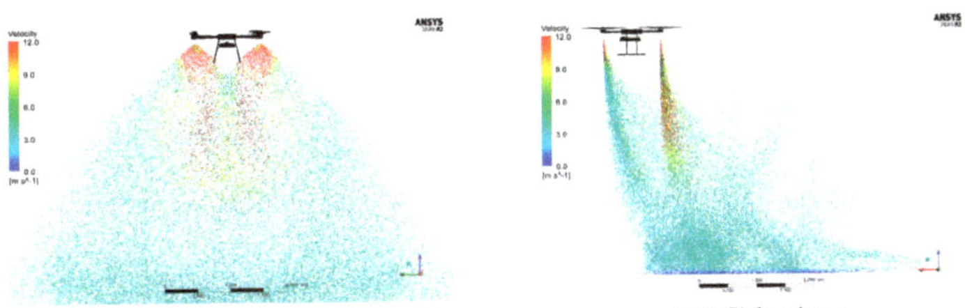

(**a1**) Frontal view (**a2**) Side view

(**a**) The movement distribution of droplets at a vertical distance of 200 mm

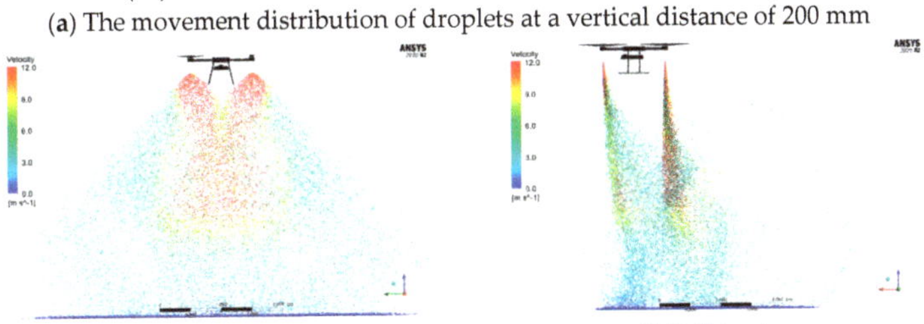

(**b1**) Frontal view (**b2**) Side view

(**b**) The movement distribution of droplets at a vertical distance of 280 mm

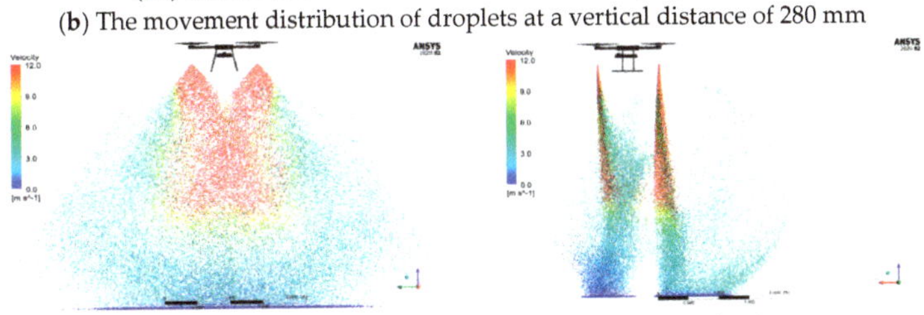

(**c1**) Frontal view (**c2**) Side view

(**c**) The movement distribution of droplets at a vertical distance of 360 mm

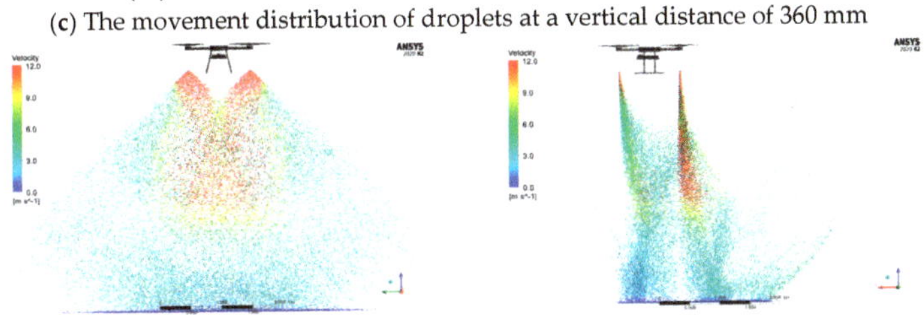

(**d1**) Frontal view (**d2**) Side view

(**d**) The movement distribution of droplets at a vertical distance of 440 mm

Figure 5. The movement distribution of droplets at different vertical distances.

It can be seen from Figure 5 that the velocity of droplets after leaving the nozzle was mainly affected by rotor airflow, and the velocity of droplets moving closer to the center of the rotor was the highest. With the further deposition of droplets to the ground, the influence of rotor airflow on the movement of droplets was weakened, and the movement speed of droplets gradually decreased under the influence of air resistance. By comparing the four side views of the movement of droplets, it can be seen that with the increase of rotor–nozzle distance, the average velocity of the droplet group nearest to right below the rotor increased first and then decreased. At the distances of 200, 280, 360, and 440 mm, the average velocities of droplets were 7.35, 8.12, 8.9, and 8.42 m/s, respectively. Combined with the simulation results of airflow distribution under different spatial heights, it can be seen that the airflow first increased and then gradually decreased, and the airflow intensity reached the maximum near the vertical distance of 350 mm, at which time droplets deposited on the ground under the stress of rotor airflow.

To sum up, the deposition movement of droplets would be affected by factors such as the rotor airflow, the relative wind field, and air resistance generated by flight movement. In order to ensure that droplets can obtain a satisfactory deposition effect, it can be seen that the rotor–nozzle distance should be selected as about 360 mm based on the above analysis. Droplets have a larger motion speed after leaving the nozzle and a minimal degree of drift in this condition.

4.3. Cloud Map Analysis of Droplet Deposition Concentration

In order to calculate the droplet deposition at different crop canopy heights under different rotor–nozzle distances of plant protection UAVs, the cloud map of droplet deposition concentration at different flight heights was simulated by CFD. Figure 6 shows the cloud map of droplet deposition concentration under the condition of flight heights of 1, 2, 3, and 4 m. The change in color of the icon on the left from red to blue indicates the change in the level of droplet deposition concentration. It can be seen from the figure that there were great differences in the distribution of droplet deposition concentration at different rotor–nozzle distances. In the condition of a flight height of 1 m, the cloud pattern of droplet deposition concentration at four different vertical distances between rotor and nozzle presents a narrow strip shape, indicating that the distribution range of droplets is small and mainly concentrated right below the fuselage. Furthermore, the maximum concentration of droplet deposition exceeds 0.010 kg/m^3, indicating poor distribution uniformity of droplet deposition. The main reason is that droplets cannot fully diffuse under the action of rotor airflow due to the limited space for droplet deposition. When the flight height increases to 2 m, it can be found from the cloud map of droplet deposition concentration that with the increase of deposit space, droplets begin to spread to both sides of the fuselage, which enlarges the effective deposition distribution range and improves the uniformity of droplet deposition. However, the comparison of the cloud pattern of droplet deposition concentration at four different vertical distances between rotor and nozzle showed that the droplet deposition distribution appeared in a circular arc shape along the flight direction and drifted backward in the flight direction due to the influence of the relative airflow when the vertical distance was 200, 280, and 440 mm. However, at the vertical distance of 360 mm, the droplet deposition distribution still remained in an elongated shape, with the maximum concentration of droplet deposition reaching 0.0073 kg/m^3, indicating that droplets can maintain a good deposition effect under the influence of the rotor downwash airflow. Compared with the cloud map of droplet deposition at a flight height of 3 m, it can be seen that the shape of deposition distribution changed less, but droplets were further diffused. Droplets began to drift to both sides of the fuselage, and the concentration of droplets decreased significantly at the vertical distances of 200 and 440 mm. Only a small volume of droplets gathered under the fuselage, and most of the droplets had drifted, so the spraying effect was poor.

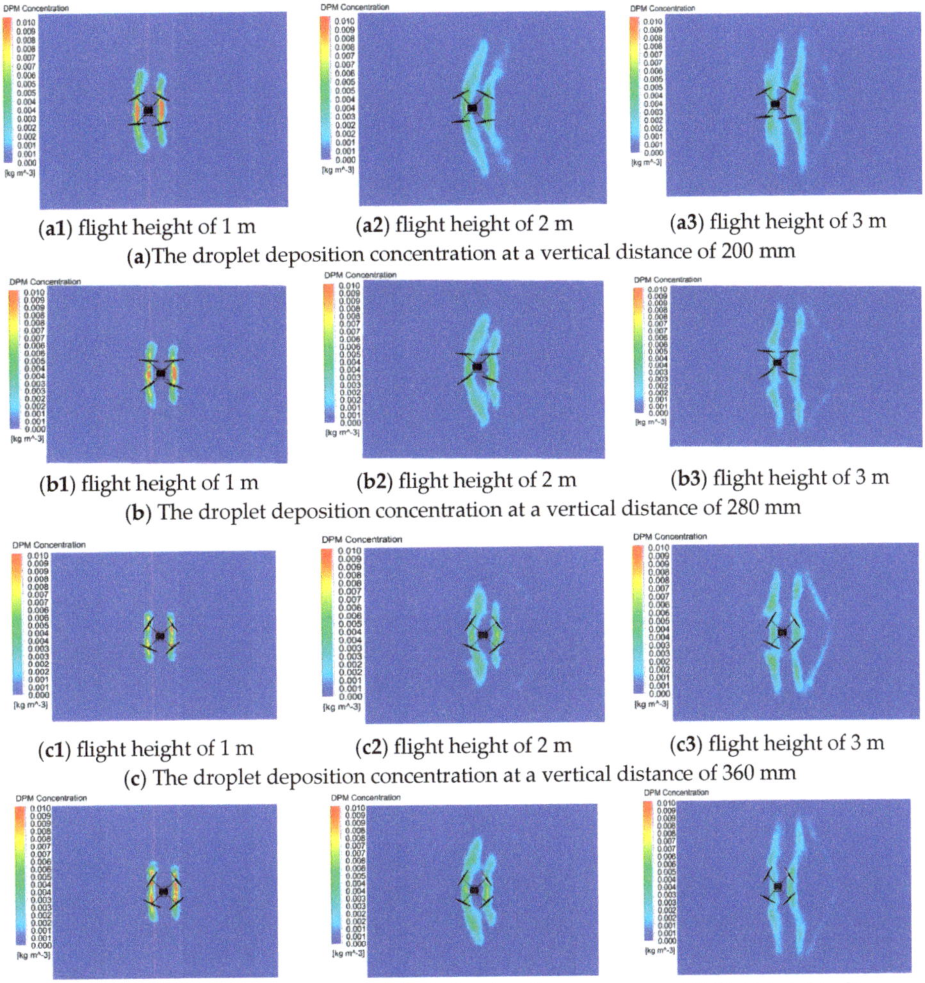

(**a1**) flight height of 1 m (**a2**) flight height of 2 m (**a3**) flight height of 3 m

(**a**)The droplet deposition concentration at a vertical distance of 200 mm

(**b1**) flight height of 1 m (**b2**) flight height of 2 m (**b3**) flight height of 3 m

(**b**) The droplet deposition concentration at a vertical distance of 280 mm

(**c1**) flight height of 1 m (**c2**) flight height of 2 m (**c3**) flight height of 3 m

(**c**) The droplet deposition concentration at a vertical distance of 360 mm

(**d1**) flight height of 1 m (**d2**) flight height of 2 m (**d3**) flight height of 3 m

(**d**) The droplet deposition concentration at a vertical distance of 440 mm

Figure 6. Cloud map of droplet deposition mass concentration at different conditions.

At present, for the spraying operations of rice, corn, wheat, and other major crops, the suitable flight height recommended by the UAV enterprise is generally 2 m. In this condition, the effective deposition distribution range of droplets sprayed by plant protection UAVs is relatively large, and the deposition uniformity of droplets is better. However, due to the influence of rotor downwash airflow and relative wind field caused by flight motion, droplets will still drift partially. According to the analysis of droplet deposition concentration at different rotor–nozzle distances, it can be seen that the effect of droplet deposition distribution was better at the vertical distance of about 360 mm, with the droplets on both sides drifting less, which would result in a better spraying effect.

5. Field Trial Validation

5.1. Materials and Methods

5.1.1. Instrument and Equipment

In order to verify the simulation results, the EFT-410S four-rotor plant protection UAV was used for the field spray test, which was consistent with the simulation model. The nozzles were installed directly below the rotor and connected through a vertical spray rod. According to the requirements of the test parameter setting, the spray rod can be extended or shortened in the vertical direction to adjust the rotor–nozzle distance. In the test, the Lu120-02 fan-shaped nozzle was used for spraying, and the spray flow rate was 2.0 L/min.

In the test, droplet deposition data were collected using water-sensitive paper (Syngenta Plant Protection Co., Ltd., Basel, Switzerland) as droplet collection cards, with a size of 26 mm × 76 mm. A HP Scanjet200 flatbed scanner (Hewlett-Packard, Palo Alto, California, USA) was used to scan the collected water-sensitive paper to obtain a gray image of the droplets. The DepositScan software (v1.0) was used to analyze the gray image and obtain the data of droplet deposition on water-sensitive paper, including droplet deposition rate, deposition density, coverage rate, etc.

The Kestrel NK-5500 weather station (Nielsen Kellerman Company, Chandler, AZ, USA) was used to collect environmental meteorological data during the test, which was used to monitor and record environmental parameters such as ambient wind speed and wind direction in the field. In addition, the droplet collection equipment also included PVC pipe (1 m), a double-ended universal clamp, rubber gloves, sealed bags, etc.

5.1.2. Test Method

The test was conducted on 27 September 2023 and test site was located in the teaching and research base of South China Agricultural University, Guangzhou, Guangdong Province. The test scheme is shown in Figure 7. A droplet collection tape with a length of 15 m was arranged perpendicular to the flight direction of the UAV in a sufficiently large field. A target area with a width of 5 m was set in the middle of the collection tape with reference to the effective spray width of plant protection UAVs provided by the manufacturer, and 5 m wide drift areas were set on both sides of the target area. Droplet collection points with an interval of 1 m were set on the droplet collection tape. At each collection point, water-sensitive paper was fixed on a PVC round pipe with double-end clips. The water-sensitive paper was placed about 1 m away from the ground to simulate the height of a crop canopy. According to the above collection and distribution method, each collection tape had a total of 16 collection points for droplets, numbered 1#~16# from left to right. In addition, in order to reduce the possible test errors in the spraying process, three replicates of the collection tape were used, and the interval distance between each collection tape was 5 m.

The weather station was placed next to the test area, and the frequency of environmental meteorological data collection was set at 1 Hz. During the test, the ambient temperature was about 21 °C and the relative humidity of the air was 60%–63%. In particular, in order to avoid the influence of ambient wind on droplet deposition distribution, the spray test was carried out under the conditions of no wind or wind speed less than 2 m/s.

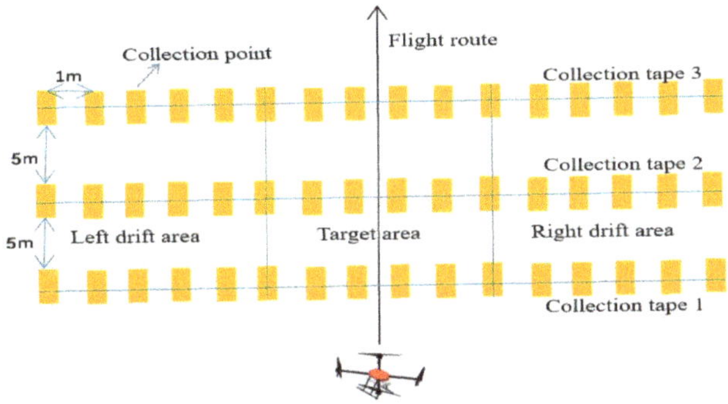

Figure 7. Schematic diagram of the test scheme.

5.1.3. Operation Parameters

The test was to study the influence of rotor airflow on droplet deposition distribution of plant protection UAVs at different rotor–nozzle distances. Therefore, the test was mainly designed for the parameter of rotor–nozzle distance. Consistent with the parameters in the simulation of Section 3, the rotor–nozzle distances were set to four groups of 200, 280, 360, and 440 mm for the field spray test. Based on the recommendation of spray operation parameters, the flight height was set to 2.5 m and the flight speed was set to 5 m/s.

During the test, the spray system was turned on when the plant protection UAV flew to a distance of about 10 m away from the first collection tape, and the spraying was stopped after flying over the droplet collection area according to the designated route, so as to reduce the impact of non-test liquid droplets on the test results. The rotor–nozzle distance was adjusted to 200, 280, 360, and 440 mm in sequence, and the spray test was repeated until these tests were completed.

5.1.4. Data Processing and Analysis

After the completion of each spray test, it is necessary to wait for the droplets on the water-sensitive paper to dry fully. These water-sensitive papers were packed in a sealed bag with a label according to the sequence of collection points and brought back to the laboratory for data processing. These water-sensitive papers were scanned by a scanner one by one. Then the scanned images were processed and analyzed by the image processing software DepositScan.

In order to characterize the droplet drift of plant protection UAVs at different rotor–nozzle distances, the droplet drift rate was used to assess droplet drift volume. The calculation formula for droplet drift rate is as follows:

$$R_{\mathrm{d}} = T_N/(T_E + T_N) \times 100\% \tag{10}$$

where R_d represents the droplet drift rate, %; T_N represents the total volume of droplets deposited in the non-target area, μL·cm^{-2}; and T_E represents the total volume of droplets deposited in the target area, μL·cm^{-2}.

In addition, to further demonstrate the influence of rotor airflow at different rotor–nozzle distances on the deposition distribution of droplets in aerial spraying, significance of difference analysis and one-way ANOVA were conducted on the test results using SPSS software (v25.0), and their significance was tested ($p < 0.05$).

5.2. Test Results and Analysis

5.2.1. Analysis of Droplet Deposition Distribution in the Target Area

As shown in Table 2, the results of droplet deposition collected in the target area in four group tests with the rotor–nozzle distances of 200, 280, 360, and 440 mm are presented. The average volume of droplets deposited in the target area in the four group tests were 0.398, 0.560, 0.766, and 0.406 $\mu L \cdot cm^{-2}$, respectively. The amount of droplet deposition varied with the different rotor–nozzle distances. With the increase in vertical distance, the number of droplets deposited in the target area increased first. However, when the distance increased from 360 mm to 440 mm, the amount of droplet deposition decreased sharply from 0.766 $\mu L \cdot cm^{-2}$ to 0.406 $\mu L \cdot cm^{-2}$, a decrease of about 47%. Based on the analysis of the simulation results in Section 3, it can be concluded that the reason for this phenomenon is the difference in airflow intensity under the rotor. In the range of 0–350 mm below the rotor, the rotor downwash airflow velocity gradually increases, while when the vertical distance exceeds 350 mm, the rotor downwash airflow velocity gradually decreases. The velocity of droplet deposition was affected by the rotor airflow intensity, and droplets with greater velocity were deposited in the target area in a shorter time, thereby affecting the distribution characteristics of droplet deposition. With the increase of the rotor–nozzle distance, the airflow forcing the downward movement of droplets first increased and then weakened, and the amount of droplet deposition in the target area also first increased and then decreased. The maximum airflow intensity was located at about 350 mm below the rotor, which forced more droplets to deposit in the target area.

Table 2. Droplet deposition in the target area.

Distance/mm	Collection Tape	Total Droplet Deposition/($\mu L \cdot cm^{-2}$)	Average Droplet Deposition/($\mu L \cdot cm^{-2}$)
200	1	0.425	0.398 ± 0.025
	2	0.404	
	3	0.365	
280	1	0.589	0.560 ± 0.075
	2	0.634	
	3	0.457	
360	1	0.761	0.766 ± 0.012
	2	0.754	
	3	0.782	
440	1	0.401	0.406 ± 0.004
	2	0.411	
	3	0.407	

Note: The mean ± SD (standard deviation) is used to describe the central tendency and dispersion of the data.

In order to further analyze whether there are significant differences in the droplet deposition at different rotor–nozzle distances, a significant analysis was conducted on the average amount of droplet deposition in the target area, and the results are shown in Figure 8. As can be seen from the figure, there were significant differences in droplet deposition between the vertical distances of 200, 280, and 360 mm, ($p < 0.05$) while there was no significant difference in droplet deposition between the vertical distances of 200 and 440 mm ($p > 0.05$). The results were consistent with the above analysis; that is, the different rotor–nozzle distances led to a different intensity of rotor downwash airflow, which resulted in a difference in the volume of droplets deposited in the target area.

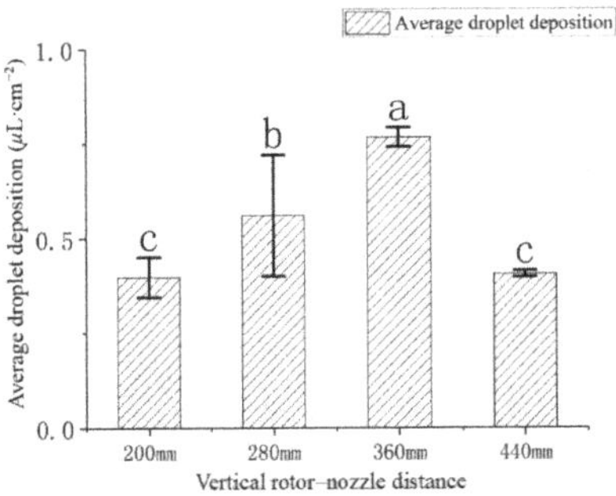

Figure 8. Droplet deposition at different rotor–nozzle distances. Note: Letters a, b, and c are used to indicate statistically significant differences between experimental groups.

5.2.2. Analysis of Droplet Drift

Table 3 shows the droplet drift of plant protection UAVs at four different rotor–nozzle distances. It can be seen that the volume of droplets deposited in the drift area was different at different vertical distances. In the four tests, the average amount of droplet drift in the drift area was 0.546, 0.536, 0.235 and 0.617 $\mu L \cdot cm^{-2}$, respectively. With the increase of rotor–nozzle distance, the volume of droplets deposited in the drift area first decreased and then increased. When the vertical distance increased from 200 to 360 mm, the drift rate of droplets decreased from 57.87% to 23.31%. As the vertical distance increased to 440 mm, the drift rate of droplets increased to 60.27%, and the maximum amount of droplet drift was reached. The phenomenon of droplet drift was consistent with the droplet deposition in the target area. Based on the simulation results of rotor airflow distribution and the droplet deposition cloud map in Section 3, it can be seen that the rotor airflow intensity was enhanced when the vertical distance increased to 360 mm. The enhanced rotor airflow significantly promoted the downward movement of droplets, resulting in more droplets depositing in the target area and fewer droplets drifting. However, as the vertical distance increased to 440 mm, the rotor airflow intensity and the downward movement of droplets were also weakened. The result was that droplets easily drifted a lot under the influence of various external wind fields or airflows.

Table 3. Droplet deposition in drift area.

Distance/mm	Collection Tape	Total Droplet Drift/($\mu L \cdot cm^{-2}$)	Average Droplet Drift/($\mu L \cdot cm^{-2}$)	Drift Rate/%
200	1	0.560	0.546 ± 0.015	57.87
	2	0.553		
	3	0.525		
280	1	0.497	0.536 ± 0.048	49.12
	2	0.507		
	3	0.603		
360	1	0.299	0.235 ± 0.051	23.31
	2	0.231		
	3	0.175		
440	1	0.625	0.617 ± 0.031	60.27
	2	0.576		
	3	0.652		

Note: The mean ± SD (standard deviation) is used to describe the central tendency and dispersion of the data.

Similarly, in order to further analyze whether there are significant differences in the droplet drift at different rotor–nozzle distances, a significance analysis was conducted on the average drift rate of droplets in the drift area, and the results are shown in Figure 9. It can be seen that there were significant differences in droplet drift between the vertical distances of 200, 280, and 360 mm ($p < 0.05$), while there was no significant difference in droplet drift between the vertical distances of 200 and 440 mm ($p > 0.05$). The results were consistent with the analysis of droplet deposition in the target area; there were significant differences in droplet deposition and drift at different rotor–nozzle distances.

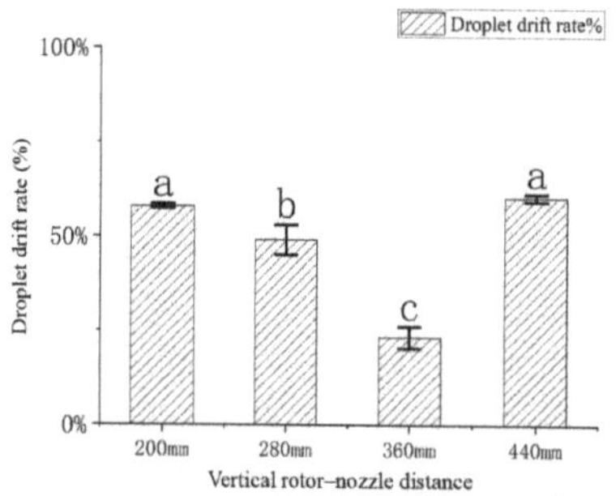

Figure 9. Droplet drift at different rotor–nozzle distances. Note: Letters a, b, and c are used to indicate statistically significant differences between experimental groups.

5.3. Comparison of Simulation and Field Test Results

Combined with the simulated results of droplet deposition concentration, the simulation data of droplet deposition on the cross-section with the effective spray width of 5 m and the spray height of 3 m in the numerical simulation were statistically analyzed, and the simulation results were compared with the field test results, as shown in Figure 10. There was a certain deviation between the droplet deposition results of the field test and that of the numerical simulation at different rotor–nozzle distances, and the amount of droplet deposition in the numerical simulation was lower than that of field test. The main cause of the deviation is primarily the difference in spray application rates, and field trials are susceptible to interference from multiple factors. However, it can be seen from the line chart that the droplet deposition trends of the two have a good consistency. As the rotor–nozzle distance increased from 200 to 360 mm, the volume of droplets deposited in the target area increased. However, when the distance increased to 440 mm, the volume of droplets deposited in the target area decreased sharply. Although the numerical simulation results of droplet deposition have some deviation from the field test results, they can still guide the development of field tests and the reasonable setting of operation parameters to a certain extent, thereby achieving the goal of precise spray operation.

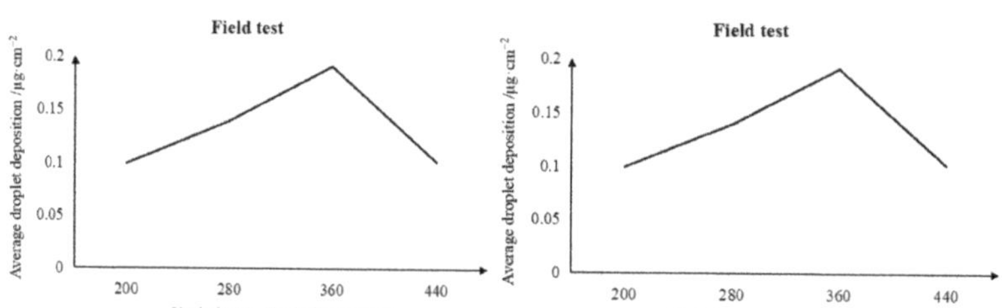

Figure 10. Comparison of simulation and field test results.

6. Conclusions

In this study, the rotor–nozzle distance of plant protection UAVs was taken as the research object; the distribution of rotor airflow and its effects on the droplet deposition of plant protection UAVs under various rotor–nozzle distances were analyzed and verified by numerical simulation and field tests. The main conclusions were as follows:

(1) The intensity of rotor airflow showed a trend of first strengthening and then weakening with the increase of the distance from the rotor, which was relatively high within the range of 300–400 mm below the rotor, and the maximum velocity of airflow could reach 8.1 m/s.

(2) The average velocity of the droplet groups followed a unimodal distribution with increasing rotor–nozzle distance, peaking at 8.9 m/s with a 360 mm vertical distance. At this optimal distance, enhanced deposition velocity near the ground promoted target crop coverage while minimizing drift losses.

(3) Droplet deposition concentration varied significantly across rotor–nozzle distances ($p < 0.05$). Optimal deposition efficiency was achieved at 360 mm, with a minimum drift rate of 23.31%.

(4) There was a certain deviation between the droplet deposition results of the field test and that of the numerical simulation, but the droplet deposition trends have a good consistency. Consequently, the simulation results can effectively inform field test design and operational parameter optimization to enhance precision spraying performance.

Author Contributions: Conceptualization, S.C. and Y.L.; methodology, X.X. and Z.L.; validation, X.X. and Z.W.; formal analysis, X.X. and Y.T.; investigation, X.X. and S.H.; resources, S.C. and Y.L.; writing—original draft preparation, X.X.; writing—review and editing, S.C.; visualization, Z.W., Y.T., and S.H.; supervision, S.C. and Y.L.; project administration, S.C.; funding acquisition, Y.L. All authors have read and agreed to the published version of the manuscript.

Funding: This study was funded by the Key R&D Project of Ningxia Hui Autonomous Region (2024BBF01013), the National Key Research and Development Plan Project (2023YFD2000200), and the 111 Project (D18019).

Institutional Review Board Statement: Not applicable for studies not involving humans or animals.

Data Availability Statement: The raw data supporting the conclusions of this article will be made available by the authors on request.

Acknowledgments: We deeply thank reviewers and editors for giving relevant revision advice for improvement of the paper.

Conflicts of Interest: The authors declare no conflicts of interest.

References

1. Hu, S.; Xu, X.; Liu, J.; Guo, J.; Guan, R.; Zhou, Z.; Lan, Y.; Chen, S. Movement Characteristics of Droplet Deposition in Flat Spray Nozzle for Agricultural UAVs. *Agriculture* **2024**, *14*, 1994. [CrossRef]
2. Zhou, Q.; Zhang, S.; Lin, T.; Jiao, Y.; Cai, C.; Xue, C.; Ye, J.; Xue, X. The Impact of Fluroxypyr Drift on Soybean Phytotoxicity and the Safety Drift Thresholds. *Agriculture* **2024**, *14*, 2203. [CrossRef]
3. Tang, Q.; Zhang, R.; Chen, L.; Xu, G.; Deng, W.; Ding, C.; Xu, M.; Yi, T.; Wen, Y.; Li, L. High-accuracy, high-resolution downwash flow field measurements of an unmanned helicopter for precision agriculture. *Comput. Electron. Agric.* **2020**, *173*, 105390. [CrossRef]
4. Jin, Z.; Guo, S.; Li, S.; Yu, F.; Xu, T. Research on the rice fertiliser decision-making method based on UAV remote sensing data assimilation. *Comput. Electron. Agric.* **2024**, *216*, 108508. [CrossRef]
5. Yu, F.; Xiang, S.; Xu, C.; Jin, Z. PIOSL-PRO: Construction of the PIOSL Model Considering the Distribution of Multiple Elements. *IEEE T. Geosci. Remote.* **2024**, *62*, 1–12.
6. Huang, J.; He, W.; Yang, D.; Lin, J.; Ou, Y.; Jiang, R.; Zhou, Z. Quantity Monitor Based on Differential Weighing Sensors for Storage Tank of Agricultural UAV. *Drones* **2024**, *8*, 92. [CrossRef]

7. Zhang, H.; Qi, L.; Wu, Y.; Musiu, E.; Cheng, Z.; Wang, P. Numerical simulation of airflow field from a six–rotor plant protection drone using lattice Boltzmann method. *Biosyst. Eng.* **2020**, *197*, 336–351. [CrossRef]
8. Fan, G.; Liu, Z.; Qin, Y.; Long, B.; Li, H.; Li, J. Airflow characteristics of rotorcraft plant protection UAV operating in rice fields. *Biosyst. Eng.* **2023**, *226*, 209–222. [CrossRef]
9. Wei, X.; Zhang, Z.; Li, H.; Wu, H.; Lv, J.; Wu, L.; Zhou, M.; Li, J. Influences of wind vortex intensity of rotor UAV on rice morphology and yield. *Precis. Agric.* **2023**, *24*, 1766–1791. [CrossRef]
10. Zhang, J.; He, X.; Song, J.; Zeng, A.; Liu, Y.; Li, X. Influence of spraying parameters of unmanned aircraft on droplets deposition. *Trans. Chin. Soc. Agric. Mach.* **2012**, *43*, 94–96, (In Chinese with English Abstract).
11. Qiu, B.; Wang, L.; Cai, D.; Wu, J.; Ding, G.; Guan, X. Effects of flight altitude and speed of unmanned helicopter on spray deposition uniform. *Trans. Chin. Soc. Agric. Eng.* **2013**, *29*, 25–32, (In Chinese with English Abstract).
12. Qin, W.; Xue, X.; Zhou, L.; Zhang, S.; Sun, Z.; Kong, W.; Wang, B. Effects of spraying parameters of unmanned aerial vehicle on droplets deposition distribution of maize canopies. *Trans. Chin. Soc. Agric. Eng.* **2014**, *30*, 50–56, (In Chinese with English Abstract).
13. Qin, W.; Xue, X.; Zhang, S.; Gu, W.; Chen, C. Optimization and test of spraying parameters for P20 multi-rotor electric unmanned aerial vehicle based on response surface method. *J. Jiangsu Univ.* **2016**, *37*, 548–555, (In Chinese with English Abstract).
14. Zhang, H.; Qi, L.; Wu, Y.; Cheng, Z.; Liu, W.; Elizabeth, M.; Xiao, Y.; Yang, Z. Distribution characteristics of rotor downwash airflow field under spraying on orchard using unmanned aerial vehicle. *Trans. Chin. Soc. Agric. Eng.* **2019**, *35*, 44–54, (In Chinese with English Abstract).
15. Lian, Q. *Study on the Variation of Downwash and the Installation Position of Nozzles in a Six-Rotor Plant Protection Drone*; Heilongjiang Bayi Agricultural University: Mishan, China, 2019.
16. Xie, Y.; Wang, G.; Wang, B.; Shang, C.; Lan, Y. Selection of nozzle type and parameter optimization in herbicide spraying process of plant protection UAV. *J. Chin. Agric. Mach.* **2021**, *42*, 61–69, (In Chinese with English Abstract).
17. Wang, C.; He, X.; Bonds, J.; Qi, P.; Yang, Y.; Gao, W. Effect of Downwash Airflow Field of 8-rotor Unmanned Aerial Vehicle on Spray Deposition Distribution Characteristics under Different Flight Parameters. *Smart Agric.* **2020**, *2*, 124–136, (In Chinese with English Abstract).
18. Chen, S.; Lan, Y.; Li, J.; Zhou, Z.; Liu, A.; Mao, Y. Effect of wind field below unmanned helicopter on droplet deposition distribution of aerial spraying. *Int. J. Agric. Biol. Eng.* **2017**, *10*, 67–77.
19. Yang, F.; Xue, X.; Cai, C.; Zhou, Q. Effect of down wash airflow in hover on droplet motion law for multi-rotor unmanned plant protection machine. *Trans. Chin. Soc. Agric. Eng.* **2018**, *34*, 64–73, (In Chinese with English Abstract).
20. Zhan, Y.; Chen, P.; Xu, W.; Chen, S.; Han, Y.; Lan, Y.; Wang, G. Influence of the downwash airflow distribution characteristics of a plant protection UAV on spray deposit distribution. *Biosyst. Eng.* **2022**, *216*, 32–45. [CrossRef]
21. Wang, L.; Zhang, Q.; Hou, Q.; Chen, D.; Wang, S. Vertical distribution law of six-rotor plant protection UAV based on multi-feature parameters. *Trans. Chin. Soc. Agric. Mach.* **2022**, *53*, 75–83, (In Chinese with English Abstract).
22. Li, J.; Guo, S.; Yao, W.; Zhan, Y.; Li, Y. Distribution characteristics of droplet size in rice field and wind tunnel simulation test under airflow operation. *Trans. Chin. Soc. Agric. Mach.* **2019**, *50*, 148–156, (In Chinese with English Abstract).
23. He, Y.; Xiao, S.; Fang, H.; Dong, T.; Tang, Y.; Nie, P.; Wu, J.; Luo, S. Development situation and spraying decision of spray nozzle for plant protection UAV. *Trans. Chin. Soc. Agric. Eng.* **2018**, *34*, 113–124, (In Chinese with English Abstract).

agriculture

MDPI

Article

YOLOv8n-SSDW: A Lightweight and Accurate Model for Barnyard Grass Detection in Fields

Yan Sun [1,2,3], Hanrui Guo [1,2,3], Xiaoan Chen [1,2,3], Mengqi Li [1,2,3], Bing Fang [4] and Yingli Cao [1,2,3,*]

1 School of Information and Electrical Engineering, Shenyang Agricultural University, Shenyang 110866, China; sunyan0530@stu.syau.edu.cn (Y.S.)
2 National Digital Agriculture Regional Innovation Center (Northeast), Shenyang 110866, China
3 Key Laboratory of Smart Agriculture Technology in Liaoning Province, Shenyang 110866, China
4 Department of Foreign Language Teaching, Shenyang Agricultural University, Shenyang 110866, China
* Correspondence: caoyingli@syau.edu.cn

Abstract: Barnyard grass is a major noxious weed in paddy fields. Accurate and efficient identification of barnyard grass is crucial for precision field management. However, existing deep learning models generally suffer from high parameter counts and computational complexity, limiting their practical application in field scenarios. Moreover, the morphological similarity, overlapping, and occlusion between barnyard grass and rice pose challenges for reliable detection in complex environments. To address these issues, this study constructed a barnyard grass detection dataset using high-resolution images captured by a drone equipped with a high-definition camera in rice experimental fields in Haicheng City, Liaoning Province. A lightweight field barnyard grass detection model, YOLOv8n-SSDW, was proposed to enhance detection precision and speed. Based on the baseline YOLOv8n model, a novel Separable Residual Coord Conv (SRCConv) was designed to replace the original convolution module, significantly reducing parameters while maintaining detection accuracy. The Spatio-Channel Enhanced Attention Module (SEAM) was introduced and optimized to improve sensitivity to barnyard grass edge features. Additionally, the lightweight and efficient Dysample upsampling module was incorporated to enhance feature map resolution. A new WIoU loss function was developed to improve bounding box classification and regression accuracy. Comprehensive performance analysis demonstrated that YOLOv8n-SSDW outperformed state-of-the-art models. Ablation studies confirmed the effectiveness of each improvement module. The final fused model achieved lightweight performance while improving detection accuracy, with a 2.2% increase in mAP_50, 3.8% higher precision, 0.6% higher recall, 10.6% fewer parameters, 9.8% lower FLOPs, and an 11.1% reduction in model size compared to the baseline. Field tests using drones combined with ground-based computers further validated the model's robustness in real-world complex paddy environments. The results indicate that YOLOv8n-SSDW exhibits excellent accuracy and efficiency. This study provides valuable insights for barnyard grass detection in rice fields.

Keywords: in-field barnyard grass detection; YOLOv8n-SSDW; lightweight model; deep learning; object detection

1. Introduction

Weed infestation in paddy fields continues to be a major factor limiting rice yield and quality improvement in global agricultural production. Statistics indicate that weeds in rice fields reduce yields by 10% to 30% annually globally, with losses being even greater in areas

https://doi.org/10.3390/agriculture15141510

that are most affected [1,2]. In addition to competing with rice for nutrients, water, and sunlight, weeds also spread pests and diseases, which interferes with rice's natural growth and development [3]. For example, the common malignant weed in paddy fields, barnyard grass, grows quickly and is highly adaptive. When it coexists with rice, it drastically lowers the number of grains per panicle and effective tillering, which eventually lowers yield [4].

Chemical herbicides, mechanical weeding, and hand weeding are the mainstays of traditional weed control techniques [5]. Even though manual weeding is accurate, it is not appropriate for large-scale agricultural production due to its high labor intensity, high costs, and inefficiency [6]. The efficacy of mechanical weeding is constrained by crop growth stages and terrain, potentially resulting in unintended harm to rice plants [7]. Chemical weeding is favored for its effectiveness and convenience; yet, prolonged and improper use of herbicides can result in issues such as environmental contamination and the emergence of weed resistance [8].

The collection of data on weed quantity and spatial arrangement in agricultural fields is increasingly common with the advancement of precision farming techniques. These data play a crucial role in enabling precise herbicide application and targeted weeding efforts, ultimately enhancing weed control efficiency, minimizing pesticide wastage, and reducing environmental harm. A critical aspect of implementing this approach successfully is the precise identification of weeds in rice paddies [9]. Conventional weed recognition techniques, which are typically based on manual feature extraction, heavily rely on human expertise or basic morphological assessments. These approaches are not only subjective but also inefficient, posing challenges for effective operation in dynamic and intricate field conditions [10].

Weed detection techniques using deep learning models offer precise identification in challenging environments by autonomously learning intricate weed attributes [11]. Detection speed and accuracy have advanced consistently, evolving from single-stage algorithms such as the YOLO series [12–14] to two-stage detectors like Faster R-CNN [15]. Nevertheless, existing models often feature excessive configurations, making them impractical for field use and hindering real-time operation on low-power agricultural devices such as drones and portable field terminals [16–18].

Researchers in weed detection have explored various methods to enhance model precision and effectiveness, such as adapting current object detection frameworks or creating new structures customized for specific weed types and environmental settings [19]. Because of its high accuracy and rapid detection speed, the YOLO series has gained recognition in the weed detection industry [20]. For example, YOLOv5 does well in identifying a variety of common weeds [21]. However, increasing model complexity lowers operational efficiency on lightweight devices (like drone-mounted systems), where limited computational resources compromise real-time monitoring capabilities. Similarly, the Region Proposal Network (RPN) of Faster R-CNN offers high precision, but it is not appropriate for lightweight devices due to its large computational overhead caused by its many convolutional, pooling, and fully connected layers [22]. The SSD model is ineffective on edge devices and has trouble detecting small weeds, even with the use of multi-scale feature maps to speed up detection [23].

There are still issues with deep learning-based weed detection. Early weed control is delayed by models' incapacity to differentiate between morphologically similar weeds, like barnyard grass and rice [24]. Second, robustness under complicated field conditions (like overlapping and occluded weeds) and generalization across different regions and growth stages are still lacking [25]. Third, high model parameters and computational demands hinder deployment on edge devices. To tackle these issues, this study introduces YOLOv8n-SRCConv-SEAM-Dysample-WIoU (YOLOv8n-SSDW), a lightweight in-field barnyard grass detection model designed for accurate and efficient detection in complex paddy environments. The main contributions are as follows:

(1) A novel module, SRCConv, was developed to decrease the parameter count; an enhanced SEAM attention mechanism was incorporated to boost feature sensitivity; and the Dysample dynamic upsampling module was integrated to enhance feature map resolution. Consequently, the lightweight YOLOv8n-SSDW model was introduced for barnyard grass detection, offering a fresh method for developing lightweight weed detection models.
(2) Images of barnyard grass in rice experimental fields were collected, and a barnyard grass detection dataset was established through processing, labeling, and augmentation. A redesigned loss function using WIoU was employed to train the YOLOv8n-SSDW model, effectively improving its ability to distinguish barnyard grass.
(3) Validation of the proposed model's efficacy was confirmed via various experiments. YOLOv8n-SSDW outperformed other models in comparative evaluations, exhibiting higher precision, recall, and mAP scores, alongside reduced loss values. Ablation studies elucidated the functions of individual modules, emphasizing the model's superiority over alternative approaches.
(4) The model was deployed on a drone for practical field testing. Although accuracy experienced a slight decline due to vibrations and airflow, the overall precision met the required standards, thereby validating the model's feasibility.

2. Materials and Methods

2.1. Data Acquisition and Processing

This study focuses on barnyard grass detection in paddy fields. Data collection was conducted in May 2022 in a 17,724.4 m^2 experimental rice field at Shenyang Agricultural University, Haicheng City, Liaoning Province, China. The site features flat terrain with complex conditions, including concealed weeds, mutual occlusion, and dim backgrounds. To ensure high-quality data acquisition, a DJI Matrice 300 RTK drone equipped with a Zenmuse P1 camera (45-megapixel resolution, 35.9 × 24 mm sensor, 4.4 μm pixel size, F2.8 aperture; the manufacturer is DJI Innovation Technology Co., Ltd., headquartered in Shenzhen, China) was deployed under calm, clear weather conditions. Images were captured at a 30 m altitude with a vertical viewing angle, yielding 8192 × 5460-pixel images at a ground sampling distance (GSD) of 0.38 cm/pixel.

To address annotation inconsistencies due to substantial image overlap, we utilized DJI Terra (v3.4.4) for aligning and merging images. The resultant images were then cropped into 640 × 640-pixel sub-images without overlap. Subsequently, 728 valid images were obtained after manual screening to exclude those lacking barnyard grass. Annotation was performed using LabelMe (v4.5.6), followed by data augmentation techniques such as random translation, flipping, rotation, and scaling to expand the dataset threefold. The final dataset was divided into distinct training (70%), validation (20%), and test (10%) sets. The effect of data augmentation is shown in Figure 1.

2.2. Baseline Model Selection

The YOLO series, renowned for real-time performance and detection efficiency, has become a benchmark in computer vision. Its single-stage detection architecture reformulates object detection as a regression problem, achieving high accuracy with rapid inference [26]. Iterative updates enhance robustness for small objects and adaptability to complex scenarios. After evaluating lightweight YOLO variants (Table 1), YOLOv8n demonstrated superior performance.

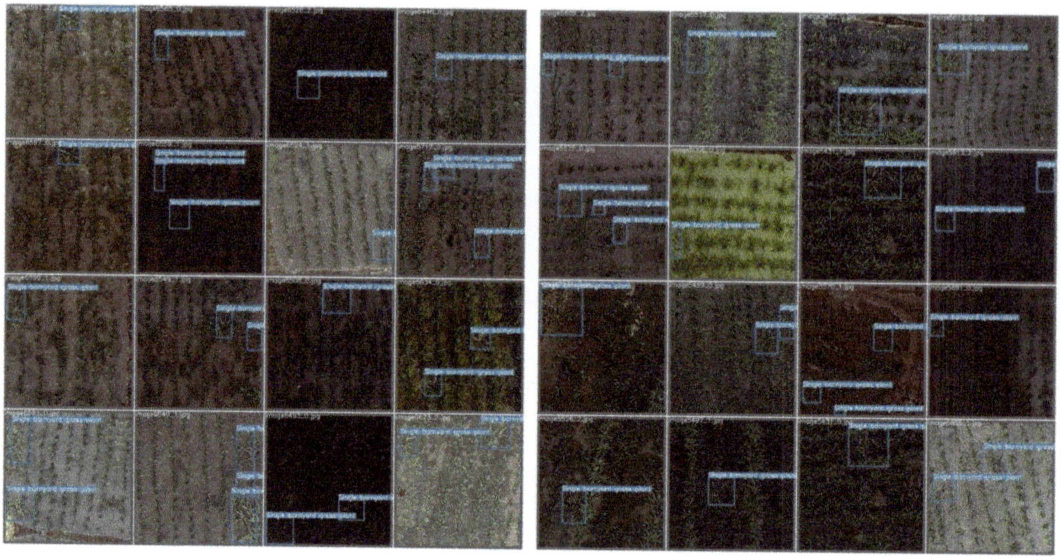

Figure 1. Effect of data augmentation on images.

Table 1. Comparison of detection performance of YOLO series models.

Baseline Model	Precision	Recall	F1	mAP_50	Parameters (M)	FLOPs (G)	Model Size (MB)	Inference Time (ms)
YOLOv5n	0.769	0.769	0.769	0.804	2.51	7.1	5.3	14.6
YOLOv7-Tiny	0.752	0.709	0.730	0.752	6.01	13.0	12.3	12.7
YOLOv8n	0.829	0.749	0.787	0.829	3.01	8.2	6.3	13.6
YOLOv9-Tiny	0.806	0.760	0.782	0.809	2.01	7.8	4.7	37.2
YOLOv10n	0.781	0.745	0.763	0.804	2.70	8.3	5.8	18.7
YOLOv11n	0.803	0.756	0.779	0.816	2.91	7.6	6.1	15.4

As evidenced by the comparative analysis, YOLOv8n demonstrates comprehensive advantages across key metrics. It achieves the highest precision (0.829) and mAP_50 (0.829) in the evaluation, indicating superior detection accuracy and overall performance. The model also attains the highest F1-score (0.787), reflecting an optimal balance between precision and recall. While its recall (0.749) is marginally lower than YOLOv5n (0.769), the superior precision and mAP_50 hold greater practical significance for minimizing false positives of barnyard grass.

In terms of efficiency, YOLOv8n maintains lightweight characteristics with a parameter count of 3.01 million and a computational load of 8.2 GFLOPs, comparable to YOLOv5n and substantially lower than YOLOv7-Tiny (6.01 M parameters). Its inference speed (13.6 ms) matches the fastest models while retaining a compact architecture (6.3 MB) suitable for resource-constrained environments. In contrast, other models exhibit critical trade-offs: YOLOv5n and YOLOv10n show compromised accuracy metrics, while YOLOv7-Tiny (excessive parameters) and YOLOv9-Tiny (37.2 ms latency) fail to achieve comparable efficiency. These results validate YOLOv8n as the optimal baseline model for paddy barnyard grass detection.

2.3. Proposed YOLOv8n-SSDW

In natural rice fields, rice and barnyard grass exhibit remarkable similarities in color and morphology, which poses significant challenges for distinguishing between the two.

However, a detailed observation of the acquired images of barnyard grass reveals a distinct growth pattern: it predominantly clusters in the inter-row areas of the rice field. Furthermore, mature barnyard grass typically demonstrates a superior growth posture compared to rice, with noticeably taller plant appearances.

Based on these unique growth characteristics and visual features of barnyard grass, we propose a novel structure for precise identification of barnyard grass in complex environments, leveraging YOLOv8n, which we designate as YOLOv8n-SSDW, as illustrated in Figure 2. Firstly, we designed a lightweight spatial location attention convolution module, termed SRCConv, which significantly reduces the model's parameter count without compromising the effectiveness of barnyard grass location feature extraction. Additionally, by introducing and improving the SEAM attention module, we greatly enhance the model's sensitivity to the edge features of barnyard grass. Furthermore, by embedding a more lightweight and efficient Dysample dynamic upsampling module, we further improve the resolution of the feature maps, enabling the model to capture the detailed characteristics of barnyard grass more accurately. Finally, we redesigned the loss function and adopted WIoU as the method for loss calculation, which greatly enhances the regression accuracy of the model's detection boxes, ensuring the accuracy and reliability of the identification results.

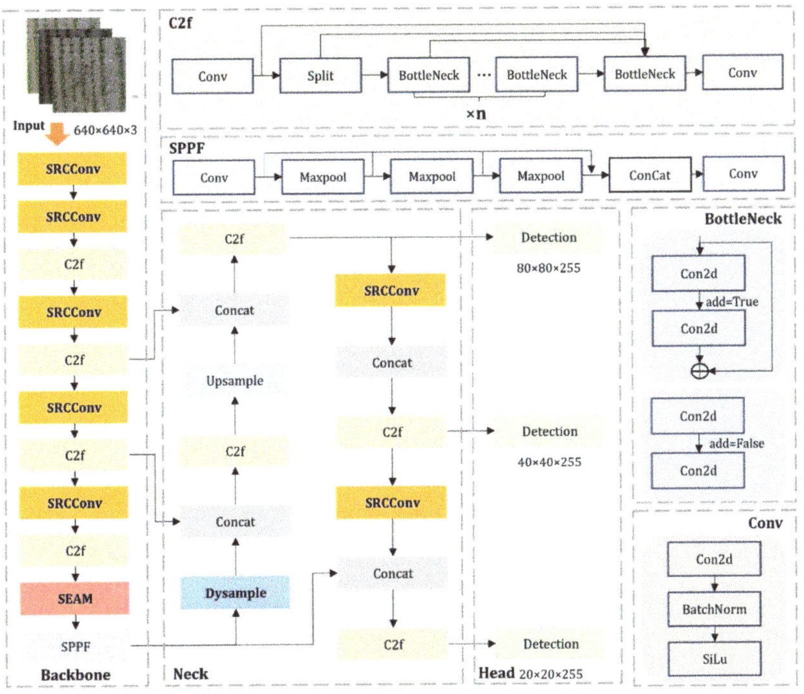

Figure 2. Structural diagram of YOLOv8n-SSDW.

2.3.1. The Newly Designed SRCConv

The growth environment of barnyard grass is complicated by the presence of rice, soil, and debris, resulting in a complex background. Additionally, barnyard grass closely resembles rice in morphology, leading to a high degree of overlap in their visual features, which makes differentiation based solely on appearance quite challenging. Moreover, during actual growth, barnyard grass and rice sometimes intertwine, resulting in instances of overlap and occlusion, further complicating the identification process. Traditional convolution operations reveal significant shortcomings in addressing such complex scenarios.

They apply uniform processing to every region of the image, lacking the ability to focus on key feature areas, which hampers the effective highlighting of subtle differences between barnyard grass and rice in a complex background, thus making it difficult to achieve the required identification accuracy.

Coordinate convolution has improved this situation to some extent by incorporating coordinate information into the convolution process, improving the ability of the model to perceive the target's location, and exhibiting certain advantages when dealing with objects that have similar shapes and overlapping situations [27]. However, coordinate convolution still has its limitations. For example, its accuracy and robustness in feature extraction when handling complex backgrounds and highly overlapping areas need further improvement, and its relatively high computational cost may be constrained by hardware resources in practical applications. In light of these shortcomings, we propose Separable Residual Coord Conv (SRCConv), the structure of which is illustrated in Figure 3. This novel convolution method optimizes the coordinate convolution structure by employing separable convolutions to reduce computational complexity while also introducing residual connections to enhance feature propagation. This approach stabilizes the extraction of barnyard grass features in complex backgrounds, reducing computational costs while ensuring identification accuracy, thereby making the model more lightweight and efficient.

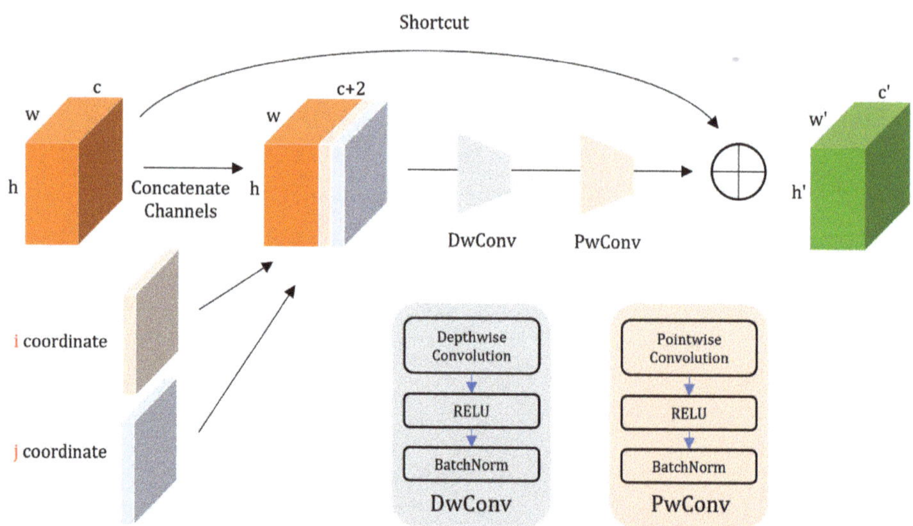

Figure 3. Structural diagram of SRCConv.

The advantage of SRCConv lies in the integration of three approaches: position awareness, efficient computation, and residual connections. This enables the network to extract features using depthwise separable convolutions based on the addition of coordinate information while also enhancing information transfer and network performance through residual connections. The overall formula is as follows:

$$F = X_{conv}(X_{coords}(X)) + X_{shortcut}(X) \tag{1}$$

To incorporate coordinate information, the generated xx_{batch} and yy_{batch} channels are concatenated with the input tensor X along the channel dimension. This process enhances the spatial awareness capability of the tensor.

$$X_{coords} = X \oplus xx_{batch} \oplus yy_{batch} \tag{2}$$

where X_{coords} represents the output after the addition of coordinate information, while X denotes the initial input tensor. xx_{batch} and yy_{batch} represent the x-coordinate matrix and y-coordinate matrix, respectively, both having the same batch size as the input tensor X. The symbol $\oplus$ denotes the concatenation operation.

Regarding depthwise separable convolution, it is applied to the tensor X_{coords} that has incorporated coordinate information. Depthwise separable convolution decomposes standard convolution into two steps: depthwise convolution and pointwise convolution, thereby reducing the number of parameters and computational load.

$$\begin{cases} X_{conv}(c', h, w) = \sum_{c=0}^{C'_{in}-1} X_{depth}(c, h, w) \times K_{point}(c', c, 0, 0) \\ X_{depth}(c, h, w) = \sum_{i=0}^{k-1} \sum_{j=0}^{k-1} X_{coords}(c, h+i, w+j) \times K_{depth}(c, 0, i, j) \end{cases} \tag{3}$$

where $X_{depth}(c, h, w)$ denotes the output of the depthwise convolution, and $X_{conv}(c', h, w)$ represents the output of the pointwise convolution. K_{point} refers to the kernel used for the pointwise convolution, while K_{depth} represents the kernel used for the depthwise convolution. X_{coords} indicates the output after including coordinate information. c and c' are the indices for input and output channels, respectively. h and w denote the height and width of the feature map, respectively. C'_{in} is the number of input channels, and k signifies the size of the convolutional kernel. Respectively, i and j are the indices along the width and height dimensions of the feature map.

For the shortcut connection, the channel dimension of the X tensor is adjusted using the shortcut connection to facilitate the addition operation.

If $C_{in} \neq C_{out}$ or the stride $s \neq 1$,

$$X_{shortcut} = Conv_{1\times1}(X), \tag{4}$$

or

$$X_{shortcut} = X \tag{5}$$

where $X_{shortcut}$ denotes the output of the skip connection. $Conv_{1\times1}(X)$ represents the output of the pointwise convolution. X refers to the output of the identity mapping. C_{in} indicates the count of input channels. C_{out} denotes the count of output channels.

2.3.2. Improved SEAM Attention Mechanism

The growth environment of barnyard grass in fields is extremely complex, with severe environmental noise interference. Additionally, mutual occlusion and morphological overlap between barnyard grass and rice plants often occur, making it difficult to extract key feature information. The YOLOv8 algorithm has inherent limitations when dealing with such complex scenarios, struggling to accurately locate and identify the critical feature regions of barnyard grass. However, the Spatio-Channel Enhanced Attention Module (SEAM) structure can effectively compensate for this shortcoming [28]. Through a dual attention mechanism in both spatial and channel dimensions, SEAM enables refined feature screening of images: on one hand, the spatial attention module can precisely locate key regions in areas of mutual occlusion between barnyard grass and rice, eliminating background noise interference; on the other hand, the channel attention module enhances the weight of unique feature channels of barnyard grass while suppressing interference from similar features of rice plants. The model's ability to focus on the most discriminative information is significantly enhanced by the synergistic effect of this dual mechanism, leading to the improved detection accuracy and robustness of barnyard grass in complex overlapping scenarios.

Within the channel attention mechanism of SEAM, global average pooling is employed for dimensionality reduction of the feature maps. Although this operation effectively aggregates global feature information and achieves channel-wise compression, it has certain limitations: On one hand, global average pooling assigns equal weights to all spatial position features, which can dilute critical feature information with background noise or redundant information, making it difficult to accurately capture the unique salient features of barnyard grass in scenarios where there is mutual occlusion and morphological overlap with rice. On the other hand, the smoothing effect reduces the local contrast between features, diminishing the model's responsiveness to slight feature distinctions. This poses a challenge when interference factors like uneven field lighting and comparable leaf textures are present, potentially impacting the model's capacity to distinguish target feature channels effectively. Consequently, this research substitutes global average pooling with global max pooling, enhancing the SEAM structure, as depicted in Figure 4. By selecting the maximum value from each channel, this approach enhances the response of critical features, highlighting the unique textures and morphological contours of barnyard grass leaves, thereby aiding the model in rapidly identifying barnyard grass plants that may be morphologically confused with rice in complex environments.

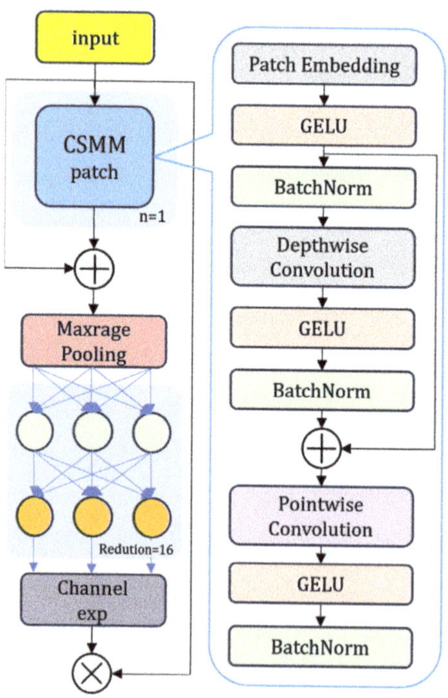

Figure 4. Structural diagram of SEAM.

2.3.3. Lightweight Dysample Upsampling

In the task of barnyard grass recognition, accurately identifying the detailed features of barnyard grass is crucial. YOLOv8 typically employs traditional upsampling methods, such as bilinear interpolation. These methods simply perform interpolation calculations on pixels when enhancing feature resolution, lacking the ability to perceive the content of the image. For example, when processing barnyard grass images with complex textures or details, these methods may fail to accurately restore detailed features at high resolutions, leading to the loss of subtle structural information. The DySample module, depicted in Figure 5, can enhance the resolution of feature maps, allowing the model to capture more detailed structural and textural characteristics of barnyard grass, like its serrated edges or leaf lines, hence boosting the precision of barnyard grass identification [29]. Moreover, through the upsampling process, DySample can better integrate feature information from different levels on high-resolution feature maps. This helps the model learn more representative features, such as the morphological characteristics of barnyard grass at different growth stages and contextual information from the surrounding environment, improving the ability of the model to express the barnyard grass' features and thereby allowing for more accurate differentiation between barnyard grass and other plants.

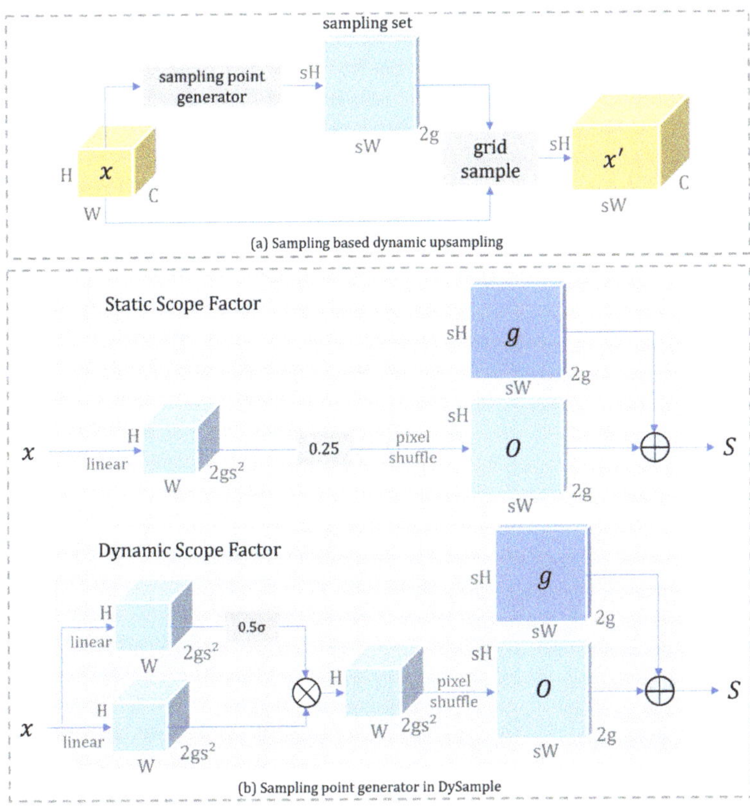

Figure 5. Structural diagram of DySample.

However, the features generated by DySample may exhibit some redundancy. Overuse can cause the model to acquire numerous redundant features, consuming computational resources unnecessarily and potentially impeding the model's grasp of essential features. In some cases, there may even be conflicts between features generated by different DySample modules, affecting the model's accuracy and stability. Therefore, this paper replaces the first upsampling process with DySample to achieve optimal results.

2.3.4. Loss Function Design

YOLOv8n employs the CIoU loss for bounding box regression, which is an extension of the IoU loss [30]. The principle of IoU's calculation of losses is shown in Figure 6. This loss function incorporates factors such as center distance and aspect ratios to accurately measure the differences between predicted and ground truth boxes by considering their intersection. Its formula is as follows:

$$\begin{cases} L_{CIoU} = 1 - IoU + \frac{\left((x-x_{gt})^2+(y-y_{gt})^2\right)}{\left(C_w^2+C_h^2\right)} + \alpha v \\ \alpha = \frac{v}{(1-IoU)+v} \\ v = \frac{4}{\pi^2}\left(actan\frac{w_{gt}}{h_{gt}} - actan\frac{w}{h}\right)^2 \\ IoU = \frac{wh+w_{gt}h_{gt}-2W_iH_i}{wh+w_{gt}h_{gt}-W_iH_i} \end{cases} \tag{6}$$

where the CIoU loss value, denoted as L_{CIoU}, quantifies the discrepancy between predicted and actual boxes. α is a coefficient for adjusting the impact of aspect ratio loss. v evaluates the aspect ratio consistency. IoU gauges the overlap between predicted and actual boxes. w and h represent the predicted box's width and height, respectively, while w_{gt} and h_{gt} indicate the actual box's width and height, respectively. W_i and H_i denote the width and height of the overlapping area, respectively. x and y are the predicted box's center coordinates, while x_{gt} and y_{gt} are the actual box's center coordinates. C_w and C_h, respectively, represent the width and height of the minimum enclosing rectangle that can contain both the predicted and ground truth boxes.

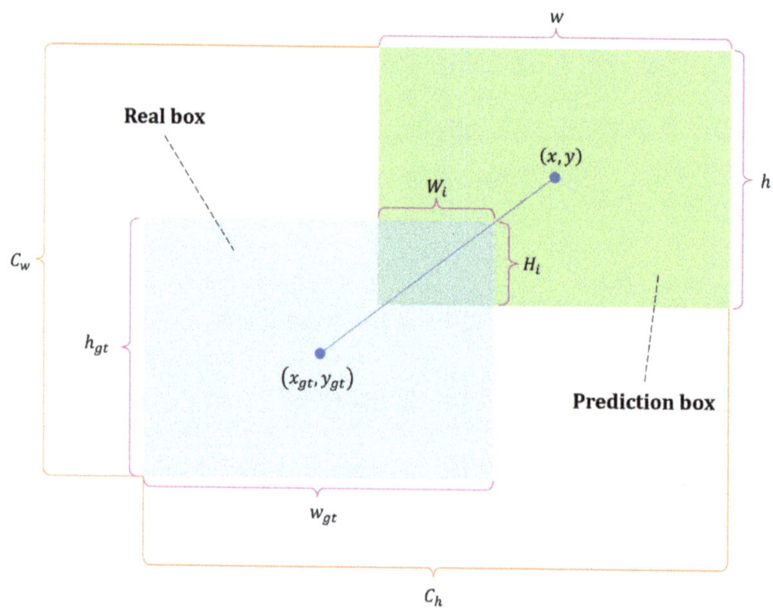

Figure 6. The principle of IoU loss in boundary box regression.

The predicted bounding box's aspect ratio and the ground truth box are restricted in CIoU loss computation, which may cause gradient instability. Significant aspect ratio differences can result in abrupt gradient changes, impacting model convergence and stability [31]. Additionally, CIoU considers the distance between the ground truth box's and the predicted box's center points, but this evaluation may lack completeness in complex scenarios [32]. It easily leads to worse bounding box regression and reduced detection accuracy, making the task of weed recognition in complex environments even more difficult. WIoU presents a novel weight system that adapts weights based on the correlation between the predicted box and the ground truth box. This mechanism addresses concerns about gradient instability observed in CIoU, especially regarding aspects like aspect ratio, promoting more stable convergence of the model during training and minimizing oscillations [33]. Furthermore, the WIoU gradient demonstrates improved stability, thereby enhancing its ability to accurately depict the difference between the predicted box and the actual box. By employing WIoU as the loss function, the model generally achieves quicker convergence to the best solution, thereby diminishing training duration [34]. Consequently, this study opts for the *WIoU* loss function, defined as:

$$\begin{cases} L_{WIoU} = r \cdot R_{WIoU} \cdot L_{IoU} \\ R_{WIoU} = exp\left(\frac{(x-x_{gt})^2+(y-y_{gt})^2}{(C_w^2+C_h^2)}\right) \\ L_{IoU} = (1 - IoU) \\ r = \frac{\lambda}{\delta\alpha^{\beta-\delta}} \\ \beta = \frac{L_{IoU}}{\overline{L_{IoU}}} \epsilon [0, +\infty) \end{cases} \tag{7}$$

where L_{WIoU} represents the total loss value of the overall loss function. R_{WIoU} is a penalty term that imposes a penalty based on the displacement between the predicted and ground truth bounding box centroids. Here, (x and y) and (x_{gt} and y_{gt}) correspond to the predicted and actual box center coordinates, respectively. The variables C_w and C_h indicate the dimensions of the minimal enclosing rectangle containing both boxes. The *IoU* loss (L_{IoU}) optimizes alignment by maximizing the intersection area. The weighting factor r balances contributions, whereas λ, δ, and α are tunable hyperparameters—with λ regulating the scaling magnitude. Parameter δ selection depends on the task requirements and dataset characteristics, while α determines the exponential influence of δ. The role of β is to normalize L_{IoU} across different samples, with $\overline{L_{IoU}}$ representing the mean of L_{IoU}.

2.4. Experimental Environment and Evaluation Metrics

The hardware components involved in this experiment include an Intel® Xeon® w5-2465X CPU (the manufacturer is Intel, in Santa Clara, CA, USA) with a clock speed of 3.10 GHz, 128 GB of RAM, and an NVIDIA RTX A5500 GPU with 24 GB of video memory. The software environment utilized Windows 11 as the operating system, and the network model training was conducted using Python version 3.10.5, along with the PyTorch (version 1.13.1) deep learning framework. In this experiment, the hyperparameters of the network were balanced and optimized, with a total training epoch set to 200 and a batch size of 64 for each training epoch. The initial learning rate, which affects the speed of network weight updates, was set to 0.01, with a decay rate of 0.1. Under these conditions, optimal training performance was achieved.

A scientifically valid assessment tool may efficiently confirm the detection capability of deep learning models. This work chooses six important criteria to thoroughly evaluate the detection capability of the model. The particular indicators are the number of parameters: F1 score, R (recall), P (precision), mAP (mean average precision), Weight (model size), and GFLOPs (floating-point operations per second, often used to assess a model's computational complexity). These indicators provide a detailed way to measure how well the model performs in real detection tasks by looking at different aspects, like how accurate it is, how well it can find things, how fast it processes information, and how efficiently it uses resources.

$$P = \frac{TP}{TP+FP} \tag{8}$$

$$R = \frac{TP}{TP+FN} \quad (9)$$

$$F1 = \frac{2 \cdot P \cdot R}{P+R} \quad (10)$$

$$AP = \int_0^1 PdR \quad (11)$$

$$mAP = \frac{1}{M}\sum_{k=1}^{M} AP(k) \times 100\% \quad (12)$$

where AP is the area under the precision–recall (P-R) curve. mAP is the average of the AP values for every class. TP represents accurate predictions of positive samples as barnyard grass images. FP indicates incorrect predictions of background or rice as barnyard grass. FN indicates predictions of barnyard grass as background or rice.

3. Experimental Results and Analysis

3.1. Training Curve Comparative Analysis

Figure 7 presents the training results of YOLOv8n and the proposed YOLOv8n-SSDW under identical experimental settings. The accuracy curve illustrates the proportion of correctly identified positive samples out of all samples predicted as positive. The recall curve illustrates the model's capability to identify true positive samples, while the mAP curve assesses the model's mean detection precision across diverse targets at varying IoU thresholds. Among them, Figure 7a shows the precision and recall curves recorded during the training process, while Figure 7b displays the mAP curve recorded during training.

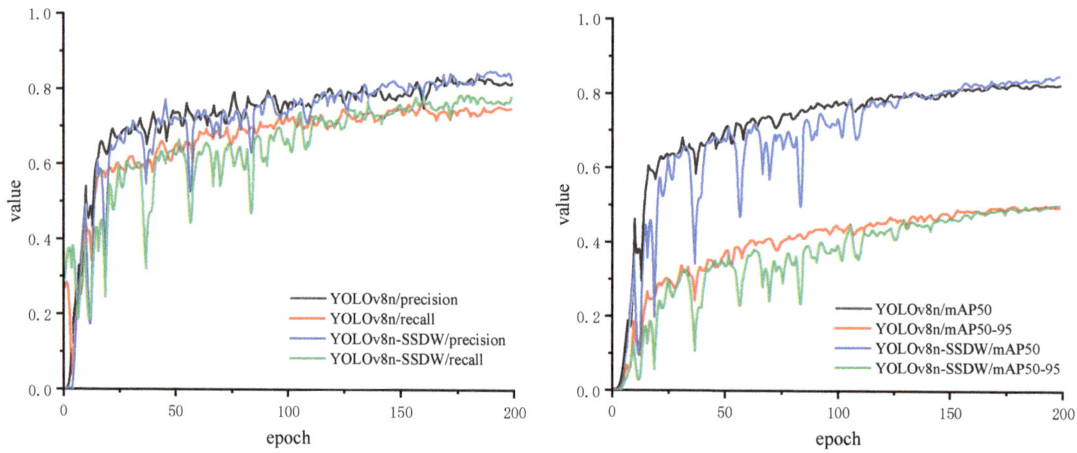

(**a**) P, R curve comparison (**b**) mAP curve comparison

Figure 7. P, R curves and mAP curves for YOLOv8n and YOLOv8n-SSDW.

For Figure 7a, the precision curves of YOLOv8n and YOLOv8n-SSDW (in black and blue) exhibit significant fluctuations in the initial stages. This is because the model is just beginning to train and has not yet fully learned the data features. As the number of epochs increases, both curves show an overall upward trend and gradually stabilize. The precision curve of YOLOv8n-SSDW is slightly higher than that of YOLOv8n for most of the epochs, indicating that YOLOv8n-SSDW has a relatively higher proportion of correct predictions when identifying positive samples. For instance, after epoch 100, the precision of YOLOv8n-SSDW stabilizes at a higher level than that of YOLOv8n, suggesting fewer misclassifications in target recognition. The recall curves of YOLOv8n and YOLOv8n-SSDW (in red and green, respectively) also show significant fluctuations at the beginning. As training progresses, the recall gradually improves. The recall curve of YOLOv8n-SSDW is also higher than that of YOLOv8n in most cases, meaning that YOLOv8n-SSDW can detect more actual targets, resulting in fewer missed detections of real targets. For example, throughout the training process, the recall growth trend of YOLOv8n-SSDW is superior, and the advantage is more pronounced at higher epochs, indicating better completeness in target detection.

For Figure 7b, mAP_50 measures the average precision of detection results at an IoU threshold of 0.5. The mAP_50 curves of YOLOv8n and YOLOv8n-SSDW (black and blue, respectively) start at relatively low values and gradually increase with epochs. However, the mAP_50 curve of YOLOv8n-SSDW rises more rapidly and ultimately surpasses that of YOLOv8n after training stabilizes. This indicates that under the IoU threshold of 0.5, YOLOv8n-SSDW achieves higher detection accuracy for various targets and can identify objects more precisely. mAP_50-95 represents the average precision of detection results across IoU thresholds ranging from 0.5 to 0.95, providing a more comprehensive evaluation of model performance. The mAP_50-95 curves of YOLOv8n and YOLOv8n-SSDW (red and green, respectively) exhibit trends similar to their mAP_50 curves, with YOLOv8n-SSDW demonstrating a steeper ascent and higher final values. This suggests that even under stricter IoU threshold criteria, YOLOv8n-SSDW maintains superior object detection accuracy and overall performance compared to YOLOv8n.

3.2. Loss Curve Comparative Analysis

Figure 8 illustrates the training outcomes of YOLOv8n and the suggested YOLOv8n-SSDW in identical experimental settings. The loss graph indicates the variance between the model's predicted and actual values. Smaller values indicate better model performance (the loss curves in the figure include box_loss and cls_loss). Figure 8a presents the loss curves recorded on the training dataset, while Figure 8b shows the loss curves recorded on the validation dataset.

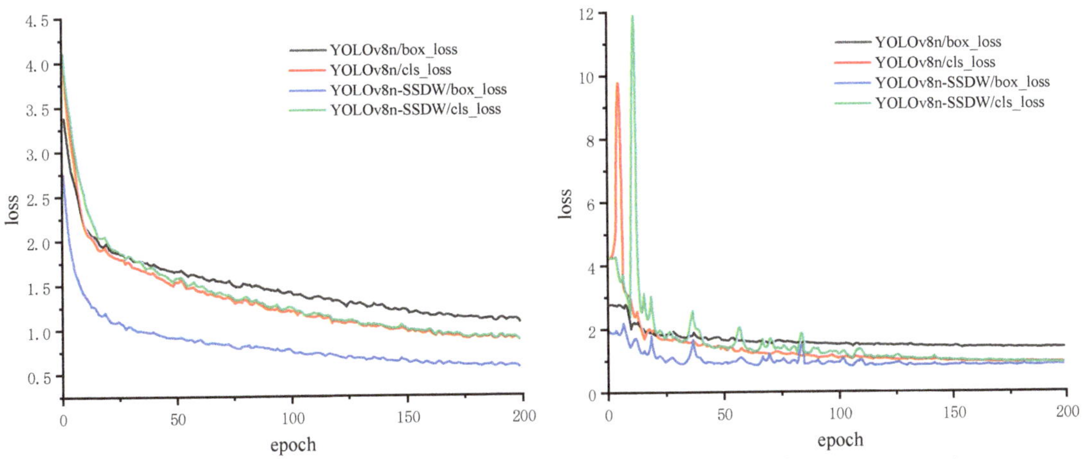

(**a**) Training loss curve comparison (**b**) Validation loss curve comparison

Figure 8. Loss curves for YOLOv8n and YOLOv8n-SSDW.

For Figure 8a, in the early stages of training, the loss values of all four curves are relatively high. YOLOv8n has a higher initial value for both box_loss and cls_loss, while YOLOv8n-SSDW has a relatively lower initial value for box_loss. As the epochs increase, all four curves exhibit a declining trend, suggesting ongoing optimization of the model throughout training, leading to a gradual reduction in the disparity between predicted and actual values. The box_loss of YOLOv8n-SSDW decreases relatively quickly, creating a gap with the box_loss of YOLOv8n early on. The cls_loss of YOLOv8n-SSDW also shows a notable downward trend, maintaining a certain distance from the cls_loss of YOLOv8n during the descent. By the time the epoch approaches 200, the downward trend of all four curves slows, gradually stabilizing, which indicates that the model is converging in the later stages of training. The stabilized loss values of box_loss and cls_loss for YOLOv8n-SSDW are relatively lower than those of YOLOv8n.

For Figure 8b, in the early stages of training, the four curves exhibit significant fluctuations, especially the cls_loss of both YOLOv8n and YOLOv8n-SSDW, which show noticeable peaks. This is due to the model not having fully learned yet in the initial phase, leading to unstable predictions. As the epochs progress, the curves gradually descend and stabilize. The box_loss and cls_loss of YOLOv8n-SSDW demonstrate relatively better performance during the decline, showing smaller fluctuations, and the stabilized loss values are lower than those of YOLOv8n. Approaching 200 epochs, all loss curves stabilize, with YOLOv8n-SSDW displaying lower box_loss and cls_loss on the validation set compared to YOLOv8n. This indicates that YOLOv8n-SSDW performs better on the validation set, potentially exhibiting stronger model generalization capabilities. The significant difference in box_loss between the two figures also validates the effectiveness of the improvements made to the loss function.

Overall, YOLOv8n-SSDW shows lower box_loss and cls_loss on both the training set and validation set compared to YOLOv8n, demonstrating better convergence and exhibiting superior performance under the same experimental conditions.

3.3. *Ablation Study of YOLOv8n-SSDW*

Table 2 shows the outcomes of the ablation experiments for the improved modules of YOLOv8n. This experiment uses YOLOv8n as the baseline model and sequentially incorporates four improved modules: Dysample, WIoU, SRCConv, and SEAM. Comparing the performance metrics of each variant reveals that Dysample, as a foundational improvement, has a minimal impact on model performance: only a slight rise of 0.005 in mAP_50. However, it lays the groundwork for the optimization of subsequent modules. The introduction of WIoU leads to the most significant improvement in accuracy, with precision rising from 0.826 to 0.873, and recall and mAP_50 increasing by 0.012 and 0.007, respectively. This indicates its effectiveness in bounding box regression, possibly by adjusting the weights of easy and hard samples, allowing the model to focus more on high-quality detections. SRCConv demonstrates excellent lightweight characteristics, reducing computational complexity by 12.2% (with FLOPs decreasing from 8.2G to 7.2G) and model size by 14.3% (from 6.3 MB to 5.4 MB) while still maintaining a high precision of 0.872, with only minor fluctuations in mAP_50. This showcases its effective balance between model performance and size during the lightweighting process. Finally, the addition of the SEAM attention mechanism further elevates mAP_50 to 0.851. Although this results in a slight increase in computational cost, it significantly enhances the overall detection performance through feature focusing.

The enhanced model demonstrates an obvious performance boost compared to YOLOv8n. The final integrated model YOLOv8n-SSDW (YOLOv8n-SRCCConv-SEAM-Dysample-WIoU) results in an increase in mAP_50 from 0.829 to 0.851, representing a 2.2% improvement, marking comprehensive optimization in object detection accuracy. Precision improves from 0.829 to 0.867, effectively reducing the false detection rate. Recall rises from 0.749 to 0.755, enhancing the model's ability to capture targets.

Moreover, YOLOv8n-SSDW achieves a balance between lightweight design and efficiency optimization. Although the SEAM module introduces additional computational overhead, the SRCConv module streamlines parameters, resulting in a 14.3% reduction in the overall model size and a 12.2% decrease in the computational load, ensuring deployment flexibility. This indicates that the improved model surpasses the baseline in detection accuracy while concurrently achieving dual enhancements in performance and efficiency, making it more competitive in the application scenario of detecting barnyard grass in rice fields.

Table 2. Ablation study results.

Baseline Model	P	R	mAP_50	Params (M)	FLOPs (G)	Weight (MB)
YOLOv8n	0.829	0.749	0.829	3.01	8.2	6.3
YOLOv8n-Dysample	0.826	0.748	0.834	3.02	8.2	6.3
YOLOv8n-Dysample-WIoU	0.873	0.760	0.841	3.02	8.2	6.3
YOLOv8n-Dysample-WIoU-SRCConv	0.872	0.767	0.837	2.58	7.2	5.4
YOLOv8n-Dysample-WIoU-SRCConv-SEAM	0.867	0.755	0.851	2.69	7.4	5.6

3.4. Quantitative Comparison of Various Object Detection Models

To validate this improvement, we conducted a comparative experiment under identical conditions. The results are shown in Table 3. This experiment includes several popular YOLO series object detection models, such as different variants of YOLOv5, YOLOv7, YOLOv8, YOLOv9, YOLOv10, and YOLOv11.

Table 3. Results of the comparison among different models.

Model	Precision	Recall	F1	mAP_50	Parameters (M)	FLOPs (G)	Model Size (MB)	Infer Time (ms)
YOLOv5n	0.769	0.769	0.769	0.804	2.51	7.1	5.3	14.6
YOLOv5s	0.824	0.791	0.807	0.840	9.12	24.0	18.5	15.6
YOLOv5m	0.817	0.773	0.794	0.825	25.1	64.2	50.5	17.1
YOLOv7-Tiny	0.752	0.709	0.730	0.752	6.01	13.0	12.3	12.7
YOLOv7	0.771	0.757	0.764	0.783	36.5	103.2	74.8	14.5
YOLOv7x	0.83	0.709	0.765	0.787	70.8	188.0	142.1	17.5
YOLOv8n	0.829	0.749	0.787	0.829	3.01	8.2	6.3	13.6
YOLOv8s	0.841	0.786	0.813	0.841	11.1	28.6	22.5	14.8
YOLOv8m	0.861	0.791	0.825	0.843	25.9	79.0	52.0	17.6
YOLOv9t	0.806	0.760	0.782	0.809	2.01	7.8	4.7	37.2
YOLOv9s	0.823	0.757	0.789	0.815	7.29	27.4	15.3	39.6
YOLOv9m	0.841	0.784	0.812	0.840	20.2	77.5	40.9	41.3
YOLOv10n	0.781	0.745	0.763	0.804	2.70	8.3	5.8	18.7
YOLOv10s	0.849	0.768	0.806	0.839	8.05	24.6	16.5	19.1
YOLOv10m	0.833	0.765	0.798	0.839	16.5	63.8	33.5	21.8
YOLOv11n	0.803	0.756	0.779	0.816	2.91	7.6	6.1	15.4
YOLOv11s	0.869	0.742	0.801	0.832	10.7	26.5	21.8	16.9
YOLOv11m	0.819	0.775	0.796	0.831	23.9	85.4	48.1	18.5
YOLOv8n-SSDW	0.867	0.755	0.807	0.851	2.69	7.4	5.6	15.3

From the perspective of detection performance, the proposed YOLOv8n-SSDW achieves the highest mAP_50 value at 0.851, which is clearly better than other models. YOLOv8s and YOLOv8m also perform well, with mAP_50 values of 0.841 and 0.843, respectively. YOLOv11s has a mAP_50 of 0.832, but its recall rate is only 0.742. This low recall may reduce the effectiveness of target detection in real-world applications. In the YOLOv5 series, YOLOv5s has a mAP_50 of 0.840, which is better than both YOLOv5n and YOLOv5m. The overall performance of the YOLOv7 series is poor, especially for YOLOv7-Tiny, which has a mAP_50 of only 0.752. This disadvantage may be due to the model's structure, which weakens its ability to extract features. The larger versions of YOLOv9 and YOLOv10 show relative advantages. For the F1 score, YOLOv8s and YOLOv8m have high values of 0.813 and 0.825, respectively. The proposed YOLOv8n-SSDW has an F1 score of 0.807, which is also excellent. In contrast, YOLOv7-Tiny has the lowest F1 score at only 0.730.

In terms of model lightweighting, the different YOLO series models show various characteristics. In terms of parameter count, YOLOv9t has the fewest parameters at 2.01M, making its structure the most streamlined. YOLOv5n follows with 2.51M parameters. Our proposed YOLOv8n-SSDW has a parameter count of 2.69M, which is a slight increase. At the same time, YOLOv7x has a high parameter count of 70.8 million. This indicates that it has a more complex model structure. YOLOv5n leads in computational complexity with a value of 7.1G. This means it has the highest computational efficiency. YOLOv8n-SSDW has a complexity of 7.4G, and YOLOv11n has 7.6G. In contrast, YOLOv7x reaches 188.0G. The complexity means it requires a lot of computational resources for practical use. YOLOv9t is the smallest model in terms of size, weighing just 4.7 MB. YOLOv5n is slightly larger at 5.3 MB, while YOLOv8n-SSDW is 5.6 MB. In contrast, YOLOv7x has a size of 142.1 MB, which demands more storage resources. The newer models, YOLOv10 and YOLOv11, have advantages in lightweighting while maintaining high detection performance compared to earlier versions.

In general, different YOLO series models show clear differences in performance and resource needs. YOLOv8n-SSDW is the best choice among all the models because of its outstanding overall performance.

3.5. *Qualitative Comparison of Various Object Detection Models*

To visually compare the overall performance of different YOLO series object detection models, we conducted a set of qualitative comparison tests. The outcomes are displayed in Figure 9a–d each display a radar chart. In these charts, each vertex represents a different performance metric. The specific metrics include the F1 score, which assesses the equilibrium between recall and precision. They also include mAP, or mean average precision at 50, which assesses the model's detection accuracy. We also have 1/Params, which is the inverse of the number of parameters and shows the model's lightweighting. A higher value indicates fewer parameters. We also have 1/FLOPs, which represents the inverse of the number of floating-point operations. This variable reflects the consumption of computational resources, where a higher value means less computation is needed. Lastly, we consider 1/Weight, which is inversely related to the model's weights. This indicator reflects the storage space used, where a smaller value is better. The different colors of the lines in the charts represent different models. All metric values represent normalized results. The size of the area formed by the lines reflects the overall performance of the models across these metrics. A larger area indicates better overall performance for that model.

When we compare the mini versions of the models, such as the n or tiny versions shown in Figure 9a, we find that they perform impressively in lightweighting. However, they do not perform well in detection accuracy. Among these models, YOLOv9t shows the most significant lightweight advantage. Its values for 1/Params and 1/Weight are noteworthy, but its F1 score and mAP are lacking. As a result, its overall performance is lower than that of YOLOv8n-SSDW. Next, we look at the small versions of the models, such as the s versions shown in Figure 9b. We see an improvement in detection accuracy, but these models do not have advantages in lightweighting. Their overall performance is not satisfactory. Then, we compare the medium versions of the models, such as the m or x versions shown in Figure 9c. We observe that these models have a slight improvement in detection accuracy. However, their lightweighting performance worsens, leading to lower overall performance. Finally, when we compare YOLOv8n to YOLOv8n-SSDW, as shown in Figure 9d, we see that their performance is relatively balanced across different metrics.

However, YOLOv8n is slightly weaker in some indicators compared to YOLOv8n-SSDW. The overall area it encloses is smaller, which reflects that its overall performance is inferior.

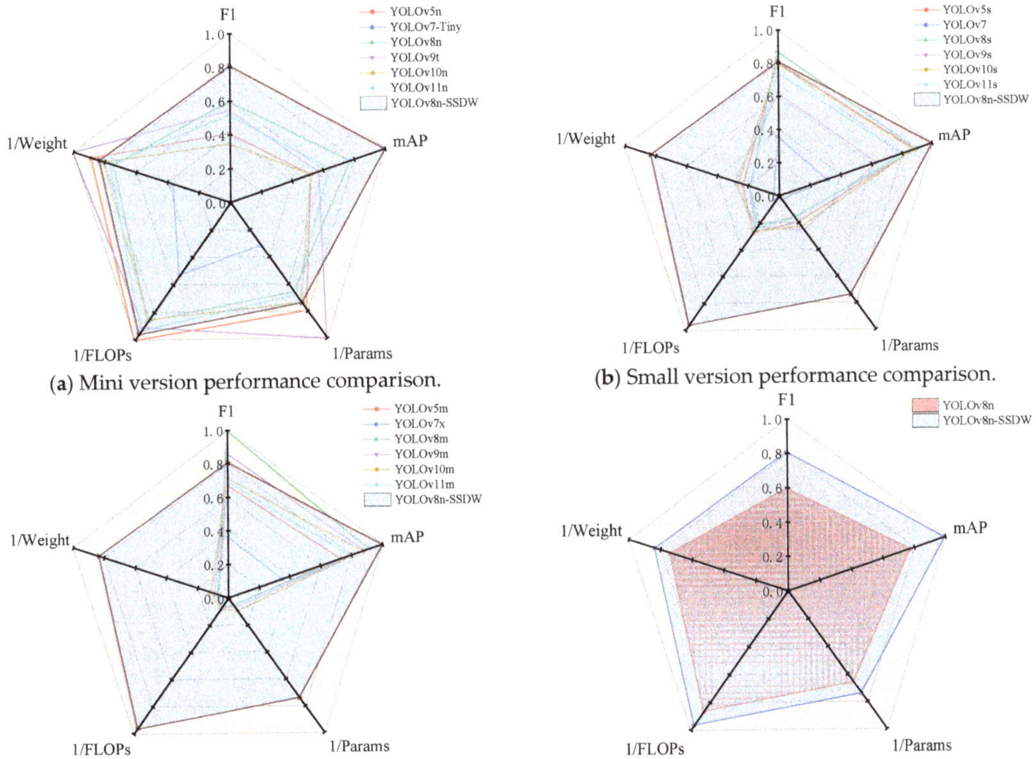

(**a**) Mini version performance comparison. (**b**) Small version performance comparison. (**c**) Middle version performance comparison. (**d**) Comparison of YOLOv8n-SSDW and YOLOV8n.

Figure 9. Radar charts comparing the performance of different YOLO series object detection models.

In summary, the YOLOv8n-SSDW proposed in this study shows the best overall performance. It performs impressively in both detection accuracy and model lightweighting. This study demonstrates its potential for use in detecting barnyard grass in rice fields.

3.6. Evaluation of Detection Outcomes

Figure 10 displays the results of identifying barnyard grass images in rice fields using the YOLOv8n model and the new YOLOv8n-SSDW model. The images present various complex situations. They include brightness differences in different lighting conditions, which may affect the overall visual quality. They also contain barnyard grass targets of different sizes, which can increase the difficulty of detection. The barnyard grass appears randomly between rice crops and has no specific distribution. There are also cases of obstruction and overlapping grass. The images are arranged in three rows. The first row is labeled "Original image". It shows five unprocessed images of barnyard grass in rice fields. In these images, you can see neatly arranged rice crops and the barnyard grass that may be present among them. The second row is labeled "YOLOv8n". This row presents the target detection outcomes using the YOLOv8n model on the corresponding original images. Detected targets and their names are highlighted in blue boxes and text. The model's accuracy in identifying barnyard grass is illustrated in this visual representation. Errors made by the model during detection are denoted by pink boxes. The "YOLOv8n-SSDW" row showcases the detection outcomes using the YOLOv8n-SSDW model, which also highlights barnyard grass targets with blue boxes and text. A comparison of the detection performance between the two models can be observed by examining the three rows of images. This evaluation encompasses successful detection rates and the accuracy of target localization. Figure 10a–e are assigned to different image numbers to differentiate the detection outcomes of distinct groups.

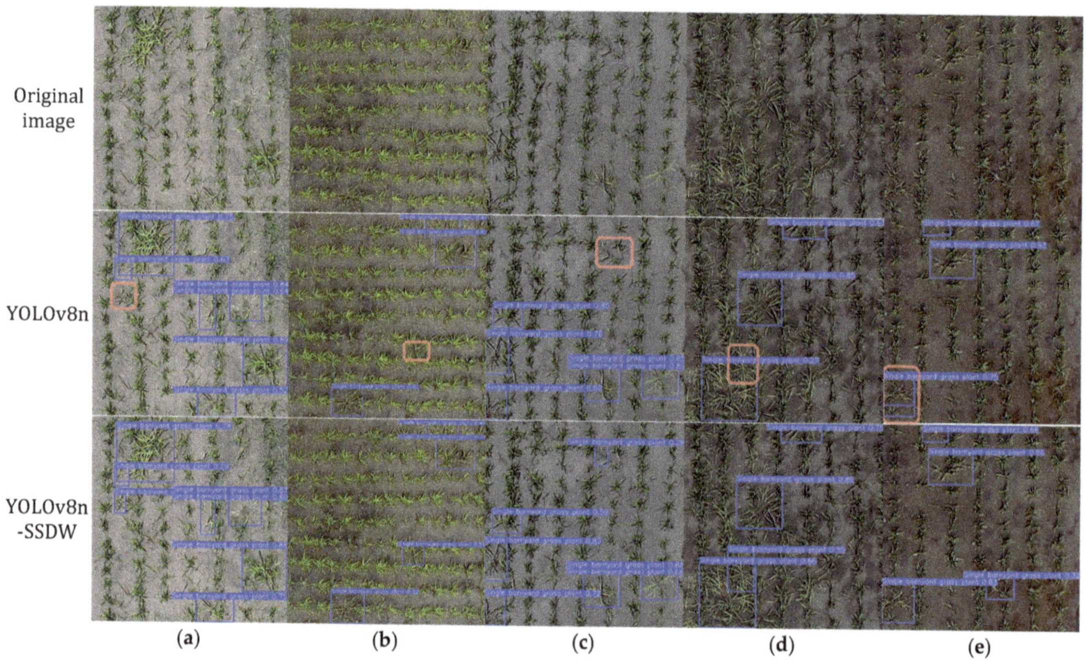

Figure 10. Detection results of barnyard grass using YOLOv8n and YOLOv8n-SSDW.

Discrepancies in missed and false detections between YOLOv8n and YOLOv8n-SSDW are evident in the comparison of images. In Figure 10a, the missed detection by YOLOv8n could be attributed to the diminutive size of the barnyard grass targets. Their similarity to the surrounding crops might cause the model to struggle in distinguishing the targets from the background. In Figure 10b, YOLOv8n misses some detections. This could be because the barnyard grass is in a darker area, making it challenging for the model to capture the target's features accurately. In Figure 10c, the missed detection might happen because the barnyard grass is somewhat hidden among the rice plants. This partial obstruction can interfere with the detection process of the model. In Figure 10d, YOLOv8n faces missed detections due to overlapping targets. The model may have trouble distinguishing between the different targets in this case. In Figure 10e, YOLOv8n shows a false detection issue. This problem may occur because similar-looking leaves mislead the model, leading to duplicate detections. In contrast, YOLOv8n-SSDW performs much better in these complex situations. This model can identify barnyard grass targets more accurately, showing greater robustness and detection accuracy.

3.7. *Heatmap Analysis of Different Detection Layers*

The heatmap visualizes the model's attention to different regions of the image through color intensity, where brighter colors (e.g., yellow) indicate higher attention, and darker colors (e.g., blue) represent lower attention. By comparing the original image with the heatmap, one can intuitively understand the model's focus on targets across different layers, aiding in the analysis of feature extraction and target detection mechanisms. Figure 11 consists of two main parts: the original field image during testing and the heatmaps of different layers generated by the YOLOv8n-SSDW model when detecting this image. The left panel (a), labeled "Original image", displays a paddy field with neatly arranged green plants, likely rice or barnyard grass. The right panel (b), labeled "Heatmaps of different layers", presents multiple heatmaps from various layers.

In the original image, the plants exhibit a certain regularity, representing crop rows of rice in the field. Among them, plants with slight variations in size and morphology, including rice and barnyard grass, are present. This complex vegetation distribution in the field poses challenges for target detection models, as similarities in appearance, dense arrangements, and natural lighting variations may interfere with accurate target identification. From a holistic perspective, the image contains areas of brightness and darkness caused by natural lighting, which may affect the color and contrast of targets, thereby influencing the model's visual feature-based detection performance.

The heatmaps illustrate the attention levels of the YOLOv8n-SSDW model across different layers. The results demonstrate that the proposed algorithm effectively focuses on regions containing barnyard grass. Shallower heatmaps (from left to right and top to bottom, the layers progressively deepen) tend to emphasize local details, such as leaf shapes and textures, with relatively dispersed and fine-grained color distributions, reflecting the extraction of basic visual features. In contrast, deeper heatmaps show more concentrated color distributions around specific barnyard grass targets, indicating that as the network layers deepen, the model integrates shallow features and gradually shifts focus toward holistic target recognition and localization, prioritizing positional and categorical information of barnyard grass. In some heatmaps, distinct yellow-highlighted regions are clearly concentrated on specific plants, suggesting that the YOLOv8n-SSDW model successfully captures key features of target barnyard grass at these layers, directing attention accordingly for accurate detection. However, certain heatmaps exhibit dispersed highlights or incomplete coverage of targets, possibly due to the model's attention to background features in some layers.

3.8. Field Counting Test

Figure 12 illustrates the weed counting test conducted in a field using a drone. This section aims to validate the predictive efficiency of the proposed YOLOv8n-SSDW method through online detection tests deployed in a complex field environment. The actual field conditions present numerous interfering factors, such as background noise and uneven lighting. The principle and process of the drone weed counting test are depicted in Figure 12. The drone is equipped with a camera that captures real-time images of the field. It utilizes wireless equipment to transmit relevant information to a ground computer, which assists in processing the results. The drone primarily carries a lens, an image processor, communication devices, and a power supply, with detailed specifications of each component listed in Table 4.

The drone's flight speed was set at 2 m per second, with a continuous forward-flight duration of 3 min, covering an approximate distance of 360 m. Manual counting revealed that the number of barnyard grasses was 643, with an average detection accuracy of 85.9%, while the average detection accuracy from laboratory tests was 86.7%. The decrease in average detection accuracy may be attributed to vibrations during the drone's flight and interference from complex airflow in the field affecting image capture. In this field test, the average detection time for a single image was 0.05 s. Overall, the results were largely in line with expectations, indicating that the YOLOv8n-SSDW model demonstrates reliable feasibility in handling the complexities of actual rice paddy environments. Although the detection accuracy declined, it also provides a clear direction for subsequent optimization.

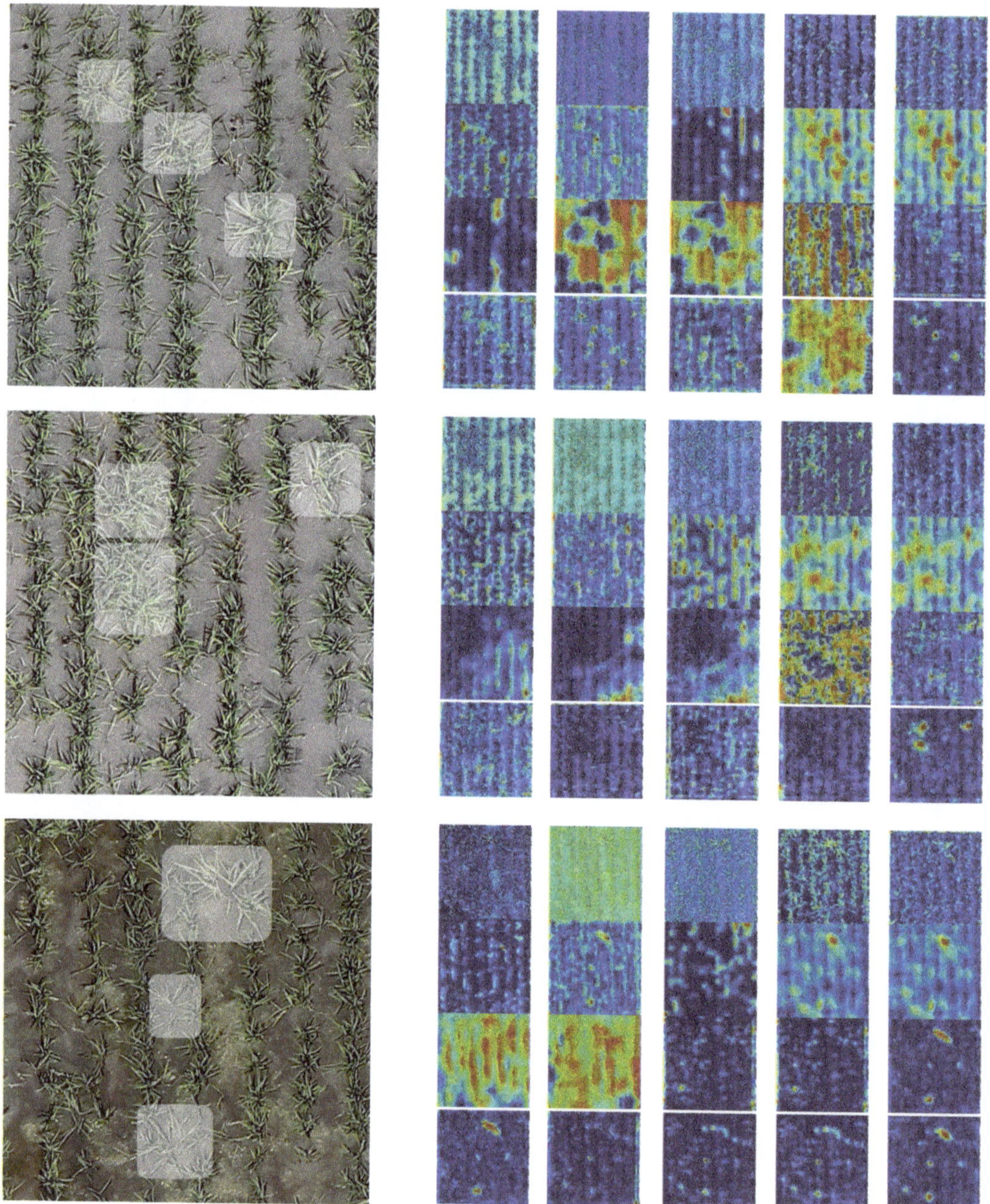

(a) Original image (b) Heatmaps of different layers

Figure 11. Heatmaps of different detection layers of YOLOv8n-SSDW alongside the original image.

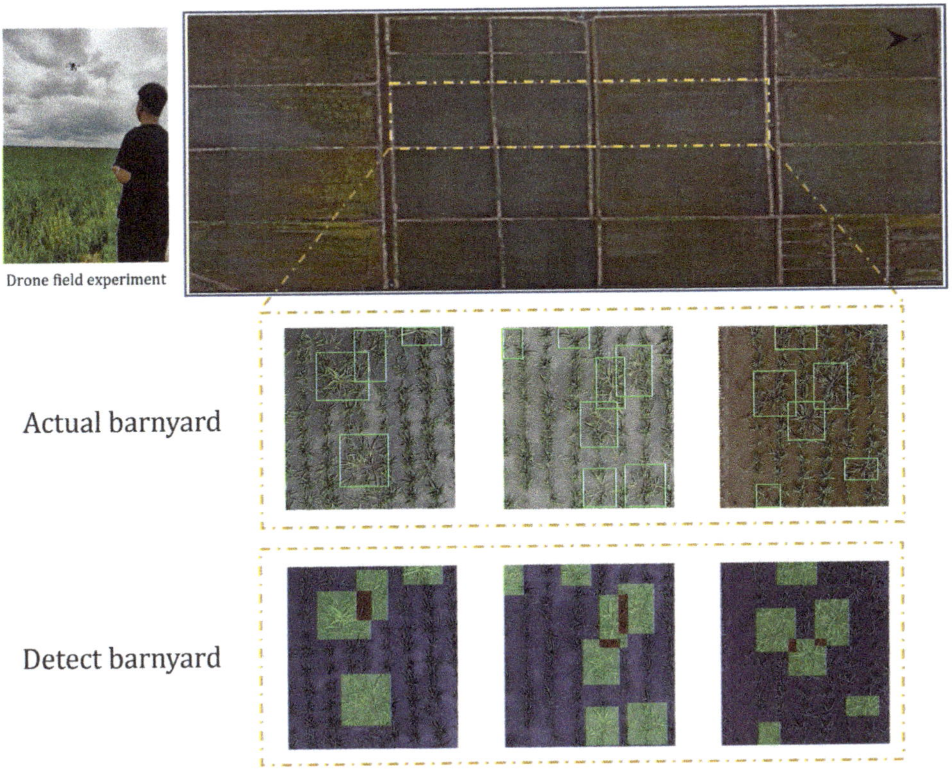

Figure 12. Drone-based field weed counting test.

Table 4. Main payload equipment of the UAV.

Devices	Related Description
Camera lens	Zenmuse P1 lens for field barnyard grass images
Image processor	Jetson nano B01 used to detect barnyard grass in the field
4G/5G network connection end point	Based on DJI airborne SDK development, real-time transmission of collected image data to the ground
Power supply	TB60 smart flight battery for UAV power supply

4. Discussion

The YOLOv8n-SSDW model proposed in this research offers advantages over existing YOLO models for barnyard grass detection in rice fields. It demonstrates enhancements in various metrics, such as F1 score, mAP, parameters, and FLOPs, compared to the original YOLOv8n model. Through the ablation study, the improved modules each contributed uniquely to the model's performance. The incorporation of the WIoU loss function notably improved the model's precision and mAP, consistent with prior findings by Wang et al., highlighting the effectiveness of adaptive weighting mechanisms in optimizing bounding box regression outcomes [35]. Additionally, the SEAM attention mechanism improved the model's ability to focus on barnyard grass features amidst complex backgrounds. Similar attention mechanisms have been shown to enhance model performance effectively in other studies on plant disease detection [36]. The SRCConv module, featuring a unique design for coordinate convolution and incorporating residual connections, maintains high detection accuracy despite its lightweight nature. This finding aligns with Hu and colleagues' assertion that separable convolutions and residual connections can improve model efficiency and stability [37].

However, the model still exhibits certain limitations. Decreasing model parameters results in lower recognition accuracy, despite optimization in the SRCConv module, suggesting potential for enhancement. Under complex field conditions, such as extreme weather events involving strong winds or dust storms that severely degrade image quality, the model's detection accuracy and robustness are significantly compromised. This observation aligns with the findings by Chen et al. regarding the sensitivity of deep learning models to environmental variations [38]. Additionally, while the model performs well on the dataset constructed in this study, its generalization capability across different regions and rice varieties requires further validation. Factors such as varying soil colors, rice planting densities, and weed species distributions may influence model performance [39].

To address these challenges, future research could focus on the following directions. First, further optimization of lightweight convolutional modules could be pursued by exploring more efficient architectural designs that minimize parameter counts while preserving feature information, potentially drawing inspiration from novel lightweight network structures [40]. Second, to enhance the model's adaptability to complex environments, training datasets could be augmented with images captured under various extreme conditions, enabling the model to learn more diverse features and improve robustness [41]. Concurrently, field tests across multiple regions and rice varieties could be conducted to collect more heterogeneous data for model refinement and enhanced generalization.

Moreover, integrating the proposed model with other advanced technologies presents a promising research avenue. For instance, improvements in UAV flight control systems or the development of anti-vibration imaging techniques could mitigate the impact of flight-induced vibrations on image quality. Alternatively, combining spectral feature-based weed detection methods with the current model [42] may leverage unique spectral signatures to improve accuracy, particularly in distinguishing morphologically similar weeds. The integration of the model with IoT technologies could also enable real-time, remote monitoring and management of field weeds, thereby advancing smart agricultural practices [43]. In summary, the YOLOv8n-SSDW model proposed in this study offers a novel solution for barnyard grass detection in paddy fields, yet continuous refinement is necessary to better meet the practical demands of agricultural production.

5. Conclusions

In response to the prevalent issues of insufficient accuracy, large parameter counts, and high computational complexity in existing weed detection models, this study constructed a barnyard grass detection dataset and proposed a lightweight field barnyard grass detection model—YOLOv8n-SSDW. A novel SRCConv was designed to replace the convolution modules of the original model. By incorporating coordinate details into the convolution process, this design improves the model's target localization capabilities. The utilization of separable convolutions decreases computational complexity and incorporates residual connections to enhance feature propagation. This approach ensures the stability of barnyard grass feature extraction in complex backgrounds, maintaining recognition accuracy while lowering computational costs, thereby making the model more lightweight and efficient. The sensitivity of the model to edge detail features of barnyard grass was enhanced by introducing the SEAM attention mechanism and upgrading the global average pooling layer to a global max pooling layer. Moreover, a lightweight and efficient upsampling module, Dysample, was incorporated to enhance the resolution of feature maps. The loss function for the training model was redefined as *WIoU* to improve the classification and regression accuracy of detection boxes. The efficacy of the model was confirmed through various experimental cohorts. The mAP_50 of the YOLOv8n-SSDW model reached 0.851, with a parameter count of 2.69M and FLOPs of 7.4G, resulting in an 11.1% reduction in model size to only 5.6 MB. YOLOv8n-SSDW outperformed the baseline model, exhibiting a higher accuracy, recall rate, and mAP, along with reduced loss values. When compared to other state-of-the-art models in the YOLO series, YOLOv8n-SSDW exhibited the highest overall performance. On-site tests conducted by combining drones with ground-based computers and using the YOLOv8n-SSDW model show that due to vibration and airflow, the accuracy slightly decreased. However, the overall performance met standards, preliminarily verifying its feasibility for barnyard grass detection in complex rice field scenarios. Future research could further optimize the model structure or enhance the shock resistance of drone image acquisition to improve the adaptability in complex environments, thereby promoting the continuous development of weed detection technology in rice paddies to better serve agricultural production practices.

Author Contributions: Conceptualization, Y.S.; data curation, H.G., X.C. and M.L.; formal analysis, Y.S. and Y.C.; investigation, H.G., X.C. and M.L.; methodology, Y.S.; resources, Y.C.; software, Y.S.; supervision, Y.S.; validation, Y.C.; visualization, Y.S.; writing—original draft, Y.S.; writing—review and editing, Y.C. and B.F. All authors have read and agreed to the published version of the manuscript.

Funding: This research was funded by the Key Research Project of the Liaoning Provincial Department of Education (JYTZD2023123).

Data Availability Statement: The data presented in this study can be requested from the corresponding author. The data are not currently available for public access because they are part of an ongoing research project.

Acknowledgments: The authors would like to thank the anonymous reviewers for their critical comments and suggestions for improving the manuscript.

Conflicts of Interest: The authors declare no conflicts of interest.

References

1. Alagbo, O.O.; Akinyemiju, O.A.; Chauhan, B.S. Weed Management in Rainfed Upland Rice Fields under Varied Agro-Ecologies in Nigeria. *Rice Sci.* **2022**, *29*, 328–339. [CrossRef]
2. Yuan, Q.; Tian, Z.; Lv, W.; Huang, W.; Sun, X.; Lv, W.; Bi, Y.; Shen, G.; Zhou, W. Effects of common rice field weeds on the survival, feeding rate and feeding behaviour of the crayfish Procambarus clarkii. *Sci. Rep.* **2021**, *11*, 19327. [CrossRef]
3. Singh, M.; Bhullar, M.S.; Gill, G. Integrated weed management in dry-seeded rice using stale seedbeds and post sowing herbicides. *Field Crops Res.* **2018**, *224*, 182–191. [CrossRef]
4. Feng, T.; Sun, W.; Wang, J.; Lei, T.; Wang, L.; Xie, Y.; Zhou, H.; Zhu, F.; Ma, H. Susceptibility monitoring and metabolic resistance study of *Echinochloa crus-galli* to three common herbicides in rice regions of the Mid-Lower Yangtze, China. *Crop Prot.* **2025**, *191*, 107108. [CrossRef]
5. Dass, A.; Shekhawat, K.; Choudhary, A.K.; Sepat, S.; Rathore, S.S.; Mahajan, G.; Chauhan, B.S. Weed management in rice using crop competition-a review. *Crop Prot.* **2017**, *95*, 45–52. [CrossRef]
6. Zhang, Z.; Li, R.; Zhao, C.; Qiang, S. Reduction in weed infestation through integrated depletion of the weed seed bank in a rice-wheat cropping system. *Agron. Sustain. Dev.* **2021**, *41*, 10. [CrossRef]
7. Ju, J.; Chen, G.; Lv, Z.; Zhao, M.; Sun, L.; Wang, Z.; Wang, J. Design and experiment of an adaptive cruise weeding robot for paddy fields based on improved YOLOv5. *Comput. Electron. Agric.* **2024**, *219*, 108824. [CrossRef]
8. Hadayat, A.; Zahir, Z.A.; Cai, P.; Gao, C. Integrated application of synthetic community reduces consumption of herbicide in field *Phalaris minor* control. *Soil Ecol. Lett.* **2024**, *6*, 230207. [CrossRef]
9. Rai, N.; Zhang, Y.; Ram, B.G.; Schumacher, L.; Yellavajjala, R.K.; Bajwa, S.; Sun, X. Applications of deep learning in precision weed management: A review. *Comput. Electron. Agric.* **2023**, *206*, 107698. [CrossRef]
10. Sun, Y.; Li, M.; Liu, M.; Zhang, J.; Cao, Y.; Ao, X. A statistical method for high-throughput emergence rate calculation for soybean breeding plots based on field phenotypic characteristics. *Plant Methods* **2025**, *21*, 40. [CrossRef]
11. Ur Rehman, M.; Eesaar, H.; Abbas, Z.; Seneviratne, L.; Hussain, I.; Chong, K.T. Advanced drone-based weed detection using feature-enriched deep learning approach. *Knowl. Based Syst.* **2024**, *305*, 112655. [CrossRef]

12. Ren, S.; He, K.; Girshick, R.; Sun, J. Faster R-CNN: Towards real-time object detection with region proposal networks. *IEEE Trans. Pattern Anal. Mach. Intell.* **2017**, *39*, 1137–1149. [CrossRef]
13. Redmon, J.; Farhadi, A. YOLO9000: Better, faster, stronger. *arXiv* **2016**, arXiv:1612.08242.
14. Redmon, J.; Divvala, S.; Girshick, R.; Farhadi, A. You only look once: Unified, real-time object detection. In Proceedings of the IEEE Conference on Computer Vision and Pattern Recognition, Las Vegas, NV, USA, 27–30 June 2016; IEEE: Piscataway, NJ, USA, 2016; pp. 779–788.
15. Varghese, R.; Sambath, M. YOLOv8: A novel object detection algorithm with enhanced performance and robustness. In Proceedings of the International Conference on Advances in Data Engineering and Intelligent Computing Systems, Chennai, India, 18–19 April 2024; IEEE: Piscataway, NJ, USA, 2024; pp. 1–6. [CrossRef]
16. Guo, Z.; Cai, D.; Zhou, Y.; Xu, T.; Yu, F. Identifying rice field weeds from unmanned aerial vehicle remote sensing imagery using deep learning. *Plant Methods* **2024**, *20*, 105. [CrossRef]
17. Farooq, U.; Rehman, A.; Khanam, T.; Amtullah, A.; Bou-rabee, M.A.; Tariq, M. Lightweight deep learning model for weed detection for IoT devices. In Proceedings of the 2022 2nd International Conference on Emerging Frontiers in Electrical and Electronic Technologies, Patna, India, 24–25 June 2022; IEEE: Piscataway, NJ, USA, 2022; pp. 1–6.
18. Prasad, D. Real-time weed detection and classification using deep learning models and IoT-based edge computing for social learning applications. In *Augmented and Virtual Reality in Social Learning: Technological Impacts and Challenges*; De Gruyter: Berlin, Germany; Boston, MA, USA, 2024; pp. 241–268. [CrossRef]
19. Ma, C.; Chi, G.; Ju, X.; Zhang, J.; Yan, C. YOLO-CWD: A novel model for crop and weed detection based on improved YOLOv8. *Crop Prot.* **2025**, *192*, 107169. [CrossRef]
20. Tang, B.; Zhou, J.; Pan, Y.; Qu, X.; Cui, Y.; Liu, C.; Li, X.; Zhao, C.; Gu, X. Recognition of maize seedling under weed disturbance using improved YOLOv5 algorithm. *Measurement* **2025**, *242 Pt B*, 115938. [CrossRef]
21. Fan, X.; Sun, T.; Chai, X.; Zhou, J. YOLO-WDNet: A lightweight and accurate model for weeds detection in cotton field. *Comput. Electron. Agric.* **2024**, *225*, 109317. [CrossRef]
22. Saleem, M.H.; Potgieter, J.; Arif, K.M. Weed Detection by Faster RCNN Model: An Enhanced Anchor Box Approach. *Agronomy* **2022**, *12*, 1580. [CrossRef]
23. Peng, H.; Li, Z.; Zhou, Z.; Shao, Y. Weed detection in paddy field using an improved RetinaNet network. *Comput. Electron. Agric.* **2022**, *199*, 107179. [CrossRef]
24. Liu, T.; Zhao, Y.; Wang, H.; Wu, W.; Yang, T.; Zhang, W.; Zhu, S.; Sun, C.; Yao, Z. Harnessing UAVs and deep learning for accurate grass weed detection in wheat fields: A study on biomass and yield implications. *Plant Methods* **2024**, *20*, 144. [CrossRef]
25. Chen, H.; Zhang, Y.; He, C.; Chen, C.; Zhang, Y.; Chen, Z.; Jiang, Y.; Lin, C.; Ma, R.; Qi, L. PIS-Net: Efficient weakly supervised instance segmentation network based on annotated points for rice field weed identification. *Smart Agric. Technol.* **2024**, *9*, 100557. [CrossRef]
26. Dang, F.; Chen, D.; Lu, Y.; Li, Z. YOLOWeeds: A novel benchmark of YOLO object detectors for multi-class weed detection in cotton production systems. *Comput. Electron. Agric.* **2023**, *205*, 107655. [CrossRef]
27. Liu, R.; Lehman, J.; Molino, P.; Petroski Such, F.; Frank, E.; Sergeev, A.; Yosinski, J. An intriguing failing of convolutional neural networks and the CoordConv solution. *arXiv* **2018**, arXiv:1807.03247.
28. Wang, Y.; Zhang, J.; Kan, M.; Shan, S.; Chen, X. Self-supervised equivariant attention mechanism for weakly supervised semantic segmentation. In Proceedings of the IEEE/CVF Conference on Computer Vision and Pattern Recognition, Seattle, WA, USA, 13–19 June 2020; IEEE: Piscataway, NJ, USA, 2020; pp. 12235–12244. [CrossRef]
29. Liu, W.; Lu, H.; Fu, H.; Cao, Z. Learning to upsample by learning to sample. In Proceedings of the IEEE/CVF International Conference on Computer Vision, Paris, France, 1–6 October 2023; IEEE: Piscataway, NJ, USA, 2023; pp. 6004–6014. [CrossRef]
30. Zheng, Z.; Wang, P.; Liu, W.; Li, J. Enhancing geometric factors in model learning and inference for object detection and instance segmentation. *IEEE Access* **2022**, *52*, 8574–8586. [CrossRef]
31. Du, S.; Zhang, B.; Zhang, P. Scale-Sensitive IoU Loss: An Improved Regression Loss Function in Remote Sensing Object Detection. *IEEE Access* **2021**, *9*, 141258–141272. [CrossRef]
32. Jin, S.; Cao, Q.; Li, J.; Wang, X.; Li, J.; Feng, S.; Xu, T. Study on lightweight rice blast detection method based on improved YOLOv8. *Pest Manag. Sci.* **2025**. [CrossRef]
33. Tong, Z.; Chen, Y.; Xu, Z.; Yu, R. Wise-IoU: Bounding Box Regression Loss with Dynamic Focusing Mechanism. *arXiv* **2023**, arXiv:2301.10051. [CrossRef]
34. San, K.H.; Kondo, T.; Maruka Tat, S.; Hara-Azumi, Y. A Comparative Study of Loss Functions for Arbitrary-Oriented Object Detection in Aerial Images. In Proceedings of the 2024 21st International Joint Conference on Computer Science and Software Engineering (JCSSE), Phuket, Thailand, 19–22 June 2024; IEEE: Piscataway, NJ, USA, 2024; pp. 1–8. [CrossRef]
35. Wang, J.; Tan, D.; Sui, L.; Guo, J.; Wang, R. Wolfberry recognition and picking-point localization technology in natural environments based on improved Yolov8n-Pose-LBD. *Comput. Electron. Agric.* **2024**, *227 Pt 1*, 109551. [CrossRef]

36. Alirezazadeh, P.; Schirrmann, M.; Stolzenburg, F. Improving Deep Learning-based Plant Disease Classification with Attention Mechanism. *Gesunde Pflanz.* **2023**, *75*, 49–59. [CrossRef]
37. Hu, Y.; Huang, Y.; Zhang, K. Multi-scale information distillation network for efficient image super-resolution. *Knowl. Based Syst.* **2023**, *275*, 110718. [CrossRef]
38. Chen, Z.; Liu, H.; Xu, C.; Wu, X.C.; Liang, B.; Cao, J.; Chen, D. Modeling vegetation greenness and its climate sensitivity with deep-learning technology. *Ecol. Evol.* **2021**, *11*, 7335–7345. [CrossRef] [PubMed]
39. Xia, X.; Wang, M.; Shi, Y.; Huang, Z.; Liu, J.; Men, H.; Fang, H. Identification of white degradable and non-degradable plastics in food field: A dynamic residual network coupled with hyperspectral technology. *Spectrochim. Acta Part A Mol. Biomol. Spectrosc.* **2023**, *296*, 122686. [CrossRef] [PubMed]
40. Ouyang, M.; Chen, Z. JPEG Quantized Coefficient Recovery via DCT Domain Spatial-Frequential Transformer. *IEEE Trans. Image Process.* **2024**, *33*, 3385–3398. [CrossRef] [PubMed]
41. Lee, H.; Kang, S.; Chung, K. Robust Data Augmentation Generative Adversarial Network for Object Detection. *Sensors* **2023**, *23*, 157. [CrossRef]
42. Zhang, Y.; Gao, J.; Cen, H.; Lu, Y.; Yu, X.; He, Y.; Pieters, J.G. Automated spectral feature extraction from hyperspectral images to differentiate weedy rice and barnyard grass from a rice crop. *Comput. Electron. Agric.* **2019**, *159*, 42–49. [CrossRef]
43. Boursianis, A.D.; Papadopoulou, M.S.; Diamantoulakis, P.; Liopa-Tsakalidi, A.; Barouchas, P.; Salahas, G.; Karagiannidis, G.; Wan, S.; Goudos, S.K. Internet of Things (IoT) and Agricultural Unmanned Aerial Vehicles (UAVs) in smart farming: A comprehensive review. *Internet Things* **2022**, *18*, 100187. [CrossRef]

agriculture

MDPI

Article

Improving Winter Wheat Yield Estimation Under Saline Stress by Integrating Sentinel-2 and Soil Salt Content Using Random Forest

Chuang Lu [1,2], Maowei Yang [3,*], Shiwei Dong [1,2,*], Yu Liu [2], Yinkun Li [1] and Yuchun Pan [2]

1 Beijing PAIDE Science and Technology Development Co., Ltd., Beijing 100097, China; luc@nercita.org.cn (C.L.); liyk@nercita.org.cn (Y.L.)
2 Research Center of Information Technology, Beijing Academy of Agriculture and Forestry Sciences, Beijing 100097, China; liuyu@nercita.org.cn (Y.L.); panyc@nercita.org.cn (Y.P.)
3 Shandong Provincial Geo-Mineral Engineering Exploration Institute (801 Institute of Hydrogeology and Engineering Geology, Shandong Provincial Bureau of Geology & Mineral Resources), Jinan 250014, China
* Correspondence: 15866631839@163.com (M.Y.); dongsw@nercita.org.cn (S.D.)

Abstract: Accurate estimation of winter wheat yield under saline stress is crucial for addressing food security challenges and optimizing agricultural management in regional soils. This study proposed a method integrating Sentinel-2 data and field-measured soil salt content (SC) using a random forest (RF) method to improve yield estimation of winter wheat in Kenli County, a typical saline area in China's Yellow River Delta. First, feature importance analysis of a temporal vegetation index (VI) and salinity index (SI) across all growth periods were achieved to select main parameters. Second, yield models of winter wheat were developed in VI-, SI-, VI + SI-, and VI + SI + SC-based groups. Furthermore, error assessment and spatial yield mapping were analyzed in detail. The results demonstrated that feature importance varied by growth periods. SI dominated in pre-jointing periods, while VI was better in the post-jointing phase. The VI + SI + SC-based model achieved better accuracy (R^2 = 0.78, RMSE = 720.16 kg/ha) than VI-based (R^2 = 0.71), SI-based (R^2 = 0.69), and VI + SI-based (R^2 = 0.77) models. Error analysis results suggested that the residuals were reduced as the input parameters increased, and the VI + SI + SC-based model showed a good consistency with the field-measured yields. The spatial distribution of winter wheat yield using the VI + SI + SC-based model showed significant differences, and average yields in no, slight, moderate, and severe salinity areas were 7945, 7258, 5217, and 4707 kg/ha, respectively. This study can provide a reference for winter wheat yield estimation and crop production improvement in saline regions.

Keywords: yield estimation; saline stress; growth period; vegetation index; salt index; random forest

1. Introduction

Soil salinization has emerged as a global environmental and ecological challenge, particularly prevalent in the arid and semi-arid regions of Northern China. The Yellow River Delta in China represents a prominent case where pedogenic environments and anthropogenic inputs have contributed to extensive soil salinization. Since the 1970s, decreased river discharge combined with seawater intrusion has disrupted the terrestrial water–salt balance, establishing a characteristic coastal salinization zone. This phenomenon has induced soil degradation and constrained crop productivity, posing serious challenges to agricultural sustainability and regional economic development [1]. Recent years have

https://doi.org/10.3390/agriculture15141544

witnessed agricultural transformation in this region driven by labor shortages and policy reforms. Notably, cultivation areas of salt-tolerant crops (e.g., cotton) have markedly decreased, while less salt-tolerant crops, particularly winter wheat, have indicated consistent annual expansion [2]. However, suboptimal resource allocation has resulted in the substantial reduction of winter wheat yields in saline areas. Given the national food security strategies and sustainable saline land utilization policies [3], accurate and timely winter wheat yield estimation has become crucial for informing production management decisions, guiding soil remediation efforts, and optimizing cropping patterns.

Compared with traditional manual crop yield assessment method, remote sensing technology is an efficient approach for improving regional yield estimation due to the significant advantages in non-contact, large-scale monitoring capabilities. Various vegetation indexes (VI), including the Normalized Difference Vegetation Index (NDVI), Enhanced Vegetation Index (EVI), Chlorophyll Reflection Index (CCRI), and Normalized Difference Water Index (NDWI), have been extensively and effectively applied in crop yield estimation in typical saline and other areas. Zhu et al. [4] identified EVI during the booting-filling period as the most effective parameter for winter wheat yield estimation in saline areas. Similarly, Satir et al. [5] achieved reliable wheat yield prediction in Mediterranean saline areas using NDVI, NDWI, and other parameters with stepwise linear regression. Shi et al. [6] employed NDVI for evaluating soil improvement and wheat growth under saline stress. To reflect the cumulative growth process of crops, Chen et al. [7] integrated vegetation indexes from multiple periods to establish a summer maize yield model. Zhao et al. [8] further advanced time-series modeling approaches for maize yield estimation. These methods had demonstrated reasonable estimation accuracy, but they often ignored critical growth-limiting factors. Existing studies have enhanced model generalization by incorporating soil variables. For instance, Farhat et al. [9] improved potato yield estimation accuracy by integrating vegetation indexes with soil conductivity and moisture content. Han et al. [10] achieved an accurate estimation at a county level by combining remote sensing and soil data. Mustafa et al. achieved satisfactory prediction accuracy using vegetation and soil data analysis [11]. Addressing field measurement limitations, Karimli et al. [12] inverted soil parameters (salinity, texture, organic carbon) from remote sensing data and achieved a high accuracy for winter wheat yield estimation by integrating these parameters.

Crop yield estimation using remote sensing methods is characterized by three distinctive features: integration of multiple remote sensing parameters, utilization of multi-source data, and utilization of long-term series analysis. In saline areas, crop productivity is constrained by salt stress, which adversely affects dry matter allocation and harvest index [13] to complicate the relationship between vegetation indexes and yield formation. The spatiotemporal heterogeneity of soil salinity further exacerbates this challenge due to its impact on crops varies substantially across different regions and growth periods [14]. These stress factors often lead to estimation errors when relying solely on single parameters. Field surveys of soil salt data can provide valuable parameters, but they are limited when widely promoted and applied. The soil salinity index (SI) is a quantitative descriptor of surface soil salinity for different areas, e.g., the Yellow River Delta, China [15], Nile Delta, and Egypt [16], and various crop growth periods ranging from bare soil periods [17] to vegetation-covered phases [18]. The integration of vegetation indexes, salinity indexes, and soil salt content parameters offer potential for enhancing information dimensionality and complementary advantages [19]. However, the use of salinity indexes and soil salt content as yield estimation components remains relatively insufficient. In this study, based on the relationships between the multiple parameters (e.g., vegetation indexes, salinity indexes, soil salt content) and wheat yield, we employed a random forest regression method, and integrated Sentinel-2 and soil salt content data to improve winter wheat yield estimation under saline stress in a typical coastal saline agricultural region, namely, Kenli County in the Yellow River Delta, China.

2. Materials and Methods

2.1. Study Area

The study area is located in Kenli County, Shandong Province, China, geographically located at 117°90′–119°82′ E and 37°01′–37°99′ N (Figure 1a). The topography is characterized by flat terrain with a gradual southwest-to-northeast slope. This region has a warm temperate semi-humid continental monsoon climate, exhibiting distinct seasonal variations. The area experiences a mean annual temperature of 13.5 °C and receives an average annual precipitation of 555.9 mm. The area has an annual evaporation rate of approximately 1885.0 mm, and the evaporation-to-precipitation ratio reaches about 3.5:1, indicating significant water deficit conditions. This agricultural region primarily cultivates wheat, corn, and cotton. The parent material primarily consists of Yellow River-derived alluvial deposits exhibiting light texture, while surface soils are predominantly classified as sandy loam and light loam. The study area features fluvo-aquic and saline-alkali soils, with chlorides as the dominant salt species. Pronounced spatial heterogeneity has resulted in substantial spatial differences in crop yield distribution. Therefore, we selected this typical county with a distinct environmental gradient for estimating winter wheat yield under saline stress.

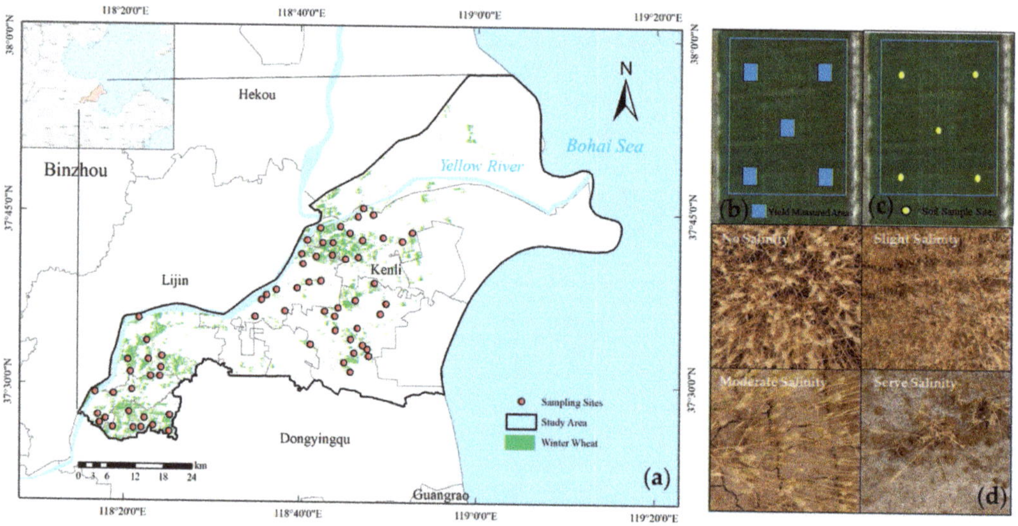

Figure 1. Distribution of winter wheat and sampling sites in the study area. (**a**) Study area; (**b**) winter wheat sampling; (**c**) soil sampling; (**d**) landscape photos of different salinity levels.

2.2. Data Acquisition and Processing

2.2.1. Sampling and Analysis of Winter Wheat and Soil

To ensure an even distribution of samples and meet the request to express spatial variability of soil salinity at county scale, a 10 km^2 square grid was established to select test plots at the center of each grid cell [20]. For each test plot, winter wheat and soil samples were achieved in June 2024.

Winter wheat yield data were measured in a 10 m × 10 m area to match pixel resolution of remote sensing data, using a five sub-samples quincunx sampling pattern with 1 m^2 harvest areas per sub-sample (Figure 1b). Winter wheat samples were collected from 68 test plots, and corresponding geographical coordinates were recorded. The harvested winter wheat samples were sun-dried, threshed, and weighed. Then, the yield of per sub-sample was calculated, and the average value was taken as the yield for each sample.

For soil sampling, surface soil samples (0–20 cm depth) were collected at the center location of each sampling grid of winter wheat, as shown in Figure 1c. The collected soil samples were air-dried, passed through a 2 mm sieve, and subsequently prepared as soil-water extracts with a soil-to-water ratio of 5:1. After shaking for 5 min and standing for 8 h, the electrical conductivity (EC) of the soil extracts was measured using a Mettler Toledo FE38 (Mettller Toledo Fe38, Zurich, Swiss) instrument. The measured EC values (mS/cm) were converted to soil salt content (SC, g/kg) according to the conversion formula [21]. Based upon the Chinese soil salinity classification standards [22], the soil salinity levels were categorized as no salinity (<1 g/kg), slight salinity (1–2 g/kg), moderate salinity (2–4 g/kg), and severe salinity (>4 g/kg). The spatial distribution of soil salinity was achieved using an ordinary Kriging interpolation method from the Geostatistical Analyst module in ArcGIS 10.8 (Esri, Redlands, CA, USA) (Figure 2). A Gaussian semivariogram model generated optimal performance (nugget = 0.27727, sill = 0.38282, range = 10.2 km). Model validation using 20% holdout sampling demonstrated satisfactory accuracy (R^2 = 0.688, RMSE = 0.45 g/kg). While stationarity assumptions may be challenged by the Yellow River Delta's complex depositional patterns, the sampling design (10 km^2 grids) captured major salinity gradients. Landscape photos of different salinity levels are shown in Figure 1d and suggested that different salinity levels affected the growth and yield of winter wheat. The sampling sites, soil salt content, and winter wheat yield for each category are indicated in Table 1.

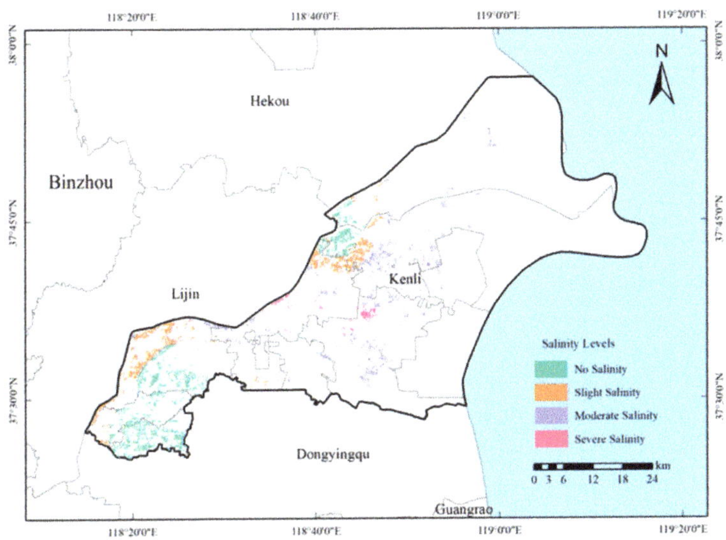

Figure 2. Spatial distribution of soil salinity.

Table 1. Sample statistic values of different salinity levels.

Salinity Level	Samples	Soil Salt Content (SC) (g/kg)			Winter Wheat Yield (kg/ha)		
		Min	Max	Mean	Min	Max	Mean
No	26	0.30	0.99	0.72	6502.23	9904.48	8252.94
Slight	19	1.01	1.98	1.50	4918.38	8641.58	6795.65
Moderate	19	2.01	3.94	2.80	1928.61	8260.78	5368.14
Severe	4	4.38	7.39	5.79	1519.96	3559.61	2660.83

2.2.2. Remote Sensing Data

Sentinel-2A/B has a high resolution and revisit period of 5 days. As presented in Table 2, the primary payload consists of an MSI multispectral imager that covers a spectral range from 440 to 2200 nm and ground resolutions of 10 m (4 bands), 20 m (6 bands), and 60 m (3 bands). Based on the GEE platform (https://earthengine.google.com/ (accessed on 15 November 2024)), 96 images of the 5-day time series of Sentinel-2 from October 2023 to June 2024 were obtained and processed, covering the entire growth cycle of winter wheat. JavaScript programming was employed to calculate Bit10 and Bit11 values in the QA60 cloud information band to obtain the cloud mask and remove cloud interference of remote sensing images.

Table 2. Spectral bands of the Sentinel-2 sensor.

Bands	Center Wavelength/nm	Resolution/m
Band 1—Coastal aerosol	443	60
Band 2—Blue	490	10
Band 3—Green	560	10
Band 4—Red	665	10
Band 5—Red-edge1	705	20
Band 6—Red-edge2	740	20
Band 7—Red-edge3	783	20
Band 8—NIR	842	10
Band 8A—Narrow NIR	865	20
Band 9—Water Vapor	945	60
Band 10—SWIR Cirrus	1380	60
Band 11—SWIR1	1610	20
Band 12—SWIR2	2190	20

According to the phenological characteristics of winter wheat in the study area, the growth periods were divided into six periods named P1 to P6 (Table 3), including seeding-tiller, dormancy, regreening, jointing, booting-flowering, and filling periods. The median synthesis method was used to calculate remote sensing parameters for each growth period.

Table 3. The number of images used for growth periods of winter wheat.

Growth Periods	Time	Images
P1 (seeding-tiller)	15 October 2023–30 November 2023	25
P2 (dormancy)	9 December 2023–24 February 2024	31
P3 (regreening)	1 March 2024–31 March 2024	15
P4 (jointing)	5 April 2024–20 April 2024	8
P5 (booting-flowering)	26 April 2024–8 May 2024	5
P6 (filling)	12 May 2024–31 May 2024	12

Vegetation indexes (VIs) can enhance the accuracy of spectral inversion for physiological vegetation and comprehensively reflect information related to crop growth, biomass, and coverage that are associated with crop yield. Six vegetation indexes were calculated from the 13 original bands according to winter wheat characteristics and existing research findings, as depicted in Table 4. NDVI and EVI primarily reflected the growth status and nutritional conditions. The chlorophyll absorption reflectance index (CARI) and CCRI were effective in indicating chlorophyll content of crops [23]. The normalized difference moisture index (NDMI) and NDWI performed well in identifying canopy moisture content. The inversion of soil salinity can be indirectly achieved through spectral reflectance. Existing studies have demonstrated that the shortwave infrared and green bands showed high sensitivity to soil salinity, and their combination with the red band could effectively construct a salinity index (SI) that accurately reflect variations of soil salt content. Another SI calculated based on the spectral reflectance of red, blue, and green bands is used to indicate soil salinization in vegetated areas.

Table 4. Vegetation indexes and salinity indexes.

Parameters		Formula	References
Vegetation Index (VI)	NDVI	$\frac{(B8-B4)}{(B8+B4)}$	[6]
	EVI	$\frac{2.5 \times (B8-B4)}{(B8+6 \times B4-7.5 \times B2+1)}$	[4]
	CARI	$(B5-B4)-0.2 \times (B5-B3)$	[24]
	CCRI	$B8/B5-1$	[25]
	NDMI	$\frac{(B8-B11)}{(B8+B11)}$	[26]
	NDWI	$\frac{(B3-B8)}{(B3+B8)}$	[27]
Salinity Index (SI)	SI1	$\sqrt{(B2 \times B4)}$	[15]
	SI2	$\sqrt{(B3^2+B4^2)}$	[28]
	SI3	$B11/B8$	[28]
	SI4	$\frac{(B4-B11)}{(B4+B11)}$	[29]
	CRSI	$\sqrt{\frac{(B8 \times B4)-(B3 \times B2)}{(B8 \times B4)+(B3 \times B2)}}$	[29]

2.2.3. Spatial Distribution Data of Winter Wheat

An investigation of land cover distribution in the study area was conducted in April 2024 using a grid-based sampling method. A total of 146 winter wheat samples and 285 non-winter wheat samples were collected, the latter comprising 124 cotton samples, 108 rice samples, and various other land cover types (forest, grassland, and water). All samples were distributed across the main cultivated areas. Based on feature variables (the difference between November NDVI and May NDVI of the following year, NDVI values for May, and the difference between May NDVI and June NDVI), the spatial distribution data of winter wheat in Kenli County in 2024 were produced using a random forest method using data derived from Sentinel-2 temporal variations from Beijing Academy of Agriculture and Forestry Sciences. It can effectively differentiate winter wheat from other vegetation and identify weak information of winter wheat in saline stress areas [30,31]. The confusion matrix is shown in Table A1. The results suggested that the overall accuracy was 92.45% and the Kappa coefficient was 0.85.

2.3. Method

The flowchart for winter wheat yield estimation in saline stress is illustrated in Figure 3. Using a random forest algorithm, feature importance analysis on vegetation indexes and salinity indexes across various growth periods was performed to select optimal remote sensing parameters. By integrating field-measured soil salt content data, yield estimation models of winter wheat were developed using four variable combinations: VI, SI, VI + SI, and VI + SI + SC. Model accuracy was assessed using the leave-one-out cross validation method, and a comprehensive analysis of estimation residuals was achieved at different salinity levels.

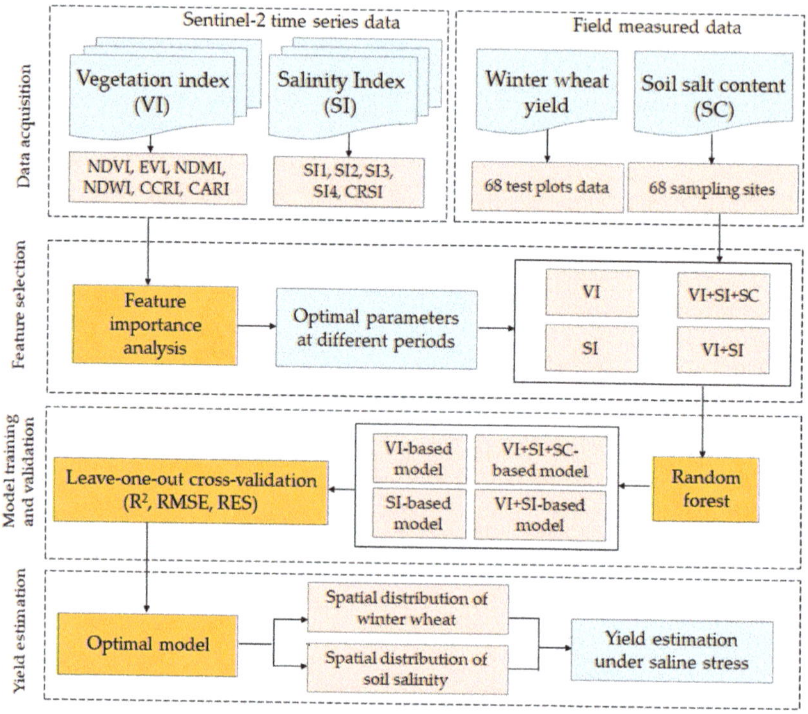

Figure 3. Flowchart of the winter wheat yield estimation method.

2.3.1. Random Forest

Random forest (RF) is an advanced statistical method based on machine learning, which has exceptional capability in handling high-dimensional datasets and high accuracy of the estimated results [32,33]. Variable importance analysis of random forest provided a robust framework for quantifying the relative contributions of independent parameters [34]. The importance of each parameter on model estimation accuracy was directly quantified using a permutation approach, with lower importance values indicating minor impacts on model performance and higher values reflecting greater influence. While the other three algorithms, namely, XGBoost (eXtreme Gradient Boosting), PLSR (Partial Least Squares Regression), and LSTM (Long Short-Term Memory), offer similar feature analysis, they may suffer from noise sensitivity, inadequate nonlinear modeling, overfitting risks, or computational inefficiencies. RF reduces variance and enhances stability through its Bagging ensemble techniques and random feature selection, demonstrating greater advantages over other methods in small-sample scenarios. In this study, random forest models were employed to select feature parameters and estimate yield of winter wheat.

We established a winter wheat yield estimation model that integrated multiple remote sensing parameters, providing a reliable framework for crop yield estimation. The RF models were implemented using MATLAB software 2016b (MathWorks, Natick, MA, USA). As shown in Table 5, the random forest models for all variants were implemented with consistent hyperparameters: 100 decision trees (ntree), which ensured error stabilization; a minimum leaf size (nodesize) of three to capture detailed patterns while preventing overfitting; and the default mtry value calculated as floor ($p/3$), where p represents the number of predictors.

Table 5. Random forest parameters by model variant.

Model Variant	Predictors	mtry	ntree	Nodesize
VI-based model	18	6	100	3
SI-based model	13	4	100	3
VI + SI-based model	31	10	100	3
VI + SI + SC-based model	32	10	100	3

2.3.2. Model Validation Method

Given the limited sample size, we employed the leave-one-out cross validation method for model validation. The method offered significant advantages for the limited datasets and maximized data utilization for training to generate robust classifiers [35]. This rigorous approach used a single sample for validation, and the remaining samples were adopted for model training, iterating this process across all samples data. The simulated outputs were subsequently compared with measured values using comprehensive statistical analysis. Model performance was quantitatively assessed using the determination coefficient (R^2), root mean square error (RMSE), and residual error (RES), as calculated using the following formulas:

$$R^2 = \frac{\sum_{i=1}^{n}(\hat{y}_i - \overline{y})^2}{\sum_{i=1}^{n}(y_i - \overline{y})^2} \tag{1}$$

$$\text{RMSE} = \sqrt{\frac{1}{n}\sum_{i=1}^{n}(\hat{y}_i - y_i)^2} \tag{2}$$

$$\text{RSE} = \hat{y}_i - y_i \tag{3}$$

where n is the total number of samples, and y_i, $\hat{y}_i$, and $\overline{y}$ represent the measured value, estimated value, and the average of the measured values for the samples, respectively.

3. Results

3.1. Feature Parameter Selection in Different Periods

Importance analysis of eleven remote sensing parameters for winter wheat was calculated and sorted in descending order, as shown in Figure 4. The results suggested that the importance of parameters in different growth periods presented distinct patterns. During the seedling-tiller period, SI3 (0.46), SI1 (0.36), NDVI (0.31), and SI2 (0.26) collectively accounted for 73.24% of the total importance. The importance of CCRI, CARI, and CRSI reflected low sensitivity during sparse vegetation periods. For the dormancy period, NDVI (0.46), SI1 (0.44), EVI (0.42), SI2 (0.41), and SI4 (0.29) were key estimative indicators. In the regreening period, SI2, SI3, NDVI, EVI, NDMI, and CCRI all exceeded 0.30 and collectively represented 71.13% of the total importance. In the jointing period, NDMI (0.71), NDWI (0.68), and CRSI (0.37) were identified as primary estimative indicators, showing increased sensitivity during vegetation development. For the booting-flowering period, NDVI (0.68) and EVI (0.64) were characterized by dominance. Finally, CRSI (0.71), SI2 (0.64), NDMI (0.52), NDWI (0.48), SI3 (0.41), and SI1 (0.39) collectively contributed 73.38% of the total importance in the grain filling period.

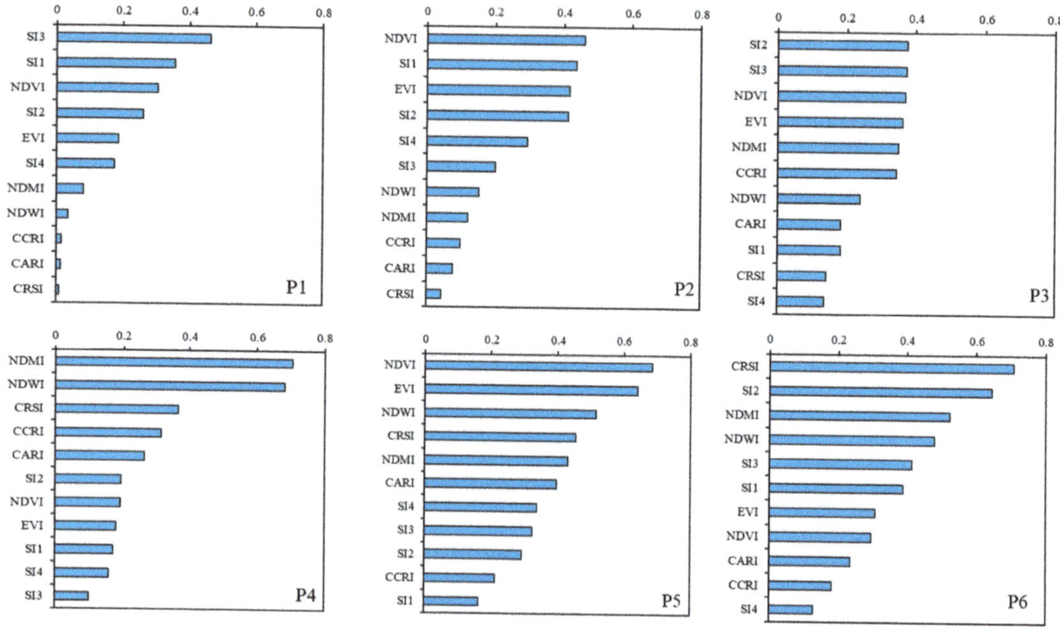

Figure 4. The importance of parameters in different growth periods. **(P1)**, seeding-tiller; **(P2)**, dormancy; **(P3)**, regreening; **(P4)**, jointing; **(P5)**, booting-flowering; **(P6)**, filling.

We performed feature parameter selection for each growth period based on their importance values to mitigate overfitting risks of information redundancy. Table A2 showed the cumulative contribution rate. The rate of parameters exceeding 70% were selected and systematically grouped into three combinations, including vegetation indexes alone, salinity indexes alone, and their combinations (VI + SI) as independent variables on yield estimation. The selection results are depicted in Table 6 and revealed distinct patterns. The results demonstrated that salinity indexes were dominant during P1 and P6 periods, while vegetation indexes showed greater sensitivity during P4 and P5 periods. During P2, although the NDVI demonstrated the highest sensitivity, indices SI1, SI2, and SI4 accounted for a substantial proportion of the cumulative contribution rate, demonstrating their complementary role in capturing soil stress during this critical overwintering phase when vegetation signals were attenuated.

Table 6. Feature parameter selection results from different periods.

Growth Periods	Vegetation Index	Salinity Index
P1	NDVI	SI1, SI2, SI3
P2	NDVI, EVI	SI1, SI3, SI4
P3	NDVI, EVI, NDMI, CCRI	SI2, SI3
P4	NDMI, NDWI, CCRI, CARI	CRSI
P5	NDVI, EVI, NDMI, NDWI, CARI	CRSI
P6	NDMI, NDWI	CRSI, SI2, SI3

3.2. Winter Wheat Yield Estimation Using Random Forest

As shown in Figure 5, single temporal remote sensing parameter-based wheat yield estimation modeling revealed period-dependent performance: the VI-based group model achieved optimal results during P5 (R^2 = 0.64, RMSE = 1268.2 kg/ha), while the SI-based model performed better in P6 (R^2 = 0.56, RMSE = 1465.6 kg/ha). Notably, the VI + SI-based model demonstrated promising performance in P5 (R^2 = 0.65, RMSE = 1214.5 kg/ha).

To enhance yield estimation accuracy across growth periods, we employed a progressive time-step approach (P1, P1–P2, P1–P3, P1–P4, P1–P5, P1–P6) to investigate information contribution. Using the random forest regression method, we analyzed VI-, SI-, and VI + SI-based group models and compared R^2 and RMSE. The results demonstrated the consistent superiority of VI + SI-based models over single-index methods in all periods.

The R^2 values of different groups exhibited the order of VI + SI > SI > VI during pre-jointing growth periods (P1–P3). Compared to R^2 of P1, R^2 of integrated P1–P2 increased from 0.12 to 0.27 for the VI-based model, 0.15 to 0.37 for the SI-based model, and reached 0.43 for the VI + SI-based model. For P3, R^2 of the VI + SI-based model achieved 0.55, demonstrating a 22.53% accuracy advantage over the VI-based model. R^2 exhibited a hierarchy of VI + SI > VI > SI due to increased vegetation coverage during post-jointing growth periods. R^2 of the VI + SI-based model maintained substantial improvements: 14.33% and 18.81% higher values than VI and SI across P1–P4, respectively, with an R^2 of 0.75 (VI + SI-based model) versus 0.71 (VI-based model) and 0.65 (SI-based model) at P1–P5. Across the complete growth periods (P1–P6), the R^2 (0.77) and RMSE (762.33 kg/ha) of the VI + SI-based model demonstrated consistent improvements over those of the VI-based model (R^2 = 0.71, RMSE = 867.17 kg/ha) and SI-based model (R^2 = 0.69, RMSE = 900.04 kg/ha), with R^2 gains of 8.45% and 11.59%, respectively.

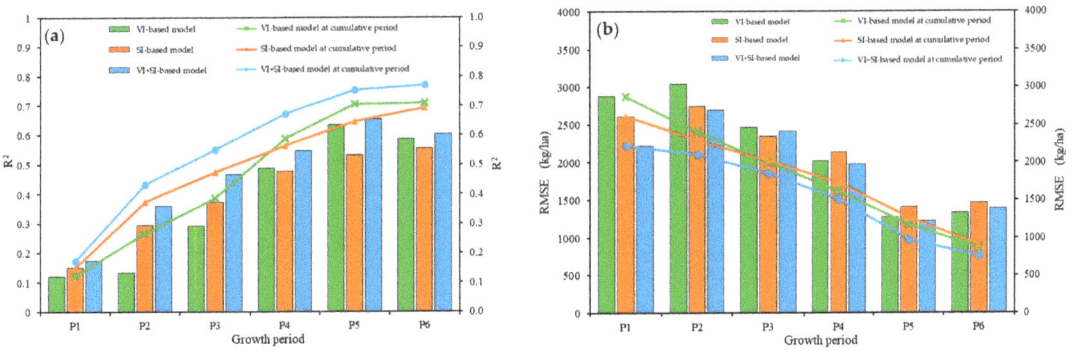

Figure 5. R^2 (**a**) and RMSE (**b**) of different yield estimation models for each single and cumulative growth period. P1, seeding-tiller; P2, dormancy; P3, regreening; P4, jointing; P5, booting-flowering; P6, filling.

The model in the VI + SI-based group achieved a good performance across the P1–P6 periods. To further enhance accuracy, we integrated field-measured soil salt content (SC) data to establish a VI + SI + SC-based composite model. As illustrated in Figure 6d, the integration of field soil parameters improved the estimative capability, and the R^2 and RMSE in the VI + SI + SC-based model were 0.78 and 720.16 kg/ha, respectively. Compared with VI-based, SI-based, and VI + SI-based models, the R^2 in VI + SI + SC-based group increased by 9.86%, 13.04%, and 1.30%, respectively.

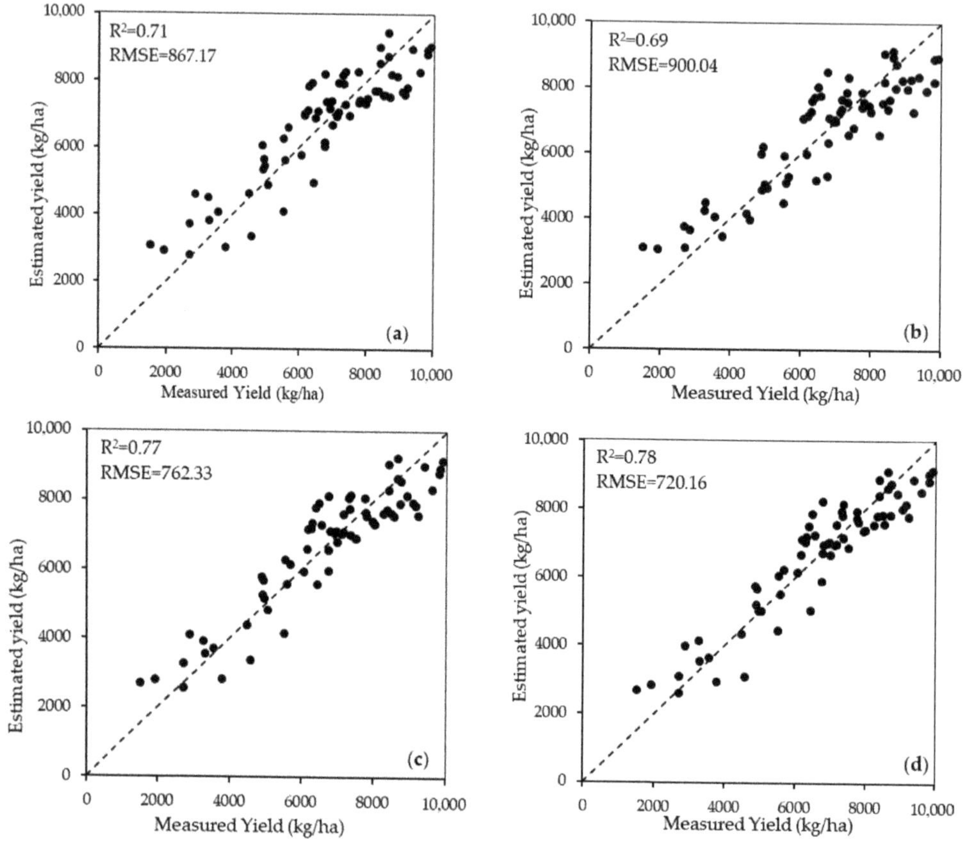

Figure 6. The R^2 and RMSE of winter wheat yield estimations in the VI-based (**a**), SI-based (**b**), VI + SI-based (**c**), VI + SI + SC-based (**d**) groups.

3.3. Estimation Error Under Different Salinity Levels

We analyzed the residuals of estimated and field-measured yields at different salinity levels (Table 1) to evaluate model generalization across salinity gradients, as shown in Figure 7. Positive residuals indicated overestimation, while negative values suggested underestimation. In general, the results in slight salinity demonstrated optimal performance (mean residual under all groups: 0.42 kg/ha), and the yields in moderate and severe salinity were overestimated (corresponding mean residual: 281.65, 920.84 kg/ha, respectively).

Detailed model performance analysis showed variations across salinity gradients. At the no salinity level, compared to VI-based and SI-based models, the VI + SI-based model reduced estimation errors, and the residual ranged from −1651.08 to 1405.48 kg/ha. The VI + SI + SC-based model exhibited a residual with a value of −1429.79 to 1466.41 kg/ha, which maintained a relatively lower mean residual. For the slight salinity level, both VI + SI-based and VI + SI + SC-based models exhibited tighter residual distributions for better capturing yield variations. At the moderate salinity level, the estimated accuracy improved progressively with model complexity, as shown by decreasing mean residuals from 385.09 kg/ha (VI-based model) and 373.36 kg/ha (SI-based model) to 220.83 kg/ha (VI + SI-based model) and finally 147.30 kg/ha (VI + SI + SC-based model). At the severe salinity level, the mean residual of VI + SI + SC-based model was 696.01 kg/ha, representing reductions of 43.01%, 28.77%, and 11.77% compared with VI-based, SI-based, and VI + SI based models.

The comprehensive analysis results demonstrated that the VI + SI + SC-based model showed distinct advantages in feature extraction across high salinity gradients and effectively integrated crop and soil factors to achieve more accurate yield estimation.

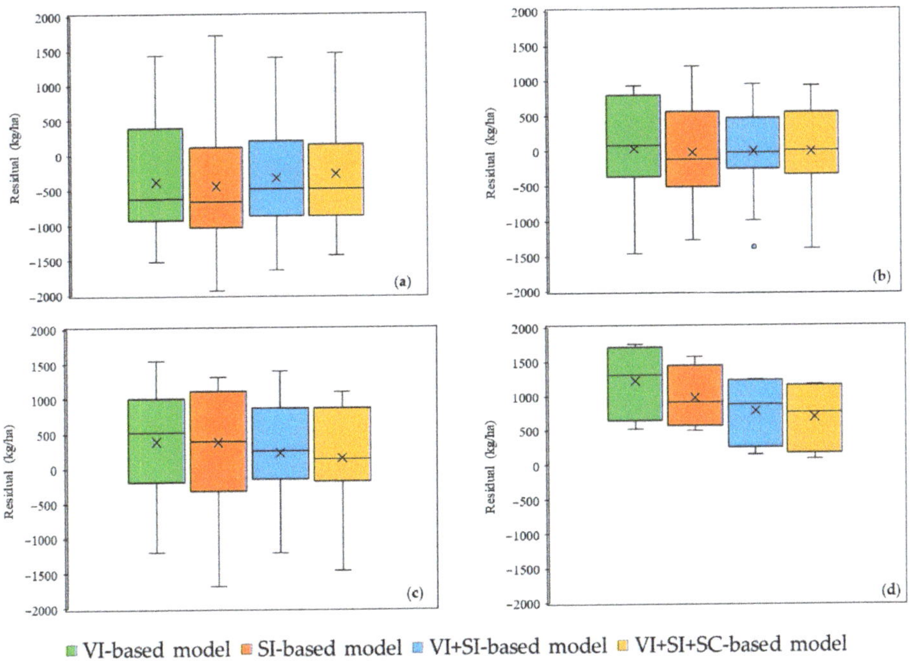

Figure 7. Residual box diagram of different models under no salinity (**a**), slight salinity (**b**), moderate salinity (**c**), and severe salinity (**d**).

3.4. Winter Wheat Yield Mapping and Feature Analysis

Based on the previous analysis and results, we employed the VI + SI + SC-based model using random forest to generate a county-level yield map of winter wheat by integrating its spatial distribution data, as shown in Figure 8. The estimated wheat yield ranged from 2100 to 10,310 kg/ha (mean = 6771 kg/ha), which was consistent with the statistical data from the Kenli government during the same period.

Winter wheat yield maps using VI-based, SI-based, and VI + SI-based models were also produced, and yield map comparisons of the subsets are presented in Figure 9. In no salinity areas, all models showed minor spatial variation of winter wheat yield. In saline-affected regions, the VI-based model demonstrated limited sensitivity to salinity-induced yield changes, while the VI + SI-based and VI + SI + SC-based models effectively captured critical yield-related information using multi-parameter integration and time-series analysis to outperform single-parameter models.

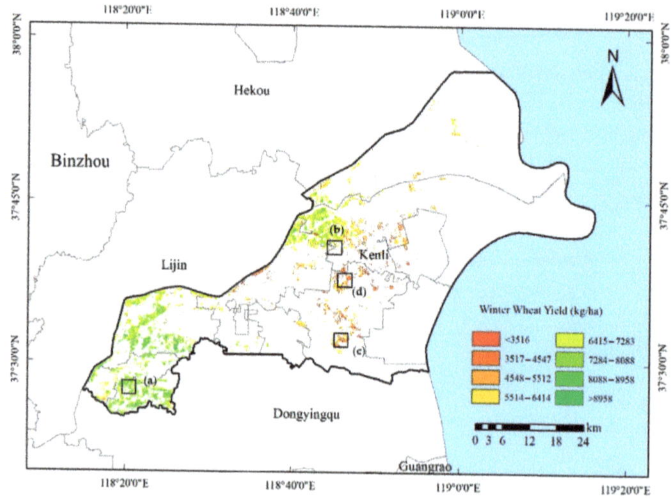

Figure 8. Spatial distribution of winter wheat yield using the VI + SI + SC-based model. The subsets (a–d) are used for detailed exhibition in Figure 9.

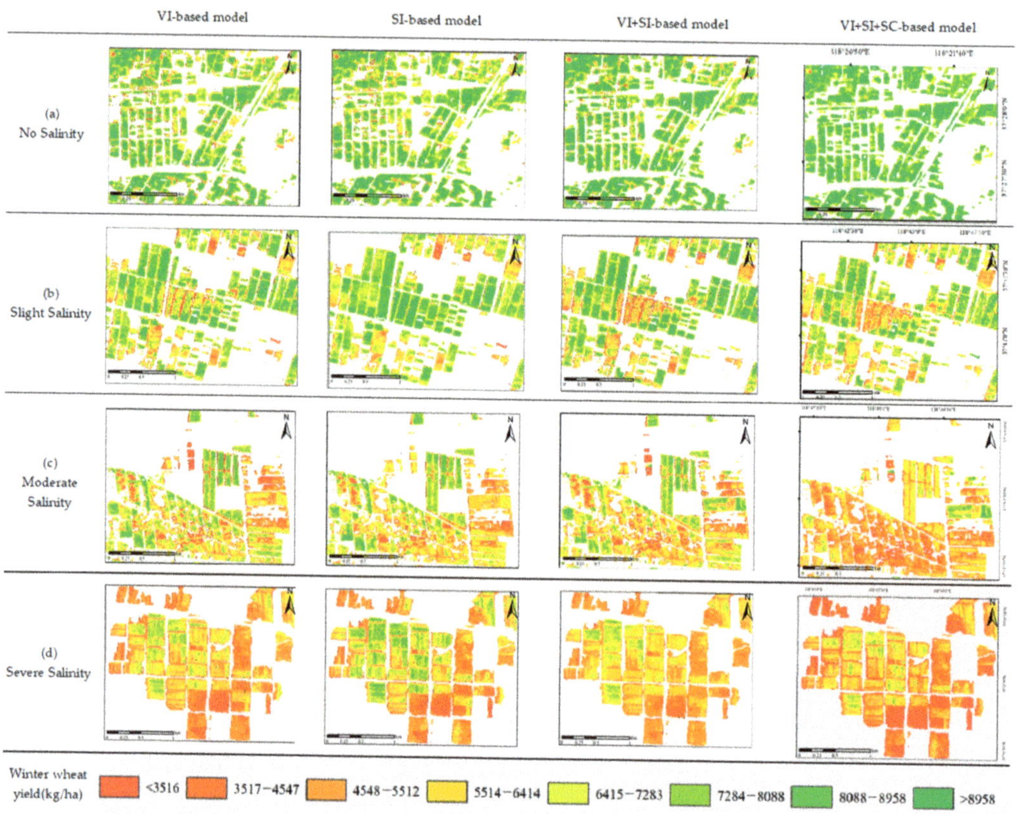

Figure 9. Comparison of winter wheat yield estimation results using different models at different salinity levels located in the subsets in Figure 8.

Compared with the soil salinity interpolation results in Figure 2, the spatial distribution of winter wheat yield in Figure 8 strongly correlated with soil salinity levels. High yields were concentrated in western regions, and low yields clustered in the central and eastern areas. According to the violin plot of the yield data distribution shown in Figure 10, the average yield in the no salinity areas mainly distributed in southwest and north was 7945 kg/ha, and most yields fell within the range of 7200–8800 kg/ha. Slight saline areas were predominantly distributed along the Yellow River in the western region, with an average yield of 7258 kg/ha. Moderate and severe saline areas in central regions showed reduced yields of 5217 kg/ha and 4707 kg/ha, respectively.

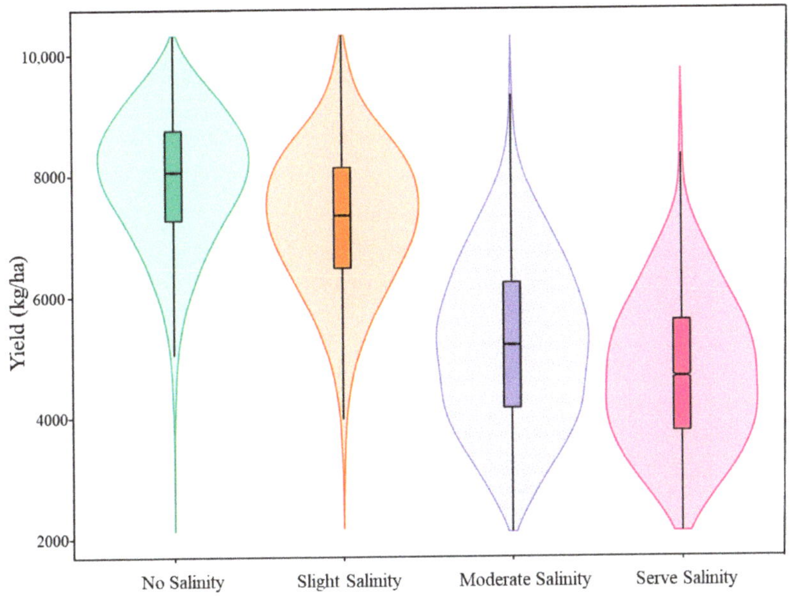

Figure 10. Violin plots of winter wheat yield for different salinity levels.

4. Discussion

4.1. Importance Analysis of Parameters in Each Period

Feature selection for input parameters of yield models is very important due to significant improvements in model accuracy and computational efficiency [36,37]. Given the dynamic accumulation process of wheat growth and its varied tolerance to seasonal soil salinity fluctuations, which are characterized by spring salt accumulation, summer leaching desalination, autumn re-accumulation via evaporation, and winter stabilization [38], in this study, period-specific feature selection of remote sensing parameters for winter wheat were implemented. This process qualitatively identifies key feature factors and quantitatively analyzes parameter importance for yield estimation. During early growth periods (seedling—dormancy), VI demonstrated relatively weak predictive performance due to insufficient dry matter accumulation. Conversely, multiple SI demonstrated higher predictive importance due to wheat's heightened sensitivity to saline stress during initial growth phases [39]. However, early-period soil feature extraction may be influenced by tillage practices, potentially causing instability of individual estimative features. To address this, multiple indexes (SI1, SI3, and SI4) were integrated to enhance the stability and reliability of parameter–soil salinity correlations. During the jointing period, when wheat experiences peak water demand and concurrent topsoil salt accumulation, canopy moisture indexes (NDWI and NDMI) exhibited better yield prediction performance. This enhancement may be attributed to their capacity to monitor irrigation-driven water availability under saline stress, a critical factor for final yield formation [40,41]. In addition, chlorophyll parameters (CARI and CCRI) showed increased estimative importance due to their sensitivity to salinity-induced chlorophyll degradation [42]. The booting-flowering period, when spike number per unit area is determined and leaf area stabilizes, showed the highest predictive utility of vegetation indexes (NDVI, EVI, NDMI, NDWI, CARI). This critical phase affects final grain weight and spike fertility, explaining the high accuracy regression models, which were consistent with established physiological principles [43,44]. During grain filling, although chlorophyll degradation and leaf senescence reduce VI predictive capacity, data integration remains essential due to salinity's potential impact on dry matter partitioning. Notably, post-vegetative growth period analysis revealed weaker yield correlations for SI1 and SI4, while CRSI maintained stronger correlations. By analyzing vegetation canopy spectral responses to salt stress, CRSI effectively integrates vegetation indexes and soil salinity characteristics, accurately reflecting the impacts of soil salinity on vegetation growth [45].

4.2. Comparisons of Different Parameter Combinations

Saline stress impairs yield formation through multiple mechanisms: inhibiting leaf expansion, weakening chlorophyll synthesis, accelerating foliar water loss, and restraining grain filling [46]. While vegetation indexes (e.g., NDVI, CARI) effectively characterize canopy structure and growth status, their utility is limited under saline conditions due to reduced dry matter allocation to reproductive growth [47,48], potentially leading to yield estimation inaccuracies. The VI + SI + SC-based model developed in this study enhanced yield estimation accuracy across varying salinity levels. The model's effectiveness stems from two key aspects. On the one hand, soil salt content data, which demonstrated a strong negative correlation with yield ($r = -0.77$, Figure 11), were incorporated. This integration improved physiological state representation, reducing estimation errors in moderate-to-severe salinity levels. Similar benefits were observed in Lebrija's saline farmland, where combining soil electrical conductivity with NDVI imagery enhanced spatial assessment of crop growth impacts during tomato–cotton–sugar rotation seasons [49]. On the other hand, salinity index integration provided crucial soil salinity information, particularly during low vegetation cover periods when VI was weak. This complement effectively addressed early growth period monitoring limitations under saline stress, corroborating findings from Karimli's high-precision wheat yield estimation in Jalilabad [12] and Li et al.'s successful soil salinity inversion [28]. Notably, the integration of SC into the VI + SI-based model resulted in only marginal improvement (R^2 increasing from 0.77 to 0.78), which may be explained by the following factors including the temporal mismatch between soil salinity sampling and crop growth dynamics, compensatory effects between SC and SI, and spatial resolution limitations inherent in the 10 km^2 interpolation approach. Despite these limitations, the inclusion of SC provided essential soil constraints that significantly reduced model residuals under our experimental conditions. For other soil types exhibiting lower risk thresholds [50], the model's performance improvement with SC incorporation may be more pronounced. From a practical standpoint, soil data integration offers valuable yield estimation corrections, especially for smaller study areas where such data are readily available. However, extensive sampling and mapping requirements make this approach impractical for larger regions. In such cases, the VI + SI-based model demonstrates reasonable estimation capability through mutual complementarity.

Model validation revealed that in saline-affected areas, poor canopy structure indicated by low VI values led to overestimation. The integrated model effectively captured yield variations across salinity gradients, enabling accurate yield mapping. Regional analysis showed progressive yield reductions of 8.65%, 34.33%, and 40.76% in slight, moderate, and severe saline areas compared to no salinity conditions, highlighting wheat's limited tolerance to moderate and severe saline stress. The results had practical significance for both operational forecasting and precision management. The model's ability to achieve moderate early-season accuracy (Figure 5) at 10 m resolution enables timely identification of salinity stress hotspots before irreversible yield loss occurs. Farmers could leverage this for targeted irrigation scheduling at the field scale. The spatial yield-salinity deviation maps (Figures 8 and 9) facilitate zone-specific interventions. Severe salinity zones (SC > 4 g/kg, and yield <4707 kg/ha) may require land rehabilitation, subsurface drainage, or alternative crops to mitigate high-salinity stress risks. Moderate salinity zones will benefit from soil amendments such as gypsum or organic matter, while slight salinity zones can adopt preventive measures like salt-tolerant cultivars. For policymakers, the results offer a scalable framework to monitor salinity's impact on productivity as part of strategies for safeguarding food security, aligning with China's 'Saline Soil Utilization' policy.

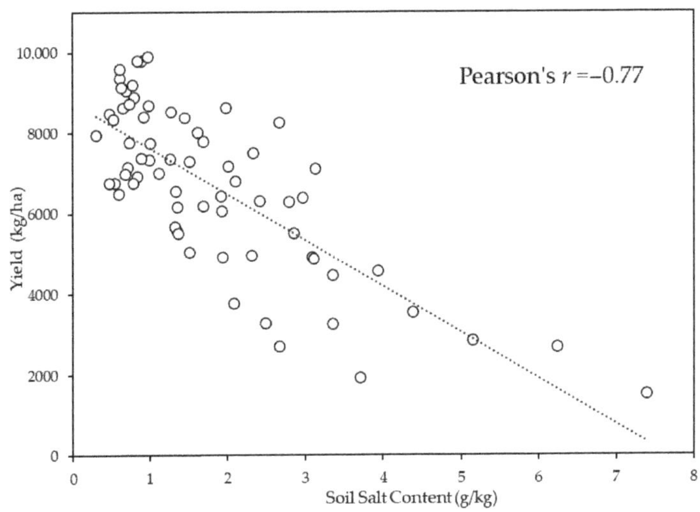

Figure 11. Correlation analysis of winter wheat yield and soil salt content in 2024.

4.3. Uncertainty Analysis

As shown in Figure 12, a comparison experiment demonstrates that RF and XGBoost consistently outperformed other methods across all combinations (VI-based model, SI-based model, VI + SI-based model, and VI + SI + SC-based model; P1~P6 cumulative periods). For the VI + SI + SC-based model, both RF and XGBoost algorithms achieved superior performance with R^2 values of 0.78 and 0.79 and RMSE values of 720.16 and 712.89 kg/ha, respectively, significantly surpassing PLSR (R^2 = 0.69) and LSTM (R^2 = 0.74). In the VI + SI-based model, RF achieved comparable performance to XGBoost (R^2 = 0.77). Although XGBoost exhibited marginally higher accuracy, RF was selected based on comprehensive evaluation of prediction stability, computational efficiency, and model explainability. Moreover, given our limited sample size (n = 68), RF's inherent mechanisms including out-of-bag error estimation and bootstrap aggregation provide robust performance validation and prevent overfitting, as evidenced by previous studies using small datasets [51]. In comparative experiments of various yield estimation modeling approaches, RF demonstrated superior stability [32,52,53]. However, the model was developed and validated using data from a single growing season. Given the interannual variations in precipitation, soil salinity, and management, its applicability to other years may be limited. Future studies should incorporate multi-year datasets to enhance validation reliability and address potential uncertainties in the algorithm's extrapolation performance across broader agricultural contexts.

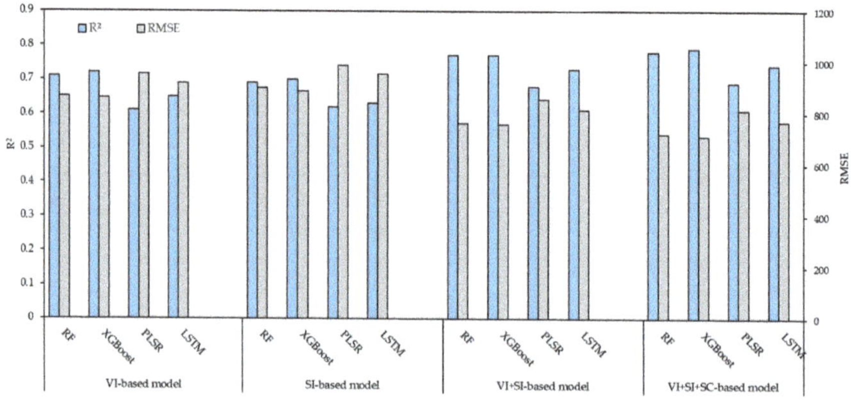

Figure 12. Comparison results of different methods.

Data sources used in this study have two primary limitations. First, the even sampling density across heterogeneous salinity distributions resulted in imbalanced sample representativeness, particularly with limited data from severe salinity areas to potentially affect estimation accuracy. Second, soil salt content data measured in the harvest period provide general plot-level salinity characterization, representing relationships between parameters at different periods (Figure 13), but they cannot fully capture the dynamic salinity variations. These limitations highlight the need for further validation of temporal relationships among soil salt content, salinity indexes, and crop yield using comprehensive multi-source datasets. In digital soil salinity mapping, future research would benefit from incorporating regression Kriging or co-Kriging methodologies.

Regarding regional specificity, the model was developed based on loam and sandy loam textured soils and did not incorporate different soil texture parameters. These parameters are known to affect salinity tolerance through their influence on soil structure, porosity, and hydraulic properties [54]. This texture-specific development may constrain the model's transferability to other saline regions with distinct soil matrices. Future studies will integrate water and salt transport characteristics across varying soil textures and implement stress risk calibration. Furthermore, while the winter wheat distribution map demonstrated good accuracy, it must be acknowledged that classification uncertainty may propagate to the yield estimation. The robustness of our yield model (R^2 = 0.78) and the leave-one-out cross-validation approach likely helped mitigate some classification-related uncertainties. Residual analysis showed no strong systematic patterns attributable to classification errors, although we cannot completely rule out some localized effects. We will further discuss these limitations and suggest methods to reduce uncertainties in future studies.

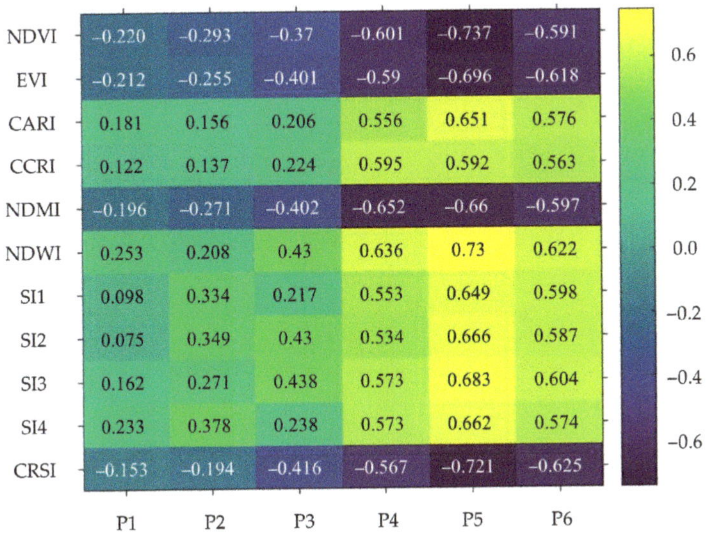

Figure 13. Correlation of remote sensing parameters in different periods with soil salt content in harvest period.

5. Conclusions

This study investigated winter wheat yield estimation in salinity areas of Kenli County, Yellow River Delta, China, by developing random forest regression models incorporating vegetation indexes, salinity indexes derived from Sentinel-2 images, and surface soil salt content. The results and findings are outlined as follows:

(1) The dominant yield estimation parameters varied across growth periods. SI (SI1, SI2, SI3) had higher feature importance in pre-jointing periods, while VI (e.g., NDMI) demonstrated greater estimative importance for winter wheat yield in post-jointing periods.

(2) The combined VI + SI-based method within the RF framework demonstrated a good wheat yield estimation performance during the wheat flowering stage among single-temporal analyses (R^2 = 0.65, RMSE = 1214.5 kg/ha). In the cumulative period, the VI + SI-based model (R^2 = 0.77, RMSE = 762.33 kg/ha) significantly outperformed individual VI-based or SI-based models, and its R^2 correspondingly improved by 8.45% and 11.59%, respectively. The VI + SI + SC-based model achieved the optimal estimation accuracy, and the R^2 improved by 9.86%, 13.04%, and 1.30% compared to VI-based, SI-based, and VI + SI-based models, respectively.

(3) Salinity stress affected yield estimation accuracy. The incorporation of SI and SC data played a crucial role in error reduction. At the moderate salinity level, mean residuals decreased from 385.09 kg/ha (VI-based) to 220.83 kg/ha (VI + SI-based) and 147.30 kg/ha (VI + SI + SC-based). At the severe salinity level, although all models exhibited overestimation, the VI + SI + SC-based model showed the closest approximation to measured yields (mean residual = 696.01 kg/ha), representing a 43.01% reduction versus the VI-based model.

The results demonstrated the effectiveness of multi-source parameters for accurate estimation of winter wheat yield across no salinity (7945 kg/ha), slight (7258 kg/ha), moderate (5217 kg/ha), and severe (4707 kg/ha) salinity areas in 2024, providing a critical reference for refining planting strategies and decision making. Future research should develop alternative regression algorithms and incorporate dynamic soil salinity data to further enhance estimation accuracy.

Author Contributions: Conceptualization, C.L. and S.D.; investigation, C.L. and Y.L. (Yu Liu); writing-original draft preparation, C.L.; writing—review and editing, C.L., M.Y. and S.D.; project administration, Y.L. (Yinkun Li); supervision, Y.P.; funding acquisition, S.D. All authors have read and agreed to the published version of the manuscript.

Funding: This research was funded by the National Key R & D Program of China (Grant Number 2023YFD2001401) and the National Natural Science Foundation of China (Grant Number 32201442).

Institutional Review Board Statement: Not applicable.

Data Availability Statement: The data presented in this study are available on request from the corresponding author due to privacy.

Conflicts of Interest: Author Chuang Lu, Shiwei Dong and Yinkun Li was employed by the company Beijing PAIDE Science and Technology Development Co., Ltd. The remaining authors declare that the research was conducted in the absence of any commercial or financial relationships that could be construed as a potential conflict of interest.

Appendix A

Table A1. Confusion matrix.

Classes	Winter Wheat	Non-Winter Wheat	Producer Accuracy/%	User Accuracy/%	Overall Accuracy/%	Kappa
Winter wheat	132	18	90.41	88.00	92.45	0.85
Non-winter wheat	14	260	93.53	94.89		

Table A2. The cumulative contribution rate (CCR) of importance in different periods.

P1		P2		P3		P4		P5		P6	
Variable	CCR/%	Variable	CCR/%	Variable	CCR/%	Variable	CCR/%	Variable	CCR/%	Variable	CCR/%
SI3	24.38	NDVI	16.97	SI2	12.27	NDMI	21.24	NDVI	15.35	CRSI	16.40
SI1	43.26	SI1	33.07	SI3	24.49	NDWI	41.81	EVI	29.70	SI2	31.39
NDVI	59.40	EVI	48.37	NDVI	36.58	CRSI	52.80	NDWI	41.26	NDMI	43.58
SI2	73.24	SI2	63.53	EVI	48.44	CCRI	62.33	CRSI	51.46	NDWI	54.71
EVI	82.93	SI4	74.37	NDMI	59.87	CARI	70.33	NDMI	61.10	SI3	64.34
SI4	91.99	SI3	81.76	CCRI	71.13	SI2	76.11	CARI	70.02	SI1	73.38
NDMI	96.20	NDWI	87.39	NDWI	78.95	NDVI	81.83	SI4	77.62	EVI	80.51
NDWI	98.05	NDMI	91.86	CARI	84.96	EVI	87.19	SI3	84.93	NDVI	87.39
CCRI	98.81	CCRI	95.50	SI1	90.93	SI1	92.29	SI2	91.52	CARI	92.84
CARI	99.53	CARI	98.39	CRSI	95.54	SI4	97.03	CCRI	96.31	CCRI	97.04
CRSI	100.00	CRSI	100.00	SI4	100.00	SI3	100.00	SI1	100.00	SI4	100.00

References

1. Guo, B.; Liu, Y.; Fan, J.; Lu, M.; Zang, W.; Liu, C.; Wang, B.; Huang, X.; Lai, J.; Wu, H. The salinization process and its response to the combined processes of climate change–human activity in the Yellow River Delta between 1984 and 2022. *Catena* **2023**, *231*, 107301. [CrossRef]
2. Chen, X.; Huang, Q.; Xiong, Y.; Yang, Q.; Li, H.; Hou, Z.; Huang, G. Tracking the spatio-temporal change of the main food crop planting structure in the Yellow River Basin over 2001–2020. *Comput. Electron. Agr.* **2023**, *212*, 108102. [CrossRef]
3. Su, W.; Magdziarczyk, M.; Smolinski, A. Increasing overall agricultural productivity in the Yellow River Delta Eco-economic Zone in China. *Reg. Environ. Change* **2024**, *24*, 64. [CrossRef]
4. Zhu, W.; Li, S.; Zhang, X.; Li, Y.; Sun, Z. Estimation of winter wheat yield using optimal vegetation indices from unmanned aerial vehicle remote sensing. *Trans. Chin. Soc. Agric. Eng.* **2018**, *34*, 78–86.
5. Satir, O.; Berberoglu, S. Crop yield prediction under soil salinity using satellite derived vegetation indices. *Field Crops Res.* **2016**, *192*, 134–143. [CrossRef]

6. Shi, F.; Wang, R.; Li, Y.; Yan, H.; Zhang, X. LAI estimation based on multi-spectral remote sensing of UAV and its application in saline soil improvement. *Sci. Agric. Sin.* **2020**, *53*, 1795–1805.
7. Chen, Y.; Zhao, G.; Chang, C.; Wang, Z.; Li, Y.; Zhao, H.; Pan, J. Grain yield estimation of wheat-maize rotation cultivated land based on Sentinel-2 multi-spectral image: A case study in Caoxian County, Shandong, China. *Chin. J. Appl. Ecol.* **2023**, *34*, 3347–3356.
8. Zhao, L.; Hua, L.; Hui, C.; Zhang, S. Maize yield forecasting and associated optimum lead time research based on temporal remote sensing data and different model. *Spectrosc. Spect. Anal.* **2023**, *43*, 2627–2637.
9. Abbas, F.; Afzaal, H.; Farooque, A.A.; Tang, S. Crop yield prediction through proximal sensing and machine learning algorithms. *Agronomy* **2020**, *10*, 1046. [CrossRef]
10. Han, J.; Zhang, Z.; Cao, J.; Luo, Y.; Zhang, L.; Li, Z.; Zhang, J. Prediction of winter wheat yield based on multi-source data and machine learning in China. *Remote Sens.* **2020**, *12*, 236. [CrossRef]
11. Mustafa, G.; Moazzam, M.A.; Nawaz, A.; Ali, T.; Alsekait, D.M.; Alattas, A.S.; AbdElminaam, D.S. ECP-IEM: Enhancing seasonal crop productivity with deep integrated models. *PLoS ONE* **2025**, *20*, e316682.
12. Karimli, N.; Selbesoğlu, M.O. Remote sensing-based yield estimation of winter wheat using vegetation and soil indices in Jalilabad, Azerbaijan. *ISPRS. Int. J. Geo-Inf.* **2023**, *12*, 124. [CrossRef]
13. Mahboob, W.; Rizwan, M.; Irfan, M.; Hafeez, O.B.A.; Sarwar, N.; Akhtar, M.; Munir, M.; Rani, R. Salinity tolerance in wheat: Responses, mechanisms and adaptation approaches. *Appl. Ecol. Env. Res.* **2023**, *21*, 5299–5328. [CrossRef]
14. Wang, W.; Zou, J.; Zhang, Y.; Niu, L.; Yu, L.; Wang, Z.; Wang, F.; Zhang, S.; Yang, X. Salinity stress phenotyping of wheat germplasm under multiple growth conditions and transcriptomic analysis of two wheat varieties contrasting in their salinity stress tolerance. *Plant Growth Regul.* **2025**, *105*, 739–757. [CrossRef]
15. Zhang, Z.; Fan, Y.; Zhang, A.; Jiao, Z. Baseline-Based Soil Salinity Index (BSSI): A novel remote sensing monitoring method of soil salinization. *IEEE J. Stars.* **2023**, *16*, 202. [CrossRef]
16. Aboelsoud, H.M.; AbdelRahman, M.A.E.; Kheir, A.M.S.; Eid, M.S.M.; Ammar, K.A.; Khalifa, T.H.; Scopa, A. Quantitative estimation of saline-soil amelioration using remote-sensing indices in arid land for better management. *Land* **2022**, *11*, 1041. [CrossRef]
17. Cui, X.; Han, W.; Zhang, H.; Dong, Y.; Ma, W.; Zhai, X.; Zhang, L.; Li, G. Estimating and mapping the dynamics of soil salinity under different crop types using Sentinel-2 satellite imagery. *Geoderma* **2023**, *440*, 116738. [CrossRef]
18. Liu, X.; Hu, Y.; Zhang, S.; Bai, Y.; Zhang, H. Comparison of different salinity estimation models for salinized soils on south bank of Yellow River in Dalat Banner. *Trans. Chin. Soc. Agric. Mach.* **2024**, *55*, 360–370.
19. Wang, J.; Ding, J.; Ge, X.; Peng, J.; Hu, Z. Monitoring soil salinization on the basis of remote sensing and proximal soil sensing: Progress and perspective. *Nat. Remote Sens. Bull.* **2024**, *28*, 2187–2208.
20. Zhang, X.; Wang, Z.; Song, X.; Liu, P.; Li, S.; Yang, X. Effect of sampling on spatial variability in soil salinity in the Yellow River Delta Area. *Resour. Sci.* **2016**, *38*, 2375–2382.
21. Zhang, Z.; Song, Y.; Zhang, H.; Li, X.; Niu, B. Spatiotemporal dynamics of soil salinity in the Yellow River Delta under the impacts of hydrology and climate. *Chin. J. Appl. Ecol.* **2021**, *32*, 1393–1405.
22. Technical Regulations and Specifications for the Third National Soil Census (Revised Edition). Available online: http://www.moa.gov.cn/ztzl/dscqgtrpc/zywj/202307/t20230720_6432535.htm (accessed on 7 July 2023).
23. Yu, F.; Bai, J.; Fang, J.; Guo, S.; Zhu, S.; Xu, T. Integration of a parameter combination discriminator improves the accuracy of chlorophyll inversion from spectral imaging of rice. *Agric. Commun.* **2024**, *2*, 100055. [CrossRef]
24. Sellami, M.H.; Albrizio, R.; Čolović, M.; Hamze, M.; Cantore, V.; Todorovic, M.; Piscitelli, L.; Stellacci, A.M. Selection of hyperspectral vegetation indices for monitoring yield and physiological response in sweet maize under different water and nitrogen availability. *Agronomy* **2022**, *12*, 489. [CrossRef]
25. Gitelson, A.; Merzlyak, M. Remote estimation of chlorophyll content in higher plant leaves. *Int. J. Remote Sens.* **1997**, *18*, 2691–2697. [CrossRef]
26. Solgi, S.; Ahmadi, S.H.; Seidel, S.J. Remote sensing of canopy water status of the irrigated winter wheat fields and the paired anomaly analyses on the spectral vegetation indices and grain yields. *Agric. Water Manag.* **2023**, *280*, 108226. [CrossRef]
27. Jin, X.; Kumar, L.; Li, Z.; Xu, X.; Yang, G.; Wang, J. Estimation of winter wheat biomass and yield by combining the AquaCrop model and field hyperspectral data. *Remote Sens.* **2016**, *8*, 972. [CrossRef]
28. Li, Y.; Chang, C.; Wang, Z.; Zhao, G. Remote sensing prediction and characteristic analysis of cultivated land salinization in different seasons and multiple soil layers in the coastal area. *Int. J. Appl. Earth Obs.* **2022**, *111*, 102838. [CrossRef]
29. Scudiero, E.; Skaggs, T.H.; Corwin, D.L. Regional scale soil salinity evaluation using Landsat 7, western San Joaquin Valley, California, USA. *Geoderma Reg.* **2014**, *2*, 82–90. [CrossRef]

30. Zhou, K.; Liu, L.; Zhang, Y.; Miao, R.; Yang, Y. Area Extraction and growth monitoring of winter wheat in Henan province supported by Google Earth Engine. *Sci. Agric. Sin.* **2021**, *54*, 2302–2318.
31. Zhang, D.; Ying, C.; Wu, L.; Meng, Z.; Wang, X.; Ma, Y. Using time series sentinel images for object-oriented crop extraction of planting structure in the Google Earth Engine. *Agronomy* **2023**, *13*, 2350. [CrossRef]
32. Jabed, M.A.; Azmi Murad, M.A. Crop yield prediction in agriculture: A comprehensive review of machine learning and deep learning approaches, with insights for future research and sustainability. *Heliyon* **2024**, *10*, e40836. [CrossRef] [PubMed]
33. Feng, H.; Fan, Y.; Yue, J.; Ma, Y.; Liu, Y.; Chen, R.; Fu, Y.; Jin, X.; Bian, M.; Fan, J.; et al. Enhancing potato leaf protein content, carbon-based constituents, and leaf area index monitoring using radiative transfer model and deep learning. *Eur. J. Agron.* **2025**, *166*, 127580. [CrossRef]
34. Wang, Y.; Chen, H.; Chen, J.; Wang, H.; Xing, Z.; Zhang, Z. Comparation of rice yield estimation model combining spectral index screening method and statistical regression algorithm. *Trans. Chin. Soc. Agric. Eng.* **2021**, *37*, 208–216.
35. Qader, S.H.; Dash, J.; Atkinson, P.M. Forecasting wheat and barley crop production in arid and semi-arid regions using remotely sensed primary productivity and crop phenology: A case study in Iraq. *Sci. Total Environ.* **2018**, *613*, 250–262. [CrossRef] [PubMed]
36. Fan, Y.; Liu, Y.; Yue, J.; Jin, X.; Chen, R.; Bian, M.; Ma, Y.; Yang, G.; Feng, H. Estimation of potato yield using a semi-mechanistic model developed by proximal remote sensing and environmental variables. *Comput. Electron. Agr.* **2024**, *223*, 109117. [CrossRef]
37. Li, Z.; Zhou, X.; Cheng, Q.; Zhai, W.; Mao, B.; Li, Y.; Chen, Z. An integrated feature selection approach to high water stress yield prediction. *Front. Plant Sci.* **2023**, *14*, 1289692. [CrossRef] [PubMed]
38. Fu, T. The Temporal and Spatial Variation of Soil Salinization in Typical Coastal Area and Application Research of the Monitoring System. Ph.D. Thesis, Chinese Academy of Sciences, Beijing, China, 2015.
39. Saddiq, M.S.; Iqbal, S.; Hafeez, M.B.; Ibrahim, A.M.H.; Raza, A.; Fatima, E.M.; Baloch, H.; Jahanzaib; Woodrow, P.; Ciarmiello, L.F. Effect of Salinity stress on physiological changes in winter and spring wheat. *Agronomy* **2021**, *11*, 1193. [CrossRef]
40. Yue, J.; Li, T.; Feng, H.; Fu, Y.; Liu, Y.; Tian, J.; Yang, H.; Yang, G. Enhancing field soil moisture content monitoring using laboratory-based soil spectral measurements and radiative transfer models. *Agric. Commun.* **2024**, *2*, 100060. [CrossRef]
41. Wang, T.; Xu, Z.; Pang, G. Effects of Irrigating with Brackish Water on soil moisture, soil salinity, and the agronomic response of winter wheat in the Yellow River Delta. *Sustainability* **2019**, *11*, 5801. [CrossRef]
42. Shah, S.; Houborg, R.; McCabe, M. Response of Chlorophyll, Carotenoid and SPAD-502 measurement to salinity and nutrient stress in wheat (*Triticum aestivum* L.). *Agronomy* **2017**, *7*, 61. [CrossRef]
43. Cai, Y.; Guan, K.; Lobell, D.; Potgieter, A.B.; Wang, S.; Peng, J.; Xu, T.; Asseng, S.; Zhang, Y.; You, L.; et al. Integrating satellite and climate data to predict wheat yield in Australia using machine learning approaches. *Agr. Forest Meteorol.* **2019**, *274*, 144–159. [CrossRef]
44. Li, Y.; Zhao, B.; Wang, J.; Li, Y.; Yuan, Y. Winter wheat yield estimation based on multi-temporal and multi-sensor remote sensing data fusion. *Agriculture* **2023**, *13*, 2190. [CrossRef]
45. Wang, D.; Yang, H.; Qian, H.; Gao, L.; Li, C.; Xin, J.; Tan, Y.; Wang, Y.; Li, Z. Minimizing vegetation influence on soil salinity mapping with novel bare soil pixels from multi-temporal images. *Geoderma* **2023**, *439*, 116697. [CrossRef]
46. Rani, S.; Sharma, M.K.; Kumar, N.; Neelam. Impact of salinity and Zinc application on growth, physiological and yield traits in wheat. *Curr. Sci.* **2019**, *116*, 1324–1330. [CrossRef]
47. Feng, H.; Fan, Y.; Yue, J.; Bian, M.; Liu, Y.; Chen, R.; Ma, Y.; Fan, J.; Yang, G.; Zhao, C. Estimation of potato above-ground biomass based on the VGC-AGB model and deep learning. *Comput. Electron. Agr.* **2025**, *232*, 110122. [CrossRef]
48. Zhao, L.; Li, F.; Chang, Q. Review on crop type identification and yield forecasting using remote sensing. *Trans. Chin. Soc. Agric. Mach.* **2023**, *54*, 1–19.
49. Gómez Flores, J.L.; Ramos Rodríguez, M.; González Jiménez, A.; Farzamian, M.; Herencia Galán, J.F.; Salvatierra Bellido, B.; Cermeño Sacristan, P.; Vanderlinden, K. Depth-Specific soil electrical conductivity and NDVI elucidate salinity effects on crop development in reclaimed marsh soils. *Remote Sens.* **2022**, *14*, 3389. [CrossRef]
50. Dai, X.; Huo, Z.; Wang, H. Simulation for response of crop yield to soil moisture and salinity with artificial neural network. *Field Crops. Res.* **2011**, *121*, 441–449. [CrossRef]
51. Gómez, D.; Salvador, P.; Sanz, J.; Casanova, J.L. Potato yield prediction using machine learning techniques and sentinel 2 data. *Remote Sens.* **2019**, *11*, 1745. [CrossRef]
52. Khodjaev, S.; Bobojonov, I.; Kuhn, L.; Glauben, T. Optimizing machine learning models for wheat yield estimation using a comprehensive UAV dataset. *Model. Earth Syst. Environ.* **2025**, *11*, 15. [CrossRef]

53. Subhashree, S.N.; Marcaida, M.; Sunoj, S.; Kindred, D.R.; Thompson, L.J.; Ketterings, Q.M. Exploring the use of high-resolution satellite images to estimate corn silage yield within field. *Remote Sens.* **2024**, *16*, 4081. [CrossRef]
54. Zhang, X.; Zuo, Y.; Wang, T.; Han, Q. Salinity effects on soil structure and hydraulic properties: Implications for pedotransfer functions in coastal areas. *Land* **2024**, *13*, 2077. [CrossRef]

agriculture

MDPI

Article

Wheat Powdery Mildew Severity Classification Based on an Improved ResNet34 Model

Meilin Li [1], Yufeng Guo [1], Wei Guo [1], Hongbo Qiao [1], Lei Shi [1], Yang Liu [2], Guang Zheng [1], Hui Zhang [1] and Qiang Wang [1,*]

[1] College of Information and Management Sciences, Henan Agricultural University, Zhengzhou 450046, China; limeilin@stu.henau.edu.cn (M.L.); guoyufeng@henau.edu.cn (Y.G.); guowei@henau.edu.cn (W.G.); qiaohb@126.com (H.Q.); shilei@henau.edu.cn (L.S.); zhengguang@henau.edu.cn (G.Z.); huizi@henau.edu.cn (H.Z.)

[2] Key Lab of Smart Agriculture System, Ministry of Education, China Agricultural University, Beijing 100083, China; liuyanghe810@cau.edu.cn

* Correspondence: wqhda@henau.edu.cn

Abstract: Crop disease identification is a pivotal research area in smart agriculture, forming the foundation for disease mapping and targeted prevention strategies. Among the most prevalent global wheat diseases, powdery mildew—caused by fungal infection—poses a significant threat to crop yield and quality, making early and accurate detection crucial for effective management. In this study, we present QY-SE-MResNet34, a deep learning-based classification model that builds upon ResNet34 to perform multi-class classification of wheat leaf images and assess powdery mildew severity at the single-leaf level. The proposed methodology begins with dataset construction following the GBT 17980.22-2000 national standard for powdery mildew severity grading, resulting in a curated collection of 4248 wheat leaf images at the grain-filling stage across six severity levels. To enhance model performance, we integrated transfer learning with ResNet34, leveraging pretrained weights to improve feature extraction and accelerate convergence. Further refinements included embedding a Squeeze-and-Excitation (SE) block to strengthen feature representation while maintaining computational efficiency. The model architecture was also optimized by modifying the first convolutional layer (conv1)—replacing the original 7 × 7 kernel with a 3 × 3 kernel, adjusting the stride to 1, and setting padding to 1—to better capture fine-grained leaf textures and edge features. Subsequently, the optimal training strategy was determined through hyperparameter tuning experiments, and GrabCut-based background processing along with data augmentation were introduced to enhance model robustness. In addition, interpretability techniques such as channel masking and Grad-CAM were employed to visualize the model's decision-making process. Experimental validation demonstrated that QY-SE-MResNet34 achieved an 89% classification accuracy, outperforming established models such as ResNet50, VGG16, and MobileNetV2 and surpassing the original ResNet34 by 11%. This study delivers a high-performance solution for single-leaf wheat powdery mildew severity assessment, offering practical value for intelligent disease monitoring and early warning systems in precision agriculture.

Keywords: wheat powdery mildew; deep learning; disease severity; image recognition; QY-SE-MResNet34 model

1. Introduction

Wheat powdery mildew, caused by *Blumeria graminis* f. sp. *tritici*, is a devastating fungal disease that severely impacts global wheat production. By impairing leaf photosynthesis, the disease causes premature plant senescence, reduces grain filling efficiency, and leads to significant yield losses ranging from 10% to 50% [1], along with substantial deterioration in grain quality. The pathogen also decreases thousand-grain weight by 10–20% [2], compromises flour quality, and reduces the nutritional value and market competitiveness of wheat grains. Effective disease control requires an integrated strategy incorporating resistant cultivars, optimized field management, and timely fungicide application. Precise identification and severity assessment of powdery mildew infection are particularly critical, enabling farmers to minimize yield losses, optimize control measures, improve pesticide application efficiency, and prevent reductions in thousand-grain weight [3]. Furthermore, accurate disease evaluation facilitates the development of resistant varieties, supports precision agriculture implementation, and enhances the economic sustainability of wheat production systems. Current disease severity grading methods, while fundamental for diagnosis and control decisions, predominantly rely on manual visual assessment [4]. These conventional approaches are not only time-consuming and labor-intensive but also subjective and inconsistent, making them unsuitable for large-scale cultivation systems requiring rapid and accurate disease diagnosis. This pressing challenge highlights the urgent need for innovative solutions leveraging advanced computer vision and deep learning technologies to revolutionize disease identification and severity assessment in modern agriculture.

The rapid evolution of artificial intelligence and deep learning technologies has brought transformative progress to agricultural disease identification [5]. This field has witnessed a paradigm shift from manual assessment to automated, intelligent detection systems. Modern image recognition techniques, powered by machine learning and deep learning architectures, can efficiently process large-scale image datasets [6], offering unprecedented advantages in terms of processing speed, detection accuracy, operational objectivity, and non-destructive analysis [7]. These capabilities provide essential technological foundations for real-time disease monitoring and assessment. Current methodologies in plant disease image recognition primarily fall into two categories: traditional machine learning and deep learning approaches [8]. The conventional machine learning pipeline involves manual feature extraction, where experts identify and isolate key visual characteristics such as color histograms, texture patterns, and edge contours from images [9]. These handcrafted features are then processed using various machine learning algorithms, including principal component analysis (PCA) for dimensionality reduction, support vector machines (SVM) for classification, AdaBoost for ensemble learning, and K-means clustering for pattern recognition [10–13], ultimately enabling automated disease identification and severity assessment. For instance, Sowmiya et al. [14] proposed an Improved Quantum Whale Optimization Algorithm integrated with Principal Component Analysis (IQWO-PCA) to analyze tomato disease image datasets using a machine learning (ML) model, thereby facilitating the adoption of effective preventive measures against this agricultural threat. Piyush et al. [15] attained a diagnostic accuracy of 98% in the automated identification of apple fruit and apple tree diseases by integrating a comprehensive feature extraction module with a Support Vector Machine (SVM) model encoded by an optimally constrained Restricted Boltzmann Machine (RBM). Shedthi et al. [16] developed a plant disease recognition framework that leveraged image processing and machine learning techniques. Their system employed a hybrid clustering algorithm—combining a Genetic Algorithm with K-means—for image segmentation and utilized an Artificial Neural Network (ANN) for disease classification. Although these approaches based on handcrafted feature extraction have achieved notable improvements in plant disease detection, they still exhibit inherent limitations. These include a strong reliance on manual feature engineering, difficulties in handling high-dimensional and sparse data, limited ability to model complex non-linear relationships, poor scalability to large datasets, and dependence on extensive labeled data for training.

In recent years, with the rapid advancement of deep learning technologies, models such as UNet [17], ResNet [18], and L-CSMS [19] have been increasingly employed in crop disease recognition. These methods enable the autonomous extraction of image features and optimize the training process, thereby significantly enhancing the performance and accuracy of plant disease identification tasks [20]. For example, Deng et al. [21] proposed a leaf blight segmentation model based on an improved VCDM-UNet. By analyzing the segmentation output, they quantified the proportion of diseased areas relative to total leaf area to perform disease severity grading, achieving an average grading accuracy of 83.95%. Zhang et al. [22] introduced the GhostNetV2 feature extraction module into the YOLOv8 architecture and constructed the GSGF model for grape leaf disease recognition, which attained an accuracy of 97.1% in tomato disease classification. Jiang et al. [23] developed a tea leaf disease detection method based on an enhanced Faster R-CNN algorithm, utilizing ResNet50 as the backbone integrated with a Feature Pyramid Network (FPN), achieving an average precision (PmA) of 88.06%. Yang [24] employed a combination of MobileNetV2 and the Large Margin Nearest Neighbor (LMNN) algorithm for wheat blast severity classification, resulting in a 3.5% improvement in accuracy over the baseline MobileNetV2 model. Similarly, Picon et al. [25] applied an improved ResNet architecture for the classification of European wheat diseases, achieving an accuracy of 87%. These studies demonstrate that deep learning approaches—through architectural augmentations—significantly improve the model's capability to autonomously learn complex and subtle disease features, thereby eliminating the need for labor-intensive manual feature engineering that is typical in traditional machine learning methods [26]. This principle underpins the methodology adopted in this study for the classification of wheat powdery mildew severity levels.

The primary objective of this study was to accurately classify the severity levels of wheat powdery mildew on individual leaf blades, with particular emphasis on the early detection of infections when visible symptoms are minimal or absent. To this end, a dataset comprising 532 RGB images of single wheat leaves was collected using a digital mobile phone during the irrigation stage. These images were annotated and categorized based on the severity grading standard defined in GBT 17980.22-2000 [27,28]. Considering the relatively limited size of the dataset, data augmentation techniques were employed as a preprocessing step to increase the number of training samples, thereby improving model robustness and generalization. The ResNet34 [29] model was adopted as the backbone for automated feature extraction. To accelerate the training process and enhance feature representation, a transfer learning strategy was incorporated by initializing the network with weights pre-trained on large-scale datasets. Additionally, the Squeeze-and-Excitation (SE) attention mechanism [30] was integrated into the architecture to improve the model's sensitivity to salient disease-related features. Meanwhile, the convolutional layer conv1 was modified from 7×7 to 3×3 with a stride of 1 and padding of 1, in order to better capture the texture and edge details of wheat leaves. Subsequently, the optimal training strategy was determined through hyperparameter tuning experiments, and GrabCut-based background processing along with data augmentation was introduced to enhance the model's robustness. In addition, interpretability techniques such as channel masking and Grad-CAM were employed to visualize the model's decision-making process. Based on these augmentations, the QY-SE-MResNet34 model was developed to classify the input leaf images according to powdery mildew severity levels. The model's performance was evaluated using four metrics: precision (1), recall (2), accuracy (3), and balanced F-score (4) [31]. The recognition performance of the proposed QY-SE-MResNet34 model was systematically compared with four mainstream deep learning models: ResNet34, ResNet50,

VGG16, and MobileNetV2, in order to assess its effectiveness and identify the optimal model for powdery mildew severity classification.

2. Materials and Methods

2.1. Research Area and Data Sources

2.1.1. Overview of the Research Area

The study was conducted at the demonstration base of Henan Agricultural University, located in the Pingyuan New District of Yuanyang County, Xinxiang City (113.956° E, 35.114° N). This region experiences a temperate continental monsoon climate, characterized by distinct seasonal variation. The average annual temperature is 14.2 °C, and precipitation is primarily concentrated in the summer and autumn months, with an annual average of approximately 680 mm. These climatic conditions are favorable for wheat cultivation: the cold winter temperatures promote wheat dormancy, while the warming trend in spring supports vegetative growth and development. In addition to its favorable climate, the region also possesses highly suitable soil resources for wheat production. The soil is fertile, with a deep profile and high organic matter content, providing an optimal environment for root development and nutrient uptake, thereby supporting healthy wheat growth throughout the growing season. The location of the research area is shown in Figure 1.

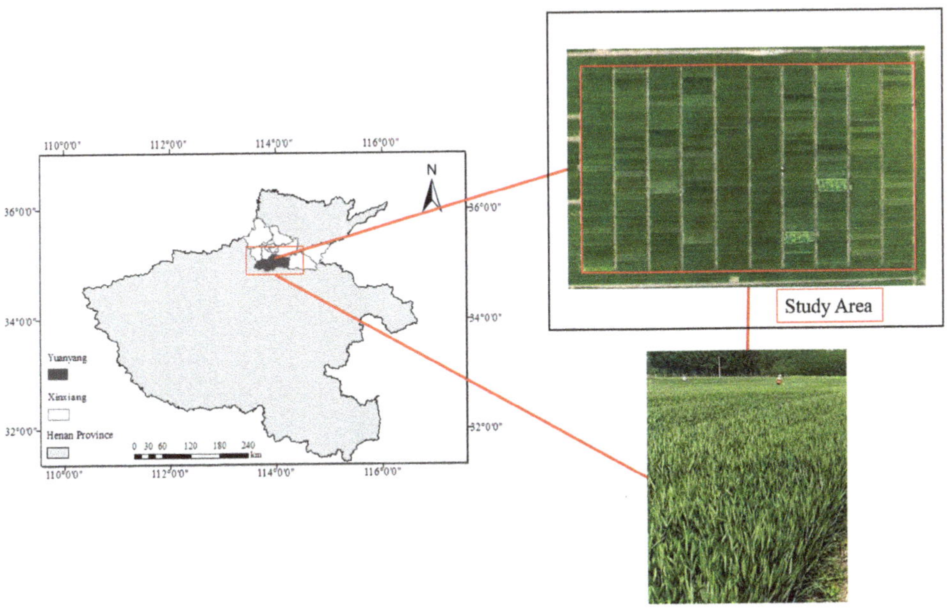

Figure 1. Geographical location of the study area.

2.1.2. Wheat Leaf Powdery Mildew Image Collection

The wheat leaf powdery mildew images were collected in early May 2024. The image acquisition process involved carefully detaching intact leaves from wheat plants grown in an outdoor experimental field. These leaves were then photographed vertically under controlled indoor conditions to ensure consistency in lighting and background. During image capture, the distance between the camera and the leaf surface was maintained within a range of 0.2 to 0.5 m. All photographs were taken between 14:00 and 16:30, a time window selected to ensure optimal natural lighting for high-quality imaging. The images were captured using an iPhone 14 Pro (Apple Inc., Cupertino, CA, USA), which is equipped with a rear triple-camera system comprising a 48 MP main sensor, a 12 MP ultra-wide sensor, and a 12 MP telephoto lens. All images were acquired at a resolution of 3024 × 4036 pixels and saved in JPG format. Based on the statistical analysis of the collected samples, the dataset includes both healthy wheat leaves and leaves exhibiting varying severity levels of powdery mildew infection, thus providing a diverse and representative foundation for the development and evaluation of classification models.

2.1.3. Wheat Powdery Mildew Dataset Construction and Image Preprocessing

According to the agricultural industry standard GBT 17980.22-2000 *Guidelines for Pesticide Field Efficacy Tests (I): Fungicide Control of Gramineae Powdery Mildew*, the collected wheat leaf samples were graded under the guidance of experts specializing in wheat powdery mildew resistance breeding [32]. Each image was sequentially numbered and assigned a corresponding label based on disease severity. The grading criteria for wheat powdery mildew severity are presented in Table 1. A total of 531 field sample images were collected for this study, comprising 43 images of healthy leaves, 137 images classified as grade 1, 117 as grade 3, 68 as grade 5, 76 as grade 7, and 90 as grade 9. Representative images for each disease severity level are illustrated in Figure 2.

Table 1. Wheat powdery mildew disease severity grading standards.

Disease Severity Levels	Symptom Characteristics
0	No disease
1	Disease spots cover less than 5% of the total leaf area
3	Disease spots cover 6% to 15% of the total leaf area
5	Disease spots cover 16% to 25% of the total leaf area
7	Disease spots cover 26% to 50% of the total leaf area
9	Disease spots cover more than 50% of the total leaf area

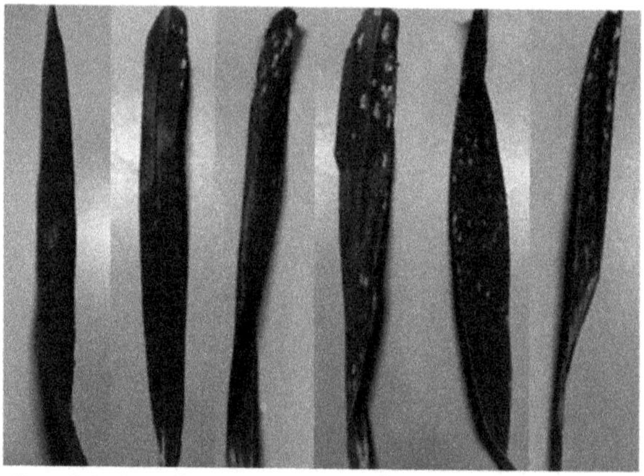

Figure 2. Wheat powdery mildew dataset legend.

To facilitate network training and support efficient convolution operations, the wheat leaf powdery mildew images were standardized to a uniform size [33]. As the primary disease-related features are predominantly concentrated in the central regions of the leaf images [34], resizing—via either upscaling or downscaling—was conducted in a manner that preserved the integrity of key visual information while reducing redundant background content. In this study, Python (3.12) scripts were developed to automate the image preprocessing workflow, aiming to eliminate irrelevant information and improve the computational efficiency of the model training process [35]. To address the risk of overfitting associated with the limited dataset size, data augmentation techniques such as horizontal and vertical flipping, random rotation, and color space transformations were employed [36]. The final dataset was divided into a training set and a validation set using a 9:1 ratio to support model evaluation and generalization testing.

2.2. Research Method

To evaluate the generalization capability of the wheat powdery mildew dataset across deep learning models, the proposed improved residual network model (QY-SE-MResNet34) was benchmarked against four widely adopted mainstream architectures: ResNet34, ResNet50, VGG16, and MobileNetV2. These models have been extensively employed in image recognition research due to their robust performance, ability to capture complex feature representations, and suitability for transfer learning [37]. Each model embodies distinct architectural characteristics and design principles. ResNet34, a classic residual network, effectively mitigates the vanishing gradient problem through identity shortcut connections. ResNet50, with its deeper architecture, offers a balance between computational efficiency and model complexity, making it suitable for scenarios with limited resources or requiring rapid inference [38]. VGG16 is characterized by a deep, uniform convolutional structure that facilitates progressive, layer-wise feature extraction. MobileNetV2, designed with efficiency in mind, excels in real-time computer vision applications and lightweight detection tasks due to its inverted residual blocks and linear bottlenecks.

2.2.1. ResNet Backbone Network

ResNet (Residual Network) is among the most widely adopted deep neural network architectures in tasks such as image classification, object detection, and semantic segmentation. Its core innovation, the residual structure, is depicted in Figure 3. The key advancement introduced by ResNet lies in the use of residual connections [39], which establish direct cross-layer pathways within the network to effectively alleviate issues of gradient vanishing and exploding during training. This design enables the construction of deeper and wider networks, thereby significantly enhancing model expressiveness and generalization ability [40].

Specifically, the residual connection in ResNet involves adding shortcut connections that bypass one or more layers, forming residual blocks where the output of a preceding layer is directly added to the output of a subsequent layer [41]. The fundamental principle of this mechanism is to learn residual functions—that is, the difference between the desired output and the input—rather than the direct mapping itself [42]. This approach facilitates the learning of identity mappings, which mitigates gradient degradation problems [43], and allows for the effective training of very deep networks with improved robustness and convergence behavior. In addition to residual connections, ResNet incorporates techniques such as batch normalization and pretraining [44] to further enhance training stability and generalization performance [45]. Batch normalization accelerates convergence and reduces internal covariate shift, thereby improving generalization, while pretraining leverages knowledge from large-scale datasets to initialize network parameters, boosting both accuracy and robustness [46].

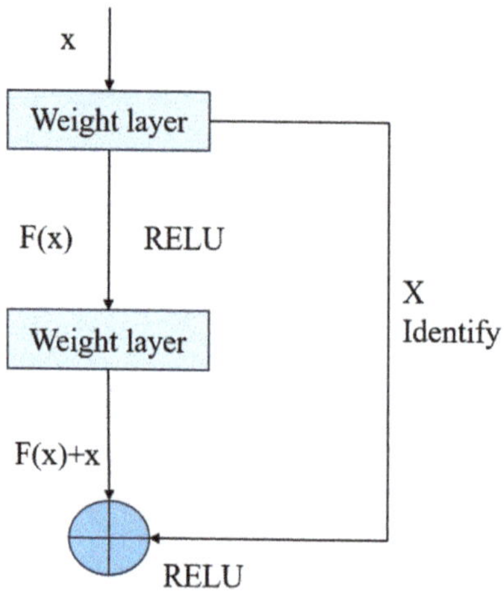

Figure 3. Residual structure diagram.

2.2.2. QY-SE-MResNet34 Network Model

To more effectively capture the subtle features of wheat powdery mildew lesions and improve the discrimination of disease severity levels, we propose the QY-SE-MResNet34 model, an enhanced version of ResNet34. Our approach integrates transfer learning and incorporates the Squeeze-and-Excitation (SE) attention module into the backbone network [47] alongside a modification of the initial convolutional layer (Conv1). Transfer learning is employed by initializing ResNet34 with weights pre-trained on large-scale datasets, thereby leveraging universal feature representations to accelerate convergence, boost classification performance, and mitigate overfitting—particularly beneficial when training data are limited. The SE module consists of two components: a "Squeeze" operation that aggregates spatial information via global average pooling, and an "Excitation" operation that models channel-wise dependencies through a lightweight gating mechanism. By learning inter-channel relationships, SE adaptively recalibrates channel feature responses, enhancing the network's focus on diagnostically relevant patterns while retaining original feature integrity. Furthermore, Conv1's original 7 × 7 kernel (stride = 2, padding = 3) is replaced with a 3 × 3 kernel (stride = 1, padding = 1) to facilitate finer-grained extraction of local texture and edge information critical for early-stage lesion detection. The architecture of the SE module is illustrated in Figure 4, highlighting its role in channel-wise feature reweighting.

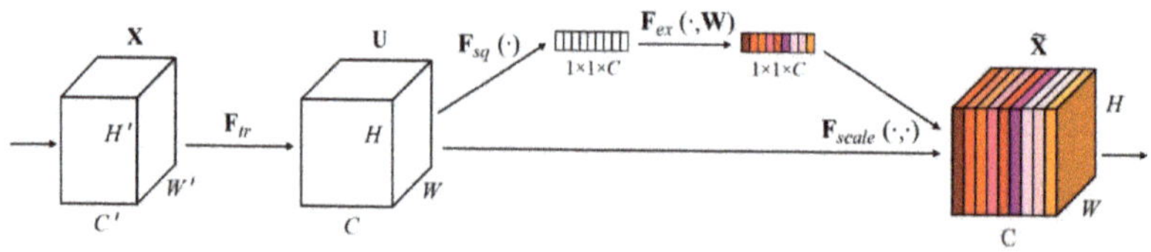

Figure 4. Squeeze-and-Excitation (SE) block: global average pooling of input **F** (H × W × C) yields channel-wise weights **s** (1 × 1 × C) via two 1 × 1 convolutions and Sigmoid, which then scale **F** to produce output F_{scale}.

In the ResNet34 architecture, a 3 × 3 convolutional kernel with a stride of 1 is employed to extract disease-related features from input wheat leaf images. This initial operation is followed by successive convolutional layers and activation functions, constituting the main processing pathway. The output of this pathway is then added to the original input features to form a residual, which is subsequently combined with the input to generate the final output of the residual block. Considering the high similarity of visual patterns across different severity levels of wheat powdery mildew, integrating attention mechanisms alongside additional convolutional kernels allows dynamic adjustment of the receptive field size. This facilitates the extraction of more fine-grained and discriminative features pertinent to disease severity. The overall architecture of the proposed QY-SE-MResNet34 residual network model is depicted in Figure 5. The transfer learning strategy initializes the model weights with parameters pretrained on the ImageNet dataset (source domain), while fine-tuning is performed using the preprocessed wheat powdery mildew images (target domain). The incorporated Squeeze-and-Excitation (SE) module enables adaptive modeling of inter-channel dependencies and weighted feature fusion, thereby enhancing the network's capacity to emphasize critical disease-related features and improve classification performance. Additionally, the adoption of smaller convolutional kernels reduces the number of parameters, leading to improved computational efficiency and optimized parameter learning, ultimately contributing to superior network performance.

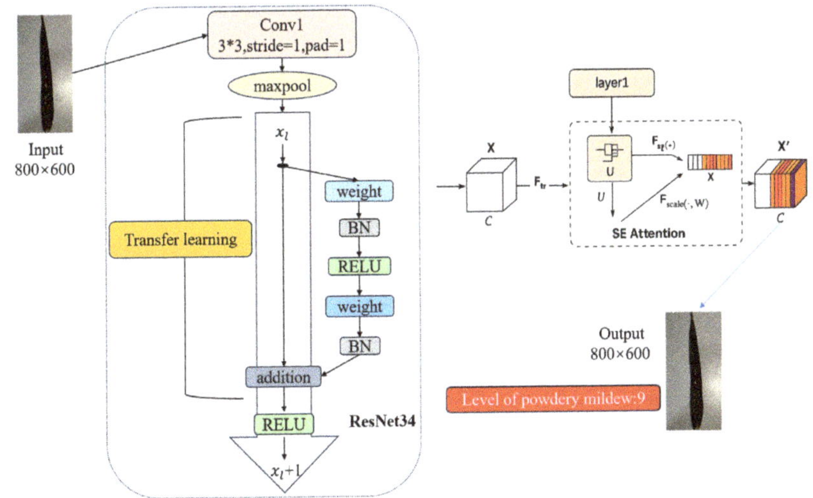

Figure 5. QY-SE-M-ResNet34 model.

2.3. Model Operating Environment

The model was implemented using the PyTorch (v2.x) deep learning framework. The hardware environment consisted of 16 virtual CPUs (Intel® Xeon® Gold 6430), 120 GB of RAM, and an NVIDIA RTX 4090 GPU with 24 GB of VRAM. The software environment included Python 3.12, CUDA 12.4, and the Ubuntu 22.04 Linux operating system. During the training process, the deep neural network model was trained for 200 epochs with a batch size of 32 and an initial learning rate set to 0.01.

2.4. Model Evaluation Metrics

To evaluate the performance of the experimental model in wheat powdery mildew disease severity classification, the following metrics were used: Precision (P) (1), Recall (R) (2), Accuracy (Acc) (3), and F-score (4). The formulas for these metrics are as follows:

$$P = \frac{TP}{TP+FP} \quad (1)$$

$$R = \frac{TP}{TP+FN} \quad (2)$$

$$\mathrm{Acc} = \frac{\mathrm{TP}+\mathrm{TN}}{\mathrm{TP}+\mathrm{FP}+\mathrm{TN}+\mathrm{FN}} \quad (3)$$

$$\mathrm{Micro} - \mathrm{F1} = 2\frac{\mathrm{P}*\mathrm{R}}{\mathrm{P}+\mathrm{R}} \quad (4)$$

In the formula:

TP (True Positive)—The number of samples correctly classified as positive by the model and that are indeed positive.

TN (True Negative)—The number of samples correctly classified as negative by the model and that are indeed negative.

FP (False Positive)—The number of samples incorrectly classified as positive by the model but that are actually negative.

FN (False Negative)—The number of samples incorrectly classified as negative by the model but that are actually positive.

P (Precision)—The proportion of samples classified as positive by the model that are truly positive.

R (Recall)—The proportion of all actual positive samples that are correctly classified as positive by the model.

Acc (Accuracy)—The proportion of all samples that are correctly classified by the model, which serves as a measure for evaluating the overall performance of the model.

F (F-score)—A metric that balances precision and recall; a higher F-score indicates superior model performance.

3. Results and Analysis

Section 3 focuses on the training process, performance evaluation, and in-depth analysis of the proposed model. Section 3.1 introduces the hyperparameter tuning process and identifies key training configurations. Section 3.2 compares the classification performance of various models to assess the effectiveness of the proposed improvements. Section 3.3 discusses the impact of image preprocessing and data augmentation on model performance, including background removal, specific parameter settings, and visualized results. Section 3.4 presents and analyzes the classification results of different models on wheat powdery mildew severity levels. Section 3.5 conducts ablation experiments to verify the contribution of each improvement module. Finally, Section 3.6 explores the model's interpretability and input feature sensitivity through channel masking and Grad-CAM visualization, providing further insights into the model's decision-making mechanism and feature dependencies.

3.1. Hyperparameter Tuning Experiments

To achieve optimal model training performance, this study conducted tuning experiments on the key hyperparameters of the deep learning model. The setting of hyperparameters significantly affects the stability, convergence speed, and final accuracy of model training. Based on the ResNet34 architecture, we performed a series of combination experiments on three key parameters: learning rate, batch size, and number of epochs. In the tuning process, the accuracy on the validation set was used as the evaluation metric to objectively reflect the model's generalization ability and avoid overfitting that may result from relying solely on training set performance.

The initial parameter settings were as follows: epoch = 100, batch size = 64, and learning rate = 0.01. On this basis, different combinations of these parameters were adjusted to observe their impact on model performance. The hyperparameter tuning process is shown in Table 2. From the experimental results, it can be seen that as the number of epochs increases and the batch size and learning rate are adjusted, the model's accuracy on the validation set gradually improves. Among the tested combinations, the configuration of epoch = 200, batch size = 32, and learning rate = 0.001 achieved the best performance, with a validation accuracy of 76.74%. Therefore, this set of parameters was ultimately adopted for formal training and model comparison experiments.

Table 2. Hyperparameter optimization.

No.	Epoch	Batch Size	Learning Rate	Validation Accuracy/%
1	100	64	0.01	63.83
2	100	32	0.001	68.58
3	200	64	0.001	72.61
4	200	32	0.001	76.74

3.2. Different Models' Accuracy Analysis

To assess the performance of deep learning models in classifying the severity levels of wheat powdery mildew, a comparative experiment was conducted involving five models: ResNet34, ResNet50, VGG16, MobileNetV2, and the proposed QY-SE-MResNet34. The variations in accuracy and loss values across training epochs for each model are depicted in Figure 6. As shown, model accuracy generally increases while loss decreases with the number of training epochs, eventually stabilizing as the models converge. This trend reflects the models' ability to progressively learn discriminative features from the input data, thereby enhancing their classification and recognition capabilities. Among the models evaluated, QY-SE-MResNet34 exhibits the fastest convergence, attaining high accuracy and low loss within approximately 80 epochs. The ResNet34 model follows closely, achieving similar performance after around 90 epochs. In contrast, ResNet50, VGG16, and MobileNetV2 require nearly 100 epochs to reach comparable results. Analysis of the relationship between training iterations and performance metrics reveals that QY-SE-MResNet34 achieves the lowest loss value among all models. This suggests that its design—featuring weighted feature fusion and convolutional kernels of different sizes—enhances the network's capacity to extract edge details and disease-specific features from wheat leaf images. Consequently, the model demonstrates an improved ability to focus on key regions and capture fine-grained variations across different severity levels, thereby boosting its classification performance in wheat powdery mildew severity identification tasks.

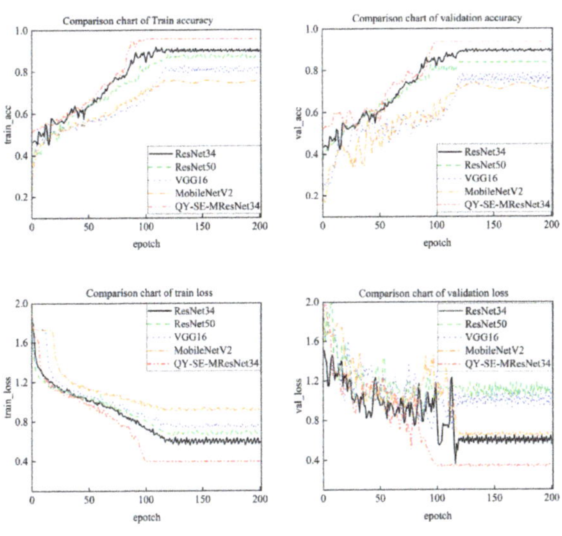

Figure 6. The accuracy of training and validation of each models' changes.

During training, the dataset was divided into a training set and a validation set at a ratio of 9:1. Figure 6 clearly illustrates the trends of accuracy and loss on both the training and validation sets across different epochs for each model. The performance of the models on the validation set remained consistent with that on the training set, demonstrating good generalization ability and indicating that no significant overfitting occurred during training.

Although the QY-SE-MResNet34 model tended to stabilize around the 80th epoch, considering the different convergence speeds of the models and to ensure comparability under consistent training settings, the Early Stopping mechanism was not applied. Instead, all models were trained for a fixed number of 200 epochs, allowing for a complete observation of the learning process and performance differences. This setting helps to comprehensively evaluate convergence trends and provides a more intuitive basis for performance comparison between models.

Table 3 summarizes the accuracy and loss values of each model following 200 training epochs. As shown, the proposed QY-SE-MResNet34 model outperforms the other architectures, achieving the highest training accuracy of 89% and validation accuracy of 87%. These results indicate that the model possesses strong generalization capability and is highly effective in identifying fine-grained features related to disease severity. In addition, the QY-SE-MResNet34 model records the lowest training and validation loss values, at 0.6925 and 0.6771, respectively, further demonstrating its robustness and superior performance in wheat powdery mildew severity classification.

Table 3. Accuracy and loss values of each model.

Network Model	Training Accuracy/%	Validation Accuracy/%	Training Loss/%	Validation Loss/%
ResNet34	78	76	0.8245	0.8268
ResNet50	74	72	0.8743	1.1738
VGG16	67	63	0.9588	1.0913
MobileNetV2	65	60	1.0912	0.9805
QY-SE-MResNet34	89	87	0.6925	0.6771

3.3. *The Impact of Data Augmentation on Improving Model Performance*

3.3.1. Image Preprocessing (Background Removal)

To further enhance the model's robustness and avoid background interference during feature extraction, background removal was performed on the original images before data augmentation. Given the relatively uniform imaging environment of wheat powdery mildew samples—typically photographed against a white canvas or background board under controlled lighting conditions—the foreground mainly consisted of a single leaf, and the background was relatively simple. However, since the color of powdery mildew lesions often closely resembles the background, simple color thresholding or binarization methods may lead to the loss of lesion information or incomplete foreground contours, ultimately affecting the model's ability to learn disease-related features.

Therefore, this study adopted a semi-automatic foreground extraction method based on GrabCut to effectively separate the leaf region from the background. The GrabCut algorithm uses Gaussian Mixture Models (GMM) to model foreground and background pixels and classifies them based on the min-cut principle, enabling fine segmentation of complex foregrounds. Specifically, the original image was first resized to 20% of its original size. Then, a rectangle was drawn around the leaf region to initialize GrabCut, ensuring that lesion areas were included in the foreground modeling and reducing the impact of background lighting variations on edge segmentation. The resulting foreground images retained the complete leaf contours and lesion areas while effectively removing background pixels.

Figure 7 presents a comparison between the original images and those processed using GrabCut. As shown, background information was effectively eliminated, while the leaf contours and disease regions were preserved, providing cleaner input data for subsequent data augmentation and model training.

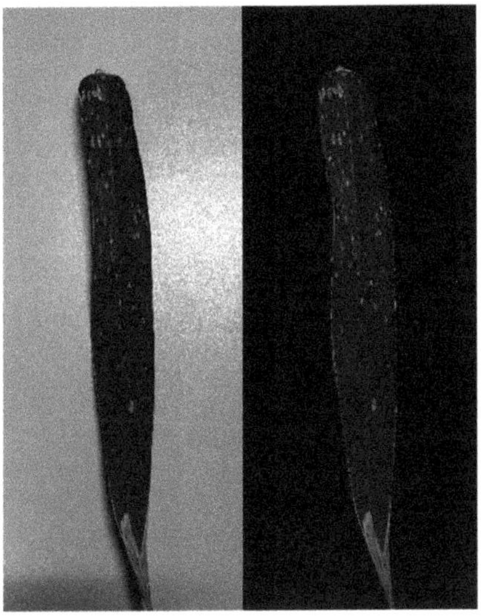

Figure 7. Comparison of original and background-removed leaf images using the GrabCut algorithm.

Although this study attempted to apply GrabCut-based background removal during the image preprocessing stage, the collected images featured clean and uniform backgrounds. Moreover, the model achieved a relatively high classification accuracy of 89% even without background removal, indicating that the background had minimal impact on feature extraction. Considering that background removal may lead to the loss of lesion edge information and incurs a high computational cost when applied to large-scale datasets, this operation was performed only on a subset of images for illustrative purposes rather than on the entire dataset. Nevertheless, this method may serve as a useful reference for lesion recognition in more complex background scenarios in future studies.

3.3.2. Data Augmentation Methods and Parameters

To expand the training dataset and enhance the model's generalization ability, the following data augmentation methods and corresponding parameters were applied:

- Horizontal flip: 100% probability
- Random rotation: Angle range of $\pm 50^\circ$, uniformly sampled
- Image translation: Random horizontal and vertical shifts of $\pm 10\%$ of the image width/height
- Brightness adjustment: Randomly adjusted with a brightness factor between 0.8 and 1.2
- Hue adjustment: Hue shift range of $\pm 10^\circ$
- Contrast adjustment: Contrast factor randomly set between 0.8 and 1.2
- Sharpness adjustment: Sharpness augmentation factor ranging from 0.5 to 1.5

Figure 8 shows illustrative examples of the different types of data augmentation.

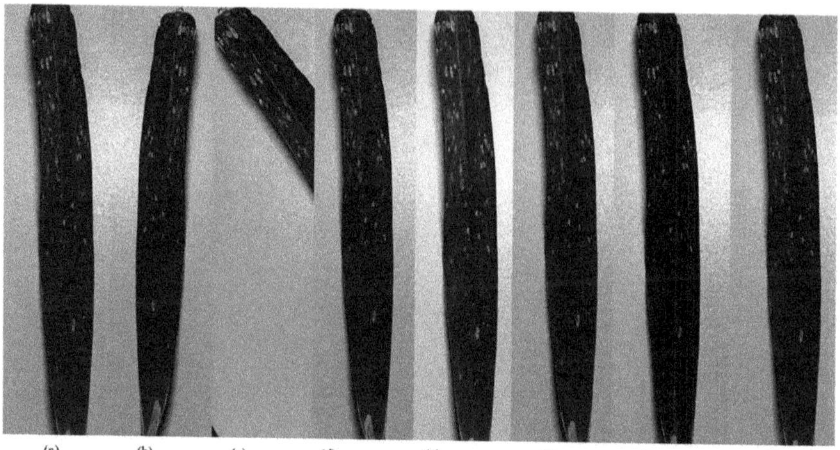

Figure 8. Enhanced results of wheat powdery mildew image data.

3.3.3. Visualization and Comparison of Data Augmentation Effects

After applying data augmentation, the training samples were balanced and used for training experiments on both the training and validation sets. The results are shown in Table 4. As observed, the training and validation accuracy after data augmentation reached 89.9% and 87.6%, respectively, whereas without data augmentation, the training and validation accuracy were 86.4% and 83.7%, respectively. Data augmentation thus improved the training and validation accuracy by 3.5% and 3.9%, respectively. Moreover, the gap between training and validation accuracy was smaller in the augmented dataset compared to the non-augmented one.

Table 4. Comparison of model recognition accuracy before and after image augmentation.

Method	Training Set Accuracy	Validation Set Accuracy
data not augmentation	86.4%	83.7%
data augmentation	89.9%	87.6%

These results indicate that using data augmentation techniques—such as flipping, rotation, translation, and color transformations—to generate a more diverse training dataset effectively reduces model overfitting and enhances its robustness and generalization capability in the wheat powdery mildew severity classification task.

To more intuitively demonstrate the impact of data augmentation, Figure 9 presents the training and validation accuracy curves over epochs for models trained with and without data augmentation. As shown in Figure 9, the model trained with data augmentation exhibits more stable training behavior, faster accuracy improvement, and consistently higher validation accuracy compared to the model without augmentation. This indicates that data augmentation effectively alleviates overfitting and enhances the model's generalization ability.

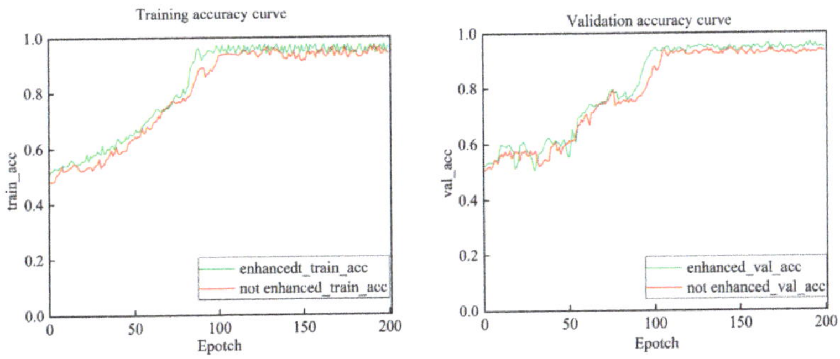

Figure 9. Effect of data augmentation on training and validation accuracy.

3.4. Different Models' Disease Severity Recognition Results and Analysis

Figure 10 presents the confusion matrices for the various models. As shown, the QY-SE-MResNet34 model exhibits superior performance in classifying the severity levels of wheat powdery mildew compared to other models. For the 0-level disease, the QY-SE-MResNet34 model achieves a perfect recognition rate of 1.00, whereas other models—except for ResNet34, which attains an accuracy of 0.86—show relatively low recognition rates. In the 1-level category, only the QY-SE-MResNet34 and ResNet34 models surpass a recognition rate of 0.80, while the remaining models fluctuate around 0.70. These results indicate that the QY-SE-MResNet34 and ResNet34 models are particularly effective in identifying the early stages (0 and 1 level) of the disease. For the 3-level disease, the QY-SE-MResNet34 model achieves the highest recognition rate of 0.96, in stark contrast to MobileNetV2, which records the lowest at 0.48. The recognition accuracies of the other three models range between 0.60 and 0.70. Except for the QY-SE-MResNet34 model, the remaining models demonstrate limited effectiveness in identifying the mid-severity levels (3-, 5-, and 7-level). Notably, 5-level diseases are frequently misclassified as 3-level, and 7-level diseases are often confused with 5-level, due to the high similarity in visual features such as white lesions and leaf yellowing. These overlapping characteristics make it challenging for the models to distinguish between varying degrees of leaf necrosis and discoloration. Regarding the 9-level disease, the MobileNetV2 model again shows the lowest recognition rate (0.42), while ResNet34, ResNet50, and VGG16 achieve approximately 0.70. In contrast, the QY-SE-MResNet34 model reaches the highest recognition rate of 0.97. Overall, the QY-SE-MResNet34 model demonstrates the most consistent and accurate performance across all severity levels. The confusion matrix clearly illustrates the model's superior ability to extract fine-grained features and distinguish between subtle inter-class differences, thereby significantly enhancing classification performance in wheat powdery mildew severity identification tasks.

Table 5 summarizes the performance metrics of each model in recognizing different severity levels of wheat powdery mildew. As shown, the QY-SE-MResNet34 model consistently outperforms the other models across all severity levels in terms of precision, recall, and balanced F-score. These results highlight the model's superior capability in accurately identifying and distinguishing fine-grained disease features, thereby enhancing the overall classification effectiveness for wheat powdery mildew severity assessment.

As shown in Table 6, the QY-SE-MResNet34 model achieved the highest performance across all evaluation metrics for wheat powdery mildew severity classification, with precision, recall, F1-score, and accuracy reaching 88.6%, 85.83%, 86.17%, and 87%, respectively. In contrast, the MobileNetV2 model exhibited the lowest performance, with corresponding values of 60.7%, 61.0%, 59.7%, and 60.5%, followed by the VGG16 model, which yielded values of 64.1%, 62.7%, 63.6%, and 63.4%, respectively.

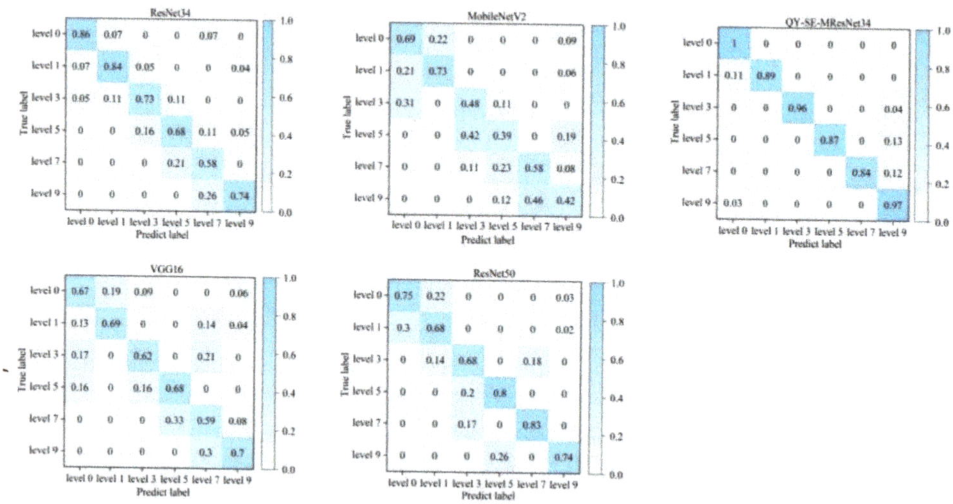

Figure 10. Confusion matrix of each model.

Table 5. Analysis of prediction results of each network model.

Network Model	Evaluation Index	Evaluation Index Result					
		0	**1**	**3**	**5**	**7**	**9**
ResNet34	Precision recall F-score	0.84 0.91 0.88	0.83 0.83 0.83	0.82 0.82 0.82	0.82 0.85 0.84	0.58 0.59 0.59	0.74 0.68 0.71
ResNet50	Precision recall F-score	0.73 0.57 0.66	0.66 0.73 0.70	0.66 0.55 0.61	0.78 0.66 0.71	0.81 0.81 0.81	0.72 0.75 0.73
VGG16	Precision recall F-score	0.67 0.39 0.51	0.61 0.71 0.66	0.54 0.65 0.59	0.74 0.25 0.38	0.37 0.49 0.42	0.69 0.71 0.70
MobileNetV2	Precision recall F-score	0.67 0.60 0.63	0.77 0.66 0.70	0.45 0.43 0.44	0.37 0.36 0.36	0.55 0.63 0.59	0.44 0.44 0.44
QY-SE-MResNet34	Precision recall F-score	1.00 0.66 0.79	0.85 0.96 0.90	0.95 0.89 0.92	0.86 0.76 0.81	0.81 0.92 0.86	0.95 0.96 0.95

Table 6. Classification test results of wheat powdery mildew in each network model.

Network Model	Precision	Recall	F-Score	Accuracy
ResNet34	76.30%	76.41%	75.80%	76.20%
ResNet50	72.67%	68.83%	70.30%	69.00%
VGG16	64.10%	62.70%	63.60%	63.40%
MobileNetV2	60.70%	61.00%	59.80%	60.50%
QY-SE-MResNet34	88.60%	85.83%	86.17%	87.00%

Notably, the QY-SE-MResNet34 model outperformed the baseline ResNet34 model by a margin of 10.8% in classification accuracy (76.2%), demonstrating the substantial improvements achieved through the integration of transfer learning, the incorporation of the SE attention module, and the optimization of the first convolutional layer (Conv1). The use of convolutional kernels with varying sizes further enhanced the model's ability to capture fine-grained features across different disease severity levels, thereby enriching the image feature representations and improving classification precision.

Although the ResNet50 model showed moderate performance, its effectiveness in identifying fine-grained features was relatively limited. Despite offering benefits such as reduced parameter count and lower computational complexity, its reliance on lightweight operations—such as depthwise separable convolutions—may constrain its representational capacity, rendering it less effective for detailed classification tasks like wheat powdery mildew severity assessment.

3.5. Ablation Experiment

To validate the effectiveness of integrating ResNet34 with transfer learning, the SE attention mechanism, and Conv1 layer optimization, an ablation study was conducted. The evaluated models included the baseline ResNet34, ResNet34 with transfer learning (QY-ResNet34), ResNet34 incorporating the SE module (SE-ResNet34), ResNet34 with Conv1 optimization (MResNet34), and a combined model integrating all three improvements (QY-SE-MResNet34). These models were assessed using four evaluation metrics: precision, recall, accuracy, and balanced F-score.

The results of the ablation experiment are summarized in Table 7. Compared with the baseline ResNet34, the QY-ResNet34 model showed improvements in precision (1.9%), recall (2.75%), F-score (2.7%), and accuracy (2.8%). These gains suggest that incorporating transfer learning enables the model to effectively leverage prior knowledge from pre-trained networks, thereby accelerating convergence and reducing computational costs. The SE-ResNet34 model achieved notable improvements—5.81% in precision, 8.6% in recall, 7.98% in F-score, and 4.8% in accuracy—demonstrating that the inclusion of the SE module strengthens the model's ability to emphasize disease-relevant features, thereby enhancing classification performance. The MResNet34 model, which modifies the Conv1 layer, achieved performance gains of 3.01% in precision, 5.91% in recall, 4.85% in F-score, and 3.8% in accuracy. These results indicate that optimizing the initial convolutional layer enables the network to extract more detailed spatial features and better capture subtle differences in disease severity levels. Among all tested configurations, the QY-SE-MResNet34 model outperformed the others across all metrics, confirming that the synergistic integration of transfer learning, SE attention, and Conv1 optimization significantly enhances the model's ability to recognize wheat powdery mildew severity. These results demonstrate the effectiveness of the proposed augmentations in improving both the robustness and precision of fine-grained disease classification.

Table 7. Ablation experiment results.

Network Model	Precision	Recall	F-Score	Accuracy
ResNet34	76.30%	76.41%	75.80%	76.20%
QY-ResNet34	78.20%	79.16%	78.50%	79.00%
SE-ResNet34	82.11%	85.01%	83.78%	81.00%
MResNet34	79.31%	82.32%	80.65%	80.00%
QY-SE-MResNet34	88.60%	85.83%	86.17%	87.00%

3.6. Model Interpretability and Feature Sensitivity Analysis

3.6.1. Channel Masking Sensitivity Analysis

To further investigate the model's sensitivity to different input color channels, this study designed and conducted a channel masking sensitivity experiment. The experiment involved individually masking the red, green, and blue channels of the input images by setting the pixel values of the corresponding channel to zero. The goal was to observe the change in the model's classification performance when information from a single channel was missing, thereby revealing the model's dependency on each channel and its impact on the disease severity recognition results.

Specifically, based on the preprocessed RGB images, the pixel values of one color channel were set to zero to generate masked images, which were then fed into the trained QY-SE-MResNet34 model for prediction. By comparing the predicted classes and confidence scores before and after masking, the contribution of each channel's information to the model's decision-making was evaluated. Figure 11 shows the visual comparison between the original and masked images, while Table 8 summarizes the predicted classes and confidence scores under different masking conditions.

Figure 11. Visual comparison of the original image and images with masked color channels.

Table 8. Predicted classes and confidence scores of the model under different channel masking conditions.

Masked Channel	Predicted Class	Confidence
Original	9	94.80%
Blue	9	88.50%
Green	9	93.68%
Red	9	93.75%

The experimental results show that after masking the blue channel, the model's predicted classes and confidence scores exhibited significant changes, with a notable decline in performance. In contrast, masking the red and green channels resulted in relatively stable predictions, with only slight decreases in confidence. Combined with the visual changes in the masked images (where masking the blue channel caused the image to appear yellowish, and masking the red and green channels resulted in magenta and cyan hues, respectively), these findings indicate that the model relies more heavily on features from the blue channel for classifying powdery mildew severity.

In summary, the channel masking sensitivity analysis verifies the model's differential responses to individual input channels, providing intuitive insights into its decision-making process. This analysis also offers valuable guidance for future model optimization and data augmentation strategy design.

3.6.2. Visualization of Model Attention Regions (Grad-CAM)

To further explore the decision basis and interpretability of the proposed QY-SE-MResNet34 model in the task of wheat powdery mildew severity classification, this study adopts Grad-CAM (Gradient-weighted Class Activation Mapping) to visualize the model's attention regions.

Grad-CAM is a gradient-based interpretability technique that generates heatmaps by computing the gradients of the model's output with respect to the feature maps of a selected convolutional layer. These heatmaps highlight the regions in the input image that the model focuses on when making predictions. This method does not require modification of the model architecture and is applicable to various convolutional neural networks, making it effective for identifying whether the model attends to task-relevant areas.

In this study, two representative images with severity levels 3 and 9 were selected for visualization. The original images were overlaid with their corresponding Grad-CAM heatmaps for analysis. As shown in Figure 12, the model primarily focuses on regions with dense lesion distribution during prediction, and in images with higher severity, the activation regions are more pronounced. This indicates that the model does not simply rely on background or leaf contour information but effectively captures fine-grained differences in diseased areas, demonstrating a reliable decision basis and interpretability.

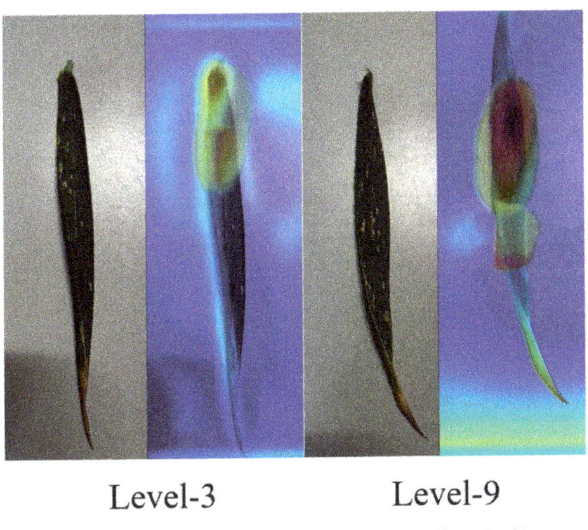

Figure 12. Visualization of attention regions on wheat leaf images with severity levels of 3 and 9 using Grad-CAM.

The visualization results indicate that the proposed model can effectively distinguish diseased areas from background noise, thereby enhancing its interpretability and practical value, and providing strong support for its deployment in real-world agricultural applications. In this section, two representative samples with correct model predictions—leaf images corresponding to powdery mildew severity levels 3 and 9—are selected. Grad-CAM is used to generate heatmaps to observe whether the model's attention is focused around the lesion areas. Only these two typical severity levels are presented here, as the Grad-CAM visualizations of other severity levels exhibit similar attention patterns, reflecting a consistent focus trend of the model.

4. Discussion

Current research on wheat diseases primarily concentrates on disease type classification, with convolutional neural networks (CNNs) widely applied in agricultural disease identification tasks. Backbone architectures such as ResNet and VGG have demonstrated outstanding performance in the classification of various wheat disease images. For instance, Feng et al. [48] employed a transfer learning strategy by setting all layers of a lightweight CNN model as trainable, thereby developing a wheat leaf disease recognition model that exhibits high accuracy, strong generalization capability, and suitability for deployment on mobile platforms. The model was trained on a dataset encompassing three major wheat leaf diseases: powdery mildew, stripe rust, and leaf rust. Similarly, Lou et al. [49] proposed WDMNet, a lightweight wheat disease recognition network based on multi-scale attention, designed to identify six common wheat diseases. By integrating a multi-scale attention mechanism, the model effectively enhances the extraction of key disease features, such as lesion location, shape, and color. In parallel, data sources for wheat disease detection have become increasingly diverse. Gao et al. [50] introduced a novel approach for the rapid and non-destructive monitoring of wheat Fusarium head blight (FHB), combining low-altitude remote sensing using unmanned aerial vehicles (UAVs) with multispectral imaging and incorporating spectral and textural analysis techniques.

Although previous studies have made significant advances in wheat disease recognition, their focus has largely been on multi-disease classification tasks [51]. In contrast, this study specifically addresses the automated severity grading of wheat powdery mildew at the leaf level. By enhancing the ResNet34 model and benchmarking it against several mainstream deep learning architectures, we achieved effective classification of powdery mildew severity levels. Specifically, we developed an advanced model, QY-SE-MResNet34, built upon the ResNet34 backbone. This model retains the original network's residual learning capability while integrating transfer learning to accelerate convergence and improve generalization performance. Additionally, squeeze-and-excitation (SE) attention modules are embedded within each residual block, enabling the model to better focus on critical lesion regions. Given the characteristics of wheat leaf disease images, such as small lesion sizes and blurred edges, the original 7×7 convolution kernel in ResNet34's first layer was replaced with a 3×3 kernel to more effectively capture fine-grained local features. Then, the optimal training strategy was determined through hyperparameter tuning experiments, further improving the model's performance. To address the issue of image backgrounds, the GrabCut method was introduced for background processing, enhancing the model's focus on key regions and its robustness. Combined with data augmentation techniques, the positive impact on model performance was demonstrated through visual comparisons. Finally, interpretability techniques such as channel masking and Grad-CAM were employed to analyze the model's decision-making process, revealing the model's sensitivity to different input channels and image regions, thereby deepening the understanding of its discriminative mechanisms. Furthermore, in accordance with the national standard (GBT 17980.22-2000), we constructed a six-level severity image dataset of single wheat leaves affected by powdery mildew, thereby enhancing the model's capability to distinguish subtle differences in disease severity under real-world conditions. Unlike many existing studies that focus primarily on binary classification (diseased vs. healthy), our work tackles a more granular severity grading problem. Through architectural optimization and a careful balance between performance and model complexity, the proposed QY-SE-MResNet34 outperformed baseline models in accuracy, recall, and F1-score, demonstrating strong practical applicability and scalability.

This study acknowledges several limitations that warrant further attention. First, the enhanced QY-SE-MResNet34 model exhibited superior performance compared to the baseline ResNet34 on our self-constructed wheat powdery mildew dataset. This improvement may be partly attributed to the image acquisition process, where wheat leaf images were captured outdoors using smartphones after manual collection. This approach effectively reduced interference from factors such as background occlusion, plant growth position, and solar altitude angle, resulting in more consistent leaf contours and geometric features across images, which contributed to stable grading results. However, in real-world applications, wheat leaves are often subject to uncontrollable environmental factors that cause greater variability in contour and geometric characteristics, potentially leading to decreased grading accuracy. The dataset used in this study contains images with relatively clean backgrounds and uniform lighting, resulting in limited sample complexity that cannot fully represent the diversity of real-world environments. Consequently, the model's generalization ability in practical scenarios remains insufficient. Although GrabCut background processing and data augmentation methods were introduced to improve model robustness, the actual effectiveness of these preprocessing and augmentation strategies still needs to be further validated under more complex and natural conditions. Additionally, this study focuses primarily on improving the deep neural network architecture and algorithmic enhancements, without addressing model deployment. Finally, the current model only performs powdery mildew severity classification on wheat leaves and does not cover diseases on stems and spikes; future work should expand the application scope and improve the model's applicability.

Therefore, addressing these challenges in future research is of paramount importance. On one hand, it is essential to evaluate the model's performance under complex environmental conditions and in the presence of co-occurring wheat diseases. Future studies should also extend severity classification to additional plant organs such as stems and ears to enhance the model's applicability. Simultaneously, balancing model complexity with generalization capability remains a critical consideration. Incorporating lightweight modules—such as the Convolutional Block Attention Module (CBAM) or depthwise separable convolutions—could improve feature extraction efficiency while maintaining manageable computational complexity. In this study, the SE attention mechanism was employed to strengthen the model's focus on salient lesion features and facilitate fine-grained feature extraction across varying severity levels of powdery mildew, thereby enriching the model's representational capacity. On the other hand, future research should also emphasize real-time deployment and large-scale application of the model in conjunction with emerging technological advancements. As deep learning technologies continue to evolve and computational resources become increasingly accessible, it is critical for models to transition from controlled experimental settings to practical, real-world agricultural environments. The proposed QY-SE-MResNet34 model, which incorporates SE attention mechanisms and modified convolutional layers based on transfer learning, has shown significant improvements in the accuracy and efficiency of powdery mildew severity classification. Nevertheless, practical deployment requires further attention to computational efficiency, hardware compatibility, and adaptability to diverse environmental conditions. Future efforts will focus on optimizing the model's computational performance, enhancing inference speed on edge devices, and adopting model compression and acceleration techniques to ensure stable operation in low-resource settings. Moreover, additional augmentations will be necessary to accommodate the complexity and variability of different agricultural scenarios, thereby improving the model's robustness and generalization. This will ultimately enable large-scale disease monitoring and support the implementation of precision agriculture practices. To address this, future research will focus on collecting wheat leaf images under natural field conditions with diverse angles, complex backgrounds, and at multiple time periods, in order to systematically evaluate the model's adaptability and robustness in real-world environments.

5. Conclusions

This study enhances the ResNet34 model and compares its performance with that of several mainstream deep learning architectures, including ResNet34, ResNet50, VGG16, and MobileNetV2. Among these, the proposed QY-SE-MResNet34 model demonstrated the best overall performance in identifying the severity levels of wheat powdery mildew, thereby significantly improving both the accuracy and efficiency of severity classification.

The conclusions of this research are as follows.

- The deep learning model autonomously learns and extracts subtle disease features from a large number of wheat leaf images, enabling precise classification of powdery mildew severity. To improve model robustness and generalization, data augmentation techniques were applied to expand the training dataset. Following augmentation, the training and validation accuracy reached 89.9% and 87.6%, respectively, representing improvements of 3.5% and 3.9% compared to the non-augmented datasets. These results confirm that data augmentation effectively enhances the model's recognition performance, aligning with findings from previous studies.
- Comparative analysis of the models revealed that ResNet34 achieves relatively high accuracy in recognizing wheat powdery mildew severity levels. This suggests that the residual connections in ResNet34 effectively mitigate issues such as gradient vanishing and model degradation, thereby enhancing model trainability and accelerating convergence. Consequently, ResNet34 is particularly well-suited for fine-grained classification tasks that require complex feature extraction. Notably, in the early identification of wheat powdery mildew, ResNet34 exhibits strong sensitivity to mild symptoms due to its efficient feature learning capabilities.
- The QY-SE-MResNet34 model achieved the highest training and validation accuracy on the wheat powdery mildew dataset, reaching 89% and 87%, respectively, along with the lowest corresponding loss values of 0.6925 and 0.6771. Compared to the original ResNet34 model, both training and validation accuracy improved by 11%, and the loss values were significantly reduced, demonstrating the enhanced model's superior capacity to recognize disease features and achieve faster convergence during training. In terms of evaluation metrics, the QY-SE-MResNet34 model achieved a precision of 88.6%, recall of 85.83%, balanced F-score of 86.17%, and overall accuracy of 87%. These represent substantial improvements over the baseline models, with accuracy gains of 10.8%, 18%, 23.6%, and 26.5% compared to ResNet34, ResNet50, VGG16, and MobileNetV2, respectively. These results highlight the model's effectiveness in fine-grained recognition of wheat powdery mildew severity.
- Key architectural modifications—specifically, the optimization of the first convolutional layer (Conv1) and the integration of the SE attention mechanism—played a critical role in enhancing model performance. Ablation studies confirmed the individual and combined effectiveness of these augmentations. Incorporating the SE (Squeeze-and-Excitation) module into the ResNet34 backbone with transfer learning improved the model's ability to focus on important channel-wise features, thereby enhancing its capacity for fine-grained disease severity recognition. This allowed the model to extract more detailed representations of lesion characteristics across different severity levels, resulting in improved classification accuracy. These findings

are consistent with prior studies demonstrating the benefits of attention mechanisms in enhancing model generalization and interpretability. Furthermore, modifying the Conv1 layer by replacing the original 7 × 7 kernel with a 3 × 3 kernel preserved higher spatial resolution in the early feature maps. This change retained more local detail and improved sensitivity to subtle visual differences, while also reducing computational complexity. Together, these augmentations contribute to the improved performance and practical applicability of the proposed model for automated severity grading of wheat powdery mildew.

- In addition, to enhance the interpretability of the model and its understanding of input features, this study implemented multiple visualization and sensitivity analysis experiments. In the image preprocessing stage, the GrabCut background removal method was introduced. By modeling foreground and background pixels using Gaussian Mixture Models (GMM) and applying the min-cut principle, effective separation between leaf regions and background was achieved. Experimental results showed that GrabCut could accurately preserve leaf contours and diseased areas while eliminating background pixels, thereby providing cleaner input data for the model. Although the overall classification accuracy was already high, indicating minimal background interference, this method offers a feasible solution for future disease recognition under complex field conditions. Regarding input feature sensitivity, a channel-masking experiment was conducted to evaluate the model's dependence on the RGB color channels. The results revealed that masking the blue channel significantly altered the predicted class and confidence, indicating that the model relies heavily on features contained in the blue channel for disease severity classification. In contrast, masking the red or green channels had a relatively minor impact, reflecting selective channel dependency in the model's recognition process. Finally, the Grad-CAM technique was applied to visualize the model's decision-making regions using heatmaps. Results demonstrated that the model primarily focused on areas of dense disease presence on the leaf surface. Moreover, samples of different severity levels exhibited distinct activation intensities and locations, suggesting that the model effectively distinguishes between fine-grained differences in disease severity. These visualizations confirmed that the model's attention is concentrated on key regions rather than background information, providing interpretable evidence for the model's decision-making process and enhancing its reliability and practical applicability.

Author Contributions: Conceptualization, M.L., Q.W. and H.Z.; data curation, M.L.; formal analysis, M.L.; funding acquisition, Q.W.; investigation, M.L.; methodology, Q.W. and H.Z.; project administration, Q.W. and H.Z.; resources, Q.W.; software, Q.W.; supervision, H.Q. and W.G.; validation, Y.G., L.S. and Y.L.; visualization, G.Z.; writing—original draft, M.L.; writing—review and editing, Q.W. All authors have read and agreed to the published version of the manuscript.

Funding: This research was funded by the National Natural Science Foundation of China (No. 32271993), Joint Fund of Advantageous Discipline Cultivation Project of the Henan Science and Technology Research and Development Program (No. 222301420114), Henan Science and Technology Tackling Project (No. 252102110367), Henan International Scientific and Technological Cooperation Project (No. 242102521027) and the Natural Science Foundation of Henan Province (No. 242301420143).

Institutional Review Board Statement: Not applicable.

Informed Consent Statement: Not applicable.

Data Availability Statement: The datasets presented in this article are not readily available because the data are part of an ongoing study. Requests to access the datasets should be directed to wqhda@henau.edu.cn.

Acknowledgments: The authors thank the College of Information and Management Sciences of Henan Agricultural University.

Conflicts of Interest: The authors declare no conflicts of interest.

References

1. Lv, Z.; Yang, S.; Ma, S.; Wang, Q.; Sun, J.; Du, L.; Han, J.; Guo, Y.; Zhang, H. Efficient Deployment of Peanut Leaf Disease Detection Models on Edge AI Devices. *Agriculture* **2025**, *15*, 332. [CrossRef]
2. Wang, Y.M.; Zhang, Z.; Feng, L.W.; Ma, Y.; Du, Q. A new attention-based CNN approach for crop mapping using time series Sentinel-2 images. *Comput. Electron. Agric.* **2021**, *184*, 106090. [CrossRef]
3. Yele, V.P.; Sedamkar, R.R.; Alegavi, S. Systematic Analysis of Effective Segmentation and Classification for Land Use Land Cover in Hyperspectral Image using Deep Learning Methods: A Review of the State of the Art: Reviewing Deep Learning Techniques for Land Use and Cover in Hyperspectral Images. In Proceedings of the 2024 20th CSI International Symposium on Artificial Intelligence and Signal Processing (AISP), Babol, Iran, 21 February 2024; pp. 1–8.
4. Liu, J.; Meng, H. Research on the maturity detection method of korla pears based on hyperspectral technology. *Agriculture* **2024**, *14*, 1257. [CrossRef]
5. Wang, S.; Xu, D.; Liang, H.; Bai, Y.; Li, X.; Zhou, J.; Su, C.; Wei, W. Advances in Deep Learning Applications for Plant Disease and Pest Detection: A Review. *Remote Sens.* **2025**, *17*, 698. [CrossRef]
6. Zhao, C.; Li, C.; Wang, X.; Li, C.; Wang, X.; Wu, X.; Du, Y.; Chai, H.; Cai, T.; Xiang, H.; et al. Plant Disease Segmentation Networks for Fast Automatic Severity Estimation Under Natural Field Scenarios. *Agriculture* **2025**, *15*, 583. [CrossRef]
7. Zhang, M.; Liu, C.; Li, Z.; Yin, B. From Convolutional Networks to Vision Transformers: Evolution of Deep Learning in Agricultural Pest and Disease Identification. *Agronomy* **2025**, *15*, 1079. [CrossRef]
8. Ren, Z.; Liang, K.; Liu, Y.; Wu, X.; Zhang, C.; Mei, X.; Zhang, Y. A Neural Network with Multiscale Convolution and Feature Attention Based on an Electronic Nose for Rapid Detection of Common Bunt Disease in Wheat Plants. *Agriculture* **2025**, *15*, 415. [CrossRef]
9. Zhao, X.; Li, K.; Li, Y.; Ma, J.; Zhang, L. Identification method of vegetable diseases based on transfer learning and attention mechanism. *Comput. Electron. Agric.* **2022**, *193*, 106703. [CrossRef]
10. Hao, X.; Wang, Z.; Zhang, Y.; Li, F.; Wang, M.; Li, J.; Mao, R. Detecting wheat yellow dwarf disease by employing a Dual-Branch multiscale model from UAV multispectral images. *Comput. Electron. Agric.* **2025**, *230*, 109898. [CrossRef]
11. Bao, W.; Yang, Z.; Zhang, P.; Hu, f.; Hu, G.; Huang, L.; Yang, X. A domain adaptive wheat scab detection method for UAV images. *Comput. Electron. Agric.* **2025**, *233*, 110081. [CrossRef]
12. Xu, K.; Hou, Y.; Sun, W.; Chen, D.; Lv, D.; Xing, J.; Yang, R. A Detection Method for Sweet Potato Leaf Spot Disease and Leaf-Eating Pests. *Agriculture* **2025**, *15*, 503. [CrossRef]
13. Aloyce, A.A. Climate change and its impact on wheat stem rust disease dynamics in Tanzania. *Discov. Agric.* **2025**, *3*, 1–12. [CrossRef]
14. Sowmiya, M.; Krishnaveni, S. IoT enabled prediction of agriculture's plant disease using improvedϖ quantum whale optimization DRDNN approach. *Meas. Sens.* **2023**, *27*, 100812. [CrossRef]
15. Sharma, P.; Sharma, P.D.; Bansal, S. Optimum RBM encoded SVM model with ensemble feature Extractor-based plant disease prediction. *Chemom. Intell. Lab. Syst.* **2025**, *258*, 105319. [CrossRef]
16. Shabari, B.S.; Siddappa, M.; Surendra, S.; Vidyasagar, S.; Suresh, R. Detection and classification of diseased plant leaf images using hybrid algorithm. *Multimed. Tools Appl.* **2023**, *82*, 32349–32372.
17. He, P.; Li, X.; Shen, W.; Deng, S.; Xiao, L.; Zhang, Y. Traceability and analysis method for measurement laboratory testing data based on intelligent Internet of Things and deep belief network. *J. Intell. Syst.* **2024**, *33*, 20240076. [CrossRef]
18. Zhang, C.; Ni, R.; Mu, Y.; Sun, Y.; Thobela, L. Lightweight Multi-scale Convolutional Neural Network for Rice Leaf Disease Recognition. *Comput. Mater. Contin.* **2023**, *74*, 983–994.
19. Bai, Y.P.; Feng, Y.K.; Li, G.H.; Zhao, M.; Zhou, H.; Hou, Z. Algorithm of wheat disease image identification based on Vision Transformer. *J. Chin. Agric. Mech.* **2024**, *45*, 267.
20. Sun, X.; Li, G.; Qu, P.; Xie, X.; Pan, X.; Zhang, W. Research on plant disease identification based on CNN. *Cogn. Robot.* **2022**, *2*, 155–163. [CrossRef]
21. Deng, Y.; Wang, X.; Long, C.; Liu, J.; Zhu, X.; Tan, S. Rice leaf blast lesion segmentation and disease severity grading based on VCDM-UNet. *Trans. Chin. Soc. Agric. Eng.* **2024**, *40*, 190–198.
22. Zhang, H.; Dai, C.; Ren, J.; Wang, G.; Teng, F.; Wang, D. Research on grape disease identification method based on GhostNetV2 improved YOLO v8 model. *J. Agric. Mech.* **2025**, *15*, 1–11.
23. Jiang, S.; Cao, Y.; Liu, Z.; Zhao, S.; Zhang, Z.; Wang, W. Tea leaf disease identification based on improved Faster RCNN. *J. Huazhong Agric. Univ.* **2024**, *43*, 41–50.

24. Yang, X. *Research on Wheat Disease Identification and Severity Grading Method Based on Convolutional Neural Networks*; Anhui University: Hefei, China, 2022.
25. Picon, A.; Alvarez-Gila, A.; Seitz, M.; Ortiz-Barredo, A.; Echazarra, J.; Johannes, A. Deep convolutional neural networks for mobile capture device-based crop disease classification in the wild. *Comput. Electron. Agric.* **2019**, *161*, 280–290. [CrossRef]
26. Wu, Y.; Wu, Y.; Wang, B.; Yang, H. A Remote Sensing Method for Crop Mapping Based on Multiscale Neighborhood Feature Extraction. *Remote Sens.* **2022**, *15*, 47. [CrossRef]
27. Zhang, Y.; Zhang, N.; Zhu, J.; Sun, T.; Chai, X.; Dong, W. Efficient Triple Attention and AttentionMix: A Novel Network for Fine-Grained Crop Disease Classification. *Agriculture* **2025**, *15*, 313. [CrossRef]
28. *GB/T 17980.22—2000*; Pesticide—Guidelines for the Field Efficacy Trials (I)—Fungicides Against Cereal Powdery Mildew. Standardization Administration of China: Beijing, China, 2000.
29. Singh, R.N.; Krishnan, P.; Bharadwaj, C.; Das, B. Improving prediction of chickpea wilt severity using machine learning coupled with model combination techniques under field conditions. *Ecol. Inform.* **2023**, *73*, 101933. [CrossRef]
30. Di, J.; Li, Q. A method of detecting apple leaf diseases based on improved convolutional neural network. *PLoS ONE* **2022**, *17*, e0262629. [CrossRef] [PubMed]
31. Zhang, D.; Hou, L.; Lv, L.; Qi, H.; Sun, H.; Zhang, X.; Li, S.; Min, J.; Liu, Y.; Tang, Y.; et al. Precision Agriculture: Temporal and Spatial Modeling of Wheat Canopy Spectral Characteristics. *Agriculture* **2025**, *15*, 326. [CrossRef]
32. Al-Gaashani, M.S.; Shang, F.; Abd El-Latif, A.A. Ensemble Learning of Lightweight Deep Convolutional Neural Networks for Crop Disease Image Detection. *J. Circuits Syst. Comput.* **2023**, *32*, 2350086. [CrossRef]
33. Nirmal, R.; Senthil, P.; Sanjay, S.; Grish, K.S.; Shamimul, Q.; Prabhu, C.A. Computer aided agriculture development for crop disease detection by segmentation and classification using deep learning architectures. *Comput. Electr. Eng.* **2022**, *103*, 108357. [CrossRef]
34. Feng, G.; Gu, Y.; Wang, C.; Zhang, D.; Xu, R.; Zhu, Z.; Luo, B. Wheat Fusarium head blight severity grading using generative adversarial networks and semi-supervised segmentation. *Comput. Electron. Agric.* **2025**, *229*, 109817. [CrossRef]
35. Liu, Y.; Ma, X.; An, L.; Sun, H.; Zhao, F.; Yan, X.; Ma, Y.T.; Li, M. Exploring UAV narrow-band hyperspectral indices and crop functional traits derived from radiative transfer models to detect wheat powdery mildew. *Int. J. Appl. Earth Obs. Geoinf.* **2025**, *141*, 104627. [CrossRef]
36. Wang, B. Zero-exemplar deep continual learning for crop disease recognition: A study of total variation attention regularization in vision transformers. *Front. Plant Sci.* **2024**, *141*, 1283055. [CrossRef] [PubMed]
37. Quach, N.T.; Vu, T.H.N.; Nguyen, T.T.A.; Le, P.C.; Do, H.G.; Nauyen, T.D.; Thao, P.T.H.; Nguyen, T.T.L.; Chu, H.H.; Phi, Q.-T. Metabolic and genomic analysis deciphering biocontrol potential of endophytic Streptomyces albus RC2 against crop pathogenic fungi. *Braz. J. Microbiol.* **2023**, *54*, 2617–2626. [CrossRef] [PubMed]
38. Mohaimin, A.Z.A.; Krishnamoorthy, S.; Shivanand, P. A critical review on bioaerosols—Dispersal of crop pathogenic microorganisms and their impact on crop yield. *Braz. J. Microbiol.* **2024**, *55*, 587–628. [CrossRef] [PubMed]
39. Ghazanfar, L.; Abdelhamid, S.E.; Mallouhy, R.E.; Alghazo, J.; Kazimi, Z.A. Deep Learning Utilization in Agriculture: Detection of Rice Plant Diseases Using an Improved CNN Model. *Plants* **2022**, *11*, 2230. [CrossRef] [PubMed]
40. Gunawan, M.Z.; Sihombing, P.; Sutarman. Optimization of the CNN model for smart agriculture. *IOP Conf. Ser. Mater. Sci. Eng.* **2021**, *1088*, 012029. [CrossRef]
41. Vasiliki, M.S.; Theodora, S.; Argyrios, S.; Minas, D. An Efficient Hybrid CNN Classification Model for Tomato Crop Disease. *Technologies* **2023**, *11*, 10. [CrossRef]
42. Mallick, M.D.T.; Biswas, S.; Das, A.K.; Saha, H.N.; Chakrabarti, A.; Deb, N. Deep learning based automated disease detection and pest classification in Indian mung bean. *Multimed. Tools Appl.* **2023**, *82*, 12017–12041. [CrossRef]
43. Fu, Y.; Guo, L.; Huang, F. A lightweight CNN model for pepper leaf disease recognition in a human palm background. *Heliyon* **2024**, *10*, e33447. [CrossRef] [PubMed]
44. Saleh, A.; Momina, M. Efficient attention-based CNN network (EANet) for multi-class maize crop disease classification. *Front. Plant Sci.* **2022**, *13*, 1003152.
45. Jose, G.E.; Margarita, G.; Melitsa, T.T.; Natasha, M.; Juan, C.; Calabria, S.; Romany, F.M. Intelligent Sine Cosine Optimization with Deep Transfer Learning Based Crops Type Classification Using Hyperspectral Images. *Can. J. Remote Sens.* **2022**, *48*, 621–632.
46. Woźniak, A.; Haliniarz, M. Response of winter wheat to 35-year cereal monoculture. *Agriculture* **2025**, *15*, 489. [CrossRef]
47. Tao, J.; Li, X.; He, Y.; Islam, M.A. CEFW-YOLO: A High-Precision Model for Plant Leaf Disease Detection in Natural Environments. *Agriculture* **2025**, *15*, 833. [CrossRef]
48. Feng, X.; Li, D.; Wang, W.; Zheng, G.; Liu, H.; Sun, Y.; Liang, S.; Yang, Y.; Zang, H. Wheat leaf disease image recognition based on lightweight convolutional neural network and transfer learning. *Henan Agric. Sci.* **2021**, *50*, 174–180.
49. Lou, G.Z.; Zhang, L.L.; Guo, Z.H.; Bi, X.; Zhao, K. Lightweight wheat disease recognition network based on multi-scale attention. *J. Inn. Mong. Agric. Univ. (Nat. Sci. Ed.)* **2025**, 1–14.

50. Gao, C.; Ji, X.; He, Q.; Gong, Z.; Sun, H.; Wen, T.; Guo, W. Monitoring of wheat fusarium head blight on spectral and textural analysis of UAV multispectral imagery. *Agriculture* **2023**, *13*, 293. [CrossRef]
51. Gamal, N.R.; Fattah, A.A.; El-Rashidy, M.A.; El-Rashidy, A.E.; EI-Sayed, A.; Hemdan, E. E-D. An Efficient Plant Disease Recognition System Using Hybrid Convolutional Neural Networks (CNNs) and Conditional Random Fields (CRFs) for Smart IoT Applications in Agriculture. *Int. J. Comput. Intell. Syst.* **2022**, *15*, 65.

agriculture

Article

Maize Leaf Area Index Estimation Based on Machine Learning Algorithm and Computer Vision

Wanna Fu [1], Zhen Chen [1], Qian Cheng [1], Yafeng Li [1,2], Weiguang Zhai [1], Fan Ding [1], Xiaohui Kuang [1], Deshan Chen [1] and Fuyi Duan [1,*]

1 Institute of Farmland Irrigation, Chinese Academy of Agricultural Sciences, Xinxiang 453002, China; 82101235622@caas.cn (W.F.); chenzhen@caas.cn (Z.C.); chengqian@caas.cn (Q.C.); 212204020029@home.hpu.edu.cn (Y.L.); zhaiweiguang@caas.cn (W.Z.); 82101231074@caas.cn (F.D.); kuangxiaohui@henu.edu.cn (X.K.); 2023055908@nwafu.edu.cn (D.C.)

2 School of Surveying and Land Information Engineering, Henan Polytechnic University, Jiaozuo 454003, China

* Correspondence: duanfuyi@caas.cn

Abstract: Precise estimation of the leaf area index (LAI) is vital in efficient maize growth monitoring and precision farming. Traditional LAI measurement methods are often destructive and labor-intensive, while techniques relying solely on spectral data suffer from limitations such as spectral saturation. To overcome these difficulties, the study integrated computer vision techniques with UAV-based remote sensing data to establish a rapid and non-invasive method for estimating the LAI in maize. Multispectral imagery of maize was acquired via UAV platforms across various phenological stages, and vegetation features were derived based on the Excess Green (ExG) Index and the Hue–Saturation–Value (HSV) color space. LAI standardization was performed through edge detection and the cumulative distribution function. The proposed LAI estimation model, named VisLAI, based solely on visible light imagery, demonstrated high accuracy, with R^2 values of 0.84, 0.75, and 0.50, and RMSE values of 0.24, 0.35, and 0.44 across the big trumpet, tasseling–silking, and grain filling stages, respectively. When HSV-based optimization was applied, VisLAI achieved even better performance, with R^2 values of 0.92, 0.90, and 0.85, and RMSE values of 0.19, 0.23, and 0.22 at the respective stages. The estimation results were validated against ground-truth data collected using the LAI-2200C plant canopy analyzer and compared with six machine learning algorithms, including Gradient Boosting (GB), Random Forest (RF), Ridge Regression (RR), Support Vector Regression (SVR), and Linear Regression (LR). Among these, GB achieved the best performance, with R^2 values of 0.88, 0.88, and 0.65, and RMSE values of 0.22, 0.25, and 0.34. However, VisLAI consistently outperformed all machine learning models, especially during the grain filling stage, demonstrating superior robustness and accuracy. The VisLAI model proposed in this study effectively utilizes UAV-captured visible light imagery and computer vision techniques to achieve accurate, efficient, and non-destructive estimation of maize LAI. It outperforms traditional and machine learning-based approaches and provides a reliable solution for real-world maize growth monitoring and agricultural decision-making.

Keywords: unmanned aerial vehicle; vegetation indices; machine learning; computer vision; leaf area index

1. Introduction

The leaf area index (LAI) is an essential agronomic indicator, significantly influencing maize development and its photosynthetic efficiency. It is essential for evaluating maize

 https://doi.org/10.3390/agriculture15121272

development, photosynthetic efficiency, and ecological functions. The magnitude of the LAI directly affects the efficiency of photosynthesis, influencing maize growth rates, yield, and resilience to environmental stresses. As a fundamental vegetation structural parameter, the LAI is extensively used in the fields of ecology, agriculture, and climate change research. It is a unitless metric used to express the total single-sided leaf surface area per unit ground area and is widely used as an important parameter in ecological and climate models. The LAI serves as a key indicator for maize variety improvement, agricultural management, ecological monitoring, and decision-making processes in agriculture. Therefore, timely and precise LAI estimation plays a crucial role in monitoring maize development, predicting yield, and guiding field management [1].

Traditional approaches to estimating the LAI are generally categorized into direct and indirect approaches. Direct measurements require destructive sampling to obtain the maize's leaf area. Although this approach provides high accuracy, its applicability for large-scale field monitoring is constrained by the inherently destructive nature of the sampling process and the substantial costs associated with it [2]. In contrast, the indirect measurement method determines the LAI using optical instruments (such as the LAI-2200C or fisheye cameras), allowing for non-destructive, repeatable measurements and dynamic monitoring of the maize over time, but its accuracy can also be affected by human and environmental factors. He et al. [3] demonstrated that when the natural canopy structure of cotton fields is altered, the LAI-2200C measurements tend to underestimate the true LAI, especially in relatively high-density cotton fields.

Recently, the utilization of unmanned aerial vehicles(UAVs) has been rapidly expanding across the agricultural sector, particularly for observing maize growth stages, identifying crop diseases, and conducting other agronomic evaluations, due to their efficiency in acquiring high-resolution canopy images within a short timeframe. Zhang et al. [4] employed wavelength feature selection along with machine learning techniques to develop a model for estimating the leaf area index based on hyperspectral data derived from images acquired by unmanned aerial vehicles (UAVs). Analysis revealed a correlation coefficient greater than 0.99 between UAV-based imagery and Analytical Spectral Devices' (ASDs) hyperspectral measurements, accompanied by an R^2 value of 0.89. UAV-based remote sensing offers substantial advantages for large-scale agricultural monitoring, including efficient, real-time, or periodic monitoring, non-destructive sampling, and the acquisition of multispectral data, thus providing precise data support for maize growth assessment. The UAV platform can be equipped with various camera sensors, such as red green blue (RGB), multispectral, and hyperspectral. Such sensors enable the collection of imagery with fine spatial and temporal resolution, allowing for the detection of gradual variations in maize development across time [5].

In contrast to satellite-based methods, low-altitude UAV remote sensing enables the collection of fine-scale data with superior temporal and spatial resolution. Jin et al. [6] utilized UAV-mounted hyperspectral sensors in combination with radiative transfer modeling (RTM) and machine learning algorithms to estimate rice canopy leaf area index (LAI) and leaf chlorophyll content (LCC). Their findings indicated that the extreme learning machine (ELM)-based models trained with the RPIOSL-UBM dataset, yielded the best performance, achieving RMSE values of 0.6357 and 6.0101 $\mu g \cdot cm^{-2}$ for LAI and LCC, respectively, outperforming models based on the PROSAIL dataset. The improvement over PROSAIL-based models was reflected in RMSE reductions of 0.1076 and 6.3297 $\mu g \cdot cm^{-2}$, respectively. Du et al. [7] constructed a nitrogen-stress-specific LAI estimation model by fusing UAV-acquired multi-source data and applying several machine learning algorithms. It was observed that the integration of diverse data sources led to a noticeable improvement in the model's prediction accuracy, outperforming models built on single-source features.

By integrating average spectral reflectance (ASR), vegetation indices (VIs), and texture features, the Random Forest (RF)model achieved optimal performance, with $R_P{}^2$ and RMSEP values of 0.78 and 0.49, respectively.

In recent years, increasing scholarly interest has been directed toward the use of computer vision techniques for tasks such as visual recognition and target identification [8]. From a technical standpoint, image processing is intrinsically linked to computer vision [9]. Image processing techniques provide significant flexibility and efficiency, facilitating the accurate extraction of maize phenotypic features, such as canopy height and leaf area, through methods including image segmentation, edge detection, and object recognition. These techniques, particularly effective in detail recognition and feature extraction, address the limitations of remote sensing technologies and are less prone to interference from large-scale environmental changes. Leveraging image processing, computer vision can accurately differentiate maize from the background using data from RGB and grayscale images, thus mitigating interference from factors such as clouds and shadows in remote sensing data. Elinisa et al. [10] employed a U-Net-based deep learning model for semantic segmentation to enable the early identification and delineation of Fusarium wilt and black Sigatoka disease in bananas. Experimental results indicated that the model achieved a Dice coefficient of 96.45% and an Intersection over Union (IoU) of 93.23%. Sun et al. [11] proposed a sample-independent approach for delineating crop field boundaries by combining super-resolution image enhancement with a dual edge-refined Segment Anything Model (SAM). The super-resolution component enhanced the clarity of PS and S2 imagery, resulting in a 10% improvement in Intersection over Union (IoU) for boundary extraction. Furthermore, the dual edge-refined SAM demonstrated superior performance compared to conventional edge detection and multi-scale segmentation methods, with the IoU of SIDEST improving by 8.1% over state-of-the-art deep learning-based farmland classification models on publicly available datasets. Lu et al. [12] applied computer vision techniques to explore threshold-based image segmentation approaches for measuring tea leaf area, incorporating grayscale, RGB, and HSV color space features. Their findings showed that the HSV-based segmentation algorithm yielded over 94% accuracy in estimating tea leaf area. Additionally, image processing techniques can be integrated with machine learning algorithms to automatically extract various maize growth parameters by learning from and training on large datasets, thereby enabling real-time monitoring and analysis.

Integrating UAV-based remote sensing technology and computer vision offers a promising and efficient solution for LAI estimation in agricultural production. By leveraging image processing and analysis, computer vision methods can autonomously extract maize characteristics, thereby enabling precise and efficient LAI estimation. These methods are less prone to human errors and environmental variations, thereby enhancing the reliability of the results. While preliminary studies have explored machine vision-based techniques for LAI estimation, challenges remain regarding accuracy, cost-effectiveness, and the wide-spread applicability of these methods [13].

In conclusion, the VisLAI system is designed to automatically estimate the LAI using computer vision technology and UAV-based remote sensing imagery. By deploying UAVs to capture orthophotos of maize fields, the system applies advanced image processing techniques to autonomously identify maize areas and compute the LAI. The main goal is to improve the precision and efficiency of LAI estimation, overcoming the inherent limitations of conventional measurement techniques. This system aims to provide a real-time, efficient solution for LAI monitoring in precision agriculture, offering valuable technical support for maize growth assessment, precision irrigation and fertilization, and crop yield forecasting.

2. Materials and Methods

2.1. Overview of the Study Area

The experimental site is located at the Xinxiang Comprehensive Experimental Base of the Chinese Academy of Agricultural Sciences, Xinxiang City, Henan Province (113°45′42″ E, 35°08′05″ N). This region is characterized by a temperate continental monsoon climate, with an average annual rainfall of approximately 500 mm. The abundant summer rainfall creates an ideal environment for maize cultivation. The soil in the experimental area is classified as light loam, and irrigation is conducted using large-scale center-pivot sprinklers. The experiment comprised 56 plots, and each plot had dimensions of 3 m × 2 m, with a row spacing of 0.6 m and a plant spacing of 0.25 m. The layout of the experimental plots is illustrated in Figure 1.

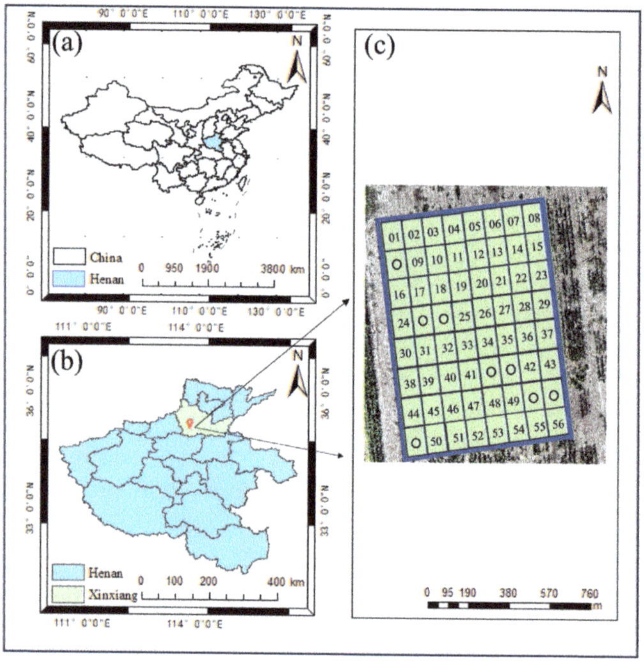

Figure 1. Location and experimental design of the study area. (**a**) Location of Henan in China; (**b**) boundary of Henan province; (**c**) maize experiment in the study area. ○, indicates that the maize in the plot has not emerged.

2.2. Data Acquisition

2.2.1. Field Data Acquisition

Data collection was conducted during critical growth stages of maize, such as the big trumpet stage, tasseling–silking, and grain filling stages, through a combination of UAV imagery and field instrument measurements. Meanwhile, the BBCH scale and description [14] corresponding to the three periods are shown in Table 1. Ground-level LAI data were collected using the LAI-2200C Plant Canopy Analyzer (LI-COR, USA), hereafter referred to as measured LAI. Three measurements were obtained from various positions within each plot, spanning both horizontal and vertical directions, and the plot's LAI was determined by averaging the recorded measurements. For each growth stage, data collection was conducted on a single day. A summary of the statistical information of the maize LAI parameters is presented in Table 2.

Table 1. The BBCH scale and description of the relevant phenological stage of maize.

Phenology Stage	BBCH Scale	Description
Principal growth stage 3: stem elongation	39	Nine or more nodes detectable
Principal growth stage 5: inflorescence emergence, heading	51	Beginning of tassel emergence: tassel detectable at top of stem
Principal growth stage 6: flowering, anthesis	61	Male: stamens in middle of tassel visible Female: tip of ear emerging from leaf sheath
Principal growth stage 7: development of fruit	71	Beginning of grain development: kernels at blister stage, approximately 16% dry matter

Table 2. Statistics of LAI parameters of maize at different growth stages.

Growth Stages	Data	Sample Size	Leaf Area Index (LAI)			
			Min	Max	Mean	Standard Deviation
Big trumpet stage	25 July 2024	56	0.48	2.36	1.46	0.43
Tasseling–silking stage	5 August 2024	56	0.50	2.42	1.59	0.47
Grain filling stage	20 August 2024	56	0.47	2.19	1.30	0.39

2.2.2. Acquisition and Preprocessing of UAV Remote Sensing Data

This study utilized the DJI Mavic 3M UAV (SZ DJI Technology Co., Shenzhen, China) to collect aerial data on the same day as ground data collection. The visible light camera equipped on this model has a sensor size of 17.3 mm × 13.0 mm, a resolution of 5280 × 3956 pixels, 20 million effective pixels, and an equivalent focal length of 24 m. The multispectral camera features a 5-megapixel effective resolution and an equivalent focal length of 25 mm. It captures spectral data across four bands: Green (G: 560 ± 16 nm), Near-Infrared (NIR: 860 ± 26 nm), Red Edge (RE: 730 ± 16 nm), and Red (R: 650 ± 16 nm).

The DJI Mavic 3M UAV was deployed for low-altitude flights at 5 m above ground level over the experimental area to acquire RGB images for model development. For the collection of multispectral imagery used in vegetation index calculation, flight missions were planned using DJI Pilot 2 software (SZ DJI Technology Co., Shenzhen, China). The camera was maintained in a nadir orientation, and the flight altitude was set at 30 m above ground level. Both the forward and side overlap rates were configured at 80%, ensuring high-quality image mosaicking and accurate feature identification. To minimize the influence of solar angle on image quality, data acquisition was conducted under clear and windless weather conditions. All UAV flights were scheduled between 11:00 a.m. and 2:00 p.m. Beijing time, corresponding to the period of relatively high and stable solar elevation, which helps reduce shadow effects and ensures consistent illumination across the study area, as shown in Figure 2.

After completing the UAV flight missions, the multispectral images were stitched using Pix4Dmapper 4.5.6 (Pix4D, Lausanne, Switzerland) to generate orthomosaic images. The image processing workflow included key steps such as importing ground control points (GCPs), image registration, alignment, dense point cloud generation, and radiometric correction. Subsequently, ArcGIS 10.6 (Environmental Systems Research Institute, Redlands, CA, USA) was used to georeferenced UAV images acquired at different growth stages. Vegetation indices were extracted by delineating polygon vectors for each plot.

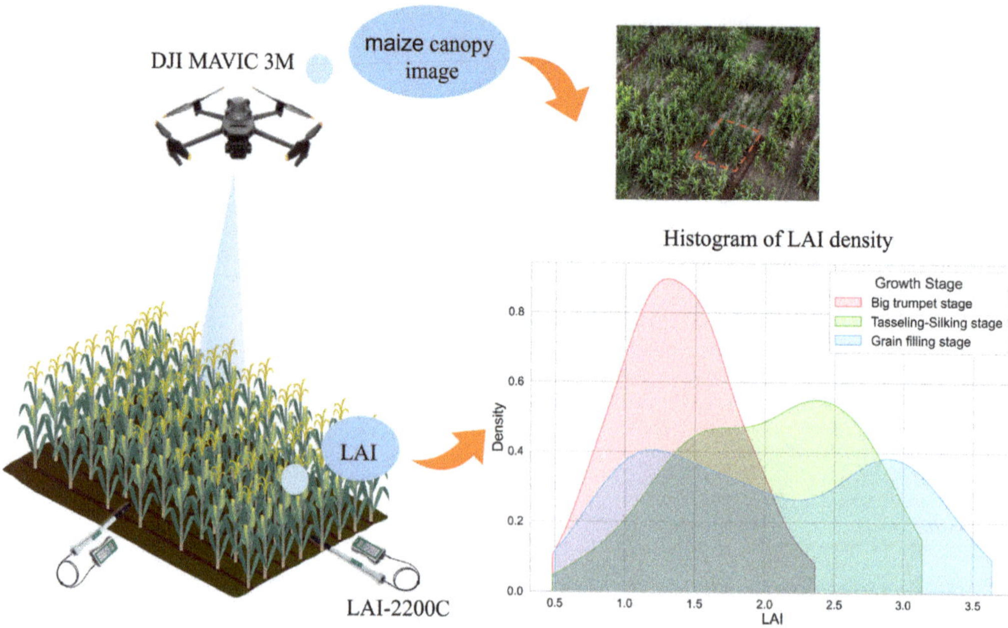

Figure 2. Schematic of UAV data and LAI data collection. The red box indicates the shooting area.

2.2.3. Vegetation Indices Extraction

Vegetation indices are derived by combining data from various spectral bands to emphasize vegetation characteristics and objectively differentiate between vegetation and soil [15]. It effectively reduces the impact of factors like land surface types, and atmospheric conditions on vegetation reflectance, facilitating precise monitoring of subtle variations in maize biochemical markers [16,17]. Building on previous studies [18–38], this study identified and computed various vegetation indices, with the corresponding formulas listed in Table 3.

Table 3. List of vegetation indices (VIs) considered for analysis, their formula, and their source.

VI	Formula	Source
Normalized difference vegetation index (NDVI)	$(\mathrm{NIR}-\mathrm{R})/(\mathrm{NIR}+\mathrm{R})$	[18]
Renormalized difference vegetation index (RDVI)	$(\mathrm{NIR}-\mathrm{R})/\sqrt{(\mathrm{NIR}+\mathrm{R})}$	[19]
Excess green index (ExG)	$2*\mathrm{G}-\mathrm{R}-\mathrm{B}$	[20]
Kernel normalized difference vegetation index (kNDVI)	$\tanh\left(\left(\frac{\mathrm{NIR}-\mathrm{R}}{2\sigma}\right)^2\right)$	[21]
Ratio vegetation index (RVI)	NIR/R	[22]
Optimization of soil regulatory vegetation index (OSAVI)	$1.16*[(\mathrm{NIR}-\mathrm{R})/(\mathrm{NIR}+\mathrm{R}+0.16)]$	[23]
Modified ratio vegetation index (MSR)	$\mathbf{(NIR/R-1)SQRT(NIR/R+1)}$	[24]
Modified greenness ratio vegetation index (MSR_G)	$\mathbf{(NIR/G-1)SQRT(NIR/G+1)}$	[25]
Nonlinear vegetation index (NLI)	$\left(\mathrm{NIR}^2-\mathrm{R}\right)/\left(\mathrm{NIR}^2+\mathrm{R}\right)$	[26]
Optimal vegetation index (Vlopt)	$1.45*\left(\mathrm{NIR}^2+1\right)/(\mathrm{R}+0.45)$	[27]
Red edge normalized difference vegetation index (RENDVI)	$(\mathrm{RE}-\mathrm{R})/(\mathrm{RE}+\mathrm{R})$	[28]
Red edge ratio vegetation index (RESR)	RE/R	[29]
Modified nonlinear vegetation index (MNLI)	$1.5\left(\mathrm{NIR}^2-\mathrm{R}\right)/\left(\mathrm{NIR}^2+\mathrm{R}+0.5\right)$	[30]
Wide dynamic range vegetation index (WDRVI)	$(a*\mathrm{NIR}-\mathrm{R})/(a*\mathrm{NIR}+\mathrm{R})$	[31]
Green chlorophyll vegetation index (GCVI)	$\mathrm{NIR}/\mathrm{G}-1$	[32]

Table 3. *Cont.*

VI	Formula	Source
Modified double-difference vegetation index (MDD)	$(NIR - RE) - (RE - G)$	[33]
Modified chlorophyll absorption reflectance index (MCARI1)	$[(NIR - RE) - 0.2 * (NIR - R)](NIR/RE)$	[34]
Modified transformed chlorophyll absorption reflectance index (MTCAR)	$3[(NIR - RE) - 0.2 * (NIR - R)](NIR/RE)$	[35]
Difference vegetation index (DVI)	$NIR - R$	[36]
Soil-adjusted vegetation index (SAVI)	$(NIR - R)(1 + l)/(NIR + R + l)(l = 0.5)$	[37]
Modified soil-adjusted vegetation index (MSAVI2)	$\left(2 * NIR + 1 - SQRT\left((2 * NIR + 1)^2 - 8 * (NIR - R)\right)\right)/2$	[38]

a = 0.12, σ = 0.5(NIR + R). R: red band reflectivity; G: green band reflectivity; B: blue band reflectivity; NIR: near-infrared band reflectivity.

2.3. Image Processing Principles and Methods

2.3.1. Principles of Image Processing

Image analysis technology is an advanced technique that leverages digital image processing and computer vision. It enhances information and extracts key features through the processing and analysis of image data [39]. A digital image consists of numerous pixels, and the representation and encoding of these pixels are essential elements in image analysis [40]. Therefore, by calculating the physical area represented by each pixel, the actual leaf area can be estimated by counting the pixels corresponding to the leaf in the image.

2.3.2. Determining the Actual Size of the Cell Based on the Field of View Angle

Accurate calculation of the actual leaf area of maize requires consideration of the field of view (FOV), as it influences both the range of leaves captured by the camera and the assessment of lighting conditions. FOV is determined by the lens focal length and the size of the image sensor [41]. By considering the distance between the object and the camera, the pixel size in the image can be estimated, which enables the calculation of the plot dimensions, as illustrated in Figure 3.

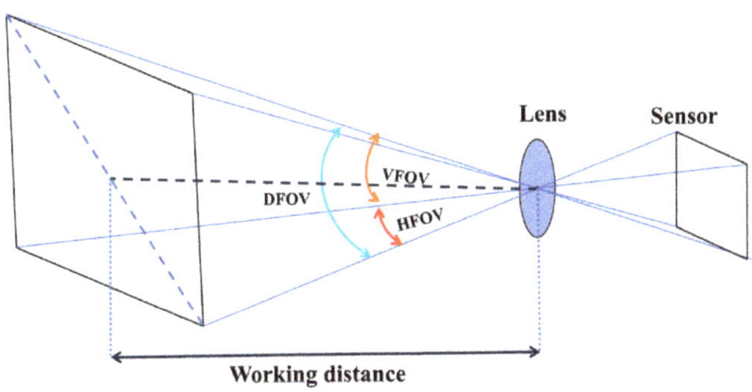

Figure 3. Field of view (FOV) diagram. HFOV: horizontal field of view; VFOV: vertical field of view; DFOV: diagonal field of view.

2.3.3. Segmentation Method Based on RGB and HSV Images

Image segmentation is a crucial preprocessing step in image recognition and computer vision. By extracting regions of interest, it enhances analysis efficiency and provides a foundation for feature extraction and subsequent applications [42]. The OTSU algorithm, also known as Otsu's method, is a widely used global thresholding technique for image binarization, introduced by Otsu [43]. The algorithm analyzes the grayscale histogram of the image to select a threshold value K, which divides the image into a foreground and background by maximizing the inter-class variance between the two [44]. A larger inter-class variance indicates a more distinct separation between the foreground and background, thereby improving the accuracy of segmentation.

The definition of the between-class variance of its target O and background B:

$$e^2(K) = P_O(\mu - \mu_o')^2 + P_b(\mu - \mu_b')^2 \quad (1)$$

In the formula, μ represents the mean grayscale value of the image, μ_o' and μ_b' represent the mean values of the target O and the background B, respectively. When the value of K maximizes $e^2(K)$, K is the optimal threshold.

The Excess Green Index (ExG) effectively differentiates vegetation from soil backgrounds in RGB images [45]. Based on the OSTU algorithm, threshold segmentation to separate the maize from the background in an RGB image, generating a grayscale image.

$$ExG = 2G - R - B \quad (2)$$

In the formula, G represents the green component in an RGB image, R represents the red component, while B represents the blue component.

This approach forms the basis of the VisLAI-RGB model, which estimates the LAI using vegetation indices derived exclusively from the RGB color space. To enhance the robustness and accuracy of LAI estimation, we propose an improved model, VisLAI-HSV. Unlike the conventional VisLAI-RGB model—which relies solely on RGB-based indices (ExG)—the VisLAI-HSV model integrates additional spectral information by transforming RGB images into the hue–saturation–value (HSV) color space. This transformation improves segmentation and feature extraction, particularly under varying illumination conditions and across different phenological stages of maize.

Compared to the RGB model, the hue–saturation–value (HSV) model more closely aligns with human color perception, making it better suited for color contrast and object segmentation [46]. In image processing, the HSV model effectively separates color information, enhancing the stability of object detection. It is particularly useful in monitoring the transition of maize leaves from green to yellow, aiding in the assessment of plant growth and health [47].

Converting from the RGB color model to the HSV model requires calculating the RGB values of each pixel to determine the corresponding hue, saturation, and value [48], the corresponding conversion formula is as follows:

$$V = \max(R, G, B) \quad (3)$$

$$S = \begin{cases} \frac{V - \min(R,G,B)}{V}, & V \neq 0 \\ 0, & \text{other} \end{cases} \quad (4)$$

$$H = \begin{cases} 60 * \frac{G-B}{V-\min(R,G,B)}, & V = R \\ 120 + 60 * \frac{B-R}{V-\min(R,G,B)}, & V = G \\ 240 + 60 * \frac{R-G}{V-\min(R,G,B)}, & V = B \end{cases} \quad (5)$$

In the formula, R: red band reflectivity; G: green band reflectivity; B: blue band reflectivity.

2.3.4. Edge Detection Based on the Canny Algorithm

The Canny edge detection algorithm, proposed by John F. Canny in 1986, is a multi-stage method for edge detection that effectively extracts valuable structural information from images [49]. It is widely employed in various computer vision systems. The algorithm begins with image smoothing using Gaussian filtering to remove noise, followed by the calculation of the image gradient. The magnitudes and directions of the gradient along the horizontal and vertical axes are then determined through differential operations. Edge refinement is achieved through non-maximum suppression, and a dual-thresholding technique is utilized to eliminate false edges while retaining true edges. The final processed image is then output [50]. The algorithm is distinguished by its simplicity and efficiency, effectively detecting edges in an image with a low error rate, while minimizing the influence of noise on the edge detection process.

2.3.5. The Standardized Estimation of LAI Based on the G Function

In image processing, the G function represents an application of the cumulative distribution function (CDF). By providing information on the distribution of leaf area density across various distance ranges, it mitigates biases arising from variations in field of view or observation conditions, thereby enabling the standardized calculation of the LAI [51].

$$G(d) = \frac{\sum_{i=1}^{j} \text{hist}(i)}{\sum_{i=1}^{N} \text{hist}(i)} \quad (6)$$

In the formula, d represents the distance, hist(i) denotes the count of the i-th bin in the histogram, and N is the total count.

Based on the above concepts, this paper proposes a method for the identification and extraction of LAI using computer vision techniques. The proposed method integrates UAV-based remote sensing imagery and processes multiple digital images, thereby enabling more accurate estimations of plant leaf area. By employing techniques such as image segmentation, feature extraction, color space transformation, and edge detection, the method effectively identifies and extracts the plant's leaf area, facilitating the calculation of its surface area. Additionally, the approach incorporates adjustments to FOV and auxiliary calculations utilizing the G function. This ensures standardized processing under various conditions, thereby enhancing the accuracy and comparability of LAI estimates, while also demonstrating robustness across different scenarios.

Figure 4 illustrates the experimental workflow of this study. In this process, the OTSU algorithm is utilized for threshold segmentation, while the ExG Index is employed to differentiate vegetation from the background. The HSV color space is used to monitor leaf chlorosis, and Canny edge detection aids in the precise extraction of leaf contours. Finally, the G function is applied to normalize the calculation of the LAI. Given VisLAI's ability to efficiently and accurately estimate the LAI under complex conditions, it offers a valuable technical reference for advancing the development of smart agriculture.

2.4. *Data Analysis and Evaluation*

2.4.1. Construction of Machine Learning-Based Model for Inversion of LAI

This study utilizes multispectral remote sensing data to develop inversion models for an LAI based on vegetation indices such as the NDVI and EVI. Using the LAI-2200C observation protocol, a correlation was established between the vegetation indices derived from UAV-based multispectral remote sensing observations. Furthermore, the study investigates the dynamic changes in the LAI at the field scale, facilitating the rapid assessment of maize growth through the integration of canopy analysis with UAV spectral technology. Pearson correlation analysis was employed to identify the independent variables most strongly correlated with the dependent variable. To enhance the stability and robustness of the model, the dataset was divided into a training set (80%) and a testing set (20%). Six machine learning algorithms—Gradient Boosting (GB), Ridge Regression (RR), Lasso Regression (Lasso), Linear Regression (LR), SVR, and RF—were employed to construct LAI inversion models for different growth stages.

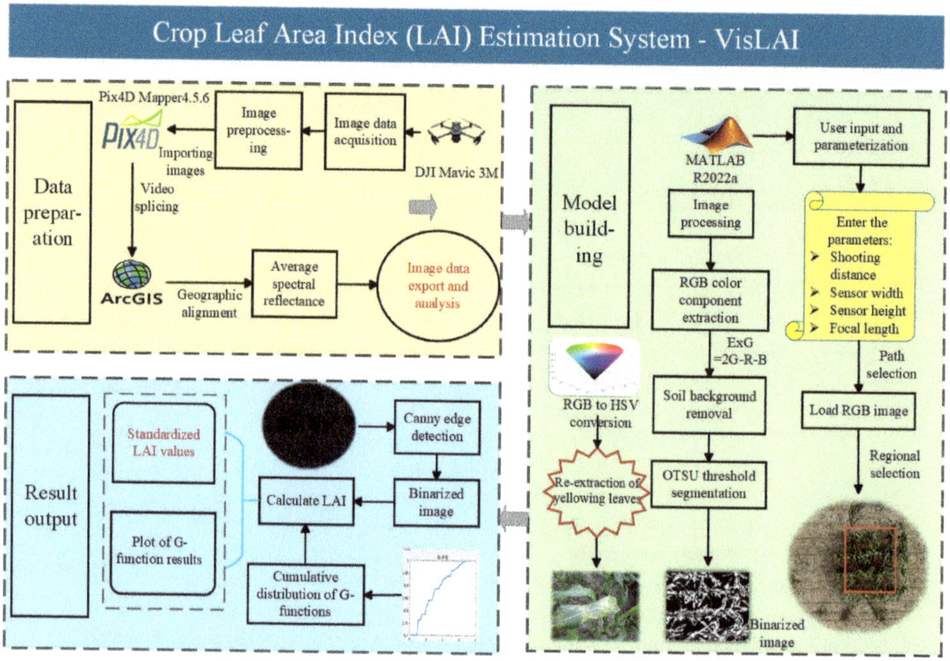

Figure 4. Technical workflow diagram of this experiment. ExG: Excess Green Index. The red box indicates the shooting area.

LR is a widely used statistical method for modeling the quantitative relationships between variables. It predicts the value of the target variable by identifying the optimal linear relationship between the independent and dependent variables [52,53]. RR is an improved version of Linear Regression that reduces model overfitting by adding a regularization term to the ordinary least squares (OLS) regression. This regularization term constrains the magnitude of the model parameters, thereby improving the model's performance on new, unseen data. RR is particularly effective in addressing multicollinearity, a common issue in many research contexts [54]. Lasso achieves regularization by applying a penalty function that shrinks the coefficients of the variables in the regression model, thereby preventing overfitting and mitigating issues of severe multicollinearity [55]. RF constructs a forest composed of numerous decision trees built in a random manner, where the trees are independent of each other. Each decision tree generates a prediction, and the final prediction for the observed data is obtained by averaging all the individual predictions [56]. SVR is a prominent technique for addressing regression problems, where the prediction speed is directly related to the sparsity of support vectors [57]. GB is an ensemble learning method that combines multiple weak classifiers or regressors to form a strong classifier or regressor, thereby enhancing predictive performance. The core idea of the GB algorithm is to use the negative gradient of the loss function as an approximation of the residuals. A base learner is then trained to fit these residuals, and its predictions are added to the previous model, iteratively reducing the value of the loss function [58].

To enhance the performance of LAI prediction, a grid search approach is adopted within the vegetation index inversion framework to determine the most effective set of hyperparameters for the six regression models. Each iteration of the grid search incorporates five-fold cross-validation to evaluate the generalizability of the model. This method involves partitioning the dataset into multiple subsets, allowing for a robust assessment of model stability and reliability. Following the tuning process, the optimized models were employed to estimate the LAI across different developmental stages of summer maize.

2.4.2. Construction of LAI Inversion Model Based on Machine Vision

This study developed an automatic estimation model for LAI extraction (VisLAI) based on UAV remote sensing imagery and computer vision technology. By applying median filtering to denoise the image, the RGB color space components are extracted. The ExG and Otsu algorithms are used for thresholding, generating a binarized ExG image. To further improve the accuracy of leaf region identification, the RGB image is converted to the HSV color space, effectively capturing yellowing leaves at different growth stages. This is combined with the initial segmentation results to generate a new binary image. Simultaneously, the Canny edge detection algorithm and the cumulative distribution function (CDF) are used to standardize the calculation of leaf area.

The model uses low-altitude UAV-acquired imagery of individual plots as input to estimate the leaf area index (LAI), and the predicted results are compared with ground-truth measurements obtained using the LAI-2200C plant canopy analyzer.

2.4.3. Model Accuracy Evaluation

This study employs the coefficient of determination (R^2), root mean square error (RMSE), and normalized root mean square error (NRMSE) as metrics for assessing the model's accuracy. A value of R^2 closer to 1 indicates a better fit of the model to the data. Lower values of RMSE and NRMSE correspond to higher accuracy in the model's predictions.

$$R^2 = \frac{\left(\sum_{i=1}^{n} y_i - \bar{y}\right)^2}{\left(\sum_{i=1}^{n} x_i - \bar{y}\right)^2} \tag{7}$$

$$RMSE = \sqrt{\frac{\sum_{i=1,j=1}^{n} (x_i - y_j)^2}{n}} \tag{8}$$

$$NRMSE = \frac{RMSE}{y_{max} - y_{min}} \tag{9}$$

In the formula, x_i represents the observed LAI values of maize, y_i denotes the estimated LAI values of maize, i and j are sample identifiers, n is the total number of samples, and $\bar{y}$ is the mean of the observed values.

3. Results

3.1. Correlation Analysis

The correlation analysis between vegetation indices at various growth stages and the LAI values measured by the LAI-2200C plant canopy analyzer is presented in Figure 5. The Pearson correlation coefficients between the selected vegetation indices and the measured LAI during the big trumpet stage range from 0.85 to 0.93, whereas the coefficients during the tasseling–silking and grain filling stages range from 0.71 to 0.86 and 0.33 to 0.74, respectively. Based on the correlations between the vegetation indices and the measured LAI across different growth stages, the top 20 vegetation indices—such as NDVI, RDVI, MSR, RVI, MSR-G, NLI, OSAVI, GCVI, kNDVI, RENDVI, RESR, WDRVI, MDD, MCARI1, MRETVI, MTCARI, DVI, SAVI, and MSAVI2—demonstrating the most optimal performance were selected as input variables. The measured LAI values served as the output variable. Subsequently, six machine learning algorithms—LR, RR, Lasso, RF, SVR, and GB—were employed to develop LAI inversion models for summer maize across different growth stages.

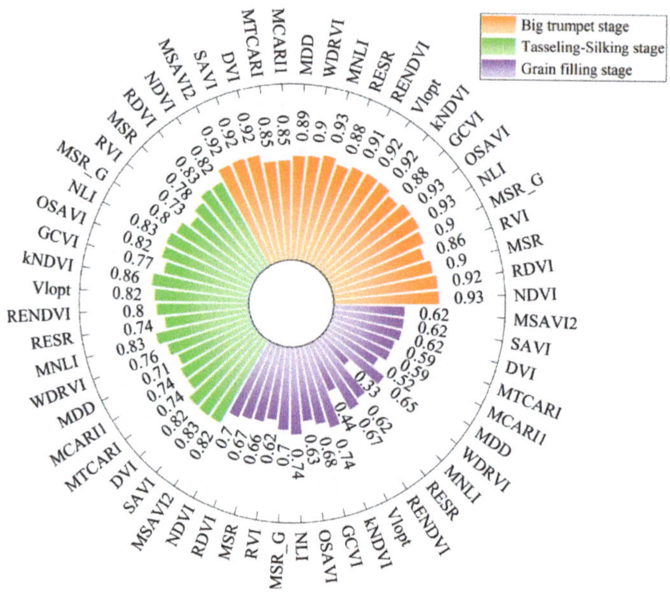

Figure 5. Correlation coefficients between vegetation indices and measured LAI at three different stages.

The correlation coefficient between the LAI estimated by VisLAI and the measured LAI during the big trumpet stage is 0.95, while the coefficients for the tasseling–silking and grain filling stages are 0.93 and 0.92, respectively. These results indicate a strong correlation between the LAI of summer maize estimated by VisLAI and the observed LAI across different growth stages.

3.2. Comparison of Accuracy Across Different Estimation Models

LAI inversion for summer maize was conducted using six distinct machine learning algorithms, with the inversion accuracy results presented in Table 4. The models exhibited lower predictive accuracy during the grain filling stage, while higher accuracy was observed during the big trumpet and tasseling–silking stages. This pattern aligns with the variations in the correlation of individual vegetation indices, thereby further validating the robustness of the model construction.

As presented in Table 4, when evaluating the inversion performance across the three growth stages, the model constructed using the GB algorithm demonstrates the best overall performance. During the big trumpet, tasseling–silking, and grain filling stages, the R^2 of the GB algorithm on the test set ranged from 0.78 to 0.82. In comparison, the R^2 for LR, RR, Lasso, RF, and SVR were marginally lower than those of the GB. Furthermore, the corresponding RMSE (0.26–0.34) and NRMSE (15–16%) for the GB algorithm were consistently lower than those observed for the other models. In conclusion, the model built using the GB algorithm outperforms all other models across the three growth stages and is therefore selected for LAI prediction.

The R^2 for the VisLAI model based on visible light imagery during the big trumpet, tasseling–silking, and grain filling stages are 0.84, 0.75, and 0.50, respectively, with corresponding RMSE values of 0.24, 0.35, and 0.44. In contrast, the R^2 for the HSV-optimized VisLAI are 0.92, 0.90, and 0.85, with RMSE values of 0.19, 0.23, and 0.22. The accuracy of the HSV-optimized VisLAI model significantly outperforms that of the VisLAI model based solely on visible light imagery, particularly during the grain filling stage, where the R^2 improved by 0.08, 0.15, and 0.35, and the RMSE decreased by 0.05, 0.12, and 0.22, respectively. These results indicate that the HSV-optimized VisLAI model is more effective at accurately identifying yellowing leaves and enhancing the precision of LAI estimation. The estimation accuracy of maize LAI using both the VisLAI model based on visible light imagery and the HSV-optimized VisLAI model is summarized in Table 5.

Table 4. Estimation accuracy of maize LAI using different machine learning algorithms.

Machine Learning	Growth Stages	Big Trumpet Stage			Tasseling–Silking Stage			Grain Filling Stage		
	Metric	R^2	RMSE	NRMSE (%)	R^2	RMSE	NRMSE (%)	R^2	RMSE	NRMSE (%)
GB	Training set	0.94	0.15	6%	0.90	0.21	9%	0.89	0.18	8%
	Test set	0.82	0.26	16%	0.78	0.34	15%	0.78	0.28	15%
LR	Training set	0.90	0.20	8%	0.79	0.31	13%	0.69	0.30	14%
	Test set	0.79	0.28	17%	0.55	0.48	21%	0.59	0.38	20%
RR	Training set	0.87	0.22	9%	0.74	0.34	14%	0.52	0.38	17%
	Test set	0.78	0.29	17%	0.68	0.41	18%	0.60	0.37	20%
Lasso	Training set	0.85	0.24	10%	0.74	0.34	14%	0.47	0.40	18%
	Test set	0.79	0.28	17%	0.72	0.38	16%	0.54	0.40	21%
RF	Training set	0.90	0.19	8%	0.80	0.30	12%	0.84	0.21	10%
	Test set	0.81	0.27	16%	0.75	0.36	15%	0.71	0.32	17%
SVR	Training set	0.88	0.21	9%	0.74	0.34	14%	0.61	0.34	15%
	Test set	0.80	0.27	16%	0.70	0.40	17%	0.67	0.34	18%

Table 5. Estimation accuracy of two methods for extracting maize LAI.

Method	Big Trumpet Stage			Tasseling–Silking Stage			Grain Filling Stage		
	R^2	RMSE	NRMSE (%)	R^2	RMSE	NRMSE (%)	R^2	RMSE	NRMSE (%)
VisLAI-RGB	0.84	0.24	14%	0.75	0.35	14%	0.50	0.44	23%
VisLAI-HSV	0.92	0.19	8%	0.90	0.23	9%	0.85	0.22	10%

The regression plots of the maize LAI predicted for all plots during the big trumpet, tasseling–silking, and grain filling stages, using the more accurate VisLAI model (VisLAI-HSV) and the GB algorithm, are presented in Figure 6. The R^2 of the vegetation indices inversion model during the big trumpet stage, tasseling–silking stage, and grain filling stage are 0.88, 0.88, and 0.65, respectively. The corresponding RMSE values are 0.22, 0.25 and 0.34, while the NRMSE values are 9%, 10%, and 15%, respectively. The estimation results from the vegetation indices inversion model indicate that R^2 is highest during the big trumpet stage and tasseling–silking stage. At the same time, the RMSE and NRMSE are smallest during the big trumpet stage.

The accuracy analysis of the VisLAI-predicted summer maize LAI and the measured LAI is presented in Figure 6. R^2 is highest during the big trumpet stage, reaching 0.92, followed by the tasseling–silking stage and the grain filling stage, with R^2 values of 0.90 and 0.85, respectively. The RMSE is lowest during the big trumpet stage, at 0.19, while it is 0.23 for both the tasseling–silking and grain filling stages. Similarly, the NRMSE is also minimal during the big trumpet stage, with a value of 3%, compared to 9% and 10% for the tasseling–silking and grain filling stages, respectively. During the big trumpet, tasseling–silking, and grain filling stages of summer maize, the LAI estimated by VisLAI demonstrates higher accuracy and smaller errors compared to the LAI derived from the vegetation indices inversion model. Especially during the grain filling stage, R^2 of the LAI estimated by VisLAI is significantly higher than that of the LAI derived from the vegetation indices inversion model, while the accuracy of the vegetation indices inversion-based LAI is the lowest during the grain filling stage.

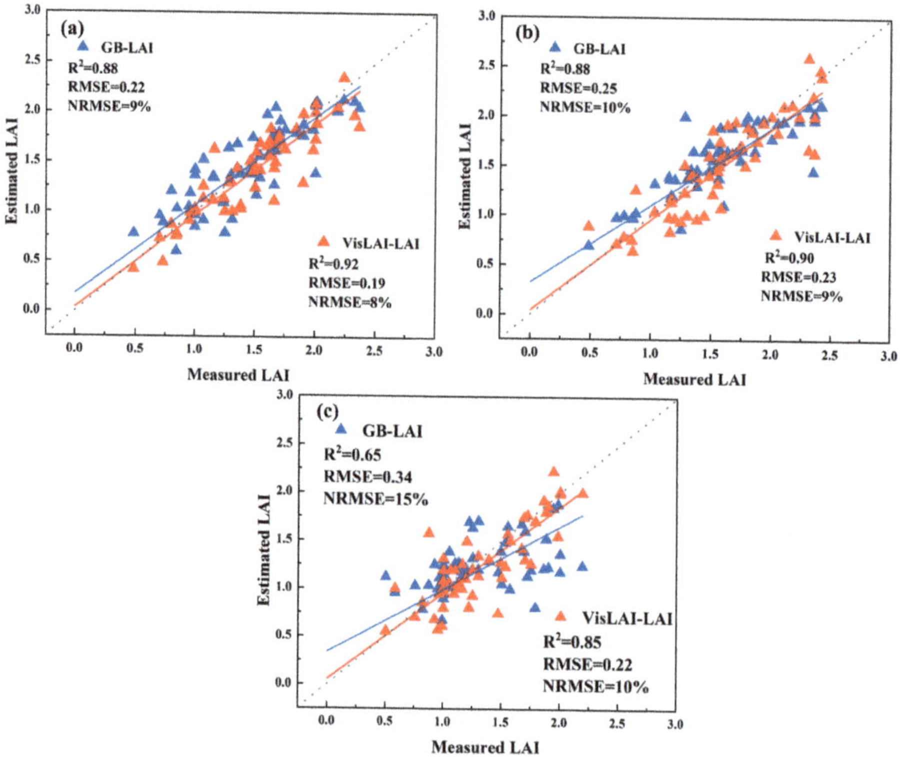

Figure 6. Regression scatter plot of measured LAI versus estimated LAI using GB model and VisLAI model. (**a**) Big trumpet stage; (**b**) tasseling–silking stage; (**c**) grain filling stage. The dashed line represents the 1:1 diagonal. GB-LAI: LAI estimated by the GB model; VisLAI-LAI: LAI estimated by the VisLAI model.

3.3. *Changes in Model Accuracy at Different Fertility Stages*

Figure 7 illustrates the accuracy of LAI estimation by different models across various growth stages. The results highlight the differing performance of machine learning-based algorithms and the VisLAI model, which utilizes UAV imagery and computer vision techniques, in estimating maize LAI during the three growth stages. During the big trumpet stage, R^2 values range from 0.78 to 0.92, with RMSE ranging from 0.19 to 0.29 and NRMSE ranging from 8% to 17%. In the tasseling–silking stage, R^2 values range from 0.55 to 0.90, with RMSE ranging from 0.23 to 0.48 and NRMSE ranging from 9% to 21%. During the grain filling stage, R^2 values range from 0.54 to 0.85, with RMSE ranging from 0.22 to 0.40 and NRMSE ranging from 10% to 21%. The results highlight that, compared to the grain filling and tasseling–silking stages, the models exhibit superior performance during the big trumpet stage, demonstrating their capacity to provide more accurate and precise LAI estimates.

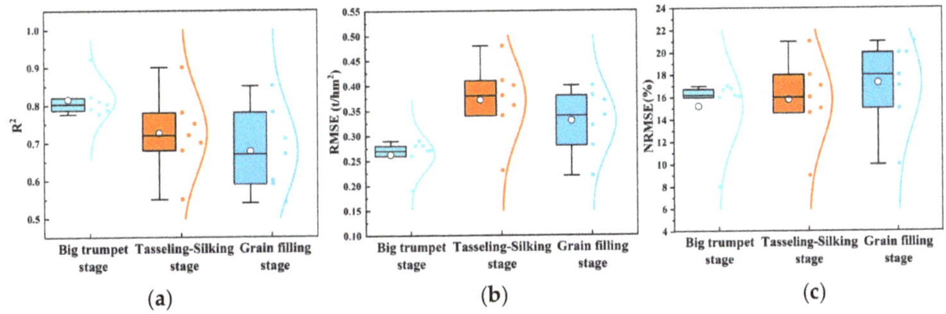

Figure 7. LAI estimation accuracy across different growth stages. (**a**) R^2; (**b**) RMSE; (**c**) NRMSE.

3.4. Spatial Distribution of LAI in Summer Maize

Figure 8 presents the LAI distribution maps for the three growth stages of maize, based on the optimal LAI estimation model (VisLAI). The results of this study indicate that, as maize progresses through its growth stages, the LAI values generally show an initial increase, followed by a subsequent decrease. The average LAI during the big trumpet stage is 1.22, during the tasseling–silking stage is 1.32, and during the grain filling stage is 1.07. During the big trumpet stage, maize experiences rapid growth, with the LAI exhibiting a sharp upward trend, peaking at this stage. As maize enters the grain filling stage, physiological senescence processes such as chlorophyll degradation and reduced photosynthetic activity begin to occur in the leaves. This leads to gradual leaf aging and noticeable shrinkage, leading to a decline in the LAI.

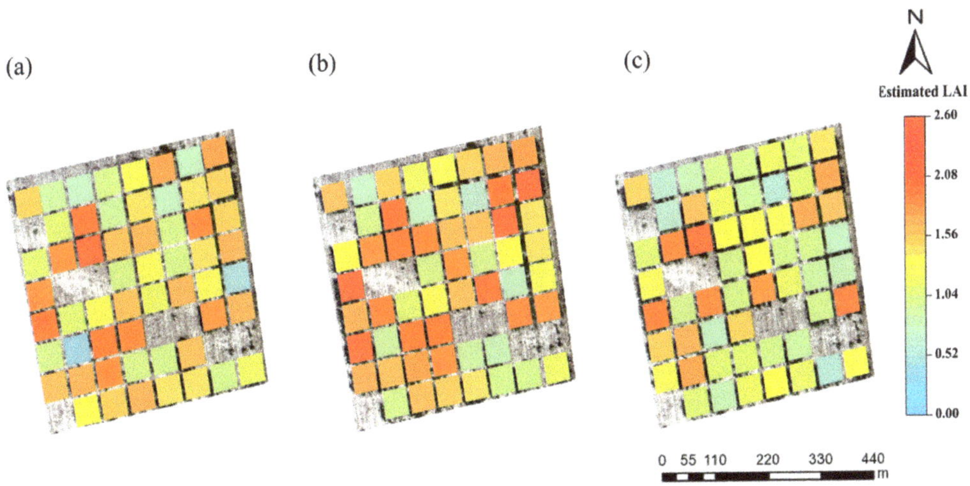

Figure 8. Spatiotemporal distribution of LAI in summer maize across different growth stages. (**a**) Big trumpet stage; (**b**) tasseling–silking stage; (**c**) grain filling stage.

4. Discussion

4.1. Comparison of Different Machine Learning Algorithms

Different machine learning algorithms exhibit varying levels of performance in predicting the LAI of summer maize. GB outperforms all other models, followed by RF. The nonlinear regression model demonstrates significantly higher accuracy than the LR model, as remote sensing data often reveal complex, nonlinear relationships with biomass [17]. LR methods, which rely on linear assumptions, perform poorly in this context because they cannot effectively capture the nonlinear characteristics of the data during the fitting process, resulting in lower prediction accuracy [59]. In contrast, decision tree-based ensemble learning methods exhibit strong robustness and stability when handling high-dimensional data and complex nonlinear relationships.

RF and GB models, by integrating multiple decision trees, progressively mitigate overfitting and enhance the model's generalization ability, resulting in higher prediction accuracy. In contrast, LR and RR models exhibit relatively poor performance in remote sensing data processing, primarily due to their assumption of a linear relationship between input features and the target variable, which makes it difficult to effectively capture complex nonlinear variations. Additionally, LR is highly sensitive to outliers, which can lead to significant prediction errors in remote sensing data. Although RR reduces overfitting through regularization, it still struggles to capture nonlinear relationships effectively, leading to generally inferior performance compared to decision tree-based ensemble learning methods. SVR models, while effective for certain problems [60], are sensitive to the choice of parameters and kernel functions. When handling complex nonlinear relationships, SVR models tend to be less robust than ensemble learning methods. Comparative analysis demonstrates that decision tree-based ensemble learning methods, such as GB and RF, offer a significant advantage in remote sensing data inversion for LAI estimation. These methods excel at handling nonlinear relationships, resulting in higher accuracy and greater robustness.

4.2. LAI Estimation of Summer Maize Based on VisLAI

With the continuous advancements in computer technology, VisLAI has demonstrated exceptional performance in handling dynamic datasets and real-time processing tasks, underscoring its robust adaptability and flexibility. Dorj et al. [61] utilized image processing to estimate citrus orchard yields through fruit detection and counting. Niu et al. [62] fixed fisheye cameras in maize, soybean, and caragana plots to regularly capture canopy images and utilized image processing software to analyze the data and estimate the LAI. While considerable research has been conducted on estimating the LAI, studies focused on enhancing the accuracy of LAI estimation through soil-adjusted vegetation indices, such as the ExG Index, HSV re-extraction, and modifications to the aggregation index G function, remain relatively limited. The ExG Index is widely used as it effectively differentiates between vegetation and soil, demonstrating a strong correlation with the LAI across all three growth stages. However, ExG images often contain erroneous data due to stray light or shadows, especially when the boundary between soil and vegetation is unclear. The application of median filtering for denoising and Gaussian filtering for smoothing proves effective in removing such noise, thereby improving image quality. These findings align with those of Yamaguchi et al. [63].

The conversion from the RGB color space to the HSV color space provides more accurate color information for subsequent image analysis, particularly concerning variations in hue and saturation. At different growth stages, the color of maize leaves undergoes significant changes. During the early growth phase, the plants exhibit healthy leaf development, with the maize leaves in the experimental area fully extended and displaying a vibrant, bright hue. However, as the growth stage progresses, the maize leaves gradually become yellow, showing various shades of brown and reddish-brown. Additionally, the proportion of exposed soil in the experimental area increases. This change forms the theoretical foundation for extracting information from the Hue (H) and Saturation (S) channels in the HSV color space, enabling more precise capture of color variations in the vegetation across different stages. By setting a specific hue range, this study facilitates the re-extraction of leaves exhibiting yellowing and wilting at various growth stages. This method effectively filters out such leaves, thereby improving the accuracy of leaf area estimation. In contrast to the studies by Lu et al. [12] and Niu et al. [62], this research not only focuses on the green portions of the leaves but also incorporates color changes during the leaf senescence stage. This approach enhances the model's adaptability and accuracy in capturing the various stages throughout the maize's growth cycle.

4.3. Advantages and Disadvantages of VisLAI Compared to Machine Learning Algorithms

Image processing techniques enable real-time processing of UAV-captured images, facilitating the rapid calculation of the LAI. Through automated image analysis workflows, large-scale image datasets can be processed efficiently, making this approach particularly suitable for the rapid monitoring and assessment of maize growth conditions. Users need only to configure the photography parameters and define the maize ping area to quickly obtain the LAI of the target region. Although vegetation indices-based inversion methods can estimate the LAI with reasonable accuracy, they rely on external data and involve complex data processing. This is especially true when large sample datasets are required, as training the model can be time-consuming. In contrast, image processing methods enable real-time analysis using existing UAV image data, offering greater flexibility and applicability. By integrating ExG, HSV re-extraction, and G-function normalization, the image processing method effectively mitigates interference from soil background, stray light, and leaf degradation, allowing for a clearer distinction between vegetation and background areas, thereby achieving high-precision region extraction. Vegetation indices are typically estimated based on pixel-level averages to assess vegetation growth status. However, during different growth stages, particularly under more complex conditions such as leaf wilting or yellowing, the inversion accuracy of vegetation indices may be compromised. While machine learning methods can improve prediction accuracy, the processes of model training, validation, and tuning require significant time and computational resources. Furthermore, machine learning models may be prone to overfitting or underfitting, necessitating continuous optimization and updates [64]. In contrast, VisLAI demonstrates a distinct advantage in estimating the LAI for summer maize, exhibiting high stability and robustness. It effectively handles environmental disturbances, resulting in superior accuracy.

4.4. Estimation Accuracy of LAI at Different Growth Stages

As the growing season progresses, the R^2 for both models gradually declines. This decrease can be attributed to the later stages of maize growth, particularly during the maize reproductive phase, when significant changes in leaf color occur, transitioning to yellow [65]. These dynamic variations in leaf color influence the models' prediction accuracy. During the maturity phase, the complexity of photosynthesis and changes in leaf pigments further reduce the models' interpretability, leading to a decline in the R^2 value. The RMSE initially increases before decreasing, with this fluctuation likely resulting from variations in maize growth at different stages, especially during transitional stages when uneven growth rates and biomass distribution introduce errors. During the early and mid-growth stages, maize development is relatively uniform, leading to smaller errors. In contrast, as maize approaches maturity in the later stages, factors such as leaf yellowing [66], biomass changes [65], and increased uncertainty in observational data contribute to higher RMSE values. However, as the model adapts to these changes, error values decrease, resulting in a subsequent reduction in RMSE. The NRMSE shows a gradual increase across the three growth stages. This trend suggests that, as the maize progresses through its growth stages, the model progressively adapts to the dynamic changes, becoming more capable of addressing the complexities and evolving characteristics of the growth process in the later stages.

4.5. The Significance and Limitations of This Study

Image processing technology, with its advantages of real-time performance, automation, and convenience, has been extensively applied in maize information extraction, providing timely and accurate decision support for crop growth monitoring and agricultural management [67]. The LAI of summer maize, as estimated by VisLAI, undergoes median filtering, thresholding, and edge extraction through its built-in image processing toolbox, resulting in high estimation accuracy. However, this method currently addresses only three key growth stages of maize: the big trumpet stage, the tasseling–silking stage, and the grain filling stage, which may not fully capture the dynamic variations across the entire maize growth cycle. To address this limitation, future research should broaden the analysis to encompass image data from the entire maize growth cycle, incorporating dynamic change analysis based on time-series data to more accurately capture the temporal variations in crop development. Additionally, the degree of leaf yellowing or wilting varies significantly across maize cultivars, highlighting the importance of validating the model across multiple maize varieties [68]. While the VisLAI model primarily relies on static image processing techniques, which are susceptible to variations in image quality and external environments, and its robustness needs to be improved. To enhance the model's adaptability in complex environments, subsequent research can introduce dynamic and adaptive image processing methods, combined with multi-angle image fusion technology, to improve its stability and accuracy.

From a broader application perspective, VisLAI, especially the optimized version of HSV, has good migratory properties and has the potential to be extended to satellite remote sensing platforms. Satellite imagery (e.g., Sentinel-2) currently provides the basis for scaling up from the localized scope of UAVs to regional or even national scales. However, the application of satellite platforms still faces challenges such as scale conversion and low resolution. Under low resolution conditions, the ability of HSV color space to express detailed features such as leaf yellowing may be reduced. Therefore, the future should focus on exploring the adaptation of VisLAI in satellite remote sensing platforms.

5. Conclusions

This study evaluates the accuracy of various methods for estimating the LAI at different growth stages of maize and compares the performance of the VisLAI method with six machine learning algorithms for LAI retrieval. The key conclusions drawn from this study are as follows:

(1) Vegetation indices and the LAI exhibit a strong correlation, with the highest correlation observed during the big trumpet and tasseling–silking stages of maize, and a lower correlation during the grain filling stage. The performance of different machine learning algorithms in estimating maize LAI varies, with the GB algorithm achieving the highest estimation accuracy.

(2) Compared to the VisLAI model based on visible light imagery, the HSV-optimized VisLAI model demonstrates superior accuracy. In cases of crop leaf senescence, the re-extraction of senescent leaves using HSV significantly enhances the precision of VisLAI extraction.

(3) The VisLAI model demonstrates significantly higher accuracy than the machine learning algorithms in estimating maize LAI. The R^2 for VisLAI at the three growth stages are 0.92, 0.90, and 0.85, respectively, highlighting its superior performance in capturing the variations in maize LAI across different growth phases.

In summary, compared to traditional machine learning algorithms, the VisLAI model demonstrates superior accuracy and robustness in estimating LAI for maize. Its capability to dynamically monitor crop growth provides critical insights, thereby supporting the advancement of precision agriculture.

Author Contributions: Conceptualization, W.F.; methodology, F.D. (Fuyi Duan), Z.C. and Q.C.; software, W.F. and Y.L.; validation, W.F., F.D. (Fuyi Duan), Y.L., W.Z. and X.K.; formal analysis, W.F.; writing—original draft preparation, W.F.; writing—review and editing, W.F., Z.C., Q.C. and Y.L.; visualization, W.F. and F.D. (Fan Ding); supervision, Z.C., F.D. (Fan Ding) and Q.C.; project administration, W.F., Y.L., Z.C., Q.C., W.Z., X.K. and D.C.; funding acquisition, F.D. (Fuyi Duan), Z.C. and Q.C. All authors have read and agreed to the published version of the manuscript.

Funding: This research was funded by the National Key R&D Program of China (2023YFD1900701) and the Central Public-interest Scientific Institution Basal Research Fund (No. IFI2024-01).

Institutional Review Board Statement: Not applicable.

Data Availability Statement: Data available on request from the authors.

Acknowledgments: The authors would like to thank the anonymous reviewers for their kind suggestions and constructive comments.

Conflicts of Interest: The authors declare no conflicts of interest.

References

1. Fang, H.L.; Baret, F.; Plummer, S.; Schaepman-Strub, G. An Overview of Global Leaf Area Index (LAI): Methods, Products, Validation, and Applications. *Rev. Geophys.* **2019**, *57*, 739–799. [CrossRef]
2. Tooley, G.; Nippert, J.B.; Ratajczak, Z. Evaluating methods for measuring the leaf area index of encroaching shrubs in grasslands: From leaves to optical methods, 3-D scanning, and airborne observation. *Agric. For. Meteorol.* **2024**, *349*, 109964. [CrossRef]
3. He, K.; Du, M.; Tian, X.; Xu, D.; Yin, X.; Li, Z. Effect of Cotton Planting Density on the Estimation of Leaf Area Index Using the LAI-2200 Plant Canopy Analyzer. *Crops* **2015**, *5*, 123–127. [CrossRef]
4. Zhang, J.J.; Cheng, T.; Guo, W.; Xu, X.; Qiao, H.B.; Xie, Y.M.; Ma, X.M. Leaf area index estimation model for UAV image hyperspectral data based on wavelength variable selection and machine learning methods. *Plant Methods* **2021**, *17*, 49. [CrossRef]
5. Chatterjee, S.; Baath, G.S.; Sapkota, B.R.; Flynn, K.C.; Smith, D.R. Enhancing LAI estimation using multispectral imagery and machine learning: A comparison between reflectance-based and vegetation indices-based approaches. *Comput. Electron. Agric.* **2025**, *230*, 109790. [CrossRef]
6. Jin, Z.Y.; Liu, H.Z.; Cao, H.N.; Li, S.L.; Yu, F.H.; Xu, T.Y. Hyperspectral Remote Sensing Estimation of Rice Canopy LAI and LCC by UAV Coupled RTM and Machine Learning. *Agriculture* **2025**, *15*, 11. [CrossRef]
7. Du, X.Y.; Zheng, L.Y.; Zhu, J.P.; He, Y. Enhanced Leaf Area Index Estimation in Rice by Integrating UAV-Based Multi-Source Data. *Remote Sens.* **2024**, *16*, 1138. [CrossRef]
8. Xue, W.; Xia, X.Y.; Wan, P.C.; Zhong, P.; Zheng, X. Adversarial Attack on Object Detection via Object Feature-Wise Attention and Perturbation Extraction. *Tsinghua Sci. Technol.* **2025**, *30*, 1174–1189. [CrossRef]
9. Chen, B.; Wu, Z.; Li, H.; Wang, J. Research of machine vision technology in agricultural application: Today and the future. *Sci. Technol. Rev.* **2018**, *36*, 54–65.
10. Elinisa, C.A.; Maina, C.W.; Vodacek, A.; Mduma, N. Image Segmentation Deep Learning Model for Early Detection of Banana Diseases. *Appl. Artif. Intell.* **2025**, *39*, e2440837. [CrossRef]
11. Sun, H.R.; Wei, Z.J.; Yu, W.G.; Yang, G.X.; She, J.N.; Zheng, H.B.; Jiang, C.Y.; Yao, X.; Zhu, Y.; Cao, W.X.; et al. SIDEST: A sample-free framework for crop field boundary delineation by integrating super-resolution image reconstruction and dual edge-corrected Segment Anything model. *Comput. Electron. Agric.* **2025**, *230*, 109897. [CrossRef]
12. Lu, D.Y.; Jin, Z.J.; Lu, L.; He, W.Z.; Shu, Z.F.; Shao, J.N.; Ye, J.H.; Liang, Y.R. Exploratory study on the image processing technology-based tea shoot identification and leaf area calculation. *J. Tea Sci.* **2023**, *43*, 691–702.
13. Müller, M.; Casser, V.; Lahoud, J.; Smith, N.; Ghanem, B. Sim4CV: A Photo-Realistic Simulator for Computer Vision Applications. *Int. J. Comput. Vis.* **2018**, *126*, 902–919. [CrossRef]
14. Feng, Z.; Cheng, Z.; Ren, L.; Liu, B.; Zhang, C.; Zhao, D.; Sun, H.; Feng, H.; Long, H.; Xu, B.; et al. Real-time monitoring of maize phenology with the VI-RGS composite index using time-series UAV remote sensing images and meteorological data. *Comput. Electron. Agric.* **2024**, *224*, 109212. [CrossRef]

15. Ji, L.; Zhang, L.; Rover, J.; Wylie, B.K.; Chen, X.X. Geostatistical estimation of signal-to-noise ratios for spectral vegetation indices *Isprs J. Photogramm. Remote Sens.* **2014**, *96*, 20–27. [CrossRef]
16. Cheng, Q.; Xu, H.; Cao, Y.; Duan, F.; Chen, Z. Grain Yield Prediction of Winter Wheat Using Multi-temporal UAV Based on Multispectral Vegetation Index. *Trans. Chin. Soc. Agric. Mach.* **2021**, *52*, 160–167.
17. Zhai, W.G.; Li, C.C.; Fei, S.P.; Liu, Y.H.; Ding, F.; Cheng, Q.; Chen, Z. CatBoost algorithm for estimating maize above-ground biomass using unmanned aerial vehicle-based multi-source sensor data and SPAD values. *Comput. Electron. Agric.* **2023**, *214*, 108306. [CrossRef]
18. Li, X.; Xu, J.W.; Jia, Y.Y.; Liu, S.; Jiang, Y.D.; Yuan, Z.L.; Du, H.Y.; Han, R.; Ye, Y. Spatio-temporal dynamics of vegetation over cloudy areas in Southwest China retrieved from four NDVI products. *Ecol. Inform.* **2024**, *81*, 102630. [CrossRef]
19. Pullanagari, R.R.; Yule, I.J.; Hedley, M.J.; Tuohy, M.P.; Dynes, R.A.; King, W.M. Multi-spectral radiometry to estimate pasture quality components. *Precis. Agric.* **2012**, *13*, 442–456. [CrossRef]
20. Perez, O.; Diers, B.; Martin, N. Maturity Prediction in Soybean Breeding Using Aerial Images and the Random Forest Machine Learning Algorithm. *Remote Sens.* **2024**, *16*, 4343. [CrossRef]
21. Wang, Q.; Moreno-Martinez, A.; Munoz-Mari, J.; Campos-Taberner, M.; Camps-Valls, G. Estimation of vegetation traits with kernel NDVI. *Isprs J. Photogramm. Remote Sens.* **2023**, *195*, 408–417. [CrossRef]
22. Zhou, Z.J.; Jabloun, M.; Plauborg, F.; Andersen, M.N. Using ground-based spectral reflectance sensors and photography to estimate shoot N concentration and dry matter of potato. *Comput. Electron. Agric.* **2018**, *144*, 154–163. [CrossRef]
23. Qiao, L.; Tang, W.J.; Gao, D.H.; Zhao, R.M.; An, L.L.; Li, M.Z.; Sun, H.; Song, D. UAV-based chlorophyll content estimation by evaluating vegetation index responses under different crop coverages. *Comput. Electron. Agric.* **2022**, *196*, 106775. [CrossRef]
24. Zhou, Q.F.; Liu, Z.Y.; Huang, J.F. Detection of nitrogen-overfertilized rice plants with leaf positional difference in hyperspectral vegetation index. *J. Zhejiang Univ.-Sci. B* **2010**, *11*, 465–470. [CrossRef]
25. Cao, Q.; Miao, Y.X.; Wang, H.Y.; Huang, S.Y.; Cheng, S.S.; Khosla, R.; Jiang, R.F. Non-destructive estimation of rice plant nitrogen status with Crop Circle multispectral active canopy sensor. *Field Crops Res.* **2013**, *154*, 133–144. [CrossRef]
26. Huang, X.; Lin, D.; Mao, X.M.; Zhao, Y. Multi-source data fusion for estimating maize leaf area index over the whole growing season under different mulching and irrigation conditions. *Field Crops Res.* **2023**, *303*, 109111. [CrossRef]
27. Chen, R.; Han, L.; Zhao, Y.H.; Zhao, Z.L.; Liu, Z.; Li, R.S.; Xia, L.F.; Zhai, Y.M. Extraction and monitoring of vegetation coverage based on uncrewed aerial vehicle visible image in a post gold mining area. *Front. Ecol. Evol.* **2023**, *11*, 1171358.
28. Elsayed, S.; Rischbeck, P.; Schmidhalter, U. Comparing the performance of active and passive reflectance sensors to assess the normalized relative canopy temperature and grain yield of drought-stressed barley cultivars. *Field Crops Res.* **2015**, *177*, 148–160. [CrossRef]
29. Erdle, K.; Mistele, B.; Schmidhalter, U. Comparison of active and passive spectral sensors in discriminating biomass parameters and nitrogen status in wheat cultivars. *Field Crops Res.* **2012**, *124*, 74–84. [CrossRef]
30. Feng, W.; Wu, Y.P.; He, L.; Ren, X.X.; Wang, Y.Y.; Hou, G.G.; Wang, Y.H.; Liu, W.D.; Guo, T.C. An optimized non-linear vegetation index for estimating leaf area index in winter wheat. *Precis. Agric.* **2019**, *20*, 1157–1176. [CrossRef]
31. Cao, Y.; Li, G.L.; Luo, Y.K.; Pan, Q.; Zhang, S.Y. Monitoring of sugar beet growth indicators using wide-dynamic-range vegetation index (WDRVI) derived from UAV multispectral images. *Comput. Electron. Agric.* **2020**, *171*, 105331. [CrossRef]
32. Huang, X.; Vrieling, A.; Dou, Y.; Belgiu, M.; Nelson, A. A robust method for mapping soybean by phenological aligning of Sentinel-2 time series. *Isprs J. Photogramm. Remote Sens.* **2024**, *218*, 1–18. [CrossRef]
33. Lu, J.; Miao, Y.; Shi, W.; Li, J.; Yuan, F. Evaluating different approaches to non-destructive nitrogen status diagnosis of rice using portable RapidSCAN active canopy sensor. *Sci. Rep.* **2017**, *7*, 14073. [CrossRef]
34. Zhang, H.Y.; Zhang, Y.; Liu, K.D.; Lan, S.; Gao, T.Y.; Li, M.Z. Winter wheat yield prediction using integrated Landsat 8 and Sentinel-2 vegetation index time-series data and machine learning algorithms. *Comput. Electron. Agric.* **2023**, *213*, 108250. [CrossRef]
35. Meng, Q.Y.; Dong, H.; Qin, Q.M.; Wang, J.L.; Zhao, J.H. MTCARI: A Kind of Vegetation Index Monitoring Vegetation Leaf Chlorophyll Content Based on Hyperspectral Remote Sensing. *Spectrosc. Spectr. Anal.* **2012**, *32*, 2218–2222.
36. Wu, G.J.; Zhou, Z.F.; Zhao, X.; Huang, D.H.; Long, Y.Y.; Peng, R.W. Study on correlation between crop optical vegetation index and radar parameters and its influencing factors based on plot unit. *Geocarto Int.* **2025**, *40*, 2453621. [CrossRef]
37. Silva, D.C.; Madari, B.E.; Carvalho, M.D.S.; Costa, J.V.S.; Ferreira, M.E. Planning and optimization of nitrogen fertilization in corn based on multispectral images and leaf nitrogen content using unmanned aerial vehicle (UAV). *Precis. Agric.* **2025**, *26*, 30. [CrossRef]
38. Laosuwan, T.; Uttaruk, P. Estimating Tree Biomass via Remote Sensing, MSAVI 2, and Fractional Cover Model. *Iete Tech. Rev.* **2014**, *31*, 362–368. [CrossRef]
39. Du, Z.Y.; Yuan, J.; Zhou, Q.Y.; Hettiarachchi, C.; Xiao, F.P. Laboratory application of imaging technology on pavement material analysis in multiple scales: A review. *Constr. Build. Mater.* **2021**, *304*, 124619. [CrossRef]

40. Meng, X.Y.; Xu, Q.H.; Xiao, S.D.; Li, Y.; Zhao, B.; Li, G.H. Performance of Sub-Pixel Displacement Iterative Algorithm Based on Digital Image Correlation Method. *Acta Opt. Sin.* **2024**, *44*, 0312003.
41. Yuan, L.Z.; Li, J.Y.; Fan, Y.; Shi, J.L.; Huang, Y.M. Enhancing pointing accuracy in Risley prisms through error calibration and stochastic parallel gradient descent inverse solution method. *Precis. Eng.-J. Int. Soc. Precis. Eng. Nanotechnol.* **2025**, *93*, 37–45. [CrossRef]
42. Liu, G.S.; Tian, S.K.; Wang, Q.; Wang, H.Z.; Kong, L.W. High-resolution measurement of moisture filed at soil surface with interfered image processing method and machine learning techniques. *J. Hydrol.* **2025**, *652*, 132623. [CrossRef]
43. Houssein, E.H.; Mohamed, G.M.; Ibrahim, I.A.; Wazery, Y.M. An efficient multilevel image thresholding method based on improved heap-based optimizer. *Sci. Rep.* **2023**, *13*, 9094. [CrossRef] [PubMed]
44. Zhou, H.K.; Yang, J.H.; Lou, W.D.; Sheng, L.; Li, D.; Hu, H. Improving grain yield prediction through fusion of multi-temporal spectral features and agronomic trait parameters derived from UAV imagery. *Front. Plant Sci.* **2023**, *14*, 1217448. [CrossRef]
45. Guo, B.; Xu, M.; Zhang, R.; Lu, M. Dynamic monitoring of rocky desertification utilizing a novel model based on Sentinel-2 images and KNDVI. *Geomat. Nat. Hazards Risk* **2024**, *15*, 2399659. [CrossRef]
46. Feng, H.K.; Tao, H.L.; Li, Z.H.; Yang, G.J.; Zhao, C.J. Comparison of UAV RGB Imagery and Hyperspectral Remote-Sensing Data for Monitoring Winter Wheat Growth. *Remote Sens.* **2022**, *14*, 3811. [CrossRef]
47. Zhang, H.; Yan, J. Low-light image enhancement guided by semantic segmentation and HSV color space. *J. Image Graph.* **2024**, *29*, 966–977. [CrossRef]
48. Orka, N.A.; Haque, E.; Uddin, M.N.; Ahamed, T. Nutrispace: A novel color space to enhance deep learning based early detection of cucurbits nutritional deficiency. *Comput. Electron. Agric.* **2024**, *225*, 109296. [CrossRef]
49. Xiao, Y.; Zhou, J. Overview of Image Edge Detection. *Comput. Eng. Appl.* **2023**, *59*, 40–54.
50. Ma, H.; Zhao, W.J.; Yu, H.Y.; Yang, P.T.; Yang, F.Q.; Li, Z.L. Diagnosis alfalfa salt stress based on UAV multispectral image texture and vegetation index. *Plant and Soil.* **2025**. [CrossRef]
51. Shahrestani, S.; Sanislav, I. Delineation of geochemical anomalies through empirical cumulative distribution function for mineral exploration. *J. Geochem. Explor.* **2025**, *270*, 107662. [CrossRef]
52. Korkmaz, M. A study over the general formula of regression sum of squares in multiple linear regression. *Numer. Methods Partial Differ. Equ.* **2021**, *37*, 406–421. [CrossRef]
53. Huang, H.; Liu, Y.; Ma, Y.H.; Xiang, S.H.; He, J.N.; Wang, S.T.; Guo, J.X. Prediction of Soluble Solid Contents in Apples Using Vis-NIRS and Functional Linear Regression Model. *Spectrosc. Spectr. Anal.* **2024**, *44*, 1905–1912.
54. Li, W.; Huang, J.; Qi, Y.; Liu, X.; Liu, J.; Mao, Z.; Gao, X. Meta-analysis of Soil Microbial Biomass Carbon Content and Its Influencing Factors under Soil Erosion. *Ecol. Environ. Sci.* **2023**, *32*, 47–55.
55. Ahrens, A.; Hansen, C.B.; Schaffer, M.E. lassopack: Model selection and prediction with regularized regression in Stata. *Stata J.* **2020**, *20*, 176–235. [CrossRef]
56. Zhang, H.Z.; Zhou, A.M.; Zhang, H. An Evolutionary Forest for Regression. *Ieee Trans. Evol. Comput.* **2022**, *26*, 735–749. [CrossRef]
57. Bellocchio, F.; Ferrari, S.; Piuri, V.; Borghese, N.A. Hierarchical Approach for Multiscale Support Vector Regression. *Ieee Trans. Neural Netw. Learn. Syst.* **2012**, *23*, 1448–1460. [CrossRef]
58. Zhang, G.; Liu, J.; Jia, H. The Application of Stochastic Gradient Boosting to the Analysis on Metabolomics Data. *Chin. J. Health Stat.* **2013**, *30*, 323–326.
59. Li, Y.F.; Li, C.C.; Cheng, Q.; Chen, L.; Li, Z.P.; Zhai, W.G.; Mao, B.H.; Chen, Z. Precision estimation of winter wheat crop height and above-ground biomass using unmanned aerial vehicle imagery and oblique photoghraphy point cloud data. *Front. Plant Sci.* **2024**, *15*, 1437350. [CrossRef]
60. Li, Y.F.; Li, C.C.; Cheng, Q.; Duan, F.Y.; Zhai, W.G.; Li, Z.P.; Mao, B.H.; Ding, F.; Kuang, X.H.; Chen, Z. Estimating Maize Crop Height and Aboveground Biomass Using Multi-Source Unmanned Aerial Vehicle Remote Sensing and Optuna-Optimized Ensemble Learning Algorithms. *Remote Sens.* **2024**, *16*, 3176. [CrossRef]
61. Dorj, U.O.; Lee, M.; Yun, S.S. An yield estimation in citrus orchards via fruit detection and counting using image processing. *Comput. Electron. Agric.* **2017**, *140*, 103–112. [CrossRef]
62. Niu, X.T.; Fan, J.; Wang, S.; Wang, Q.M. Measuring the dynamics of leaf area index of vegetation using fisheye camera. *Ying Yong Sheng Tai Xue Bao = J. Appl. Ecol.* **2018**, *29*, 3183–3190.
63. Yamaguchi, Y.; Yoshida, I.; Kondo, Y.; Numada, M.; Koshimizu, H.; Oshiro, K.; Saito, R. Edge-preserving smoothing filter using fast M-estimation method with an automatic determination algorithm for basic width. *Sci. Rep.* **2023**, *13*, 5477. [CrossRef] [PubMed]
64. Singh, H.; Kommuri, S.V.R.; Kumar, A.; Bajaj, V. A new technique for guided filter based image denoising using modified cuckoo search optimization. *Expert Syst. Appl.* **2021**, *176*, 114884. [CrossRef]
65. Meng, L.; Yin, D.M.; Cheng, M.H.; Liu, S.B.; Bai, Y.; Liu, Y.; Liu, Y.D.; Jia, X.; Nan, F.; Song, Y.; et al. Improved Crop Biomass Algorithm with Piecewise Function (iCBA-PF) for Maize Using Multi-Source UAV Data. *Drones* **2023**, *7*, 254. [CrossRef]

66. Zhao, R.L.; Wang, Y.H.; Yu, X.F.; Liu, W.M.; Ma, D.L.; Li, H.Y.; Ming, B.; Zhang, W.J.; Cai, Q.M.; Gao, J.L.; et al. Dynamics of Maize Grain Weight and Quality during Field Dehydration and Delayed Harvesting. *Agriculture* **2023**, *13*, 1357. [CrossRef]
67. Appiah, O.; Hackman, K.O.; Diakalia, S.; Codjia, A.K.D.; Bebe, M.; Ouedraogo, V.; Diallo, B.A.A.; Gandji, K.; Abdoul-Karim, D.; Ogunjobi, K.O.; et al. TOM2024: Datasets of tomato, onion, and maize images for developing pests and diseases AI-based classification models. *Data Brief* **2025**, *59*, 111357. [CrossRef]
68. Li, Z.M.; Yuan, C.; Li, S.D.; Zhang, Y.; Bai, B.; Yang, F.P.; Liu, P.P.; Sang, W.; Ren, Y.; Singh, R.; et al. Genetic Analysis of Stripe Rust Resistance in the Chinese Wheat Cultivar Luomai 163. *Plant Dis.* **2024**, *108*, 3550–3561. [CrossRef]

agriculture

MDPI

Review

Research Status and Development Trends of Deep Reinforcement Learning in the Intelligent Transformation of Agricultural Machinery

Jiamuyang Zhao [1], Shuxiang Fan [2,*], Baohua Zhang [3], Aichen Wang [1,4], Liyuan Zhang [1] and Qingzhen Zhu [1,4,*]

1 School of Agricultural Equipment Engineering, Jiangsu University, Zhenjiang 212013, China; 2222416076@stmail.ujs.edu.cn (J.Z.); acwang@ujs.edu.cn (A.W.); liyuan.zhang@ujs.edu.cn (L.Z.)
2 School of Technology, Beijing Forestry University, Beijing 100083, China
3 College of Artificial Intelligence, Nanjing Agricultural University, Nanjing 210031, China; bhzhang@njau.edu.cn
4 Key Laboratory for Theory and Technology of Intelligent Agricultural Machinery and Equipment of Jiangsu University, Zhenjiang 212013, China
* Correspondence: fansx@bjfu.edu.cn (S.F.); qingzhen_zhu@ujs.edu.cn (Q.Z.)

Abstract: With the acceleration of agricultural intelligent transformation, deep reinforcement learning (DRL), leveraging its adaptive perception and decision-making capabilities in complex environments, has emerged as a pivotal technology in advancing the intelligent upgrade of agricultural machinery and equipment. For example, in UAV path optimization, DRL can help UAVs plan more efficient flight paths to cover more areas in less time. To enhance the systematicity and credibility of this review, this paper systematically examines the application status, key issues, and development trends of DRL in agricultural scenarios, based on the research literature from mainstream Chinese and English databases spanning from 2018 to 2024. From the perspective of algorithm–hardware synergy, the article provides an in-depth analysis of DRL's specific applications in agricultural ground platform navigation, path planning for intelligent agricultural end-effectors, and autonomous operations of low-altitude unmanned aerial vehicles. It highlights the technical advantages of DRL by integrating typical experimental outcomes, such as improved path-tracking accuracy and optimized spraying coverage. Meanwhile, this paper identifies three major challenges facing DRL in agricultural contexts: the difficulty of dynamic path planning in unstructured environments, constraints imposed by edge computing resources on algorithmic real-time performance, and risks to policy reliability and safety under human–machine collaboration conditions. Looking forward, the DRL-driven smart transformation of agricultural machinery will focus on three key aspects: (1) The first aspect is developing a hybrid decision-making architecture based on model predictive control (MPC). This aims to enhance the strategic stability and decision-making interpretability of agricultural machinery (like unmanned tractors, harvesters, and drones) in complex and dynamic field environments. This is essential for ensuring the safe and reliable autonomous operation of machinery. (2) The second aspect is designing lightweight models that support edge-cloud collaborative deployment. This can meet the requirements of low-latency responses and low-power operation in edge computing scenarios during field operations, providing computational power for the real-time intelligent decision-making of machinery. (3) The third aspect is integrating meta-learning with self-supervised mechanisms. This helps improve the algorithm's fast generalization ability across different crop types, climates, and geographical regions, ensuring the smart agricultural machinery system has broad adaptability and robustness and accelerating its application in various agricultural settings. This paper proposes research directions from three key dimensions-"algorithm capability enhancement, deployment architecture optimization, and generalization ability

 https://doi.org/10.3390/agriculture15111223

improvement"-offering theoretical references and practical pathways for the continuous evolution of intelligent agricultural equipment.

Keywords: deep reinforcement learning (DRL); agricultural machinery; agricultural intelligence; agricultural machinery navigation; path planning; UAV operations

1. Introduction

With advancements in cloud positioning and collaborative precision positioning (collaborative precision positioning refers to the technology permitting multiple positioning devices or systems to work together to achieve more accurate positioning information) technologies, agricultural automation is transitioning from single-dimensional navigation tasks to multidimensional intelligent operations, significantly reducing labor intensity and enhancing production efficiency [1–3]. Modern agricultural automation has evolved under the impetus of precision agriculture [4], which is closely tied to efficient and intelligent navigation systems for agricultural machinery. High-precision positioning and navigation are prerequisites for agricultural robots to perform autonomous field operations [5]. During navigation, robots must first determine their absolute or relative positions to facilitate subsequent path planning and trajectory tasks [6,7]. Unlike navigation scenarios for pedestrians, mobile robots, vehicles, or UAVs [8–12], agricultural environments feature unstructured terrain, including uneven soil, dynamic crop distributions (e.g., varying plant heights during growth cycles), and transient obstacles (e.g., fallen branches or irrigation tools); unmanned agricultural machinery imposes higher demands on navigation due to operational speed and equipment action requirements [13]. Consequently, there is a pressing need to develop instruction-based navigation methods for agricultural machinery to achieve efficient full-field coverage [14]. Current autonomous driving technologies for agricultural machinery, leveraging high-precision positioning and path planning, have markedly improved efficiency in tasks such as plowing and sowing. Furthermore, meeting the diverse demands of delicate operations, such as fruit picking and field weeding, relies on the flexible control of intelligent agricultural end-effectors. Recent breakthroughs in sensor technology, materials science, and computer science have driven innovations in decision-making, perception and localization, structural optimization, intelligent control, and operational management for these end-effectors, which are critical to enhancing harvesting efficiency [15–18]. Additionally, the application of low-altitude UAV technology in agriculture has emerged as a transformative practice, injecting new momentum into agricultural production through data-driven models [19]. In scenarios such as precision pesticide spraying and crop growth monitoring, UAVs have demonstrated remarkable advantages in autonomous decision-making [20]. However, the unique complexity of agricultural production environments poses multidimensional challenges to traditional automation technologies:

(1) Dynamic environmental factors (e.g., changing crop distributions, sudden obstacles) demand real-time perception and adaptive responses.
(2) Hybrid task requirements (e.g., coupling continuous control with discrete decision-making) necessitate the development of hybrid intelligent decision systems.
(3) Resource constraints (e.g., limited computational power and energy consumption) impose stricter demands on system efficiency.

In agricultural environments, traditional methods struggle to handle real-time environmental changes and are highly sensitive to sensor noise and uncertainties. To address these limitations, researchers are actively exploring the adaptability of intelligent algorithms in agricultural scenarios. While deep learning (DL), a representative perception intelligence technology, excels in feature extraction and complex data processing, its reliance on extensive training data and high computational costs in dynamic environments (e.g., orchards and crop fields) limit its practicality. In contrast, reinforcement learning (RL), which relies on environmental interaction and trial-and-error learning, demonstrates unique advantages in addressing dynamic and stochastic challenges [21–23]. Nevertheless, traditional RL algorithms face dimensional catastrophe in real-world control tasks due to constrained action and sample spaces in complex agricultural environments (e.g., narrow passages, dense crop obstructions, and dynamic obstacles). To bridge these gaps, researchers proposed deep reinforcement learning (DRL) [24], which integrates the perceptual capabilities of DL with the decision-making strengths of RL in unknown environments. In summary, compared to traditional rule-based automation, DRL overcomes the rigidity limitations of rule systems in real-time environmental changes by integrating dynamic perception with autonomous decision-making. It can adaptively address the complexity, uncertainty, and resource constraints of agricultural scenarios, achieving more flexible and efficient intelligent decision-making. DRL, through the deep coupling of perception and decision-making, offers innovative strategies to resolve the dilemma of "environmental dynamism, task complexity, and resource constraints" in agricultural scenarios.

This paper reviews the recent literature to provide a comprehensive understanding of DRL advancements in agricultural production environments. We first introduce DRL fundamentals and classifications, then analyze its applications, challenges, and future directions, aiming to guide further research and deployment of DRL in agriculture.

2. Deep Reinforcement Learning Technology Framework and Algorithm Architecture

2.1. Deep Reinforcement Learning Algorithm Framework

DRL, the integration of deep learning (DL) and reinforcement learning (RL), aims to address intelligent decision-making in complex environments. Its core lies in end-to-end learning, which eliminates the need for labeled data. Instead, agents learn action policies by interacting with the environment through raw input information, refining strategies via trial-and-error to develop highly adaptive intelligence [25].

DRL encompasses a wide range of algorithms [26], including classical frameworks such as Deep Q-Networks (DQNs) [27], Deep Deterministic Policy Gradient (DDPG) [28], and Twin Delayed Deep Deterministic Policy Gradient (TD3) [29]. DQNs use deep networks to handle high-dimensional states (limited to discrete actions); DDPG outputs continuous actions via Actor–Critic but suffers from overestimation; TD3 introduces dual Critics, delayed updates, and policy smoothing to reduce variance and error, resulting in greater stability. Depending on whether environmental models are explicitly constructed during training, DRL algorithms can be categorized into model-based and model-free approaches [30–33] (Figure 1) (Table 1). Model-based DRL algorithms seek optimal policies based on learned environmental dynamics, encompassing methods like fine-tuning algorithms [34] and augmented intelligence frameworks [35]. In contrast, model-free DRL algorithms acquire optimal policies through direct agent–environment interactions, broadly divided into value function-based and policy gradient-based methods [36]. Compared to model-based approaches, model-free DRL avoids constructing explicit environmental dynamics, learning directly from interactions, making it more suitable for high-dimensional, dynamic, or unknown agricultural scenarios. This section focuses on model-free DRL algorithms, specifically value function and policy gradient variants.

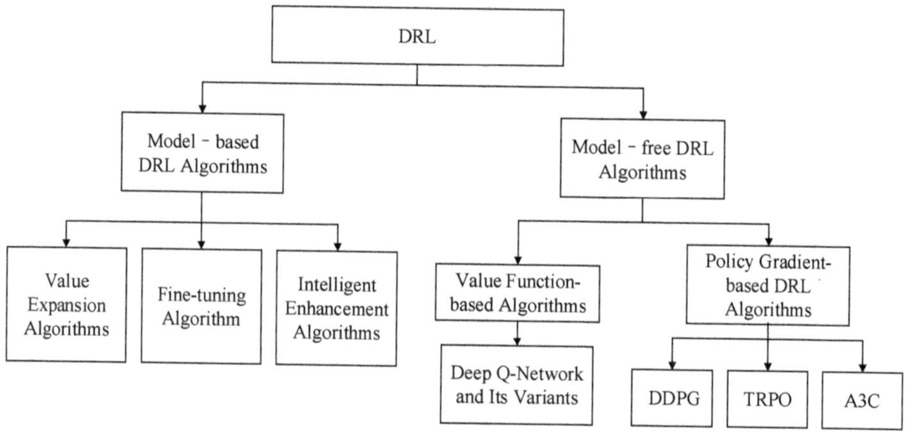

Figure 1. Schematic diagram of DRL algorithm classification.

Table 1. Comparison of model-based vs. model-free deep reinforcement learning algorithms.

Attribute	Model-Based DRL	Model-Free DRL
Core Concept	Builds a model of environment dynamics for policy optimization	Learns optimal policy directly through interaction with environment
Sample Efficiency	High—can generate abundant data via the learned model	Low—requires large amounts of real-world interaction
Generalization Ability	Strong—suitable for transfer and multi-task learning	Moderate—relies on experience replay or exploration mechanisms
Typical Application Scenarios	Structured environments (e.g., greenhouse climate control)	Complex, unstructured environments (e.g., field navigation)
Representative Algorithms	PILCO [37], MBPO [38], Dreamer [39]	DQN, DDPG, TD3
Major Challenges	Model error accumulation, increased training complexity	High data demand, unstable convergence
Agricultural Use Cases	Crop growth modeling, irrigation/fertilization control	Tractor path tracking, UAV spraying missions

2.1.1. Value Function-Based DRL Algorithms

The DQN algorithm, a widely adopted RL variant, has been successfully applied to robot path planning and similar fields [40–42]. In DQNs, agents utilize neural networks to approximate the optimal action value function, mapping states to the expected long-term rewards of actions. The network is trained through a variant of Q-learning, where agents learn from state transitions and rewards [43–45]. When applying a DQN to robot path planning, agents are first trained on a set of sample environments. During training, agents explore the environment and learn to select optimal actions for each state. Performance is evaluated based on their ability to navigate to target locations while avoiding obstacles [46–48]. However, a traditional DQN's single-network architecture is prone to Q-value overestimation, potentially destabilizing policy convergence. This limitation has driven researchers to propose improved frameworks like Double Q-learning.

To mitigate overfitting caused by a single Q-network, Hasselt et al. [49] introduced a Double Q-learning structure combined with deep learning, outperforming standard DQNs. Building on Double-DQNs, Zhang et al. [50] developed a path smoothing and tracking control method capable of tracking linear and polygonal paths. Compared to traditional pure pursuit control (PPC), their approach significantly reduced stabilization time and corner overshoot in high-speed scenarios. Yue et al. [51] employed a Double-DQN architecture to design a reinforcement learning-based obstacle avoidance controller for agricultural robots, achieving efficient and reliable autonomous navigation in complex farm environments. Zhigang Ren et al. [52] implemented a Double-DQN-based path-tracking control algorithm for orchard traction spray robots, demonstrating superior path-tracking accuracy and stability compared to conventional control algorithms. These studies confirm that value function-based DRL algorithms effectively reduce errors caused by inaccurate environmental modeling in agriculture, thereby enhancing operational efficiency.

2.1.2. Policy Gradient-Based DRL Algorithms

Policy gradient-based DRL algorithms primarily include DDPG, Trust Region Policy Optimization (TRPO) [53], and Asynchronous Advantage Actor–Critic (A3C) [54] (Figure 2). The core idea of these algorithms is to adjust policy parameters via gradient ascent to maximize the expected long-term cumulative reward. Owing to their flexibility and adaptability, policy gradient-based DRL has become a critical branch of DRL, particularly excelling in complex control tasks.

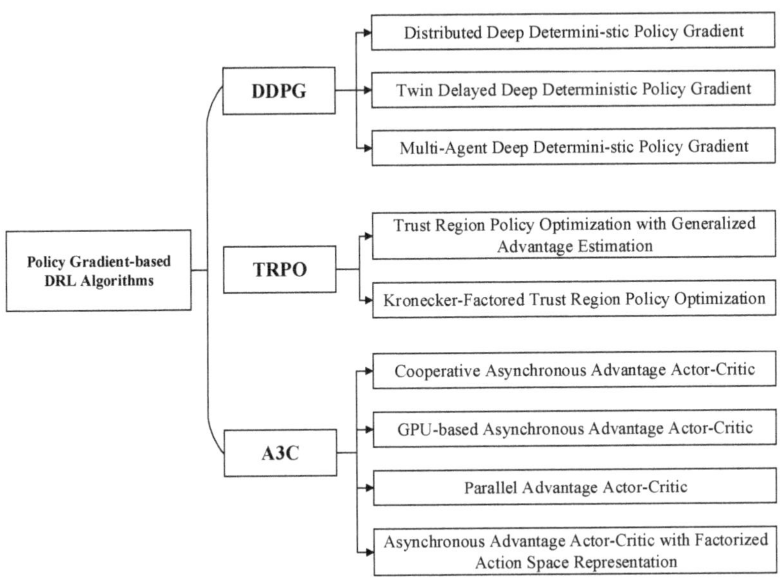

Figure 2. Classification of DRL algorithms based on gradient policies.

Designing effective reward mechanisms and strategies for multi-agent collaboration and competition remains challenging due to intricate relationships between agents. For instance, Hu et al. [55] enhanced the DDPG algorithm by designing reward functions based on COLREGs (Collision Avoidance Regulations) and introducing potential-based reward shaping to guide agents toward optimal policies. Takahashi et al. [56] proposed a Multi-Agent Deep Deterministic Policy Gradient (MADDPG) method to learn near-optimal solutions from prior knowledge. Ye et al. [57] integrated an ε-greedy exploration strategy into MADDPG to balance exploration and exploitation during training, accelerating convergence and improving performance. Dynamic environments pose another significant challenge, as traditional deep learning models trained in static settings struggle to adapt to real-time changes. To address this, Chen et al. [58] improved the reward–penalty mechanism of DDPG by incorporating adaptive artificial potential fields (APF-DDPG). This enhancement boosted learning speed, obstacle avoidance success rates, and continuous information utilization during training. For efficient computational resource utilization, Yoko Sasaki et al. [59] developed an A3C-based motion learning algorithm for autonomous mobile robots, reducing training costs and simplifying collision avoidance design. In summary, researchers have made notable progress in reward design for multi-agent systems, policy stability, and dynamic environment adaptability. These advancements not only enhance learning efficiency and decision-making precision in complex scenarios but also provide foundational insights for future explorations in multi-objective collaborative optimization and robust policy design under non-stationary conditions.

Compared to value function-based DRL algorithms, policy gradient-based approaches directly search for optimal policies in the policy space through end-to-end learning. Their simpler architecture makes them more suitable for handling continuous and high-dimensional action spaces.

3. Applications of DRL in Agricultural Production Environments

With the rapid advancement of artificial intelligence, DRL has been widely adopted in agricultural production environments due to its robust learning and decision-making capabilities [60]. For instance, DRL-powered agricultural transplanting robots have reduced mechanical seedling damage rates to 2.82% through multi-agent collaborative path optimization. Meanwhile, DRL-enhanced plant protection drones achieved a 41.68% improvement in pesticide deposition coverage rate while reducing operational path overlap to 5.56%, enabled by dynamic environment modeling and action space adaptation. This section explores its applications in three key areas: agricultural ground platform navigation, motion planning for intelligent agricultural end-effectors, and low-altitude UAV operations, highlighting the technical strengths and operational advantages of smart agricultural systems to support the development of an intelligent agricultural ecosystem.

3.1. Agricultural Ground Platform Navigation

3.1.1. Application Background

Agricultural ground platforms, including autonomous tractors and combine harvesters, face significant navigation challenges in unstructured farmland environments characterized by uneven crop distributions, soil undulations, and transient obstacles. These dynamic, unstructured environments demand robust navigation systems to handle variable conditions while improving operational efficiency and reducing energy consumption. Although traditional navigation technologies have made progress through sensor fusion and algorithm enhancements, their inherent limitations become evident in agricultural scenarios. For example, Freitas et al. [61] developed an orchard obstacle detection system that identifies obstacles over 15 cm when unobscured by grass and adjusts vehicle speed based on proximity yet fails to detect smaller obscured obstacles. Blok et al. [62] achieved lateral deviations below 5 cm at 0.5 m/s speeds using a particle filter with laser beam modeling but showed limited adaptability in high-speed or sudden obstacle scenarios. Wang et al. [63] improved the A*-SVR method to reduce lateral deviations by 29.57% to 6.90 cm between tree rows, though performance degrades significantly under model mismatches due to reliance on precise environmental modeling. These methods generally suffer from static environmental perception and rigid algorithmic adjustments, struggling to adapt to real-time agricultural dynamics. In contrast, DRL overcomes dependence on preset models through autonomous environmental interaction and policy optimization, offering a novel pathway to break through traditional navigation limitations in unstructured agricultural settings.

3.1.2. DRL-Based Solution and Key Advantages

In the field of precision agriculture navigation, traditional end-to-end decision-making frameworks based on multi-sensor fusion (e.g., vision/LiDAR/GNSS integration) can achieve basic path tracking but face challenges such as complex parameter tuning and insufficient environmental adaptability, particularly under dynamic scenarios like uneven crop distributions, undulating terrain, or sudden obstacles [64]. To address these complex control issues, DRL is emerging as a core technology for intelligent navigation in agricultural machinery, leveraging its autonomous decision-making advantages through environmental interactions. In agricultural ground vehicle control, innovations in DRL algorithms primarily focus on dynamic performance optimization and system lightweighting. For instance, Zhang et al. [50] pioneered the application of Double-DQNs to agricultural vehicle navigation. By integrating nonlinear normalization and reward function design, they optimized dynamic path-tracking performance, overcoming the limitations of traditional methods in sharp-turning and high-speed scenarios. Yan et al. [65] proposed a lightweight, portable DRL control algorithm. By incorporating path curvature states, the algorithm enhanced control accuracy in curved and high-curvature paths, demonstrating centimeter-level precision and robust performance in both simulations and field trials. This method has been successfully applied to unmanned agricultural machinery for straight-line operations and headland turning. To meet the multidimensional demands of smart agriculture, DRL technology is expanding into multi-agent collaboration and specialized environmental adaptation. Examples of this include the following: Fan et al. [66] developed an SMO-Rainbow strategy for UAV path planning in smart tourism agriculture. By combining hierarchical reinforcement learning (HRL) with techniques like Double-DQN and Dueling DQN, they reduced model complexity and improved performance, addressing inefficiencies in data collection, training complexity, and dynamic adaptability. Hu [67] introduced a DRL-based navigation method for orchard inspection robots using the Soft Actor–Critic (SAC) algorithm. Ordered stochastic curriculum learning was employed to resolve GPS inaccuracy, sparse rewards, and environmental adaptability challenges. Furthermore, DRL is demonstrating significant potential beyond physical navigation, extending into the core decision-making and resource optimization layers of smart agriculture systems. Devarajan et al. [68] proposed a two-stage DRL framework (DONSA$/MACO-DQN + RL-DQN) for intelligent agricultural management. The first stage employs an Ant Colony Optimization-enhanced Deep Q-Network (MACO-DQN) to optimally offload diverse monitoring tasks (e.g., fire/pest detection, irrigation scheduling, soil/climate monitoring) to edge, fog, or cloud computing nodes based on latency, energy consumption, and computing power. The second stage utilizes a reinforcement learning-enabled DQN (RL-DQN) model for the actual prediction and monitoring of these agricultural activities. This approach demonstrated superior performance (98.5% precision, 99.1% recall, 98.1% F-measure, and 98.5% accuracy) and faster convergence compared to traditional methods, highlighting DRL's capability in optimizing complex system-level tasks and resource allocation within the smart agriculture paradigm. Table 2 compares agricultural machinery navigation methods. Next, we introduce several typical agricultural ground platform algorithms:

- Double-DQN algorithm (Figure 3a): The Double-DQN is an enhanced algorithm developed from the foundation of DQNs, with the primary objective of addressing the issue of Q-value overestimation inherent in DQNs [49]. The central principle involves decoupling the evaluation of Q-values from the selection of actions, employing two distinct neural networks to execute these tasks independently. This separation enhances the precision of Q-value estimation, thereby enabling the agent to learn an optimal policy with greater stability throughout the decision-making process. As depicted in the leftmost input section of the accompanying figure, the input comprises speed and two error terms. These elements collectively characterize the agent's current environmental state, serving as the foundational basis for subsequent decision-making. The central component of the figure, the deep network, constitutes the critical processing unit of the Double-DQN. This network accepts the input state and processes it through a multi-layer neural network architecture, performing feature extraction and transformation to map the relationship between states and Q-values. The network's parameters are iteratively updated to progressively approximate the true Q-value function. In the output phase, the action yielding the highest Q-value is designated as the final decision action. This selection is executed via a "max" operation, identifying the optimal action that drives the agent to perform the corresponding operation within the environment, subsequently receiving a reward, and transitioning to the next state. The figure provides a clear illustration of this workflow: from the input state, through deep network processing to derive Q-values, to the ultimate selection of actions based on these Q-values. This visualization encapsulates the fundamental operational framework and decision-making paradigm of Double-DQNs.

- Soft Actor–Critic (SAC) algorithm (Figure 3b): The SAC algorithm is a policy gradient method rooted in maximum entropy reinforcement learning [69]. Its core principle involves not only pursuing high cumulative rewards during policy optimization but also maximizing the entropy (uncertainty) of the policy. This encourages the agent to thoroughly explore the environment while maintaining effective control. During training, the agent executes actions determined by the current policy (output by the Actor network), interacts with the environment, and collects experiential data (such as states, actions, and rewards), which is stored in a replay buffer. Data sampled from this replay buffer is then used to update the networks.
- SMO-Rainbow strategy (Figure 3c): The rainbow algorithm integrates multiple improved algorithms into the DQN algorithm [70]. The network architecture uses a fully connected neural network with two hidden layers and a dueling layer, as shown in Figure 2. The network input is the environment state S, with 1024 and 512 neurons in the hidden layers, respectively. The dueling layer includes both a value function network and an advantage function network, which together output the predicted Q-values for each option. The hidden layers and the dueling layer use ReLU (rectified linear unit) activation functions, and the loss function is Huber loss.

These studies collectively reveal the technological breakthrough trajectory of DRL in agricultural navigation: through adaptive state representation construction (such as the introduction of curvature parameters), hierarchical policy optimization (such as the SMO-Rainbow framework), and innovative training mechanisms (such as curriculum learning), they systematically address inherent deficiencies of traditional methods in dynamic environment perception, multi-objective optimization, and hardware adaptation. With the integration and evolution of lightweight deployment and edge computing technologies, DRL-driven high-precision navigation is reshaping the operational paradigms of precision agriculture, providing core technological support for low-consumption and efficient unmanned farm operations.

Table 2. Comparison of performance of agricultural machinery path planning methods.

Method	Path Accuracy	Adaptability	Computational Load	Suitable Terr
PPC	Medium	Low	Low	Flat Fields
MPC	High	Medium	High	Greenhouses
DRL(DQN,PPO)	High	High	Medium	Unstructured fields

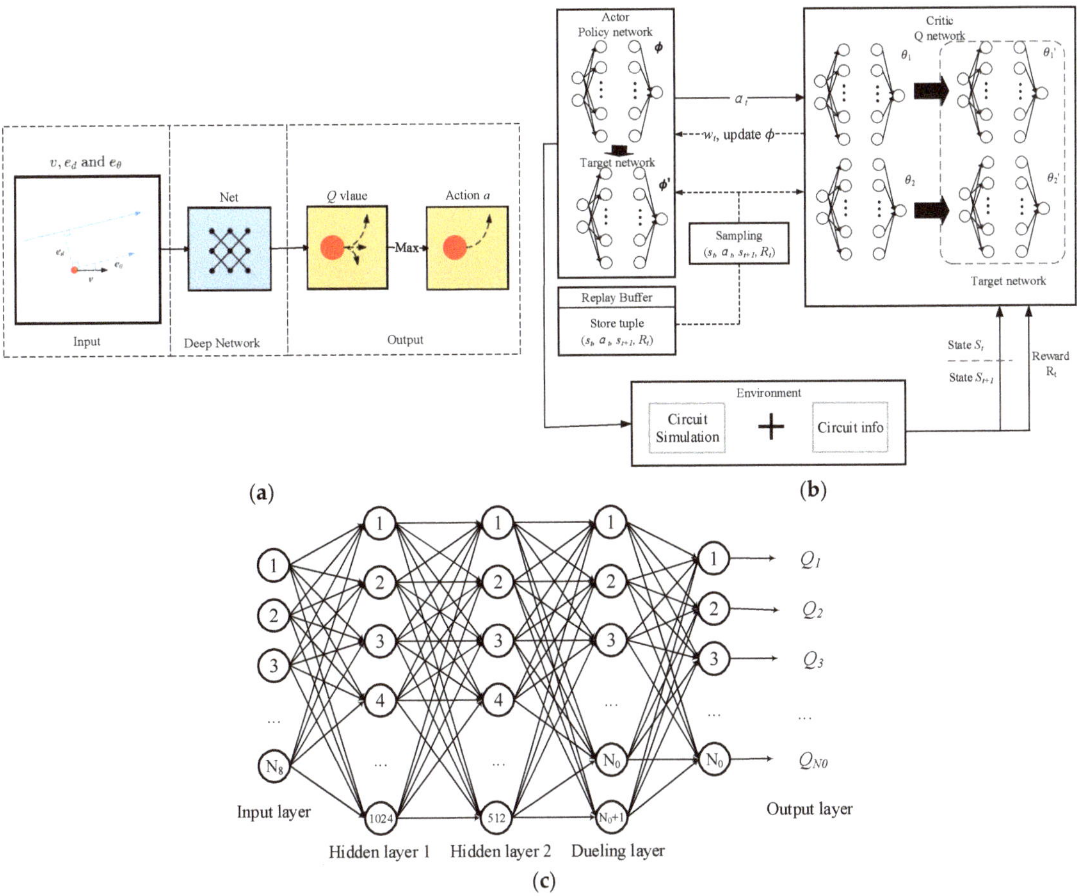

Figure 3. Diagram of the algorithm framework for agricultural ground platform navigation. (**a**) Double-DQN algorithm topology diagram; (**b**) Actor–Critic network architecture; (**c**) SMO-Rainbow strategy network architecture.

3.2. Motion Planning for Intelligent Agricultural End-Effectors

3.2.1. Application Background

In recent years, DRL has demonstrated significant advantages in motion planning for intelligent agricultural end-effectors. However, fruit harvesting and weeding require the precision control of manipulators in dynamic environments with occlusions and soft targets—challenges where rule-based control falls short. By leveraging autonomous agent–environment interaction mechanisms, DRL effectively addresses the limitations of traditional methods in dynamic environmental adaptability and complex constraint handling. From fruit picking to field weeding, and from multi-end-effector collaboration to dynamic path planning, DRL is rapidly advancing agricultural robots toward intelligent operation.

3.2.2. DRL-Based Solution and Key Advantages

As a core driver for the intelligent upgrade of agricultural robotic arms, DRL's capabilities in autonomous environmental interaction and dynamic policy optimization are progressively overcoming the technical bottlenecks of traditional motion planning in complex farmland scenarios. In perception modeling, researchers construct high-dimensional state spaces through multi-source heterogeneous data fusion. For example, Zhang et al. [71]

employed the SAC algorithm to develop a 6-degree-of-freedom (6-DOF) robotic arm assembly system. By integrating multi-source data such as end-effector pose, joint angles, and contact forces into the state space, they achieved a 93% success rate in flexible assembly tasks for 3C products. To address the morphological diversity of crops, Sheng et al. [72] innovated a joint framework combining point cloud feature extraction and grasp evaluation networks, enabling the stable grasping of irregular targets like tomatoes and peppers. This advances DRL's adaptation from general-purpose robotic manipulation to specialized agricultural scenarios. As perception modeling matures, real-time responsiveness in dynamic environments has become a focal point. Xuan et al. [73] modeled dynamic target grasping using Markov decision processes, incorporating Kalman filtering for trajectory prediction and Proximal Policy Optimization (PPO) for 6-DOF robotic arm control. Their approach improved success rates by 21% compared to traditional methods. Simultaneously, Liu et al. [74] proposed a safety verification mechanism, building a closed-loop system (trajectory prediction-collision detection-dynamic replanning) on the TD3 framework. This enabled robotic arms to generate dynamic obstacle avoidance paths within 12.1 milliseconds, achieving a 3.7-fold speed improvement over Rapidly Exploring Random Trees (RRTs). For multi-robot collaborative tasks with complex constraints, DRL exhibits robust optimization capabilities. With advancements in single-robot intelligence, distributed decision-making frameworks are emerging to address multi-agent coordination challenges. Xie et al. [75] constructed a multi-agent Markov game model, coordinating a four-robot harvesting system via self-attention mechanisms. This reduced task completion time by 10.7% in scenarios involving 50 targets. Bu et al. [76] combined artificial potential fields with DDPG, designing a multi-level reward function incorporating obstacle avoidance penalties and contact force constraints. Their method reduced seedling damage rates to 2.82% in inter-row weeding tasks. These studies demonstrate that explicit constraint integration into reward functions allows DRL to balance operational efficiency and safety metrics effectively. To tackle the inherent uncertainties of agricultural environments, successful deployment relies on breakthroughs in simulation-to-reality transfer. Current research utilizes high-fidelity digital twin systems built on physics engines like MuJoCo and PyBullet. By introducing over 20 domain randomization parameters—such as wind disturbances and soil adhesion—the generalization capabilities of robotic arms trained in virtual environments are significantly enhanced. From multimodal perception to swarm collaboration, and from dynamic obstacle avoidance to virtual–real migration, DRL not only elevates robotic arm precision by orders of magnitude but also redefines the technological paradigm of agricultural automation. It shifts mechanical systems from rigid program execution to autonomous environmental cognition, injecting core momentum into fully autonomous operations for fruit picking, precision spraying, and beyond. A representative framework diagram of motion planning algorithms for intelligent agricultural robotic end-effectors is illustrated in Figure 4:

- Twin Delayed Deep Deterministic Policy Gradient (TD3) (Figure 4a): TD3 is an improved deterministic policy gradient algorithm. Its core idea involves enhancing the stability of reinforcement learning by integrating dual critic networks, smooth target network updates, and delayed policy updates. During execution, the agent executes actions ("a") according to the policy output by the "Actor Network π_0", interacts with the environment, and observes the next state ("s′"). These experiences—including the current state, action, and next state—are then stored (typically in a replay buffer for practical applications).
- A deep reinforcement learning network with self-attention (Figure 4b): This deep reinforcement learning network incorporates a self-attention mechanism. Its core idea is to leverage the self-attention mechanism to capture global dependencies among

different features within the input observations, thereby extracting more effective features for value estimation and action selection in reinforcement learning. The agent acquires observational data from the environment and inputs it into a feature extractor. The data first undergo FNC and ReLU processing, performing preliminary feature extraction and nonlinear transformation on the raw observations. The self-attention mechanism then processes these initially extracted features, computing correlation weights between features. By comparing each feature against others, the self-attention mechanism determines the importance of each feature, ultimately generating a new feature representation that highlights the most critical features for the task.

- Deep Deterministic Policy Gradient (DDPG) algorithm (Figure 4c): The DDPG algorithm is a reinforcement learning method that combines the Q-learning and policy gradient techniques [28]. It employs two neural networks—a policy network (Actor) and a value network (Critic)—to represent the policy and value function, respectively, utilizing experience replay and target networks to stabilize the training process. At its core, DDPG optimizes the value function via a deterministic policy to identify optimal policies in continuous action spaces. The agent executes actions generated by the online policy network πθ (st) during environmental interaction, observing the next state (s_{t+1}) and receiving an immediate reward (r_t). These experiences (s_t, a_t, r_t, and s_{t+1}) are stored in an experience replay buffer. Through continuous updates to the online networks and soft updates to the target networks, the agent learns an effective policy to maximize cumulative rewards.

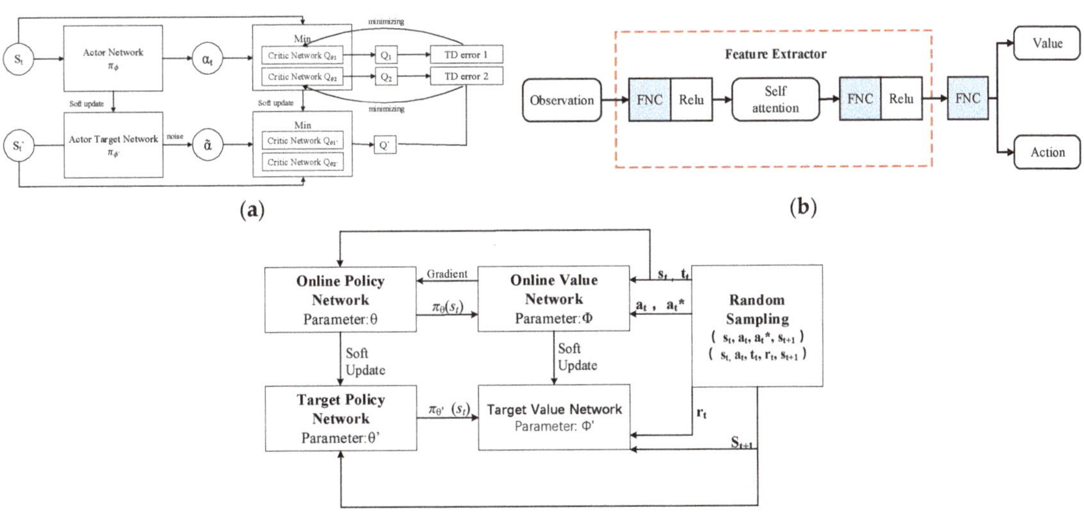

Figure 4. Diagram of the motion planning algorithm framework for intelligent agricultural end-effectors. (**a**) TD3 framework; (**b**) a deep reinforcement learning network with self-attention mechanism; (**c**) flowchart of the DDPG algorithm.

DRL overcomes the limitations of traditional agricultural robotic arms by enabling autonomous environmental interaction and dynamic policy optimization, which is crucial for complex farmland scenarios. Its multidimensional perception decision loop integrates robot dynamics with environmental physics, achieving real-time responses such as millisecond obstacle avoidance. Table 3 summarizes the performance comparison between DRL schemes and traditional methods in robot task scenarios.

Table 3. DRL Gains in Agricultural Manipulator Tasks.

Metric	Traditional	DRL Solution
Obstacle reaction time	42 ms	12.1 ms
Multi-target success rate	65%	87%
Multi-arm task time	120 s	107 s

3.3. *Agricultural Low-Altitude Drone Operations*

3.3.1. Application Background

As aerial platforms for agricultural intelligence, unmanned aerial vehicles (UAVs) have witnessed rapid adoption in modern farming systems, driven by their low-cost deployment and operational flexibility. Currently, UAVs are undergoing a paradigm shift—transitioning from mechanized task execution to autonomous decision-making—through the integration of DRL. This evolution enables UAVs to dynamically optimize mission parameters (e.g., flight altitude, spraying intensity, and obstacle avoidance) in response to real-time field conditions, thereby enhancing both task adaptability and resource-use efficiency [77,78] (Figure 5). By leveraging the state representation capabilities of deep neural networks and the dynamic policy optimization mechanisms of reinforcement learning, DRL has successfully addressed core challenges faced by traditional UAVs in complex farmland scenarios, such as delayed environmental responses and difficulties in multi-objective coordination. Significant breakthroughs have been achieved in critical areas, including pesticide spraying, path planning, and dynamic perception.

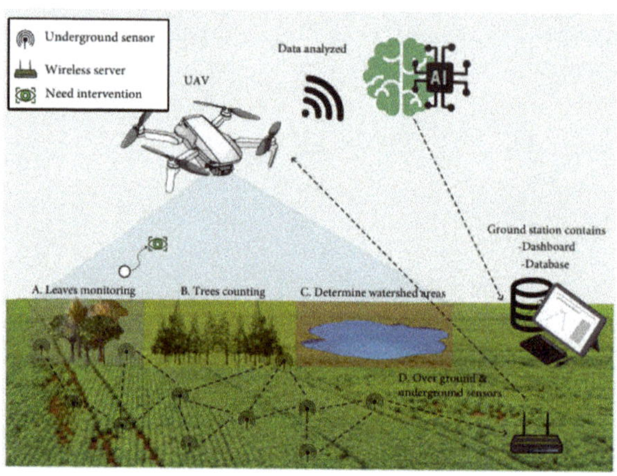

Figure 5. Common drone system architectures [79].

3.3.2. DRL-Based Solution and Key Advantages

In pesticide spraying scenarios, DRL has enabled a transformative leap from static path execution to dynamic trajectory optimization. For instance, Hu et al. [80] designed a wireless sensor network (WSN)-assisted UAV trajectory correction system that integrates real-time wind speed and direction data from ground sensors. By employing a dual-algorithm framework combining a DQN and Particle Swarm Optimization (PSO), they generated optimal spraying paths. Experimental results demonstrated a 41.68% increase in pesticide settlement coverage and a reduction in overlapping coverage to 5.56%. Fu et al. [81] further enhanced traditional DQNs by introducing a Bidirectional Long Short-Term Memory (Bi-LSTM) network to construct a BL-DQN model. This approach achieved 19.9% fewer steps for efficient coverage in a 10 × 10 grid map, validating DRL's robustness in pesticide spraying across complex terrains. Path planning technologies have also evolved significantly, showcasing DRL's advantages in multi-physics coupled environments. Kang et al. [82] proposed a control frequency adaptive (CFA) scheduling method, where a reinforcement learning agent dynamically adjusts PID-based attitude and position control frequencies. Under sudden wind disturbances, this method, combined with quadrotor dynamics and Q-learning, reduced waypoint tracking time by 12.8%. Huang et al. [83] addressed obstacle avoidance in mountainous orchards by developing a 3D path planning system using deep Q-learning. A multi-tiered reward mechanism—incorporating terrain slope, crop density, and pest distribution weights—reduced path redundancy by 31.4% and saved battery consumption by 18.2%. Agricultural UAVs not only address the limitations of satellite-based remote sensing (e.g., temporal resolution constraints and cloud interference) but also demonstrate superior operational advantages, including real-time responsiveness, cost-effectiveness, and operator-friendly simplicity [84]. Furthermore, DRL integration is driving the evolution of agricultural UAVs toward embodied intelligence—a paradigm characterized by self-adaptive decision loops and enhanced environment–body–task integration through sensorimotor learning. Almalki et al. [79] developed a dual-cognition UAV system that integrates DRL for autonomous navigation and Faster R-CNN for vegetation detection, achieving 98% detection accuracy in Saudi Arabia's arid valleys. Chen et al. [85] proposed the MTPI-MTSA hybrid algorithm, which optimizes network initialization parameters through transfer learning and automatically enhances datasets using multi-Thompson sampling reinforcement learning. This method reduced vegetation segmentation network training time by 93.7% and improved the Intersection over Union (IoU) metric to 90.9%. Additionally, Gözen and Özer [86] innovated action-sequence reward functions and introduced diagonal movement commands for UAV visual tracking, boosting tracking accuracy by 3.87% on the VisDrone dataset and effectively resolving challenges such as small-target occlusion and scale variations. Collectively, these advancements outline a clear trajectory for DRL-powered agricultural UAVs: transitioning from single-task optimization (e.g., spray coverage) to multi-objective synergy (e.g., balancing energy efficiency and precision) and evolving from discrete functional modules (perception, planning, control) to intelligent closed-loop systems. This progression establishes a comprehensive technical framework that integrates environmental perception, dynamic decision-making, and precise execution into a unified continuum. With ongoing breakthroughs in 3D path planning and multimodal perception fusion, DRL-driven UAVs are redefining operational paradigms in precision plant protection and ecological monitoring, offering scalable, intelligent solutions to support global agricultural transition toward low-carbon practices. A representative algorithmic framework for low-altitude agricultural UAV operations is depicted in Figure 6:

- Neural network-based value function approximator of reinforcement learning (Figure 6a): Hu et al.'s neural network architecture, as shown in Figure 3, consists of two fully connected layers instead of the convolutional layers found in typical Deep Q-Networks. Additionally, the rectified linear unit (ReLU) is used as the activation function, with each layer having 32 neurons. The input is the state $S = (U, X_W, w)$, and the output is the corresponding Q-value.
- QFP and CFA models (Figure 6b): QFP is trained to predict the next position of a quadcopter controlled by PID in an environment free from external influences. After training, the estimated next state by QFP is used as input for CFA. Then, CFA is trained to adjust the position and attitude control frequencies against external influences by maximizing a given reward function. The approximate external influence is calculated as the difference between the current state (enclosed in a red dashed box) and the estimated state (enclosed in a green dashed box). CFA is trained to balance the position and attitude control frequencies to achieve time-optimal waypoint tracking control.

- Multi-Task State Aggregation (MTSA) algorithm (Figure 6c): The MTSA algorithm aims to enhance the efficiency and performance of reinforcement learning by combining multi-task learning with state aggregation techniques. Its core principle leverages shared information across tasks to accelerate learning while reducing state space complexity through state aggregation, enabling more effective handling of complex environments. The agent interacts with the environment, selecting actions based on the current state. These actions are generated by a Q-network, which guides the agent's behavior by estimating the value of state–action pairs. During training, state-aggregated training is accelerated using MPI (Message Passing Interface). This approach enables efficient processing of large-scale state spaces.

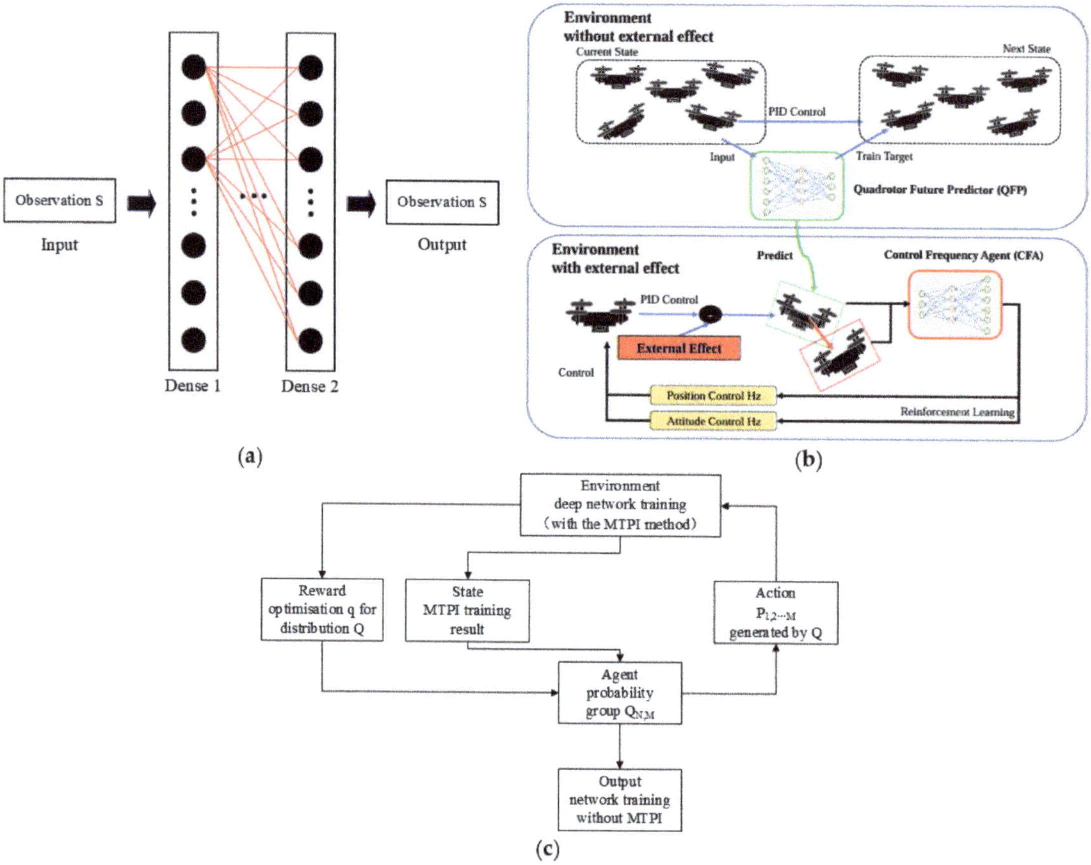

Figure 6. Agricultural low-altitude drone algorithm framework diagram. (**a**) Neural network-based value function approximator of reinforcement learning. (**b**) The proposed QFP and CFA models [82]. (**c**) The block diagram of MTSA reinforcement learning.

4. Key Challenges of DRL in Agricultural Applications

DRL has shown significant advantages in agricultural ground platform navigation, robotic arm motion planning, and low-altitude drone operations, it still faces numerous severe challenges during practical implementation. Overall, these challenges mainly manifest in three dimensions: environmental complexity, limitations of algorithms and computational resources, and issues of safety and reliability. The following analysis will delve into each dimension in detail.

4.1. Environmental Complexity Issues

Agricultural production sites are typically unstructured environments characterized by high dynamism and uncertainty. Regarded as semi-natural systems, agricultural settings inherently involve numerous stochastic and seasonal factors [15], posing significant challenges for autonomous agricultural systems [87]. For instance, variations in crop growth cycles, undulating terrain, climatic conditions, and sudden weather disturbances impose heightened adaptability requirements on automated equipment for navigation and task execution. Particularly in highly dynamic and unstructured agricultural environments—which may include obstacles of varying sizes (e.g., branches, leaves), gusts of wind, multi-obstacle occlusions, and fluctuating light conditions [88]—the unpredictable distribution of crops, diverse topography, and erratic obstacles render traditional experience- or rule-based methods inadequate in addressing these environmental complexities.

The technical bottlenecks of path planning in dynamic environments are further exacerbated under such conditions. In dynamic scenarios, if sensors detect unexpected obstacles, path planning systems must rapidly recalculate trajectories to avoid collisions while progressing toward the target location [89]. Conventional path planning approaches often struggle to deliver satisfactory performance under these constraints. Although DRL technology offers adaptive learning capabilities, continuously evolving dynamic factors in real-world environments (e.g., crop growth stages, sudden weather changes) can cause trained policies to become obsolete quickly, compromising long-term stability. Table 4 summarizes the strengths and weaknesses of contemporary path planning methods.

The above content categorizes and summarizes various path planning methods, but their application advantages, limitations, and suitability in specific agricultural scenarios still require further exploration. Below, we analyze the applicability and challenges of different methods by combining three typical scenarios proposed in this paper: navigation for agricultural ground platforms, motion planning for intelligent agricultural end-effectors, and low-altitude drone operations. For agricultural ground platform navigation, the core requirements include dynamic path planning, real-time obstacle avoidance, high-precision path tracking, and adaptability to unstructured farmland environments (such as crop growth interference and terrain undulations), as shown in Table 5. However, its limitations lie in the fact that dynamic farmland environments (such as crop growth interference and sudden obstacles) cause traditional methods (like RRT and A*) to fail; while DRL methods (such as TD3 and SAC) are more adaptable, they rely on high-performance computing devices, making it difficult to deploy them in edge environments in real time. For intelligent agricultural end-effector motion planning, the core requirements include high-precision trajectory control, dynamic obstacle avoidance (such as moving crops), multi-arm collaboration, and real-time response (<50 ms), as shown in Table 6. However, its limitations are that agricultural end-effectors need to balance efficiency and safety at millimeter-level precision, which traditional methods (like APF) cannot meet under dynamic constraints; although DRL methods (such as MADDPG) support collaborative optimization, they require high-precision simulation environment migration support. For low-altitude drone operations, the core requirements include multi-objective coordination (such as balancing coverage and energy consumption), 3D path planning, wind disturbance resistance, and real-time decision-making (<100 ms), as shown in Table 7. However, its limitations are that drones need to achieve multi-objective optimization under resource constraints, which traditional methods (like genetic algorithms) cannot respond to online;

hybrid architectures (such as DQN + PSO) improve performance but depend on high-precision environmental modeling and edge-cloud collaborative computing.

Table 4. Advantages and disadvantages of path planning methods.

Method	Advantages	Disadvantages	Reference
RRT	Simple, low computation	Static-only; non-optimal paths	Yang et al. [90]
A*	Fast search	Static-only; high computational burden; non-smooth	Hart et al. [91]
APF	Fast convergence	Local minima problem	Chen & Zhang [92]
Dijkstra's Alg	Easy implementation	High complexity; static-only	Dijkstra et al. [93]
PRM	Handles complex spaces	Static-only; non-optimal; time-consuming	Yan et al. [94]
Genetic Alg	Solves NP-hard and multi-objective	High complexity; premature convergence	Tsai et al. [95]
CNN	Handles dynamic, unknown	High complexity; many hyperparameters; non-optimal	Wu et al. [96]
DQN	Adaptive	Non-optimal; hard to implement	Tong et al. [97]
DDPG	Supports continuous action spaces; suitable for high-dimensional control	Unstable training; high computational resource demands	Tian et al. [98]
TD3	Improved stability over DDPG; reduces overestimation	Complex parameter tuning; insufficient real-time performance	Liu et al. [74]
SAC	Balances exploration-exploitation; adapts to complex dynamic environments	High algorithmic complexity; long training time	Haarnoja et al. [99]
PPO	Stable training; suitable for multi-task scenarios	Requires fine hyperparameter tuning; slow convergence	Baumgartner et al. [100]

In summary, in terms of agricultural ground platforms, DRL methods such as TD3 and SAC are gradually replacing traditional rule-based algorithms but need to address edge computing bottlenecks. For agricultural end-effectors, multi-agent DRL like MADDPG is driving collaborative automation but relies on high-fidelity simulation-to-reality transfer. In the case of low-altitude agricultural drones, hybrid architectures combining DRL with optimization algorithms have become mainstream but require breakthroughs in lightweight deployment and cross-scenario generalization. Notably, even if path planning algorithms can handle dynamic environments, agricultural automation systems face another fundamental challenge: technical limitations in data acquisition and processing. Agricultural operations rely heavily on data from vision systems, LiDAR, GNSS, and environmental sensors, which are often plagued by noise and latency. Moreover, significant disparities in data formats, accuracy, and update frequencies across different sensors complicate multi-sensor data fusion. While DRL algorithms approximate Q-value functions via deep neural networks during training, enabling agents to learn and optimize path planning strategies [101], they must process high-dimensional and imperfect state information. This compromises model convergence and decision robustness, particularly in scenarios involving transient obstacles or abrupt local environmental changes. Future research must therefore prioritize breakthroughs in sensor fusion and noise-resistant algorithm design to enhance model adaptability.

Table 5. Advantages and limitations of agricultural ground platform navigation.

Method	Advantages	Limitations	Applicability Case
RRT	Simple, low computation	Only suitable for static environments, the path is not optimal, and it cannot handle dynamic obstacles	For initial path exploration of static obstacles in farmland (such as avoiding fixed gullies); it should be combined with other methods to optimize the path.
A*	Fast search	Training is unstable, requires high computational resources, and has limited real-time performance	For initial global path planning of agricultural machinery; it needs to be combined with local dynamic adjustments.
DDPG	Supports continuous action spaces; suitable for high-dimensional control	Parameter tuning is complex, and hardware compatibility is poor	Zhang et al. used DDPG to optimize tractor dynamic path tracking, improving response speed by 30%.
TD3	Improved stability over DDPG; reduces overestimation	High algorithm complexity and long training cycles	Liu et al. implemented dynamic obstacle avoidance path generation for agricultural machinery based on TD3, reducing the response time to 12.1 milliseconds.
SAC	Balances exploration–exploitation; adapts to complex dynamic environments	Only applicable for static maps; path is not smooth; high computational burden	Hu adopted an SAC-designed orchard inspection robot navigation strategy to address the issue of sparse GPS signals.

Table 6. Advantages and limitations of motion planning for intelligent agricultural end-effectors.

Method	Advantages	Limitations	Applicability Case
PPO	Training is stable and suitable for multi-task scenarios	Requires fine-tuning of parameters, with slow convergence speed	Xu et al. achieved dynamic grasping with a 6-degree-of-freedom robotic arm using PPO, improving the success rate by 21%
DQN	Strong adaptive learning ability; suitable for discrete action spaces (such as decision-making)	Difficult to handle continuous actions	For discrete task selection of end-effectors (such as spray switch control); it needs to be combined with policy gradient methods
MADDPG	Supports multi-agent collaboration	High risk of strategy drift requires complex reward function design	Xie et al. developed a multi-robotic arm Markov game model, reducing task completion time by 10.7%
APF	Converges quickly; suitable for local obstacle avoidance	Prone to becoming stuck in local minima; unable to handle complex constraints	Chen et al. combined APF with DDPG to design an obstacle avoidance reward mechanism, reducing the seedling damage rate to 2.82%

Table 7. Advantages and limitations of agricultural low-altitude drone operations.

Method	Advantages	Limitations	Applicability Case
Genetic Alg	Suitable for multi-objective optimization	High computational complexity; prone to premature convergence	For offline global path planning (such as large field area division); but it needs to be combined with online DRL dynamic adjustment
DQN + PSO	Combining the adaptability of DQN with the global search capability of PSO to enhance path optimality	Implementation is complex and requires data fusion from multiple sensors	Hu et al. designed a drone trajectory correction system assisted by WSN, which increased pesticide deposition coverage by 41.68%
TD3	Adapt to continuous action space	Insufficient real-time performance; difficulties in deploying at the edge	For drone attitude control in simulation environments, a lightweight model such as TinyDRL is needed to adapt to actual hardware
SAC	Supports complex dynamic environments (such as sudden changes in wind speed), with high efficiency	The need for extensive training data makes it difficult to quickly transfer to new scenarios	Almalki et al. combined SAC with Faster R-CNN to achieve vegetation detection in arid river valleys with an accuracy of 98%

4.2. Algorithm and Computational Resource Limitations

Despite demonstrating theoretical potential in agricultural automation, the practical deployment of DRL faces systematic challenges arising from computational constraints, data acquisition, and real-time responsiveness.

First, computational resource bottlenecks directly limit algorithmic performance. DRL's training and inference heavily rely on GPU parallel computing capabilities [102]. However, field operation platforms must simultaneously process multimodal data streams, including multispectral imaging (crop vitality assessment [103]), thermodynamic analysis (water stress detection [104]), computer vision (pest/disease detection [105]), and LiDAR point clouds (vegetation density reconstruction [106]). These demands impose stringent requirements on edge computing devices, with existing agricultural machinery often suffering from delayed policy updates due to insufficient computational power. For instance, during fruit harvesting operations using agricultural robotic end-effectors, oscillations of target fruits during the grasping process may significantly increase the computational load of motion planning algorithms. This elevated demand for real-time processing could induce mechanical blockages (e.g., delayed actuator responses or trajectory conflicts), thereby compromising the practical utility of automated harvesting systems in field applications [107].

Second, high data acquisition costs and simulation-to-reality transfer hurdles exacerbate deployment difficulties. DRL's reliance on extensive trial-and-error interactions compels researchers to use virtual simulation platforms like MuJoCo and PyBullet as substitutes for costly field trials. However, discrepancies persist between simulated and real-world environments in terms of lighting randomness, soil physical properties, and other factors. Even with domain randomization strategies to inject perturbed parameters, path planning errors in simulation-to-reality transfer remain unresolved. Furthermore, the massive computational resources required for simulation further elevate technical barriers to application.

More critically, real-time decision-making poses a pressing contradiction. Traditional DRL frameworks, designed to balance multi-objective optimization (e.g., waypoint tracking and sudden obstacle avoidance), often employ complex neural networks and multi-level reward functions. This leads to latency in online computation and decision-making during real-world operations. In high-speed scenarios, such as hilly terrain operations, such delays can trigger cumulative trajectory deviations or even cascading control failures. Thus, reducing computational complexity and energy consumption while maintaining decision accuracy is a critical breakthrough point for future research.

4.3. Safety and Reliability Issues

Agricultural automation equipment must not only perform tasks efficiently but also ensure the safety of on-site personnel and crops. Consequently, safety and reliability issues have emerged as a core challenge in technology promotion. In recent years, agricultural machinery accidents have occurred frequently in China. Statistical data indicate that 220 agricultural machinery incidents were reported nationwide in 2021, resulting in 46 fatalities and significant economic losses [108]. These recurring accidents highlight that the safety and reliability of automated agricultural equipment have become critical factors constraining the development of agricultural modernization.

In practical applications, agricultural robots often operate in human–robot collaborative environments. For example, when deploying spraying drones in complex agricultural settings, it is critical to account for obstacles such as heavy machinery, moving vehicles, and coexisting robotic agents to prevent collisions while simultaneously fulfilling the dual requirements of "precision spraying" and "safety" [109]. In tasks such as autonomous navigation and robotic arm grasping, inaccurate risk quantification in decision-making mechanisms may lead to erroneous device actuation, potentially causing crop damage or operator injuries. Therefore, safety verification and confidence estimation for DRL strategies, combined with real-time fault detection modules, are imperative for reliable operations. Furthermore, long-term deployed agricultural equipment often exhibits policy drift—a phenomenon where initially trained strategies gradually deteriorate due to dynamic environmental changes and evolving task requirements. This necessitates continuous online learning or periodic policy updates. Achieving adaptive adjustments while maintaining system stability (i.e., avoiding cascading erroneous decisions) has emerged as a key research frontier. Potential solutions include structured stochastic curriculum learning, transfer learning, and online adaptation algorithms; however, their practical efficacy remains to be empirically validated under real-world agricultural scenarios.

5. Future Research Directions for DRL in Agricultural Applications

With AI's evolution, DRL applications in agriculture will rapidly advance toward higher efficiency, intelligence, and integration. Although DRL has demonstrated significant potential in the intelligentization of agricultural machinery, its practical deployment still faces three major technical barriers: First, the contradiction between complex neural network structures and the edge computing resources of agricultural machinery results in existing systems struggling to meet real-time response requirements in actual operations. Second, the black-box nature of strategies fundamentally conflicts with the safety requirements of human–machine coexistence scenarios in farmland, and the lack of quantitative verification mechanisms may lead to catastrophic failures. Third, the differences in physical properties between simulation environments and real farmland make virtual training strategies frequently ineffective in field applications, as evidenced by repeated cases. To overcome these bottlenecks, coordinated innovation across the three dimensions of algorithm–architecture–verification must be pursued:

(1) Complex Hybrid Architectures and Algorithmic Innovations: Develop hybrid decision frameworks combining model predictive control with DRL to enhance stability and

interpretability; innovate algorithms merging value and policy methods (e.g., SAC + DQN) to boost convergence and generalization; introduce attention mechanisms and multi-scale state representations to improve strategy expressiveness in complex scenarios.

(2) Edge-Cloud Collaborative Computing and Lightweight Deployment: Establish edge-cloud collaborative architectures, training complex models in the cloud while deploying lightweight, quantized models (e.g., TinyDRL, ONNX-quantized) on edge devices for low latency and energy efficiency. Leveraging 5G/6G networks enables real-time model updates and strategy synchronization, reconstructing intelligent farm IT infrastructure.

(3) Meta-Learning and Self-Supervised DRL for Rapid Adaptation: Integrate meta-learning and self-supervised tasks to enable few-shot policy generalization across crop varieties, climates, and regions. Construct self-supervised tasks from historical trajectories and visual representations to achieve plug-and-play agricultural agents.

In summary, DRL's future in agriculture lies in simultaneous breakthroughs in algorithmic depth and application breadth. Through algorithm innovation, system integration, and computing architecture collaboration, DRL will become the core engine driving smart agriculture toward higher efficiency, lower carbon emissions, and increased precision, providing key technology support for sustainable global agriculture.

6. Conclusions

DRL, as a cutting-edge artificial intelligence technology, has emerged as a core driver of the intelligent transformation of agricultural machinery, demonstrating significant potential for decision optimization in complex and dynamic farmland environments. This paper systematically reviews the research progress of DRL in the autonomous navigation of agricultural machinery, motion planning for intelligent robotic arms, and optimization of low-altitude unmanned aerial vehicle (UAV) operations, highlighting its technical advantages in enhancing agricultural automation efficiency and adaptability. Key challenges and future directions for practical applications are also identified. Key findings include the following:

- Autonomous Navigation and Path Planning: Hybrid DRL algorithms integrating value function and policy gradient approaches (e.g., Double-DQN and DDPG) have achieved centimeter-level precision in agricultural vehicle path tracking (e.g., reducing errors to ± 3 cm in [44]). Dynamic state representations (e.g., path curvature parameters) significantly improved robustness in complex farmland scenarios. However, the long-term stability of high-precision path tracking requires further validation, particularly under dynamic conditions such as crop growth interference and sudden obstacles.
- UAV Operation Optimization: Multi-objective reward mechanisms (e.g., balancing coverage efficiency and energy consumption) demonstrated preliminary success in pesticide spraying tasks (e.g., a 41.68% increase in coverage in [67]). However, their generalization across heterogeneous farmland scenarios necessitates further validation through cross-regional and multi-crop experiments.
- Multi-Agent Collaboration: Distributed DRL frameworks with attention mechanisms (e.g., MADDPG) reduced task completion time by 10.7% in collaborative harvesting scenarios ([63]). Yet, real-time responsiveness and safety of multi-agent systems require systematic optimization under hardware constraints.

Nevertheless, the practical deployment of DRL in agriculture faces persistent challenges, including unstructured environmental dynamics, real-time algorithmic constraints, and safety risks in human–machine collaboration. Future research should prioritize the following:

- Hybrid DRL architectures coupled with model predictive control to enhance decision interpretability and robustness;
- Edge-cloud collaborative computing frameworks for deploying lightweight models with low-latency field response and high energy efficiency;
- Cross-scene adaptive agents developed through meta-learning and self-supervised mechanisms to advance agricultural machinery from task-specific to generalized intelligence.

In conclusion, by synergizing algorithmic depth and systemic breadth, DRL is poised to resolve the trilemma of "complex environmental conditions, multitask coordination, and computing resources" in agriculture, serving as a core engine to propel smart agriculture toward sustainable, low-carbon, and fully autonomous practices. This evolution will provide critical technological support for global food security and agricultural modernization.

Author Contributions: Conceptualization, Q.Z. and J.Z.; methodology, J.Z. and S.F.; validation, B.Z.; formal analysis, A.W. and L.Z.; investigation, J.Z. and B.Z.; resources, S.F. and Q.Z.; data curation, Q.Z. and S.F.; writing—original draft preparation, J.Z.; writing—review and editing, Q.Z. and S.F. All authors have read and agreed to the published version of the manuscript.

Funding: This work was supported by the Natural Science Foundation of Jiangsu Province (Grant No. BK20230548), the National Natural Science Foundation of China (Grant No. 32301712), and the Project of Faculty of Agricultural Equipment of Jiangsu University (Grant No. NGXB20240203).

Institutional Review Board Statement: Not applicable.

Data Availability Statement: No new data were created or analyzed in this study. Data sharing is not applicable to this article.

Conflicts of Interest: The authors declare no conflicts of interest.

References

1. Yin, X.; Wang, Y.X.; Chen, Y.L.; Jin, C.Q.; Du, J. Development of autonomous navigation controller for agricultural vehicles. *Int. J. Agric. Biol. Eng.* **2020**, *13*, 70–76. [CrossRef]
2. Wu, C.C.; Fang, X.M. Development of precision service system for intelligent agriculture field crop production based on BeiDou system. *Smart Agric.* **2019**, *1*, 83–90.
3. Sun, J.L.; Wang, Z.; Ding, S.H.; Xia, J.; Xing, G.Y. Adaptive disturbance observer-based fixed time nonsingular terminal sliding mode control for path-tracking of unmanned agricultural tractors. *Biosyst. Eng.* **2024**, *246*, 96–109. [CrossRef]
4. Hu, J.T.; Gao, L.; Bai, X.P.; Li, T.C.; Liu, X.G. Review of research on automatic guidance of agricultural vehicles. *Trans. Chin. Soc. Agric. Eng.* **2015**, *31*, 1–10.
5. Cui, B.; Cui, X.; Wei, X.; Zhu, Y.; Ma, Z.; Zhao, Y.; Liu, Y. Design and Testing of a Tractor Automatic Navigation System Based on Dynamic Path Search and a Fuzzy Stanley Model. *Agriculture* **2024**, *14*, 2136. [CrossRef]
6. Duan, J.; Wang, M.L.; Jiang, Y.; Zhao, J.B.; Tang, Y.W. A Compound Fuzzy Control Method for Agricultural Machinery Automatic Navigation Based on Genetic Algorithm. In Proceedings of the IEEE 2nd Information Technology, Networking, Electronic and Automation Control Conference (ITNEC), Chengdu, China, 15–17 December 2017; pp. 1663–1666.
7. Hameed, I.A. Intelligent Coverage Path Planning for Agricultural Robots and Autonomous Machines on Three-Dimensional Terrain. *J. Intell. Robot. Syst.* **2014**, *74*, 965–983. [CrossRef]
8. Gong, J.L.; Wang, W.; Zhang, Y.F.; Lan, Y.B. Cooperative working strategy for agricultural robot groups based on farmlandenvironment. *Trans. Chin. Soc. Agric. Eng.* **2021**, *37*, 11–19.
9. Li, Y.W.; Xu, J.J.; Wang, M.F.; Liu, D.X.; Sun, H.W.; Wang, X.J. Development of autonomous drivingtransfer trolley on field roads and its visual navigation system for hilly areas. *Trans. Chin. Soc. Agric. Eng.* **2019**, *35*, 52–61.
10. Wan, J.; Sun, W.; Ge, M.; Wang, K.H.; Zhang, X.Y. Robot Path Planning Based on Artificial Potential Field Method with Obstacle Avoidance Angles. *J. Agric. Mach.* **2024**, *55*, 409–418.
11. Zheng, Z.; Yang, S.H.; Zheng, Y.J.; Liu, X.X.; Chen, J.; Su, D.B.L.G. Obstacle avoidance path planning algorithm for multi-rotor UAVs. *Trans. Chin. Soc. Agric. Eng.* **2020**, *36*, 59–69.
12. Zhang, X.H.; Fan, C.G.; Cao, Z.Y.; Fang, J.L.; Jia, Y.J. Novel obstacle-avoiding path planning for crop protection UAV using optimized Dubins curve. *Int. J. Agric. Biol. Eng.* **2020**, *13*, 172–177. [CrossRef]

13. Wu, C.C.; Wang, D.X.; Chen, Z.B.; Song, B.B.; Yang, L.L.; Yang, W.Z. Autonomous driving and operation control method for SF2104 tractors. *Trans. Chin. Soc. Agric. Eng.* **2020**, *36*, 42–48.
14. Lu, E.; Xu, L.Z.; Li, Y.M.; Tang, Z.; Ma, Z. Modeling of working environment and coverage path planning method of combine harvesters. *Int. J. Agric. Biol. Eng.* **2020**, *13*, 132–137. [CrossRef]
15. Jin, Y.C.; Liu, J.Z.; Xu, Z.J.; Yuan, S.Q.; Li, P.P.; Wang, J.Z. Development status and trend of agricultural robot technology. *Int. J. Agric. Biol. Eng.* **2021**, *14*, 1–19. [CrossRef]
16. Kang, H.W.; Chen, C. Fruit detection, segmentation and 3D visualisation of environments in apple orchards. *Comput. Electron. Agric.* **2020**, *171*, 105302. [CrossRef]
17. Kim, W.S.; Lee, D.H.; Kim, Y.J.; Kim, T.; Hwang, R.Y.; Lee, H.J. Path detection for autonomous traveling in orchards using patch-based CNN. *Comput. Electron. Agric.* **2020**, *175*, 105620. [CrossRef]
18. Li, T.; Yu, J.P.; Qiu, Q.; Zhao, C.J. Hybrid Uncalibrated Visual Servoing Control of Harvesting Robots With RGB-D Cameras. *IEEE Trans. Ind. Electron.* **2023**, *70*, 2729–2738. [CrossRef]
19. Aguilar, W.G.; Luna, M.A.; Moya, J.F.; Abad, V.; Parra, H.; Ruiz, H. Pedestrian detection for UAVs using cascade classifiers with Meanshift. In Proceedings of the 11th IEEE International Conference on Semantic Computing (ICSC), San Diego, CA, USA, 30 January–1 February 2017; pp. 509–514.
20. Liao, M.; Sen, T.; Elasser, Y.; Al Hassan, H.A.; Pigney, A.; Knapp, E.; Chen, M.J. UAV Fleet Charging on Telecom Towers with Differential Capacitive Wireless Power Transfer. *IEEE Trans. Power Electron.* **2025**, *40*, 6370–6384. [CrossRef]
21. Zhao, D.B.; Shao, K.; Zhu, Y.H.; Li, D.; Chen, Y.R.; Wang, H.T.; Liu, D.R.; Zhou, T.; Wang, C.H. Review of deep reinforcement learning and discussions onthe development of computer Go. *Control Theory Appl.* **2016**, *33*, 701–717.
22. Farias, G.; Garcia, G.; Montenegro, G.; Fabregas, E.; Dormido-Canto, S.; Dormido, S. Reinforcement Learning for Position Control Problem of a Mobile Robot. *IEEE Access* **2020**, *8*, 152941–152951. [CrossRef]
23. Gao, J.L.; Ye, W.J.; Guo, J.; Li, Z.J. Deep Reinforcement Learning for Indoor Mobile Robot Path Planning. *Sensors* **2020**, *20*, 5493. [CrossRef] [PubMed]
24. Liu, Q.; Zhai, J.W.; Zhang, Z.Z.; Zhong, S.; Zhou, Q.; Zhang, P.; Xu, J. A Survey on Deep Reinforcement Learning. *Chin. J. Comput.* **2018**, *41*, 1–27.
25. Wen, H.; Li, H.; Wang, Z.; Hou, X.; He, K. Application of DDPG-based Collision Avoidance Algorithm in Air Traffic Control. In Proceedings of the 2019 12th International Symposium on Computational Intelligence and Design (ISCID), Hangzhou, China, 14–15 December 2019; pp. 130–133.
26. Zhang, J.; Lu, S.; Zhang, Z.; Yu, J.; Gong, X. Survey on Deep Reinforcement Learning Methods Based on Sample Efficiency Optimization. *J. Softw.* **2022**, *33*, 4217–4238.
27. Mnih, V.; Kavukcuoglu, K.; Silver, D.; Rusu, A.A.; Veness, J.; Bellemare, M.G.; Graves, A.; Riedmiller, M.; Fidjeland, A.K.; Ostrovski, G.; et al. Human-level control through deep reinforcement learning. *Nature* **2015**, *518*, 529–533. [CrossRef]
28. Lillicrap, T.P.; Hunt, J.J.; Pritzel, A.; Heess, N.; Erez, T.; Tassa, Y.; Silver, D.; Wierstra, D. Continuous control with deep reinforcement learning. *arXiv* **2015**, arXiv:1509.02971.
29. Fujimoto, S.; van Hoof, H.; Meger, D. Addressing Function Approximation Error in Actor-Critic Methods. In Proceedings of the 35th International Conference on Machine Learning (ICML), Stockholm, Sweden, 10–15 July 2018.
30. Luo, L.; Li, L.; Yang, R.; Chen, L.L. Vector Antenna Neighborhood Search Tuning Algorithm. *Commun. Technol.* **2019**, *52*, 1800–1803.
31. Yan, D.; Weng, J.Y.; Huang, S.Y.; Li, C.X.; Zhou, Y.C.; Su, H.; Zhu, J. Deep reinforcement learning with credit assignment for combinatorial optimization. *Pattern Recogn.* **2022**, *124*, 108466. [CrossRef]
32. Shi, X.T.; Li, Y.J.; Du, C.L.; Shi, Y.; Yang, C.H.; Gui, W.H. Fully Distributed Event-Triggered Control of Nonlinear Multiagent Systems Under Directed Graphs: A Model-Free DRL Approach. *IEEE Trans. Autom. Control* **2025**, *70*, 603–610. [CrossRef]
33. Zhou, Y.; Zhou, L.C.; Yi, Z.H.; Shi, D.; Guo, M.J. Leveraging AI for Enhanced Power Systems Control: An Introductory Study of Model-Free DRL Approaches. *IEEE Access* **2024**, *12*, 98189–98206. [CrossRef]
34. Herrera, E.M.; Calvet, L.; Ghorbani, E.; Panadero, J.; Juan, A.A. Enhancing carsharing experiences for Barcelona citizens with data analytics and intelligent algorithms. *Computers* **2023**, *12*, 33. [CrossRef]
35. Liu, J.W.; Gao, F.; Luo, X.L. Survey of Deep Reinforcement Learning Based on Value Function and Policy Gradient. *Chin. J. Comput.* **2019**, *42*, 1406–1438.
36. Bravo-Arrabal, J.; Toscano-Moreno, M.; Fernández-Lozano, J.J.; Mandow, A.; Gomez-Ruiz, J.A.; García-Cerezo, A. The internet of cooperative agents architecture (X-ioca) for robots, hybrid sensor networks, and mec centers in complex environments: A search and rescue case study. *Sensors* **2021**, *21*, 7843. [CrossRef]
37. Deisenroth, M.P.; Rasmussen, C.E. *PILCO: A Model-Based and Data-Efficient Approach to Policy Search*; Omnipress: Madison, WI, USA, 2011.

38. Janner, M.; Fu, J.; Zhang, M.; Levine, S. When to Trust Your Model: Model-Based Policy Optimization. In Proceedings of the Advances in Neural Information Processing Systems 32, Volume 16 of 20: 32nd Conference on Neural Information Processing Systems (NeurIPS 2019), Vancouver, CA, USA, 8–14 December 2019; Neural Information Processing Systems Foundation, Inc. (NeurIPS): La Jolla, CA, USA, 2020.
39. Bellemare, M.G.; Naddaf, Y.; Veness, J.; Bowling, M. The Arcade Learning Environment: An Evaluation Platform for General Agents. *J. Artif. Intell. Res.* **2013**, *47*, 253–279. [CrossRef]
40. Bae, S.-Y.; Lee, J.; Jeong, J.; Lim, C.; Choi, J. Effective data-balancing methods for class-imbalanced genotoxicity datasets using machine learning algorithms and molecular fingerprints. *Comput. Toxicol.* **2021**, *20*, 100178. [CrossRef]
41. Choi, S.; Park, S. Development of Smart Mobile Manipulator Controlled by a Single Windows PC Equipped with Real-Time Control Software. *Int. J. Precis. Eng. Manuf.* **2021**, *22*, 1707–1717. [CrossRef]
42. Liu, Z.T.; Shi, Y.H.; Chen, H.W.; Qin, T.X.; Zhou, X.J.; Huo, J.; Dong, H.; Yang, X.; Zhu, X.D.; Chen, X.N.; et al. Machine learning on properties of multiscale multisource hydroxyapatite nanoparticles datasets with different morphologies and sizes. *npj Comput. Mater.* **2021**, *7*, 142. [CrossRef]
43. Chen, K.Y.; Liang, Y.F.; Jha, N.; Ichnowski, J.; Danielczuk, M.; Gonzalez, J.; Kubiatowicz, J.; Goldberg, K. FogROS: An Adaptive Framework for Automating Fog Robotics Deployment. In Proceedings of the 17th IEEE International Conference on Automation Science and Engineering (CASE), Lyon, France, 23–27 August 2021; pp. 2035–2042.
44. Ou, J.J.; Guo, X.; Lou, W.J.; Zhu, M. Learning the Spatial Perception and Obstacle Avoidance with the Monocular Vision on a Quadrotor. In Proceedings of the IEEE International Conference on Mechatronics and Automation (IEEE ICMA), Takamatsu, Japan, 8–11 August 2021; pp. 582–587.
45. Saeedvand, S.; Mandala, H.; Baltes, J. Hierarchical deep reinforcement learning to drag heavy objects by adult-sized humanoid robot. *Appl. Soft. Comput.* **2021**, *110*, 107601. [CrossRef]
46. Jembre, Y.Z.; Nugroho, Y.W.; Khan, M.T.R.; Attique, M.; Paul, R.; Shah, S.H.A.; Kim, B. Evaluation of reinforcement and deep learning algorithms in controlling unmanned aerial vehicles. *Appl. Sci.* **2021**, *11*, 7240. [CrossRef]
47. Timmis, I.; Paul, N.; Chung, C.J. Teaching Vehicles to Steer Themselves with Deep Learning. In Proceedings of the IEEE International Conference on Electro Information Technology (EIT), Mount Pleasant, MI, USA, 14–15 May 2021; pp. 419–421.
48. Yuhas, M.; Feng, Y.L.; Ng, D.J.X.; Rahiminasab, Z.; Easwaran, A. Embedded Out-of-Distribution Detection on an Autonomous Robot Platform. In Proceedings of the Design Automation for CPS and IoT, Nashville, TN, USA, 18 May 2021; pp. 13–18.
49. van Hasselt, H.; Guez, A.; Silver, D. Deep Reinforcement Learning with Double Q-Learning. In Proceedings of the 30th Association-for-the-Advancement-of-Artificial-Intelligence (AAAI) Conference on Artificial Intelligence, Phoenix, AZ, USA, 12–17 February 2016; pp. 2094–2100.
50. Zhang, W.Y.; Gai, J.Y.; Zhang, Z.G.; Tang, L.; Liao, Q.X.; Ding, Y.C. Double-DQN based path smoothing and tracking control method for robotic vehicle navigation. *Comput. Electron. Agric.* **2019**, *166*, 104985. [CrossRef]
51. Yu, Y.; Liu, Y.F.; Wang, J.C.; Noguchi, N.; He, Y. Obstacle avoidance method based on double DQN for agricultural robots. *Comput. Electron. Agric.* **2023**, *204*, 107546. [CrossRef]
52. Ren, Z.G.; Liu, Z.J.; Yuan, M.X.; Liu, H.; Wang, W.; Qin, J.F.; Yang, F.Z. Double-DQN-Based Path-Tracking Control Algorithm for Orchard Traction Spraying Robot. *Agronomy* **2022**, *12*, 2803. [CrossRef]
53. Schulman, J.; Levine, S.; Abbeel, P.; Jordan, M.; Moritz, P. Trust region policy optimization. In Proceedings of the International Conference on Machine Learning, Lille, France, 7–9 July 2015; pp. 1889–1897.
54. Mnih, V.; Badia, A.P.; Mirza, M.; Graves, A.; Harley, T.; Lillicrap, T.P. Asynchronous Methods for Deep Reinforcement Learning. In Proceedings of the 33rd International Conference on Machine Learning, New York, NY, USA, 20–22 June 2016.
55. Hu, Z.Y.; Wang, Y. A deep deterministic policy gradient method for collision avoidance of autonomous ship. *Command Control Simul.* **2024**, *46*, 37–44.
56. Takahashi, K.; Tomah, S. Online optimization of AGV transport systems using deep reinforcement learning. *Bull. Netw. Comput. Syst. Softw.* **2020**, *9*, 53–57.
57. Ye, X.F.; Deng, Z.Y.; Shi, Y.J.; Shen, W.M. Toward Energy-Efficient Routing of Multiple AGVs with Multi-Agent Reinforcement Learning. *Sensors* **2023**, *23*, 5615. [CrossRef]
58. Chen, Y.; Schomaker, L.; Cruz, F. Boosting Reinforcement Learning Algorithms in Continuous Robotic Reaching Tasks Using Adaptive Potential Functions. In Proceedings of the Australasian Joint Conference on Artificial Intelligence, Melbourne, Australia, 25–29 November 2024; pp. 52–64.
59. Sasaki, Y.; Matsuo, S.; Kanezaki, A.; Takemura, H. A3C Based Motion Learning for an Autonomous Mobile Robot in Crowds. In Proceedings of the IEEE International Conference on Systems, Man and Cybernetics (SMC), Bari, Italy, 6–9 October 2019; pp. 1036–1042.
60. Lyu, S.; Gong, X.Y.; Zhang, Z.H.; Han, S.; Zhang, J.W. Survey of Deep Reinforcement Learning Methods with Evolutionary Algorithms. *Chin. J. Comput.* **2022**, *45*, 1478–1499.

61. Freitas, G.; Hamner, B.; Bergerman, M.; Singh, S. A practical obstacle detection system for autonomous orchard vehicles. In Proceedings of the IEEE/RSJ International Conference on Intelligent Robots & Systems, Tokyo, Japan, 3–7 November 2013.
62. Blok, P.M.; Kwon, S.H.; Boheemen, K.v.; Hakjin, K. Autonomous In-Row Navigation of an Orchard Robot with a 2D LIDAR Scanner and Particle Filter with a Laser-Beam Model. *Inst. Control Robot. Syst.* **2018**, *24*, 726–735. [CrossRef]
63. Wang, M.; Xu, J.; Zhang, J.C.; Cui, Y. An autonomous navigation method for orchard rows based on a combination of an improved a-star algorithm and SVR. *Precis. Agric.* **2024**, *25*, 1429–1453. [CrossRef]
64. Kiumarsi, B.; Vamvoudakis, K.G.; Modares, H.; Lewis, F.L. Optimal and Autonomous Control Using Reinforcement Learning: A Survey. *IEEE Trans. Neural Netw. Learn. Syst.* **2018**, *29*, 2042–2062. [CrossRef]
65. Yang, Y.; Zhang, R.R.; Zhang, L.H.; Chen, L.P.; Yi, T.C.; Wu, M.Q.; Yue, X.L. DQN-based Path Tracking Control for Intelligent Agricultural Machinery. *J. Agric. Mech. Res.* **2025**, *47*, 28–34. [CrossRef]
66. Zhang, F.; Wan, X.F.; Cui, J.; Liu, H.D.; Cai, T.T.; Yang, Y. UAV path planning strategy for smart tourism agriculture. *Comput. Eng Des.* **2022**, *43*, 1905–1914. [CrossRef]
67. Hu, G.M. Research on Navigation of Orchard Inspection Robot Based on Deep Reinforcement Learning. *Mod. Inf. Technol.* **2021**, *5*, 154–156+160. [CrossRef]
68. Devarajan, G.G.; Nagarajan, S.M.; Alnumay, G.W. DDNSAS: Deep reinforcement learning based deep Q-learning network for smart agriculture system. *Sustain. Comput.-Infor.* **2023**, *39*, 100890. [CrossRef]
69. Haarnoja, T.; Zhou, A.; Abbeel, P.; Levine, S. Soft Actor-Critic: Off-Policy Maximum Entropy Deep Reinforcement Learning with a Stochastic Actor. In Proceedings of the 35th International Conference on Machine Learning, Stockholm, Sweden, 10–15 July 2018.
70. Hessel, M.; Modayil, J.; Van Hasselt, H.; Schaul, T.; Ostrovski, G.; Dabney, W.; Horgan, D.; Piot, B.; Azar, M.; Silver, D. Rainbow: Combining Improvements in Deep Reinforcement Learning. In *Thirty-Second AAAI Conference on Artificial Intelligence*; AAAI: Philadelphia, PA, USA, 2017; Volume 32.
71. Zhang, Y.H.; Chen, W.B.; Zhang, J.Q.; Ma, H. A flexible assembly strategy for a 6-DOF robotic arm based on deep reinforcement learning. *J. Chongqing Univ. Technol. (Nat. Sci.)* **2024**, *38*, 148–154.
72. Zhang, S.; Shen, J.; Cao, K.; Dai, H.S.; Li, T. Research on 6D Robotic Arm Grasping Method Based on Improved DDPG. *Comput. Eng. Appl.* **2025**, 1–10.
73. Zhang, X.; Lu, H.M.; Ren, J.K.; Mo, X.M.; Xiao, H.R.; Zhang, W.J.; Yang, X. A Dynamic Target Grasping Method for Manipulator Based on Deep Reinforcement Learning. *Ordnance Ind. Autom.* **2024**, *43*, 91–96.
74. Liu, J.; Yap, H.J.; Khairuddin, A.S.M. Path Planning for the Robotic Manipulator in Dynamic Environments Based on a Deep Reinforcement Learning Method. *J. Intell. Robot. Syst.* **2024**, *111*, 3. [CrossRef]
75. Xie, F.; Guo, Z.; Li, T.; Feng, Q.; Zhao, C. Dynamic Task Planning for Multi-Arm Harvesting Robots Under Multiple Constraints Using Deep Reinforcement Learning. *Horticulturae* **2025**, *11*, 88. [CrossRef]
76. Yang, B.; Wu, X.; Zhang, M.L.; Feng, S.K. Path Planning of Weeding Robot Arm Based on Deep Reinforcement Learning. *J. Agric. Mech. Res.* **2025**, *47*, 15–21. [CrossRef]
77. Zhang, S.C.; Xue, X.Y.; Chen, C.; Sun, Z.; Sun, T. Development of a low-cost quadrotor UAV based on ADRC for agricultural remote sensing. *Int. J. Agric. Biol. Eng.* **2019**, *12*, 82–87. [CrossRef]
78. Shi, Q.; Liu, D.; Mao, H.; Shen, B.; Li, M. Wind-induced response of rice under the action of the downwash flow field of a multi-rotor UAV. *Biosyst. Eng.* **2021**, *203*, 60–69. [CrossRef]
79. Almalki, F.A.; Salem, S.M.; Fawzi, W.M.; Alfeteis, N.S.; Esaifan, S.A.; Alharthi, A.S.; Alnefaiey, R.Z.; Naith, Q.H. Coupling an Autonomous UAV With a ML Framework for Sustainable Environmental Monitoring and Remote Sensing. *Int. J. Aerosp. Eng.* **2024**, *2024*. [CrossRef]
80. Hu, J.; Wang, T.; Yang, J.C.; Lan, Y.B.; Lv, S.L.; Zhang, Y.L. WSN-Assisted UAV Trajectory Adjustment for Pesticide Drift Control. *Sensors* **2020**, *20*, 5473. [CrossRef] [PubMed]
81. Fu, H.T.; Li, Z.; Zhang, W.J.; Feng, Y.X.; Zhu, L.; Fang, X.; Li, J. Research on Path Planning of Agricultural UAV Based on Improved Deep Reinforcement Learning. *Agronomy* **2024**, *14*, 2669. [CrossRef]
82. Kang, C.; Park, B.; Choi, J. Scheduling PID Attitude and Position Control Frequencies for Time-Optimal Quadrotor Waypoint Tracking under Unknown External Disturbances. *Sensors* **2022**, *22*, 150. [CrossRef]
83. Huang, Y.Y.; Li, Z.W.; Yang, C.H.; Huang, Y.M. Automatic Path Planning for Spraying Drones Based on Deep Q-Learning. *J. Internet Technol.* **2023**, *24*, 565–575. [CrossRef]
84. Zhu, W.; Feng, Z.; Dai, S.; Zhang, P.; Wei, X. Using UAV Multispectral Remote Sensing with Appropriate Spatial Resolution and Machine Learning to Monitor Wheat Scab. *Agriculture* **2022**, *12*, 1785. [CrossRef]
85. Chen, Y.Y.; Zhou, B.B.; Chen, X.P.; Ma, C.K.; Cui, L.; Lei, F.; Han, X.J.; Chen, L.J.; Wu, S.S.; Ye, D.P. A method of deep network auto-training based on the MTPI auto-transfer learning and a reinforcement learning algorithm for vegetation detection in a dry thermal valley environment. *Front. Plant Sci.* **2025**, *15*, 1448669. [CrossRef] [PubMed]
86. Gözen, D.; Özer, S. Visual Object Tracking in Drone Images with Deep Reinforcement Learning. In Proceedings of the 25th International Conference on Pattern Recognition (ICPR), Milan, Italy, 10–15 January 2021; pp. 10082–10089.

87. Lytridis, C.; Kaburlasos, V.G.; Pachidis, T.; Manios, M.; Vrochidou, E.; Kalampokas, T.; Chatzistamatis, S. An Overview of Cooperative Robotics in Agriculture. *Agronomy* **2021**, *11*, 1818. [CrossRef]
88. Delavarpour, N.; Koparan, C.; Nowatzki, J.; Bajwa, S.; Sun, X. A Technical Study on UAV Characteristics for Precision Agriculture Applications and Associated Practical Challenges. *Remote Sens.* **2021**, *13*, 1204. [CrossRef]
89. Miao, H.; Tian, Y.C. Dynamic robot path planning using an enhanced simulated annealing approach. *Appl. Math. Comput.* **2013**, *222*, 420–437. [CrossRef]
90. Yang, K.J.; Sukkarieh, S. REAL-TIME Continuous Curvature Path Planning of Uavs in Cluttered Environments. In Proceedings of the 5th International Symposium on Mechatronics and its Applications, Amman, Jordan, 27–29 May 2008; pp. 1–6.
91. Hart, P.E.; Nilsson, N.J.; Raphael, B. A Formal Basis for the Heuristic Determination of Minimum Cost Paths. *IEEE Trans. Syst. Sci. Cybern.* **1968**, *4*, 100–107. [CrossRef]
92. Chen, X.; Zhang, J. The Three-Dimension Path Planning of UAV Based on Improved Artificial Potential Field in Dynamic Environment. In Proceedings of the 2013 5th International Conference on Intelligent Human-Machine Systems and Cybernetics, Hangzhou, China, 26–27 August 2013; pp. 144–147.
93. Dijkstra, E.W. A note on two problems in connexion with graphs. *Numer. Math.* **1959**, *1*, 269–271. [CrossRef]
94. Yan, F.; Liu, Y.S.; Xiao, J.Z. Path Planning in Complex 3D Environments Using a Probabilistic Roadmap Method. *Int. J. Autom. Comput.* **2013**, *10*, 525–533. [CrossRef]
95. Tsai, J.T.; Chou, J.H.; Liu, T.K. Tuning the structure and parameters of a neural network by using hybrid Taguchi-genetic algorithm. *IEEE Trans. Neural Netw.* **2006**, *17*, 69–80. [CrossRef]
96. Wu, K.Y.; Esfahani, M.A.; Yuan, S.H.; Wang, H. TDPP-Net: Achieving three-dimensional path planning via a deep neural network architecture. *Neurocomputing* **2019**, *357*, 151–162. [CrossRef]
97. Guo, T.; Jiang, N.; Biyue, L.I.; Zhu, X.; Wenbo, D.U. UAV navigation in high dynamic environments: A deep reinforcement learning approach. *Chin. J. Aeronaut.* **2020**, *34*, 479–489. [CrossRef]
98. Tian, S.S.; Li, Y.X.; Zhang, X.; Zheng, L.; Cheng, L.H.; She, W.; Xie, W. Fast UAV path planning in urban environments based on three-step experience buffer sampling DDPG. *Digit. Commun. Netw.* **2024**, *10*, 813–826. [CrossRef]
99. Haarnoja, T.; Zhou, A.; Hartikainen, K.; Tucker, G.; Ha, S.; Tan, J.; Kumar, V.; Zhu, H.; Gupta, A.; Abbeel, P. Soft Actor-Critic Algorithms and Applications. *arXiv* **2018**, arXiv:1812.05905.
100. Baumgartner, J.; Petric, T.; Klancar, G. Potential Field Control of a Redundant Nonholonomic Mobile Manipulator with Corridor-Constrained Base Motion. *Machines* **2023**, *11*, 293. [CrossRef]
101. Li, L.Y.; Wu, D.F.; Huang, Y.Q.; Yuan, Z.M. A path planning strategy unified with a COLREGS collision avoidance function based on deep reinforcement learning and artificial potential field. *Appl. Ocean Res.* **2021**, *113*, 102759. [CrossRef]
102. Cao, K.; Zhu, Y.; Gao, Q.; Liu, J.H. Research status and prospect of deep reinforcement learning in automatic control. *J. Drain. Irrig. Mach. Eng.* **2023**, *41*, 638–648.
103. Choudhury, M.R.; Das, S.; Christopher, J.; Apan, A.; Chapman, S.; Menzies, N.W.; Dang, Y.P. Improving Biomass and Grain Yield Prediction of Wheat Genotypes on Sodic Soil Using Integrated High-Resolution Multispectral, Hyperspectral, 3D Point Cloud, and Machine Learning Techniques. *Remote Sens.* **2021**, *13*, 3482. [CrossRef]
104. Awais, M.; Li, W.; Cheema, M.J.M.; Zaman, Q.U.; Shaheen, A.; Aslam, B.; Zhu, W.; Ajmal, M.; Faheem, M.; Hussain, S.; et al. UAV-based remote sensing in plant stress imagine using high-resolution thermal sensor for digital agriculture practices: A meta-review. *Int. J. Environ. Sci. Technol.* **2023**, *20*, 1135–1152. [CrossRef]
105. Velusamy, P.; Rajendran, S.; Mahendran, R.K.; Naseer, S.; Shafiq, M.; Choi, J.G. Unmanned Aerial Vehicles (UAV) in Precision Agriculture: Applications and Challenges. *Energies* **2022**, *15*, 217. [CrossRef]
106. Gao, T.; Gao, Z.H.; Sun, B.; Qin, P.Y.; Li, Y.F.; Yan, Z.Y. An Integrated Method for Estimating Forest-Canopy Closure Based on UAV LiDAR Data. *Remote Sens.* **2022**, *14*, 4317. [CrossRef]
107. Zhao, D.A.; Lv, J.D.; Ji, W.; Zhang, Y.; Chen, Y. Design and control of an apple harvesting robot. *Biosyst. Eng.* **2011**, *110*, 112–122. [CrossRef]
108. Feng, R.G.; Hu, J.P.; Wang, M.J.; Niu, X.S.; Li, H.T. Key technologies and application analysis of intelligent agricultural machinery autonomous driving. *Agric. Equip. Veh. Eng.* **2024**, *62*, 15–18.
109. Ahmed, S.; Qiu, B.J.; Ahmad, F.; Kong, C.W.; Xin, H. A State-of-the-Art Analysis of Obstacle Avoidance Methods from the Perspective of an Agricultural Sprayer UAV's Operation Scenario. *Agronomy* **2021**, *11*, 1069. [CrossRef]

agriculture

MDPI

Article

An Improved YOLOv8 Model for Detecting Four Stages of Tomato Ripening and Its Application Deployment in a Greenhouse Environment

Haoran Sun [1], Qi Zheng [1], Weixiang Yao [1,*], Junyong Wang [1], Changliang Liu [1], Huiduo Yu [1] and Chunling Chen [1,2,*]

[1] College of Information and Electrical Engineering, Shenyang Agricultural University, Shenyang 110866, China; 2023240095@stu.syau.edu.cn (H.S.); 2024240171@stu.syau.edu.cn (Q.Z.); 2021189075@stu.syau.edu.cn (J.W.); liuchangliang@stu.syau.edu.cn (C.L.); 2024240121@stu.syau.edu.cn (H.Y.)
[2] Liaoning Engineering Research Center for Information Technology in Agriculture, Shenyang 110299, China
* Correspondence: yaoweixiang@syau.edu.cn (W.Y.); chenchunling@syau.edu.cn (C.C.)

Abstract: The ripeness of tomatoes is a critical factor influencing both their quality and yield. Currently, the accurate and efficient detection of tomato ripeness in greenhouse environments, along with the implementation of selective harvesting, has become a topic of significant research interest. In response to the current challenges, including the unclear segmentation of tomato ripeness stages, low recognition accuracy, and the limited deployment of mobile applications, this study provided a detailed classification of tomato ripeness stages. Through image processing techniques, the issue of class imbalance was addressed. Based on this, a model named GCSS-YOLO was proposed. Feature extraction was refined by introducing the RepNCSPELAN module, which is a lightweight alternative that reduces model size. A multi-dimensional feature neck network was integrated to enhance feature fusion, and three Semantic Feature Learning modules (SGE) were added before the detection head to minimize environmental interference. Further, Shape_IoU replaced CIoU as the loss function, prioritizing bounding box shape and size for improved detection accuracy. Experiments demonstrated GCSS-YOLO's superiority, achieving an average mean average precision mAP50 of 85.3% and F1 score of 82.4%, outperforming the SSD, RT-DETR, and YOLO variants and advanced models like YOLO-TGI and SAG-YOLO. For practical deployment, this study deployed a mobile application developed using the NCNN framework on the Android platform. Upon evaluation, the model achieved an RMSE of 0.9045, an MAE of 0.4545, and an R^2 value of 0.9426, indicating strong performance.

Keywords: tomato detection; ripeness; YOLOv8s; android deployment; greenhouse environment

1. Introduction

Tomatoes are one of the most widely cultivated and consumed vegetable crops, with an exceptionally high global production rate [1]. To meet the continuous demand for daily consumption, tomatoes are currently grown in large quantities within greenhouse environments. Typically, in such controlled settings, tomatoes ripen at an accelerated pace. However, if they become overripe, they are prone to rot, leading to significant economic losses. According to previous studies, losses caused by various diseases and rot account for approximately 30% of the total production [2]. Therefore, it is crucial to accurately classify the growth stages of tomatoes. The rapid and non-destructive identification of tomatoes at different stages of ripeness is necessary for better management of resources during

https://doi.org/10.3390/agriculture15090936

harvesting, transportation, and storage, thus reducing economic as well as labor-related losses [3].

In recent years, traditional image processing algorithms and machine learning techniques have been widely applied across various domains, such as fruit and crop analysis, where they have played a significant role. However, during the course of their application, numerous challenges and issues have also emerged. For instance, excessive reliance on human intervention and vulnerability to complex environmental conditions often result in poor generalization and limited robustness [4]. With the advancement of artificial intelligence, deep learning methods, due to their distinctive capabilities, have demonstrated remarkable efficiency in handling complex scenarios involving occlusion, illumination variation, and scale changes [5,6]. Deep learning-based object detection can be broadly classified into two categories: single-stage detection algorithms and two-stage detection algorithms. The two-stage detection approach consists of an initial stage that generates multiple candidate bounding boxes containing potential objects, followed by a second stage that refines these boxes through localization and classification. Prominent algorithms in this category include Mask R-CNN [7] and Faster R-CNN [8]. As proposed by Wang et al. [9], the MatDet model was introduced for the detection of two categories—green and ripe tomatoes—under complex environmental conditions, achieving a mean average precision (mAP) of 96.14%. Zu et al. [10] designed a Mask R-CNN network for the identification and segmentation of green tomatoes in greenhouse environments, with an F1 score of 92.0%. Furthermore, Minagawa et al. [11] integrated Mask R-CNN with clustering techniques to predict the ripening time of tomato clusters in greenhouses, achieving accuracy (ACC) rates of 80% and 92% in noisy and noise-free environments, respectively. The aforementioned studies validate the high detection accuracy of two-stage detection algorithms. However, these algorithms often overlook critical issues, such as processing time and the inherent complexity of the algorithm itself.

In recent years, single-stage algorithms have gained widespread attention across various research domains, with notable representatives including You Only Look Once (YOLO) and Single-Shot MultiBox Detector (SSD), among which the YOLO series has experienced the most rapid development. The YOLO series algorithms include YOLOv3 [12], YOLOv4 [13], YOLOv5 [14], YOLOv7 [15], YOLOv8 [16], YOLOv9 [17], YOLOv10 [18], and YOLOv11 [19]. While maintaining low complexity and high processing speed, these algorithms also exhibit high detection precision, making them widely applicable across various fields [20]. For instance, Wu et al. [21] designed an efficient object detection network that automatically assigns weights to channel features for apple detection under complex weather conditions, achieving a precision of 90.7%. Zhu et al. [22] proposed an improved network model based on YOLOv8 and applied it within a corn plantation to achieve 128.5 FPS. Additionally, Pual et al. [23] conducted a comprehensive study on peppers using various functionalities within YOLOv8, covering tasks such as recognition, segmentation, classification, and counting, and developed a corresponding Android application, ultimately achieving a detection success rate of 95%. Ren et al. [24] proposed an enhanced YOLOv8 model called YOLO-RCS, which minimizes background interference to capture the distinctive features of "Yuluxiang" pears, achieving an mAP of 88.63% with an inference time of 1.6 ms. Zhu et al. [25] designed a detection model specifically for oil tea fruits in orchards and conducted validation experiments across two datasets, resulting in an mAP of 93.18%, with a model size of only 19.82 MB. These studies demonstrate that single-stage models, while enabling real-time detection, can also maintain high accuracy and are progressively playing a significant role in the field of agricultural recognition and detection.

Recent studies have also explored the detection and classification of tomatoes. Yang et al. [26] classified tomatoes into three categories: mature, immature, and diseased. Their improved model achieved an mAP of 93.7% and a recall of 92.0% on the test set. Gao et al. [27] employed an improved YOLOv5s model for recognizing single-class tomatoes in continuous operational environments, achieving an mAP of 92.08%. Meanwhile, Sun et al. [28] achieved an average detection precision of 92.46% and an ACC of 96.60% on a public dataset, with a frame rate of 74.05 FPS. Chen et al. [29] proposed the MTD-YOLO multi-task cherry tomato network, which enables the detection of both cherry tomatoes and the maturity of fruit clusters. Notably, the model achieved an overall score of 86.6% in its multi-task learning. These diverse approaches to tomato classification provide a valuable foundation for subsequent research in the field. Although these studies are comprehensive, it is evident that there is a lack of detailed research on the finer classification of tomato fruit growth and maturity stages. Tomatoes have a short maturation period and are highly susceptible to various pathogens, often exhibiting multiple concurrent growth states. Therefore, a more rational and effective classification of tomato maturity stages is essential, particularly for accurately identifying tomatoes that are rotten due to disease. Such advancements could facilitate selective harvesting and reduce losses caused by disease-induced decay. Although the aforementioned models have achieved commendable results in detection precision and generalization capabilities, further optimization is still necessary to enhance their adaptability in complex environments. In particular, maintaining high accuracy and robustness while reducing model size will be crucial for enabling broader applications.

With the development of the deep learning embedded field, nowadays, cell phone mobile deployment has become a more popular direction, with remarkable success. The combination of the two empowers key convenient visualization capabilities, which are now widely used for various plant diseases, e.g., lightweight cotton [30] and rice [31]. Similarly, a great deal of research has been conducted on recognizing the plants themselves, such as strawberry [32], winter jujube [33], and so on. Moreover, there is currently a lack of mobile deployment applications for real-time greenhouse tomato recognition. Given the need for the efficient processing of acquired information, quick validation, and timely feedback in mobile applications, the YOLO algorithm, with its high precision, fast efficiency, and ease of lightweight deployment, is particularly well-suited to meet the real-time and practical demands of such end-user applications. Considering these reasons, developing lightweight mobile deployment applications based on the YOLO series could serve as a viable solution for achieving optimal performance on edge devices [34].

Based on the preceding analysis, the key contributions of this study are outlined as follows:

(1) A fine-grained, four-stage classification of tomato maturity (green ripe stage, turning ripe stage, fully ripe stage, and disease-related decay stage) was conducted. Additionally, a data-augmentation-based greenhouse tomato fruit dataset was constructed, encompassing the entire maturation process from the green mature to disease-related decay stages. This dataset also included real-world growth conditions of tomatoes, capturing various angles, lighting intensities, and occlusions.

(2) The GSCC-YOLO improved model was proposed, which effectively reduced computational redundancy and enhanced detection capability while meeting the requirements for real-time detection. Notably, this model demonstrated an mAP50 of 85.3% on a self-constructed dataset, showing a distinct advantage over the current models. To evaluate the model's generalization ability, validation on public datasets was conducted, achieving an mAP50 of 90.5%.

(3) A mobile application for greenhouse tomato recognition, developed based on the NCNN framework, was successfully deployed on Android devices. Through linear regression experiments and real-world applications, it was demonstrated that the application can accurately and efficiently perform detection in the complex environment of a greenhouse, achieving an R^2 value of 0.9426.

2. Materials and Methods

2.1. Dataset Composition

The dataset was primarily divided into three parts. The first part consisted of a self-constructed dataset, which was used for model training and experimentation. The second part comprised a public dataset (https://aistudio.baidu.com/datasetdetail/142431/2, (accessed on 15 December 2024)), which was utilized to validate the generalization ability of the improved model. The third part included the test set from the self-constructed dataset and real-world images captured on-site, which were used for mobile application testing.

2.2. Dataset Construction

2.2.1. Image Collection

The self-built dataset was collected at the tomato cultivation base of Shenyang Agricultural University, located in Shenyang, Liaoning Province, China (123°57′ E, 41°83′ N). The tomato variety cultivated was Dongnong727, with an average plant height of approximately 180 ± 5 cm. Due to the occlusion caused by the upper branches and leaves, it was challenging to capture tomatoes positioned higher up. To address this issue, this study employed a combined approach of using a fixed-point shooting pole and manual photography for image collection. The distance between the shooting pole and the tomato plants was set at 30 cm, with shooting heights of 45 ± 5 cm, 75 ± 5 cm, and 105 ± 5 cm above the ground. Researchers manually photographed tomatoes located outside this height range. The specific shooting positions are illustrated in Figure 1. Image collection covered three time periods: November 2023 to January 2024, July 2024 to September 2024, and December 2024 to January 2025. During each time period, images were collected at the following times: 7:00–9:00 AM, 11:00 AM–1:00 PM, and 4:00–5:00 PM.

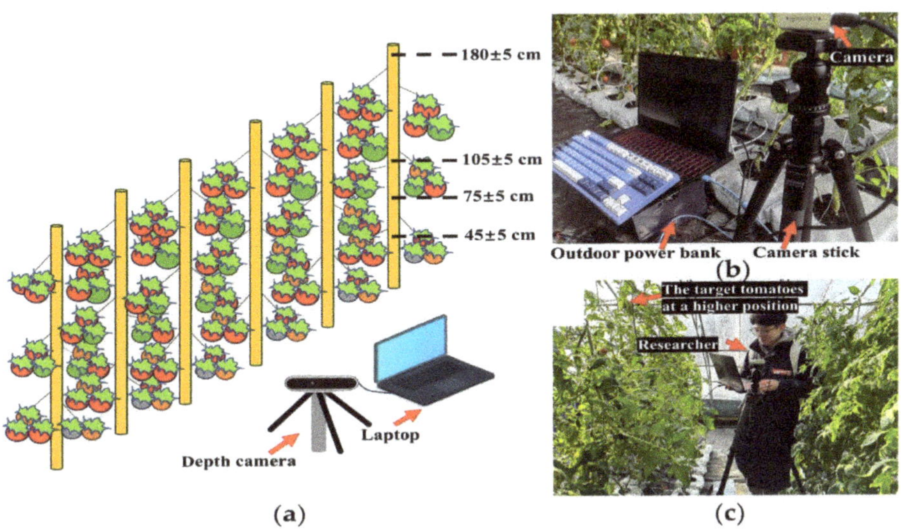

Figure 1. Dataset image collection diagram. (**a**) Overview of dataset image collection. (**b**) On-site image collection at low height, (**c**) On-site image collection at a higher distance.

To ensure the comprehensiveness and generalizability of the dataset, photographs of tomatoes in various growth stages were captured from multiple angles, as illustrated in Figure 2. A total of 723 images and 9 video clips were recorded, with the videos processed through frame extraction to generate additional images. The process resulted in a total of 763 images, all stored in JPEG format.

Figure 2. Images captured from different angles. (**a**) Front lighting; (**b**) back lighting; (**c**) front lighting with mild occlusion; (**d**) front lighting with moderate occlusion; (**e**) front lighting with heavy occlusion; (**f**) back lighting with mild occlusion; (**g**) back lighting with moderate occlusion; (**h**) back lighting with heavy occlusion.

2.2.2. Image Annotations and Dataset Composition

Our pre-experimental annotation framework implemented LabelImg to classify the tomato phenological stages into four distinct categories (Figure 3): green ripe stage (T_GreenRP), turning maturity stage (T_BetweenGMP), full maturity stage (T_MaturityP), and disease-related decay stage (T_RotP). The disease-related decay stage includes two types of rot: one caused by delayed harvesting, resulting in natural decay, and the other caused by diseases leading to rotting. The diseases primarily include issues such as wormholes and umbilical rot [35].

Figure 3. Illustrative images of tomato fruit at different stages of maturity and decay classification.

2.2.3. Handling of Imbalanced Data Distributions

Due to the rarity of disease-related decay stages in tomatoes under real-world conditions, the imbalance in the dataset may lead to reduced model accuracy and overfitting during training. To address this issue, this study first manually grouped the diseased tomatoes and then applied image processing techniques to mitigate the challenge. The procedure involved the following steps: First, pixel-level segmentation was performed on the images of decayed, disease-affected tomatoes. Second, complex background images without any tomatoes were selected from both videos and photographs. Once these steps were completed, the data synthesis process was carried out. The detailed workflow is illustrated in Figure 4. In total, 21 background images and 7 images of diseased, decayed tomatoes were used. For testing of fits to synthetic data, see Appendix A.

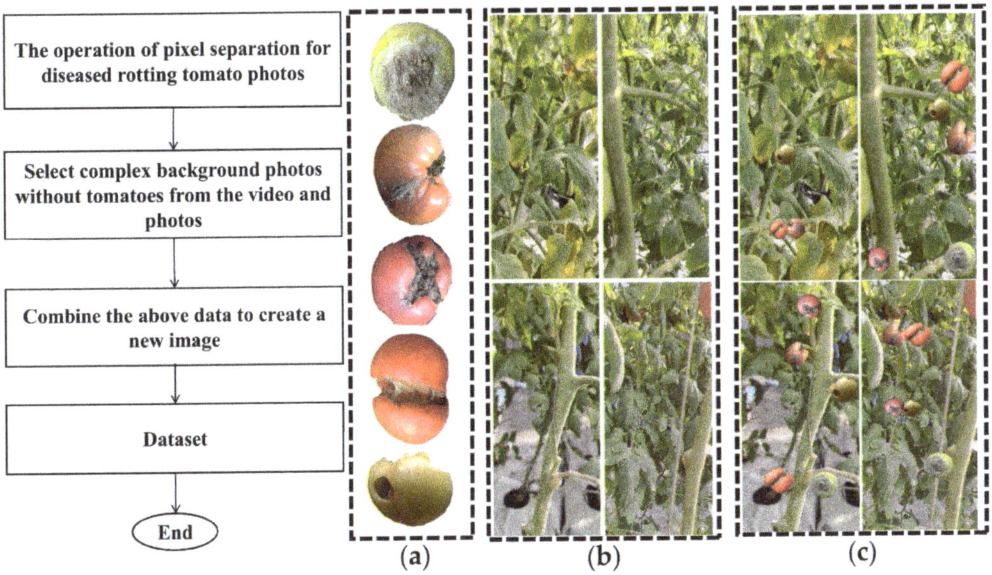

Figure 4. Dataset synthesis flowchart. (**a**) Disease-related decay of tomatoes. (**b**) Complex background without tomatoes. (**c**) Synthesized image.

2.2.4. Augmentation of the Dataset

We implemented a targeted augmentation pipeline incorporating seven transformation modalities: random translation, Gaussian noise injection, brightness modulation, random crops, rotational variance (±30°), horizontal flipping, and affine shearing. This protocol generated an enhanced dataset containing 6270 annotated samples, systematically partitioned into training (n = 4389), validation (n = 1254), and test subsets (n = 627) following a 7:2:1 stratified allocation. Table 1 quantitatively details the class distribution across maturity stages, including both image counts and their associated annotation instances.

Table 1. Detailed composition of the tomato growing period dataset.

Data Categories	Number of Images	The Number of Tag Box Selections				
		T_GreenRP	T_BetweenGMP	T_MaturityP	T_RotP	Total
Training set	4389	5268	4178	3030	3154	15,630
Validation set	1254	1632	1302	1025	504	4463
Testing set	627	891	782	575	501	2749
Integrity dataset	6270	7791	6262	4630	4159	22,642

2.3. GCSS-YOLO

YOLOv8 is a single-stage algorithm designed for tasks such as object detection, instance segmentation, and image classification. Its network architecture is composed of four main components: the input layer, backbone network, neck network, and detection head. YOLOv8 is further categorized into five different network architectures, including YOLOv8n, YOLOv8s, YOLOv8m, YOLOv8l, and YOLOv8x, based on network depth and width thresholds, with each architecture corresponding to variations in the number of submodules and kernels [36]. To address a variety of tasks, different architectural approaches were explored. In this study, YOLOv8s was chosen as the baseline model due to its relatively low parameter count, compact model size, and superior precision and detection speed compared to other architectures. The model was then adapted for effective deployment in the recognition of tomato growth and maturation stages on mobile platforms.

However, several challenges arose during practical detection, including complex branch and leaf environments, overlapping and occlusion of multiple targets, and situations where some tomatoes shared similar colors with the branches or leaves. These issues impeded the model's ability to extract features effectively. In light of these challenges, the YOLOv8s network was specifically improved to ensure both lightweight deployment and efficient, accurate extraction of the growth features of tomatoes at each stage. The modified model was referred to as the GCSS-YOLO model, and its structure is illustrated in Figure 5.

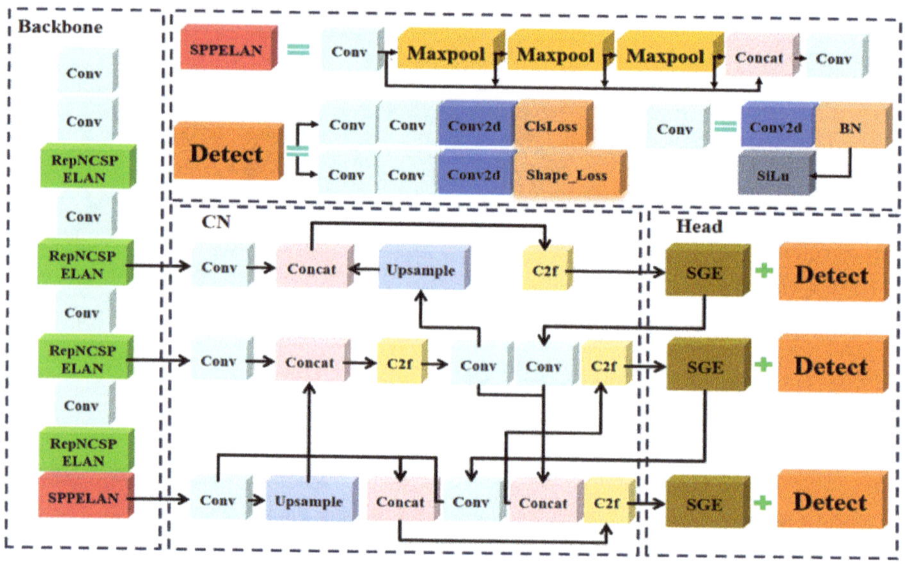

Figure 5. GCSS-YOLO network architecture diagram.

Specifically, to enhance the backbone network's ability to focus on the tomato regions in the input images, the lightweight multi-feature decomposition module (RepNCSPELAN) was employed to replace the original C2f structure in the backbone. For the neck network, the PAN structure was retained while the input and output channel dimensions were adjusted to reduce computational redundancy. However, the lightweight modification of the neck network led to an imbalance in the extraction of semantic and spatial features during detection. To address this issue, a Semantic Feature Learning module (SGE) was integrated into the network prior to the detection head. Finally, to improve the localization accuracy of target boundaries and enhance the model's convergence, the Shape_IoU loss function was introduced at the output stage.

2.3.1. Lightweight Multi-Feature Decomposition Module

Tomatoes grown in greenhouse environments are often subjected to complex background conditions, which increase the difficulty and instability of accurate tomato recognition. This instability interferes with the backbone network's ability to extract tomato features, resulting in fragmented feature representations during global feature extraction and consequently increasing the difficulty of tomato recognition. To mitigate this issue, a lightweight multi-feature decomposition module was introduced into the network. The global and local tensor information of the input image was integrated and processed to enhance the completeness of the target feature representation. The structure of the RepNCSPELAN module is illustrated in Figure 6.

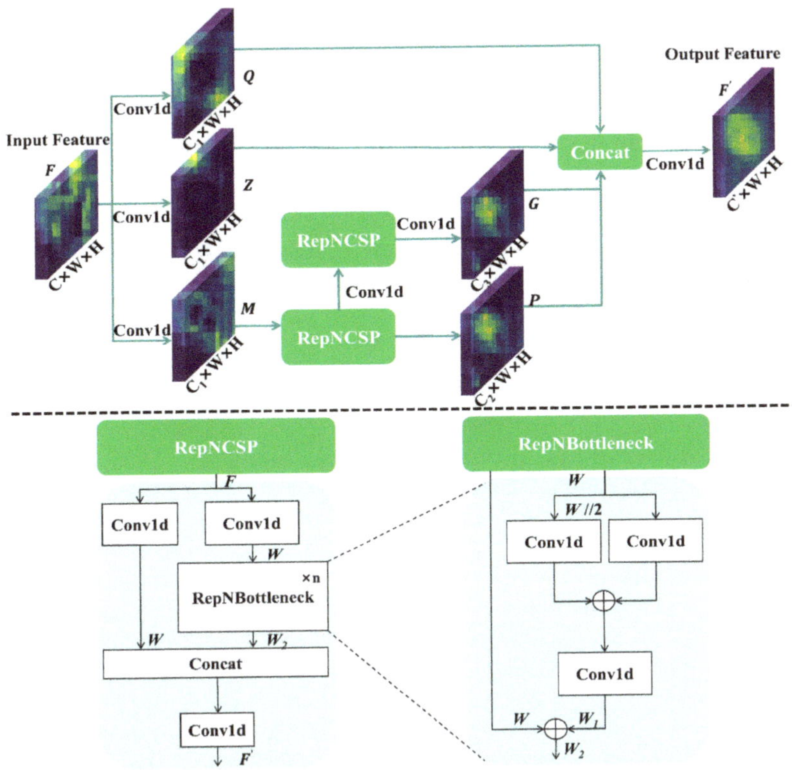

Figure 6. Structure of RepNCSPELAN.

As shown in Figure 6, the enhanced YOLOv8s backbone network processes input features $F \in R^{C \times W \times H}$ through three parallel 1×1 convolutional ($Conv1d$) layers, adjusting the channel dimension to C_1, and generates three intermediate feature maps: Q, Z, and $M \in R^{C_1 \times W \times H}$. Among these, Q and Z retain the original filtered features, while M is processed by a dedicated spatial feature enhancement module. This module employs multiple $Conv1d$ to progressively transform the channel dimensions into C_2 and C_3, prouducing refined feature maps $G \in R^{C_2 \times W \times H}$ and $P \in R^{C_3 \times W \times H}$. The spatial enhancement process strengthens the model's focus on critical regions and improves the adaptability of spatial feature representations. Finally, a multi-channel dimensional fusion operation integrates the refined features into a globally coherent representation $F' \in R^{C' \times W \times H}$, enabling more effective target characterization. The overall workflow is mathematically formalized in Equations (1) and (2).

$$Q = Conv1d_{1\times1}(F), Z = Conv1d_{1\times1}(F), M = Conv1d_{1\times1}(F) \tag{1}$$

$$G = Conv1d_{C_2}(M), P = Conv1d_{C_3}(G), F' = Concat(Q, Z, G, P) \tag{2}$$

where $Q, Z, M \in R^{C'\times W\times H}$, $C' = C_1 + C_2 + C_3$, and $F' \in R^{C'\times W\times H}$.

In the RepNCSPELAN module, the RepNCSP component enhances feature dimensionality by convolving contracted features, as detailed in Equations (3)–(5).

$$W = Conv1d_{1\times1}(F) \tag{3}$$

$$W_2 = \sum_{i=1}^{n} Concat(Conv1d_{1\times1}(W, W_1)) \tag{4}$$

$$F' = Conv1d_{1\times1}(Concat(W, W_2)) \tag{5}$$

In the above equations, F denotes the feature nodes derived from the multi-scale decomposition of high-dimensional input features. W_1 and W represent the multi-scale features obtained through hierarchical scale-aware decomposition. These features are processed through n stacked 1×1 convolutional layers to generate low-dimensional embeddings W_2. Finally, F' represents the refined features obtained by integrating differential characteristics across scales, thereby enhancing representational coherence. This process ensures adaptive feature optimization while preserving essential spatial and semantic information.

2.3.2. Lightweight Multi-Dimensional Feature Network Structure Reconstruction

After being processed by the RepNCSPELAN module in the backbone network, the multi-dimensional refined features are forwarded to into the neck network. However, the original neck network lacks the capacity to effectively process multi-dimensional features. To address this issue, a novel neck architecture, termed the C-Neck (CN) network, was proposed in this study.

The proposed approach incorporates a convolutional module within the feature decoupling region to expand the receptive field of the convolutional kernels. This not only enables the capture of richer local information but also adjusts the input and output channel dimensions of the convolutional module. The original neck network adopts a progressive strategy for channel dimension adjustment. In this study, the original progressive channel dimensions were replaced with fixed values of 128 and 256 at the corresponding level. Additionally, the decoupling strategy of the convolutional modules in the up-sampling path was modified. In the Bottleneck module of the C2f structure, the transition from low-dimensional to high-dimensional representations may result in feature redundancy. To address this issue, the number of Bottleneck modules was adjusted to achieve an optimal balance for feature extraction. This approach effectively eliminates computational redundancy while consistently extracting more comprehensive and efficient features, thereby retaining a greater amount of relevant information. The specific structure of the neck network is illustrated in Figure 7, with detailed parameter specifications provided in Section 2.4.

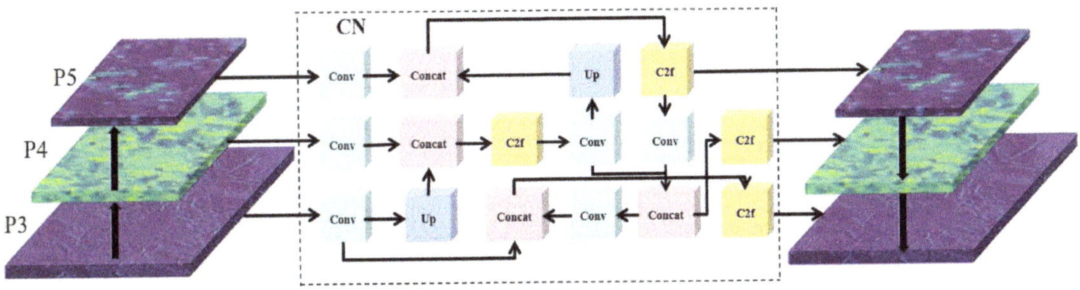

Figure 7. The structure of the CN network.

2.3.3. Adding Semantic Feature Learning into the Detection Model

Due to interference from tomato foliage, stems, and occlusions between fruits in the greenhouse, the convolutional kernels in the neck network may encounter environmental noise when extracting image features. This results in disturbances within the feature space across channels, thereby degrading the quality of the extracted features and ultimately reducing recognition accuracy. To address this issue, the Spatial Group-wise Enhance (SGE) [37] module was introduced. The SGE module is a lightweight, channel-independent mechanism designed to generate attention factors at each spatial location within each semantic group, thus enabling dynamic adjustment of sub-features. When integrated with convolutional neural networks, it enhances feature correlations across channels, reduces the impact of noise interference in real-world scenarios, and facilitates the acquisition of comprehensive spatial and semantic information.

First, the $H \times W \times C$ features in the spatial domain are divided into G groups. Spatial vectors are then used to represent the vectors at any position within the space. To mitigate noise interference with global spatial features, each vector in the global space undergoes a normalization process, as shown in Equations (6) and (7).

$$X = \{x_1 \ldots m\}, x_i \in R^{\frac{C}{G}}, m = H \times W \tag{6}$$

$$g = F_{gp}(X) = \frac{1}{m}\sum_{i=1}^{m} x_i \tag{7}$$

where x_i represents an arbitrary vector in the local space, where i denotes the spatial feature index $i = (i_H, i_W, i_G)$, and R is the set of global spatial vector feature groups. $F_{gp}(\cdot)$ represents the spatial averaging function, and g is the semantic vector of the group after normalization, approximated accordingly.

To establish the relationship between the global semantic and the normalized global features, feature enhancement is performed using the coefficients between the global semantic and the local features, as shown in Equations (8) and (9).

$$c_i = g \cdot x_i \tag{8}$$

$$\hat{c_i} = \frac{c_i - \mu_c}{\sigma_c + \varepsilon}, \mu_c = \frac{1}{m}\sum_{j}^{m} c_j, \sigma_c^2 = \frac{1}{m}\sum_{j}^{m}(c_j - \mu_c)^2 \tag{9}$$

where c_i represents the corresponding feature coefficient and $\hat{c}_i$ denotes the normalized (enhanced) feature coefficient. μ_i and σ_i represent the mean and variance of the corresponding feature coefficients, respectively, and ε is the constant added to stabilize the coefficients.

To ensure the identity transformation of feature coefficient normalization in the network, a pair of parameters, γ and β, are introduced, with the same number as group G, to shift and scale the normalized values a_i. Finally, the spatial vector x_i is combined with the sigmoid function $\sigma(\cdot)$ to generate the enhanced feature vector $\hat{x}_i$, as shown in Equations (10) and (11).

$$a_i = \gamma\hat{c}_i + \beta \tag{10}$$

$$\hat{x}_i = x_i \cdot \sigma(a_i) \tag{11}$$

The structure of the SGE model is shown in Figure 8. SGE focuses on mapping point features to global features, significantly reducing the environmental interference in individual spatial features. This, in turn, enhances the model's adaptability and generalization ability in complex environments.

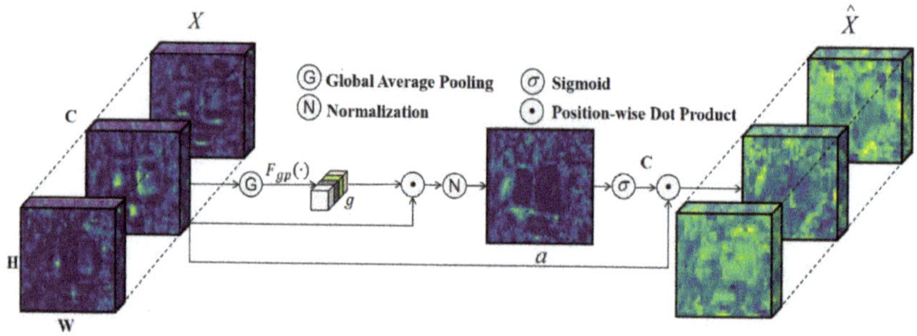

Figure 8. The structure of the SGE model.

2.3.4. Shape_IoU Loss Function

The original YOLOv8 model employs a loss function that primarily addresses the geometric relationship between ground truth boxes and predefined anchor boxes, utilizing a shape-aware loss term to minimize their spatial discrepancies. However, this approach exhibits two critical limitations in practical agricultural detection scenarios.

For bounding box regression samples with identical nominal dimensions, subtle shape variations between anchor boxes and ground truth boxes (e.g., aspect ratio differences in tomato clusters) can disproportionately affect Intersection over Union (IoU) calculations, resulting in suboptimal localization accuracy. During the initial phases of tomato development, the chromatic similarity between immature green tomatoes and surrounding foliage induces anchor box misprioritization in the feature matching process, thereby propagating localization errors in detection outputs.

Therefore, this paper adopted Shape_IoU as the model's edge loss function. This loss function places greater emphasis on the shape and size of the bounding boxes themselves, reducing the training loss by leveraging their properties. To address the feature insensitivity problem of the green ripe stage, the dynamic weighting of green ripe tomatoes was improved based on Shape_IoU. When the target is "T_GreenRP", the ratio of the target to the entire image is adjusted, and the compliance value is modified to break the intrinsic value and achieve higher sensitivity. The specific formula for Shape_IoU is given by Equations (12)–(14):

$$distance^{shape} = \frac{2 \times (h^{gt})^{scale} \times \left(x_c - x_c^{gt}\right) + 2 \times (w^{gt})^{scale} \times \left(y_c - y_c^{gt}\right)}{(w^{gt})^{scale} + (h^{gt})^{scale}} \Big/ c^2 \tag{12}$$

$$\Omega^{shape} = \sum_{t=w,h} \left(1 - e^{-\omega t}\right)^{\theta}, \theta = 4 \tag{13}$$

$$L_{Shape_{IoU}} = 1 - IoU + distance^{shape} + 0.5 \times \Omega^{shape} \tag{14}$$

where *scale* represents the scaling factor, which is related to the target size in the dataset. ww and hh represent the weighting coefficients in the horizontal and vertical directions, respectively, with their values depending on the size of the ground truth boxes. Ω denotes the shape loss. $h^{gt}, w^{gt}, w,$ and$h$ represent the length and height of the ground truth box and the anchor box, respectively.

As shown in Figure 9, Shape_IoU gives more detailed attention to the shape and size of the anchor boxes and the ground truth bounding boxes, thereby enhancing the accuracy of bounding box regression. This enhances the model's generalization ability and robustness in complex environments.

Figure 9. Schematic diagram of Shape_IoU parameters. b^{gt} represents the center position of the ground truth box, b denotes the center position of the anchor box, $\left(x_c^{gt}, y_c^{gt}\right)$ refers to the centroid coordinates of the ground truth box, and (x_c, y_c) represents the centroid coordinates of the anchor box.

2.4. Network Architecture Parameters

Statistical experiments on the number of parameters and FLOPs for each network were conducted for the GCSS-YOLO (Layers [0:29]). First, for the backbone network (Layers [0:9]), replacing the RepNCSPELAN module reduced the FLOPs to 9.892 G and the number of parameters to 1.166 M. Second, the neck network (Layers [10:28]), which consisted of the proposed CN network, differed from the previous neck network. This network reduces the repetition of the C2f module, performing it only once. The input and output thresholds of the Conv module were uniformly set to 128, while those of the C2f module were changed to 128 and 256. These adjustments reduced the FLOPs of the neck network to 3.543 G and the number of parameters to 0.886 M. Lastly, for the detection head (Layers [29]), due to changes in the input and output channel thresholds in the neck network, the computational size of the previous model was reduced, with FLOPs decreasing to 7.054 G and the number of parameters to 1.262 M.

Overall, the number of layers in the network was slightly increased compared to the original model. However, computational redundancy was reduced by adjusting the feature-aware region module of the backbone network and the structure of the neck network. As a result, the computational complexity of the network was significantly reduced, providing an excellent foundation for the subsequent application in the mobile app. For specific experiments, please refer to Section 3.4 on the ablation experiment.

2.5. Deployment of the Model on a Mobile Device

To validate the performance of the improved YOLOv8s model on mobile devices, the baseline YOLOv8s model was also deployed on the mobile platform for comparison. First, the weight files (.pt files) of both models were saved. When deploying models on mobile or embedded platforms, it is typically necessary to use the model's static graph representation, which includes the complete model files.

In light of this issue, the .pt files were converted to .onnx format to enable cross-framework compatibility. To optimize the interfering operators in the .onnx file, the onnx-simplifier tool was employed. Subsequently, the structure was converted using the NCNN framework. NCNN is an open-source, efficient neural network inference framework, specifically optimized for mobile devices. It facilitates the seamless migration of deep learning models to mobile platforms without relying on third-party dependencies, thereby promoting the efficient development of AI applications [38]. Subsequently, the .onnx format was converted into the structure (.bin) and parameter (.param) files required by the NCNN framework. Finally, the model was compiled and debugged within the Android Studio environment, and the APK file was generated for installation on Android devices. The specific application interface is shown in Figure 10.

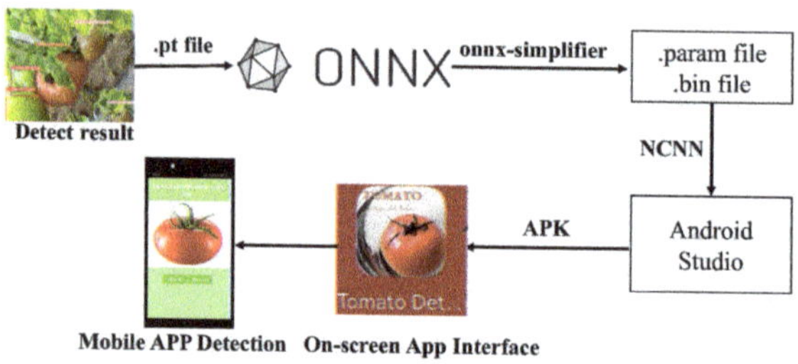

Figure 10. App technology process flowchart.

2.6. Experiment Platform

The models in this experiment were trained and validated under the same environment. The system configuration included a 13th Gen Intel® Core™ i9-13900KF processor (Intel, Santa Clara, CA, USA), paired with an RTX 4080 GPU with 32 GB of memory (NVIDIA, Santa Clara, CA, USA). The deep learning framework used for this experiment was PyTorch (Version 2.6.0), with implementation carried out using CUDA 11.0, Python 3.8, and cuDNN version 8.0.5.39. The training parameters were set as follows: a batch size of 8, 200 iterations, an initial learning rate of 0.01, Automatic Mixed Precision (AMP) set to False, a momentum factor of 0.937, and an input image resolution of 640 × 640 pixels. All compared models were trained with identical hyperparameters. For training parameter tests, see Appendix B.

2.7. Model Evaluation Metrics

This study utilized precision (P), recall (R), mean average precision (mAP), and the F1 score to evaluate the model's performance. mAP represents the mean of the average precision (AP) values for the detected objects, indicating the average detection precision for tomatoes at four stages of maturity. The number of parameters (Params) and the number of floating-point operations (FLOPs) were used to measure the model's complexity. The final model's accuracy was evaluated using metrics such as Mean Absolute Error (MAE),

Root Mean Squared Error (RMSE), and the Coefficient of Determination (R^2). The specific formulas for the metrics are as follows:

$$P = \frac{TP}{TP + FP} \tag{15}$$

$$R = \frac{TP}{TP + FN} \tag{16}$$

$$mAP = \frac{1}{n}\sum_{i=1}^{n} AP_i \tag{17}$$

$$F1\ score = \frac{2PR}{P + R} \tag{18}$$

$$MAE = \frac{1}{n}\sum_{i-1}^{n}\left|\left(\overset{\wedge}{x_i}\right) - x_i\right| \tag{19}$$

$$RMSE = \sqrt{\frac{\sum_{i-1}^{n}\left(x_i - \overset{\wedge}{x_i}\right)^2}{n}} \tag{20}$$

$$R^2 = 1 - \frac{\sum_i\left(x_i - \overset{\wedge}{x_i}\right)^2}{\sum_i (x_i - \overline{x})^2} \tag{21}$$

In the above formulas, TP refers to the number of tomato objects in the sample that are correctly labeled and detected by the model, FP denotes the number of tomatoes in the sample that the model incorrectly detects, and FN represents the number of tomato samples that the model fails to detect. The variable n represents the total number of tomato sample categories, x_i denotes the actual count of tomatoes, $\hat{x}_i$ represents the number of tomatoes counted by the model, and $\overline{x}$ denotes the average of the actual tomato count.

3. Experimental Results

3.1. Analysis of the Attention Modules

To mitigate the impact of environmental factors on feature extraction, attention mechanisms were incorporated to enhance the network's ability to focus on relevant features. This section discusses various attention mechanisms and their respective contributions to enhancing feature extraction. Given the presence of tomatoes at different growth stages and varying pixel resolutions in the detected images, additional models were incorporated before the detection head, as illustrated in Figure 11.

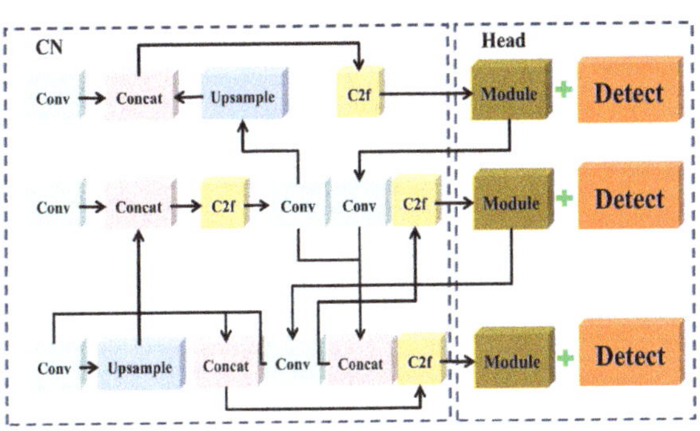

Figure 11. The attention module integrated into the CN network.

The attention mechanism module includes TripleAttention [39], SGE, StokenAttention [40], EMAttention [41], LSK [42], and NAMAttention [43]. The experimental results are summarized in Table 2.

Table 2. Comparison of training results of models with different attention mechanisms.

Model	P/%	R /%	mAP50 /%	Params /M	FLOPs/G	Model Size/MB	F1 Score/%
YOLOv8s	83.7	77.9	83.9	11.127	28.4	21.5	80.7
+Triple Attention	82.4	78.2	82.8	11.128	28.7	21.5	80.3
+Stoken Attention	84.2	76.3	79.1	12.504	29.5	24.1	80.1
+EM Attention	81.5	78.8	84.4	11.181	29.3	21.6	80.1
+LSK	84.0	78.7	84.1	11.713	29.6	22.6	81.3
+NAM Attention	81.3	80.5	83.3	11.128	28.5	21.5	80.9
+SGE	83.8	80.2	84.6	11.127	28.4	21.5	81.9

As shown in Table 2, the baseline YOLOv8s model achieved an mAP50 of 83.9%, an F1 score of 80.7%, a model size of 21.5 MB, and 28.4 GFLOPs. In terms of the mAP50, the models incorporating EMAttention, LSK, and SGE demonstrated improvements of 0.5%, 0.2%, and 0.7%, respectively, over the baseline. However, while the EMAttention module led to a 0.6% decrease in the F1 score compared to YOLOv8s, the SGE-enhanced model achieved increases of 0.2% in the mAP50 and 1.8% in the F1 score, indicating a more balanced performance improvement. The model incorporating the LSK module achieved an mAP50 that was 0.2% higher than that of the YOLOv8s baseline. However, the model with the LSK module incurred a 1.1% increase in model size and an additional 1.2 GFLOPs compared to the YOLOv8s baseline. In terms of the mAP50 and the F1 score, it underperformed relative to the SGE-enhanced model by 0.5% and 0.6%, respectively. Although the model incorporating the TripleAttention module showed no significant increases in parameter count, FLOPs, or model size compared to the YOLOv8s baseline, its mAP50 and F1 score decreased by 1.1% and 0.4%, respectively. The model incorporating the NAMAttention module achieved a 2.6% improvement in recall and a 0.2% increase in the F1 score compared to the YOLOv8s baseline. However, it also showed a 0.6% decline in the mAP50 and a 2.4% drop in precision relative to the YOLOv8s model. Finally, the model with the StokenAttention module achieved a 0.5% improvement in precision over the YOLOv8s model and a 0.4% increase compared to the SGE-based model. However, this enhancement came with a 1.04× increase in FLOPs, a 2.6 MB larger model size, and an additional 1.4 million parameters relative to YOLOv8s. Overall, the model incorporating the SGE module showed the smallest increases in model size, FLOPs, and parameter count. Additionally, its mAP50 outperformed that of the YOLOv8s model and those incorporating TripleAttention, StokenAttention, EMAttention, LSK, and NAMAttention by 0.7%, 1.8%, 5.4%, 0.2%, 0.5%, and 1.3%, respectively, achieving the best balance between model compactness and high accuracy. Therefore, the SGE module was selected for this study.

3.2. Analysis of Boundary Loss Functions

To examine the impact of boundary loss functions on the convergence of the network model, this study conducted experimental analyses using various boundary loss functions: CIoU [44], WIoU [45], MPDIoU [46], Inner_IoU [47], and Shape_IoU [48]. Since the loss function had minimal impact on the model's complexity, experiments and discussions on the parameter count, floating-point operations, and model size were omitted. The detailed experimental data are presented in Table 3.

Table 3. Results of the loss function performance experiment.

Loss Function	P/%	R/%	mAP50/%	F1 Score/%
CIoU	83.7	77.9	83.9	80.7
Shape_IoU	84.5	78.3	84.1	81.3
Inner_IoU	82.4	77.9	82.0	80.1
MPDIoU	83.4	78.8	83.0	81.0
WIoU	81.9	80.5	83.9	81.2

As shown in Table 3, introducing the Inner_IoU boundary loss function led to a 1.9% reduction in the mAP50 and a 0.6% reduction in the F1 score compared to the YOLOv8s model. After introducing the WIoU and MPDIoU boundary loss functions, the model's F1 score improved by 0.3% and 0.5%, respectively, compared to the original loss function. When referring to the mAP50, the MPDIoU showed a 0.9% decrease compared to the original loss function, while WIoU remained unchanged but was lower than the model with Shape_IoU. Specifically, the model with Shape_IoU outperformed CIoU (by 0.2% in the mAP50 and 0.6% in the F1 score), Inner_IoU (by 2.1% in the mAP50 and 1.2% in the F1 score), MPDIoU (by 1.1% in the mAP50 and 0.3% in the F1 score), and WIoU (by 0.2% in the mAP50 and 0.1% in the F1 score). In summary, by placing greater emphasis on bounding box accuracy, the model with Shape_IoU effectively reduced interference from complex greenhouse environments, allowing it to more accurately focus on extracting tomato features.

3.3. Toward an Adaptive Experiment for Neck Networks

To verify whether the parallel channel causes different levels of imbalance compared to the adaptive channel, a comparison between the C-Neck and adaptive channel assignment modules was conducted for the target test. The experimental results are shown in Table 4. It can be observed that compared to the cross-layer channels of BiFPN, the efficient feature up-sampling of the CARAFE module and the intensive information exchange of potential semantics at different spatial scales in GFPN, C-Neck maintained a large portion of the feature surface while reducing the model size, without losing most of the features. In general, C-Neck is the most effective when the application side is the target.

Table 4. Neck network adaptive experiment.

Neck Model	P/%	R/%	mAP50 /%	Params /M	FLOPs/G	Model Size/MB	Reference Time/ms
C-Neck	83.5	77.7	83.8	7.3	23.0	14.0	2.2
BiFPN	84.6	76.8	83.3	11.2	28.8	22.1	2.6
GFPN	82.6	79.5	84.0	12.2	29.5	23.5	2.4
CARAFE	84.9	77.5	84.1	11.6	30.8	24.8	2.7

3.4. Ablation Experiment

The ablation study was conducted based on the original YOLOv8s model. First, the C2f module in the backbone network was replaced with the RepNCSPELAN module. Next, the original neck network was modified to the CN network. Subsequently, the SGE module was added, and, finally, the Shape_IoU loss function was incorporated into the boundary loss function. The results are shown in Table 5.

Table 5. Ablation experiment results for each improved module.

No.	A	B	C	D	P/%	R/%	mAP50 /%	Params /M	FLOPs /G	Model Size /MB	F1 Score/%	Reference Time/ms
1					83.7	77.9	83.9	11.1	28.4	21.5	80.7	2.3
2	√				83.3	78.8	83.2	7.7	25.3	14.9	81.0	2.1
3		√			83.5	77.7	83.8	7.3	23.0	14.0	80.5	2.2
4			√		83.8	80.2	84.6	11.1	28.4	21.5	81.9	2.0
5				√	84.5	78.3	84.1	11.1	28.4	21.5	81.3	2.0
6	√	√			82.9	80.5	84.4	4.0	20.4	8.0	81.7	3.3
7	√	√	√		84.5	79.6	84.8	4.0	20.4	8.0	82.0	2.6
8	√	√	√	√	84.6	80.3	85.3	4.0	20.4	8.0	82.4	2.2

"A" represents the RepNCSPELAN module, "B" represents the CN network, "C" represents the SGE module, and "D" represents the Shape_IoU loss function. "√" means that the module is added. Experiment 1 was the YOLOv8s model. Experiment 8 was the final GCSS-YOLO model.

As shown in Table 5, after replacing the C2f module in the original backbone network with the RepNCSPELAN module, the mAP50 decreased by 0.7% compared to the original model. However, the number of parameters and model size were reduced by 3.4 M and 6.6 MB, respectively, while the F1 score increased by 0.3% compared to the original YOLOv8s model. In addition, when using the CN network alone, although the mAP50 and F1 score decreased by 0.1% and 0.2%, respectively, compared to the original YOLOv8s model, it also reduced the model complexity. Subsequently, the addition of the SGE module improved the mAP50 and F1 score of the original model by 0.7% and 1.2%, respectively, indicating a reduction in the interference of environmental noise on the model's feature extraction. After replacing the boundary loss function Shape_IoU, the mAP50 and F1 score increased by 1.2% and 1.1%, respectively, compared to the original model. This indicated that while maintaining the model size, detection precision is significantly improved. After adding the CN network in addition to replacing the RepNCSPELAN module, the number of parameters decreased by 55.9%, and the model size was reduced by 61.9% compared to the original model. Simultaneously, the model's mAP50 and F1 score increased by 0.5% and 1.0%, respectively. This demonstrated that the CN network can more effectively process the refined multi-dimensional features. However, due to the increase in the number of layers, the model's inference time also increased by 1.0 ms. Furthermore, when the SGE module was added in addition to this, it reduced the interference caused by environmental factors during the model's feature processing. As a result, the mAP50 and F1 score increased by 0.4% and 0.3%, respectively, compared to the previous model, while the inference time decreased by 0.7 ms. After incorporating the lightweight boundary loss function Shape_IoU, the model achieved an mAP50 of 85.3% and an F1 score of 82.4%, representing improvements of 1.4% and 1.7%, respectively, compared to the original YOLOv8s model. Finally, the improved model reduced the number of parameters, FLOPs, and model size to 36.9%, 71.8%, and 37.2% of the original model, respectively, while also decreasing the inference time by 0.1 ms. The detailed results of the comparative experiments between the original model and the improved model for the four-stage object categories are shown in Table 6.

The analysis was conducted based on the model optimization data. (Since the F1 score is derived from precision and recall, it was excluded from the analysis. For more details, refer to Formula (18)). The results are illustrated in Figure 12. The comprehensive analysis results indicated that the improved model achieved a higher precision across the green ripe, turning ripe, fully ripe, and disease-related decay stages. This result further validates the effectiveness of the improved modules in enhancing tomato object detection performance.

Table 6. Comparison between the improved model and the original model.

Category	Evaluation Indicators	YOLOv8s	GCSS-YOLO
T_GreenRP	P/%	81.2	81.7 (+0.5)
	R/%	61.0	64.0 (+3.0)
	AP50/%	71.5	74.5 (+3.0)
	F1 score/%	69.7	71.8 (+2.1)
T_BetweenP	P/%	77.9	78.7 (+0.8)
	R/%	76.0	78.9 (+2.9)
	AP50/%	81.0	82.1 (+1.1)
	F1 score/%	76.9	78.0 (+1.1)
T_MaturityP	P/%	83.0	85.2 (+2.2)
	R/%	76.5	79.3 (+2.8)
	AP50/%	86.1	86.8 (+0.7)
	F1 score/%	79.6	82.1 (+2.5)
T_RotP	P/%	92.6	92.7 (+0.1)
	R/%	98.1	99.1 (+1.0)
	AP50/%	97.5	98.0 (+0.5)
	F1 score/%	95.3	95.8 (+0.5)

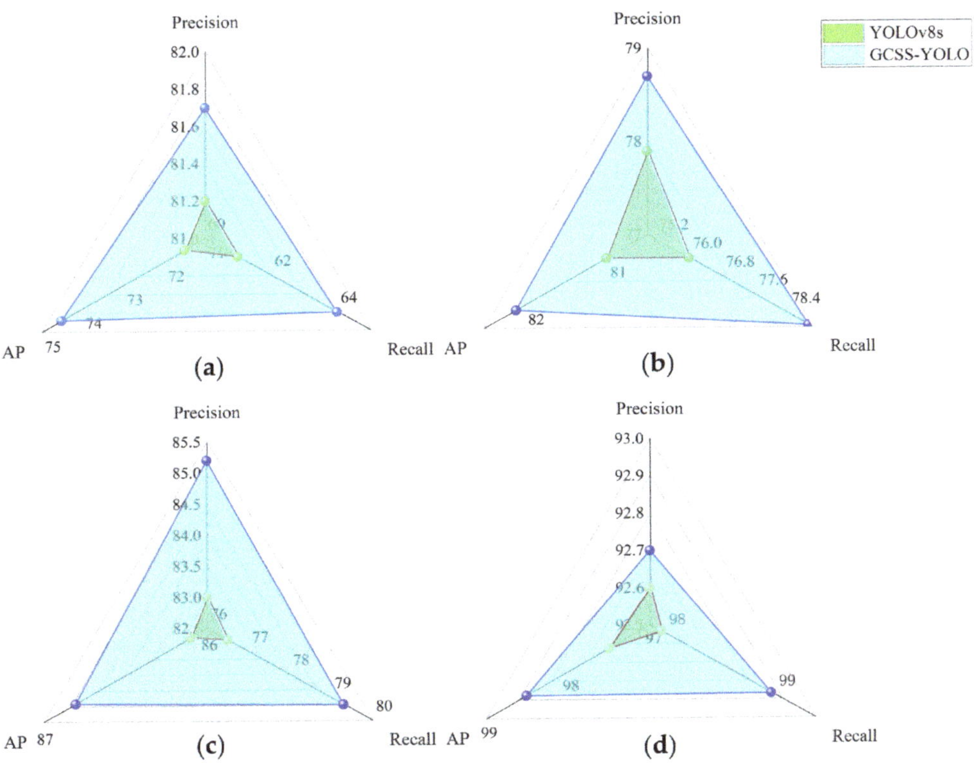

Figure 12. Radar chart. (**a**) The green ripe stage. (**b**) The turning ripe stage. (**c**) The fully ripe stage. (**d**) The disease-related decay stage.

3.5. Detection Heatmap Analysis

To further evaluate the performance of the improved model in complex greenhouse environments, Figure 13 presents the heatmap visualizations generated using Gradient-weighted Class Activation Mapping (Grad-CAM) for both GCSS-YOLO and YOLOv8s. It is worth noting that in the heatmap visualization results, warmer colors indicate the degree of contribution of the region to the detection outcomes. The deeper the warm color, the greater the contribution of that region.

Figure 13. Heatmap analysis of different models. (**a**) Minimal fruit occlusion. (**b**) Substantial tomato fruit occlusion. (**c**) Tomatoes partially occluded by branches and leaves. (**d**) Significant occlusion by branches and leaves. (**e**) Rotting tomato.

There were regions outside the target area that exhibited warm colors, as shown in Figure 13a. This suggested that the YOLOv8s model failed to effectively capture the key semantic information of the tomatoes in the spatial domain, resulting in the center of the target area displaying cool colors, while the edge regions exhibited warmer colors in the heatmap. Similarly, when the heat distribution of different parts of the tomato target in the heatmap is uneven, it indicates that the model exhibits biases during the detection process, which may lead to the omission of certain regions of the target. This is evident in Figure 13b,c. The excessive concentration of warm colors or an inconsistent warm–cool color distribution further highlights the model's limitations in extracting representative features of tomatoes. In contrast, as shown in Figure 13d,e, although the model demonstrated some detection ability, its feature extraction capability was weaker compared to the GCSS-YOLO model. Particularly in Figure 13e, when facing tomatoes with distinct decay features, the model's detection results exhibit color discrepancies, failing to effectively improve the model's performance on such targets. In summary, GCSS-YOLO demonstrates stronger interpretability, better adaptability, and more robust feature extraction performance than the original model when addressing the diverse semantic characteristics of tomatoes at different ripening stages.

3.6. Comparison of Different Detection Algorithms

This study selected several widely used detection algorithms, including the single-stage SSD, YOLO series, and transformer-based RT-DETR [49] model. A comparative experiment was then conducted between these models and the improved model using the test set of a self-constructed dataset. The final results demonstrated that the improved model is effective. Specifically, the GCSS-YOLO model outperformed SSD (11.2%, 26.4%), YOLOv3 (7.7%, 10.9%), YOLOv4 (10.2%, 8.1%), YOLOv5 (2.6%, 1.5%), YOLOv7 (3.4%, 4.2%), YOLOv8 (1.4%, 1.7%), RT-DETR (6.4%, 2.4%), YOLOv9 (0.4%, 1.0%), YOLOv10 (2.4%, 1.2%), and YOLOv11 (3.7%, 2.7%) in terms of the mAP50 and F1 score. The specific performance metrics for each model are shown in Table 7.

Table 7. Comparison of model performance.

Model	AP/%				mAP 50/%	P /%	R /%	Params /M	FLOPs /G	Model Size /MB	F1 Score /%	Inference Time/ms
	G	B	M	R								
SSD	54.1	69.2	78.3	94.9	74.1	**93.6**	36.6	24.0	274.4	92.1	56.0	5.5
YOLOv3	61.7	72.2	80.4	96.1	77.6	84.4	63.7	61.5	65.6	235.0	71.5	7.3
YOLOv4	64.7	68.8	73.1	93.7	75.1	82.4	62.3	64.0	59.9	244.0	74.3	6.4
YOLOv5	68.9	81.3	84.3	96.1	82.7	83.7	78.3	21.0	50.3	42.5	80.9	**2.0**
YOLOv7	70.4	76.9	83.8	96.4	81.9	81.7	78.3	36.5	103.2	74.8	78.2	4.5
RT-DETR	68.8	73.7	75.6	97.4	78.9	85.4	75.3	31.9	102.0	66.1	80.0	7.8
YOLOv9	**75.8**	81.2	84.4	98.3	84.9	82.6	80.2	60.8	264.9	122.4	81.4	9.9
YOLOv10	72.1	76.3	84.6	**98.4**	82.9	83.0	77.6	8.0	24.5	16.6	80.2	2.9
YOLOv11	72.9	76.1	81.3	96.2	81.6	79.8	79.4	9.4	21.3	19.2	79.7	2.1
YOLOv8	71.5	81.0	86.1	96.9	83.9	83.9	77.9	11.1	28.4	21.5	80.7	2.3
GCSS-YOLO	74.5	**82.1**	**86.8**	98.0	**85.3**	84.6	**80.3**	**4.0**	**20.3**	**8.0**	**82.4**	2.2

"G" represents the green ripe stage, "B" represents the turning ripe stage, "M" represents the fully ripe stage, and "R" represents the disease-related decay stage. Bolding represent optimal values.

As shown in Table 7, the YOLOv8s model surpassed most other models on the test set in terms of the mAP50 and F1 score. However, its mAP50 and F1 score values were 0.7% and 0.2% lower, respectively, than those of the YOLOv9 model, and its F1 score was 0.2% lower than the YOLOv5 model. Nevertheless, the YOLOv9 and YOLOv5 models were too large and unsuitable for deployment on mobile devices. Considering both accuracy and the need for lightweight models, the YOLOv8s model was clearly the best choice. The comparison also revealed that the SSD model achieved the highest precision among the 11 models, reaching 93.6%, which is 9% higher than that of the GCSS-YOLO model. However, due to its considerably low recall rate, the SSD model carried a high risk of missing a large number of targets during the training process. As a result, the SSD model was not suitable for the subsequent visualization experiments. In terms of the average precision, although the GCSS-YOLO model did not achieve the best performance during the green ripe stage and the disease-related decay stage, being 1.3% lower than the YOLOv9 model in the green ripe stage and 0.4% lower than the YOLOv10 model in the disease-related decay stage, it reduced the number of parameters and model size by 56.8 M and 114.4 MB compared to YOLOv9 and by 4 M and 8.6 MB compared to YOLOv10. Although the inference time of the GCSS-YOLO model was 0.1 ms longer than YOLOv11 and 0.2 ms longer than YOLOv5, its precision was significantly higher than both. Overall, the GCSS-YOLO model successfully reduces inference time and computational complexity while maintaining high precision, recall, and mAP50, demonstrating superior resource utilization efficiency and model optimization capabilities. As a result, it offers excellent advantages in handling tasks within complex environments.

To further evaluate the performance of the GCSS-YOLO model, a visualization experiment was conducted, comparing it with the models listed in Table 7, including YOLOv3,

YOLOv4, YOLOv5, YOLOv7, YOLOv8, RT-DETR, YOLOv9, YOLOv10, and YOLOv11. The results of the experiment are shown in Figure 14.

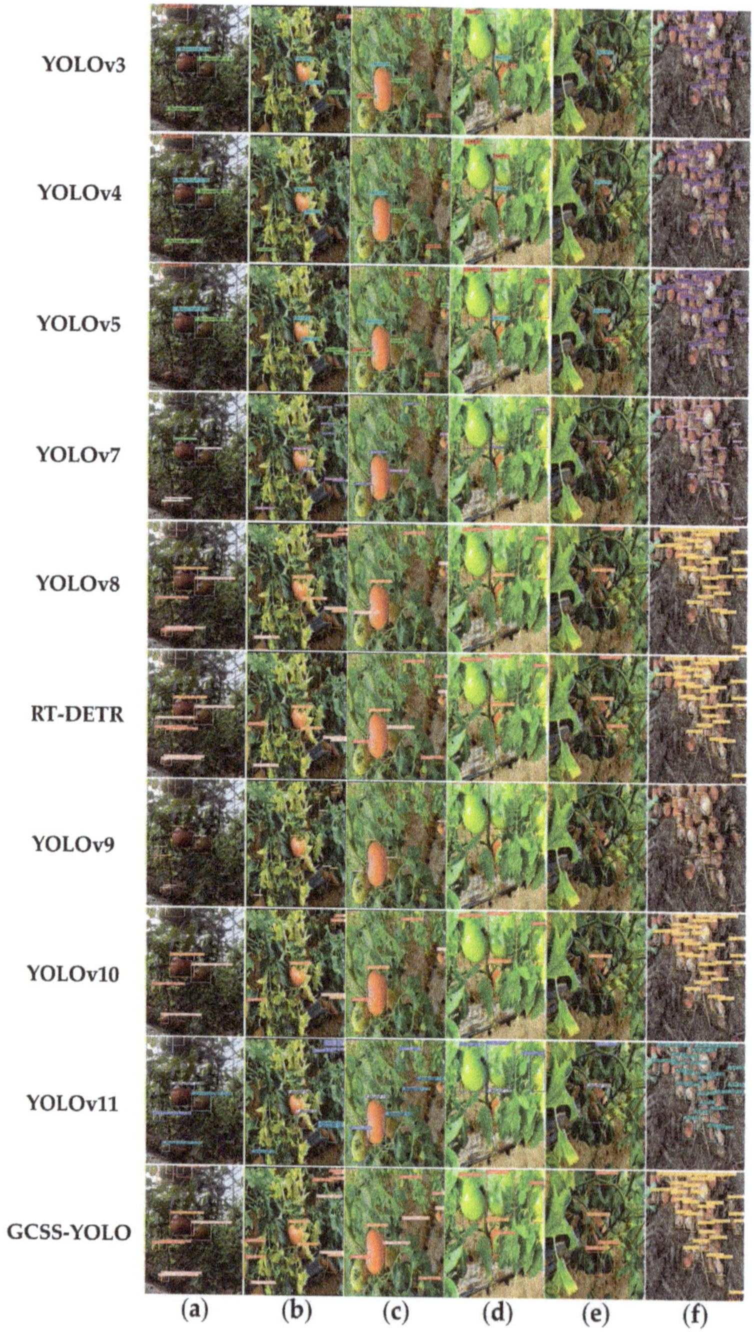

Figure 14. Visualization results of each model: (**a**) The backlight conditions with multiple ripe stages coexisting. (**b**) The front light environment with multiple ripe stages coexisting. (**c**) Mild occlusion. (**d**) Moderate occlusion. (**e**) Heavy occlusion. (**f**) Multiple stages of disease-related decay.

From the analysis of Figure 14, it can be observed that under backlight conditions, where multiple ripe stages coexist, the YOLOv9 model missed detecting only one green ripe tomato, whereas the GCSS-YOLO model missed detecting only one turning ripe tomato. The other models exhibited varying degrees of missed detections. In the downlight environment with multiple coexisting ripeness stages, except for the GCSS-YOLO model, which missed the detection of one fully mature tomato, the other models still exhibited a significant number of missed detections. In environments with varying levels of occlusion, the GCSS-YOLO model was the only one capable of successfully detecting all the tomatoes. In contrast, the performance of the other models was hindered by the complex conditions, leading to ineffective feature extraction and missed detections. In particular, as shown in Figure 14e, the green ripe tomatoes exhibited a color remarkably similar to that of the branches and stems. In the real-world scenario, four tomatoes were present; however, most of the other models only detected one or two. The GCSS-YOLO model was the only one that effectively overcame environmental interference and accurately detected all the tomatoes. Figure 14f illustrates the excellent capability of the GCSS-YOLO model in the environment with multiple stages of disease-related decay. Compared to most of the other models, it successfully identified 35 out of a total of 38 tomatoes, despite detecting 2 fewer than the RT-DETR model. The GCSS-YOLO model demonstrated exceptional performance in accurately identifying tomatoes at various ripe stages, particularly in scenarios involving overlapping and occlusion.

Collectively, the enhanced backbone network demonstrates superior efficiency compared to previous YOLO variants: YOLOv3 (complex single-residual linking), YOLOv4 and YOLOv5 (staged feature merging), YOLOv7 (stacked channel reorganization), YOLOv8 and YOLOv11 (cross-stage residual combining), YOLOv9 (multipath reparameterization), and YOLOv10 (deep pointwise convolutional substitution). The cross-dimensional residual combination enhances feature representation while minimizing computational redundancy. Furthermore, the proposed lightweight parallel-parameter neck network outperforms recurrent neck structures in the existing models by reducing feature loss during training and improving stability. In greenhouse environments with complex interference, traditional localization loss functions (CIoU, MPDIoU, SIoU, EIoU) fail to address prediction deviations effectively. By prioritizing target-centric optimization, GCSS-YOLO significantly mitigates localization misalignment and reduces false detection rates. Overall, GCSS-YOLO achieves an optimal balance among model size, inference speed, and accuracy, surpassing existing models and providing robust support for mobile deployment in real-world scenarios.

3.7. Comparison of Different Improved Models

This study conducted comparative experiments between the proposed model and those developed in recent years within the relevant field. The selected models were chosen based on their primary focus on tomato detection, aligning with the objectives of this study, including YOLO-TGI [50], LACTA [51], and MTS-YOLO [52]. Additionally, objects with characteristics similar to tomatoes, such as apples in DNE-YOLO [21] and the Tomato Yellow Leaf Curl Virus (TYLCV) in YOLO-CDSA-BiFPN [53], were also selected for comparison. The final choice selected the SAG-YOLO model [54], which was specifically designed for wildlife detection. This choice was made due to the high diversity, complex color patterns, and distinct features exhibited by wildlife species, making this model particularly well-suited for such tasks. The comparative results of each model are presented in Table 8.

Table 8. Comparison of experimental results for the improved model at the current stage.

Model	AP/%				mAP 50/%	P /%	R /%	Params /M	FLOPs /G	Model Size /MB	F1 Score /%	Inference Time/ms
	G	B	M	R								
DNE-YOLO	74.2	79.7	86.1	95.9	84.0	84.5	78.0	10.5	25.5	21.3	81.0	4.5
YOLO-CDSA-BiFPN	70.6	78.8	85.9	97.8	83.3	83.1	78.6	7.7	26.1	15.8	80.8	2.8
SAG-YOLO	72.7	81.2	85.1	96.1	83.8	85.0	77.7	11.4	24.7	23.0	80.8	2.3
MTS-YOLO	71.0	78.5	86.1	98.8	83.6	82.6	78.1	7.9	23.6	16.2	80.3	2.1
LACTA	70.0	80.5	68.5	94.1	83.5	82.1	80.2	3.5	19.4	7.4	81.1	9.9
YOLO-TGI	64.0	76.6	84.8	95.8	80.3	82.9	76.9	5.4	12.2	11.1	79.8	1.8
GCSS-YOLO	74.5	82.1	86.8	98.0	85.3	84.6	80.3	4.0	20.3	8.0	82.4	2.2

By comprehensively comparing the lightweight metrics of various models, although the GCSS-YOLO model had 0.5 M more parameters, 0.7 G more FLOPs, and 0.6 MB larger model size than the LACAT model, it achieved an improvement of 1.8% in the mAP50 and 1.1% in the F1 score while reducing the processing time by 7.7 ms compared to LACAT. Compared to the lightweight YOLO-TGI model, the GCSS-YOLO model, despite an increase of 8.1 G in FLOPs and 0.4 ms in processing time, exceeded YOLO-TGI by 5% in the mAP50 and 2.6% in the F1 score. Overall, both of the aforementioned models reduced the model size excessively, neglecting essential tomato features in the process. From the perspective of precision metrics, the GCSS-YOLO model exhibited a 0.4% lower precision compared to the SAG-YOLO model, but it outperformed it by 1.7% in the mAP50 and 1.6% in the F1 score while also featuring a more lightweight model size. The GCSS-YOLO model proposed in this study demonstrates considerable advantages, achieving higher mAP50 and F1 scores compared to DNE-YOLO (by 1.3% and 1.4%, respectively), YOLO-CDSA-BiFPN (by 2.0% and 1.6%), SAG-YOLO (by 1.5% and 1.6%), MTS-YOLO (by 1.7% and 2.1%), LACTA (by 1.8% and 1.3%), and YOLO-TGI (by 5.0% and 2.6%).

Although the SAG-YOLO model was designed for multi-feature target detection, its AIFI module failed to mitigate environmental interference effectively. Additionally, the model's overall parameter size increased significantly compared to the SGE module, which compromised its deployment efficiency. Similarly, while DNE-YOLO and YOLO-CDSA-BiFPN demonstrated partial capability in recognizing tomato-like objects, their WIOU and Inner-CIoU loss functions suffered from localization failures under environmental disturbances. Furthermore, LACTA's AFEN feature extraction network lacked a crucial feature preservation mechanism, unlike the CN network proposed in this study, which resulted in limited robustness. The lightweight YOLO-TGI model reduced the parameters substantially but lost critical functionality in extracting tomato ripeness features. In contrast, the GCSS-YOLO framework proposed in this study achieved high-precision detection with shorter inference time, demonstrating superior performance and practicality over the existing models.

3.8. Public Dataset Validation Generalizability Test

To validate the generality and effectiveness of the improved model, this study conducted experiments using two public tomato datasets, including both regular tomatoes and cherry tomatoes. The dataset consists of 1297 images, which were split into training, validation, and test sets in a 7:2:1 ratio. The experimental setup was consistent with that described in Section 2.6. Additionally, to verify whether the improved model maintains its advantage in tomato feature extraction at a larger scale, the YOLOv8s architecture was selected for the generalization experiment. The experimental results are presented in Table 9.

Table 9. Comparison of results between the improved model and the original model on public datasets.

Model	P/%	R/%	mAP50 /%	Params/M	FLOPs/G	Model Size/ MB	F1 Score /%	Inference Time/ms
YOLOv8s	85.8	83.1	89.9	11.1	28.6	21.4	84.4	4.7
GCSS-YOLOv8s	85.5	83.6	90.1	4.0	20.4	8.0	84.5	2.8

It can be observed that the improved model reduced the model size by 62.6% compared to the original model, with a decrease of 8.2 G in FLOPs and a reduction of 7.1 M in the number of parameters. Although the precision was 0.3% lower than that of the original YOLOv8s model, the mAP50 was 0.2% higher, while the inference time was reduced by 1.9 ms. The fluctuations in the precision, recall, mAP50, and mAP50:95 during the training process for both models are shown in Figure 15.

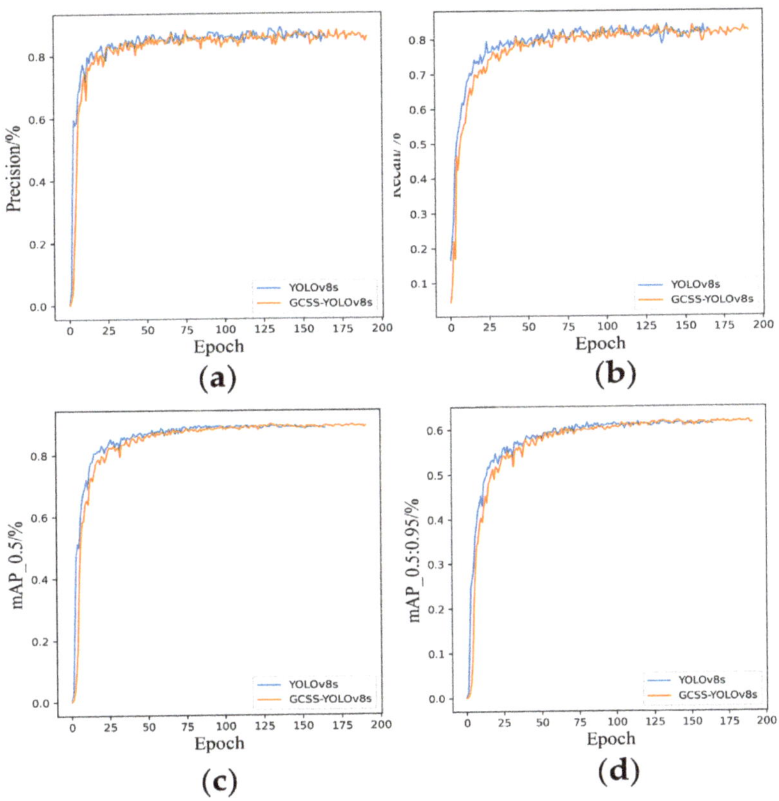

Figure 15. Variation plots of various metrics during training. (**a**) The fluctuation in precision during training. (**b**) The fluctuation in recall during training. (**c**) The fluctuation in mAP50 during training, (**d**) The fluctuation in mAP50:95 during training.

It can be observed that the original model terminates training early to prevent overfitting, while the improved model, benefiting from greater generalization capability, continues to show a steady improvement in performance throughout training. Based on the comparative analysis above, it can be concluded that the GCSS-YOLO model performs excellently on public datasets as well. Specifically, the improved model demonstrates higher prediction confidence, fewer false positives, and a lower likelihood of false negatives, further validating the effectiveness of the proposed approach.

3.9. Generalizability Experiments in a Real Greenhouse Environment

To verify the generalization ability of the model in real-world environments, 550 tomato datasets were collected from tomato greenhouses in Liao-Zhong District, Liaoning Province, with the variety being Legend 91. The datasets were divided into training, validation, and test sets and trained according to the parameters outlined in Section 2.6. The results are shown in Table 10. The improved model achieved a lightweight design while improving the F1 score and mAP50 by 1.1% and 0.3%, respectively, compared with the original model.

Table 10. Comparative table of generalizability tests in real greenhouse environments.

Model	P/%	R/%	mAP 50 /%	Model Size/ MB	F1 Score /%	Inference Time/ms
YOLOv8s	90.1	81.6	87.4	21.4	85.6	6.3
GCSS-YOLOv8s	88.9	84.7	87.7	8.0	86.7	3.5

To further verify the model's performance, the visualization results of this part of the dataset are provided in Figure 16. The visualization results are compared to the original model. As shown in Figure 16b, both of them missed the detection phenomenon, but the improved model reduced the error to a certain extent and avoided the phenomenon of missed detection and re-detection to a great extent.

Figure 16. Visualization of test charts in a real environment. (**a**) Increased testing accuracy. (**b**) Reduced missed tests. (**c**) Reduced repeated tests.

3.10. Comparison of the Application-Side Experiment

This section evaluates the application's ability to perform high-precision detection by adding an object-counting function for the objects in the detected images. A total of 150 images from the test set and 50 real-world captured images were used for comprehensive testing, with the detection results shown in Figure 17.

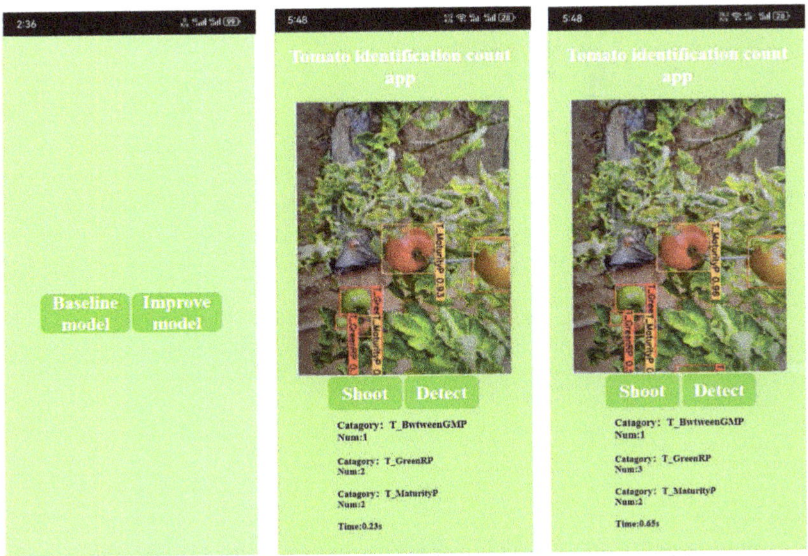

(a) (b) (c)

Figure 17. Example of the app interface. (**a**) The interface allows users to choose between the baseline and the improved model. (**b**) Detection results using the improved model, showing the generated category detection count and detection time. (**c**) Detection results using the original model.

A statistical comparison of the predicted and actual quantities on the application side is shown in Figure 18. The horizontal axis in the figure represents the true quantities, the vertical axis represents the predicted quantities. The closer the fitted line is to the diagonal, the more accurately the model estimates the true values. Additionally, the fitted points correspond to the pairings of the true and predicted values for each quantity. It can be observed that the GCSS-YOLO model is closer to the central axis compared to the original model. Moreover, the R^2 value increased by 0.0489, reaching 0.9426, indicating a better fit of the regression line. The RMSE value decreased by 0.3232, and the MAE value reduced by 0.2528, both demonstrating improvements over the original YOLOv8s model. The overall performance confirms that the application-side predictions are more accurate with the improved model.

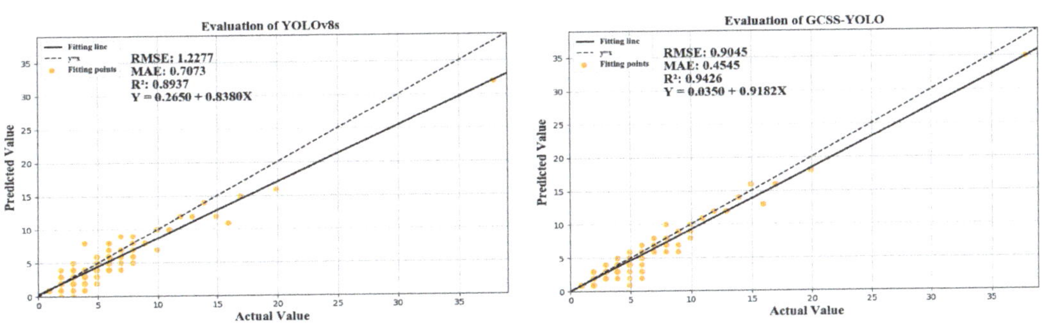

(a) (b)

Figure 18. Quantity statistics chart. (**a**) The linear statistical results of the original model. (**b**) The linear statistical results of the improved model.

3.11. Mobile Application Performance Experiment

3.11.1. Related Agricultural APP Function Experiment

To assess the practicality of the mobile app functionality in this study, functional comparison experiments were conducted with apps proposed by other researchers, as well as with the corresponding recognition networks. As can be seen in Table 11, although the improved model is slightly larger than most recognition networks in terms of model size, its processing time is significantly better, enhancing the timeliness of the app. Meanwhile, in terms of application functions, the app proposed in this study offers stage-by-stage counting, a function that provides convenience for subsequent precision agriculture yield estimation.

Table 11. Comparison table of the functionality of related agricultural mobile apps.

APP	Model Performance		Mobile Deployment
	Mobile Size/MB	**Inference Time/ms**	**Application Function**
Cotton Disease	3.69	-	Detection
Rice Disease	6.97	-	Detection
Strawberry	15.3	2.6	Detection Overall number of counts
Winter Jujube	4.36	13.49	Detection Overall number of counts
Ours	8.0	2.2	Detection Stepwise graded counting

3.11.2. Effect of Different Levels of Light and Shading on Modeling

To verify the feasibility of the improved app as well as the model in practical applications, we performed additional experiments on a partial subset of the test machine. The images were first categorized based on lighting conditions into two groups, i.e., smooth light and backlight, with 20 images each. Secondly, they were categorized according to different occlusion degrees from small to large, specifically into light occlusion, medium occlusion, and heavy occlusion, with 25 images each. These subsets were evaluated using the YOLOv8 model, the proposed GCSS-YOLO model, and the corresponding app. The analysis results are presented in Table 12.

Table 12. Comparison table of tests with different light conditions and shading conditions.

Dataset	Model	Model Indicator	Application Indicators	
		mAP50/%	**Successful Detection Rate/%**	**Average Detection Time/s**
Sunbeam dataset	YOLOv8s	84.4	91.2%	1.14 s
	GCSS-YOLO	86.7	95.6%	0.73 s
Backlight dataset	YOLOv8s	83.3	89.6%	1.77 s
	GCSS-YOLO	85.6	92.2%	0.97 s
Lightly occluded dataset	YOLOv8s	84.2	90.0%	0.93 s
	GCSS-YOLO	86.6	96.7%	0.67 s
Moderately occluded dataset	YOLOv8s	83.5	88.5%	1.66 s
	GCSS-YOLO	85.8	92.3%	0.91 s
Heavily occluded dataset	YOLOv8s	82.7	81.2%	1.83 s
	GCSS-YOLO	85.5	90.4%	1.01 s

As shown in Table 12, the experimental results demonstrate the performance patterns of the models and their associated applications under varying lighting and occlusion cases. Both models perform better under smooth lighting and light occlusion scenarios. However, in the backlight and moderate and heavy occlusion cases, YOLOv8s has a certain degree of degradation, but the GCSS-YOLO model resists the interference caused by the environment, and both mAP50 values are improved. Regarding application-level performance, the detection times for the improved model in most environments remain under 1 s, and the successful detection rates consistently exceed 90%. These results indicate greater stability and higher detection accuracy compared to the original model, further validating the improved model's robustness and reliability in uncertain real-world environments.

4. Discussion

This study explored four ripe stages of tomatoes in a complex greenhouse environment. Drawing on recent advancements in the field of computer vision, this study proposed the GCSS-YOLO model, specifically designed for tomato detection. The model incorporated an attention mechanism, the RepNCSPELAN module, a boundary-aware loss function, and a lightweight, multi-dimensional feature fusion neck network to enhance detection performance. It is noteworthy that this study innovatively combined multi-dimensional features to enhance the precision of tomato detection. The experimental results demonstrated that with a model size of only 8.0 MB, the AP for fruits in the green ripe, turning ripe, fully ripe, and disease rot stages reached 74.5%, 82.1%, 86.8%, and 98.0%, respectively. The optimization effectively addressed the issue of color similarity between different maturity stages and surrounding complex branches and leaves while also reducing the impact of lighting and occlusion factors in the greenhouse environment on the model. When deploying the designed model to the application side, several challenges remain. In addition to detection precision, detection speed and the number of detections are equally critical. In contrast to evaluating detection speed through FPS on GPUs, this study assessed detection speed based on the time consumed during the detection process. Additionally, this study conducted a statistical analysis of tomato targets in each ripe stage using real-time detection and compared the results with those obtained using the original model. By developing a dedicated application, this research enhanced the intuitive experience for researchers, contributing to the advancement of smart agriculture, particularly in the deployment of edge devices.

Despite the promising results achieved in this study, several limitations remain. Notably, this article does not provide a comparative analysis between the default data augmentation techniques integrated within the YOLOv8 framework and the custom enhancements proposed herein. This aspect warrants further investigation and will be explored in our future work.

Meanwhile, even though the GCSS-YOLO model outperforms other models, its model size is still too large compared to the nano version. Our future research will focus on model pruning and refinement techniques to reduce computational redundancy, thereby enhancing its applicability for deployment on embedded and mobile platforms.

In addition, although the improved model improved the detection accuracy at all stages, it was lower at the green ripening stage compared to the remaining three periods of tomatoes. This is precisely because green ripening tomatoes in an actual greenhouse are too similar to the branch and leaf colors and share the same feature regions. This suggests that in future model optimization, we can minimize the environmental spatial interference, which can be dealt with by adding domain discriminators, performing adversarial training, and employing dynamic tuning strategies during the training process. In the future, we will aim to improve the accuracy and stability of the tomato classification task and ultimately improve the model's adaptability to specific agricultural data.

5. Conclusions

To address the challenges of tomato ripe stage detection in complex greenhouse environments, this study proposes an improved, lightweight YOLOv8s detection model (GCSS-YOLO). While ensuring high precision, the model also enables real-time detection on Android devices. In this study, an image augmentation technique involving random image stitching is employed to enhance the diversity of the tomato dataset and improve the model's generalization capability. The C2f module in the backbone network is replaced with the RepNCSPELAN module, which not only reduces the model size but also decreases the inference time. Three SGE modules are introduced in the neck network detection head to reduce the interference of environmental factors on the feature extraction channels of the model. A CN network is designed for multi-dimensional feature fusion, enabling the capture of more effective semantic information in the spatial domain. The Shape_IoU loss function is adopted to replace the original model's convergence method, effectively addressing the challenges posed by tomato detection in real-world environments.

Based on validation conducted on a self-constructed dataset, the GCSS-YOLO model in this study achieved an accuracy of 84.6%, a recall rate of 80.3%, an mAP50 of 85.3%, and an F1 score of 82.4%. Additionally, it demonstrated a detection speed of only 2.2 ms, with 4.0 M parameters, 20.3 GFLOPs, and a model size of 8.0 MB. The improved model surpassed the current state-of-the-art models, public benchmark evaluations, and real-world experiments, which validated the model's generalization capability across diverse scenarios. Furthermore, the algorithm was successfully implemented on mobile platforms, enabling rapid and reliable in-field detection. While this study establishes a foundation for tomato maturity recognition systems in greenhouse settings, future efforts should focus on enhancing algorithmic robustness and expanding domain-specific datasets to address edge cases. Such advancements will drive the evolution of scalable, adaptive solutions for precision agriculture, bridging the gap between theoretical research and practical agricultural automation.

Author Contributions: Conceptualization, W.Y. and H.S.; methodology, H.S.; software, H.S. and Q.Z.; validation, H.S.; formal analysis, H.S. and J.W.; investigation, H.S.; resources, C.C.; data curation, H.S., Q.Z., H.Y. and C.L.; writing—original draft preparation, H.S.; writing—review and editing, H.S.; supervision, W.Y.; project administration H.S.; funding acquisition, C.C. All authors have read and agreed to the published version of the manuscript.

Funding: This research was funded by the Liaoning Provincial Department of Education Fund, Precision Agriculture Aerospace and Smart Farm Key Technology R&D Platform Project (grant number: JYTPT2024002).

Institutional Review Board Statement: This study involved only observational data and did not involve any handling of animals; therefore, ethical approval was not required.

Data Availability Statement: The data underlying the results presented in this paper are not publicly available at this time but may be obtained from the authors upon reasonable request.

Acknowledgments: The authors would like to acknowledge Shenyang Agricultural University and Liaoning Engineering Research Center for Information Technology in Agriculture for their continuous support of our research, as well as the editors and reviewers for their careful review and valuable suggestions on this article.

Conflicts of Interest: The authors declare no conflicts of interest.

Appendix A Cross-Domain Performance Experiment for Synthetic Datasets

In order to further verify whether the synthetic data of the disease-related decay stage would cause the model overfitting phenomenon, an incremental test of its original data and synthetic data was carried out. The specific operation process is as follows. Firstly, the test was conducted based on the original data, and, secondly, some of the synthesized tests were added sequentially in the database until they were completely increased. The final test results are shown in the table below:

As shown in Table A1, both the mAP50 and F1 scores of the model gradually increased with the addition of the synthetic dataset. Compared to the model trained solely on the original dataset, the performance improved by 5.8% in the mAP50 and 7.7% in the F1 score. Meanwhile, the mAP50 of the model stabilized when the synthetic dataset was increased by more than 90%, indicating that the addition of a moderate amount of synthetic data does not cause overfitting problems, and the addition of synthetic data improves the robustness capability of the model.

Table A1. Synthetic dataset validation test table.

Dataset	P/%	R/%	mAP50/%	F1 Score/%
Raw data	85.7	90.6	92.7	88.1
Raw data vs. 30% synthesized data	88.9	92.2	94.1	90.5
Raw data vs. 50% synthetic data	88.4	93.7	95.7	91.0
Raw data vs. 70% synthetic data	90.1	96.5	97.1	93.2
Raw data vs. 90% synthetic data	92.8	97.1	98.2	94.9
Raw data vs. 100% synthetic data	92.6	98.1	98.5	95.8

Appendix B Training Parameter Experiences

Appendix B includes information on part of the training parameters for some of the relevant tests. In preparation for training, necessary parameter screening was required. First, for the AMP test, the results are shown in Table A2. From the table, it can be seen that after turning off the AMP, the F1 score increased by 0.5% and the mAP50 increased by 0.7% compared with the original setting. Turning off the AMP reduced the processing time by 0.1 ms but made the model smoother to train and reduced the loss caused by the gradient change.

Table A2. AMP parameter experiment.

Mode	P/%	R/%	mAP50/%	F1 Score/%	Inference Time/ms
AMP = True	81.8	78.6	83.2	80.2	2.2
AMP = False	83.7	77.9	83.9	80.7	2.3

The detailed test results are presented in Table A3. The initial learning rate tests were conducted with Automatic Mixed Precision (AMP) disabled. The results indicate that adjusting the initial learning rate to 0.001 or increasing it to either 0.05 or 0.1 resulted in lower mAP50 and F1 scores compared to the baseline learning rate of 0.01. A learning rate that is too low can unnecessarily prolong the training process by increasing the number of required epochs. Conversely, an excessively high learning rate may cause drastic weight oscillations, overfitting, or premature convergence, ultimately compromising the model's performance.

Table A3. Initial learning rate parameter experimentation.

Initial Learning Rate	P/%	R/%	mAP50/%	F1 Score/%
0.001	82.2	78.6	81.7	80.4
0.01	83.7	77.9	83.9	80.7
0.05	81.7	78.3	83.1	80.0
0.1	83.9	77.2	83.7	80.4

References

1. Song, J.; Kim, D.; Jeong, E.; Park, J. Determination of Optimal Dataset Characteristics for Improving YOLO Performance in Agricultural Object Detection. *Agriculture* **2025**, *15*, 731. [CrossRef]
2. Cama-Pinto, D.; Damas, M.; Holgado-Terriza, J.A.; Gómez-Mula, F.; Cama-Pinto, A. Path Loss Determination Using Linear and Cubic Regression Inside a Classic Tomato Greenhouse. *Int. J. Environ. Res. Public Health* **2019**, *16*, 1744. [CrossRef] [PubMed]
3. Meng, Z.; Du, X.; Xia, J.; Ma, Z.; Zhang, T. Real-time statistical algorithm for cherry tomatoes with different ripeness based on depth information mapping. *Comput. Electron. Agric.* **2024**, *220*, 108900. [CrossRef]
4. Yu, F.; Bai, J.; Fang, J.; Guo, S.; Zhu, S.; Xu, T. Integration of a Parameter Combination Discriminator Improves the Accuracy of Chlorophyll Inversion from Spectral Imaging of Rice. *Agric. Commun.* **2024**, *2*, 100055. [CrossRef]
5. Yue, X.; Qi, K.; Na, X.; Zhang, Y.; Liu, Y.; Liu, C. Improved YOLOv8-Seg Network for Instance Segmentation of Healthy and Diseased Tomato Plants in the Growth Stage. *Agriculture* **2023**, *13*, 1643. [CrossRef]
6. Yue, J.; Li, T.; Feng, H.; Fu, Y.; Liu, Y.; Tian, J.; Yang, H.; Yang, G. Enhancing Field Soil Moisture Content Monitoring Using Laboratory-Based Soil Spectral Measurements and Radiative Transfer Models. *Agric. Commun.* **2024**, *2*, 100060. [CrossRef]
7. He, K.; Gkioxari, G.; Dollár, P.; Girshick, R. Mask r-cnn. In Proceedings of the IEEE International Conference on Computer Vision, Venice, Italy, 22–29 October 2017; pp. 2961–2969.
8. Ren, S.; He, K.; Girshick, R.; Sun, J. Faster R-CNN: Towards Real-Time Object Detection with Region Proposal Networks *IEEE Trans. Pattern Anal. Mach. Intell.* **2017**, *39*, 1137–1149. [CrossRef]
9. Wang, Z.; Ling, Y.; Wang, X.; Meng, D.; Nie, L.; An, G.; Wang, X. An improved Faster R-CNN model for multi-object tomato maturity detection in complex scenarios. *Ecol. Inform.* **2022**, *72*, 101886. [CrossRef]
10. Zu, L.; Zhao, Y.; Liu, J.; Su, F.; Zhang, Y.; Liu, P. Detection and Segmentation of Mature Green Tomatoes Based on Mask R-CNN with Automatic Image Acquisition Approach. *Sensors* **2021**, *21*, 7842. [CrossRef]
11. Minagawa, D.; Kim, J. Prediction of Harvest Time of Tomato Using Mask R-CNN. *AgriEngineering* **2022**, *4*, 356–366. [CrossRef]
12. Redmon, J.; Farhadi, A. YOLOv3: An Incremental Improvement. *arXiv* **2018**, arXiv:1804.02767.
13. Bochkovskiy, A.; Wang, C.-Y.; Liao, H.-Y.M. YOLOv4: Optimal Speed and Accuracy of Object Detection. *arXiv* **2020**, arXiv:2004.10934.
14. Hussain, M. YOLOv5, YOLOv8 and YOLOv10: The Go-To Detectors for Real-time Vision. *arXiv* **2024**, arXiv:2407.02988.
15. Wang, C.; Bochkovskiy, A.; Liao, H.-Y.M. YOLOv7: Trainable Bag-of-Freebies Sets New State-of-the-Art for Real-Time Object Detectors. In Proceedings of the IEEE/CVF Conference on Computer Vision and Pattern Recognition (CVPR), Vancouver, BC, Canada, 17–24 June 2023; pp. 7464–7475. [CrossRef]
16. Varghese, R.; Sambath, M. YOLOv8: A Novel Object Detection Algorithm with Enhanced Performance and Robustness. In Proceedings of the 2024 International Conference on Advances in Data Engineering and Intelligent Computing Systems, Chennai, India, 18–19 April 2024; pp. 1–6. [CrossRef]
17. Wang, C.Y.; Yeh, I.H.; Liao, H.-Y.M. YOLOv9: Learning What You Want to Learn Using Programmable Gradient Information. *arXiv* **2024**, arXiv:2402.13616.
18. Wang, A.; Chen, H.; Liu, L.; Chen, K.; Lin, Z.; Han, J.; Ding, G. YOLOv10: Real-Time End-to-End Object Detection. *arXiv* **2024**, arXiv:2405.14458.
19. Khanam, R.; Hussain, M. YOLOv11: An Overview of the Key Architectural Enhancements. *arXiv* **2024**, arXiv:2410.17725.
20. Liu, J.; Wang, X. EggplantDet: An efficient lightweight model for eggplant disease detection. *Alex. Eng. J.* **2025**, *115*, 308–323. [CrossRef]
21. Wu, H.; Mo, X.; Wen, S.; Wu, K.; Ye, Y.; Wang, Y.; Zhang, Y. DNE-YOLO: A method for apple fruit detection in Diverse Natural Environments. *J. King Saud. Univ.—Comput. Inf. Sci.* **2024**, *36*, 102220. [CrossRef]
22. Zhu, R.; Hao, F.; Ma, D. Research on Polygon Pest-Infected Leaf Region Detection Based on YOLOv8. *Agriculture* **2023**, *13*, 2253. [CrossRef]
23. Paul, A.; Machavaram, R.; Ambuj; Kumar, D.; Nagar, H. Smart Solutions for Capsicum Harvesting: Unleashing the Power of YOLO for Detection, Segmentation, Growth Stage Classification, Counting, and Real-Time Mobile Identification. *Comput. Electron. Agric.* **2024**, *219*, 108832. [CrossRef]

24. Ren, R.; Zhang, S.; Sun, H.; Wang, N.; Yang, S.; Zhao, H.; Xin, M. YOLO-RCS: A method for detecting phenological period of 'Yuluxiang' pear in unstructured environment. *Comput. Electron. Agric.* **2025**, *229*, 109819. [CrossRef]
25. Zhu, X.; Chen, F.; Zheng, Y.; Chen, C.; Peng, X. Detection of Camellia oleifera fruit maturity in orchards based on modified lightweight YOLO. *Comput. Electron. Agric.* **2024**, *226*, 109471. [CrossRef]
26. Yang, G.; Wang, J.; Nie, Z.; Yang, H.; Yu, S. A Lightweight YOLOv8 Tomato Detection Algorithm Combining Feature Enhancement and Attention. *Agronomy* **2023**, *13*, 1824. [CrossRef]
27. Gao, G.H.; Shuai, C.Y.; Wang, S.Y.; Ding, T. Using improved YOLO V5s to recognize tomatoes in a continuous working environment. *Signal Image Video Process.* **2024**, *18*, 4019–4028. [CrossRef]
28. Sun, X.Y. Enhanced tomato detection in greenhouse environments: A lightweight model based on S-YOLO with high accuracy. *Front. Plant Sci.* **2024**, *15*, 1451018. [CrossRef]
29. Chen, W.; Liu, M.; Zhao, C.; Li, X.; Wang, Y. MTD-YOLO: Multi-task deep convolutional neural network for cherry tomato fruit bunch maturity detection. *Comput. Electron. Agric.* **2024**, *216*, 108533. [CrossRef]
30. Liao, J.; He, X.; Liang, Y.; Wang, H.; Zeng, H.; Luo, X.; Li, X.; Zhang, L.; Xing, H.; Zang, Y. A Lightweight Cotton Verticillium Wilt Hazard Level Real-Time Assessment System Based on an Improved YOLOv10n Model. *Agriculture* **2024**, *14*, 1617. [CrossRef]
31. Li, Y.; Chen, X.; Yin, L.; Hu, Y. Deep Learning-Based Methods for Multi-Class Rice Disease Detection Using Plant Images. *Agronomy* **2024**, *14*, 1879. [CrossRef]
32. Tao, Z.; Li, K.; Rao, Y.; Li, W.; Zhu, J. Strawberry Maturity Recognition Based on Improved YOLOv5. *Agronomy* **2024**, *14*, 460. [CrossRef]
33. Yu, C.; Feng, J.; Zheng, Z.; Guo, J.; Hu, Y. A Lightweight SOD-YOLOv5n Model-Based Winter Jujube Detection and Counting Method Deployed on Android. *Comput. Electron. Agric.* **2024**, *218*, 108701. [CrossRef]
34. Chen, C.; Zheng, Z.; Xu, T.; Guo, S.; Feng, S.; Yao, W.; Lan, Y. YOLO-Based UAV Technology: A Review of the Research and Its Applications. *Drones* **2023**, *7*, 190. [CrossRef]
35. Li, J.; Qiao, Y.; Liu, S.; Zhang, J.; Yang, Z.; Wang, M. An Improved YOLOv5-Based Vegetable Disease Detection Method. *Comput. Electron. Agric.* **2022**, *202*, 107345. [CrossRef]
36. Liu, Y.H.; Huang, Z.H.; Song, Q.; Bai, K. PV-YOLO: A lightweight pedestrian and vehicle detection model based on improved YOLOv8. *Digit. Signal Process.* **2025**, *156*, 104857. [CrossRef]
37. Li, X.; Hu, X.; Yang, J. Spatial Group-wise Enhance: Improving Semantic Feature Learning in Convolutional Networks. *arXiv* **2019**, arXiv:1905.09646.
38. Zaferani, H.; Kiani, K.; Rastgoo, R. Real-Time Face Verification on Mobile Devices Using Margin Distillation. *Multimed. Tools Appl.* **2023**, *82*, 44155–44173. [CrossRef]
39. Misra, D.; Nalamada, T.; Arasanipalai, A.U.; Hou, Q. Rotate to Attend: Convolutional Triplet Attention Module. *arXiv* **2020**, arXiv:2010.03045.
40. Huang, H.; Zhou, X.; Cao, J.; He, R.; Tan, T. Vision Transformer with Super Token Sampling. *arXiv* **2024**, arXiv:2211.11167.
41. Ouyang, D.; He, S.; Zhang, G.; Luo, M.; Guo, H.; Zhan, J.; Huang, Z. Efficient Multi-Scale Attention Module with Cross-Spatial Learning. *arXiv* **2023**, arXiv:2305.13563.
42. Li, Y.; Hou, Q.; Zheng, Z.; Cheng, M.-M.; Yang, J.; Li, X. Large Selective Kernel Network for Remote Sensing Object Detection. *arXiv* **2024**, arXiv:2303.09030.
43. Liu, Y.; Shao, Z.; Teng, Y.; Hoffmann, N. NAM: Normalization-based Attention Module. *arXiv* **2021**, arXiv:2111.12419.
44. Zheng, Z.; Wang, P.; Liu, W.; Li, J.; Ye, R.; Ren, D. Distance-IoU Loss: Faster and Better Learning for Bounding Box Regression. *Proc. AAAI Conf. Artif. Intell.* **2020**, *34*, 12993–13000. [CrossRef]
45. Tong, Z.; Chen, Y.; Xu, Z.; Yu, R. Wise-IoU: Bounding Box Regression Loss with Dynamic Focusing Mechanism. *arXiv* **2023**, arXiv:2301.10051.
46. Ma, S.; Xu, Y. MPDIoU: A Loss for Efficient and Accurate Bounding Box Regression. *arXiv* **2023**, arXiv:2307.07662.
47. Zhang, H.; Xu, C.; Zhang, S. Inner-IoU: More Effective Intersection over Union Loss with Auxiliary Bounding Box. *arXiv* **2023**, arXiv:2311.02877.
48. Zhang, H.; Zhang, S. Shape-IoU: More Accurate Metric considering Bounding Box Shape and Scale. *arXiv* **2024**, arXiv:2312.17663.
49. Zhao, Y.; Lv, W.; Xu, S.; Wei, J.; Wang, G.; Dang, Q.; Liu, Y.; Chen, J. DETRs Beat YOLOs on Real-Time Object Detection. In Proceedings of the 2024 IEEE/CVF Conference on Computer Vision and Pattern Recognition (CVPR), Seattle, WA, USA, 16–22 June 2024; Volume 35, pp. 16965–16974. [CrossRef]
50. Kang, R.; Huang, J.; Zhou, X.; Ren, N.; Sun, S. Toward Real Scenery: A Lightweight Tomato Growth Inspection Algorithm for Leaf Disease Detection and Fruit Counting. *Plant Phenomics* **2024**, *6*, 0174. [CrossRef]
51. Gao, J.; Zhang, J.; Zhang, F.; Gao, J. LACTA: A Lightweight and Accurate Algorithm for Cherry Tomato Detection in Unstructured Environments. *Expert. Syst. Appl.* **2024**, *238*, 122073. [CrossRef]
52. Wu, M.; Lin, H.; Shi, X.; Zhu, S.; Zheng, B. MTS-YOLO: A Multi-Task Lightweight and Efficient Model for Tomato Fruit Bunch Maturity and Stem Detection. *Horticulturae* **2024**, *10*, 1006. [CrossRef]

53. Mo, H.; Wei, L. Tomato Yellow Leaf Curl Virus Detection Based on Cross-Domain Shared Attention and Enhanced BiFPN *Ecol. Inform.* **2024**, *85*, 102912. [CrossRef]
54. Chen, L.; Li, G.; Zhang, S.; Mao, W.; Zhang, M. YOLO-SAG: An Improved Wildlife Object Detection Algorithm Based on YOLOv8n. *Ecol. Inform.* **2024**, *83*, 102791. [CrossRef]

agriculture

MDPI

Article

Estimation of Leaf Chlorophyll Content of Maize from Hyperspectral Data Using E2D-COS Feature Selection, Deep Neural Network, and Transfer Learning

Riqiang Chen [1,2,3], Lipeng Ren [2,4], Guijun Yang [2], Zhida Cheng [2], Dan Zhao [2], Chengjian Zhang [2,3], Haikuan Feng [1,2,5], Haitang Hu [1,2] and Hao Yang [2,*]

1 Nongxin Science & Technology (Beijing) Co., Ltd., Beijing 100097, China; chenriqiang1995@bjfu.edu.cn (R.C.); fenghk@nercita.org.cn (H.F.); huht@nercita.org.cn (H.H.)
2 Key Laboratory of Quantitative Remote Sensing in Agriculture of Ministry of Agriculture and Rural Affairs, Information Technology Research Center, Beijing Academy of Agriculture and Forestry Sciences, Beijing 100097, China; 212204020096@home.hpu.edu.cn (L.R.); yanggj@nercita.org.cn (G.Y.); 22210226120@stu.xust.edu.cn (Z.C.); 2020200006@stu.syau.edu.cn (D.Z.); chengjian_zhang@bjfu.edu.cn (C.Z.)
3 School of Information Science and Technology, Beijing Forestry University, Beijing 100083, China
4 Research Institute of Quantitative Remote Sensing and Smart Agriculture, School of Surveying and Mapping Land Information Engineering, Henan Polytechnic University, Jiaozuo 454000, China
5 College of Agriculture, Nanjing Agricultural University, Nanjing 210095, China
* Correspondence: yangh@nercita.org.cn

Abstract: Leaf chlorophyll content (LCC) serves as a vital biochemical indicator of photosynthetic activity and nitrogen status, critical for precision agriculture to optimize crop management. While UAV-based hyperspectral sensing offers maize LCC estimation potential, current methods struggle with overlapping spectral bands and suboptimal model accuracy. To address these limitations, we proposed an integrated maize LCC estimation framework combining UAV hyperspectral imagery, simulated hyperspectral data, E2D-COS feature selection, deep neural network (DNN), and transfer learning (TL). The E2D-COS algorithm with simulated data was used to identify structure-resistant spectral bands strongly correlated with maize LCC: Big trumpet stage: 418 nm, 453 nm, 506 nm, 587 nm, 640 nm, 688 nm, and 767 nm; Spinning stage: 418 nm, 453 nm, 541 nm, 559 nm, 688 nm, 723 nm, and 767 nm. Combining the E2D-COS feature selection with TL and DNN significantly improves the estimation accuracy: the R^2 of the proposed Maize-LCNet model is improved by 0.06–0.11 and the RMSE is reduced by 0.57–1.06 g/cm compared with LCNet-field. Compared to the existing studies, this study not only clarifies the spectral bands that are able to estimate maize chlorophyll, but also presents a high-performance, lightweight (fewer input) approach to achieve the accurate estimation of LCC in maize, which can directly support growth monitoring nutrient management at specific growth stages, thus contributing to smart agricultural practices.

Keywords: maize; chlorophyll; radiative transfer model; feature selection; transfer learning

1. Introduction

Leaf chlorophyll content (LCC) is an important biochemical indicator of a crop's photosynthetic capacity, nitrogen status, and overall plant health, and is a key biochemical parameter in precision smart agriculture [1,2]. For maize, a staple crop that is critical for global food security, accurate LCC information can help with interventions (fertilizer application, irrigation, etc.), optimizing yields and resource use efficiency [3,4]. Therefore, an accurate and timely estimation of maize LCC serves as a cornerstone for precision fertilization, directly informing nutrient management decisions that balance yield optimization with environmental sustainability. With maize leaf chlorophyll information, growers can optimize fertilization strategies with crop requirements, while ensuring optimal plant development and preventing resource overuse and ecological damage.

Traditional LCC quantification methods, such as destructive experimental analysis methods or handheld SPAD instrumental measurements, suffer from space constraints, labor-intensive work, and poor scalability that prevent them from being applicable to large-scale, dynamic in situ measurements [5]. In contrast, remote sensing technologies, particularly UAV-based imaging hyperspectral technologies, offer unprecedented opportunities for nondestructive, high-resolution, and spatially-inspired LCC estimation [6]. UAV hyperspectral technology has also now been widely used in several aspects of crop agronomic parameter estimation, such as above-ground biomass (AGB) [7], chlorophyll [8,9], and yield estimation [10].

Hyperspectral imaging captures reflectance in hundreds of narrow bands, providing a wealth of information on spectral data. These have now been successfully applied to wheat yield [11], biomass [12], and many other types of agronomic parameters estimation [13]. In addition to the drawback of high redundancy of spectral information, there is a key challenge with hyperspectral data: the spectral overlap situation, where multiple agronomic parameters (chlorophyll, nitrogen) share sensitive spectral regions, leads to feature ambiguity with reduced model specificity [14,15]. Effective band selection is therefore critical to identify features that are sensitive to chlorophyll while suppressing irrelevant variability. Existing approaches broadly fall into three categories: firstly, principle of information content: prioritizing bands with high variance or entropy, such as optimal index factor [16]. This method will retain informative bands, but these methods usually select features that are statistically salient but biologically irrelevant to the target parameter. For example, highly informative bands do not work well for estimating wheat LAI [16]. Secondly, goal-directed principle: focuses on bands that have a significant impact on the estimation model, e.g., Boruta [17], regression feature elimination method [18]. The advantages of this method automatically screen redundant features without presetting the direction of the features. For example, the partial least squares method with a variety of feature optimization methods was used to specify the bands that are sensitive to maize chlorophyll and accurately estimate the chlorophyll content [19]. However, the method has high computational complexity, strong model dependence, and is prone to the risk of local overfitting, and these drawbacks may ultimately lead to poor migration ability of the model [20,21]. Both of these estimation LCC methods do not consider the influence of spectral overlap effects on the estimation results. Thirdly, correlation analysis method: focuses on identifying bands that have strong statistical relationships with the target covariates [22]. For example, the Pearson correlation analysis method, mutual correlation information method [23], etc. The advantage of this method is high efficiency and simple realization. However, this simple statistical analysis method struggles to address spectral overlap, fails to accurately identify individual components, and lacks sensitivity to subtle spectral changes and inter-wavelength relationships, hindering in-depth understanding of spectral responses. For example, the highly informative short-wave infrared spectra are simultaneously related to vegetation nitrogen and moisture [14], and this coupling effect will greatly reduce the accuracy of the model. Recently, it has been shown that the inclusion of a second data dimension can effectively suppress the interference of other parameters in a parameter-specific oriented band selection task [24,25], and the core of the method is mainly to combine multiple data dimensions to generate a two-dimensional correlation matrix that quantifies wavelength-to-wavelength interactions as a way of separating out the dominant spectral response region for a specific parameter [26]. The method has been applied to wheat pigment estimation [24]. This approach provides ideas for selecting bands that are sensitive to LCC and resistant to the effects of canopy structure for maize chlorophyll estimation tasks.

Remote sensing-driven crop parameter estimation models are primarily categorized into three approaches: empirical models, physically-based mechanistic models, and hybrid models. Empirical models, such as linear regression for potato AGB estimation and random forest (RF) for assessing nitrogen [27], establish statistical relationships between field-measured parameters and spectral data using machine learning techniques [28]. However, empirical methods suffer from the drawbacks of low accuracy and poor model applicability and interpretability. In contrast, physically-based mechanistic models, exemplified by look-up table (LUT) methods, derive parameter–spectra relationships from radiative transfer theory [29]. For example, Cheng et al. [30] developed a joint inversion model constrained by prior knowledge, demonstrating accurate canopy chlorophyll estimation via LUT-based optimization. Despite their strong physical interpretability, such models face computational bottlenecks and susceptibility to local optima during inversion, particularly when handling high-dimensional hyperspectral data [29].

Hybrid models bridge this gap by integrating physical constraints with data-driven methods [31]. A notable example is Zhao et al.'s framework combining 3D radiative transfer simulations with convolutional neural networks (CNNs) to estimate maize leaf biomass [32]. Similar methods have also been applied to diverse crops, including rice AGB [32], wheat biochemical parameter [33], and grassland AGB estimation [34]. There are fewer studies on hybrid models for estimating chlorophyll in maize leaves using hybrid models. The hybrid model proceeds in two ways: Simulation-Based Training (SBT); and Simulation-Real Transfer Learning (SRTL). The former suffers from the problem of local non-adaptation, which requires the model to be very consistent with the local data [35]. The latter approach, which is also known as transfer learning, can solve the problem of local non-adaptation and learn the physical laws at the same time [36]. In summary, the hybrid modeling approach combining simulated and measured data has a great advantage in improving crop parameter estimation accuracy and provides an opportunity for parameter estimation in precision agriculture [37]. When dealing with massive model data, traditional machine learning methods such as random forests have many advantages, but they also have significant shortcomings: low computational efficiency, and limited processing of complex and high-dimensional data features [38]. Deep learning can effectively make up for the shortcomings of traditional machine learning methods in large-scale data processing due to its advantages of automated feature selecting [39], efficient processing of massive data, and complex modeling capabilities [40]. Thus, the development of deep learning has given convenience to the processing of huge amounts of simulation data. For example, when modeling and processing for large amounts of data (114,048 × 2101), the CNN framework developed by Yue et al. [41] can also cope with it easily.

In summary, the problems of unclear overlap of sensitive spectra and unsatisfactory model accuracy are still present in the current study of maize chlorophyll estimation using remote sensing. Therefore, to solve the above problems, this paper proposed an integrated approach combining enhanced two-dimensional correlation spectroscopy (E2D-COS), hyperspectral data (simulated and field data), and transfer learning-optimized deep neural networks (TL-DNNs) for the accurate UAV-based estimation of maize leaf chlorophyll content (LCC). The main contributions are (1) to specify the spectral bands that are sensitive to chlorophyll and resistant to canopy structure interference using E2D-COS with simulated data, and (2) to improve the estimation performance of maize LCC by combining radiative transfer modeling and migration learning. This study not only clarifies the spectral bands that are able to estimate maize chlorophyll, which provides a reference for other studies, but also presents a method for estimating chlorophyll which can provide a basis for decision-making in growth monitoring and nutrient management in smart agricultural production.

2. Materials and Methods

2.1. Study Area and Data

2.1.1. Study Area

The field experiment was conducted at the Smart Agriculture Demonstration Base of the Chinese Academy of Agricultural Sciences in Xinxiang County, Xinxiang City, Henan Province, China (35.2° N, 113.8° E; see Figure 1). The terrain in this region is predominantly flat, with a gentle rise from north to south. Geographically, the site forms part of the highly productive North China Plain, which is well known for intensive cereal cropping. The local climate is classified as a warm-temperate continental monsoon climate, with mean annual temperatures ranging from 14 °C to 27.3 °C and an average annual precipitation of approximately 573 mm. Notably, precipitation exhibits a strong seasonal pattern, with most rainfall occurring during the summer months.

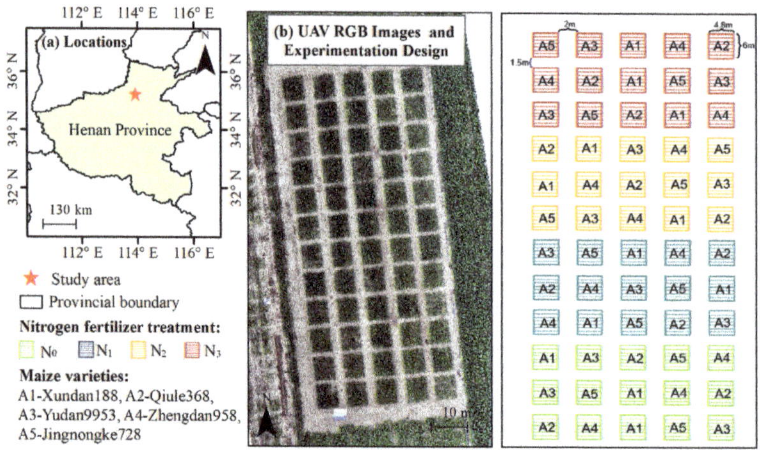

Figure 1. Overview of the study area. (**a**) Location of the study area; (**b**) UAV images and experimentation design of study area.

The experiment was conducted during the 2024 summer maize growing season, which commenced with sowing in June and concluded with harvesting in October. Four nitrogen (N) fertilizer treatments were established along a north-to-south gradient, arranged in descending order of application rate: N_0: 0 kg N per mu, N_1: 5 kg N per mu, N_2: 10 kg N per mu, N_3: 15 kg N per mu. The experimental field was divided into 60 plots in a 12-row by 5-column arrangement, where every three rows constituted one N treatment zone. Each plot measured 4.8 m × 6.0 m, with buffer zones of 2.0 m between plots in the east–west direction and 1.5 m in the north–south direction to minimize edge effects. Five maize varieties were selected to represent a range of genetic backgrounds and agronomic characteristics (A1: Xundan188, A2: Qiule368, A3: Yudan9953, A4: Zhengdan958, and A5: Jingnongke728). Within each nitrogen treatment, each variety was replicated three times, ensuring robust statistical analyses of treatment effects. Figure 1 provides an illustrative overview of the experimental layout and plot arrangement.

2.1.2. UAV-Canopy Hyperspectral Data

A HeadWall MV.C VNIR hyperspectral imaging system (HeadWall Photonics, Bolton, MA, USA) served as the primary sensor for this study. The VNIR camera operates over a spectral range of 400–1000 nm, encompassing 342 distinct spectral channels, each at 1.75 nm sampling intervals and with a full-width-at-half-maximum (FWHM) of approximately 6 nm. Equipped with a CMOS detector, the camera provides a spatial resolution of 1024 pixels. Its fully reflective, concentric-aberration-corrected optical design (f/2.5) enhances imaging fidelity by minimizing optical distortions and maximizing signal throughput. Data transmission for the VNIR camera is supported via a USB 3.1 interface. The hyperspectral camera was mounted on a DJI Matrice 300 RTK (M300 RTK, Shenzhen, China), a quadcopter UAV system widely used for precision agricultural applications. The UAV's dimensions are 810 mm × 670 mm × 430 mm (length × width × height), with a diagonal motor wheelbase of 895 mm. Its base weight, including dual batteries, is 6.3 kg, while the maximum takeoff weight can reach 9 kg. With a single-gimbal damping assembly capable of carrying up to 930 g, the platform readily accommodates the hyperspectral payload required for field-scale data acquisition.

Multi-temporal hyperspectral imagery was collected at two critical growth stages of maize during the 2024 growing season, namely the big trumpet stage (6 August) and the spinning stage (14 August). These particular phenological periods were chosen because they represent key developmental phases for maize, where physiological changes are most pronounced and therefore most informative for remote sensing–based assessments. To ensure data quality and inter-comparability, all flights were conducted under clear skies with wind speeds below 3 m/s, typically between 11:00 and 14:00 local time. This timing ensured optimal solar altitude angles, thereby minimizing shadow effects and maximizing reflectance signal consistency across the study plots. Such multi-temporal measurements are vital for capturing the dynamics of maize growth, facilitating advanced studies on crop stress, nutrient status, and yield estimation under different management regimes.

After capturing the initial hyperspectral UAV imagery, a structured series of preprocessing operations is essential to obtain reliable reflectance data for each maize plot. First, the high-accuracy onboard GPS/IMU data are combined with uniformly distributed ground control points (GCPs) to perform rigorous geometric and orthorectification corrections, ensuring centimeter-level positional precision. Following this, a comprehensive radiometric calibration and atmospheric correction is carried out to convert raw digital number (DN) values into surface reflectance. During this phase, reference panel measurements (recorded prior to takeoff) are used to correct for sensor-specific biases, thereby generating hyperspectral reflectance images that closely capture the actual spectral signatures of the canopy. Subsequently, ENVI software (Version 5.3.1) is employed to delineate each experimental plot as the fundamental unit of analysis. By aggregating all pixels within a plot boundary and computing their average reflectance value, representative canopy-level spectra are derived for each plot. The ratio of field training to validation set was 2:1, the number of training samples was 40, and the number of validation samples was 20 based on randomization.

2.1.3. Leaf Chlorophyll Content and Other Data

In this study, a spectrophotometric (chemical) method was employed to measure the chlorophyll levels in maize leaves, thereby providing both highly precise reference data and rapid field-based assessments. Chemical (Spectrophotometric) Method: Following standard procedures, two representative plants were selected from each experimental plot. From each plant, the third, seventh, and eleventh functional leaves (counted from the top) were sampled to capture potential vertical variations in chlorophyll content. To ensure sample consistency, 48 leaf discs (each 6 mm in diameter) were punched from the central portion of each leaf, avoiding the main vein, for a total leaf disc area of approximately 14 cm^2 per leaf position. These discs were immediately placed in 80 mL of 75% ethanol and kept under dark conditions for 5–6 days to facilitate complete chlorophyll extraction. Chlorophyll absorbance was measured using a 752 UV–Vis spectrophotometer (Hinotek, Ningbo, China). Prior to data collection, the instrument was warmed up for 30 min to achieve thermal equilibrium. The absorbance of each extract (in triplicate) was measured at 645 nm and 663 nm. The total chlorophyll content (C_{ab}) was computed using Equation (1), where the individual chlorophyll a (C_a) and chlorophyll b (C_b) concentrations were obtained via Equations (2) and (3) [42]:

$$C_{ab} = C_a + C_b \tag{1}$$

$$C_a = (12.72A_{663} - 2.59A_{645}) \times [V/(1000 \times W)] \tag{2}$$

$$C_b = (22.88A_{645} - 4.67A_{663}) \times [V/(1000 \times W)] \tag{3}$$

where A_{645}, A_{663} are the absorbances at 645 nm and 663 nm, respectively, V is the volume of the extract (mL), and W is the total area (cm^2) of the leaf discs.

2.2. Overview of Methods

Figure 2 illustrates a technical flowchart of this research, as detailed below:

- **Dataset collection:** UAV hyperspectral systems and spectrophotometers were used to obtain a total of 120 canopy spectral data (Section 2.1.2) and leaf chlorophyll data (Section 2.1.3) over two fertility stages. The PROSAIL model was used to simulate leaf spectral data (Section 2.3).
- **Band selection:** To identify bands that are sensitive to LCC and resistant to structural effects, the E2D-COS method (Section 2.4) was used and analyzed in combination with radiative transfer model simulation data (Section 2.3).
- **Model pre-training:** The simulated spectral data was employed to pre-train the DNN model to learn the potential knowledge of spectral versus vegetation traits, i.e., to get the model weights of the pre-trained model (Sections 2.5.1 and 3.3.1).
- **Model fine-tuning based on transfer learning:** The weights of the pre-trained model are used as initial values for the model, which is again de-trained based on the field measured spectral data to fine-tune the part parameters of model (Sections 2.5.2 and 3.3.2).
- **Comparison of other methods:** This study compared the performance of (1) the Mazie-LCNet trained on simulated and field measured data, (2) LCNet model trained on simulated dataset, (3) an Maize-LCNet-Field trained on field measured data, and (4) traditional statistical regression methods in estimating the maize LCC (Sections 2.5.3 and 3.3.3).

2.3. Maize Canopy Spectral Simulation Using PROSAIL

The PROSAIL model, widely regarded as a foundational tool for simulating vegetation canopy spectra, couples the PROSPECT leaf optical properties model with the SAIL bidirectional reflectance canopy model [43,44]. In this study, we employed version 2.0.5 of the PROSAIL Python library (Version 2.0.5) to generate simulated canopy spectra of maize at multiple growth stages, aligning with the requirements bands selection (sensitive band screening (Sections 2.4 and 3.1), structural interference spectral analysis (Sections 2.4 and 3.2) and transfer learning (Sections 2.5 and 3.3) of the research. The reason for choosing PROSAIL is that this model has been successfully used in many tasks of estimating physiological and biochemical parameters of crops, such as leaf area index [45], chlorophyl [46], and nitrogen [47]. At the same time, compared with some complex radiative transfer models (e.g., the LESS model [48]), the PROSAIL model is computationally efficient and has a low parameter requirement. Key model parameters—such as leaf area index (LAI), leaf angle distribution (LAD), and leaf chlorophyll content—were set according to field-based biophysical measurements and established references [24,32], ensuring that the simulations closely reproduced in situ spectral characteristics of maize canopies. Moreover, site-specific soil reflectance spectra, obtained directly from the experimental field, were incorporated to enhance both the realism and regional applicability of the results. Detailed model parameter values for big-bell-mouth stage and silking stage are given in Table 1.

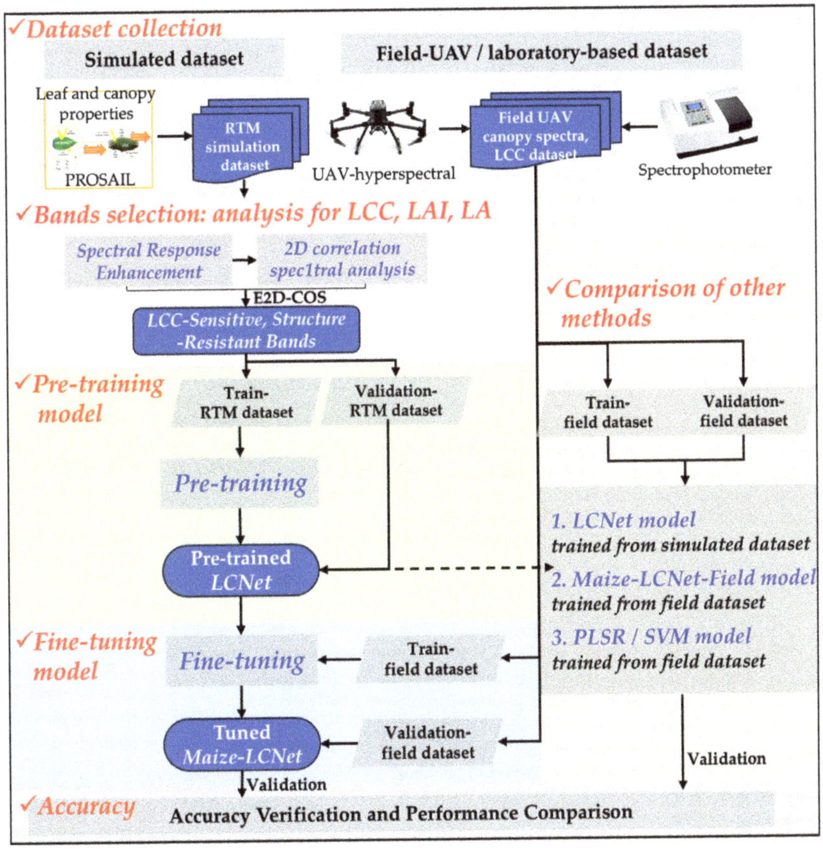

Figure 2. Schematic diagram of this study.

After parameterizing the model, a simulated dataset of 190,512 (Big trumpet stage) and 132,192 (Spinning stage) samples was generated. Each simulation included a high-resolution canopy reflectance spectrum and corresponding leaf biochemical parameters. A comprehensive quality-control procedure was carried out to remove any data points that did not conform to empirical observations. From each of the two growth stages, in order to increase the training efficiency of the model and reduce the computational performance requirements, 10,000 spectra were randomly selected to pre-train a neural network using transfer learning techniques. The ratio of training to validation set was 2:1, the number of training samples was 6666 and the number of validation samples was 3334 based on randomization. To facilitate two-dimensional correlation spectroscopy analyses, representative simulations were selected to investigate how leaf chlorophyll content

(LCC) responds to variations in biophysical parameters under different canopy conditions. Specifically, (1) Screening of LCC sensitive bands using fixed-LAI and LA spectral data: big trumpet stage (LAI = 2.5, LA = 45°) and spinning period (LAI = 4, LA = 45°); (2) Band screening for resistance to structural interference using fixed-field measured spectral data of non-structural parameters (LAI and LA): for LAI, big trumpet stage (N = 1.5, C_w = 0.018, C_m = 0.008, LA = 45°, LAI = 1:8) and spinning period (N = 1.7, C_w = 0.08, C_m = 0.012, LA = 45°, LAI = 1:8). For LA, big trumpet stage (N = 1.5, C_w = 0.018, C_m = 0.008, LA = 10:60°, LAI = 2.5) and spinning period (N = 1.7, C_w = 0.08, C_m = 0.012, LA = 10:60°, LAI = 4). The resulting two-dimensional correlation spectra were analyzed to identify stable spectral regions that are minimally affected by changes in canopy structure. These stable regions can serve as robust spectral indices for LCC estimation, even when the canopy structure is subject to significant variation.

Table 1. Settings of the PROSAIL.

Parameters	Units	Big Trumpet Stage		Spinning Stage	
		Transfer Learning	Bands Selection	Transfer Learning	Bands Selection
Leaf structure index (N)	unitless	1.2–1.6 (0.2)	1.5	1.2–1.8 (0.3)	1.7
Chlorophyll a + b content (Chl)	$\mu g/cm^2$	20–90 (2)			
Carotenoid content (Car)	$\mu g/cm^2$	Cab/5			
Equivalent water thickness (C_w)	cm	0.015–0.025 (0.002)	0.018	0.02–0.035 (0.002)	0.022
Dry matter content (C_m)	g/cm^2	0.003–0.009 (0.001)	0.008	0.006–0.012 (0.002)	0.012
Leaf area index (LAI)	m^2/m^2	2–5 (0.5)	1.0–8.0 (1)	2.5–5 (0.5)	1.0–8.0 (1)
Average leaf inclination angle (LA)	Deg (°)	10–60 (10)	10–80 (10)	10–60 (10)	10–80 (10)
Solar zenith angle (SZA)	Deg (°)	45			
Observer zenith angle (OZA)	Deg (°)	0			

2.4. *Enhanced Two-Dimensional Correlation Spectral Analysis (E2D-COS)*

To select the sensitive spectral bands, E2D-COS is chosen for band screening in this paper. The reason for the selection is that it not only has the advantages of high efficiency and simple implementation, but also the method is highly sensitive to subtle spectral variations and can accurately quantify the interactions between bands for the purpose of separating sensitive bands [25,26]. The method has been successfully used in a variety of parameter estimation studies [24]. The specific steps are as follows: we first apply the spectral enhancement methods from Section 2.4.1 to preprocess the spectral data. Then, the 2D Correlation Spectroscopy Analysis plug-in is used to generate synchronous (Synchronous 2D-COS) and asynchronous (Asynchronous 2D-COS) spectra (Section 3.2.2). The resulting technique, termed enhanced two-dimensional correlation spectroscopy analysis (E2D-COS), combines these 2D correlation analyses with the improved spectral data.

2.4.1. Spectral Response Enhancement

Building on the classical two-dimensional correlation spectroscopy (2D-COS), Zhang et al. [24] proposed an amplitude- and shape-enhanced 2D-COS analysis approach (E2D-COS) to increase the sensitivity of hyperspectral data to external perturbations (e.g., changes in LCC, LAI, and LA). By jointly considering both the reflectance amplitude and the first derivative (i.e., the shape) of the hyperspectral curve, this method highlights subtle spectral features that may be overlooked if only a single facet of the spectrum is analyzed. The enhanced approach consists of four main steps:

✓ Spectral Normalization

To control for the constant incremental changes in the perturbation variable (LCC), raw hyperspectral reflectance values are normalized using the min–max method, as shown in Equation (4):

$$a_i = \frac{r_i - r_{min}}{r_{max} - r_{min}} \tag{4}$$

where r_i is the reflectance at the i-th band, and r_{min} and r_{max} are the minimum and maximum reflectance within that specific spectrum, respectively.

✓ First Derivative of the Spectrum

The first derivative of the normalized reflectance spectrum captures changes in slope and helps reduce the influence of background noise. Using the finite difference method, the first derivative (θ) at i-th band is calculated as in Equation (5):

$$\theta = \frac{a_{i+1} - a_i}{\lambda_{i+1} - \lambda_i} \tag{5}$$

where a_{i+1} and a_i are the normalized reflectance at wavelengths λ_{i+1} and λ_i, respectively.

✓ Response Relationship Computation

Pearson correlation coefficients are then calculated to quantify (I) the relationships between the normalized reflectance (a_j) and LCC, and (II) the first derivative (θ_j) and LCC, as shown in Equations (6) and (7):

$$r_a = \frac{\Sigma_{j=1}^{n}\left[(a_j - \bar{a})(y_i - \bar{y})\right]}{\sqrt{\Sigma_{j=1}^{n}(a_j - \bar{a})^2}\sqrt{\Sigma_{j=1}^{n}(j - \bar{y})}} \tag{6}$$

$$r_\theta = \frac{\Sigma_{j=1}^{n}\left[(\theta_j - \bar{\theta})(y_i - \bar{y})\right]}{\sqrt{\Sigma_{j=1}^{n}(\theta_j - \bar{\theta})^2}\sqrt{\Sigma_{j=1}^{n}(y_i - \bar{y})^2}} \tag{7}$$

where r_a and r_θ represent the Pearson correlation coefficients of LCC with the normalized reflectance and its first derivative, respectively; a_j and θ_j are the reflectance and derivative values for j-th sample, a and b are the respective mean reflectance and mean derivative over all samples; y_i is the LCC value for sample; y is the mean LCC of the sample set; and n is the total number of samples.

✓ Enhanced Dynamic Spectrum Computation

Finally, the enhanced dynamic spectrum (D) is constructed by integrating the correlation coefficients (r_a) and first derivative (r_θ) with the original reflectance (r_i), as given in Equation (8):

$$D = r_a + r_\theta + r_i \tag{8}$$

where D is the enhanced dynamic spectrum, and r_a, r_θ and r_i represent original reflectance, the Pearson correlation coefficients of LCC with the normalized reflectance and its first derivative. This additive integration of amplitude and shape information provides a more robust and sensitive spectral measure that highlights features most responsive to chlorophyll variation, effectively improving subsequent 2D correlation analyses. By emphasizing wavebands that exhibit high sensitivity to LCC, the enhanced approach helps elucidate key spectral drivers underlying chlorophyll dynamics and enhances the reliability of downstream applications such as vegetation health assessment and biochemical parameter retrieval.

2.4.2. Two-Dimensional Correlation Spectral Analysis

Conventional one-dimensional (1D) spectral analysis has certain limitations in handling complex spectral data. First, it struggles with overlapping spectral bands arising from multiple constituents, making it difficult to accurately identify and separate individual spectral features. Second, 1D methods often exhibit insufficient sensitivity to subtle variations in spectral data, potentially overlooking important spectral information. Moreover, they cannot intuitively reveal the interrelationships among different wavelengths, which constrains deeper investigation into the underlying mechanisms of spectral response.

Two-dimensional correlation spectroscopy (2D-COS) addresses these issues by introducing a second spectral dimension, thereby uncovering additional hidden information in the data. This method consists primarily of two core components: the synchronous spectrum and the asynchronous spectrum. The synchronous spectrum reflects the similarity of intensity changes across different wavelengths, whereas the asynchronous spectrum captures the sequential order of these changes. This technique offers several advantages: (1) by expanding 1D spectra into a two-dimensional map, it significantly enhances spectral resolution and helps isolate overlapping peaks; (2) it identifies dynamic features of spectral changes, highlighting minor structural variations within the sample; and (3) it reveals correlations among different wavelengths, providing critical insights into the mechanisms that drive the observed spectral responses.

By supplying multidimensional information about molecular vibrational modes, 2D-COS can extract weak peaks, shift peaks, and overlapping peaks. According to theory, the intensity of the dynamic spectrum is represented by S, v as the variable and t as the external perturbation, measured over m steps with equal increments (Δt). The general expression is given in Equation (9):

$$S_{(v)} = \begin{pmatrix} \begin{pmatrix} y(v,t_1) \\ y(v,t_2) \end{pmatrix} \\ y(v,t_3) \\ \cdot \\ \cdot \\ \cdot \\ y(v,t_m) \end{pmatrix} \tag{9}$$

The synchronous and asynchronous 2D correlation intensities between two frequencies v_1 and v_2 are denoted by $\phi(v_1,v_2)$ and $\varphi(v_1,v_2)$, respectively, and can be computed using Equations (10) and (11):

$$\phi(v_1,v_2) = \frac{1}{m-1} s_{(v_1)}{}^{T} \cdot s_{(v_2)} \tag{10}$$

$$\varphi(v_1,v_2) = \frac{1}{m-1} s_{(v_1)}{}^{T} \cdot D \cdot s_{(v_2)} \tag{11}$$

where $w_{(v_1,v_2)}$ is the combined 2D correlation intensity obtained by multiplying the synchronous and asynchronous correlation intensities:

$$w_{(v_1,v_2)} = [\phi(v_1,v_2)] \cdot [\varphi(v_1,v_2)] \tag{12}$$

In these expressions, D_{jk} is the Hilbert–Noda transformation matrix; for row j and column k, its elements are defined as follows (Equation (13)):

$$D_{jk} = \begin{cases} 0, & j = k \\ \frac{1}{\pi(k-j)}, & j \neq k \end{cases} \tag{13}$$

Additionally, the dataset used in this study derives from both in situ measurements and PROSAIL-simulated data. The simulated dataset is leveraged to compensate for the limited LCC gradient in the measured data, ultimately improving the effectiveness of E2D-COS. Specifically, the PROSAIL dataset ranges from 20 to 90 μg/cm^2 in 2 μg/cm^2 increments of chlorophyll content, covering the majority of observed spectral scenarios. This study primarily utilizes the synchronous spectrum to identify characteristic wavelengths linked to maize canopy LCC. Through highlighting dynamically responsive spectral features, E2D-CSA deepens our understanding of canopy reflectance mechanisms and provides a basis for a more accurate retrieval of key biochemical parameters.

2.5. Modeling Methods

2.5.1. Deep Neural Network

A deep neural network (DNN) can be viewed as a multilayer feedforward neural architecture designed to capture high-level feature interactions from input data through successive layers of processing. When each layer in a DNN is fully connected, every neuron in one layer links to every neuron in the subsequent layer. By systematically increasing the number of hidden layers, the model gains the capacity to discern and learn more complex patterns, which can improve predictive performance for regression or classification tasks under certain conditions [49]. The reason for choosing DNN is that compared to currently commonly used models such as RF, and more complex DL models, DNN models adaptively extract spectral features through hierarchical non-linear transformations, overcoming the limitations of traditional methods that rely on manual feature engineering [50], while avoiding the modelling of invalid spatial correlations by complex DL networks [51].

In this work, we employed a five-layer DNN (Figure 3) to estimate the leaf nitrogen content (LNC). The structure comprises a single input layer, three hidden layers, and an output layer. All layers are fully connected; specifically, the final output layer regresses the LNC based on the feature representations obtained in the hidden layers. Since this design does not inherently utilize spatial information, the input layer accepts only one-dimensional vectors, where each sample's features (e.g., reflectance bands and other ancillary attributes) have been concatenated into a single vector. To harmonize feature magnitudes, we apply Z-score normalization, which recalibrates each feature x to $(x-\mu)/\sigma$, where μ is the mean and μ is the standard deviation. Model learning proceeds by forward propagation of inputs through each hidden layer, with intermediate activations producing non-linear transformations of the data. Ultimately, the last layer generates a linear output that corresponds to the predicted LNC. The training objective employs the root mean squared error (RMSE) as the loss function, augmented with an L2 regularization term to reduce overfitting:

$$L = \frac{1}{n}\sum_{i=1}^{n}\left(y_{true}^{i} - y_{esti}^{i}\right)^{2} + \frac{c}{2n}\|w\|_2^2 \tag{14}$$

$$\|w\|_2^2 = \sum_{j=1}^{n} w_j^2 = w^T w \tag{15}$$

where n is the number of training samples, y_{true}^{i} and y_{esti}^{i} denote the observed and predicted LNC values for sample iii, respectively, c is a penalty coefficient, and w is the vector of model weights. By backpropagating the error calculated from this loss function, the model iteratively updates its parameters.

Overfitting can arise when the model complexity is high or when the training data are insufficient. To counteract this risk, we incorporate L2 regularization alongside a dropout mechanism, both of which can limit the model's tendency to memorize training examples and enhance its ability to generalize. We also conduct grid-based tuning of the most influential hyperparameters, ensuring that the final DNN configuration strikes a balance between model capacity and robustness. The resulting architecture has proven effective for learning sophisticated feature representations from diverse spectral and auxiliary inputs, enabling precise regression of LCC values.

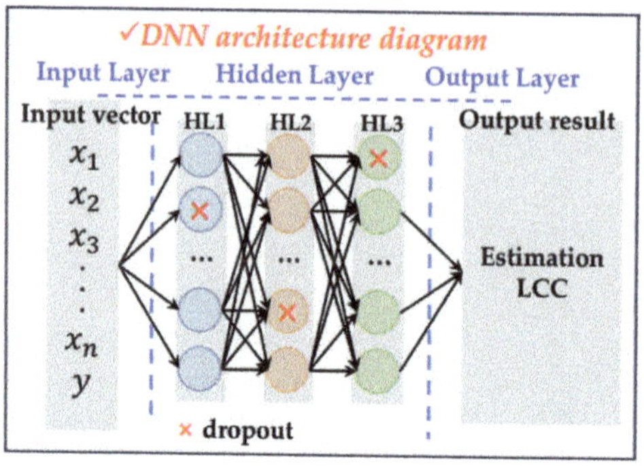

Figure 3. DNN architecture diagram.

2.5.2. Transfer Learning

Transfer learning (TL) generally describes a process wherein expertise acquired through solving one task is leveraged to enhance performance on another related task. This strategy is particularly useful for mitigating the limitations associated with applying a model trained in one setting directly to new or varying environments, a problem often termed the "domain shift." By integrating TL, researchers can minimize the reliance on extensive labeled datasets from each new context, thereby addressing discrepancies in data characteristics across different neighborhoods or study sites [52]. Over the past few years, TL has become increasingly prevalent in the remote sensing domain, proving instrumental for applications such as land cover classification [53], monitoring vegetation dynamics [36] estimating soil properties [54], and predicting disease variations [55]. In this work, we initially trained the DNN on simulated datasets generated by PROSAIL to enable the model to learn LCC estimation capabilities (LCNet). During the subsequent model adaptation, the weights of the first two hidden layers (HL1 and HL2) acquired in the pre-training phase served as fixed parameter values; and the last hidden layer (HL3) weights served as initial parameter values; these were then optimized using the field-measured spectra (Section 2.1.2), thus refining the model for practical, real-world application (Maize-LCNet).

2.5.3. Comparison of Methods

In addition to the proposed method for estimating the canopy LCC of maize, we tested the performance of the pre-trained model using simulated data (LC-Net), and PLSR/RF methods for quantitative validation.

- LCNet: Pre-trained models trained on simulated data (n = 6666) directly estimate the field validation dataset (n = 20) to evaluate their performance.
- Maize-LCNet-field methods: DNN trained on field data (n = 40) directly estimate the field validation dataset (n = 20) to evaluate their performance.
- PLSR/SVM-field methods: Based on the spectral data measured in the field (n = 40), linear and non-linear machine learning algorithms (PLSR and SVM) are used to train the model and verify its accuracy.

2.6. Assessing Accuracy

To assess the predictive quality of our model in estimating LCC, we adopted two commonly used performance metrics: the coefficient of determination (R^2), and the root means square error (RMSE). In essence, R^2 quantifies how closely the predictions align with real observations—higher values indicate a stronger match. RMSE reflects the average magnitude of errors between predicted and observed values, providing an overall sense of accuracy.

3. Results

3.1. Sensitive Bands of LCC

3.1.1. Characteristics of the Simulated Spectral Data

Figure 4 presents simulated canopy reflectance curves for the big trumpet stage and the spinning stage. These simulated spectra encompass nearly the full breadth of the in situ reflectance measurements acquired at each developmental phase. A pronounced "green peak" emerges around 550 nm, attributable to intense chlorophyll and carotenoid absorption in the blue and red bands contrasted with relatively weaker absorption in the green region. Around 690 nm, there is a marked rise in reflectance (the "red edge"), a known indicator of photosynthetic pigment content transitioning into the near-infrared reflectance plateau. An evident dip near 960 nm is further observed and is generally associated with water vapor absorption, reflecting both atmospheric effects and canopy moisture content.

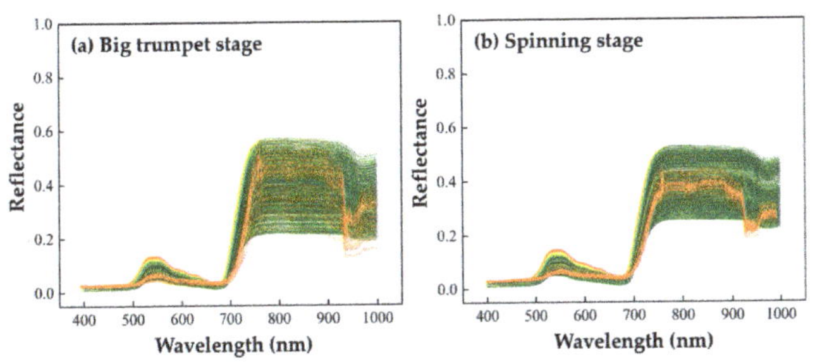

Figure 4. Comparison of simulated and measured spectra.

Figure 5 illustrates the reflectance distribution at five representative wavelengths—450 nm (blue), 550 nm (green), 650 nm (red), 740 nm (red edge), and 800 nm (near-infrared)—across each growth stage. These results confirm that the spectral variability in the simulated dataset extends to practically all reflectance values measured in the field. By spanning these critical wavebands, the simulations demonstrate broad coverage and strong representativeness of actual canopy reflectance dynamics throughout the crop growth cycle. Collectively, these findings underscore the suitability of the simulated dataset for investigating the spectral behavior of maize canopies and for supporting advanced modeling of plant physiological traits.

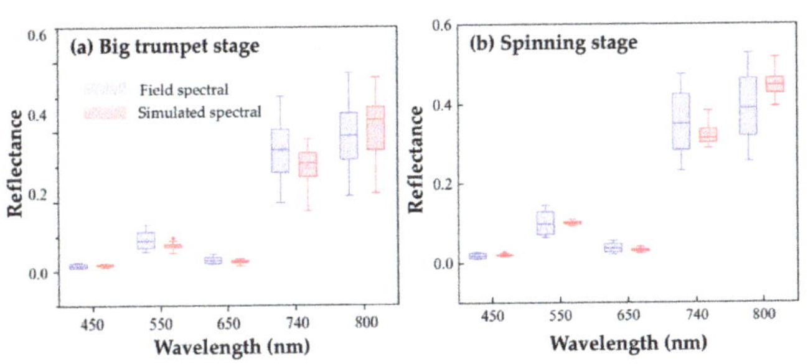

Figure 5. Box plots of reflectance distribution in key bands.

3.1.2. Enhanced Two-Dimensional Correlation Spectral Analysis of Canopy LCCs

Figure 6 presents the synchronous spectra derived from the E2D-COS methodology, shedding light on how canopy reflectance in maize responds to variations in leaf chlorophyll content (LCC) at distinct developmental phases. In the big trumpet stage, the number of self-correlation peaks increases to 11, detected at 418 nm, 453 nm, 506 nm, 566 nm, 587 nm, 640 nm, 688 nm, 767 nm, 802 nm, 829 nm, and 956 nm. Compared with the jointing stage, additional key wavelengths arise in the visible region (416–688 nm), especially in the green band (506–587 nm), suggesting that changes in LCC exert a heightened influence on reflectance in this spectral window. Likewise, the near-infrared range (767–956 nm) shows intensified correlations, reflecting more intricate canopy-level interactions as the crop transitions toward more developed structural forms. By the spinning stage, the synchronous spectrum features 11 self-correlation peaks at 418 nm, 453 nm, 541 nm, 559 nm, 688 nm, 723 nm, 767 nm, 832 nm, 878 nm, 956 nm, and 994 nm. Notably, the near-infrared interval (767–994 nm) encompasses a broader set of sensitive wavelengths, with correlation intensities reaching their highest levels. Such strong near-infrared responses likely stem from the canopy's relatively stable structure during reproductive growth, wherein variations in LCC manifest more markedly through overall reflectance changes. Additionally, the enduring sensitivity in the 688–723 nm red-edge domain highlights its ongoing prominence in tracking LCC fluctuations.

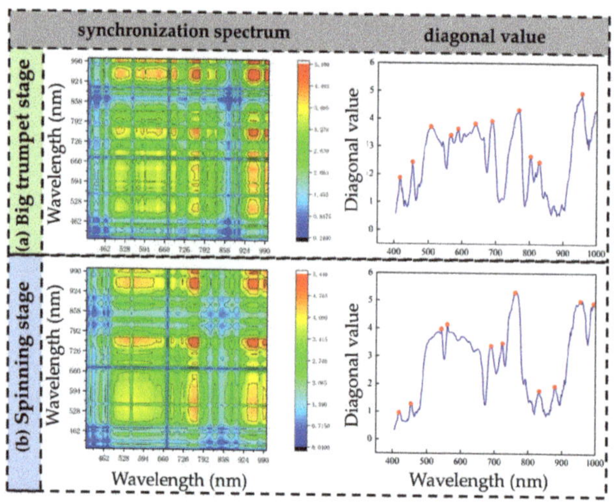

Figure 6. Enhanced E2D-COS synchronization maps for multiple fertility periods and diagonal value.

In summary, these two stages collectively illustrate a trend in which reflectance characteristics initially concentrate around the red and red-edge bands, then expand to broader spectral regions as maize development progresses. The growing importance of near-infrared features underscores the complex interplay between biochemical and structural factors in the canopy. These findings not only validate the utility of E2D-COS for delineating stage-specific responses to LCC but also offer actionable insights for selecting spectral features of the estimation model aimed at improved chlorophyll estimation in maize.

Figure 7 illustrates the asynchronous enhanced two-dimensional correlation spectroscopy (E2D-COS) outcomes, thereby revealing the sequential relationships underlying canopy reflectance variations across different maize growth stages. Comparative analysis of the three asynchronous E2D-COS maps demonstrates a clear evolution in spectral response characteristics as the crop develops. In the big trumpet stage, this alternating "red–blue" pattern becomes concentrated within a narrower 705–744 nm window, with higher correlation intensities pointing to more pronounced sequential differences among wavebands in that interval. By the spinning stage, asynchronous correlation intensities reach their highest levels (±0.05), especially between 703 nm and 735 nm, where the red–blue oscillations are most pronounced.

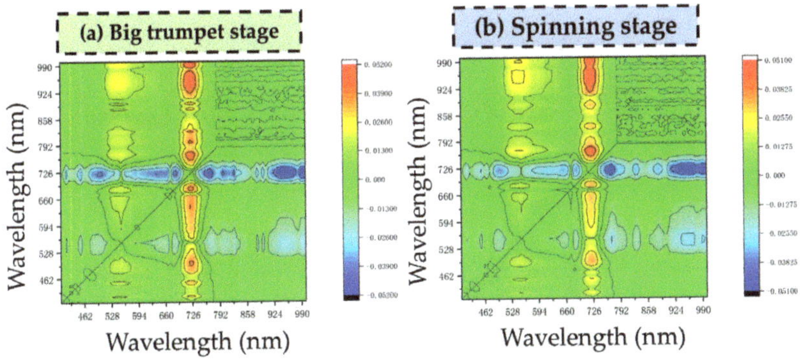

Figure 7. Enhanced E2D-COS asynchronous maps for multiple fertility periods.

This systematic progression of asynchronous correlations aligns strongly with the synchronous E2D-COS findings, reinforcing the importance of these wavebands in tracking chlorophyll dynamics. Moreover, the observed shift in the timing of spectral responses—gradually converging around the red-edge region as the plant advances through its phenological stages—highlights the crucial role of red-edge reflectance in chlorophyll estimation. These insights not only corroborate the selection of key diagnostic wavelengths but also illuminate the temporal sequencing of spectral changes, offering critical theoretical underpinnings for refining stage-specific chlorophyll inversion models in maize.

3.2. Screening Results for Structural Interference Signature Bands

3.2.1. Enhanced Two-Dimensional Correlation Spectral Analysis of LAI

In the remote sensing inversion of vegetation physiological parameters, it is crucial that waveband selection be primarily driven by the target variable rather than confounding influences. In particular, leaf chlorophyll content (LCC) and leaf area index (LAI) each govern distinct processes in photosynthesis—LCC predominantly dictates the absorption of solar radiation, whereas LAI modulates how effectively a canopy intercepts incoming light. Together, these two parameters exhibit considerable coupling effects on canopy reflectance. Consequently, identifying wavebands highly sensitive to LCC while only marginally impacted by LAI is essential for enhancing the accuracy of retrieval models.

This study employed the PROSAIL model to simulate canopy reflectance at two critical phenological stages of maize—the big trumpet stage and the spinning stage. Over an LAI range of 1–8, LCC was systematically varied from 20 to 90 μg/cm^2 in increments of 2 μg/cm^2, thereby illuminating how the spectral signatures shift in response to LCC. We then applied an enhanced two-dimensional correlation spectroscopy (E2D-COS) approach to probe the spectral response patterns under different LAI levels. Figures 8 and 9 present the synchronous E2D-COS maps generated at each growing stage, providing insights into the consistent spectral features that are most indicative of LCC changes across diverse canopy structures. These findings form a robust basis for refining inversion strategies aimed at accurately estimating LCC, even when LAI varies substantially.

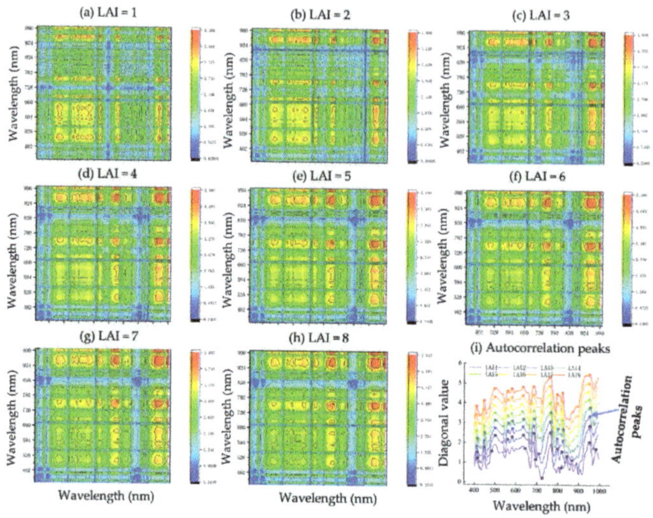

Figure 8. Enhanced two-dimensional correlation spectroscopy (E2D-COS) synchronization maps of simulated data at big trumpet stage under different leaf area indices (LAI = 1~8).

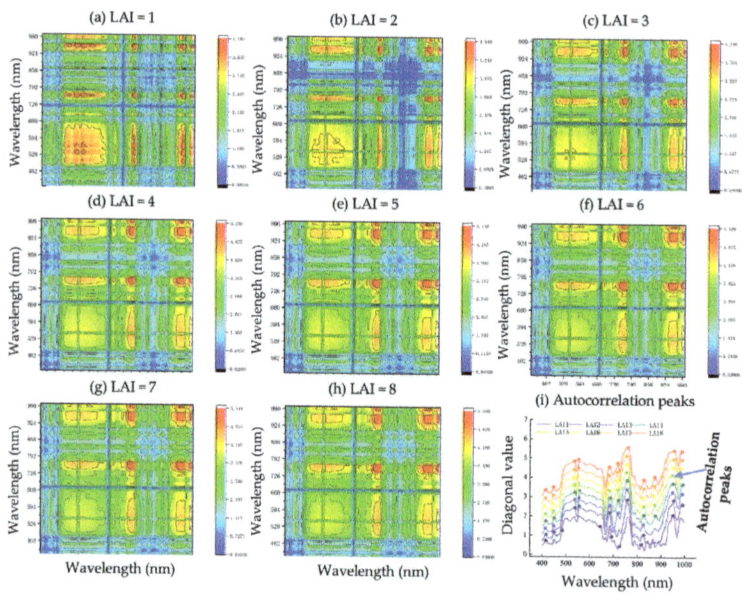

Figure 9. Enhanced two-dimensional correlation spectroscopy (E2D-COS) synchronization maps of simulated data at spinning stage under different leaf area indices (LAI = 1~8).

✓ The synchronous E2D-COS maps of the big trumpet stage with various LAIs

Figure 8i summarizes the evolution of self-correlation peak positions under different LAI conditions of the big trumpet stage. At this stage, the number of self-correlation peaks in the visible range increases substantially, producing a dense cluster of stable wavebands (418 nm, 453 nm, 506 nm, 566 nm, and 587 nm) that remain largely unaffected by changes in LAI. Compared with the jointing stage, red-edge peaks (640–688 nm) also show greater positional stability, implying that canopy structure exerts diminished influence on red-edge reflectance at this point in development. The near-infrared region evolves from multiple discrete self-correlation peaks (767–985 nm) at lower LAI values (e.g., LAI = 1 or LAI = 2) to a more concentrated set of stable peaks (767 nm, 802 nm, 829 nm, and 954 nm) at higher LAI values. Thus, LAI changes during this period mainly affect wavelengths beyond 767 nm. Consequently, the big-bell-mouth stage wavebands that demonstrate minimal LAI sensitivity include 418 nm, 453 nm, 506 nm, 587 nm, 640 nm, 688 nm, and 767 nm.

✓ The synchronous E2D-COS maps of the spinning stage with various LAIs

By the silking stage, self-correlation peaks become fewer but more robust. Although the number of peaks in the visible region (418–559 nm) declines compared to earlier stages, their stability is markedly enhanced. The red-edge domain (688–723 nm) remains nearly stationary, reflecting a relatively mature and stable canopy structure. In the near-infrared range, scattered peaks at lower LAI values (767–985 nm) coalesce into a fixed set of characteristic peaks (e.g., 767 nm, 832 nm, 878 nm, 961 nm, and 996 nm) at higher LAI levels. This pattern echoes that observed at the big-bell-mouth stage, where LAI primarily influences wavelengths above 767 nm. Consequently, the silking-stage wavebands with minimal susceptibility to LAI include 418 nm, 453 nm, 541 nm, 559 nm, 688 nm, 723 nm, and 767 nm. Figure 9i depicts the specific peak positions under varying LAI conditions.

3.2.2. Enhanced Two-Dimensional Correlation Spectral Analysis of LA

Beyond leaf area index (LAI), variations in leaf inclination also shape the overall structure of a maize canopy. To clarify the impact of leaf angle distribution (LAD) on spectral signals, we simulated canopy reflectance using the PROSAIL model with an average leaf angle (ALA) range of 10–80°; leaf chlorophyll content (LCC) was systematically varied from 20 to 90 $\mu g/cm^2$ in increments of 2 $\mu g/cm^2$. Leveraging enhanced two-dimensional correlation spectroscopy (E2D-COS), we then analyzed the spectral response patterns under these diverse LAD configurations. Figures 10 and 11 depict the synchronous E2D-COS plots for key phenological stages.

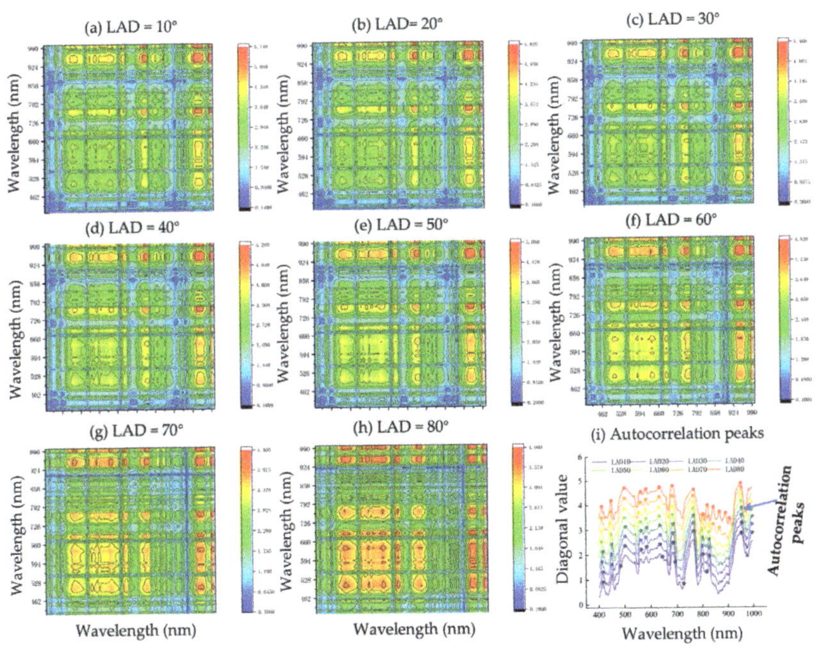

Figure 10. Enhanced two-dimensional correlation spectroscopy (E2D-COS) synchronization maps of simulated data at big trumpet stage under different LAD (10~80°).

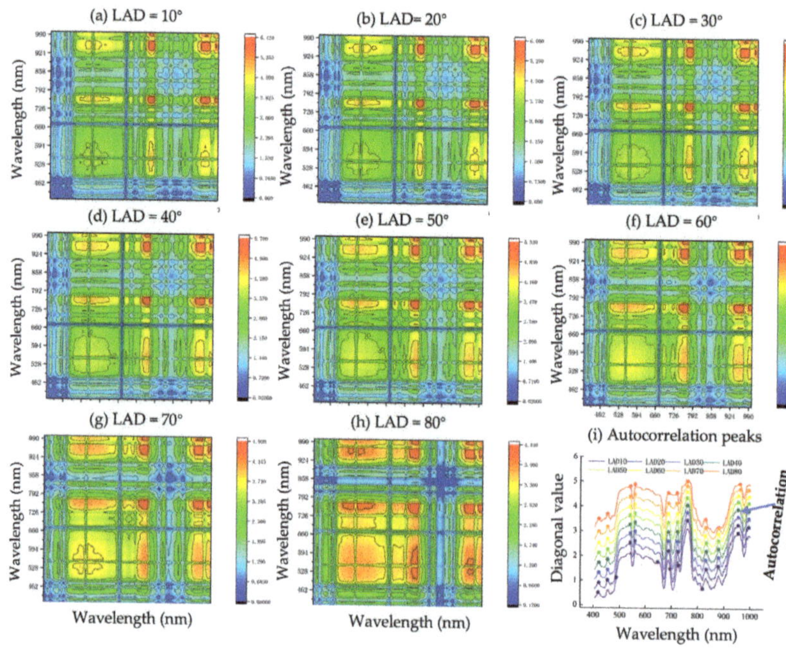

Figure 11. Enhanced two-dimensional correlation spectroscopy (E2D-COS) synchronization maps of simulated data at spinning stage under different LAD (10~80°).

✓ The synchronous E2D-COS maps of the big trumpet stage with various LADs

The big trumpet stage demonstrates notably consistent spectral features (Figure 10). When the leaf angle (LAD) varies between 10° and 60°, the visible-range peaks (418 nm, 453 nm, 506 nm, 566 nm, and 587 nm) and red-edge peaks (640 nm and 688 nm) remain stable. The near-infrared region also exhibits relatively fixed peak positions at 767 nm, 802 nm, 829 nm, 954 nm, and 998 nm. However, for LAD values above 70°, additional NIR peaks (807 nm, 825 nm, 846 nm, 871 nm, 894 nm, 910 nm, and 985 nm) emerge. Consequently, wavebands at 418 nm, 453 nm, 506 nm, 566 nm, 587 nm, 640 nm, 688 nm, and 767 nm remain largely unaffected by moderate variations in leaf angle. Figure 10i illustrates the positions of these peaks under different LAD conditions.

✓ The synchronous E2D-COS maps of the spinning stage with various LADs

By the spinning stage, self-correlation peaks exhibit greater consolidation and enhanced stability (Figure 11). In the visible spectrum, wavebands around 418 nm, 453 nm, 541 nm, and 559 nm remain robust throughout the examined LAD range. The red-to-red-edge interval (approximately 688–760 nm) similarly shows consistent behavior, with only minor shifts (723–725 nm) at its lower boundary. In the near-infrared region, peaks near 828 nm change very little as LAD increases. Meanwhile, certain longer-wavelength peaks (for example, at 956 nm and 994 nm) do shift slightly at LAD values between 10° and 70°. Overall, wavebands at 418 nm, 453 nm, 541 nm, 559 nm, 688 nm, 723 nm, 767 nm, and 832 nm demonstrate minimal sensitivity to variations in canopy structure. Figure 11i illustrates these patterns within the range of leaf angles considered.

Summarize Section 3.2: The E2D-COS analysis identifies wavebands that strongly correlate with LCC yet exhibit limited sensitivity to LAD alterations. Specifically, during the big-bell-mouth stage, the optimal set comprises 418 nm, 453 nm, 506 nm, 587 nm, 640 nm, 688 nm, and 767 nm. Finally, for spinning, wavebands at 418 nm, 453 nm, 541 nm, 559 nm, 688 nm, 723 nm, and 767 nm display robust resistance to canopy structural changes. These stable waveband combinations provide valuable guidance for improving remote-sensing models aimed at retrieving chlorophyll levels, with reduced interference from varying leaf angles and complex canopy architectures.

3.3. LCC Estimation Result

3.3.1. Pre-Training Based on Simulated Hyperspectral Reflectance Dataset

Table 2 lists the train and validation accuracy results of the LC-Net of different stages utilizing simulated spectral data. The findings indicate that all pre-trained LC-Net models successfully achieved an accurate estimation of maize LCC (R^2s above 0.94, RMSEs below 5 g/cm^2). Figure 12 illustrates the pre-training estimated outcomes of the LC-Net network for different stages utilizing simulated spectral data. Figure 12a,d presents the variation in loss across epochs of the big trumpet stage and the spinning stage. The findings suggest that loss decreases rapidly during the first 5 epochs of training; during the subsequent training sessions (5–95 epochs), the change in loss becomes slow. This indicates that the model received significant convergence in the training process. The estimates and simulated inputs of train and validation in Figure 12b,c,e,f have strong consistency (slopes > 0.90, RMSEs < 5 g/cm^2), which also indicates that the LC-Net model achieves an accurate estimation of maize LCC.

Table 2. The accuracy of simulated dataset of proposed LCNet of different stages in pre-training process of transfer learning.

Model	Stage	Train (n = 6667)		Validation (n = 3334)	
		R^2	RMSE (g/cm^2)	R^2	RMSE (g/cm^2)
Pre-trained LCNet	Big trumpet stage	0.94	4.33	0.94	4.31
	Spinning stage	0.97	3.07	0.97	3.04

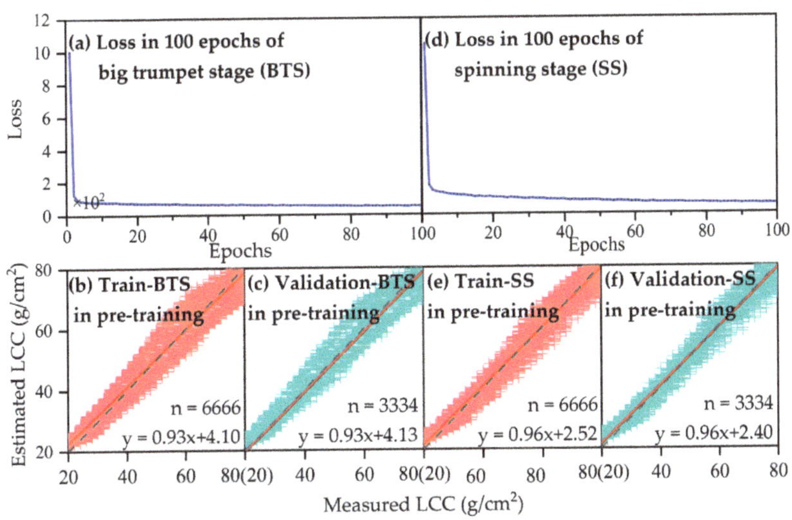

Figure 12. (**a**,**d**) are loss for 100 epochs in pre-training process of LC-Net of big trumpet stage (BTS) and spinning stage (SS), respectively; (**b**,**c**,**e**,**f**) are estimated and measured LCC of simulated data with lower loss in pre-training process of big trumpet stage and spinning stage, respectively.

3.3.2. LCC Estimation Based on Transfer Learning

Applying transfer learning, the LC-Net network obtained from pre-training is again trained with the maize field spectral data to achieve the fine-tuning of the model (Maize-LCNet). Table 3 shows the train and validation accuracy of the fine-tuned Maize-LCNet. The performance of the estimation model was superior for both growth stages; the explanatory power and goodness-of-fit of the model for LCC were higher than 54% (54% to 84%), and the RMSE was below 5 g/cm^2. Figure 13 illustrates the fitting relationship between the estimated and measured values for each model. The differences in the degree of deviation from the 1:1 line and the accuracy metrics of the curve fits of the different model estimates to the measured data are consistent. Specifically, the R^2 of the SS was greater than 0.60, the fitted curve was closer to the 1:1 line, and the fitted slope was higher than 0.50, while the R^2 of the BTS was lower than 0.60, the fitted slope was lower than 0.40, and the RMSEs that could individually represent the errors of the different periods were all very low. Overall, the estimation ability of the SS model was superior to the BTS model; the training and validation accuracies R^2 of the SS stage model were 0.21 and 0.01 higher compared to the BTS model.

Table 3. The accuracy of field dataset of proposed Maize-LCNet with different stages in fine-tuning process of transfer learning.

Model	Stage	Train (n = 40)		Validation (n = 20)	
		R^2	RMSE (g/cm^2)	R^2	RMSE (g/cm^2)
Maize-LCNet	Big trumpet stage	0.63	2.49	0.54	2.53
	Spinning stage	0.84	2.67	0.65	4.39

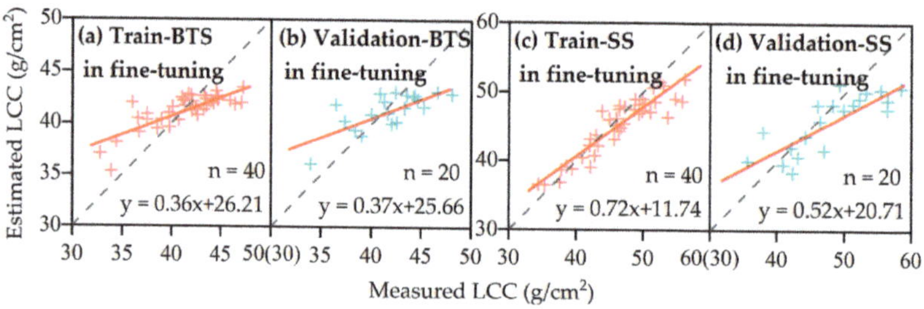

Figure 13. Estimated and field measured LPC in fine-tuning process of transfer learning with different growing stages (BTS: big trumpet stage, SS: spinning stage).

3.3.3. Estimation Results from Comparative Experiments

To demonstrate the effectiveness of the proposed model, comparison experiments were conducted and the validation accuracies of the pre-trained model (LC-Net) and the model trained using field data (PLSR-field/SVM-field) are shown in Table 4 and Figure 14. The results showed that the pre-trained models (LC-Net) for both fertility stages performed poorly, with validation R^2 lower than 0.20 and RMSE higher than 3 g/cm^2, including very large RMSE errors (65.84 g/cm^2) during the spinning stage (SS); the validation accuracies of the remaining three models (LC-Net-field, PLSR-field, and SVM-field) trained based on real data were all acceptable. The R^2 during the big trumpet stage (BTS) was greater than 0.45, and the RMSEs were all less than 4 g/cm^2, and the R^2 during the SS was all greater than 0.54, and the RMSEs were all less than 5. In contrast, the PLSR model had a higher accuracy, and both the LC-Net model and the SVM model performed poorly. The results of the estimated and measured values in Figure 14 also proved that the fitted line of the PLSR model was the closest to the 1:1 line; the fitted slopes were 0.65 to 0.72. The next best fit was Maize-

LCNet-field, with fitted slopes of 0.65 to 0.68; and the other models apparently suffered from overall underestimation (Figure 14b,e,f), or local underestimation/overestimation (Figure 14a,d); the slopes of the fits were all below 0.50.

Table 4. Validation results of multiple comparison methods.

Growth Stage	Accuracy Indicators		LCNet	Maize-LCNet-Field	PLSR-Field	SVM-Field
Big trumpet stage	Validation	R^2	0.09	0.48	0.51	0.45
		RMSE (g/cm²)	3.61	3.59	2.52	2.55
Spinning stage	Validation	R^2	0.17	0.54	0.62	0.55
		RMSE (g/cm²)	65.84	4.96	3.87	4.23

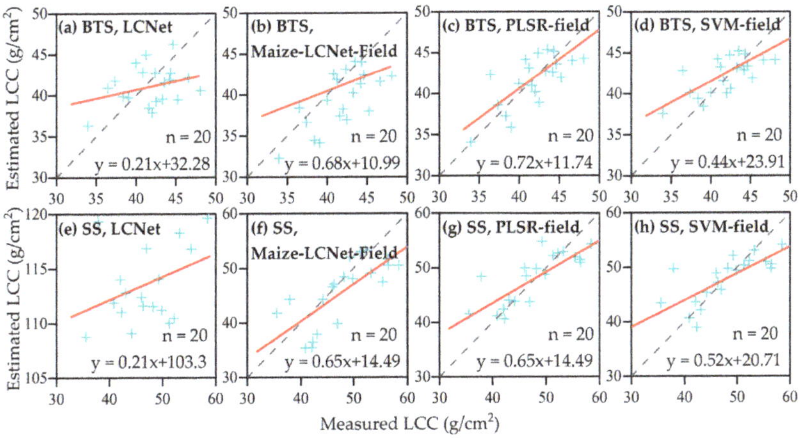

Figure 14. Estimated and field measured LCC of multiple comparison methods (BTS: big trumpet stage, SS: spinning stage).

To clarify whether the estimation results of different models are statistically significant, paired *t*-tests between the proposed Maize-LCNet model and multiple comparative models were performed, and the results are given in Table 5. The results indicated that, except for the LCNet model of the BTS and the SVM-field model of the SS, the estimation results of Maize-LCNet were significantly different from the other models, with the degree of significance reaching 5% (*p*-value: 0.000 to 0.045), and the above results proved the validity of the proposed model.

Table 5. Results of paired sample *t*-test between proposed Maize-LCNet and comparative model.

Comparison	Big Trumpet Stage		Spinning Stage	
	t	*p*-Value	t	*p*-Value
Maize-LCNet vs. LCNet	0.468	0.645	2.421	0.026
Maize-LCNet vs. Maize-LCNet-field	4.289	0.000	49.619	0.000
Maize-LCNet vs. PLSR-field	−3.772	0.045	2.256	0.036
Maize-LCNet vs. SVM-field	−4.330	0.000	−0.285	0.779

4. Discussion

4.1. Advantages of the Estimation Method

Accurate real-time chlorophyll monitoring in maize canopies is critical for precision agriculture, enhancing fertilizer efficiency and yield stability. This study introduces an innovative deep learning architecture (Maize-LCNet) that synergistically integrates physical models, deep learning, and transfer learning for enhanced chlorophyll content quantification in maize canopies. Compared with existing studies, this study not only clarifies the spectral bands that are relevant to maize chlorophyll and resistant to structural influences, but also proposes an estimation method for high-performance estimation of maize chlorophyll content, with detailed findings as follows: (1) Effective spectral band selection: The integration of physical modeling with the E2D-COS method successfully identified chlorophyll-sensitive spectral bands. These bands enabled the development of a robust PLSR-based estimation model (R^2 = 0.62 at the spinning stage), demonstrating the feasibility of using E2D-COS and simplified regression approaches for canopy chlorophyll quantification, which is consistent with existing findings (R^2 = 0.61 in heading stage of wheat) [24]. (2) Simulation-to-reality transfer: The proposed Maize-LCNet model, fine-tuned with field data, significantly outperformed the simulation-only trained baseline (CC-Net), with R^2 increasing from 0.09–0.17 to 0.54–0.65 and RMSE decreasing from 3.61–65.84 to 2.53–4.39 g/cm^2. This highlights the necessity of domain adaptation to bridge the spectral gap between synthetic and real-world data. (3) Transfer learning efficacy: Compared to field-data-trained models (LCNet-field), Maize-LCNet achieved superior accuracy with R^2 improvements of 0.06–0.11 and RMSE reductions of 0.57–1.06 g/cm^2, validating the synergistic effect of combining pre-training on simulated data with targeted fine-tuning. The above results inform future estimation studies. Transfer learning is one way to improve model performance, consistent with the advocacy of existing research [52,56]. Meanwhile, the estimation results of the proposed Maize-LCNet model have lower errors (RMSE: 2.53 in the BTS) compared to the existing methods (RMSE: 4.14~4.46) [57]. (4) Comparative method performance: Traditional methods (PLSR, SVM) exhibited comparable accuracy to deep learning models (DNN), likely due to the optimized spectral features selected through physical guidance. This suggests that feature engineering remains crucial even in deep learning frameworks. These findings collectively demonstrate that Maize-LCNet, which integrated E2D-COS, RTM, field spectroscopy, and TL, provides a reliable solution for leaf chlorophyll content (LCC) estimation in maize. The model's strong performance (R^2 = 0.65 in critical growth stages) underscores its potential for precision nitrogen management. Notably, our results align with recent studies [36,52] emphasizing that pre-training on large synthetic datasets followed by transfer learning significantly enhances model generalizability, particularly under limited field sampling conditions.

4.2. Optimized Bands for Maize Chlorophyll Estimation

The identification and optimization of sensitive spectral features play a pivotal role in ensuring robust performance for both regression and classification tasks in agricultural remote sensing. Traditional approaches, including vegetation indices [58], fractional derivative transformations [59], and recursive feature elimination [18], primarily rely on empirical spectral feature engineering derived from field measurements. While effective, these methods often face limitations in generalizability due to their dependency on site-specific data patterns. To address this challenge, our study introduces a physics-informed spectral optimization framework that synergizes enhanced E2D-COS with radiative transfer modeling, which not only ensures that the selected bands are resistant to structural influences, but at the same time responds significantly to canopy chlorophyll changes. The screened bands showed changes corresponding to the growth and development of maize: Big trumpet stage: dominated by the transition zone of the blue-green bands (418 nm, 453 nm, 506 nm), the valley of chlorophyll absorption (587 nm, 640 nm) and the early red edge (688 nm), reflecting the rapid growth of the leaves and the high demand for plant nutrients. Spinning stage: enhanced red-edge dynamics and near-infrared plateaus (688 nm, 723 nm, 767 nm), capturing canopy closure effects and photosynthetic optimization during reproductive phases. These findings of locations of chlorophyll-sensitive but resistant-to-structural-effects bands described above have similarities with existing studies (458 nm, 586 nm, 686 nm,690 nm, etc.) [60,61], but the present study uses radiative transfer modelling to clarify the rationale for the choice of this band. These bands collectively capture the spectral interplay between biochemical absorption and canopy structural development. The identification of these bands provides a reference for maize chlorophyll estimation studies.

4.3. Limitations and Future Directions

While this study demonstrates the feasibility of incorporating physical knowledge into deep neural networks (DNNs) for chlorophyll estimation, several limitations warrant attention. First, the DNN architecture may not fully capture the full complexity of radiative transfer processes, particularly the implicit parameter interactions within PROSAIL simulations. Future work should explore advanced architectures, such as convolutional neural networks (CNNs) or hybrid neural operators, to better model the hierarchical spectral–structural relationships inherent in canopy radiative transfer. Of course, although DNN model outperform the PLSR and SVM approach (Section 3.3.3), the use of DNN also increases the time and computational resources for model training, mainly because the DNN model structure is relatively complex compared to methods such as random forests, or simpler deep learning methods, and it is important to balance model complexity and cost in future research. Second, although the UAV-based hyperspectral platform meets farm-level precision agriculture requirements, its scalability to regional monitoring remains constrained. Satellite multispectral imagery—despite coarser spectral resolution—offers broader applicability. However, adapting our model to satellite data requires addressing cross-sensor generalization capabilities and atmospheric correction challenges.

5. Conclusions

The capacity to accurately monitor the health and growth of maize is of paramount importance for farmers and policymakers, as it plays a crucial role in guiding agricultural production and policy implementation. This study proposes a novel method for estimating maize leaf chlorophyll content (LCC) by integrating E2D-COS feature selection, transfer learning (simulated and field hyperspectral data), and the deep learning network (LCNet). The principal conclusions are summarized as follows: (1) The E2D-COS feature selection method combined with simulated data effectively identified structural interference-resistant spectral bands strongly correlated with maize LCC: Big trumpet stage: 418 nm, 453 nm, 506 nm, 587 nm, 640 nm, 688 nm, and 767 nm; Spinning stage: 418 nm, 453 nm, 541 nm, 559 nm, 688 nm, 723 nm, and 767 nm. (2) The E2D-COS-derived spectral bands enabled reliable LCC estimation across models, confirming the robustness of the feature selection methodology: The PLSR-based model achieved R^2 = 0.62 and RMSE = 3.87 g/cm and the CC-Net-field model yielded R^2 = 0.54 with RMSE = 4.96 g/cm. (3) The integration of E2D-COS feature selection with transfer learning and deep learning techniques significantly improved estimation accuracy: Compared to the CC-Net-field, the proposed Maize-LCNet model exhibited R^2 improvements of 0.06–0.11 and RMSE reductions of 0.57–1.06 g/cm. Compared to the existing studies, this study not only clarifies the spectral bands that are relevant to maize chlorophyll and resistant to structural influences, but also proposes an estimation method for high-performance estimation of maize chlorophyll content. The accurate estimation of chlorophyll content provides actionable insights for both farmers and policymakers. By monitoring real-time chlorophyll levels, farmers gain critical visibility into crop vitality, enabling data-driven better decisions on fertilization, irrigation, and pest management to optimize yield and resource efficiency. For governments, this information enables targeted policies to support precision agriculture and sustainable agricultural development. Certainly, the above method has limitations: the DNN may not fully capture spectral variations under chlorophyll changes, requiring more advanced architectures; UAV-based data also limits scalability, highlighting the need to address chlorophyll estimation at satellite scale in future work.

Author Contributions: Conceptualization, R.C. and L.R.; methodology, R.C. and L.R.; software, H.H. and Z.C.; validation, D.Z. and C.Z.; formal analysis, H.H. and H.F.; investigation, R.C. and L.R.; resources, G.Y. and H.Y.; data curation, L.R. and Z.C.; writing—original draft preparation, R.C. and L.R.; writing—review and editing, L.R. and H.Y.; visualization, Z.C.; supervision, G.Y.; project administration, G.Y. and H.Y.; funding acquisition, G.Y. and H.Y. All authors have read and agreed to the published version of the manuscript.

Funding: This research was supported by the National Key Research and Development Program (2024YFD1500802), the National Natural Science Foundation of China (42371373), the Beijing Academy of Agriculture and Forestry Sciences Special Fund for Technological Innovation Capacity Building (KJCX20230434), and the earmarked fund for CARS-02.

Data Availability Statement: Data will be made available on request.

Acknowledgments: We are grateful to the editors and anonymous reviewers for their constructive and helpful comments, which improved the quality of this paper.

Conflicts of Interest: Authors Riqiang Chen, Haikuan Feng and Haitang Hu were employed by the company Nongxin Science & Technology (Beijing) Co., Ltd. The remaining authors declare that the research was conducted in the absence of any commercial or financial relationships that could be construed as a potential conflict of interest.

References

1. Tanaka, A.; Ito, H. Chlorophyll degradation and its physiological function. *Plant Cell Physiol.* **2024**, *66*, 139–152. [CrossRef]
2. Gao, F.; Guo, J.; Shen, Y. Advances from chlorophyll biosynthesis to photosynthetic adaptation, evolution and signaling. *Plant Stress* **2024**, *12*, 100470. [CrossRef]
3. Singhal, G.; Choudhury, B.U.; Singh, N.; Goswami, J. An enhanced chlorophyll estimation model with a canopy structural trait in maize crops: Use of multi-spectral UAV images and machine learning algorithm. *Ecol. Inform.* **2024**, *83*, 102811. [CrossRef]
4. Guo, Y.; Chen, S.; Li, X.; Cunha, M.; Jayavelu, S.; Cammarano, D.; Fu, Y. Machine learning-based approaches for predicting SPAD values of maize using multi-spectral images. *Remote Sens.* **2022**, *14*, 1337. [CrossRef]
5. Zhang, R.; Yang, P.; Liu, S.; Wang, C.; Liu, J. Evaluation of the methods for estimating leaf chlorophyll content with SPAD chlorophyll meters. *Remote Sens.* **2022**, *14*, 5144. [CrossRef]
6. Khan, M.S.; Yadav, P.; Semwal, M.; Prasad, N.; Verma, R.K.; Kumar, D. Predicting canopy chlorophyll concentration in citronella crop using machine learning algorithms and spectral vegetation indices derived from UAV multispectral imagery. *Ind. Crops Prod.* **2024**, *219*, 119147. [CrossRef]
7. Ferreira, M.P.; Martins, G.B.; de Almeida, T.M.H.; da Silva Ribeiro, R.; da Veiga Júnior, V.F.; Paz, I.d.S.R.; de Siqueira, M.F.; Kurtz, B.C. Estimating aboveground biomass of tropical urban forests with UAV-borne hyperspectral and LiDAR data. *Urban For. Urban Green.* **2024**, *96*, 128362. [CrossRef]
8. Jiazheng, L.; Beibei, L.; Xiang, C.; Feng, S.; Juting, C.; Jing, W.; Qian, Z.; Xiefeng, Y. Monitoring of Leaf Chlorophyll Content in Flue-Cured Tobacco Based on Hyperspectral Remote Sensing of Unmanned Aerial Vehicle. *Smart Agric.* **2023**, *5*, 68.
9. Angel, Y.; McCabe, M.F. Machine learning strategies for the retrieval of leaf-chlorophyll dynamics: Model choice, sequential versus retraining learning, and hyperspectral predictors. *Front. Plant Sci.* **2022**, *13*, 722442. [CrossRef]
10. Afsar, M.M.; Iqbal, M.S.; Bakhshi, A.D.; Hussain, E.; Iqbal, J. MangiSpectra: A Multivariate Phenological Analysis Framework Leveraging UAV Imagery and LSTM for Tree Health and Yield Estimation in Mango Orchards. *Remote Sens.* **2025**, *17*, 703. [CrossRef]
11. Fei, S.; Xiao, S.; Zhu, J.; Xiao, Y.; Ma, Y. Dual sampling linear regression ensemble to predict wheat yield across growing seasons with hyperspectral sensing. *Comput. Electron. Agric.* **2024**, *216*, 108514. [CrossRef]
12. Sherstneva, O.; Abdullaev, F.; Kior, D.; Yudina, L.; Gromova, E.; Vodeneev, V. Prediction of biomass accumulation and tolerance of wheat seedlings to drought and elevated temperatures using hyperspectral imaging. *Front. Plant Sci.* **2024**, *15*, 1344826. [CrossRef] [PubMed]

13. Wieme, J.; Mollazade, K.; Malounas, I.; Zude-Sasse, M.; Zhao, M.; Gowen, A.; Argyropoulos, D.; Fountas, S.; Van Beek, J. Application of hyperspectral imaging systems and artificial intelligence for quality assessment of fruit, vegetables and mushrooms: A review. *Biosyst. Eng.* **2022**, *222*, 156–176. [CrossRef]
14. Li, D.; Wang, X.; Zheng, H.; Zhou, K.; Yao, X.; Tian, Y.; Zhu, Y.; Cao, W.; Cheng, T. Estimation of area-and mass-based leaf nitrogen contents of wheat and rice crops from water-removed spectra using continuous wavelet analysis. *Plant Methods* **2018**, *14*, 1–20. [CrossRef] [PubMed]
15. Liu, N.; Townsend, P.A.; Naber, M.R.; Bethke, P.C.; Hills, W.B.; Wang, Y. Hyperspectral imagery to monitor crop nutrient status within and across growing seasons. *Remote Sens. Environ.* **2021**, *255*, 112303. [CrossRef]
16. Chen, R.; Feng, H.; Yang, F.; Li, C.; Yang, G.; Pei, H.; Pan, L.; Chen, P. Estimation of leaf area index of winter wheat based on hyperspectral data of unmanned aerial vehicles. In Proceedings of the IGARSS 2019–2019 IEEE International Geoscience and Remote Sensing Symposium, Yokohama, Japan, 28 July–2 August 2019; pp. 1785–1788.
17. Manikandan, G.; Pragadeesh, B.; Manojkumar, V.; Karthikeyan, A.; Manikandan, R.; Gandomi, A.H. Classification models combined with Boruta feature selection for heart disease prediction. *Inform. Med. Unlocked* **2024**, *44*, 101442. [CrossRef]
18. Ji, T.; Liu, X. Establishing a Hyperspectral Model for the Chlorophyll and Crude Protein Content in Alpine Meadows Using a Backward Feature Elimination Method. *Agriculture* **2024**, *14*, 757. [CrossRef]
19. Gao, D.; Qiao, L.; An, L.; Sun, H.; Li, M.; Zhao, R.; Tang, W.; Song, D. Diagnosis of maize chlorophyll content based on hybrid preprocessing and wavelengths optimization. *Comput. Electron. Agric.* **2022**, *197*, 106934. [CrossRef]
20. Tang, J.; Alelyani, S.; Liu, H. Feature selection for classification: A review. In *Data Classification: Algorithms and Applications*; CRC Press: Boca Raton, FL, USA, 2014; Volume 37.
21. Pudjihartono, N.; Fadason, T.; Kempa-Liehr, A.W.; O'Sullivan, J.M. A review of feature selection methods for machine learning-based disease risk prediction. *Front. Bioinform.* **2022**, *2*, 927312. [CrossRef]
22. Zouhri, H.; Idri, A.; Ratnani, A. Evaluating the impact of filter-based feature selection in intrusion detection systems. *Int. J. Inf. Secur.* **2024**, *23*, 759–785. [CrossRef]
23. Gong, H.; Li, Y.; Zhang, J.; Zhang, B.; Wang, X. A new filter feature selection algorithm for classification task by ensembling pearson correlation coefficient and mutual information. *Eng. Appl. Artif. Intell.* **2024**, *131*, 107865. [CrossRef]
24. Zhang, Y.; Hui, J.; Qin, Q.; Sun, Y.; Zhang, T.; Sun, H.; Li, M. Transfer-learning-based approach for leaf chlorophyll content estimation of winter wheat from hyperspectral data. *Remote Sens. Environ.* **2021**, *267*, 112724. [CrossRef]
25. Park, Y.; Jin, S.; Noda, I.; Jung, Y.M. Continuing progress in the field of two-dimensional correlation spectroscopy (2D-COS), part II. Recent noteworthy developments. *Spectrochim. Acta Part A Mol. Biomol. Spectrosc.* **2023**, *284*, 121750. [CrossRef] [PubMed]
26. Park, Y.; Noda, I.; Jung, Y.M. Diverse Applications of Two-Dimensional Correlation Spectroscopy (2D-COS). *Appl. Spectrosc.* **2025**, *79*, 36–68. [CrossRef]
27. Thieme, A.; Jennewein, J.; Hively, W.; Lamb, B.; Whitcraft, A.; Mirsky, S.; Reberg-Horton, S.; Justice, C. Multispectral red-edge indices accurately estimate nitrogen content in winter cereal cover crops. *Agron. J.* **2025**, *117*, e70011. [CrossRef]
28. dos Santos Luciano, A.C.; Picoli, M.C.A.; Duft, D.G.; Rocha, J.V.; Leal, M.R.L.V.; Le Maire, G. Empirical model for forecasting sugarcane yield on a local scale in Brazil using Landsat imagery and random forest algorithm. *Comput. Electron. Agric.* **2021**, *184*, 106063. [CrossRef]
29. Wang, C.; Yang, C.; Zhang, J.; Kuai, J.; Xie, J.; Wu, W.; Zuo, Q.; Yan, M.; Du, H.; Ma, N. A PROSAIL model with a vegetation index lookup table optimized with in-situ statistics for rapeseed leaf area index estimation using diverse unmanned aerial vehicle sensors in the Yangtze River Basin. *Comput. Electron. Agric.* **2023**, *215*, 108418. [CrossRef]
30. Cheng, J.; Yang, H.; Qi, J.; Sun, Z.; Han, S.; Feng, H.; Jiang, J.; Xu, W.; Li, Z.; Yang, G. Estimating canopy-scale chlorophyll content in apple orchards using a 3D radiative transfer model and UAV multispectral imagery. *Comput. Electron. Agric.* **2022**, *202*, 107401. [CrossRef]
31. Bhadra, S.; Sagan, V.; Sarkar, S.; Braud, M.; Mockler, T.C.; Eveland, A.L. PROSAIL-Net: A transfer learning-based dual stream neural network to estimate leaf chlorophyll and leaf angle of crops from UAV hyperspectral images. *ISPRS J. Photogramm. Remote Sens.* **2024**, *210*, 1–24. [CrossRef]
32. Zhao, D.; Yang, G.; Xu, T.; Yu, F.; Zhang, C.; Cheng, Z.; Ren, L.; Yang, H. Dynamic Maize True Leaf Area Index Retrieval with KGCNN and TL and Integrated 3D Radiative Transfer Modeling for Crop Phenotyping. *Plant Phenomics* **2025**, *7*, 100004. [CrossRef]
33. Jiao, Q.; Sun, Q.; Zhang, B.; Huang, W.; Ye, H.; Zhang, Z.; Zhang, X.; Qian, B. A random forest algorithm for retrieving canopy chlorophyll content of wheat and soybean trained with PROSAIL simulations using adjusted average leaf angle. *Remote Sens.* **2021**, *14*, 98. [CrossRef]
34. Lu, B.; Proctor, C.; He, Y. Investigating different versions of PROSPECT and PROSAIL for estimating spectral and biophysical properties of photosynthetic and non-photosynthetic vegetation in mixed grasslands. *GISci. Remote Sens.* **2021**, *58*, 354–371. [CrossRef]

35. Ma, Y.; Song, X.; Zhang, J.; Pan, D.; Feng, H.; Yang, G.; Qiu, C.; Sun, H.; Zheng, C.; Li, P. Inversion of biophysical parameters of potato based on an active learning pool-based sampling strategy. *Int. J. Remote Sens.* **2025**, *46*, 320–339. [CrossRef]
36. Wan, L.; Zhou, W.; He, Y.; Wanger, T.C.; Cen, H. Combining transfer learning and hyperspectral reflectance analysis to assess leaf nitrogen concentration across different plant species datasets. *Remote Sens. Environ.* **2022**, *269*, 112826. [CrossRef]
37. de França e Silva, N.R.; Chaves, M.E.D.; Luciano, A.C.d.S.; Sanches, I.D.A.; de Almeida, C.M.; Adami, M. Sugarcane yield estimation using satellite remote sensing data in empirical or mechanistic modeling: A systematic review. *Remote Sens.* **2024**, *16*, 863. [CrossRef]
38. Wang, D.; Cao, W.; Zhang, F.; Li, Z.; Xu, S.; Wu, X. A review of deep learning in multiscale agricultural sensing. *Remote Sens.* **2022**, *14*, 559. [CrossRef]
39. Pichler, M.; Hartig, F. Machine learning and deep learning—A review for ecologists. *Methods Ecol. Evol.* **2023**, *14*, 994–1016. [CrossRef]
40. Avacharmal, R.; Pamulaparthyvenkata, S.; Pandiya, D.K.; Prakash, R.K.; Ranjan, P.; Balakrishnan, A.; Maheswaran, S. Comprehensive investigation on Deep learning models: Applications, Advantages, and Challenges. In Proceedings of the 2024 15th International Conference on Computing Communication and Networking Technologies (ICCCNT), Kamand, India, 24–28 June 2024; pp. 1–6.
41. Yue, J.; Yang, H.; Feng, H.; Han, S.; Zhou, C.; Fu, Y.; Guo, W.; Ma, X.; Qiao, H.; Yang, G. Hyperspectral-to-image transform and CNN transfer learning enhancing soybean LCC estimation. *Comput. Electron. Agric.* **2023**, *211*, 108011. [CrossRef]
42. Hu, B.; Huang, h.; JI, Y.; Zhao, X.; Qi, J.; Zhang, L.; Zhang, G. Evaluation of the optimum concentration of chlorophyll for determination of chlorophyll content by spectrophotometert. *Prataculturał Sci.* **2018**, *35*, 1965–1974.
43. Darvishzadeh, R.; Skidmore, A.; Schlerf, M.; Atzberger, C. Inversion of a radiative transfer model for estimating vegetation LAI and chlorophyll in a heterogeneous grassland. *Remote Sens. Environ.* **2008**, *112*, 2592–2604. [CrossRef]
44. Raya-Sereno, M.D.; Camino, C.; Pancorbo, J.L.; Alonso-Ayuso, M.; Gabriel, J.L.; Beck, P.; Quemada, M. Assessing wheat genotype response under combined nitrogen and water stress scenarios coupling high-resolution optical and thermal sensors with radiative transfer models. *Eur. J. Agron.* **2024**, *154*, 127102. [CrossRef]
45. Xu, Z.; Zhang, C.; Xiang, S.; Chen, L.; Yu, X.; Li, H.; Li, Z.; Guo, X.; Zhang, H.; Huang, X. A Hybrid Method of PROSAIL RTM for the Retrieval Canopy LAI and Chlorophyll Content of Moso Bamboo (Phyllostachys Pubescens) Forests From Sentinel-2 MSI Data. *IEEE J. Sel. Top. Appl. Earth Obs. Remote Sens.* **2024**, *18*, 3125–3143. [CrossRef]
46. Zhang, S.; Tian, J.; Lu, X.; Tian, Q.; He, S.; Lin, Y.; Li, S.; Zheng, W.; Wen, T.; Mu, X. Monitoring of chlorophyll content in local saltwort species Suaeda salsa under water and salt stress based on the PROSAIL-D model in coastal wetland. *Remote Sens. Environ.* **2024**, *306*, 114117. [CrossRef]
47. Li, D.; Wu, Y.; Berger, K.; Kuang, Q.; Feng, W.; Chen, J.M.; Wang, W.; Zheng, H.; Yao, X.; Zhu, Y. Estimating canopy nitrogen content by coupling PROSAIL-PRO with a nitrogen allocation model. *Int. J. Appl. Earth Obs. Geoinf.* **2024**, *135*, 104280. [CrossRef]
48. Qi, J.; Xie, D.; Yin, T.; Yan, G.; Gastellu-Etchegorry, J.-P.; Li, L.; Zhang, W.; Mu, X.; Norford, L.K. LESS: LargE-Scale remote sensing data and image simulation framework over heterogeneous 3D scenes. *Remote Sens. Environ.* **2019**, *221*, 695–706. [CrossRef]
49. Liu, S.; Jin, X.; Nie, C.; Wang, S.; Yu, X.; Cheng, M.; Shao, M.; Wang, Z.; Tuohuti, N.; Bai, Y. Estimating leaf area index using unmanned aerial vehicle data: Shallow vs. deep machine learning algorithms. *Plant Physiol.* **2021**, *187*, 1551–1576. [CrossRef]
50. Sharma, A.; Jain, A.; Gupta, P.; Chowdary, V. Machine learning applications for precision agriculture: A comprehensive review. *IEEe Access* **2020**, *9*, 4843–4873. [CrossRef]
51. Joshi, A.; Pradhan, B.; Gite, S.; Chakraborty, S. Remote-sensing data and deep-learning techniques in crop mapping and yield prediction: A systematic review. *Remote Sens.* **2023**, *15*, 2014. [CrossRef]
52. Ma, Y.; Chen, S.; Ermon, S.; Lobell, D.B. Transfer learning in environmental remote sensing. *Remote Sens. Environ.* **2024**, *301*, 113924. [CrossRef]
53. Tong, X.-Y.; Xia, G.-S.; Lu, Q.; Shen, H.; Li, S.; You, S.; Zhang, L. Land-cover classification with high-resolution remote sensing images using transferable deep models. *Remote Sens. Environ.* **2020**, *237*, 111322. [CrossRef]
54. Shen, Z.; Ramirez-Lopez, L.; Behrens, T.; Cui, L.; Zhang, M.; Walden, L.; Wetterlind, J.; Shi, Z.; Sudduth, K.A.; Baumann, P. Deep transfer learning of global spectra for local soil carbon monitoring. *ISPRS J. Photogramm. Remote Sens.* **2022**, *188*, 190–200. [CrossRef]
55. Jagota, M.; Ye, C.; Albors, C.; Rastogi, R.; Koehl, A.; Ioannidis, N.; Song, Y.S. Cross-protein transfer learning substantially improves disease variant prediction. *Genome Biol.* **2023**, *24*, 182. [CrossRef] [PubMed]
56. Rossel, R.A.V.; Shen, Z.; Lopez, L.R.; Behrens, T.; Shi, Z.; Wetterlind, J.; Sudduth, K.A.; Stenberg, B.; Guerrero, C.; Gholizadeh, A. An imperative for soil spectroscopic modelling is to think global but fit local with transfer learning. *Earth-Sci. Rev.* **2024**, *254*, 104797. [CrossRef]
57. Wu, B.; Ye, H.; Huang, W.; Wang, H.; Luo, P.; Ren, Y.; Kong, W. Monitoring the vertical distribution of maize canopy chlorophyll content based on multi-angular spectral data. *Remote Sens.* **2021**, *13*, 987. [CrossRef]

58. Chatterjee, S.; Baath, G.S.; Sapkota, B.R.; Flynn, K.C.; Smith, D.R. Enhancing LAI estimation using multispectral imagery and machine learning: A comparison between reflectance-based and vegetation indices-based approaches. *Comput. Electron. Agric.* **2025**, *230*, 109790. [CrossRef]
59. Dou, S.; Zhang, W.; Deng, Y.; Zhang, C.; Mei, Z.; Yan, J.; Li, M. Comparison of Citrus Leaf Water Content Estimations Based on the Continuous Wavelet Transform and Fractional Derivative Methods. *Horticulturae* **2024**, *10*, 177. [CrossRef]
60. Guo, Y.; Jiang, S.; Miao, H.; Song, Z.; Yu, J.; Guo, S.; Chang, Q. Ground-Based Hyperspectral Estimation of Maize Leaf Chlorophyll Content Considering Phenological Characteristics. *Remote Sens.* **2024**, *16*, 2133. [CrossRef]
61. Sudu, B.; Rong, G.; Guga, S.; Li, K.; Zhi, F.; Guo, Y.; Zhang, J.; Bao, Y. Retrieving SPAD values of summer maize using UAV hyperspectral data based on multiple machine learning algorithm. *Remote Sens.* **2022**, *14*, 5407. [CrossRef]

agriculture

MDPI

Article

Passion Fruit Disease Detection Using Sparse Parallel Attention Mechanism and Optical Sensing

Yajie He †, Ningyi Zhang †, Xinjin Ge , Siqi Li, Linfeng Yang, Minghao Kong, Yiping Guo and Chunli Lv *

China Agricultural University, Beijing 100083, China
* Correspondence: lvcl@cau.edu.cn
† These authors contributed equally to this work.

Abstract: A disease detection network based on a sparse parallel attention mechanism is proposed and experimentally validated in the passion fruit (*Passiflora edulis* [Sims]) disease detection task. *Passiflora edulis,* as a tropical and subtropical fruit tree, is loved worldwide for its unique flavor and rich nutritional value. The experimental results demonstrate that the proposed model performs excellently across various metrics, achieving a precision of 0.93, a recall of 0.88, an accuracy of 0.91, an mAP@50 (average precision at the IoU threshold of 0.50) of 0.90, an mAP@50–95 (average precision at IoU thresholds from 0.50 to 0.95) of 0.60, and an F1-score of 0.90, significantly outperforming traditional object detection models such as Faster R-CNN, SSD, and YOLO. The experiments show that the sparse parallel attention mechanism offers significant advantages in disease detection with multi-scale and complex backgrounds. This study proposes a lightweight deep learning model incorporating a sparse parallel attention mechanism (SPAM) for passion fruit disease detection. Built upon a Convolutional Neural Network (CNN) backbone, the model integrates a dynamically selective attention mechanism to enhance detection performance in cases with complex backgrounds and multi-scale objects. Experimental results demonstrate that the model has superior precision, recall, and mean average precision (mAP) compared with state-of-the-art detection models while maintaining computational efficiency.

Keywords: passion fruit disease detection; multi-scale detection; smart agriculture; image processing; deep learning

1. Introduction

Passion fruit (*Passiflora edulis* [Sims]), as a tropical and subtropical fruit tree, is loved worldwide for its unique flavor and rich nutritional value [1]. In recent years, with the popularization of agricultural greenhouse technology, the cultivation of passion fruit has gradually shifted towards efficient and large-scale production. However, with the expansion of cultivation scale and changes in environmental conditions, the problem of passion fruit diseases has become increasingly severe, posing a significant challenge to agricultural production [2–4]. Especially in the region where the Bayannur Wuyuan Meteorological Bureau is located, due to the area's unique climate conditions and environmental factors, the disease problems of passion fruit exhibit distinct regional characteristics. Therefore, accurately and timely detecting passion fruit diseases has become an important issue to improve agricultural production efficiency and ensure food safety. Traditional methods for passion fruit disease detection primarily rely on manual observation, traditional pathological diagnosis, and simple visual inspection [5]. Although these methods can identify disease symptoms to some extent, they have many limitations. Manual detection is not only

https://doi.org/10.3390/agriculture15070733

time-consuming and inefficient but also easily influenced by the experience and subjective factors of the inspector, leading to frequent misdiagnoses or missed diagnoses [6]. In addition, in agricultural greenhouse environments, diseases tend to spread rapidly, making it difficult for traditional methods to meet the need for timely detection and response. Therefore, the rapid development and application of disease detection technologies are crucial. Recent advancements in deep learning have significantly improved plant disease detection. Traditional object detection methods such as Faster R-CNN (Region-based Convolutional Neural Network), SSD (Single-Shot MultiBox Detector), and YOLO (You Only Look Once version) have been widely used in agricultural disease recognition [7], but their generalization ability remains limited under conditions of complex backgrounds and high visual similarity between diseased and healthy leaves. Additionally, existing models struggle with early-stage disease detection and often require high computational resources, limiting their applicability in resource-constrained environments. To address these challenges, this study introduces a lightweight detection framework incorporating a sparse parallel attention mechanism (SPAM) to improve detection accuracy and computational efficiency.

With the rapid development of deep learning and computer vision technologies, image recognition-based disease detection methods have gradually become mainstream [8]. In recent years, target detection methods based on Convolutional Neural Networks (CNNs) have achieved significant results in agricultural disease detection [9–11]. Huang et al. [12] proposed an improved YOLOv8-G algorithm to address the limitations of traditional methods. Experimental results show that the average precision (mAP) of the YOLOv8-G algorithm is 83.1%, a 3.3% improvement over the original model. Chen et al. [13] proposed a YOLOv8-MDN (Mixture Density Network)-Tiny model to improve the small-scale disease detection capability in passion fruit. Compared with YOLOv8s, their improved lightweight model achieved more accurate localization of small passion fruit targets. Specifically, the mAP50 improved by 2.2–94.8%, and accuracy and recall rates increased by 1.5% and 6.0%, respectively. However, these models still face limitations when dealing with complex backgrounds, occlusion, and multi-scale objects, especially when disease symptoms are highly similar to background objects, reducing the robustness of the models. In recent years, the application of Transformers in object detection has gradually emerged, especially with the DETR (Detection Transformer) model [14–17]. The method presented in [14] is valuable in the field of disease detection, but excessive discussion may obscure the original contributions of this paper. We have streamlined the description of this method and shifted the focus more explicitly to the innovative aspects of the sparse parallel attention mechanism proposed in our study. Chen et al. [18] proposed a Transformer model based on cyclic consistency for generating disease tomato leaf images for data augmentation. Experimental results showed that the proposed model achieved an accuracy of 99.45% on the PlantVillage dataset [19]. However, the model's robustness needs further validation to adapt to the complex and variable field environment. Li et al. [20] proposed a new object detection method called "Plant Leaf Detection transformer with Improved deNoising anchOr boxes (PL-DINO)". Experimental results demonstrated the superiority of PL-DINO compared with other advanced methods. Li et al. [21] proposed a high-precision and highly robust object detection model based on an improved real-time detector (RT-DETR) called Intelligent Multi-Scale Lychee Leaf Disease and Pest DETR (IMLL-DETR). Traditional disease detection methods rely on manual observation or pathological diagnosis, which are inefficient and prone to human error. Deep learning methods, while improving detection accuracy, still face technical challenges such as poor sensitivity to early-stage symptoms, high computational cost, and the need for substantial computational resources for field deployment. To address these issues, we propose a sparse parallel attention mechanism that reduces computational cost and improves focus on critical regions, overcoming these bottlenecks.

To overcome the limitations of traditional methods and existing deep learning approaches, this paper proposes a disease detection network based on a sparse parallel attention mechanism. The innovations of this method are as follows:

- Introduction of sparse parallel attention mechanism: This paper innovatively introduces a sparse parallel attention mechanism, optimizing the efficiency of attention computation in the Transformer model. By sparsifying the attention matrix, the computational complexity is reduced, enabling the model to focus more on feature extraction from key areas.
- Design of parallel differential loss: The proposed parallel differential loss guides the model to learn across multiple scales during training, enhancing its adaptability to diseases of varying sizes and forms. This innovative design helps the model learn features of diseases of different scales from multiple dimensions simultaneously, especially in handling multi-scale, complex-background disease data, which effectively improves detection accuracy and robustness.
- Adaptation to the diversity and complexity of agricultural greenhouse environments: The proposed method is optimized for the practical conditions in agricultural greenhouse environments, capable of handling changes in the greenhouse environment, the diversity of diseases, and the growth states of plants.

In conclusion, this study not only has theoretical significance but also strong practical value. Through field applications in the agricultural greenhouse environment of the Bayannur Wuyuan Meteorological Bureau, the proposed method can detect passion fruit diseases in real time and efficiently, helping farmers take precise preventive and control measures, thereby improving the sustainability and economic efficiency of agricultural production.

2. Related Work

2.1. CNN-Based Object Detection

Object detection, a core task in computer vision, focuses on identifying and locating objects in images [22]. CNNs, as the foundation of deep learning, have been widely used in this area. Recent advances in CNN-based object detection have led to significant performance improvements through various network architectures, training strategies, and optimization methods [23,24]. The two main frameworks for object detection are single-stage and two-stage detection.

2.1.1. Single-Stage Object Detection

YOLO (You Only Look Once) and SSD (Single-Shot MultiBox Detector) are the most representative CNN-based single-stage detection algorithms [25,26]. YOLO frames object detection as a regression problem, where the network directly predicts the object's location and class, eliminating the need for candidate boxes [27]. It predicts a fixed number of bounding boxes and their confidence scores for each grid cell. Each bounding box is represented by four parameters: (x, y, w, h), where (x, y) are the center coordinates, and w and h are the width and height. YOLO's loss function consists of localization loss and classification loss, representing the differences between predicted and actual bounding box positions and categories, respectively. The loss function in YOLO can be represented as

$$
\begin{aligned}
L =&\lambda_{\text{coord}} \sum_{i} ⊮\text{obj}\Big((x_i - \hat{x}i)^2 + (y_i - \hat{y}i)^2 + (w_i - \hat{w}i)^2 + (h_i - \hat{h}i)^2\Big) \\
&+ \lambda\text{conf} \sum i⊮\text{obj}(C_i - \hat{C}i)^2 + \lambda\text{class} \sum i⊮\text{obj} \sum_{c} (P_{i,c} - \hat{P}_{i,c})^2.
\end{aligned}
\tag{1}
$$

YOLO uses an indicator function $\mathbb{1}_{obj}$ that takes the value 1 when an object is present in the grid cell and 0 otherwise. The parameters (x_i, y_i, w_i, h_i) and $(\hat{x}_i, \hat{y}_i, \hat{w}_i, \hat{h}i)$ represent the predicted and ground-truth bounding box coordinates, respectively. C_i and $\hat{C}i$ are the predicted and ground-truth confidence scores, and Pi, c and $\hat{P}i, c$ represent the predicted and ground-truth probabilities for class c in the i-th bounding box. YOLO's advantages include speed and efficiency, as it performs object detection in a single forward pass, making it highly real-time [28].

SSD is another single-stage detection algorithm that performs object detection on feature maps at different scales, predicting bounding boxes and classes by using default boxes of various sizes [29]. Its loss function consists of localization loss, which measures the difference between predicted and true bounding box positions, and classification loss, which calculates the difference between predicted and true classes for each box. The loss function is given by

$$\begin{aligned} L = &\frac{1}{N_{obj}} \sum_i \mathbb{1}obj\left((x_i - \hat{x}i)^2 + (y_i - \hat{y}i)^2 + (w_i - \hat{w}i)^2 + (h_i - \hat{h}i)^2\right) \\ &+ \frac{1}{Nnoobj} \sum i\mathbb{1}noobj(C_i - \hat{C}i)^2 + \frac{1}{Nclass} \sum i\mathbb{1}obj \sum_c (P_{i,c} - \hat{P}_{i,c})^2, \end{aligned} \quad (2)$$

where N_{obj} and N_{noobj} represent the number of predicted boxes with and without objects, respectively; $\mathbb{1}_{obj}$ and $\mathbb{1}_{noobj}$ are the indicator functions for object presence; C_i and $\hat{C}_i$ are the predicted and ground-truth confidence scores, respectively; and $P_{i,c}$ and $\hat{P}_{i,c}$ represent the predicted and ground-truth probabilities for class c in the i-th bounding box. SSD's advantage lies in detecting objects of various sizes through multi-scale feature maps. Compared with YOLO, SSD strikes a better balance between accuracy and speed, making it more suitable for detecting dense and multi-scale objects, especially against complex backgrounds, where it excels at recognizing small objects [30].

2.1.2. Two-Stage Object Detection

Faster R-CNN is a two-stage object detection algorithm [31]. Unlike single-stage methods, it has two stages: region proposal and object classification with bounding box regression. In the region proposal stage, the RPN (Region Proposal Network) applies convolution to generate feature maps [32] and then slides a window over the feature maps to generate candidate regions, called anchor boxes. The RPN predicts the presence of objects and their positions for each anchor box. The RPN output includes the probability of an object being present and the regression offsets for adjusting the anchor boxes to better match the target's position and scale. Specifically, the RPN output can be represented as

$$\hat{p}_i = \text{sigmoid}(f(\mathbf{x}_i)), \quad (3)$$

$$\hat{t}_i = f(\mathbf{x}_i), \quad (4)$$

where $\hat{p}_i$ represents the probability that the i-th anchor box contains a target, $f(\mathbf{x}_i)$ is the output from a fully connected layer applied to feature vector $\mathbf{x}_i$ generated by the CNN, and $\hat{t}_i$ is the regression offset for the anchor box relative to the real target. In Faster R-CNN, object classification and regression are the core tasks of the second stage. The candidate regions from the RPN are input into an RoI Pooling (Region of Interest Pooling) layer for spatial alignment, followed by feature extraction through fully connected layers [33]. These features are then passed into two parallel networks: one for object classification and one for bounding box regression, where the classification network outputs probabilities for each class and the regression network predicts the location offsets between the region and the real target. The object classification and regression loss functions can be expressed as

$$L_{cls} = -\sum_{i} y_i \log(p_i), \tag{5}$$

$$L_{loc} = \sum_{i} \mathbb{1}_{[i \in \text{pos}]} \left((t_i - \hat{t}_i)^2 \right), \tag{6}$$

where y_i is the real class label of the i-th candidate region, and p_i is the predicted class probability for that region; t_i and $\hat{t}_i$ are the real and predicted regression offsets for the i-th candidate region, respectively; $\mathbb{1}_{[i \in \text{pos}]}$ is an indicator function that is 1 if the region is a positive sample and 0 otherwise. By combining the RPN with the CNN, Faster R-CNN enables end-to-end object detection, generating candidate regions and then performing classification and bounding box regression. This two-stage approach improves both the precision and efficiency of detection. Despite its success, Faster R-CNN faces challenges like high computational cost and difficulties in anchor box setting [34].

2.2. Transformer-Based Object Detection

In recent years, the success of the Transformer model in natural language processing (NLP) has led to its increasing application in computer vision (CV) tasks [35]. DETR, a Transformer-based object detection model, eliminates the need for traditional Region Proposal Networks and anchor boxes by using a global attention mechanism to directly predict object locations and classes [36]. The core idea of DETR is to leverage the Transformer architecture and its self-attention mechanism to predict the position and class of objects from the global features of the image. After the input image passes through a feature extraction network, the resulting feature map is represented as a 2D tensor $\mathbf{X} \in \mathbb{R}^{H \times W \times C}$, where H and W are the height and width and C is the number of channels. To include positional encoding, DETR introduces a positional vector $\mathbf{P} \in \mathbb{R}^{H \times W \times D}$ for each feature point, where D is the dimensionality of the positional encoding. The design of positional encoding can be implemented by using sine and cosine functions, which enables the model to effectively capture the spatial position information of feature points. The final combined representation of the image's features $\mathbf{X}$ and the positional encoding $\mathbf{P}$ can be expressed as

$$\mathbf{Z}_0 = \mathbf{X} + \mathbf{P}. \tag{7}$$

The feature vectors $\mathbf{Z}_0$ are input into the Transformer's encoder, and the output $\mathbf{Z}_1$ represents a global feature map with information from the image. This feature is used in the decoder for object detection. DETR adopts a query-based mechanism in the decoder, where queries interact with the encoder's output to generate predictions for each object. For each query q_i, the decoder's output $\mathbf{y}_i$ consists of the class prediction and bounding box regression parameters. Specifically, each query generates an output $\mathbf{y}_i \in \mathbb{R}^{1 \times (C+4)}$, where C is the number of classes and 4 represents the bounding box parameters. By introducing the self-attention mechanism of the Transformer, DETR transforms object detection into a set prediction problem, bypassing the need for candidate region generation in traditional methods [37]. DETR's strength lies in its end-to-end training and global information modeling, making it highly effective in complex scenarios. However, it still faces challenges, such as long training times and high computational costs, requiring optimization for real-time detection [38,39].

3. Materials and Methods

The objective of this section is to describe the materials and methodologies used for passion fruit disease detection in this study. It outlines the data collection process, including the dataset composition, annotation, and augmentation strategies, as well as the specific methods applied for disease detection. The section also explains the development and application of a novel disease detection network based on a sparse parallel attention mechanism, which aims to optimize computational efficiency and improve detection accuracy in complex, multi-scale agricultural environments. The methodology aims to provide a comprehensive framework for training, validating, and evaluating deep learning models in real-world agricultural settings.

3.1. Dataset Collection

In this study, passion fruit disease recognition is based on a dataset containing images of several common disease categories. To ensure the representativeness and comprehensiveness of the data, the disease dataset in this study mainly includes five common types of passion fruit diseases: ulcer disease (*Phytophthora* spp.), brown rot (*Monilinia* spp.), gray mold (*Botrytis cinerea*), anthracnose (*Colletotrichum* spp.), and late blight (*Phytophthora infestans*), as shown in Figure 1. The data collection took place in Wuyuan County, Bayannur City, Inner Mongolia, with collection occurring from July 2023 to October 2024. During the data collection process, the different types of diseases were first carefully defined and categorized to ensure that images for each disease category were accurately classified. Each disease type in the dataset contains at least 1000 images, as shown in Table 1.

Table 1. Number of images for each disease type.

Disease	Data
Ulcer disease	1092
Brown rot	1781
Gray mold	1267
Anthracnose	1514
Late blight	1339

Figure 1. Examples from dataset. (**a**) Ulcer disease, (**b**) brown rot, (**c**) gray mold, (**d**) anthracnose, and (**e**) late blight.

The data were collected by using a high-resolution DSLR camera (Digital Single Lens Reflex (Canon Inc., Tokyo, Japan)), specifically the Canon EOS 5D Mark IV, equipped with a 24-megapixel CMOS sensor, capable of capturing high-quality, detailed images. To avoid interference from environmental lighting, all images were captured under standardized lighting conditions with the aid of stable artificial light sources. The light sources used were LED photographic lamps with a CRI (Color Rendering Index) of 95 to ensure high color fidelity and reduce shadow interference. During the collection, leaf diseases were typically captured from a vertical or slightly tilted angle to ensure clear visibility of the disease spots. For fruit diseases, more attention was paid to capturing surface details in order to observe the impact of the disease on the fruit. The shooting distance was controlled between

30 cm and 50 cm to ensure that each image clearly presented both local features and the overall morphology of the disease spots. After each collection, images were subjected to preliminary screening and sorting to remove blurry, duplicate, or substandard images, ensuring high-quality final data. In terms of disease features, ulcer disease is characterized by round or irregular brown ulcer spots on the leaf and fruit surfaces, typically with a sunken center and slight decay. Brown rot is characterized by moist brown spots on the fruit, which rapidly expand, leading to soft rot on the surface. Gray mold mainly affects the fruit and leaves of the passion fruit, with spots that are typically gray or brown, often accompanied by a gray-white mold layer. Anthracnose lesions are usually round, starting as reddish brown and later becoming dark brown or black, affecting both fruit and leaves. Late blight generally appears as water-soaked lesions on the leaves, with fuzzy edges, leading to gradual leaf decay at the affected spots. Due to the variety of diseases and their diverse manifestations, images were captured at various growth stages and with different disease severities to better simulate real-world disease recognition scenarios. With this diverse set of images, the model can more accurately identify diseases and enhance its generalization ability in practical applications.

3.2. Dataset Annotation and Augmentation

3.2.1. Dataset Annotation

The task of dataset annotation typically includes two main components: the assignment of class labels to each object and the precise localization of each object through bounding boxes or polygons. Annotation is not merely an image processing task, but it directly impacts the model's ability to learn features and recognize objects during training. LabelMe is an open-source image annotation tool widely used in computer vision tasks, especially in object detection, image segmentation, and semantic segmentation, as shown in Figure 2. LabelMe supports a graphical interface that allows users to easily add labels and annotate bounding boxes for objects within images through simple interactive operations. The core functionalities of LabelMe include polygon and rectangular annotation, as well as the generation of corresponding annotation files based on user requirements. The tool stores annotation results in JSON format, containing information about the object's location, category, shape, and other details, thus greatly facilitating data management and processing. During the annotation process, it is first necessary to determine the position of each object. Traditional object detection methods typically use rectangular bounding boxes to mark object locations. The position of a rectangular box is represented by four coordinate values:

$$B = (x_{\min}, y_{\min}, x_{\max}, y_{\max}), \tag{8}$$

where B denotes the bounding box of the object, $x_{\min}$ and $y_{\min}$ represent the coordinates of the top-left corner, and $x_{\max}$ and $y_{\max}$ represent the coordinates of the bottom-right corner. This representation is concise and efficient but only captures the boundary information of the rectangular box and cannot accurately describe irregularly shaped objects. For more complex object shapes, LabelMe supports polygon annotations. In polygon annotation, the boundaries of an object are represented by a series of consecutive points $(x_1, y_1), (x_2, y_2), \ldots, (x_n, y_n)$, forming a closed polygon. The formula is expressed as

$$P = (x_1, y_1), (x_2, y_2), \ldots, (x_n, y_n), \tag{9}$$

where P denotes the polygon boundary of the object and (x_i, y_i) denotes the coordinates of the i-th point. Compared with rectangular bounding box annotation, polygon annotation can more accurately fit the shape of the object, particularly for irregularly shaped objects such as plant leaves or animals, resulting in higher annotation precision. In practical applications, LabelMe not only provides annotation tools but also integrates several convenient functions, such as the automatic saving of annotation progress, importing existing annotation data, and the batch processing of annotated images. These features not only improve annotation efficiency but also reduce human errors during the annotation process. To facilitate the operators, LabelMe also supports image scaling, rotation, and dragging, making the annotation process more flexible and efficient. Despite the convenience that LabelMe offers for data annotation, several challenges remain. First, the accuracy of the annotation data directly influences the subsequent model training performance. If the annotations are erroneous or inconsistent, the model may be disturbed by incorrect information during training, leading to a decrease in performance. Therefore, annotators must possess a certain level of expertise to ensure that each object is correctly annotated according to the task requirements.

In agricultural domains, particularly in crop disease detection and pest identification tasks, data annotation plays a crucial role. By using LabelMe, researchers can precisely annotate crop images, providing high-quality training data for deep learning models. For example, in the disease detection task in this paper, the researchers used LabelMe to annotate disease spots on passion fruit leaves and accurately marked the location and category of each spot based on the type and shape of the lesions. These annotated data will serve as the foundation for training deep learning models, helping them learn the features of various types of diseases and improving their detection accuracy.

Figure 2. Example of dataset annotation for disease detection. The ground-truth labels are illustrated.

3.2.2. Data Augmentation

Data augmentation is a crucial technique for enhancing the robustness and generalization ability of deep learning models. It involves applying various transformations to the original data during training, expanding the diversity of the dataset and effectively preventing overfitting, especially in cases with limited sample sizes. In this study, two data augmentation methods, namely, Cutout and CutMix, are employed. These methods introduce controlled pixel alterations to input images, simulating a degree of image variation, thus forcing the model to learn more robust and meaningful features. Cutout is a data augmentation method that improves model robustness by masking part of the input image [40]. Specifically, this approach involves augmenting the training dataset by randomly removing one or more rectangular regions from the image. In the implementation of Cutout, the occlusion region is determined by a rectangle located at a random position within the image, where the size and location of the rectangle can vary. The dimensions of the occlusion region, $w \times h$, are determined by a certain random distribution, typically generated by randomly selecting values for w and h within the width and height of the image. If the size of the input image is $W \times H$, Cutout will randomly select a $w \times h$ region within the image and set the pixel values of that region to zero. The mathematical expression for this operation can be represented as

$$I_{out} = I - C, \tag{10}$$

where I represents the original input image, I_{out} denotes the image augmented by Cutout, and C is a rectangular occlusion area, where the pixel values are set to zero.

CutMix is another innovative image augmentation technique that creates new training samples by mixing portions of two images [41]. Specifically, CutMix cuts two images according to a certain proportion and exchanges their regions to generate a new image. Let I_1 and I_2 represent two images, with corresponding labels y_1 and y_2. In CutMix, images I_1 and I_2 are cut and stitched together to form a new image I_{mix}. The cutting operation involves swapping a region R from image I_1 with a region of the same size from image I_2, resulting in a new image I_{mix}. The label of the mixed image, y_{mix}, is computed as a weighted average of the labels y_1 and y_2, where the weights correspond to the area proportions of the respective regions. Let λ denote the area ratio of the cut region R in image I_1; then, the label y_{mix} can be expressed as

$$y_{mix} = \lambda y_1 + (1 - \lambda) y_2. \tag{11}$$

In practice, λ is typically determined randomly, with values selected from the range $[0, 1]$.

3.3. Proposed Method

The overall structure of the proposed method begins with the processing of input data, which are passed through multiple modules for successive information extraction and processing, as shown in Figure 3. In the initial stage of the model, the data are processed through an embedding layer, followed by feature extraction via an attention mechanism and then passed to the multi-head attention layer. In this layer, the data are mapped into query (Q), key (K), and value (V) matrices and operated upon with corresponding weight matrices. Next, the data flow into the sparse parallel attention mechanism, where the attention matrix is sparsified to reduce computational complexity and enhance the model's focus. The processed features then undergo further processing through a feed-forward neural network (FNN) layer, and the output is passed to the detection head. In the output phase, after processing by multiple streaming heads, the output consists of target category and bounding box regression values, forming the final prediction result. The output of each module serves as the input for the next, refining the data layer by layer to ultimately achieve efficient disease detection for passion fruit. In this study, the sparse parallel attention mechanism optimizes attention computations by focusing on key regions of the input data, significantly reducing computational complexity. Unlike traditional fully connected attention mechanisms, our approach concentrates on the critical information in the image, enhancing computational efficiency while maintaining high accuracy. The mechanism works by using multiple sparse selectors in parallel, allowing for the simultaneous processing of multiple key regions, thus improving the model's robustness in complex environments. The dynamic selector is the core component of the sparse parallel attention mechanism. It dynamically selects the regions to be attended to based on the input data's features. Specifically, in each layer, the selector determines which areas are most important for the task based on the content of the image and the output from the previous layer, thus avoiding redundant computations and improving processing efficiency. By dynamically selecting the regions, the model can focus on key areas while adjusting its computational strategy, resulting in higher accuracy in multi-scale disease detection and complex-background environments, as shown in Table 2.

Table 2. Experimental setup table.

Item	Configuration
Hardware	NVIDIA A100 Tensor Core GPU
Operating system	Ubuntu 20.04
Software	TensorFlow 2.4, PyTorch 1.7
Development environment	Python 3.8
Training time	50 h (using a single GPU for training)
Batch size	16
Learning rate	0.0001
Optimizer	Adam optimizer
Hyperparameters	Dropout rate: 0.3; weight decay: 1×10^{-4}
Dataset	Custom passion fruit disease dataset, 10,000 images
Image resolution	512 × 512
Training epochs	50

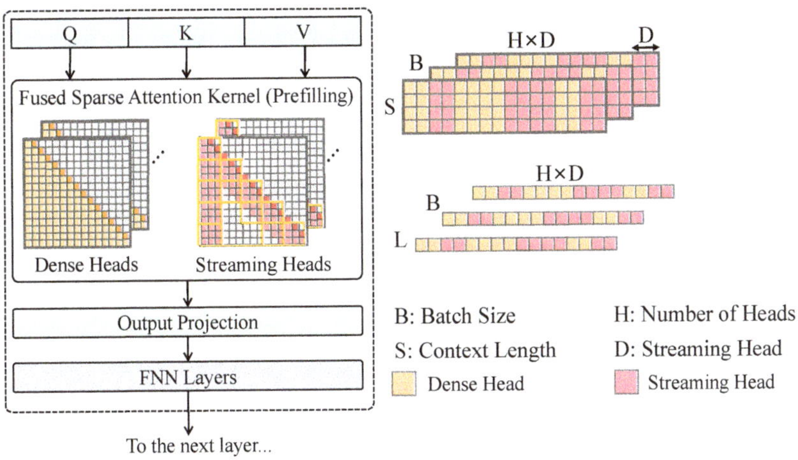

Figure 3. Overall architecture of the proposed disease detection network. The network incorporates a sparse parallel attention mechanism, which optimizes attention calculations through multiple heads and streaming heads for efficient disease feature extraction.

3.3.1. Disease Detection Network Based on Sparse Parallel Attention Mechanism

As shown in Figure 4, the proposed disease detection network based on the sparse parallel attention mechanism combines the advanced Transformer model in deep learning with sparse attention mechanisms to address the challenges of computational complexity and robustness in disease detection tasks, particularly when faced with complex backgrounds, occlusions, and multi-scale objects. The overall design concept of this network is to leverage the powerful modeling capability of the Transformer, especially the self-attention mechanism, combined with the optimization approach of sparse parallel attention, to effectively improve the model's efficiency and accuracy when processing large-scale image data. First, the input image data undergo preliminary convolutional layer processing to extract low-level features such as edges and textures. These features are then passed to the attention mechanism module. In traditional Transformer models, the attention mechanism generates attention weights by computing the relationships between the queries (Q), keys (K), and values (V), but this computation can be very costly, particularly when processing large images. To solve this problem, the sparse parallel attention mechanism is introduced, where instead of performing full connection computations for all input positions, a dynamic selection mechanism is used to compute only the important parts, thereby reducing the computational burden and increasing efficiency. Specifically, the sparse parallel attention mechanism involves multiple dynamic selectors, each responsible for selecting important regions from the input data for computation, rather than globally computing over the entire input. In each layer's processing, the selector dynamically selects the areas to focus on based on the previous layer's selection results and the current input features. This design allows the model to adaptively focus on key areas of the image while effectively avoiding the high computational complexity typically found in traditional methods. Through sparsification, the model not only improves computational efficiency but also focuses on the most information-rich parts of the image, thereby enhancing its performance.

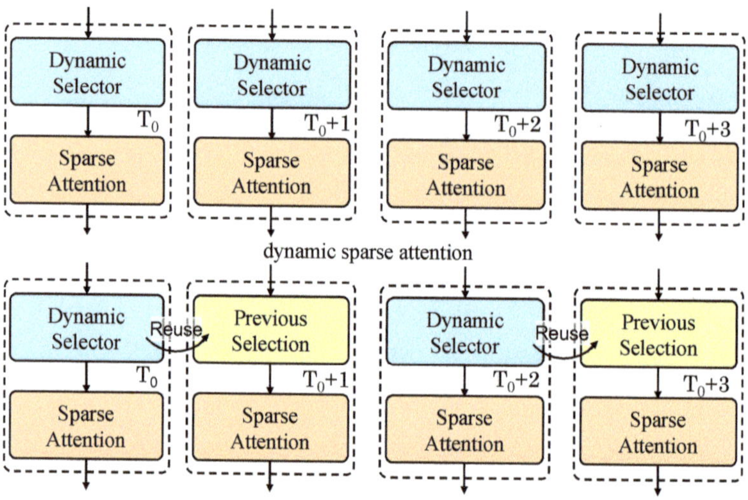

Figure 4. This diagram illustrates the architecture of the proposed disease detection network, which utilizes a sparse parallel attention mechanism. The network incorporates dynamic selectors that focus on key regions in the input data, followed by sparse attention operations.

The specific implementation of this model involves multiple sparse attention modules and an FNN. In each layer's sparse parallel attention module, the input feature map is processed by multiple dynamic selectors, with each selector performing weighted computations based on the input features. Each module outputs a sparsified attention matrix, which is weighted and passed into the next module for further processing. After several rounds of such processing, the output feature map is passed to the final detection head for disease classification and bounding box regression. Mathematically, the core idea of the sparse parallel attention mechanism is to optimize the attention computation process. However, in the sparse parallel attention mechanism, attention is computed by focusing on important query–key pairs, reducing the computational load. Through this method, the sparse parallel attention mechanism can effectively reduce computational complexity, especially when handling large-scale image data. Furthermore, to enhance the model's adaptability, a parallel differential loss design is also proposed in this work. During model training, the loss function includes not only traditional classification and regression losses but also introduces parallel differential losses targeting diseases at different scales. This design allows the model to simultaneously perform feature learning at different scales, thus improving its ability to detect multi-scale diseases. Through the parallel differential loss design, the model can perform feature extraction at multiple scales and gradually learn the key features of diseases at various scales during training.

3.3.2. Sparse Parallel Attention Mechanism

As shown in Figure 5, the sparse parallel attention mechanism is a novel method for optimizing self-attention computation, aimed at addressing the issue of excessive computational complexity in deep learning, particularly in object detection tasks. In traditional self-attention mechanisms, attention calculation is fully connected, meaning that each query (Q) is computed with every key (K), which significantly increases the computational burden as the number of input features grows. This results in the limitation of training and inference speed for the model. To overcome this issue, the sparse parallel attention mechanism introduces a sparsification operation, calculating only a subset of important attention values, thereby greatly reducing computational complexity. The core idea of the sparse parallel attention mechanism is that during attention computation, not all queries and keys are involved in the calculation. Instead, a selection mechanism is applied to choose the most relevant portions of the input features for computation. This method ensures computational efficiency while maintaining high performance. Compared with traditional self-attention mechanisms, the sparse parallel attention mechanism does not compute over the entire input but instead focuses on specific regions or features by "selectively" attending to them. This reduces the computational load and enhances the model's computational efficiency.

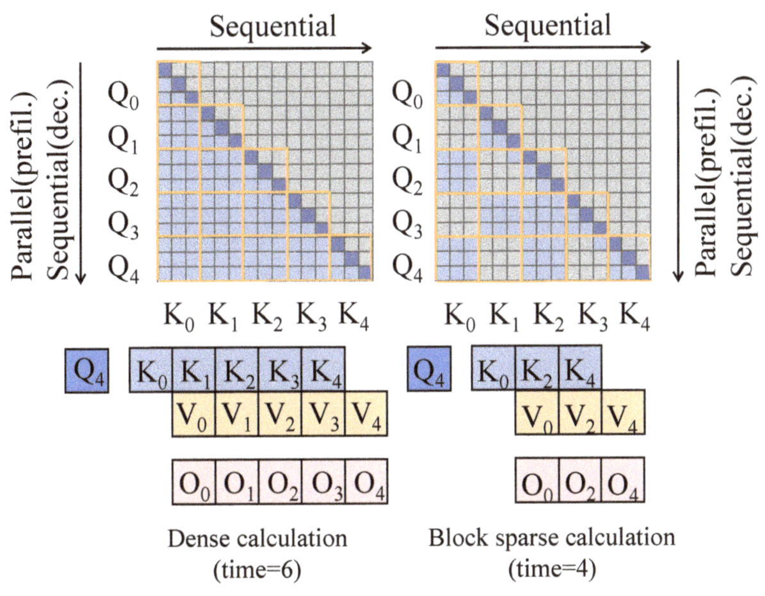

Figure 5. This diagram illustrates the computational process based on the sparse parallel attention mechanism, highlighting the comparison between traditional dense computation and sparse matrix-based computation.

In practice, the sparse parallel attention mechanism dynamically selects key regions for computation based on the output of each layer and the input features. Typically, the selection of sparsification is determined by weight values, feature importance, or a predefined selection strategy. For instance, when processing image data, the model can compute the importance of each region and perform attention calculations only on the most important areas, ignoring the influence of other regions. This enables the model to significantly improve computation speed while maintaining accuracy. Mathematically, the computation of the sparse parallel attention mechanism can be expressed as

$$A_{\text{sparse}} = \text{softmax}\left(\frac{QK_{\text{sparse}}^{T}}{\sqrt{d_k}}\right)V, \tag{12}$$

where Q represents the query matrix, K_{sparse} is the key matrix after sparse selection, V represents the value matrix, d_k is the dimension of the keys, and A_{sparse} is the computed sparse attention matrix. In traditional attention mechanisms, the K matrix contains all the key information, but in the sparse parallel attention mechanism, K_{sparse} contains only the most important parts after selection, thus reducing the computational load. The design of the sparse parallel attention mechanism offers several notable advantages. Firstly, by reducing the computation of irrelevant regions, the model can significantly improve training and inference efficiency, especially when handling large-scale data, leading to considerable speedup. Secondly, the sparsification operation helps the model focus on key feature regions, improving the model's performance, especially in complex backgrounds, where it effectively suppresses the interference from irrelevant information. The sparse parallel attention mechanism is particularly suitable for multi-scale object detection tasks. In such tasks, the size of the objects varies greatly, and the background is complex. Traditional fully connected attention mechanisms may fail to capture the features of small objects and instead increase the computational overhead. The sparse parallel attention mechanism can perform selectively computation based on the features of different objects, thus reducing computational complexity while improving the detection capability for small objects. By dynamically selecting important regions for attention calculation, the sparse parallel attention mechanism can adaptively adjust the computation process, better accommodating targets of different scales.

3.3.3. Parallel Differential Loss

In object detection tasks, traditional loss function designs are typically divided into two components: classification loss and regression loss. Classification loss is used to measure the discrepancy between the predicted and true class labels, while regression loss evaluates the error between the predicted and true bounding boxes. However, this traditional approach often optimizes for targets of a single scale and fails to effectively handle multi-scale, complex-background, and multi-form object detection problems. To address this issue, we propose a "parallel differential loss" design, which computes the loss of targets at different scales in parallel, significantly enhancing the model's adaptability to diseases of various scales. The core idea behind parallel differential loss is to guide the model to simultaneously handle classification and regression tasks at different scales during the training process, rather than relying on a single-scale loss calculation. Specifically, for each scale, classification loss and regression loss are computed for that scale; then, these losses are weighted and summed to obtain the total loss. The mathematical expression for this method can be written as

$$L_{\text{parallel}} = \sum_{i} \lambda_i \cdot \left(L_{\text{class}}(\hat{y}i, y_i) + \text{Lbbox}(\hat{b}_i, b_i)\right), \tag{13}$$

where $L_{\text{class}}(\hat{y}_i, y_i)$ represents the classification loss for the i-th target, $\hat{y}i$ is the predicted class, and y_i is the actual class; $\text{Lbbox}(\hat{b}_i, b_i)$ is the regression loss, where $\hat{b}_i$ is the predicted bounding box and b_i is the true bounding box; λ_i is the weight coefficient for the scale, responsible for balancing the contribution of losses from different scales. With parallel differential loss, the model can independently learn at each scale, integrating information from multiple scales for object detection. This method has the advantage of overcoming the limitations of traditional methods that focus on a single scale. By simultaneously optimizing multiple scales within the same training process, detection accuracy and robustness are improved. In agricultural disease detection tasks, where the shapes and sizes of diseases can vary significantly, the use of parallel differential loss allows the model to better adapt to diseases of different sizes and shapes, thereby enhancing its multi-scale disease detection capability. Traditional loss functions struggle with multi-scale targets, particularly when dealing with complex backgrounds and large variations in object sizes, which limits the model's performance. By introducing multiple scales, parallel differential loss can simultaneously focus on both large and small targets, achieving better results in multi-scale object detection. For example, when detecting diseases on passion fruit, where lesions vary in shape and size, traditional loss functions may not achieve high accuracy under diverse disease presentations. Parallel differential loss, by computing losses across multiple scales, helps the model learn the features of different disease types, thus improving its generalization ability and accuracy. Furthermore, parallel differential loss avoids the performance bottlenecks of traditional loss functions when dealing with complex scenes. In traditional methods, model training typically relies on error calculations from a single scale, and for multi-scale targets, the model is prone to false positives or missed detection results. Through multi-scale parallel computation, the model can effectively synthesize information from all scales, reducing the likelihood of errors in complex environments and enhancing disease detection accuracy.

3.4. Experimental Setup

3.4.1. Hardware/Software Platforms and Hyperparameters

As shown in Table 2, in this experiment, the hardware platform utilized is a high-performance computing cluster equipped with NVIDIA A100 Tensor Core GPUs, each possessing up to 40 GB of memory, thus enabling large-scale image processing tasks and deep learning model training. The CPU used is the Intel Xeon Gold 6248R processor, with 24 cores to support high concurrency, effectively aiding data preprocessing and parallel computing tasks. A memory configuration of 256 GB DDR4 ensures sufficient storage space when handling large datasets. The storage is managed by SSDs, offering high-speed read/write performance that enhances the data loading process. The operating system chosen is Ubuntu 20.04, known for its stability and compatibility. The network environment relies on a 10 Gbps high-speed network connection, ensuring efficient and low-latency data transmission. Regarding the software platform, TensorFlow and PyTorch were employed for the experiment. TensorFlow is primarily used for model training and inference, offering a rich API and efficient distributed training capabilities suitable for large-scale dataset training. PyTorch, on the other hand, is used for implementing the novel algorithms involved in the experiment. For experiment management and dependency handling, Anaconda was used as the package manager to ensure compatibility among various libraries. Image processing and augmentation were carried out by using OpenCV and Pillow, while LabelMe was used for annotating the dataset.

In terms of hyperparameter settings, the Adam optimizer was chosen for model training, with a learning rate set to 10^{-4}, utilizing a learning rate decay strategy to gradually decrease the learning rate for improved convergence. The loss function combines both classification and regression losses, where the classification loss is computed by using the cross-entropy loss function, and the regression loss uses the L1 loss function. A batch size of 16 was selected to balance memory usage and training speed. The training process was initialized with 5 epochs of pre-training, each consisting of 5000 iterations. To prevent overfitting, a Dropout rate of 0.5 was set, and data augmentation techniques such as Cutout and CutMix were employed. The training process spans 50 epochs, with a maximum training time of 6 h per epoch, ensuring the model achieves optimal performance within a reasonable timeframe.

3.4.2. Dataset Split

In this experiment, the dataset was divided according to the common 7:2:1 ratio, with 70% of the data allocated to the training set, 20% to the validation set, and 10% to the test set. This approach ensures that most of the data are used for model training, while retaining a portion for model evaluation and performance validation. Additionally, to further enhance the model's generalization ability and prevent overfitting, 10-fold cross-validation (*k = 10*) was employed. In this method, the dataset is divided into 10 subsets, with 9 subsets used for training and the remaining 1 used for validation. This process is repeated 10 times, each time with a different subset as the validation set, and the final model performance is evaluated by averaging the results from the 10 folds. This cross-validation technique effectively assesses the model's performance across different data subsets, enhancing the reliability and robustness of the experimental results.

In this study, we adopted a standard data partitioning method, dividing the dataset into training, validation, and test sets in a 7:2:1 ratio. Specifically, 70% of the data are allocated for model training, 20% are used for hyperparameter tuning and early stopping, and the remaining 10% are reserved for final evaluation. The primary purpose of 10-fold cross-validation is to optimize the model during training rather than for final testing. During the training phase, the training set (70%) is further divided into 10 subsets. In each fold, 9 subsets are used for training, and 1 subset is used for validation. This process is repeated 10 times, ensuring that each subset serves as a validation set once. The final model performance is evaluated by averaging the results across these folds, ensuring the robustness and generalization capability of the model. Regarding the concern about 5-fold cross-validation, we clarify that cross-validation is not applied during final testing. It is strictly used within the training phase for model optimization. After training, we use the separate 20% validation set for hyperparameter tuning and model selection. The final model evaluation is conducted on the independent 10% test set, which serves as a one-time assessment of the best-performing model selected during validation. No cross-validation is applied to the final test results.

3.4.3. Evaluation Metrics

To comprehensively and objectively evaluate the performance of the model, we used several common evaluation metrics, including precision (*p*), recall (*r*), accuracy (*acc*), F1-score (*F*1), and mAP (mean average precision). These metrics not only help assess the model's performance from different perspectives but also reveal the strengths and weaknesses of the model when dealing with different types of data. Precision (*p*) measures the proportion of true positive samples among those predicted as positive (detected as target objects). Recall (*r*) measures the proportion of actual target objects that the model successfully identifies. Accuracy (*acc*) is the proportion of correct predictions in classification tasks, applicable to classification models but also useful as a supplementary metric in object detection tasks. The *F*1-score (*F*1) is the harmonic mean of precision and recall, balancing both metrics. The *F*1-score is especially useful when the data are imbalanced, as it provides more guidance than precision and recall alone. The mAP is the core evaluation metric for object detection tasks, widely used to measure the overall performance of a model on detection tasks. *mAP* is calculated by averaging the precision (*AP*) of different target classes, where AP is calculated based on different Intersection over Union (IoU) thresholds. In this paper, both *mAP*@50 and *mAP*@50–95 are used. *mAP*@50 represents the average precision when the IoU threshold is 0.5, while *mAP*@50–95 computes the average precision over IoU thresholds from 0.5 to 0.95 (usually with a step size of 0.05) and then averages those values. Their mathematical formulas are

$$p = \frac{TP}{TP + FP}. \tag{14}$$

$$r = \frac{TP}{TP + FN}. \tag{15}$$

$$acc = \frac{TP + TN}{TP + TN + FP + FN}. \tag{16}$$

$$F1 = 2 \cdot \frac{p \cdot r}{p + r}. \tag{17}$$

$$AP = \int_0^1 p(r), dr. \tag{18}$$

$$mAP = \frac{1}{N} \sum_{i=1}^{N} AP_i. \tag{19}$$

where TP represents true positives, the number of target objects correctly identified by the model; FP represents false positives, the number of times the model incorrectly identifies background or non-target objects as target objects; FN represents false negatives, the number of target objects that the model fails to identify; TN represents true negatives, the number of background regions (non-target regions) correctly predicted by the model; $p(r)$ represents the precision corresponding to recall r; N is the number of classes; and AP_i is the average precision (AP) for the i-th class. For mAP@50, the AP is calculated at an IoU threshold of 0.5, while for mAP@50–95, it is the average of AP values over multiple IoU thresholds. These metrics effectively reflect the precision, recall, and overall performance of the object detection model.

3.5. Baseline Methods

In this study, several mainstream object detection models were selected as baseline models for performance comparison. These models include SSD [42], RetinaNet [43], YOLOv3 [44] and YOLOv4 [45], Faster R-CNN [7], and DETR [46]. SSD is an efficient single-stage object detection model that performs predictions on feature maps at different scales, using CNNs for rapid target localization and classification. RetinaNet addresses the class imbalance problem by introducing focal loss, effectively mitigating background noise commonly encountered in small-sample object detection. It improves detection capabilities for difficult samples by separately weighting low-frequency and high-frequency predictions. The YOLO series represents a class of typical single-stage object detection models. YOLOv3 and YOLOv4 further enhance the feature extraction network based on the original YOLO model, improving detection for small and dense objects. These models are widely applicable in real-time scenarios due to their high efficiency. Faster R-CNN, a classical two-stage object detection model, first generates candidate regions by using a Region Proposal Network (RPN), followed by classification and regression for each candidate region. Lastly, DETR, a novel object detection model based on the Transformer architecture, eliminates the region proposal step present in traditional models. Instead, it directly performs target detection within the global image context, using self-attention mechanisms to model targets, overcoming many local computational limitations inherent in traditional methods. The advantage of DETR lies in its ability to enhance the model's understanding of targets through global information modeling, demonstrating stronger robustness in complex scenarios. By comparing these baseline models, the advantages and shortcomings of models based on sparse parallel attention mechanisms in the context of passion fruit disease detection can be thoroughly analyzed, providing insights for further model optimization.

4. Results and Discussion

4.1. Experimental Results of Disease Detection Models

The purpose of this experiment was to evaluate the performance of various object detection models in the task of passion fruit disease detection. By comparing the detection capabilities of different models, the most optimal detection method could be selected. The experimental results for Faster R-CNN, SSD, RetinaNet, YOLOv10, DETR, YOLOv11, and the proposed model are shown in Table 3. The evaluation metrics included precision, recall, accuracy, mAP@50 (mean average precision at an IoU threshold of 0.5), mAP@50–95 (mean average precision at IoU thresholds ranging from 0.5 to 0.95), and F1-score. These metrics provide a comprehensive assessment of the models' performance in disease detection, allowing for an analysis of their strengths and weaknesses and providing theoretical guidance for practical applications.

Table 3. Experimental results of disease detection models.

Model	Precision	Recall	Accuracy	mAP@50	mAP@50–95	F1-Score	FPS
Faster R-CNN	0.84	0.79	0.81	0.80	0.50	0.82	29
SSD	0.85	0.80	0.82	0.81	0.52	0.83	25
RetinaNet	0.87	0.83	0.85	0.84	0.56	0.85	34
YOLOv10	0.88	0.84	0.86	0.86	0.56	0.86	41
DETR	0.89	0.84	0.86	0.85	0.54	0.86	39
YOLOv11	0.91	0.86	0.88	0.87	0.57	0.87	42
Proposed method	0.93	0.88	0.91	0.90	0.60	0.90	47

As shown in Table 3 and Figure 6, the proposed model performed excellently across all evaluation metrics, particularly in precision, recall, and F1-score, with values of 0.93, 0.88, and 0.90, respectively, significantly outperforming other models [47,48]. Specifically, YOLOv11 and DETR followed closely in terms of precision and recall but still lagged slightly in mAP@50–95 and F1-score, indicating that while these models perform well in certain metrics, they still face limitations in handling complex disease data, especially in terms of object detection accuracy [49]. Traditional models like Faster R-CNN and SSD performed relatively poorly, with lower precision and recall, and F1-scores not exceeding 0.83. These results suggest that although these models exhibit good performance on basic detection tasks, their detection capabilities are limited when faced with diverse and complex agricultural disease detection problems, due to their inherent model structures and learning capacities. In contrast, YOLOv10 and YOLOv11, with their optimized network structures and feature extraction methods, exhibited superior performance, particularly in achieving a good balance between precision and speed. DETR, as a Transformer-based model, was able to better understand the global information in the image through self-attention mechanisms, but its performance was slightly lower than that of YOLOv11. From a mathematical perspective, traditional CNN-based object detection models such as Faster R-CNN and SSD rely on RPNs and fixed default box strategies, which exhibit weak performance in detecting small objects and handling complex backgrounds. The region proposal process in Faster R-CNN leads to high computational complexity, and the model struggles to detect small and overlapping objects. SSD enhances detection capability through multi-scale feature maps, but still faces challenges when dealing with small and multi-scale objects, especially against complex backgrounds, where its reliance on default box strategies makes the model less robust. YOLOv10 and YOLOv11, through optimized feature extraction networks and end-to-end training, achieve a good balance between precision and speed, offering significant advantages in fast real-time detection. DETR's strength lies in the introduction of Transformer architecture, which allows for the global modeling of image information and better adapts to complex scene detection tasks. However, its high computational cost and longer training times result in slightly inferior performance compared with the YOLO series models in terms of real-time processing and multi-scale detection. The proposed sparse parallel attention mechanism optimizes the attention computation process and performs parallel computation across multiple scales, significantly enhancing model accuracy and robustness, especially in detecting targets against complex backgrounds and multi-scale scenarios, thus outperforming all other models.

Figure 6. Experimental results of different disease detection models. The proposed method is compared against SSD, RetinaNet, DETR, YOLOv11, YOLOv10, and Faster R-CNN.

4.2. Experimental Results of Disease Detection Models for Each Disease Type

The aim of this experiment was to evaluate the proposed model's ability to detect different types of diseases. By comparing the results across various disease types, the performance differences in detecting each disease type were analyzed, providing a foundation for further optimizing disease detection models. The experimental results for five types of diseases (ulcer disease, brown rot, gray mold, anthracnose, and late blight) are presented in the table. The evaluation metrics enable a comprehensive assessment of the model's performance when handling different disease types and offer theoretical support for the detection characteristics of each disease.

As shown in Table 4, the model's detection accuracy varied depending on the disease type. Late blight exhibited the best detection performance, with precision, recall, accuracy, mAP@50, and F1-score all showing the highest values of 0.97, 0.93, 0.95, 0.94, and 0.95, respectively. This indicates that the characteristics of this disease are relatively distinctive, allowing the model to effectively distinguish it. For anthracnose, gray mold, and brown rot, although detection accuracy remained high, performance was somewhat lower compared with late blight, particularly in terms of mAP@50–95 and F1-score, indicating a slight decrease in detection precision for these diseases. Ulcer disease performed relatively worse, with a precision of 0.89 and a recall of 0.85. Despite the high accuracy and F1-score, the model's ability to detect ulcer disease still showed some limitations. Theoretically, these differences can be explained by the disease's visual features and the model's learning ability. Late blight typically presents more characteristic symptoms with easily recognizable lesions that are relatively consistent in shape and size, making it easier for the model to learn the features. On the other hand, diseases like ulcer disease may have lesions that are irregular in appearance and distribution, making it more difficult for the model to capture stable features during training, which results in lower detection precision. Mathematically, the proposed model utilizes a sparse parallel attention mechanism, which effectively addresses multi-scale issues and complex backgrounds in disease detection. For diseases that are easier to detect, such as late blight, the model can quickly capture key features through global information modeling and sparse attention mechanisms, thus enhancing detection accuracy. For more difficult-to-detect diseases, like ulcer disease, where lesions have irregular shapes and distributions, the model must learn features at multiple scales. The sparse parallel attention mechanism optimizes the computation process and reduces unnecessary calculations, improving the model's ability to capture complex features. These mathematical optimizations enable the model to adapt to the diversity of different diseases, minimize background noise interference, and simultaneously improve robustness and detection accuracy.

Table 4. Experimental results of disease detection models for each disease type.

Disease Type	Precision	Recall	Accuracy	mAP@50	mAP@50–95	F1-Score	FPS
Ulcer disease	0.89	0.85	0.87	0.86	0.56	0.87	46
Brown rot	0.91	0.88	0.90	0.89	0.59	0.89	44
Gray mold	0.92	0.89	0.91	0.90	0.60	0.90	49
Anthracnose	0.94	0.91	0.93	0.92	0.63	0.92	48
Late blight	0.97	0.93	0.95	0.94	0.65	0.95	48

4.3. Ablation Experiment of Different Attention Mechanisms

The purpose of this experiment was to assess the impact of different attention mechanisms on object detection performance, particularly focusing on comparing the standard self-attention mechanism, the Convolutional Block Attention Module (CBAM), and the sparse parallel attention mechanism proposed in this study in passion fruit disease detection. Through this ablation study, a deeper understanding was gained of how each attention mechanism affects the model's detection accuracy, recall, and overall performance, providing a theoretical basis for further model optimization. The experimental results presented in the table indicate that the standard self-attention mechanism performed well, but there was still a noticeable gap compared with the proposed mechanism. The performance of the CBAM was relatively lower, suggesting that traditional convolutional attention mechanisms struggle with multi-scale and complex-background scenarios.

As shown in Table 5, it can be observed that the standard self-attention mechanism showed strong performance in precision, recall, and accuracy, particularly excelling in F1-score and mAP@50, outperforming the CBAM model. However, the mAP@50–95 of the standard self-attention mechanism was only 0.52, indicating poor robustness when dealing with multi-scale issues. While the CBAM, as a convolutional attention module, introduced spatial and channel-wise attention mechanisms, its overall performance was still inferior to the standard self-attention mechanism. This may be attributed to the limitations in the way the CBAM focuses attention when handling complex backgrounds and multi-scale objects, which hinders its ability to effectively capture detailed features. In contrast, the proposed sparse parallel attention mechanism performed the best across all evaluation metrics, especially excelling in mAP@50–95 and F1-score, indicating that this approach effectively improved detection accuracy and robustness in complex disease scenarios. From a mathematical perspective, the standard self-attention mechanism calculates the relationship between each query and all keys in a fully connected manner, which allows the model to capture global information but comes with high computational complexity, especially when processing large-scale images, causing a drastic increase in computational load. On the other hand, the sparse parallel attention mechanism reduces the computational complexity by sparsifying the attention matrix, minimizing the influence of irrelevant information, and focusing on more crucial areas of the image. This is particularly advantageous in multi-scale disease detection, where the model can efficiently capture features from lesions of varying sizes. Additionally, through parallel computing, the model can learn features from multiple dimensions simultaneously, enhancing detection accuracy. The CBAM attempts to extract more information by adding channel and spatial attention mechanisms, but due to the limitations of its mechanism, it was less efficient in improving model performance compared with the sparse parallel attention mechanism, especially when faced with complex disease features.

Table 5. Ablation experiment of different attention mechanisms.

Attention	Precision	Recall	Accuracy	mAP@50	mAP@50–95	F1-Score	FPS
CBAM	0.85	0.81	0.83	0.82	0.44	0.81	34
Standard self-attention	0.89	0.83	0.86	0.85	0.52	0.76	39
Proposed method	0.93	0.88	0.91	0.90	0.60	0.90	47

4.4. Ablation Experiment of Different Loss Functions

The purpose of this experiment was to evaluate the impact of different loss functions on the performance of the model, specifically comparing cross-entropy loss, focal loss, and the proposed loss function, in the passion fruit disease detection task. Through ablation experiments, the differences in how each loss function handles issues like sample imbalance, detection accuracy, recall, and overall performance were analyzed, providing theoretical support for selecting the most appropriate loss function. The experimental results in the table demonstrate that the cross-entropy loss showed relatively average performance, with low precision, recall, and mAP metrics, whereas focal loss exhibited significant improvements. The proposed loss function outperformed all other metrics, achieving the best overall performance.

As shown in Table 6, it can be observed that the cross-entropy loss yielded low precision (0.67), recall (0.63), accuracy (0.65), and F1-score (0.63), with mAP@50 and mAP@50–95 also at low levels. Although cross-entropy loss is well suited for some standard classification tasks, it struggles in object detection tasks, particularly in addressing class imbalance, leading to low recall and detection accuracy. Focal loss, which introduces higher weights for difficult samples, effectively improved the model's ability to detect small targets and adapt to complex backgrounds. Precision, recall, and F1-score were significantly enhanced, particularly mAP@50–95 and F1-score, which reached 0.82 and 0.82, respectively. Focal loss, by weighting easy and hard samples, forces the model to focus more on difficult samples, reducing interference from background noise. However, compared with focal loss, the proposed loss function showed even more significant improvements across all metrics, achieving a precision of 0.93, and recall and F1-score of 0.88 and 0.90, respectively, with mAP@50 and mAP@50–95 reaching 0.90 and 0.60. This demonstrates the model's powerful capability to handle complex disease data. From a mathematical perspective, cross-entropy loss typically faces challenges with class imbalance in object detection tasks. In real-world applications, background samples vastly outnumber target object samples, causing the model to focus too much on background learning, which hinders the detection of small objects. Focal loss addresses this by introducing a scaling factor that reduces the weight of easily classifiable samples and increases the attention on hard-to-classify samples, which helps improve small object detection, especially when the targets are small and difficult to detect. However, in extreme cases of sample imbalance, focal loss may still be insufficient because it only adjusts the weights of each sample, which may not capture all features effectively. In contrast, the proposed loss function not only tackles class imbalance in object detection but also introduces a parallel differential mechanism to handle multi-scale object detection. By calculating losses at multiple scales in parallel and applying weighted summation, the model optimizes detection accuracy across multiple dimensions, improving its ability to handle multi-scale targets. Additionally, by fully considering the differences between targets and backgrounds in the loss computation, the proposed loss function enhances the model's ability to recognize disease targets, particularly maintaining high detection accuracy and recall in cases with complex backgrounds and small targets.

Table 6. Ablation experiment of different loss functions.

Loss	Precision	Recall	Accuracy	mAP@50	mAP@50–95	F1-Score	FPS
Cross-entropy loss	0.67	0.63	0.65	0.64	0.32	0.63	31
Focal loss	0.85	0.80	0.83	0.82	0.43	0.82	35
Proposed method	0.93	0.88	0.91	0.90	0.60	0.90	47

4.5. Limitation and Future Work

Despite the excellent performance of the disease detection network based on the sparse parallel attention mechanism in various metrics, some limitations remain. Firstly, although the model demonstrates high accuracy and robustness in most disease detection tasks, its performance may still be affected by highly complex or heavily occluded diseases. Especially when disease symptoms closely resemble background objects, the model's discriminative ability may decrease, leading to false positives or false negatives. Additionally, due to the large variety of diseases, each with different symptoms and features, the model's training relies on a substantial number of high-quality annotated data. The accuracy and comprehensiveness of data annotation remain critical factors influencing the model's performance. In future research, the model's robustness can be further improved by expanding the dataset, introducing more types of disease images, and employing data augmentation techniques. Furthermore, for detecting complex backgrounds and small objects, more advanced attention mechanisms, such as cross-modal attention and global adaptive attention, could be considered to enhance the model's adaptability to multi-scale and multi-class diseases. Lastly, for real-time detection requirements, optimizing the model's inference speed on hardware platforms is essential to ensuring its efficiency in practical applications, such as in agricultural greenhouses.

5. Conclusions

A disease detection network based on a sparse parallel attention mechanism is proposed, aiming to address the accuracy and robustness issues in passion fruit disease detection. With the advancement of agricultural greenhouse technology, disease detection has become increasingly important, particularly when faced with complex backgrounds and multi-scale diseases, where traditional detection methods often encounter performance bottlenecks. The innovation of this study lies in the introduction of the sparse parallel attention mechanism, which optimizes the traditional self-attention mechanism, enabling the model to process multi-scale and complex backgrounds more efficiently. By performing parallel computations at multiple scales, the model can better focus on key features, reducing computational complexity while enhancing its ability to extract detailed information. Furthermore, a parallel differential loss is designed, further improving the model's adaptability to different diseases and enhancing both the accuracy and robustness of disease detection. In experiments, the proposed model achieved outstanding results in passion fruit disease detection. The model reached a precision of 0.93, a recall of 0.88, an accuracy of 0.91, an F1-score of 0.90, an mAP@50 of 0.90, and an mAP@50–95 of 0.60, outperforming other comparison models, including DETR, Faster R-CNN, YOLOv4, YOLOv3, RetinaNet, and SSD. Notably, in the presence of complex backgrounds and multi-scale lesions, the proposed sparse parallel attention mechanism performed excellently, maintaining low false detection and missed detection rates while achieving high precision and recall.

Author Contributions: Conceptualization, Y.H., N.Z., X.G. and C.L.; Data curation, S.L. and M.K.; Formal analysis, L.Y. and Y.G.; Funding acquisition, C.L.; Investigation, L.Y. and M.K.; Methodology, Y.H., N.Z. and X.G.; Project administration, C.L.; Resources, S.L. and M.K.; Software, Y.H., N.Z., X.G. and S.L.; Supervision, C.L.; Validation, L.Y. and Y.G.; Visualization, Y.G.; Writing—original draft, Y.H., N.Z., X.G., S.L., L.Y., M.K., Y.G. and C.L.; Y.H., N.Z. and X.G. contributed equally to this work. All authors have read and agreed to the published version of the manuscript.

Funding: The authors would like to express their sincere gratitude to the Computer Association of China Agricultural University (ECC) for their valuable technical support. Upon the acceptance of this paper, the project code and the dataset will be made publicly available to facilitate further research and development in this field.

Data Availability Statement: The data presented in this study are available upon request from the corresponding author.

Conflicts of Interest: The authors declare no conflicts of interest.

References

1. Asande, L.K.; Ombori, O.; Oduor, R.O.; Nchore, S.B.; Nyaboga, E.N. Occurrence of passion fruit woodiness disease in the coastal lowlands of Kenya and screening of passion fruit genotypes for resistance to passion fruit woodiness disease. *BMC Plant Biol.* **2023**, *23*, 544. [CrossRef] [PubMed]
2. Wang, Y.; Teng, Y.; Zhang, J.; Zhang, Z.; Wang, C.; Wu, X.; Long, X. Passion fruit plants alter the soil microbial community with continuous cropping and improve plant disease resistance by recruiting beneficial microorganisms. *PLoS ONE* **2023**, *18*, e0281854.
3. Do, D.H.; Chong, Y.H.; Ha, V.C.; Cheng, H.W.; Chen, Y.K.; Bui, T.N.L.; Nguyen, T.B.N.; Yeh, S.D. Characterization and detection of Passiflora mottle virus and two other potyviruses causing passionfruit woodiness disease in Vietnam. *Phytopathology®* **2021**, *111*, 1675–1685. [CrossRef]
4. Zhang, Y.; Lv, C. TinySegformer: A lightweight visual segmentation model for real-time agricultural pest detection. *Comput. Electron. Agric.* **2024**, *218*, 108740.
5. Zhang, S.; Ma, Y.; Chen, J.; Yu, M.; Zhao, Q.; Jing, B.; Yang, N.; Ma, X.; Wang, Y. Chemical composition, pharmacological effects, and parasitic mechanisms of Cistanche deserticola: An update. *Phytomedicine* **2024**, *132*, 155808.
6. Kibriya, H.; Abdullah, I.; Nasrullah, A. Plant disease identification and classification using convolutional neural network and SVM. In Proceedings of the 2021 International Conference on Frontiers of Information Technology (FIT), Islamabad, Pakistan, 13–14 December 2021; pp. 264–268.
7. Ren, S.; He, K.; Girshick, R.; Sun, J. Faster R-CNN: Towards real-time object detection with region proposal networks. *IEEE Trans. Pattern Anal. Mach. Intell.* **2016**, *39*, 1137–1149.
8. Zhang, Y.; Wa, S.; Liu, Y.; Zhou, X.; Sun, P.; Ma, Q. High-accuracy detection of maize leaf diseases CNN based on multi-pathway activation function module. *Remote Sens.* **2021**, *13*, 4218. [CrossRef]
9. Sun, Q.; Li, P.; He, C.; Song, Q.; Chen, J.; Kong, X.; Luo, Z. A lightweight and high-precision passion fruit YOLO detection model for deployment in embedded devices. *Sensors* **2024**, *24*, 4942. [CrossRef]
10. Preanto, S.A.; Ahad, M.T.; Emon, Y.R.; Mustofa, S.; Alamin, M. A Semantic Segmentation Approach on Sweet Orange Leaf Diseases Detection Utilizing YOLO. *arXiv* **2024**, arXiv:2409.06671.
11. Zhang, Y.; Wa, S.; Zhang, L.; Lv, C. Automatic plant disease detection based on tranvolution detection network with GAN modules using leaf images. *Front. Plant Sci.* **2022**, *13*, 875693. [CrossRef]
12. Huang, L.; Chen, M.; Peng, Z. Yolov8-g: An improved yolov8 model for major disease detection in dragon fruit stems. *Sensors* **2024**, *24*, 5034. [CrossRef] [PubMed]
13. Chen, D.; Lin, F.; Lu, C.; Zhuang, J.; Su, H.; Zhang, D.; He, J. YOLOv8-MDN-Tiny: A lightweight model for multi-scale disease detection of postharvest golden passion fruit. *Postharvest Biol. Technol.* **2025**, *219*, 113281.
14. Huangfu, Y.; Huang, Z.; Yang, X.; Zhang, Y.; Li, W.; Shi, J.; Yang, L. HHS-RT-DETR: A Method for the Detection of Citrus Greening Disease. *Agronomy* **2024**, *14*, 2900. [CrossRef]
15. Wang, H.; Nguyen, T.H.; Nguyen, T.N.; Dang, M. PD-TR: End-to-end plant diseases detection using a transformer. *Comput. Electron. Agric.* **2024**, *224*, 109123.
16. Zhang, Y.; Yang, X.; Liu, Y.; Zhou, J.; Huang, Y.; Li, J.; Zhang, L.; Ma, Q. A time-series neural network for pig feeding behavior recognition and dangerous detection from videos. *Comput. Electron. Agric.* **2024**, *218*, 108710.
17. Redmon, J.; Divvala, S.; Girshick, R.; Farhadi, A. You only look once: Unified, real-time object detection. In Proceedings of the IEEE Conference on Computer Vision and Pattern Recognition, Las Vegas, NV, USA, 27–30 June 2016; pp. 779–788.

18. Chen, Z.; Wang, G.; Lv, T.; Zhang, X. Using a Hybrid Convolutional Neural Network with a Transformer Model for Tomato Lea Disease Detection. *Agronomy* **2024**, *14*, 673. [CrossRef]
19. Singh, D.; Jain, N.; Jain, P.; Kayal, P.; Kumawat, S.; Batra, N. PlantDoc: A dataset for visual plant disease detection. In Proceeding of the 7th ACM IKDD CoDS and 25th COMAD; New York, NY, USA, 15 January 2020; pp. 249–253.
20. Li, W.; Zhu, L.; Liu, J. PL-DINO: An improved transformer-based method for plant leaf disease detection. *Agriculture* **2024** *14*, 691. [CrossRef]
21. Li, Z.; Shen, Y.; Tang, J.; Zhao, J.; Chen, Q.; Zou, H.; Kuang, Y. IMLL-DETR: An intelligent model for detecting multi-scale litch leaf diseases and pests in complex agricultural environments. *Expert Syst. Appl.* **2025**, *273*, 126816.
22. Kaur, R.; Singh, S. A comprehensive review of object detection with deep learning. *Digit. Signal Process.* **2023**, *132*, 103812.
23. Liu, Y.; Sun, P.; Wergeles, N.; Shang, Y. A survey and performance evaluation of deep learning methods for small object detectior *Expert Syst. Appl.* **2021**, *172*, 114602.
24. Wang, A.; Chen, H.; Liu, L.; Chen, K.; Lin, Z.; Han, J.; Ding, G. Yolov10: Real-time end-to-end object detection. *Adv. Neural Inf Process. Syst.* **2025**, *37*, 107984–108011.
25. Vijayakumar, A.; Vairavasundaram, S. Yolo-based object detection models: A review and its applications. *Multimed. Tools Appl* **2024**, *83*, 83535–83574. [CrossRef]
26. Lu, X.; Ji, J.; Xing, Z.; Miao, Q. Attention and feature fusion SSD for remote sensing object detection. *IEEE Trans. Instrum. Meas* **2021**, *70*, 1–9. [CrossRef]
27. Zhang, Z.; Lu, X.; Cao, G.; Yang, Y.; Jiao, L.; Liu, F. ViT-YOLO: Transformer-based YOLO for object detection. In Proceedings of the IEEE/CVF International Conference on Computer Vision, Montreal, QC, Canada, 10–17 October 2021; pp. 2799–2808.
28. Li, S.; Li, Y.; Li, Y.; Li, M.; Xu, X. Yolo-firi: Improved yolov5 for infrared image object detection. *IEEE Access* **2021**, *9*, 141861–141875 [CrossRef]
29. Zheng, W.; Tang, W.; Jiang, L.; Fu, C.W. SE-SSD: Self-ensembling single-stage object detector from point cloud. In Proceedings of the IEEE/CVF Conference on Computer Vision and Pattern Recognition, Nashville, TN, USA, 20–25 June 2021; pp. 14494–14503
30. Cheng, L.; Ji, Y.; Li, C.; Liu, X.; Fang, G. Improved SSD network for fast concealed object detection and recognition in passive terahertz security images. *Sci. Rep.* **2022**, *12*, 12082. [CrossRef]
31. Li, W. Analysis of object detection performance based on Faster R-CNN. *J. Phys. Conf. Ser. Iop Publ.* **2021**, *1827*, 012085. [CrossRef]
32. Qiao, L.; Zhao, Y.; Li, Z.; Qiu, X.; Wu, J.; Zhang, C. Defrcn: Decoupled faster r-cnn for few-shot object detection. In Proceedings of the IEEE/CVF International Conference on Computer Vision, Montreal, QC, Canada, 10–17 October 2021; pp. 8681–8690.
33. Avola, D.; Cinque, L.; Diko, A.; Fagioli, A.; Foresti, G.L.; Mecca, A.; Pannone, D.; Piciarelli, C. MS-Faster R-CNN: Multi-stream backbone for improved Faster R-CNN object detection and aerial tracking from UAV images. *Remote Sens.* **2021**, *13*, 1670 [CrossRef]
34. Han, G.; Huang, S.; Ma, J.; He, Y.; Chang, S.F. Meta faster r-cnn: Towards accurate few-shot object detection with attentive feature alignment. In Proceedings of the AAAI Conference on Artificial Intelligence, Online, 22 February–1 March 2022; Volume 36, pp. 780–789.
35. Li, Y.; Miao, N.; Ma, L.; Shuang, F.; Huang, X. Transformer for object detection: Review and benchmark. *Eng. Appl. Artif. Intell.* **2023**, *126*, 107021. [CrossRef]
36. Zhang, H.; Li, F.; Liu, S.; Zhang, L.; Su, H.; Zhu, J.; Ni, L.M.; Shum, H.Y. Dino: Detr with improved denoising anchor boxes for end-to-end object detection. *arXiv* **2022**, arXiv:2203.03605.
37. Pu, Y.; Liang, W.; Hao, Y.; Yuan, Y.; Yang, Y.; Zhang, C.; Hu, H.; Huang, G. Rank-DETR for high quality object detection. *Adv. Neural Inf. Process. Syst.* **2023**, *36*, 16100–16113.
38. Yao, Z.; Ai, J.; Li, B.; Zhang, C. Efficient detr: Improving end-to-end object detector with dense prior. *arXiv* **2021**, arXiv:2104.01318.
39. Ouyang, H. Deyo: Detr with yolo for end-to-end object detection. *arXiv* **2024**, arXiv:2402.16370.
40. DeVries, T.; Taylor, G.W. Improved Regularization of Convolutional Neural Networks with Cutout. *arXiv* **2017**, arXiv:1708.04552.
41. Yun, S.; Han, D.; Oh, S.J.; Chun, S.; Choe, J.; Yoo, Y. CutMix: Regularization Strategy to Train Strong Classifiers With Localizable Features. In Proceedings of the IEEE/CVF International Conference on Computer Vision (ICCV), Seoul, Korea, 27 October–2 November 2019.
42. Liu, W.; Anguelov, D.; Erhan, D.; Szegedy, C.; Reed, S.; Fu, C.Y.; Berg, A.C. Ssd: Single shot multibox detector. In Proceedings of the Computer Vision–ECCV 2016: 14th European Conference, Amsterdam, The Netherlands, 11–14 October 2016; Proceedings, Part I 14; Springer: Berlin/Heidelberg, Germany, 2016; pp. 21–37.
43. Lin, T.Y.; Goyal, P.; Girshick, R.; He, K.; Dollár, P. Focal loss for dense object detection. In Proceedings of the IEEE International Conference on Computer Vision, Venice, Italy, 22–29 October 2017; pp. 2980–2988.
44. Redmon, J.; Farhadi, A. Yolov3: An incremental improvement. *arXiv* **2018**, arXiv:1804.02767.
45. Aldakheel, E.A.; Zakariah, M.; Alabdalall, A.H. Detection and identification of plant leaf diseases using YOLOv4. *Front. Plant Sci.* **2024**, *15*, 1355941. [CrossRef]

46. Carion, N.; Massa, F.; Synnaeve, G.; Usunier, N.; Kirillov, A.; Zagoruyko, S. End-to-end object detection with transformers. In Proceedings of the European Conference on Computer Vision, Glasgow, UK, 23–28 August 2020; Springer: Berlin/Heidelberg, Germany, 2020; pp. 213–229.
47. Zhao, Z.Q.; Zheng, P.; Xu, S.T.; Wu, X. Object Detection With Deep Learning: A Review. *IEEE Trans. Neural Netw. Learn. Syst.* **2019**, *30*, 3212–3232. [CrossRef]
48. Sayed, A.; Zaki, M. Comparison of Deep Learning Models for Agricultural Disease Detection. *Int. J. Comput. Appl.* **2020**, *175*, 30–38.
49. Tay, Y.; Bahri, D.; Yang, L.; Metzler, D.; Juan, D.C. Sparse Sinkhorn Attention. In *Proceedings of Machine Learning Research, Proceedings of the 37th International Conference on Machine Learning, Red Hook, NY, USA, 13–18 July 2020*; Daume, H., III, Singh, A., Eds.; ACM Digital Library: New York, NY, USA, 2020; Volume 119, pp. 9438–9447.

agriculture

MDPI

Article

Estimation Model of Corn Leaf Area Index Based on Improved CNN

Chengkai Yang [1,†], Jingkai Lei [1,†], Zhihao Liu [1], Shufeng Xiong [1], Lei Xi [1,2], Jian Wang [1], Hongbo Qiao [1,2,*] and Lei Shi [1,2,*]

[1] College of Information and Management Science, Henan Agricultural University, Zhengzhou 450046, China; yck03185@stu.henau.edu.cn (C.Y.); ljk2000@stu.henau.edu.cn (J.L.); lzh1229@stu.henau.edu.cn (Z.L.); xsf@whu.edu.cn (S.X.); xil@henau.edu.cn (L.X.); leonw63@mail.bnu.edu.cn (J.W.)

[2] Henan Grain Crop Collaborative Innovation Center, Zhengzhou 450046, China

[*] Correspondence: qiaohb@henau.edu.cn (H.Q.); shilei@henau.edu.cn (L.S.); Tel.: +86-0371-56990030 (L.S.)

[†] These authors contributed equally to this work.

Abstract: In response to the issues of high complexity and low efficiency associated with the current reliance on manual sampling and instrumental measurement for obtaining maize leaf area index (LAI), this study constructed a maize image dataset comprising 624 images from three growth stages of summer maize in the Henan region, namely the jointing stage, small trumpet stage, and large trumpet stage. Furthermore, a maize LAI estimation model named LAINet, based on an improved convolutional neural network (CNN), was proposed. LAI estimation was carried out at these three key growth stages. In this study, the output structure was improved based on the ResNet architecture to adapt to regression tasks. The Triplet module was introduced to achieve feature fusion and self-attention mechanisms, thereby enhancing the accuracy of maize LAI estimation. The model structure was adjusted to enable the integration of growth-stage information, and the loss function was improved to accelerate the convergence speed of the network model. The model was validated on the self-constructed dataset. The results showed that the incorporation of attention mechanisms, integration of growth-stage information, and improvement of the loss function increased the model's R^2 by 0.04, 0.15, and 0.05, respectively. Among these, the integration of growth-stage information led to the greatest improvement, with the R^2 increasing directly from 0.54 to 0.69. The improved model, LAINet, achieved an R^2 of 0.81, which indicates that it can effectively estimate the LAI of maize. This model can provide information technology support for the phenotypic monitoring of field crops.

Keywords: corn; leaf area index estimation; convolutional neural network regression; LAINet

1. Introduction

Corn, as one of the world's most important staple crops, serves not only as a major food source for humans but also has extensive applications in the fields of feed and industrial raw materials. With the continuous growth of the global population and the challenges posed by climate change, enhancing the yield and quality of corn has become a significant objective in agricultural research [1,2]. The LAI is an agronomic indicator reflecting the size of the crop population, which can not only measure the growth condition of crops but is also closely related to yield calculation. The accurate acquisition of LAI is of great significance for scientific cultivation management and yield estimation [3,4]. Traditional methods for estimating LAI require specialized personnel to conduct multiple sampling measurements using instruments, which is a relatively cumbersome process. For example, LAI measurement devices such as the LAI-2200C can be used for LAI determination, but they typically require purchase and operation by trained professionals. Some LAI measurement systems, such as the LAInet leaf area index automatic monitoring system, necessitate complex installation procedures, including the placement of sensor nodes above and below the canopy, as well as regular maintenance and calibration. Most remote-sensing-based monitoring relies on satellites, unmanned aerial vehicles (UAVs), or handheld remote-sensing devices, which often involve a certain degree of lag in data inversion and processing. In contrast, smartphones are convenient, fast, and widely available. By capturing images with smartphones and leveraging deep learning models, LAI estimation can be achieved. This approach provides an intelligent and low-cost method for obtaining crop phenotypic parameters, offering a technological reference for the application of artificial intelligence in smart agriculture. Maize grows rapidly, and there are few agricultural personnel with professional knowledge and measurement instruments. Therefore, estimating maize LAI through field images can help improve monitoring efficiency and meet the practical needs of large-scale maize planting and high-frequency monitoring.

Remote-sensing platforms currently possess robust data acquisition capabilities, enabling rapid coverage of extensive areas. High-resolution imagery from satellite, drone, and ground-based remote-sensing platforms allows for the extraction of a vast amount of surface data, facilitating application research in areas such as agricultural environmental monitoring [5,6], crop-planting surveys [7,8], crop phenotyping [9–11], and monitoring and early warning of agricultural pests, diseases, and weeds [12,13]. Zhou et al. [14] used the actual measured LAI data from the United States Soil Moisture Experiment and the surface reflectance data from Landsat 7 ETM+. By optimizing the parameters of Support Vector Regression (SVR) using the Artificial Bee Colony (ABC) algorithm, they achieved a determination coefficient (R^2) of 0.775, thereby improving the inversion accuracy of LAI from remote-sensing images. He et al. [15] addressed the issue of LAI estimation for the Suaeda salsa wetlands in the Yellow River Delta. They utilized high-resolution hyperspectral remote-sensing data from drones and ground-based spectral data, combined with soil, vegetation, and image features, to propose a method based on a deep extreme-learning machine (DELM) algorithm optimized by random forest (RF) and particle swarm optimization (PSO). The final R^2 and root mean square error (RMSE) reached 0.9546 and 0.1341, respectively. Wang et al. [16] proposed a method for inverting the LAI of winter wheat by combining the PROSAIL model with the VMG multivariate regression method. This method involved constructing an RGB vegetation index model and selecting the optimal model to invert the LAI of winter wheat. Subsequently, a sensitivity analysis of the PROSAIL parameters was conducted to obtain the optimal parameter values. Finally, the two models were combined using a fast simulated annealing algorithm, achieving a R^2 of 0.8. The aforementioned methods have achieved high recognition accuracy. However, hyperspectral imaging instruments are relatively expensive, and the processing of hyperspectral data requires professionals to complete, making it difficult to achieve real-time detection in the field.

With the development of drone remote-sensing technology, drones have been widely used in precision agriculture due to their advantages of convenient operation, low cost, fast speed, high image resolution, and the ability to observe large areas [17–19]. Wittstruck et al. [20] explored the potential of using UAV-borne RGB data and convolutional neural networks (CNNs) for estimating the LAI of winter wheat during two cropping seasons, demonstrating that the combination of RGB data and plant structures provided the best overall prediction accuracy (R^2 = 0.83) compared to models with only one input source (RGB: R^2 = 0.58, nDSM: R^2 = 0.75). Liu et al. [21] utilized multispectral data from drones and estimated the LAI of maize under different stress levels of disease using machine learning algorithms. The study ultimately demonstrated that the XGBoost method achieved the highest precision in LAI estimation under different disease stress levels, with a relative root mean square error of only 12.85%. Tao et al. [22] utilized hyperspectral data from drones and established models for the LAI of winter wheat at different growth stages using three models: multiple linear regression (MLR), partial least squares regression (PLSR), and RF. They demonstrated that the MLR model provided the best modeling results, with an average determination coefficient of 0.71 on the validation set. The aforementioned studies on crop phenotyping monitoring based on drone platforms have achieved promising results. However, there is still room for improvement in the complexity of spectral feature extraction and selection, model construction, and the accuracy and efficiency of estimation.

With the development of deep learning and convolutional neural networks (CNNs), CNNs can extract deep-level features from images, providing new methods for estimating LAI. Jiang et al. [23] conducted a comprehensive study evaluating the performance of a CNN model across eleven diverse land-cover types within global terrestrial ecosystems for short-term LAI prediction. Their results showed the CNN model achieved an overall R^2 of 0.845 and RMSE of 0.301, outperforming all other baseline models. Hao et al. [24] selected ResNet, InceptionV3, and DenseNet to extract features from visible-light RGB images and used the LightGBM model for feature fusion, realizing LAI estimation for four crops—soybean, wheat, peanut, and maize—across six different growth stages. The results ultimately indicated that DenseNet had a strong feature extraction capability, with a determination coefficient reaching 0.71. Relevant studies have used deep learning to replace traditional machine learning, but still require extensive feature selection and extraction.

In real-world environments, RGB images of field crops are more easily obtained compared to spectral images. Li et al. [25] proposed a method for estimating the LAI of winter wheat based on color indices and texture features derived from RGB images captured by unmanned aerial vehicles (UAVs). By integrating multiple features from RGB images, this method enhances the accuracy of LAI estimation for winter wheat. The results indicate that the method achieves an R^2 value of 0.730 and an RMSE of 0.691. Zhang et al. [26] developed a multi-feature collaborative optimization method based on the fusion of UAV RGB data and multispectral data. This approach addressed the limitations of traditional univariate models, which often suffer from poor adaptability to different scenarios and restricted accuracy. The results demonstrated that the random forest regression (RFR) model constructed using RGB data at a flight altitude of 20 m achieved the highest accuracy (R^2 = 0.673, RMSE = 0.881). Furthermore, by integrating texture and cover features, the model's accuracy was significantly improved by 7.3%. This study aims to explore the use of CNN networks for the regression analysis of RGB images to directly estimate LAI, thereby simplifying the steps of feature extraction and selection. Unlike traditional image processing or unmanned aerial vehicle (UAV) remote-sensing methods for estimating crop LAI, this study focuses on maize canopy images conveniently obtained using smartphones and constructs a deep learning model. The objective is to identify the optimal LAI estimation model for maize-breeding materials, providing references for maize growth monitoring, the rapid acquisition of phenotypic parameters, and yield estimation. In this paper, the CNN model is improved, using ResNet50 as the baseline model. The network output layer is modified, and a Triplet module is introduced into the model to enhance feature fusion and implement self-attention mechanisms, thereby improving model accuracy. The ResNet framework is reorganized to propose a lightweight model, LAINet. Additionally, the loss function is improved during the training process to enable rapid convergence of the model. The model is ultimately applied to the digital image recognition of maize to estimate the leaf area index using images, with the aim of replacing some manual observation tasks and providing effective support for crop phenotyping monitoring.

2. Materials and Methods

2.1. Data Source

The experimental research area is located at the maize-breeding experimental field of the Yuanyang Base of Henan Agricultural University (Yuanyang County, Xinxiang City, Henan Province). The experimental field is situated at 34°83′ N latitude and 113°84′ E longitude, with an elevation of approximately 81 m. The soil type is fluvo-aquic soil, and only one season of maize-breeding materials is planted per year. The location of the data-collection area has a warm temperate climate, characterized by a semi-humid continental monsoon climate. The typical climatic features of this region include scarce rainfall and frequent winds in spring, abundant rainfall and high temperatures in summer, cool and sunny autumn, and cold and dry winter, with distinct seasons. The frost-free period is 180–240 days, the average annual temperature is about 11–17 °C, and the annual rainfall is around 650 mm, with the majority of precipitation occurring in summer, accounting for 50–60% of the annual total. Rainfall in other months is relatively low, which is suitable for the growth of maize and other food crops. The geographical location of the experimental field is shown in Figure 1.

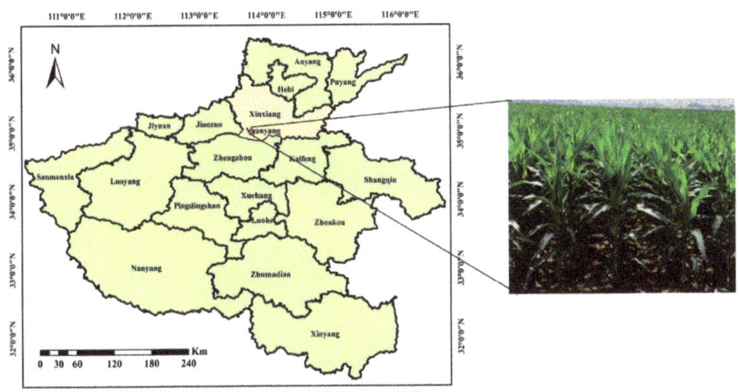

Figure 1. Geographical location of data-collection area.

The maize was sown in late June 2023. Forty days after sowing, data collection began during clear-weather periods. The experiment collected canopy RGB images of multiple categories of maize-breeding materials. Data collection took place from July to August 2023, with a total of 67 sampling grid areas selected, each measuring 1.2 m × 2.4 m. Within each sampling grid area, two 1 m × 1 m image sampling zones were established. A smartphone equipped with a 50-million-pixel Sony IMX707 sensor was used to photograph each image sampling zone. During image collection, the device was mounted on a tripod 1 m directly above the sampling zone, with the lens facing downward and the phone parallel to the ground, with the flash and optical zoom turned off. A total of 12 image collections were conducted, yielding 624 maize images with a resolution of 3072 pixels × 4080 pixels. The specific times, quantities, and growth stages of the image collections are indicated in Table 1.

Table 1. Number of images at different growth stages.

Growth Stage	Shooting Date	Number of Images
Jointing stage	21 July 2023	30
Jointing stage	23 July 2023	64
Jointing stage	27 July 2023	134
Small trumpet stage	30 July 2023	134
Small trumpet stage	6 August 2023	64
Large trumpet stage	10 August 2023	64
Large trumpet stage	13 August 2023	134

The areas for LAI data collection were the same as those for growth stage data, and the LAI of maize within the same area was measured and recorded immediately after capturing the canopy images. Some original images of maize growth stages are shown in Figure 2.

Figure 2. Raw images of corn growth stage.

2.2. Dataset Division

In this study, the expanded and augmented dataset was divided into a training set and a validation set in a ratio of 7:3. The original number of images was limited (a total of 624 images), characterized as a high-precision small-sample dataset. To expand the maize LAI image dataset, data augmentation was performed following the procedure shown in Figure 3.

For the images in the training set, after the division of the training and validation sets, image augmentation was performed. The enhancement after dataset division was to prevent any overlap between the original images of the training and validation sets, ensuring that the validation set data is cleaner. Additionally, to enhance the generalization capability of the model, random saturation enhancement and random contrast enhancement were applied to the images in the data reader, ensuring that the images for each training iteration are not identical. The number of images for each growth stage is shown in Table 2.

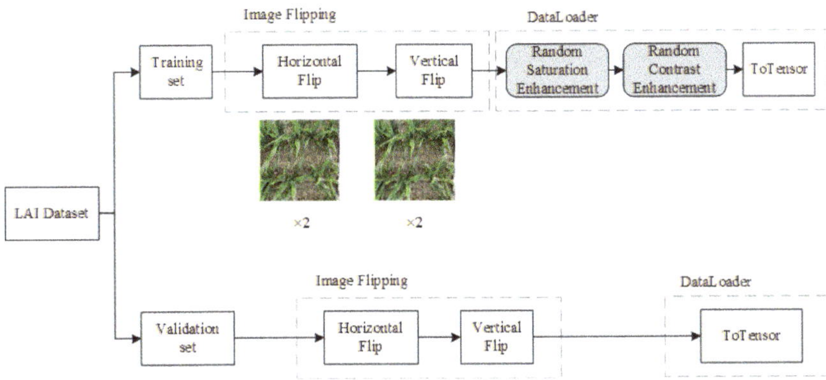

Figure 3. LAI dataset division process.

Table 2. Number of images at different growth stages.

Growth Stage	Original Image Count	Data Partitioning		Data Augmentation	
		Training Set	Test Set	Training Set	Test Set
Jointing stage	228	160	68	2560	272
Small trumpet stage	198	139	59	2224	236
Large trumpet stage	198	139	59	2224	236

2.3. CNN Model

CNNs are deep learning models particularly well-suited for processing image data. They automatically learn features from images through multiple convolutional and pooling layers, thereby extracting high-level feature representations from raw pixel values. In this study, CNN was chosen as the model for estimating maize LAI. Firstly, CNNs can learn complex features related to vegetation structure from images, which are crucial for accurately predicting LAI. Secondly, the end-to-end learning approach of CNNs allows the model to directly map from image pixels to LAI, bypassing the feature extraction and selection steps required in traditional methods. Moreover, after appropriate training, CNN models have demonstrated good generalization capabilities, enabling the accurate prediction of LAI under different regions, times, and vegetation conditions. ResNet [27] represents a significant innovation in the field of convolutional neural networks, aiming to address the training challenges that arise with increasing network depth. This study selected the classic ResNet50 as the baseline model for LAI estimation and improved the model's structure.

2.4. Improving the CNN-Based Maize LAI Estimation Model

To address the issues of low precision, large model size, and low processing efficiency caused by the complex background and large image size in field environment for maize images, improvements were made to ResNet in three aspects: network structure modification, addition of attention mechanisms, and integration of growth-stage features. Additionally, the loss function was improved during the training process.

2.4.1. Improve the Network Structure

The original ResNet was designed for classification tasks, whereas estimating LAI is a regression task. Therefore, the output layer of the ResNet network was modified. The original single-layer linear fully connected layer was changed to a three-layer linear connection, with ReLU [28] used as the activation function between the linear layers. The improved output layer structure is shown in Figure 4.

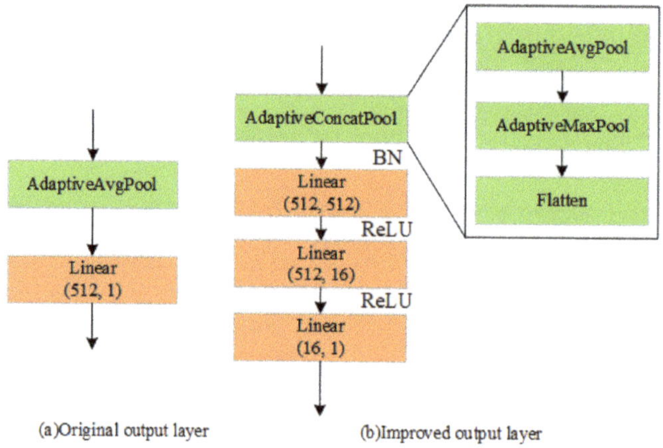

Figure 4. Improvement of output layer.

Additionally, the ResNet network was originally developed based on the ImageNet 1K dataset, with input images having a resolution of 224 pixels × 224 pixels. In contrast, the original resolution of the maize dataset is significantly higher than that of the ImageNet [29] public dataset. To better learn the features of high-resolution maize images, the ResNet Block, which is the feature extraction module of the ResNet network, was improved. A comparison between the models before and after the improvement is shown in Figure 5. After the improvement, the ResNet module is divided into two types, one of which is a convolutional module with 1 × 1 convolutions connected at the beginning and end. These two types of modules are used alternately to enhance the feature fusion between network layers.

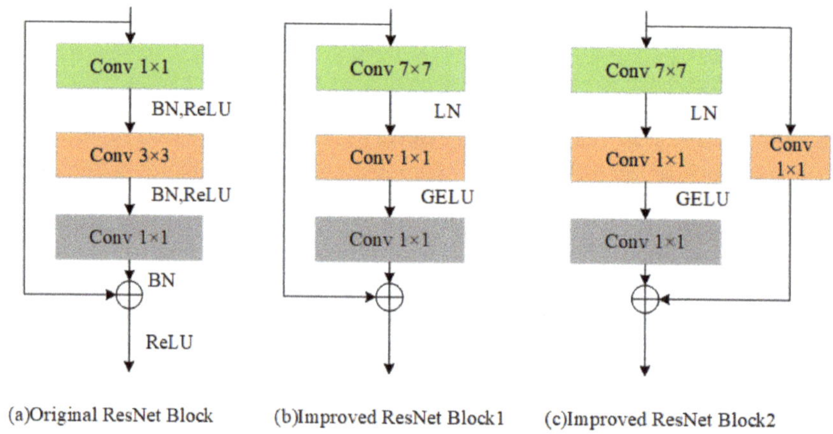

Figure 5. Improvement of ResNet Block.

2.4.2. Feature Fusion and Attention Mechanism

ResNet lacks the implementation of attention mechanisms. In the improved ResNet structure, a Triplet attention mechanism module [30] was added to achieve the fusion of multi-scale features, and the structure of the Triplet module is shown in Figure 6. This module employs a novel method of calculating attention weights by capturing cross-dimensional interactions using a three-branch structure. The input tensor is first decomposed into three distinct branches, each corresponding to the channel, height, and width dimensions. In each branch, a rotation operation is applied to the input tensor to facilitate the interaction between different dimensions. Following the rotation, shared-weight convolution operations are performed in each branch to extract feature maps that represent the interactions across the respective dimensions. These feature maps are then passed through a global-average-pooling layer to generate attention weights, which quantify the importance of each dimension in the input tensor. The attention weights are subsequently applied to the input tensor via element-wise multiplication, modulating the feature maps to emphasize salient regions and suppress irrelevant background information. Finally, the modulated feature maps from the three branches are combined through a residual connection with the original input tensor, ensuring that the output retains both the enhanced features and the original input information. This design allows the Triplet module to effectively fuse multi-scale features and implement self-attention mechanisms with a lightweight architecture, improving the model's ability to focus on critical regions of the input data. Compared to the SE module [31] and the CBAM module [32], this module can encode channel-wise and spatial information with fewer parameters, featuring high performance and lightweight characteristics.

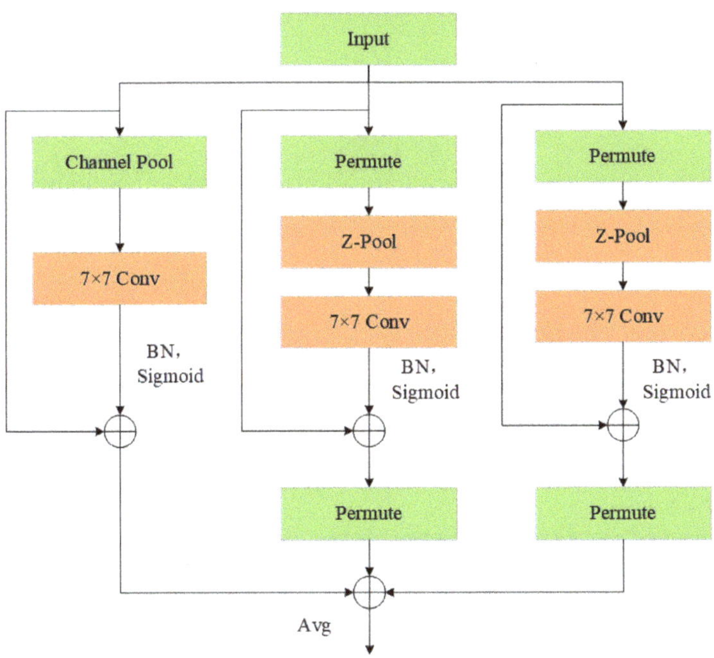

Figure 6. Structure of triplet module.

2.4.3. Integrate Phenological Information

Maize grows rapidly with significant changes in plant height. During the large trumpet stage, there is a considerable overlap of maize plant leaves, and due to the shooting angle, some leaves are occluded, leading to feature disappearance. This results in a certain deviation between the effective LAI and the actual LAI. By introducing the growth-stage number into the model, it can perform well at each growth stage. The input end of the improved ResNet model structure was modified to enable it to accept both growth-stage information and image data simultaneously. The growth-stage information was input into the network model using one-hot encoding, with the encoding for each growth stage shown in Table 3.

Table 3. One-hot coding value for different growth stages.

Growth Stage	One-Hot Encoding
Jointing stage	[1, 0, 0]
Small trumpet stage	[0, 1, 0]
Large trumpet stage	[0, 0, 1]

To incorporate one-hot encoding into the network, modifications were made to the network structure. The input data to the network includes both image data and growth stage data encoded with one-hot encoding. During input, the data are split, with the growth-stage encoding information placed after the final-average-pooling layer of the network, and a linear layer is used for fusion. The model structure is shown in Figure 7.

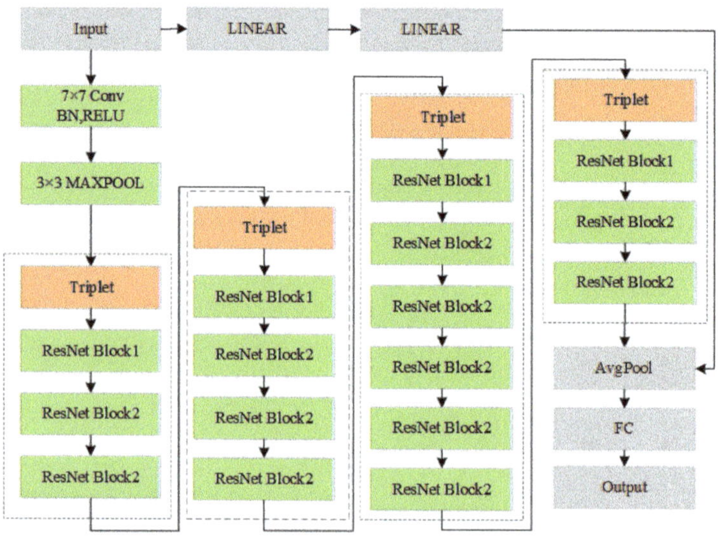

Figure 7. Structure of LAINet network.

2.4.4. Improve the Loss Function

Commonly used loss functions for regression tasks include L1Loss, L2Loss, and SmoothL1Loss [33]. L1Loss represents the mean absolute error (MAE) loss, while L2Loss represents the mean squared error (MSE) loss. L1Loss is more robust than L2Loss. L1Loss is less sensitive to outliers, with a constant derivative for the loss value. In the later stages of training, when the loss value is small and the learning rate remains unchanged, the loss function will fluctuate around a stable value, making it difficult to converge to a higher precision. L2Loss, on the other hand, tends to amplify the effect of outliers. Since L2Loss squares the error, when the error is greater than 1, it becomes significantly magnified. Models using L2Loss are more sensitive to outliers than those using L1Loss. If a sample is an outlier, the model must adjust to accommodate this single outlier, at the expense of many other normal samples. When using gradient descent for optimization, the gradients can be very large, and L2Loss may also lead to gradient explosion. SmoothL1Loss combines the advantages of L1Loss and L2Loss [34], with the calculation formula shown in Equation (1).

$$\text{SmoothL1 (x)} = \begin{cases} 0.5x^2 & (|x| < 1) \\ |x| - 0.5 & (|x| > 1) \end{cases} \quad (1)$$

Although SmoothL1Loss addresses some of the issues associated with L1Loss and L2Loss to a certain extent, in the task of estimating maize LAI, the values of LAI typically fall within a specific range, with the maximum LAI value generally not exceeding the minimum by more than 5. The range of maize LAI usually does not exceed 5, and the difference between the predicted and actual values needs to be controlled within a reasonable range. To this end, the LAILoss function is a further optimization of the SmoothL1Loss function. When the error exceeds 5, the selected function amplifies the overall error to a greater extent, facilitating the adjustment of model parameters and reducing extreme cases where the LAI value is excessively large. A comparison of the curves of LAILoss and other loss functions is shown in Figure 8. The calculation formula is given in Equation (2).

$$\text{LAILoss(x)} = \begin{cases} 0.5\text{x}^2 & (|\text{x}| < 1) \\ |\text{x}| - 0.5 & (1 \le |\text{x}| < 5) \\ 0.5\text{x}^2 - 8 & (|\text{x}| \ge 5) \end{cases} \quad (2)$$

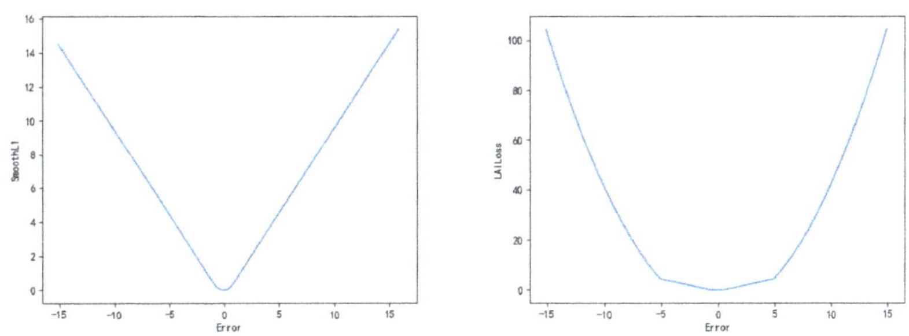

Figure 8. Function curves of LAILoss and others.

2.5. Test Environment and Parameters

The hardware environment for this experiment includes 32 GB of memory, an Intel (R) Core I7 11800F CPU, an NVIDIA V100 32GB GPU, and the operating system is Windows 11. The selected open-source deep learning framework is Pytorch, which is used to call the GPU for training different neural networks. During the experiment, the image size was fixed at 448 pixels × 448 pixels. The Lion optimizer was used, with a batch size set to 16, an initial learning rate of 0.001, and 120 iterations.

2.6. Model Evaluation Indicators

The performance of the model was evaluated using the MAE, MSE, RMSE, and R^2 on the test set of the self-constructed maize LAI dataset.

3. Results and Analysis

3.1. The Impact of Improved Network Structure on the Model

Both the improved ResNet model and the original ResNet model were trained on the training set of the maize LAI dataset. Subsequently, testing was conducted on the validation set of the maize LAI dataset. The distribution of the estimated LAI values versus the true values on the validation set is shown in Figure 9.

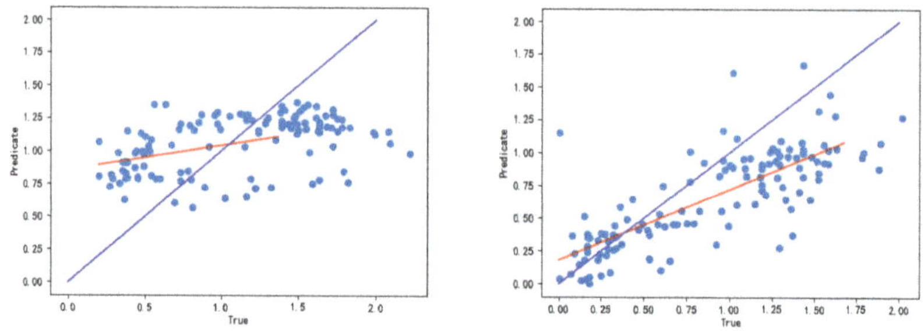

Figure 9. Result distribution using ResNet and ResNet-Reform.

As shown in Figure 9, the distribution of the predicted values versus the actual values for the original ResNet model mostly does not closely follow the blue diagonal line, indicating a poor fit of the model. In contrast, the improved ResNet model shows a significant enhancement compared to the original version, with most of the predicted values aligning more closely with the blue diagonal line. To further analyze the improvements brought by the model modifications, various regression evaluation metrics were calculated based on the predicted and actual values. The results of these evaluation metrics are presented in Table 4.

Table 4. Results between ResNet and ResNet-Reform.

Model	MSE	MAE	RMSE	R^2
ResNet	0.22	0.40	0.47	0.22
ResNet-Reform	0.10	0.23	0.32	0.54

As shown in Table 4, the R^2 of the original ResNet was only 0.22, which is almost incapable of performing the LAI estimation task. The improved ResNet model (ResNet-Reform) increased the R^2 to 0.54, and all other evaluation metrics also outperformed the original model. The reason for the improvement is that the original ResNet was designed for classification tasks, and its output fully connected layer was also designed for classification. Even though setting the output layer to 1 can endow the model with some regression analysis capabilities, the single linear layer directly maps all features to 1, resulting in a significant loss of information and an inability to effectively utilize various image features. By adding extra linear layers, the model can capture the relationship between image features and LAI. Moreover, the three linear layers not only possess linear analysis capabilities but also have some nonlinear analysis capabilities, enabling the mapping of certain hidden nonlinear relationships, thereby ultimately enhancing the model's fitting ability.

3.2. *The Impact of Adding Attention Mechanism on the Model*

After incorporating the attention mechanism module, the various errors of the model were effectively reduced. Table 5 shows the changes in model accuracy after the introduction of the attention mechanism.

Table 5. Results between ResNet-Reform and ResNet-Attention.

Model	MSE	MAE	RMSE	R^2
ResNet-Reform	0.10	0.23	0.32	0.54
ResNet-Attention	0.10	0.24	0.31	0.57

The specific distribution of predicted values versus actual values is shown in Figure 10.

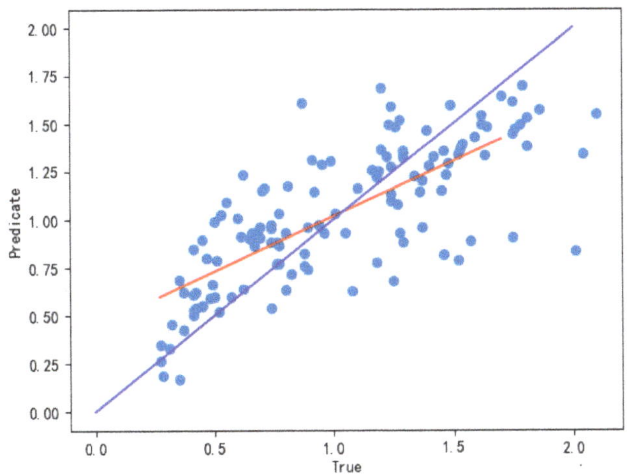

Figure 10. Result distribution using ResNet-Attention.

As shown in Table 5, after the introduction of the attention mechanism, the MAE was reduced to 0.24, and the R^2 reached 0.57, with all evaluation metrics showing significant improvement. Figure 10 indicates that compared to before the introduction of growth-stage information, the estimation accuracy has been greatly enhanced, with the distribution being closer to the diagonal line. The image with the highest improvement in estimation accuracy was selected for analysis, and a heatmap of the region of interest was drawn, as shown in Figure 11.

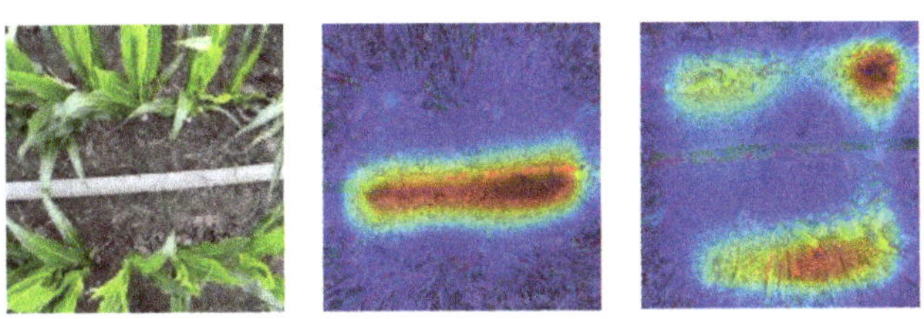

Figure 11. Changes in image regions of interest after introducing attention-mechanism modules.

As shown in Figure 11, the original images were collected in a field environment with interferences from non-crop features such as soil, rocks, irrigation pipes, and debris. The irrigation pipes, in particular, affected the region of interest (ROI) in the images. Without the attention mechanism, the ROI was influenced by the pipes in the center of the image, leading to a significant difference between the estimated and actual values. After incorporating the attention-mechanism module, the model was trained to focus on the maize plants, thereby reducing the impact of the environment. This ultimately led to an improvement in the model's accuracy.

3.3. The Impact of Integrating Phenological Information on the Model

The maize growth-stage data were encoded using one-hot encoding. Compared to not using growth-stage information, this approach led to improvements in the model's evaluation metrics. The introduction of growth-stage data effectively enhanced the model's performance. The model was ultimately validated on the validation set, with the results presented in Table 6.

Table 6. Results between ResNet and ResNet-Stage.

Model	MSE	MAE	RMSE	R^2
ResNet-Reform	0.10	0.23	0.32	0.54
ResNet-Stage	0.07	0.19	0.27	0.69

As shown in Table 6, the ResNet-Stage model, which incorporates growth-stage data, achieves superior results compared to the original ResNet model. The MAE decreased from 0.23 to 0.19, and the R^2 increased from 0.54 to 0.69. The distribution of predicted values versus actual values is illustrated in Figure 12.

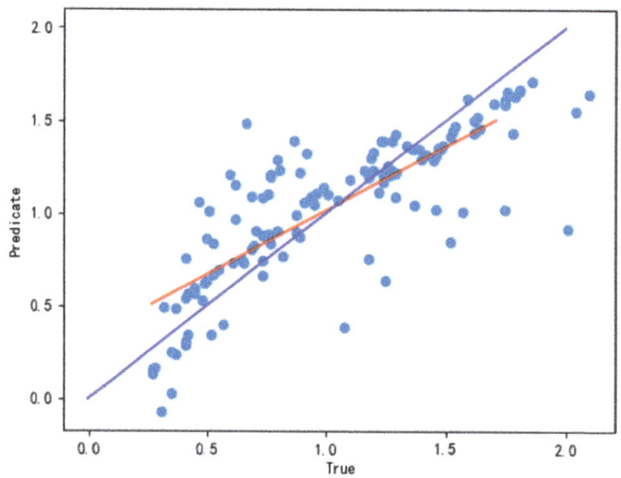

Figure 12. Result distribution using ResNet-Stage.

3.4. The Impact of Improving the Loss Function on the Model

To investigate the impact of different loss functions on the model, this study selected four loss functions—L1Loss, L2Loss, SmoothL1Loss, and LAILoss—for experimentation. The changes in MAE on the training set using the improved ResNet structure (ResNet-Reform) are shown in Figure 13.

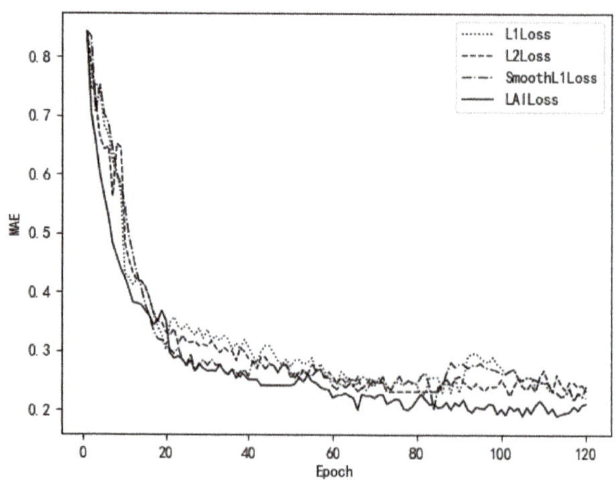

Figure 13. MAE results of using different loss functions.

As shown in Figure 13, the MAE converges more rapidly with the improved loss function compared to L1Loss, L2Loss, and SmoothL1Loss. Additionally, it avoids the sudden increase in MAE during training that can occur with L1Loss and SmoothL1Loss. The training results for different loss functions are presented in Table 7.

Table 7. Results using different loss functions.

Loss Function	MSE	MAE	RMSE	R^2
L1Loss	0.10	0.22	0.31	0.52
L2Loss	0.10	0.23	0.32	0.54
SmoothL1Loss	0.10	0.23	0.32	0.55
LAILoss	0.10	0.19	0.32	0.59

As shown in Table 7, the RMSE shows almost no significant difference when using different loss functions, while the MAE varies considerably. Using LAILoss as the loss function results in an MAE of 0.19, which is a decrease of 0.03, 0.04, and 0.04 compared to L1Loss, L2Loss, and SmoothL1Loss, respectively. The MAE reflects the situation of the average absolute error. Combining the information from Figure 13, it can be concluded that using the LAI loss function can suppress the extremely large results produced at the beginning, accelerate the convergence speed of the network, and effectively reduce the average absolute error.

3.5. Ablation Experiment

To investigate the impact of four improvement methods—improving network structure, adding attention mechanisms, integrating growth-stage information, and improving the loss function—on the final model performance, ablation studies were conducted on the maize LAI dataset. The results are shown in Table 8.

Table 8. Results of ablation experiment.

Model	Improvement Points				Evaluation Metrics			
	Structural Improvement	Attention Mechanism	Integrate Fertility Stage Information	Loss Function	MSE	MAE	RMSE	R^2
ResNet	×	×	×	×	0.22	0.40	0.47	0.22
ResNet-Reform	√	×	×	×	0.10	0.22	0.31	0.54
ResNet-Attention	√	√	×	×	0.10	0.24	0.31	0.57
ResNet-Stage	√	×	√	×	0.07	0.19	0.27	0.69
ResNet-LAILoss	√	×	×	√	0.10	0.19	0.32	0.59
LAINet	√	√	√	√	0.04	0.12	0.21	0.81

Adjusting the structure is a fundamental improvement, and all other enhancements are built upon this foundational change. As shown in Table 8, the factors that most significantly affect the R^2 of the ResNet-Reform model, in descending order, are the integration of growth-stage information, the improved loss function, and the addition of attention mechanisms. Compared to ResNet-Reform, R^2 increased by 0.15, 0.05, and 0.03, respectively. The primary reason that integrating growth-stage information has the greatest impact on model accuracy is that the relationship between images and LAI varies across different growth stages. By introducing growth-stage information through one-hot encoding, the model can to some extent fit the feature changes between images of different growth stages and the leaf area index.

3.6. Comparison of Different Regression Methods

The improved CNN model was compared with traditional machine learning models, and the results are shown in Table 9. The enhanced CNN model, referred to as LAINet, outperformed conventional machine learning methods across all evaluation metrics. Specifically, LAINet achieved an MSE of 0.04, an MAE of 0.12, an RMSE of 0.21, and an R^2 of 0.81. In contrast, the best-performing machine learning method, SVR-CC, had an MSE of 0.09, an MAE of 0.16, an RMSE of 0.40, and an R^2 of 0.77. These results indicate that LAINet has a significant advantage in prediction accuracy and model fit. This superiority can be attributed to the fact that deep learning models, such as LAINet, directly utilize images as inputs for feature learning, whereas traditional machine learning methods require the manual calculation of vegetation features and an analysis of variable correlations to establish relationships between vegetation features and LAI. The latter approach may be more susceptible to environmental influences during feature selection, potentially leading to the omission of important features.

Table 9. Results of different regression methods.

Method	MSE	MAE	RMSE	R^2
LR- TGI	0.07	0.17	0.26	0.71
LR-CC	0.07	0.16	0.40	0.78
RF- TGI	0.07	0.18	0.42	0.68
RF-CC	0.09	0.16	0.40	0.77
SVR- TGI	0.07	0.18	0.42	0.68
SVR-CC	0.09	0.16	0.40	0.77
LAINet	0.04	0.12	0.21	0.81

3.7. LAI Estimation Results Under Different Growth Stages

The LAI estimation results for different growth stages are shown in Table 10. The highest fitting degree was achieved during the small trumpet stage, with an RMSE of only 0.10 and an R^2 of 0.91. The estimation accuracy was the lowest during the large trumpet stage, with MSE, MAE, and RMSE values of 0.11, 0.19, and 0.34, respectively, and an R^2 of only 0.64.

Table 10. Results of different growth stages.

Growth Stage	MSE	MAE	RMSE	R^2
Jointing stage	0.01	0.06	0.12	0.84
Small trumpet stage	0.01	0.08	0.10	0.91
Large trumpet stage	0.11	0.19	0.34	0.64
Comprehensive Fertility Period	0.04	0.10	0.20	0.85

To further analyze the prediction results for different growth stages, each image's results were analyzed, and the differences between actual and estimated values were plotted. Using the actual values as the x coordinate and the predicted values as the y coordinate, a scatter plot was created as shown in Figure 14. The blue line in the figure represents the coincidence of predicted and actual values; points closer to the blue line indicate lower prediction deviations. Points below the blue line indicate that the predicted values are less than the actual values, while points above the blue line indicate that the predicted values are greater than the actual values. The red line represents the overall deviation of the predictions; when the red line coincides with the blue line, it indicates an overall deviation of 0. The larger the angle between the red and blue lines, the lower the fit, and the worse the overall prediction performance.

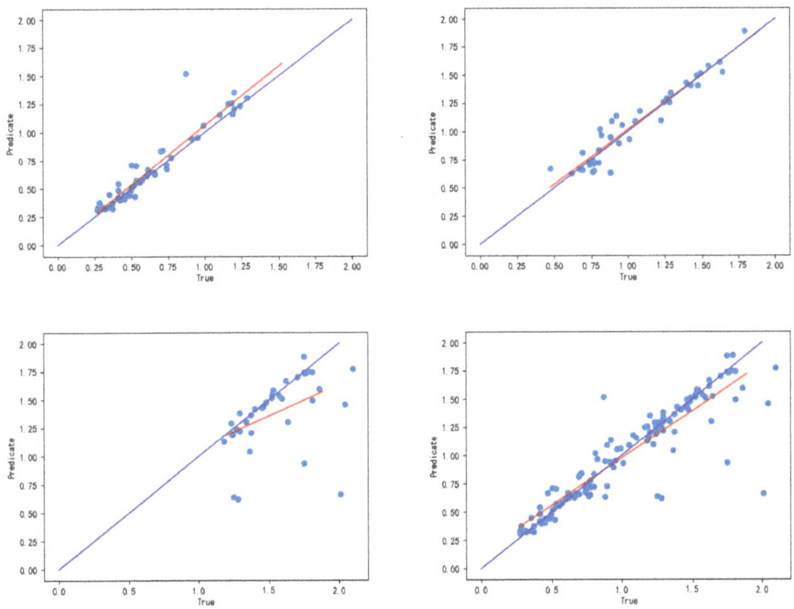

Figure 14. Result distribution on the corn growth-stage dataset.

As shown in Figure 14, the constructed network model performs the worst during the large trumpet stage. The reason for this is that as maize grows and develops, the large trumpet stage has essentially completed canopy closure, and the leaves overlap and shade each other. Additionally, when capturing images, shadows can form between upper and lower leaves, leading to low prediction accuracy for some images, which affects the overall precision of the model.

4. Discussion

The present study introduces an enhanced CNN-based model, LAINet, designed to estimate the LAI of corn, addressing the inefficiencies and complexities associated with traditional LAI measurement techniques. The model's architecture, built upon modifications to the ResNet framework, the integration of a Triplet module for feature fusion and self-attention, and the incorporation of growth-stage information alongside an optimized loss function, has demonstrated significant improvements in performance on a dataset of corn images captured across various growth stages.

The structural modifications to the ResNet output layer were foundational in enhancing the model's performance. Transitioning from a single linear fully connected layer to a three-layer linear connection, interspersed with ReLU activation functions, allowed the model to more effectively capture the intricate relationships between image features and LAI. This architectural adjustment was pivotal in elevating the model's fitting capabilities, as evidenced by the substantial increase in the R^2 value from 0.22 to 0.54. This improvement underscores the necessity of tailored network adjustments for regression tasks, particularly when dealing with the nuanced data characteristics of agricultural imagery.

The integration of attention mechanisms through the Triplet module further refined the model's precision. By enabling multi-scale feature fusion and self-attention, the model was able to concentrate on salient regions within the images, effectively mitigating the impact of background noise. This enhancement resulted in a modest yet notable increase in the R^2 value by 0.03, highlighting the value of attention mechanisms in processing complex field images. This finding is consistent with prior research that has established the efficacy of attention mechanisms in enhancing the performance of image classification and other visual tasks.

The most significant leap in performance was observed with the incorporation of growth-stage information. Utilizing one-hot encoding to introduce these data into the model allowed for a more nuanced understanding of the variations in corn characteristics across different growth stages. This modification led to a dramatic increase in the R^2 value from 0.54 to 0.69, underscoring the critical role of growth-stage information in accurate LAI estimation. The distinct structural and leaf distribution differences across growth stages provide essential cues that aid the model in more accurately predicting LAI, thereby enhancing the overall estimation accuracy.

The optimization of the loss function also played a crucial role in the model's performance. The LAILoss function, an enhancement over SmoothL1Loss, was designed to amplify errors when they exceeded a certain threshold, thereby accelerating the adjustment of model parameters and improving convergence speed. This adjustment resulted in a noticeable reduction in the MAE, indicating that the improved loss function effectively guided the training process, minimizing prediction errors.

The LAINet model proposed in this study demonstrated significant advantages in the estimation of maize LAI; compared with the BO-CNN-BiLSTM deep learning model reported in the literature [35], the LAINet model achieved an R^2 value of 0.81 through an improved CNN architecture, incorporating growth-stage information and an optimized loss function. This R^2 value is comparable to that of the BCBL model in winter-wheat yield estimation, but with a smaller RMSE. These results indicate that the LAINet model has better fitting performance. It also exhibits stronger capabilities in feature extraction and fitting when dealing with complex image data, thereby more accurately reflecting the variations in maize LAI. Shi et al. [36] proposed an automated processing pipeline that integrates deep learning and clustering algorithms for individual segmentation of soybean plants and estimation of LAI in the field. Machine learning algorithms, including RF, support vector machine (SVM), and XGBoost, were employed to construct LAI prediction models. Among these, the SVM model exhibited the best performance on the validation set, with an R^2 value of 0.79 and an RMSE of 0.47. In contrast, the LAINet model enhanced feature fusion and self-attention mechanisms by incorporating a Triplet module, thereby improving the robustness and adaptability of the model. As a result, LAINet demonstrated superior performance in estimating maize LAI across different growth stages, achieving an R^2 value of 0.81. Compared with the method based on drone-based multispectral imaging proposed in Reference [37], LAINet leverages RGB image data and employs an improved CNN architecture to achieve higher estimation accuracy (R^2 = 0.81), whereas the R^2 value for the multispectral imaging method is 0.80. In addition to its superior accuracy, the LAINet model also features low data acquisition costs and ease of large-scale application.

Despite these advancements, the model exhibited varying degrees of accuracy across different growth stages. Notably, the model's performance was least accurate during the late trumpet stage, with an R^2 value of only 0.64. This discrepancy is likely attributable to the increased complexity of image features during this stage, characterized by overlapping leaves and shadowing, which complicates feature extraction. Additionally, while the model performed well on the self-constructed dataset, its generalizability to other regions or varying planting conditions remains untested. Future research should aim to validate the model's performance on a broader range of datasets to assess its robustness and adaptability.

Looking forward, the introduction of more sophisticated image-enhancement techniques, such as random rotation, cropping, and flipping, can enhance the model's adaptability to different shooting angles and lighting conditions, thereby improving its robustness in complex environments. Additionally, in terms of model lightweighting and real-time performance, although LAINet achieves high accuracy, its computational complexity poses challenges for real-time monitoring systems. Techniques such as model pruning, quantization, and knowledge distillation could be employed to reduce the model's parameter count and computational demands, enabling deployment on edge devices for real-time crop phenotyping.

In conclusion, the LAINet model introduced in this study has shown remarkable performance in estimating corn LAI, yet it is not without limitations. Future research endeavors should focus on optimizing model architecture and training methodologies to enhance robustness and real-time capabilities, ensuring the model's applicability in practical scenarios.

5. Conclusions

This study presents a maize LAI estimation model, LAINet, based on an improved CNN. By constructing a maize image dataset across three critical growth stages of summer maize in Henan (jointing stage, small trumpet stage, and large trumpet stage), and by modifying the output structure of the ResNet architecture, incorporating a Triplet module for feature fusion and self-attention mechanisms, integrating growth-stage information, and optimizing the loss function, the model significantly enhanced the accuracy of maize LAI estimation. Compared with traditional methods, LAINet eliminates the need for multiple sampling measurements by professionals, effectively simplifies the steps of feature extraction and selection, and achieves a coefficient of determination (R^2) of 0.81 on the self-constructed dataset. It can rapidly and efficiently estimate maize LAI, providing robust technical support for crop phenotyping and monitoring. However, this study is limited to datasets from three growth stages. Future research will expand the dataset to include more growth stages, covering key nodes across the entire growth cycle, to improve the model's generalizability. Building on these findings, future work can further optimize the model architecture and training methods, introduce more advanced image-enhancement techniques to enhance the model's adaptability to different shooting angles and lighting conditions, and promote the widespread application of this model in practical agricultural production.

(1) After improving the output layer of the ResNet network, the accuracy of LAI estimation was significantly enhanced. Compared to the unimproved version, the R^2 increased from 0.22 to 0.54.
(2) A comprehensive comparison of the various improvements shows that incorporating an attention mechanism, integrating growth-stage information, and improving the loss function each increased the R^2 of the improved output layer model by 0.03, 0.15, and 0.05, respectively. Among these, the integration of growth-stage information had the most significant impact, directly increasing the R^2 from 0.54 to 0.69.
(3) Compared to machine learning, the improved CNN model is capable of automatic feature extraction, eliminating the complex steps involved in traditional feature extraction, while also achieving higher estimation accuracy.
(4) The proposed method can quickly and efficiently estimate the LAI of maize, providing a technical reference for crop phenotyping monitoring.

Author Contributions: Conceptualization, C.Y., J.L. and L.S.; methodology, C.Y., J.L. and L.S.; software, C.Y., J.L. and Z.L.; validation, C.Y., J.L. and S.X.; formal analysis, C.Y., J.L. and L.X.; investigation, J.W. and H.Q.; resources, C.Y., J.L. and L.S.; data curation, C.Y., J.L., Z.L., S.X., L.X., J.W., H.Q. and L.S.; writing—original draft preparation, C.Y., J.L. and L.S.; writing—review and editing, C.Y., J.L., Z.L., S.X., L.X., J.W., H.Q. and L.S.; visualization, C.Y., J.L. and J.W.; supervision, H.Q.; project administration, L.S.; funding acquisition, L.S. All authors have read and agreed to the published version of the manuscript.

Funding: This research was funded by the National Natural Science Foundation of China (No. 31501225); the Natural Science Foundation of Henan Province (No. 242301420143, No. 232300420146); the key research and development projects of Henan Province (No. 241111110080); the Key Scientific and Technological Project of Henan Province (No. 242102111193).

Institutional Review Board Statement: Not applicable.

Informed Consent Statement: Not applicable.

Data Availability Statement: Data will be made available on request.

Conflicts of Interest: The authors declare no conflict of interest.

References

1. Erenstein, O.; Jaleta, M.; Sonder, K.; Mottaleb, K.; Prasanna, B.M. Global maize production, consumption and trade: Trends an R&D implications. *Food Secur.* **2022**, *14*, 1295–1319. [CrossRef]
2. Wang, J.; Hu, X. Research on corn production efficiency and influencing factors of typical farms: Based on data from 12 corr producing countries from 2012 to 2019. *PLoS ONE* **2021**, *16*, e0254423. [CrossRef] [PubMed]
3. Li, H.; Zhou, Y.; Zhao, X.; Zhang, X.; Liang, S. A dataset of 0.05-degree leaf area index in China during 1983–2100 based on dee learning network. *Sci. Data* **2024**, *11*, 1122. [CrossRef]
4. Cheng, Q.; Ding, F.; Xu, H.; Guo, S.; Li, Z.; Chen, Z. Quantifying corn LAI using machine learning and UAV multispectra imaging. *Precis. Agric.* **2024**, *25*, 1777–1799. [CrossRef]
5. Xu, R.; Fan, Y.; Fan, B.; Feng, G.; Li, R. Classification and Monitoring of Salt Marsh Vegetation in the Yellow River Delta Based o Multi-Source Remote Sensing Data Fusion. *Sensors* **2025**, *25*, 529. [CrossRef] [PubMed]
6. Zhang, J.; Qi, Y.; Li, Q.; Zhang, J.; Yang, R.; Wang, H.; Li, X. Combining UAV-Based Multispectral and Thermal Images t Diagnosing Dryness Under Different Crop Areas on the Loess Plateau. *Agriculture* **2025**, *15*, 126. [CrossRef]
7. Zhang, P.; Lu, B.; Ge, J.; Wang, X.; Yang, Y.; Shang, J.; La, Z.; Zang, H.; Zeng, Z. Using UAV-based multispectral and RGB imager to monitor above-ground biomass of oat-based diversified cropping. *Eur. J. Agron.* **2025**, *162*, 127422. [CrossRef]
8. Crusiol, L.G.T.; Nanni, M.R.; Furlanetto, R.H.; Sibaldelli, R.N.R.; Cezar, E.; Sun, L.; Foloni, J.S.S.; Mertz-Henning, L.M.; Nepomu ceno, A.L.; Neumaier, N.; et al. Classification of Soybean Genotypes Assessed Under Different Water Availability and at Differen Phenological Stages Using Leaf-Based Hyperspectral Reflectance. *Remote Sens.* **2021**, *13*, 172. [CrossRef]
9. Curran, P.J. Remote sensing in agriculture: An introductory review. *J. Geogr.* **1987**, *86*, 147–156. [CrossRef]
10. Ogungbuyi, M.G.; Mohammed, C.; Fischer, A.M.; Turner, D.; Whitehead, J.; Harrison, M.T. Integration of Drone and Satellit Imagery Improves Agricultural Management Agility. *Remote Sens.* **2024**, *16*, 4688. [CrossRef]
11. Terentev, A.; Badenko, V.; Shaydayuk, E.; Emelyanov, D.; Eremenko, D.; Klabukov, D.; Fedotov, A.; Dolzhenko, V. Hyperspectra Remote Sensing for Early Detection of Wheat Leaf Rust Caused by Puccinia triticina. *Agriculture* **2023**, *13*, 1186. [CrossRef]
12. Long, L.; Chen, Y.; Song, S.; Zhang, X.; Jia, X.; Lu, Y.; Liu, G. Remote sensing monitoring of pine wilt disease based on time-serie remote sensing index. *Remote Sens.* **2023**, *15*, 360. [CrossRef]
13. Yang, C. High resolution satellite imaging sensors for precision agriculture. *Front. Agric. Sci. Eng.* **2018**, *5*, 393–405. [CrossRef]
14. Zhou, X.; Li, N.; Pan, Y.; Sun, L. Optimized SVR based on artificial bee colony algorithm for leaf area index inversion. *Nat Remote Sens. Bull.* **2022**, *26*, 766–780. [CrossRef]
15. He, S.; Zhang, S.; Tian, J.; Lu, X. UAV hyperspectral inversion of Suaeda Salsa leaf area index in coastal wetlands combined wit multimodal data. *J. Remote Sens.* **2023**, *27*, 1441–1453. [CrossRef]
16. Wang, X.; Lu, X.; Yang, Z.; Gao, Z.; Wang, L.; Zhang, B. Retrieving Method for Leaf Area Index of Winter Wheat by Combinin PROSAIL Model with VMG Model. *Trans. Chin. Soc. Agric. Mach.* **2022**, *53*, 209–216. [CrossRef]
17. Gao, C.; Ji, X.; He, Q.; Gong, Z.; Sun, H.; Wen, T.; Guo, W. Monitoring of Wheat Fusarium Head Blight on Spectral and Textura Analysis of UAV Multispectral Imagery. *Agriculture* **2023**, *13*, 293. [CrossRef]
18. Yeh, J.F.; Lin, K.M.; Yuan, L.C.; Hsu, J.M. Automatic Counting and Location Labeling of Rice Seedlings from Unmanned Aeria Vehicle Images. *Electronics* **2024**, *13*, 273. [CrossRef]

19. Wang, J.; Zhang, S.; Lizaga, I.; Zhang, Y.; Ge, X.; Zhang, Z.; Zhang, W.; Huang, Q.; Hu, Z. UAS-based remote sensing for agricultural Monitoring: Current status and perspectives. *Comput. Electron. Agric.* **2024**, *227*, 109501. [CrossRef]
20. Wittstruck, L.; Jarmer, T.; Trautz, D.; Waske, B. Estimating LAI From Winter Wheat Using UAV Data and CNNs. *IEEE Geosci. Remote Sens. Lett.* **2022**, *19*, 1–5. [CrossRef]
21. Liu, S.; Jin, X.; Feng, H.; Nie, C.; Bai, Y.; Cheng, M. Analysis of Effect of Disease Stress on Maize LAI Remote Sensing Estimation. *Trans. Chin. Soc. Agric. Mach.* **2023**, *54*, 246. [CrossRef]
22. Tao, H.; Xu, L.; Feng, H.; Yang, G.; Miao, M.; Lin, B. Estimation of plant height and biomass of winter wheat based on UAV digital image. *Trans. Chin. Soc. Agric. Mach.* **2020**, *51*, 180–191. [CrossRef]
23. Jiang, C.; Yeddula, S.D.; Ku, W.S. A convolutional neural network model for accurate short-term leaf area index prediction. *Model. Earth Syst. Environ.* **2024**, *10*, 6397–6412. [CrossRef]
24. Zi-yuan, H.; Wei, Y.; Hao, L.; Hao, Y.; Min-zan, L. Study on Prediction Models for Leaf Area Index of Multiple Crops Based on Multi-Source Information and Deep Learning. *Spectrosc. Spectr. Anal.* **2023**, *43*, 3862–3870.
25. Li, H.; Yan, X.; Su, P.; Su, Y.; Li, J.; Xu, Z.; Gao, C.; Zhao, Y.; Feng, M.; Shafiq, F.; et al. Estimation of winter wheat LAI based on color indices and texture features of RGB images taken by UAV. *J. Sci. Food Agric.* **2025**, *105*, 189–200. [CrossRef] [PubMed]
26. Zhang, Y.; Jiang, Y.; Xu, B.; Yang, G.; Feng, H.; Yang, X.; Yang, H.; Liu, C.; Cheng, Z.; Feng, Z. Study on the Estimation of Leaf Area Index in Rice Based on UAV RGB and Multispectral Data. *Remote Sens.* **2024**, *16*, 3049. [CrossRef]
27. He, K.; Zhang, X.; Ren, S.; Sun, J. Deep residual learning for image recognition. In Proceedings of the IEEE Conference on Computer Vision and Pattern Recognition, Las Vegas, NV, USA, 27–30 June 2016; pp. 770–778.
28. Maas, A.L.; Hannun, A.Y.; Ng, A.Y. Rectifier nonlinearities improve neural network acoustic models. In Proceedings of the International Conference on Machine Learning, Atlanta, GA, USA, 16–21 June 2013; Volume 30, p. 3.
29. Deng, J.; Dong, W.; Socher, R.; Li, L.J.; Li, K.; Fei-Fei, L. Imagenet: A large-scale hierarchical image database. In Proceedings of the 2009 IEEE Conference on Computer Vision and Pattern Recognition, Miami, FL, USA, 20–25 June 2009; IEEE: Piscataway, NJ, USA, 2009; pp. 248–255. [CrossRef]
30. Misra, D.; Nalamada, T.; Arasanipalai, A.U.; Hou, Q. Rotate to attend: Convolutional triplet attention module. In Proceedings of the IEEE/CVF Winter Conference on Applications of Computer Vision, Waikoloa, HI, USA, 3–8 January 2021; pp. 3139–3148. [CrossRef]
31. Hu, J.; Shen, L.; Sun, G. Squeeze-and-excitation networks. In Proceedings of the IEEE Conference on Computer Vision and Pattern Recognition, Salt Lake City, UT, USA, 18–23 June 2018; pp. 7132–7141. [CrossRef]
32. Woo, S.; Park, J.; Lee, J.Y.; Kweon, I.S. Cbam: Convolutional block attention module. In Proceedings of the European Conference on Computer Vision (ECCV), Munich, Germany, 8–14 September 2018; pp. 3–19. [CrossRef]
33. Zhao, H.; Liu, W.; Zhou, Y.; Luo, Y.; Zong, S.; Ren, L. Method for detecting pine forest discoloured epidemic wood based on semi-supervised learning. *Trans. Chin. Soc. Agric. Eng.* **2022**, *38*, 164–170. [CrossRef]
34. Tang, H.; Xiao, J.; Zhai, Y.; Yang, D. Remote sensing image matching algorithm based on cycle generative adversarial strategy. *J. Optoelectron. Laser* **2022**, *33*, 824–830. [CrossRef]
35. Zhang, L.; Li, C.; Wu, X.; Xiang, H.; Jiao, Y.; Chai, H. BO-CNN-BiLSTM deep learning model integrating multisource remote sensing data for improving winter wheat yield estimation. *Front. Plant Sci.* **2024**, *15*, 1500499. [CrossRef] [PubMed]
36. Shi, B.; Guo, L.; Yu, L. Accurate LAI estimation of soybean plants in the field using deep learning and clustering algorithms. *Front. Plant Sci.* **2025**, *15*, 1501612. [CrossRef] [PubMed]
37. Yao, X.; Wang, N.; Liu, Y.; Cheng, T.; Tian, Y.; Chen, Q.; Zhu, Y. Estimation of wheat LAI at middle to high levels using unmanned aerial vehicle narrowband multispectral imagery. *Remote Sens.* **2017**, *9*, 1304. [CrossRef]

MDPI AG
Grosspeteranlage 5
4052 Basel
Switzerland
Tel.: +41 61 683 77 34

Agriculture Editorial Office
E-mail: agriculture@mdpi.com
www.mdpi.com/journal/agriculture

www.ingramcontent.com/pod-product-compliance
Lightning Source LLC
Chambersburg PA
CBHW061758210926
51850CB00006B/589
* 9 7 8 3 7 2 5 8 6 5 4 8 2 *